1634
THE BALTIC WAR

Eric Flint
&
David Weber

1634: THE BALTIC WAR

A Baen Book

Baen Publishing Enterprises
P.O. Box 1403
Riverdale, NY 10471
www.baen.com

ISBN 10: 1-4165-5588-9
ISBN-13: 978-1-4165-5588-9

Cover art by Tom Kidd
Maps by Randy Asplund

First Baen paperback printing, November 2008

Library of Congress Control Number: 2007004705

Distributed by Simon & Schuster
1230 Avenue of the Americas
New York, NY 10020

Pages by Joy Freeman (www.pagesbyjoy.com)
Printed in the United States of America

TABLES TURNED

Maddox's second shot took out another grappling hook holder on the approaching pirate ship. Harry was at the side an instant later, bracing his left hip against the rail and firing half-sideways with a two-handed grip.

He double-tapped the pirate right across from him in the chest. Then he shifted his aim from left to right, double-tapping each target as he came to it. Speed was everything in this situation and Harry just concentrated on killing the nearest targets, whatever they had in their hands.

Swords and other hand weapons only, so far as he could see. That was what he had expected. No sensible pirate captain would arm his men with firearms just to capture an unresisting merchant vessel with a crew less than a third the size of his own. Leaving aside the ever-present risk of accidentally shooting one of your own in the excitement of the moment, loaded guns on a ship—and they'd all be matchlocks, to make it worse—posed too great a danger of starting a fire.

The pirates were shrieking now, but Harry blocked that out of his mind. There was just a row of targets, that's all. The only sounds that registered at all clearly were the sharp and unmistakable cracks of a semi-automatic rifle going into action from the stern. When his pistol ran out of ammunition, Harry just dropped it onto the deck, pulled out his backups, and kept firing at the pirate ship.

Maddox had joined Harry and Felix at the rail with her own pistol, and, not more than two seconds later, Paul Maczka was out from under the tarpaulin he'd hidden under and weighed in with his shot at the bow. Like all seventeenth-century soldiers Harry knew, Paul positively adored pump-action shotguns. *Clickety-BOOM, clickety-BOOM, clickety-BOOM*.

By the time he started reloading, the bow of the enemy's ship was a charnelhouse.

To Anna Lou Ballew McQuade

Acknowledgments

First, credit where credit is due:

As he did for us in *1633*, Mike Spehar wrote the first drafts of all the flying scenes that appear in *1634: The Baltic War*. Without his expertise as a pilot, those scenes would have necessarily lacked much of their existing detail.

Bob Gottlieb developed the industrial accident portrayed in Chapters 2 and 3 of the novel, and wrote a rough draft depicting the way it would unfold.

In addition, I'd like to thank:

Michael Barthelemy, for his gorgeous period maps of the Tower of London.

Annette Pedersen, Vincent Coljee and Jens Guld, among others, for their assistance regarding Denmark and Copenhagen in the 17th century.

And the editorial board of the *Grantville Gazette*, especially Virginia DeMarce and Paula Goodlett, for their careful scrutiny of the manuscript and spotting a number of errors and continuity lapses.

For those readers not familiar with it, the *Grantville Gazette* is an electronic magazine devoted to the 1632 series. There's an advertisement explaining how to subscribe at the end of the book.

Finally, anyone who enjoyed this book and would be interested in participating in the online discussion regarding the 1632 series are welcome to join it. You can do so as follows:

1) Go to: www.baen.com
2) Select "Baen's Bar" from the menu across the top.
3) Fill out a quick and simple registration. Thereafter, you can simply log in.
4) Once you get into the Bar, select the conference titled "1632 Tech Manual."
5) Then, lurk or post, as you choose. Most of all, enjoy yourself.

Contents

Map of the United States of Europe

As of April, 1634

Baltic Sea

Poland

Silesia

Moravia

Ottoman Empire

Brandenburg

Berlin   Saxony   Bohemia

Denmark

Luebeck

Ahrensbok

United States of Europe

Dresden   Prague   R. Elbe   Vienna

Magdeburg

Austria

Wietze Oil Fields

Grantville

Bamberg

Bavaria

Kassel   Nürnberg

Independent Principalities

Munich

Venice

R. Rhine

Venetian Republic

Amsterdam

Brussels

Disputed Territory

N. Sea

Swiss Confederation

France

Territory Controlled by Bernhard of Saxe-Weimar

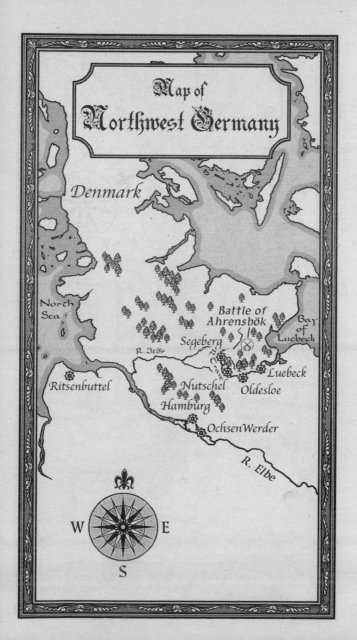

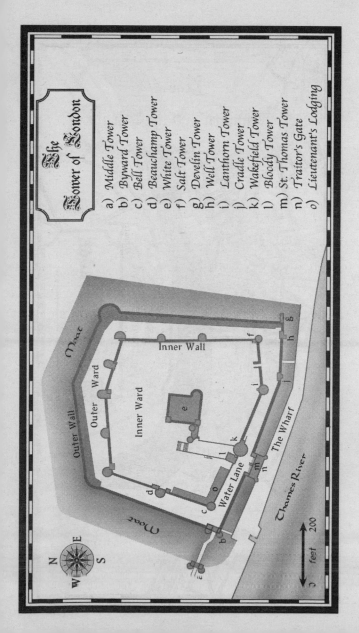

The Tower of London

a) Middle Tower
b) Byward Tower
c) Bell Tower
d) Beauchamp Tower
e) White Tower
f) Salt Tower
g) Develin Tower
h) Well Tower
i) Lanthorn Tower
j) Cradle Tower
k) Wakefield Tower
l) Bloody Tower
m) St. Thomas Tower
n) Traitor's Gate
o) Lieutenant's Lodging

Map of
Denmark and the Straits

Denmark

Sweden

Stockholm

Göteborg

Skagerrak

Kattegat

Öland
Island

The Jutland

The Great Belt

Baltic
Sea

North

Zealand
Island

Copenhagen

Øresund

Bornholm
Island

Funen
Island

Little Belt

Rugen
Island

Sea

Mecklenburg
Bay

Stralsund

Wismar

Luebeck

United States of
Europe

W — E

S

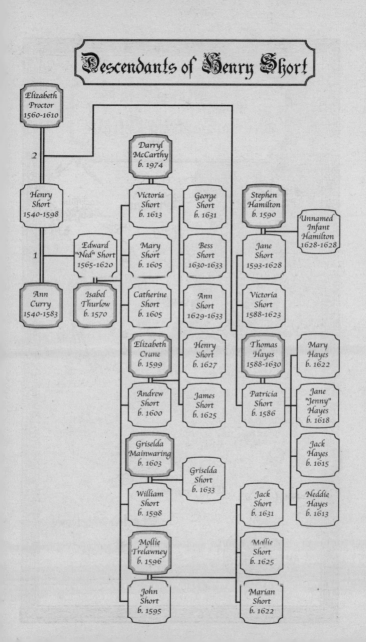

Descendants of Henry Short

- Elizabeth Proctor 1560–1610
  - 2
- Henry Short 1540–1598
  - 1
- Ann Curry 1540–1583

- Darryl McCarthy b. 1974
- Victoria Short b. 1613
- George Short b. 1631
- Stephen Hamilton b. 1590
  - Unnamed Infant Hamilton 1628–1628
- Edward "Ned" Short 1565–1620
- Mary Short b. 1605
- Bess Short 1630–1633
- Jane Short 1593–1628
- Isabel Thurlow b. 1570
- Catherine Short b. 1605
- Ann Short 1629–1633
- Victoria Short 1588–1623
- Elizabeth Crane b. 1599
- Henry Short b. 1627
- Thomas Hayes 1588–1630
- Mary Hayes b. 1622
- Andrew Short b. 1600
- James Short b. 1625
- Patricia Short b. 1586
- Jane "Jenny" Hayes b. 1618
- Griselda Mainwaring b. 1603
  - Griselda Short b. 1633
- Jack Hayes b. 1615
- William Short b. 1598
- Jack Short b. 1631
- Neddie Hayes b. 1613
- Mollie Trelawney b. 1596
- Mollie Short b. 1625
- John Short b. 1595
- Marian Short b. 1622

Part One

A mist that is like blown snow is sweeping over all

Chapter 1

Hans Richter Field
Near Grantville, in the State of Thuringia

December 1633

Colonel Jesse Wood turned off the computer in his office, removed the floppy disk and carefully slid it into its protective sleeve. It was a copy of the original disk he had already placed in an envelope and addressed to Mike Stearns, the Prime Minister of the United States of Europe. The copy itself was destined for Admiral John Simpson, Chief of Naval Operations, advisor to the head of all the USE's armed forces, and one of the chief architects of the new nation's growing industrial capability in Magdeburg.

And how he manages all three, I have no idea, Jesse thought. *Lord knows I always feel about two weeks behind in my sleep. At least this report should cheer him up.*

The thought wasn't as sour as it would have been some months earlier. In fact, it was rather respectful. Whatever Jesse thought of the way John Simpson had conducted himself in the two years following the Ring of Fire, the man's actions after Mike Stearns had put him in charge of the new little navy—especially during and after the Battle of Wismar—had pretty much washed all that old antagonism away. As it had, Jesse knew, for Stearns himself. Simpson might have been a disaster as a political leader, but there was no denying that as a pure and simple military commander he had a lot going for him. Even if his insistence on the punctilio of military protocol still rubbed Jesse the wrong way, now and then.

The colonel squinted out the window at the unseasonably bright, late afternoon sunlight, catching a glimpse of Master Sergeant Friedrich Krueger giving the welcoming briefing to a bunch of newly arrived recruits. The sergeant was not being gentle about it. A recruit was on the ground, rubbing his head, no doubt after having been instructed in some fine detail of service courtesy. The tall German NCO had well earned his nickname of *Freddy Krueger*, although Jesse doubted he understood the allusion.

He watched as the sergeant pointed to the white stripes on the sleeve of the dark brown jumpsuit that was his uniform. *Perhaps he does, though*, Jesse reflected. *God knows they made enough of those crappy movies. One's sure to be in town somewhere.*

Jesse made a mental note to ask Major Horton to have another word with the NCO about his temper. He had to admit that Krueger's techniques were highly effective, if rather crude. Still, there was no sense in beating men who had just arrived, since they probably didn't yet have enough sense to absorb the lesson. Looking at the assembled recruits, Jesse felt he knew the source of Krueger's irritation. They were a very mixed bag, as all of the latest had been. Recalling the roster on his desk, Jesse thought he could spot their origins, for the most part. Among the fifteen men, he saw several Dutch, a couple of Bavarians, other Germans of all regions and dialect, two Spanish deserters, and a Swede. One man, by his dress, appeared to be either a nobleman or the son of a rich merchant.

I wonder what he's running from? Jesse mused. *Well, it doesn't matter, he's in Freddy's gentle care, now. I'll wager not one of them knows a word of English. I wonder how many of them brought families with them?*

They were refugees for the most part, from all over Europe. The same sort of people who filled the ranks of most of the armies of the era. Mercenaries, at bottom, regardless of the official label of "citizen soldiers" they had in the United States of Europe.

Unfortunately from Jesse's point of view, although it saved him a lot of grief in other ways, the air force didn't get too many volunteers from the Committees of Correspondence. He'd been surprised by that, at first, since Hans Richter had been an airman and Hans was the poster boy for the CoCs. But after a little experience, the reason had become obvious enough. Lots of enthusiastic CoC members volunteered to become *pilots* like Hans Richter, sure enough. But in an air force that still only had a literal handful of planes, how many pilots did you need? What the air force mainly needed were people for the ground crews—and for all but a tiny number of CoC firebrands, serving behind the lines doing what they saw as mostly menial chores just didn't appeal to them. One of the many

American terms that had made its way into the hybrid mostly-German dialect of the new nation emerging in central Europe was "REMFs".

Instead, they volunteered for the new regiments in the army Gustav Adolf was creating, which were sure to see action come next spring. So, for the most part, Jesse had to make do with men—and some women, here and there—who "volunteered" out of necessity rather than political fervor. Granted, that saved Jesse from having to deal with the rambunctious politics that saturated the new army regiments and had most down-time officers tearing out their hair. Most up-time officers, for that matter, who were often just as aghast as their down-time counterparts at the radical conclusions their volunteers sometimes drew about the logic of democracy as applied to military discipline.

So, true enough, Jesse was generally spared that problem. What he faced instead were the traditional ones of maintaining efficiency and discipline in a mercenary force—a problem that officers in the new army regiments rarely had to deal with. If a recruit in one of those regiments slacked off, he'd get disciplined by his CoC mates before any officer even knew a problem existed—and the discipline could be a lot more savage than anything even a sergeant like Krueger would hand out.

Jesse rubbed his eyes, pulled his leather jacket over his own brown flying suit, and grabbed the two often-used envelopes. Sweeping up his beret with its eagle insignia off his desk, he stretched his sore back and stepped out of his office into that of his adjutant. Lieutenant Cynthia Garlow was seated behind her desk, sharpening a goose feather quill, her own computer showing a floral screen saver pattern. For reasons Jesse had never been able to grasp, she preferred using quill pens over the still-perfectly-functional modern pens that had come through the Ring of Fire in plentitude.

She didn't stand up as he entered. She couldn't, having lost the use of her legs in a riding accident on the far side of the Ring of Fire. Instead, the former CAP cadet straightened to attention in her wheelchair and looked at Jesse expectantly.

"Yes, Colonel?"

Jesse smiled. "Cynthia, how many times have I told you to save the 'attention' bit for visitors? It's just the two of us here. At ease, for Pete's sake."

Cynthia tossed her short auburn curls impatiently. "About a million times, Colonel. Almost as often as I've told you I can type faster than you, so why not just dictate to me?" She looked meaningfully at the envelopes in Jesse's hand.

Jesse laid the envelopes on her desk. "Not this time, Lieutenant. This report was a pleasure to write. I've declared the Gustav flight tests completed. Now that we've finished those, the real fun begins. With luck and good weather, we'll have half a dozen trained crews by spring. Send the original to Mike Stearns in Government House on tomorrow's courier run to Magdeburg. The copy goes to Admiral Simpson."

"Yes, sir. That's great news. Anything else?"

"Yeah, send word to Major Horton that I'd like to see him in my quarters tonight at 2030, will you? I'm going to take a turn around the base, then go home. Why don't you wrap up things here and take off?"

Cynthia gave him an impish grin. "Why, thank you

sir. Friedrich promised to take me to dinner in town,
if we both got off early enough."

Jesse nodded and wondered again at the dichotomy
of Sergeant Krueger's renowned harshness to recruits
and his obvious love for the crippled girl in the
wheelchair. His gentleness and deference to her was
an unceasing wonder to all who witnessed it. Cynthia
was lovely and doubtless her fluency in German helped,
but still . . . Jesse was glad he hadn't found the need
to institute any of the fraternization rules from the
other time line. Planting his beret on his head, eagle
shining, he moved toward the door.

"Evening, Cynthia."

"Good evening, Colonel."

Jesse stepped outside the newly constructed headquarters *cum* bachelor officers' quarters. Walking down
the ramp built for Cynthia's use, he glanced down the
side of the building. Like all the other new buildings
at the field, it was a simple wooden design, having
few windows, and without central heating—the lack
of which Jesse was feeling acutely, now that winter
had arrived.

Due to a recent heat spell—using the term "heat"
loosely—most of the snow that had covered the ground
the week before had melted. Jesse walked down the
damp, unpaved surface of Richter Avenue, doing his
best to avoid the worst patches of mud. He then
walked past the NCO quarters, the mess hall, the
married enlisted buildings, and the single enlisted
barracks, their new wooden walls already grayed by
the elements. Opposite the buildings, children were
playing in the parade ground, which was as yet unused
for its named purpose.

The snap of the flag at the top of the smooth wooden pole drew his eye and he felt suddenly better, less tired.

You should see the old field now, Hans. All because of you.

Jesse hadn't meant to capitalize on Hans' death, of course. But, once the initial shock had worn off and he'd been able to analyze the battle of Wismar, he had become angry. His anger wasn't directed at the Grantville leadership—he understood military necessity—but at the enemies who threatened to destroy all he knew and loved. The depth of his anger had surprised him. He had always been slow to anger and his ire had nearly always passed swiftly. Certainly, he'd never felt any particular hatred towards the enemies of the U.S. in the old time line. In reflection, he realized his anger was more than half fear—fear that, should these enemies win, there would be no starting over, since there was nowhere to run in this world. So, he had concentrated on the anger, had shaped it into a weapon. And in doing so, he had changed himself. Before Wismar, he had been a pilot playing the role of commander. Afterward, though he would never voice it, he *became* a commander, with a commander's view of things.

Within days, he had returned to Grantville, directing two pilots, Lieutenants Woodsill and Weissenbach, to take the *Las Vegas Belle II* and rejoin the ground contingent at Richter Field in Wismar. Woody and Ernst had been thrilled to be left with the only functioning aircraft—and within range of the enemy, at that. Jesse felt he had taken the edge off a good deal of that enthusiasm, and he was sure the two young pilots would follow his cautious operational instructions. They were to provide aerial reconnaissance for Gustavus Adolphus in Luebeck, and that was all. Even so, he had taken care to not stifle their spirit. A pilot's élan is as important as fuel.

Only in the past month, with the completion of two more Belles and Gustav production now running smoothly, had he relaxed his restrictions on the Wismar detachment. He'd allowed them to try their hand at rocket attacks on the enemy encampment, a duty the two young pilots had accepted with the eagerness of unleashed tigers.

Jesse had channeled his own efforts into convincing Grantville to give him the resources to accelerate aircraft production, to give him the tools to punish their enemies. While he talked practicalities with President Stearns, Admiral Simpson, and Hal Smith, to all others he spoke in terms of duty, sacrifice, and honor. As much as he hated public speaking, he gave speeches to citizen groups and retold the Battle of Wismar and Captain Richter's heroism countless times.

The story was certainly gripping. The account of a valiant few fighting against long odds with makeshift weapons—buying time, as Jesse put it, so their people could prepare for the inevitable onslaught—caught the imagination of the public. In Magdeburg even more than in Grantville. Before long, most who deemed themselves politicians in the newly formed United States of Europe had jumped on board.

Not that everything's gone my way, Jesse grumbled. *The frigging Kellys, for instance. What do those stupid politicians think we are, anyway? Boeing vs. Lockheed?*

The object of his ire came into view as he walked towards the flightline. On the opposite side of the field, a sizable building, smoke curling from one of its chimneys, stood in the midst of squalor, despite its newness. Junked cars, stacks of lumber, cans of waste, and piles of trash unidentifiable at this distance stood in front of the building's wide, closed doors. It was the Kellys' touted "Skunkworks," and Jesse's irritation surged as he thought of the waste involved.

He'd been shocked when, just as the politicians seemed certain to give him all he needed to build a fighting air force, a small but vocal faction had temporarily stopped everything by demanding competition in aircraft construction. He'd even complained to Mike Stearns, demanding that he intervene in the foolishness.

Only to be turned down. Stearns, though sympathetic, had given Jesse a short, painful lesson in politics. He'd pointed out that many thought it unfair for Wood and Smith to be given so much deference and support in their aircraft building business—never mind the fact that they had built aircraft that had proven themselves in combat and hadn't yet realized a dime in profit from the enterprise.

"And there are new angles involved too, Jesse," Stearns had explained. "Now that the Confederated Principalities of Europe is on the junk heap, replaced by the United States of Europe, we don't have the same autonomy we used to have. We're a province in the USE now, which has a federal structure. We're no longer the independent-in-all-but-name New United States."

"So?"

Mike rolled his eyes. "So stop it with the pigheaded 'I don't need no steenkeeng politics' routine, Jesse. What do you *think*? You know damn well that most of the principalities that Gustav Adolf roped into the USE were frog-marched into it. From the standpoint of those disgruntled little princelings, one of the few bright spots is that they can now make a claim to getting a piece of up-time technology."

It was Jesse's turn to roll his eyes. "You've got to be kidding! What? We're supposed to divert resources to having—who, for God's sake?—the Hessians? the Pomeranians?—start building airplanes?"

"Oh, it's not *that* bad. None of the important princes are dumb enough to think they can set up an aircraft industry right now, from scratch. But look at the issue of the Kellys from *their* point of view. As long as you and Hal Smith have a monopoly on aircraft construction—with your close ties to the federal authorities—they can't see any way to get a foot in edgewise."

Jesse made a face. "Hey, look, Mike. It's no secret that I don't like the Kellys, especially She-Who-Will-Not-Be-Named. But I never suggested they were traitors."

"You couldn't anyway, even if you did think it," said Mike forcefully. "What 'treason' would be involved? Moving their aircraft works from Grantville to Magdeburg or Kassel? That's just silly. It'd be like accusing Lockheed of 'treason' if they decided to move their works from Burbank, California, to somewhere else in the United States. We're a *federation* now, Jesse. If the Kellys wanted to, they'd have every right to pack up their operation and move to another city in the USE."

He ran fingers through his hair. "But that's not even the issue. So far as I know, the Kellys have no intention of leaving Grantville. The Kellys aren't really what's at stake, to begin with, from the standpoint of the down-time princelings. Right now, they simply want to break up what amounts to your semi-official monopoly over up-time aircraft technology. And there's only so far I can resist that pressure, without starting to feed the sentiment—and there's plenty of it—that we up-timers are dogs in a manger. We can afford some waste in aircraft production a lot more than we can afford *that* issue to start getting explosive. So live with it, Jesse."

Jesse had kept trying, even to the point of resigning as a partner in the aircraft firm, but it hadn't been enough. The powers-that-be, in their wisdom, had seen fit to authorize assistance to both firms in the form of "a suitable building, strategic materials, and such labor and facilities as are deemed necessary by the strategic resources board for aircraft construction." And so, while Hal and his workers had used the assistance to move construction of the "Gustav" model into high gear, the Kelly Aircraft Company had moved into their new digs—and, so far at least, had shown precious little for it.

But it was a done deal, so Jesse let it go. He turned his attention to the aircraft shelters he was passing, five completed now and one in progress. Three had aircraft in them, a Belle and two of the new Gustavs, low wing, powerful looking birds. Their ground crews were still working on them in the lowering sunlight, busy, purposeful. The Belle ground crew was fueling their aircraft from a horse drawn fuel bowser. At the next shelter over, the crewchief of *Gustav I*, Sergeant Hiram Winters, noticed Jesse and raised a hand. Jesse smiled and raised his own hand in greeting before he moved on.

Good kids, he smiled. *Good aircraft. Thank you, God, for both*.

He neared an airman lounging on a small tractor near the landing zone. With two hundred and thirty-five men and women now on the rolls, he no longer worried about manpower to work on the field, though the constant effort required brought to memory the old British secret for a nice lawn: good seed, plenty of water, and rolled daily for three hundred years. To that end, the tractor had a roller in tow. Filling in and smoothing out the ruts made in the runway's landing zone was a routine end-of-flying-day chore. He waved his hand down as the young man made to get off his machine.

"Good evening, Airman . . ." He looked for the airman's nametag.

"*Guten abend, Herr Oberst. Mein name ist* Fleischer. 'Gus' Fleischer."

"Fleischer." Jesse put his hands in the small of his back and stretched. "Waiting for the last aircraft?"

"*Jawohl* . . . I mean, 'Yes sir,'" Fleischer replied.

Jesse checked his watch. "Soon, I think. How long have you been with us, Fleischer?"

"*Drei,* uh, three month, Herr Colonel," Fleischer said slowly.

"And driving already, huh? Very good."

"Yes, sir." The young man lifted his chin. "I will be a pilot, someday." He lifted his arm and pointed. "Look, *Herr Oberst! Er kommt!*"

"Yes, he does," said Jesse, watching the *Belle III* slide over the field boundary and touch down. He clapped the airman on the shoulder. "Study hard, Gus, eh?"

"*Ja*, Colonel!" The young German nodded, started the tractor, and drove off proudly to his duty.

Chapter 2

Magdeburg, on the Elbe River
Capital of the United States of Europe

"Short handed again," Thorsten Engler muttered to himself, as he counted those still out sick. Fortunately, all they had to do at night was keep the furnace running until morning. Things were usually pretty quiet, although one time the gas had started to run out, and he'd had to scramble to unload the coke and load new coal in several retorts. That could be the case tonight, with the cold and the snow increasing demand for heat.

Being the recently promoted foreman for the night shift at the coal gas plant—which was almost as new as he was—Engler always tried to walk around the plant every hour, whether it was clear, rain, or snow. It was the only way to make sure everyone was awake, and it tended to keep him awake as well. Despite the snow falling, the plant was mostly clear. That was probably due to the heat of the furnace, and maybe some shoveling as well. He'd have to make sure that they continued that during the night, or he'd look bad in the morning when the plant manager arrived.

He walked around the plant, looking at the furnace and the machinery. As he had many times by now, he wished he knew more about the manufacturing processes involved in the operation. It had only been a month since the plant officially opened. He had trained for it and even helped build it, but no one here had ever seen such a collection of machinery before.

To make the situation worse, his training had been narrowly focused on the job of repairman he'd been originally hired on for, not the more general training a supervisor should get. Neither he nor the plant management had expected him to become a foreman almost as soon as he started. That was another effect of the influenza that was ravaging the city. The original foreman had been a much older man. He'd died from the disease just three weeks ago.

Everything looked good, though, so far as Thorsten could tell. He was about to head inside when he heard a faint high-pitched whistle. That was odd, he thought. The wind didn't seem strong enough for that.

But, not seeing anything amiss, he went into his office to catch up on his paperwork. With all the men out sick because of the influenza, the work records were more of a tangle than usual.

A couple of hours later, one of the workmen came into the office. That was Eric Krenz, who served the night shift as its crane operator. Since they still didn't have a full-time repairman on night shift, he also helped Thorsten in that capacity. Both single men in their mid-twenties, they'd become quite good friends in the short time since they'd started working together.

"Something's wrong, Thorsten," Krenz said. "The street lamps seem to be going out."

Thorsten quickly went outside. The lights were indeed dimming. Those farther away from the plant were already out.

"Shit. There'll be a lot of pissed people soon. Did we run out of gas?"

"I don't think so," said Eric. "It's only been two or three hours since we started this batch. I don't know what's going on."

Engler decided to start at the beginning, with the coal loading operation. That was being handled by Robert Stiteler these past few days. Stiteler was an Alsatian, one of the many immigrants who'd arrived in Magdeburg over the past year. He normally helped Krenz operate the steam-powered crane that moved the kegs containing the coal tar products and ammonia water. But with so many of the men off sick, he'd agreed to handle loading the coal instead. It was back-breaking work, using a shovel instead of a steam crane, but he'd done a fine job with it. He'd kept the coal going in and the coke going out, which was what mattered.

When Engler appeared in the furnace room, with Krenz in tow, Stiteler broke off from his work and leaned his shovel against one of the stanchions that supported the furnace room's walls and roof. As a safety measure, the stanchion was much thicker and sturdier than it really needed to be. The furnace "room" was really a big shed, with walls and a roof made of thin planks just thick enough to handle rain and snow.

"Evening, Thorsten," he said pleasantly. As was true of the most of the men working in the plant—anywhere in Magdeburg—the Alsatian immigrant had quickly adopted the informality favored in work places by the American up-timers. All the more so since the Committees of Correspondence who were almost a separate, informal government in the capital city insisted on it as a matter of principle. They had members everywhere, especially in the ranks of the industrial workers and their unions. Thorsten wasn't a member of the CoCs himself, simply because he'd been too busy for the meetings involved. But his friend Eric Krenz belonged, as did perhaps a fourth of the workmen in the plant.

"Evening, Robert," he said, trying to be just as pleasant but wanting to get on to the problem at hand. Normally, he would have taken the time to chat idly with Stiteler for a minute or two, just to give the man a legitimate excuse to take a rest from the grueling labor of shoveling coal down the chute into the retorts. "We seem to be losing gas somewhere along the way. Are you having any problems?"

Stiteler shook his head. "No, nothing."

Thorsten inspected the furnace, which seemed fine. Then he headed toward the gas main.

Stumbling over something, he looked down. There was a grate lying on the floor, which he hadn't spotted before because it was half-covered in the coal dust that was spread over much of room. Frowning, Thorsten looked over at the furnace again and noticed for the first time that the grate that should have been located on the coal chute was missing. Instead, the opening for the grate seemed to be covered with something solid, from what little of it Thorsten could see because of the coal dust.

He looked back down at the object he'd stumbled

over. "Robert, what is this grate doing here? And what have you got covering the hole it was on?"

Stiteler had gone back to shoveling, but now looked over. "Oh, that damned thing. I took it off two days ago and replaced it with some wood. It kept getting fouled with the smaller pieces of coal. Made it hard to shovel the coal in, because it kept catching the blade. This way works much better."

Engler hissed in a breath. "Robert, it's *supposed* to get fouled. You don't want the fine pieces . . ."

Robert was frowning at him. "Why? What's the matter?"

Truth be told, Engler wasn't sure himself why the grate was important. But he had a vague memory of one of the up-time engineers who'd designed the plant telling him that it was. If he remembered correctly, the function of the grate was to make sure that only the larger chunks of coal got into the furnace itself. If you let the coal pieces that were too fine into the furnace, especially the dust . . .

He couldn't remember what would happen. The foreman's training he'd gotten—all half a day of it—had been too quick and hurried for him to remember a lot of what he'd been told. But it was certainly nothing good.

"Put the grate back on," he ordered, "and *don't* take it off again."

Moving more urgently now, he began moving down the main, inspecting the big pipe. Eric Krenz came with him.

"The main looks wrong," Thorsten said. "See, Eric?"

Krenz nodded. "The pipe should be entirely red hot, but only the top half seems red. It stops at the bend."

There was a loud crack from inside the furnace, the sound of metal breaking.

"What was that?" half-shouted Stiteler, stumbling back and almost dropping his shovel.

"I don't know," Thorsten replied. "I've never seen something like this." He began to smell smoke. "Smoke?"

"Look, Thorsten!" said Eric. "There's your smoke!"

Sure enough. Smoke was starting to pour out of one of the short smokestacks next to the furnace.

Understanding came instantly to Thorsten. "One of the retorts must have broken, and the coal has caught fire. But why?"

He looked again at the gas main, thinking quickly. With the grate removed, small pieces of coal—a lot of it nothing more than dust—would have . . .

He wasn't sure. But with the inside of the gas main lined with coal tar, as it inevitably became . . . and as gummy as that stuff was . . . he had a bad feeling that the coal dust would have started piling up in there, constricting the main.

"There has to be a blockage," he stated firmly. "Quick, turn the gas off!"

"If the coal has caught fire in there," said Eric, "that won't do any good. We can't put that out."

Thorsten wavered for a second. He wanted to handle this problem himself, but not bringing the fire under control could be disastrous. "Yes, you're right. Run over and get the fire brigade now!"

"Please get these messages out ASAP," Mike Stearns said, handing the radio operator a sheaf of papers. "And let me know if any of the messages are not acknowledged."

"Yes, sir," the operator said. "Conditions seem pretty good tonight. I'll encrypt them and get them out. Any special priorities?"

"Not really. But send the one to my wife first, please. And make sure the one to Colonel Wood gets through. I'd like him up here tomorrow, if it's at all possible."

Mike turned and walked out of the room. The Marine on guard outside stood at attention as he walked by, and nodded in response to Mike's "good night." He was leaving the building when he heard a bell ringing in the distance and the clattering of horses. By the time he was at the entrance to the USE government's main building—the *Hans Richter Palace,* to use its official name, although most people just called it "Government House"—a dozen Marines and sailors had come out of the nearby barracks, apparently curious about what was going on.

Almost immediately, they heard the horses slow and then stop. Realizing it was close, Mike said "Let's go, guys." With his impromptu military escort, he headed toward the commotion at a brisk walk.

Thomas Kruz, Chief of the First Fire Brigade in Magdeburg, had been playing cards with several of his men when the runner arrived with the news. His men knew their jobs, and they'd quickly hitched their horses to the fire wagon and ridden out into the night. The wagon was new, a first-of-its-kind steam pump fire wagon, and he was proud of it. He and his men had trained with it over and over, until they could operate it in their sleep. He was sure beyond any doubt they were prepared for a fire.

Within a couple of minutes, they had reached the coal gas plant. When they arrived, they saw thick black smoke rising from one of the smokestacks. The snow falling everywhere else turned into steam before it struck the furnace. But, fortunately, there were no flames, no exposed fire, nothing that really screamed *Emergency!*

He saw someone running towards him. As he got closer, Kruz recognized the night shift foreman, Thorsten Engler. As it happened, they were neighbors.

"There's a fire in the furnace, Thomas," Thorsten said, "and we can't put it out. It could destroy the furnace."

Chief Kruz had toured the coal gas plant, several times, since a fire here was one of his biggest fears. Still, he really didn't know much more about it than most people did—including, unfortunately, most of the people working in the plant itself. The drive to expand industry in Magdeburg in response to the war with the League of Ostend was forcing people to take shortcuts and use makeshifts everywhere. His fire crew was actually quite exceptional in having had the time to be trained properly. Most of the factories in the city were being run by half-trained people, with foremen who often had little more training than the men they supervised.

Quickly, he looked toward the area of the plant where the vats of pitch and other flammable materials were stored. But they seemed to be safe, not being very close to the furnace. He breathed a sigh of relief that his worst fears were not realized.

"What's the problem, Thorsten?"

"I'm not sure. But I think the gas main is blocked

and the gases are backing up into the furnace. It's starting to break on the inside."

"Show me where it's blocked."

Kruz followed Engler into the furnace room. Once inside, they walked around to the other side of the furnace, and Thorsten pointed out a big wrought iron tube, the upper half of it glowing red against the dim light. "You see? That's the main. It's got to be clogged. The gasses are backing up into the furnace."

The fire chief wasn't sure what to do. He'd been trained to deal with open fires, flames. This . . .

"What can we do to help, Thorsten?"

Engler ran fingers through his thick black hair. "We have to stop the fire and cool the furnace, before there is any more damage. This plant is providing gas to light the street, to heat and run several factories here. It is important!"

"Yes, fine, but what's the best way to do that? Thorsten, we can't pump water over the furnace, because we can't keep it from hitting those metal doors." He pointed at the doors to the retorts which, like the gas main, were glowing dull red with heat. "The water could well cause them to crack."

Exasperated, Engler shook his head. "You're right. And it wouldn't put out the fire inside the furnace anyway. We have to put that out first and let things cool down."

They hurried back around to the front, where the smoke from the left smokestack was, if anything, increasing. One of the plant workers was already there. Another of Kruz's neighbors, as it happened, the crane operator Eric Krenz.

"There! The air is drawn into the furnace over there!" Krenz was pointing to a smokestack on the right. His finger moved over. "And the smoke is coming out there. We change the direction every ten minutes. We need to pump water in both."

Finally having clear directions, Kruz nodded vigorously. "You three, set up the pump," the chief instructed his men. "You two, run a canvas hose down to the river. We'll pump water from there."

He looked over the situation. Pumping water there seemed reasonable. It wouldn't hurt to try. "That furnace is very hot. Stand well back!"

Within three minutes, his men had set up the pump, attached a hose from the river and two hoses to the pump, and had the steam engine up to heat.

By now, a small crowd had gathered outside the plant, and were watching them. Kruz took a quiet pride at how his fire crew was holding up under pressure. Two men were holding each fire hose, one was stationed at the river to control the hose there, and another man reported to the Chief: "We're ready."

"Start up the pump," Kruz directed.

The Marine sergeant at Mike's side leaned over toward him. "Is there anything you want us to do, Mr. Pres—ah, I mean, Prime Minister?"

Mike had to fight down a little smile. The sergeant was an up-timer, and like most such was still getting used to peculiar "foreign" titles like prime minister instead of the familiar president. Not surprising, of course. The United States of Europe had been in existence for less than three months.

"No, Sergeant. The firemen are here and they seem

to know what they're doing. We'd just be getting in their way."

He almost ordered everyone to go back to the barracks, but . . .

Didn't. The problem was that Mike knew full well just how desperately undertrained most people were in Magdeburg's new industrial plants. The capital of the new USE was also rapidly becoming both its largest city and its major manufacturing center. Those were both developments that Mike was encouraging every way he possibly could. Grantville was simply too small and too isolated in the Thuringian hills to serve as the center for the new society coming into existence in central Europe. Nor, even if its location had been better, could it ever grow very big because of the surrounding terrain.

He'd been very cold-blooded about it all, willing to accept the risks for the benefits. However diplomatic he might be, most times, and however much he was willing to tack and veer in the requisite political maneuvers, Mike never lost sight for a moment of the fact that what he was really doing was organizing a revolution. And one of the lessons he'd taken from the voracious reading of history he'd been doing since the Ring of Fire—with advice from Melissa Mailey and his wife Rebecca, who read even more extensively than he did—was that revolutions were greatly assisted by having a big capital city that doubled as a nation's industrial center. The role that, in other revolutions in another universe, had been played by cities like Paris and "Red Berlin" and St. Petersburg, Mike intended to be played in this one by Magdeburg.

But nothing came free, and the price they paid for

that explosive growth was inevitable. Everything and everybody was stretched very thin, and they weren't so much cutting corners as lopping them off with an ax. With his own extensive experience in coal mining and stevedoring, Mike knew full well just how dangerous that could be.

So, he decided to stick around for a bit. True enough, the firemen seemed to know what they were doing. However, that could simply mean that they were efficiently going about their work, but the work itself wasn't what they should be doing.

It was hard to know. The sight in front of him, mostly in darkness with a soft snowfall obscuring everything still further, was a pretty good summary of the whole situation in Europe as the year 1633 came to a close.

Chapter 3

Within a few seconds, two thick streams of water began arching into the air and falling into the smokestacks. A thick cloud of steam flashed instantly into the air, as the water contacted the hot brick. Fortunately, the smokestacks were ten feet high, and the steam flashed above them, so the firemen weren't cooked where they stood. Courageously, they continued pumping water into the smokestacks.

Then disaster struck. The incredibly hot firebrick in the reverberatory furnace had some resistance to water at room temperature, but none at 900C. It dissolved under the impact of the water, collapsing and blocking both smokestacks, trapping high temperature steam within. The main furnace chamber, containing the retorts, held.

"My God!" the chief reacted. He looked at the foreman and the other two plant workers, who were staring, mouth open, at the damage.

"Stop the pump! Get the wagon back! Everyone get back!" he directed. He stared at the furnace. It was a ruin, obviously enough. But at least the smoke had stopped. The fire was probably out.

✧   ✧   ✧

"Hell's bells," Mike hissed, when he heard the bricks collapse. "We could use Jerry Trainer right now," he said to no one in particular.

"What's happening, sir?" the sergeant asked.

"No idea," he replied. "We'll keep the men here, though, just in case we're needed."

By now, they were in the middle of a large crowd, standing behind a very sturdy-looking waist-high brick wall that surrounded the plant everywhere except along the river. The men at the plant had ignited torches to replace the gas lamps, and the faint light and drifting snow gave the scene an eerie look.

"Do you see flames there?" One of the sailors pointed to the location where the gas main entered the furnace room.

Mike squinted, trying to see through the snowfall. It was very faint, but something did seem to be burning. And the flames were blue.

Chief Kruz and his men were also watching the furnace. "Look!" one of them yelled. From closer up, very faint blue flames were apparent where the gas main entered the furnace, and also around the doors of the retorts.

"Get the men back! Back!" Kruz had never seen flames like that, and he didn't like it.

The flames were indeed blue, the color of burning hydrogen gas. When water was pumped into the furnace, besides destroying the firebrick, it reacted with the red-hot coal in the furnace to make hydrogen and carbon monoxide. The hydrogen, being very light, pushed the coal gas down as it sought the highest elevation. It then began leaking out between the firebrick and the gas main, as well as around the retorts. When the hydrogen reached the air it burned, creating high temperature steam, which began to eat through the firebrick. The structure holding the gas main in the furnace dissolved, and the pipe shifted. When that happened, all the remaining hydrogen rushed out, and air rushed in to fill the gap, where it mixed with coal gas into an explosive mixture.

The fire chief was not positioned to see the gas main shift, but one of his men was. He saw a flash as the hydrogen escaped and exploded, and yelled "Down!" A split second later, the coal gas-oxygen mixture exploded.

The gas main pipe went flying end-over-end, spewing smaller pieces of red-hot iron and crashing into a large metal distilling vat. Some of the retorts also split, blasting out of the furnace like cannon fire. The thin walls of the furnace rooms came off, as did large sections of the roof.

One of the retorts smashed into Stiteler and slammed him into the column behind him, killing him instantly. The shovel flew from his hand and Engler and Krenz ducked to avoid being hit by it. Luckily for them, as it happened, because a second piece of wreckage hurtled right through the air where they'd been standing a second earlier.

Another piece of a retort went through the thin wall as if it weren't there and landed on the barge holding the coal for the plant. Another, much bigger one, did the same thing to a different wall—and then shattered the wall of an adjacent factory as it struck, instantly killing two workers and starting the structure on fire.

Stone, iron and coal sprayed in all directions from the impact site. In other cases, only the doors to the retorts flew out, red hot frisbees delivering death and destruction. One of these struck the fireman holding the hose by the river, cutting him in half and throwing what was left of him into the waters of the Elbe. Another flew across the street into an apartment building, starting yet another fire. Fortunately, no one was killed outright, although a young mother was badly hurt and the baby she'd been feeding would wind up losing his arm below the elbow.

The last one flew unerringly into the vats of coal tar products, badly damaging the support structure for one of the vats. At the same time, pieces of burning coal from the retorts flew into the air, bombarding those passersby not lucky or smart enough to be crouching behind the wall or under shelter.

Mike rose from behind the wall and briefly looked at his escort to make sure they were unharmed. Some of the sailors and Marines were purposefully moving to put out flames and administer first aid to bystanders who had been hit by flying coal. The coal plant itself seemed to be fairly free of flames, now. There were a few piles of flaming coal but little other damage beyond the explosion. As he watched, he saw two people come stumbling to the wall.

"What happened to the plant?" the sergeant asked them.

Now leaning with both hands on the wall, one of

the men shook his head. "I don't know. Robert . . ." He shook his head again. "Robert Stiteler. He was killed. I don't believe this."

"Do you work here?" Mike asked.

"Yes. I am the night shift foreman. Thorsten Engler." He nodded to the man next to him. "This is Eric Krenz, the crane operator."

Hearing a new sound, of collapsing metal, Engler and Krenz turned their heads around to look back. As they and Mike watched, the damaged vat began to shift, finally falling on its side. It impacted with a loud crack, and gallons of thick pitch began to ooze out.

By now, the fire chief had reorganized his men and moved to put out the fires in the adjacent factory and the apartment buildings across the street. Only one other structure was aflame, the roof of a shed near the river, away from both the coal tar and the machinery.

"What's in that shed?" Mike asked.

Engler looked over. "Nothing much," he said. "Just fertilizer. For growing plants."

Mike frowned. "Why do you have fertilizer at the coal gas plant?"

"It's very new. They call it . . . 'ammonium nitrate,' I think. Supposed to be the best fertilizer ever. We make it from some of the waste from the coal tar."

Mike would swear he could literally feel the blood draining from his face. *Ammonium nitrate, for the love of God!*

Bituminous coal mining operations rarely used explosives much, any longer, but he'd been around enough blasting operations to know what the stuff was used for besides farming.

The sergeant was staring at him. "Is it dangerous, sir?"

"Hell, yes, it's dangerous," Mike replied. "There was a cargo ship full of it in Texas City that blew up once and took out most of the town—not to mention that it was the stuff that provided most of the force for the Oklahoma City bombing."

Mike looked again at the shed. The flames had moved down from the roof to the walls, and the whole thing was being consumed. "Everybody down!" he yelled. Then, repeated the yell for the benefit of the firemen, accompanying it with frantic arm waving.

Fortunately, the fire chief wasn't pigheaded. He immediately ordered his men out of the area and behind the wall. Mike grabbed Engler and Krenz and dragged them over the wall, then dropped down himself below the top.

For perhaps twenty seconds, nothing happened. A few people started to get up, here and there. Then there was a tremendous explosion that seemed to obliterate everything in a sheer blast of noise. Half-dazed, Mike saw one of the bystanders who'd been incautious enough to raise his head over the wall get decapitated. By what, he had no idea. A piece of brick, who knew? One moment the man had a head, the next moment a corpse was collapsing to the ground with blood gushing out of a neck stump.

When it seemed to be over, Mike carefully peered over the top of the wall. There was a ten-foot crater where the shed had been. Some of its flaming remnants had apparently landed on the coal barge, and were completing its destruction.

Mike shifted his gaze, and saw that the vat that

had tipped over seemed mostly empty. However, two more of the vats had shifted from the impact, and were now also tilted.

Engler's head had come up next to his, with Krenz following a second later. Mike pointed at the vats. "What's in those vats?"

"Coal tar," said Krenz. "Different kinds. We separate them, and sell the different kinds."

"The one that fell on the ground contained pitch," Engler added. "We usually don't have more than a few days' worth; there's a lot of demand for it. That one"—he pointed to the one starting to list—"contains something called 'light benzoils.' We don't get much call for it, so we've been saving it up to sell to the Americans."

"How much of it is stored up?"

"I add a new barrel or two to that vat every day," said Krenz. "Maybe a couple of hundred barrels worth."

Mike felt his face paling again. That was the equivalent of several thousand gallons of gasoline. If it spread and ignited, half the city was likely to burn down before it was all over.

He turned to the sergeant. "Get every available man from the base."

He turned to another Marine. "See if you can find Gunther Achterhof, the CoC guy for this district. We need all the manpower we can get. Tell him to bring shovels, buckets, whatever will fight the fire."

He looked back again. Fortunately, the pitch still hadn't caught, despite the hot fragments of furnace littering the ground. "Two of you Marines get shovels and buckets and get those fragments out of here before they ignite the pitch."

Once those pressing immediate tasks were seen to,

he turned to the contingent of sailors and Marines who were gathered around him. "We've got to keep that vat from tipping over. Get some long pieces of lumber from the dockyards. Get block and tackle. Fast!"

Half a dozen sailors took off, heading for the base. As he looked again, he saw the pitch slowly oozing out of the plant and into the street. Beyond it, he saw the road leading to the open end of the sewer under construction. "Christ on a crutch," he said. "If the stuff in that vat gets in the sewers, the entire city will go."

"There isn't enough time," Engler said. "We have to get in there now." He climbed over the wall and into the plant's yard, heading for the coal tar vats. Krenz came right behind him.

Mike stared at them, decided they were right, and followed himself. His men joined him.

The ground was an obstacle course, requiring them to zigzag to avoid the still-hot debris from the explosion. They ran over to the fire chief, who was lying on the ground, stunned. "Wake up!" Mike shouted. "You've got to get your pump going."

"We still have steam, we can pump!" one of the firemen yelled, having heard him. "But we have to put out those fires now." He was pointing to the apartment buildings, and Mike could see that he was right. As tightly packed as those buildings were throughout most of Magdeburg, if a fire got out of control it would be almost impossible to stop.

One of the other firemen pulled out a knife and cut away the harness for one of the horses. The animal's back had been shattered by a big chunk of flying debris. The fire chief staggered to his feet and looked around. The first fireman ran over to him. "Sir, there are buildings on fire. We've got to put them out now!"

Mike came to a quick decision. "Go," he said. "My men and I will take care of the plant."

The fire chief nodded, and stumbled after the pump as his men led it away.

Mike continued through the obstacle course, finally arriving at the upended vat, He looked beyond it to the damaged one. It was still standing, but was now starting to leak a thin liquid on the ground.

"Make way!" Krenz yelled. He carried an empty barrel across the pitch to put it under the leak. "That won't stop it for long."

"We've got to jack up that platform, or that won't matter," one of the sailors said.

"Over there," Mike directed. "The platform for the destroyed vat. See if any of the wood can be salvaged." Several men started pulling lumber off the ground. Others pushed the grounded vat a few feet out of the way. They replaced parts of the damaged supports.

"The vat's too badly damaged," Engler said. Mike could see that he was right. The leak was increasing. They had to move the tar before it ruptured entirely. As he watched, the first barrel filled up and overflowed. The liquid quickly overtook the thick pitch in its downhill flow. A couple of men rolled the barrel out of the way, and replaced it with a new barrel.

"We can't keep this up. We don't have enough barrels." Mike glanced at the nearby steam crane and turned to Krenz. "You said you filled the vats. Can you put those barrels into other vats?"

"Yes," he replied. "But it takes time to bring the boiler to steam. We don't have enough time."

One of the Marines pointed to the burning coals scattered across the yard. "We can use that coal."

"Do it," Mike said. He directed some of the newly arrived troops to use their shovels to fill the firebox of the crane. Others, he directed to help the fire brigade put out the nearby fires.

Krenz sat down in the crane, then yelled, stood up, and batted a small lump of coal from the seat. Despite the tension of the moment, a burst of laughter went up from the men who saw. Krenz grinned himself, shaking his head ruefully, before he sat back down at the controls.

The crane lifted its bucket, which Krenz sat down next to the first barrel. By this point, there were three filled barrels, and the last one was almost full. Several men tipped one of the barrels into the bucket, which was quickly raised and poured into a different vat.

Mike looked at the barrels and the vat. "It's not going to be enough," he muttered. "It's just a finger in the dike." He called several of the men, both naval personnel and the CoC members who were starting to arrive.

"It's not enough. We've got to keep it out of the sewers." He looked around. "Some of you, fill in the end of the sewer. The rest of you, we need to direct what gets out into the river. Start a trench here."

Gunther Achterhof came running up with a number of his people. "This looks bad, Prime Minister. How can we help?"

"Could your people relieve my troops helping the fire brigade? We've got to handle this leak before it gets in the sewers."

"Yes, of course."

Mike turned back, to see that the trench was beginning to take shape. But the leak was getting worse, and
was clearly winning. He moved back to Krenz and the
crane. "The leak is speeding up; soon it'll be more than
we can stop. How can we redirect the benzoil?"

"It would take too long to use the crane to dig a
trench," Krenz said, "and this is the wrong scoop,
anyway."

"Okay, then. Can you use the crane to knock the
vat so that it goes into the river?"

Mike thought, briefly and little ruefully, of what
environmentalists in the world they'd left behind
would say to a thousand gallons or so of toxic organic
chemicals being poured into the river that ran right
through a major city. But they were three and half
centuries away in a different universe and didn't have
a town burning down around them.

"I can lift the side of the vat with the scoop. The
crane isn't strong enough to pick it up, but that might
be enough. Make a shitpot of a mess, though."

"If most of that liquid reaches the sewer, we'll have
a lot bigger mess on our hands. I'll tell the men."

Mike went over to the men desperately unload-
ing the vat. "We're going to lift that side of the vat,
and pour the liquid into the river. Get some long
pieces of lumber as levers, and we'll try to direct
which way it goes. The rest of you, get the hell out
of here. Move!"

Krenz carefully brought the scoop under the side of
the vat, and two sailors used pieces of wood to direct
it into place. Several others braced lumber against the
vat, now pouring its flammable contents at a rapid

rate onto the ground. While they did that, the people digging the ditch started running from the plant.

"Now!" Mike yelled, and the scoop lifted up. Under the combined efforts of the crane and the men, the platform started to collapse on the opposite side, and the vat slowly started to topple. A moment later, most of the contents poured out of the vat and surged towards the river. He grimaced as he saw a small stream of it heading for the base of the furnace. The chemicals lapped against the side of the furnace, where the heat caused some of it to vaporize. It touched some of the burning coal near the furnace, and there was an almost-explosion as gallons of it caught fire. Flames raced outward, following the path to the river and entering it. Only there did they stop. Other flames raced towards the other vats, but fortunately couldn't quite reach them before they burned themselves out.

It was over. Leaving behind a ruined coal gas plant and one unholy mess, true. Not to mention a number of people killed and injured. But at least an industrial accident hadn't become transformed into a city-wide catastrophe.

Mike sat down and caught his breath. Thorsten Engler sat down next to him, and a naval rating on the other side.

"What a cluster-fuck," the rating said.

Engler rubbed his face wearily. "Poor Robert. And all of it because of a stupid grate."

Mike didn't say anything. Eventually, he'd get a full report of what had caused the disaster, in considerable detail. But he already knew the gist of it.

They were pushing too hard, because of the war.

And the only way he could see to end it was to win the war as soon as possible.

When Mike got back to the government building, he went directly to the radio room.

"Did we hear anything—"

Smiling, the operator held up a sheet of paper. "Yes, Prime Minister. Your wife is fine and she says—"

"Not her," Mike said impatiently. "I meant did we get anything from Colonel Wood?"

The radio operator stared at him for a moment. Then, clearing his throat. "Ah, yes, sir. He'll fly up here tomorrow. He'll be here by noon, he says."

"Good." Seeing the operator still staring at him, Mike smiled a bit crookedly. "And, now, yes. Of course I'd like to see the message from my wife."

Chapter 4

Admiral John Chandler Simpson quietly slid himself back into his seat in the chamber of the new royal palace that was being used for public musical performances until the still-newer music center was completed. The gesture was smooth and practiced, as was his wife Mary's *sang-froid* at the abrupt departure and return of her husband in the middle of a performance. She was accustomed to the problem, and had been for decades.

True, in times past in Pittsburgh her husband would leave because some assistant whispered urgent news in his ear concerning his large petrochemical corporation—not because of an explosion so loud it had rattled the windows in the chamber. But, from Mary's viewpoint, the distinction was minor. When moving in high society, one always maintained one's cool—even if no one would think of using such a gauche term to describe the behavior. Appearances weren't everything, to be sure. But they mattered.

"An industrial accident of some sort," he whispered into her ear. "A bad one, it seems. But from what I could determine, no enemy action seems to be involved."

Her responding nod was a minute thing. To all

41

outward appearances, all her attention was focused on the performance. Which, in fact, almost all of it actually was.

Frescobaldi, for the love of God!

The man *himself,* that was to say. Truth be told, in the world somewhere on the other side of the Ring of Fire, Mary Simpson had never been all that fond of Frescobaldi's music. She hadn't been very fond of any music between that of Monteverdi and Bach, in fact. Like most classical music enthusiasts, she'd generally considered the whole seventeenth century something of a musical desert between the great eras of the High Renaissance and the Baroque. A great period in western civilization in terms of the visual arts, of course, but not music. Perhaps aficionados of the organ felt differently about the matter, she supposed, but the organ was very far from her favorite musical instrument.

But that was then and there, and this was here and now. And the fact remained that Girolamo Frescobaldi was one of the tiny number of composers whose name and music would survive for three and a half centuries. And not simply as a footnote in scholarly studies, either—some of his music was still in the standard repertoire, in the universe they'd left behind. Not much of it, true, and that almost entirely organ music. Still he was a genuine *name*—and he was here in person.

Mary was quite simply thrilled to death, whatever she thought of the man's music itself. Especially since she was pretty sure that her relentless campaign— sophisticated, suave, yes, yes, but still relentless—to persuade Frescobaldi to resign his post as organist

for the Medicis in Florence and set up in Magdeburg
was nearing success.

Fortunately, Amalie Elizabeth shared her enthusiasm for music. The landgravine of Hesse-Kassel
was even, unlike Mary, a fan of organ music. True,
her husband Wilhelm V had instituted tight budget
limits in order to pay off the debts of his profli-
gate father Moritz. But Hesse-Kassel was a wealthy
enough principality that even with limits, Amalie
Elizabeth still had some money to throw at music
and the arts. So, Mary was able to waggle a very
nice stipend under Frescobaldi's nose if he moved
to Magdeburg. That, combined with the fascination
the composer and keyboard performer had for the
new innovations brought by the up-timers ought to
do the trick. In that respect, and despite being now
middle-aged, Frescobaldi was no different than almost
all musicians of the era.

Still, she couldn't deny she was a bit relieved when
Frescobaldi finally stood up from the harpsichord
where he'd been playing what seemed like an endless series of pleasant but slight toccatas. Mary was
even less fond of the harpsichord than she was of
the organ. Why subject oneself to that damn *tinkle-
tinkle-tinkle* when you could listen to the rich sounds
of a pianoforte?

The auditorium was drowned in applause, to which
Mary added her own vigorous share. She even whistled,
something she'd never have dreamed of doing in the
concert halls she'd left behind. But she'd discovered
that seventeenth-century music patrons, from royalty
on down, had a far more raucous notion of applause
than their counterparts possessed in the twentieth

century. And, well, as a child Mary had discovered she was a superb whistler—an uncouth skill which, sadly, she'd had to abandon once she grew old enough to participate in proper society.

She caught a glimpse of her husband grimacing slightly, out of the corner of her eye.

"Hey, look," she murmured, "I'm a *great* whistler. Being able to do it again makes up for a lot. Almost makes up for seventeenth-century plumbing."

Her husband's grimace deepened. "Mary, nothing makes up for the plumbing in the here and how. But that's not why I was wincing. I simply can't for the life of me understand—never could—why anyone would applaud a performer who subjected them to that damn harpsichord. *Tinkle-tinkle-tinkle.* It's like listening to a concerto for nails-scratching-a-blackboard and orchestra."

Mary chuckled. "Well, take heart. Our very own Marla is up next."

That announcement caused John Simpson to lean back in his chair with some degree of anticipation. Mary had always had protégés in the past. Marla Linder was the latest; a young woman Mary had discovered in Grantville who, while she might not be a prodigy, was clearly gifted. She had been their guest in Magdeburg the last few weeks, preparing for this concert. Having heard her singing snippets of songs around their townhouse, John was actually looking forward to hearing her.

The harpsichord had been moved out of the way and the grand piano muscled into position. John joined the applause as Marla came out, gave a nod of her head in acknowledgment, then sat and began. Several selections followed, all sounding somewhat familiar to him, ending with a Chopin showpiece. Loud applause erupted. After it died down, John leaned over to Mary. "I think that made Signor Frescobaldi sound a bit insipid." He smiled at her frown.

Marla returned, taking a stand in front of the piano. What followed was remarkable, even to John's less than trained ears. Song followed song, lyrical, polished, enrapting; classical was followed by show tunes, ending with Christmas music. Some were sung as duets or ensembles, one with her violinist fiancé Franz Sylwester, but most were solos. The final piece was "Ave, Maria," during which John looked over to see a bit of moisture in Mary's eyes. Truth to tell, he had a bit of a lump in his own throat.

After the concert was over, John Simpson waited while his wife did her usual gadding about, congratulating the performers, chatting with—or chatting up, rather—various key members of the nobility and wealthy merchants present, comparing notes quickly with Amalie Elizabeth and the abbess of Quedlinburg. The usual conspiratorial business of the dame of Magdeburg, in her drive to turn the brand new USE's brand new capital city into one of Europe's cultural powerhouses.

To Simpson's amusement, some of the city's newspapers were already starting to use that title for her. He wondered if they'd come up with it on their own, or if somehow they'd discovered that in a different universe Pittsburgh's newspapers had often called her "the Dame of the Three Rivers" and decided it was catchy.

Whatever. Over the years, he'd learned to be patient about the whole business, even though he had very little interest in the matter himself. As one of Pittsburgh's premier industrialists, he'd found Mary's constant cultural and philanthropic enterprises had added a great deal to his own prestige and status. Now as an admiral in the USE's growing little navy—*the* admiral, really—he knew her activities would have the same effect. More so, probably, in this world than the one they'd left behind.

So, he waited. Still, it was with some relief that he was finally able to escort her out of the palace. He hadn't let any of it show, but he was actually quite concerned about that industrial accident. True, the location of it wasn't close enough to the navy yard to pose any direct threat to his own enterprises. But as stretched thin as all of Magdeburg's industries were, any major disaster would have an impact—especially since his naval building projects were the main customer for a lot of those industries.

As soon as they stepped out of the palace onto the portico, his concern spiked sharply. The portico was elevated a good fifteen feet above the rest of Magdeburg—a city whose terrain was as flat as a pancake, where it wasn't outright marshland—with a wide stone staircase descending to the street below. From that perch, they had a good view of the Elbe.

"Oh . . . my . . . God . . ." said Mary, staring.

The portico was packed with people, staring along with them.

Suddenly, Mary chuckled. Almost a giggle. "Well, we won't be able to make jokes about Cleveland any more."

The nonsensical comment jarred Simpson out of his anxiety enough to look at her. "Excuse me?"

"The Cuyahoga, remember?"

Simpson still couldn't make any sense out of what she was saying.

"The river that burned? That song by Randy Newman?"

"Oh. Yes."

He looked back. True enough, the Elbe itself seemed to be aflame. That was an illusion, he knew. Somehow a large quantity of flammable substances must have gotten spilled into the river and had caught fire. It wasn't really as dangerous as it looked, since even the slow current of the Elbe would soon enough carry it away. Assuming it hadn't burned out by then, which it probably would. Whatever was burning there had to be some sort of light oils, floating on the surface. There simply couldn't be that much of it, given the still-primitive state of the USE's petroleum industry.

Nevertheless . . . the navy yard was downstream. As dark as it was, with a light snowfall, Simpson couldn't actually see it. But he knew the location of the Yard perfectly. The edges of the flames might already have reached it by now.

"I need to get down there."

"Yes, dear, of course. I'll come with you."

With Mary in tow, Simpson shouldered his way through the little mob on the stairs, being as polite about it as he could, but not to the point of being delayed. There would be a wait anyway, to get a carriage, once they reached the street. He wanted to be one of the first in line.

As it happened, however, no wait was necessary.

By the time he got down to the street, he discovered that there was a Marine carriage already drawn up for him.

Lieutenant Franz-Leo Chomse emerged from the carriage and held the door open for them. "I assumed you'd wish to be taken to the navy yard, sir."

Simpson was pleased to see him. Partly because of his general anxiety, but also because it demonstrated once again that Chomse was turning into an excellent aide. He would have taken this initiative on his own, of course. Chomse wouldn't ever replace Eddie Cantrell somewhere in that place in Simpson's heart he almost never admitted existed, even to himself. But as an admiral's aide, he was actually better. If he had less of Eddie's occasional brilliance he had a lot more in the way of methodical thoughtfulness—and, thankfully, none of the up-time redhead's annoying rambunctiousness.

"Thank you, Lieutenant. Yes, I would, please."

John and Mary entered the carriage and took their seats. Chomse joined them on the bench opposite, after a quick command to the driver. No sooner had he closed the door than the carriage set off.

Almost immediately, Mary got jostled into her husband. "You and your blasted notions of military protocol," she muttered.

Simpson ignored the wisecrack. Like most people, Mary thought using a wheeled carriage in the streets of Magdeburg was just silly. Between the ruts and the mud and the potholes—not to mention those few stretches which had been cobblestoned, which were often worse—riding through Magdeburg in a wheeled contrivance guaranteed a rough ride. Bruises, often enough. Far better to take one of the more common conveyances, which were essentially small palanquins toted between two horses, like covered litters. Or four horses, in the case of big ones. The conveyances never had direct contact with the street, since the legs and hooves of the horses absorbed the impact.

But Simpson found the contraptions repellent and insisted on "proper" carriages for the Navy and the Marines. He wasn't sure why, actually. In public, even to Mary, he stood stoutly by his claim that the arcane demands of military protocol required wheels. But he suspected it was really an emotional residue from the Vietnam War. A war which he had faithfully served in, as a junior officer, but had detested just as much as almost anyone in the military at the time.

The seventeenth-century palanquins, in some vague way, had an oriental flavor to them. And not the Orient of Vietnam's peasants and poor town dwellers, which he had often found irritating—their consequences, rather—but had never despised. Poverty was simply what it was, no more to be sneered at than sneering at the winds or the tides. No, the palanquins some-how reminded him of South Vietnam's elite, a class of people he had come to loathe, as had most American officers. He had no desire whatever to infuse that spirit into the ranks of his new navy, even indirectly or purely symbolically. *Real* soldiers would have their teeth rattle when they rode in carriages, damnation.

Fine, it was silly. So was war, if you looked at it from a certain perspective. But war was now John Simpson's business, and he took it seriously

"What happened, Lieutenant?" he asked Chomse. "Do we know any details yet?"

"Almost all of them, sir. A large number of naval ratings and Marines were involved in dealing with the disaster at the coal gas plant. The prime minister happened to be nearby when the fire started, and he pretty much took charge of things, using sailors and Marines from the navy yard."

Quickly and precisely—by now, the lieutenant had learned to give excellent briefings—Chomse explained what had happened.

When he finished, Mary shook her head. "My God, is the man *insane*? He's the prime minister of the United States of Europe! He's got no business risking his life like that!"

Simpson looked out of the window. There was still nothing much to see, beyond an occasional street lamp in front of a tavern or one of the wealthier residences—and, then, only the old-fashioned oil lamps. None of the newer gas lights were working. As a result of the catastrophe, obviously.

He felt his wife tugging on his elbow. "John, you *must* speak to Mike about the matter. He simply can't do things like this."

Simpson thought about it for a moment. "No, Mary, I don't think I will. First, because Mike Stearns wouldn't pay any attention to me if I did. And second, because I don't really agree with you anyway."

"How can you—"

"Mary, leave off. The man is what he is. You might as well ask an iceberg to stop being chilly. Or—perhaps a better analogy—ask a general like George Patton to lead from the rear, the way a sensible general should."

His wife shook her head. "People will think he's crazy."

"*Which* people, Mary? That crowd we just left in the palace? Oh, yes, they will. Many of them, at least." He tilted his head toward the window. "But I can assure you that most of the city's residents won't have that reaction. This is a workingmen's city, dear, don't ever forget that. If the fire had spread, it would have been their modest and cramped apartments that went up in flames—along with what little they possess in the way of material goods, and quite possibly they themselves and their children."

Mary stared at him. Simpson felt an old exasperation stir a little, and suppressed it. Being fair, it wasn't that his wife was callous in her attitudes toward people of the lower classes. In fact, she was quite popular with those of them she had contact with. She was invariably gracious and the graciousness wasn't simply a façade.

Put any single person in front of Mary Simpson whom she had to deal with, and she had no difficulty at all seeing that person as an individual human being, regardless of what class they came from. And she was quite indifferent to matters of race. In fact, she was generally far more perceptive in her dealings with people than Simpson was himself.

The problem lay elsewhere. It was simply that Mary didn't deal with such people all that often, and almost never at close range except for servants. Her world—both of those worlds—had always been that of the upper crust. Whereas Simpson himself, as the CEO of a major corporation, had always had to deal with his workforce—and now, as an admiral, had to lead men into combat, almost every one of whom came from very modest circumstances. The prestigious service for seventeenth-century noblemen was the army, not the navy.

That included the young man sitting across from him, in a naval uniform that he wore all the more proudly because his father had been a simple butcher. Chomse's expression was outwardly noncommittal, but some subtlety there made it perfectly clear to Simpson that the lieutenant did not agree with the opinion of his admiral's wife. Not that he would ever say so openly, of course.

In the event, he didn't need to. Mary hadn't missed the subtleties in his expression either.

"I take it you don't agree with me either, Lieutenant Chomse?"

Franz-Leo shifted uncomfortably in his seat. "Well . . . to be honest, Mrs. Simpson, no. I don't. I understand your point of view, but . . ."

He, too, looked out of the window. In his case, not to gather his thoughts but because they'd now entered the industrial zone and were passing by an area of flat land devoted to storing timber. For the first time, they had a close-up view of the burning river, with no buildings to obstruct the view.

It was an impressive sight, in its own way. Now that they were much closer, it was obvious that Simpson's guess had been correct. The flames emerging from the river were clearly coming from a thin film of oil on the surface. The fire actually seemed less threatening from this distance, since it was clear from the dancing and flickering motion of the flames that it was literally skin-deep. There was nothing burning here that could last for all that long.

"Skin-deep," however, meant a lot of skin, spread out

of that much expanse of water. Gloomily, Simpson was quite certain that the USE had just suffered a noticeable dent in its stock of petroleum products—which had been none too extensive to begin with.

"The thing is, Mrs. Simpson," Chomse continued, "however much the prime minister might frighten many people in the nation, his own people are ferociously loyal to him." He did not need to add—in fact, Simpson was sure, didn't even think about it—that by "his own people" Chomse was referring mostly to German down-timers.

That thought was more than a bit of a rueful one, for Simpson. He knew he'd been wrong about many things, in the period after the Ring of Fire. But about nothing had he been more wrong than his assessment that seventeenth-century Germans would be oblivious to the appeal of democracy. Many of them, especially from the lower classes, had adopted Mike Stearns' ideology quite readily. Often, in fact, with a fervor that made Simpson himself uncomfortable.

"So tonight will simply deepen that loyalty," Chomse concluded. "In private, you know"—he made a little sweeping motion with his forefinger at the apartment buildings visible through the opposite window of the carriage—"these folk are more likely to call him 'Prince of Germany' than they are to use his actual title of prime minister."

Prince of Germany. Simpson had overheard the term once or twice himself, spoken by his sailors. But he hadn't realized it had become so widespread.

He had to fight down another wince. There were at least three edges to that sword. One, he approved of; one, he didn't; and of the third he wasn't sure.

The edge he approved of was the obvious one. The informal title bestowed on its prime minister was a focus of militant enthusiasm for the new nation, which translated in time of war into a determination to defeat its enemies. Simpson would be depending on that determination himself, in a few months, when he finally took the ironclads down the Elbe to deal with the Ostender fleets. If a smaller proportion of his sailors were members of the Committees of Correspondence than the volunteers in the new army regiments, they were still plenty of them—and most of the men who weren't actual CoC members shared many of their opinions.

But there was also the second edge, which worried him. Mike Stearns was leading a revolution in Europe. It was as simple as that, regardless of the fact that he was now doing it wearing his fancy dress as a head of government, and sitting in an office. And it was just a fact, attested to by all of history, that charismatic revolutionary leaders often wound up becoming tyrants. "Tyrants," in the literal and original Greek meaning of the term, which was not a sloppy synonym for dictators but a reference to men who led the lower classes in revolt and whose determination to champion their interests often led them to crush ruthlessly everything that stood in the way. You did not have to impute wicked motives to such men to understand that, carried too far, their virtues could become vices. In fact, those very virtues—real ones, undoubted ones—could make them ten times more dangerous than men whose motives were simply personal ambition.

Now that he'd gotten to know Stearns much better,

Simpson didn't believe any longer that the man's character and temperament would incline him in that direction. But a political leader's personality was only one factor in history. Given enough pressure, any personality was malleable. And there was a great deal of pressure on Mike Stearns in the last month of the year 1633—and there would be still more in the years to come.

Finally, there was the third edge. *Prince of Germany.* No other man of the time would be given that title, because there were no other princes *of* Germany. Plenty of princes *in* Germany, to be sure—or "the Germanies," as people usually expressed it. Most of those princes could even be called German princes, for that matter.

But there was no Germany, as such. In the world they'd left behind, Germany would not become a nation of its own for another quarter of a millennium. In this world, it was already emerging—largely because of Mike Stearns. And so, that third edge, that Simpson was very ambivalent about. A genuine national consciousness was emerging here, two hundred and fifty years ahead of schedule. The name for the nation might be the neutral "United States of Europe," but for all intents and purposes what was really happening was the unification of the German people and the German lands. A phenomenon that, in the universe Simpson came from, had had very mixed results indeed.

His wife, who knew far more general history than he did, was more sanguine about the matter. So, at least for the moment, he deferred to her judgment.

"Oh, don't be silly, John," she'd once said to him.

"It's inevitable that Germany is going to exist, sooner or later. Me? I'd just as soon have it emerge a lot earlier, without a chip on its shoulder, and with Mike Stearns conducting the orchestra instead of Otto von Bismarck. Fine, he's an uncouth hillbilly, a lot of the time. But at least he's never a damn *Prussian*."

They'd finally arrived at the navy yard. Chomse got out of the carriage and held the door open for the admiral and his wife.

As soon as he emerged, Simpson looked to the ironclads. They were still there, of course, although in the darkness they weren't much more than looming hulks against the piers, covered with snow. No fire such as the one that was drifting down the Elbe could really threaten the things. Still, Simpson was relieved.

The relief, combined with the sight of the great engines of war, joggled another thought forward.

"And don't forget something else, dear," he murmured to his wife. "There is at least one aristocrat in the nation who will have no trouble at all understanding what Mike did tonight—because he would have done the same. His name is Gustav Adolf, King of Sweden and Emperor of the United States of Europe, and he's the only one that really matters."

Mary chuckled. "That madman! At least he's stopped leading cavalry charges. Well. Until the campaign starts next spring, anyway. After that, we'll just have to hold our breath."

As he escorted his wife toward the naval yard's headquarters, the admiral found himself still thinking about the emperor. Because there was that, too. Yet another variable in the complex political equation. The emperor of Germany's background, training, political attitudes—not to mention the advice of his counselors—would lead him to oppose his nation's prince. But he was a strong-willed man, as much so as any European monarch of the past several centuries—and it was also a fact that he and Stearns were much alike, in many ways. If the emperor often looked askance at many of the doings of his prince, he did not distrust him. Not much, at least—and once he heard about tonight, as he surely would, whatever distrust might still be there would drop a little lower.

That might count for a lot, some day. It was hard to know.

Stearns was in the headquarters already, in the admiral's own office, sitting in one of the chairs near the desk and wiping the soot from his face with a rag. When he saw Simpson and his wife come in, he gave them a small, slightly crooked smile.

"Don't start in on me, Mary."

"I never said a word," she replied primly.

Chapter 5

"This better be goddam necessary, is all I gotta say," Jesse Wood groused as he stomped into Mike Stearns' office, still shedding a little snow from his jacket. Catching sight of the three other occupants of the room—he hadn't been expecting them—he made an attempt to retrieve the military formalities he'd so flamboyantly discarded on the way in.

A stiff little nod, to the Swedish officer sitting in a chair near the prime minister's desk. "Morning, General Torstensson." Another one, to the man sitting next to him. "Morning, Admiral." And a third to the man sitting on the other side of the room. "General Jackson."

Mike Stearns looked up from the pile of papers on his desk and grinned. So did Frank Jackson. Torstensson smiled. A bit thinly, but it was still a genuine smile. Admiral Simpson, on the other hand, was frowning. From his viewpoint, the top command of the USE's other armed forces had a terribly slack attitude when it came to military protocol.

"Well, I think it is, Jesse," Mike said, waving at an empty chair next to Jackson. "Have a seat. Want some tea?" Stearns rose and reached for the pot on the small table next to his desk.

"Thanks, I will. It's damned cold outside in mid-December, especially at eight thousand feet. It's a good thing the weather cleared or I couldn't have come at all." The flyer removed his old Nomex and leather gloves, unwrapped the scarf at his neck, and unzipped his pre-Ring of Fire leather flying jacket.

"To be more precise," said Torstensson, "the prime minister believes the matter is necessary. I've got my doubts, myself." Although Torstensson's English was still heavily accented, by now he'd not only become fluent in the language—he'd been almost fluent, anyway, when the Americans had first met him as the commander of Gustav Adolf's artillery—but was even becoming adept at American idiom. "I believe it's fair to say that Admiral Simpson thinks he's completely off his rocker."

Simpson's frown came back. "I certainly wouldn't put it that way, to the prime minister. But, yes, I think his proposal is unwise."

Stearns handed Wood a steaming mug. "Sorry about hauling you up here on such short notice. You want something to eat?"

After taking a seat, Jesse shook his head. "It'll wait. Besides, that behemoth out there you call a secretary doesn't look like he's the type to cook. Where'd you get him, anyway?"

Stearns put down the teapot and leaned back into his seat. "David? Well, believe it or not, he's a professor at the University of Jena. Or was, until he volunteered for government service. He taught rhetoric and languages. Speaks about six, near as I can tell. A very handy man."

"I don't doubt it," Jesse said. "Rhetoric, eh? He didn't get those scars declining verbs, though, did he?"

Torstensson chuckled. "He wasn't always a scholar, and today he's also one of Achterhof's people. I don't object, mind you, even if Axel would be aghast to learn that many of the USE prime minister's personal staff were hardcore CoC members." That was a reference to Axel Oxenstierna, the chancellor of Sweden, who was still fully committed to the general principles of aristocratic rule. "But—"

The Swedish general who was the top commander of the USE's army shrugged heavily. "Since one of our prime minister's many foolish whims is a distaste for having a proper military escort, I figure it's just as well to have him surrounded by people like Achterhof and Zimmermann. Any Habsburg assassin trying to get past Achterhof will need mastiffs—and to get past Zimmermann, they'll need climbing gear."

Jesse hadn't noticed Gunther Achterhof, on his way into Government House. But as one of the central organizers of the CoC for all of Magdeburg, Achterhof often had other things besides Mike Stearns' security to keep him busy. It didn't matter. Jesse hadn't spotted Achterhof himself, but he had spotted at least three other CoC members keeping an eye on the building.

He was inclined to share Torstensson's view of the matter. The special CoC unit that Achterhof had assigned to guard Stearns—as well as Admiral and Mrs. Simpson, and Frank and Diane Jackson—might lack the formal training of the up-time Secret Service, when it came to guarding dignitaries and heads of state. Not to mention lacking fancy communication gear. But Jesse thought they probably made up for it by their instant readiness to engage in what up-time spin doctors and public relations flacks might have labeled "proactive security."

The CoC didn't exactly have an iron grip on Magdeburg. Not when Torstensson had twenty thousand men in army camps just outside the city, and the CoC was maintaining good relations with him. But there wasn't much that happened in the city that they didn't find out about very quickly. Jesse had heard the rumor—never officially confirmed—that a presumed enemy assassination team had found themselves at the bottom of the Elbe less than two days after they got into the city. With weights around their ankles to keep them there.

"Presumed," because Achterhof's men had never seen any need for something as fussy and officious as pressing formal charges and holding an actual trial.

By now, Jesse was intrigued. For all the jests about Mike Stearns' recklessness, it was actually rather unusual for both Torstensson and Simpson to be this strongly opposed to something he wanted to do. Which meant this was going to be a real doozy.

"So what's on your mind, Mr. President?"

"It's 'Prime Minister,'" Simpson corrected him stiffly.

"Yeah, sorry. I forget. Whatever. What do you want, boss?"

Mike looked him right in the eye. "I want you to fly me into Luebeck, if it's at all possible."

Jesse thought about it. Not for long, however, because he'd already given the matter quite a bit of thought. Not from the standpoint of being able to fly

Stearns into Luebeck, admittedly. Jesse's concern had been whether he could fly Gustav Adolf *out*, in case the Ostender siege of the city looked to be succeeding. But the technical problems involved were the same, either way.

"Yeah, I can—provided Gustav Adolf is willing to cooperate. There's no way to land inside Luebeck itself, you understand? But if the emperor can keep a big enough field clear of enemy troops just outside the walls, we can manage it."

"That much is not a problem," said Torstensson. "Here, I will show you."

He pulled out a map from a satchel by the legs of his chair and spread it over Mike's desk, after Mike had cleared some room. Torstensson pointed to an area just outside the walls of the city and across the moat that guarded Luebeck on the east. There were field fortifications shown there, that provided something of a sheltered area because of a large bastion shown on the southern side of the field. It would be an earthen bastion, nothing fancier, but it would be enough to protect the field from the French troops who'd crossed the Trave south of the city.

"Will this be enough space?" Torstensson asked.

Jesse studied the map for about a minute. His main concern was to get a sense of how accurate the whole map was, from the standpoint of maintaining consistent measurements of distance. As a rule, especially when working on the scale of a city, seventeenth-century cartographers tended to be reasonably accurate even if they were still rarely able to use the sort of precision surveying equipment that Grantville had brought—in no great supply, alas—through the Ring of Fire.

Finally satisfied, he sat back down. By now Jesse had overflown Luebeck at least half a dozen times and the map pretty much corresponded to his own memory. As it happened, he'd noticed that field himself, on one of those flights, and had even taken the time to overfly it again as a way of getting a rough estimate of whether it would work as a landing field. He'd thought at the time that it would, although it would be a bit tight.

"That'll do," he said. "But they'll need to check it carefully to make sure there aren't any obstructions. All it takes is one good-sized rock to break the landing gear."

Torstensson nodded. "Not a problem. I doubt if there'll be much in the way of obstructions anyway. The city's residents—even some of the king's soldiers—use that area to pasture goats, since it's shielded from enemy artillery. And it's much too far from the bay for the enemy's naval forces to pose a threat." He grinned, rather wolfishly. "Needless to say, the Danes and the French don't even try to enter the river any longer. Not after His Majesty let them know that he still had his American scuba wizards residing in Luebeck."

Mike smiled, and Frank Jackson laughed outright. But Jesse noticed that Simpson didn't share in the amusement.

Neither did he, although he smiled politely. The problem was that he and Simpson led the two branches of the USE's military that dealt more closely with German artisans and craftsmen than the army did—or politicians like Mike Stearns. By now, Jesse had come to have a much deeper respect for the abilities of seventeenth-century skilled workers than he'd had in the first period after the Ring of Fire.

True enough, by the manufacturing standards of the world they'd left behind, the skilled craftsmen of the time worked very slowly. More precisely, they could only produce a small quantity of something in the same time that, back in the twentieth century, any factory could have churned out large numbers. But it was amazing what they _could_ produce, even if only in small quantities. All they really needed to know was that something was possible, and be given a rough idea of the general principles of how it worked.

Personally, he thought Gustav Adolf had been foolish to let the enemy know how his forces had destroyed the ships that the Danes had sent up the river to threaten Luebeck early in the siege. It hadn't taken more than six weeks thereafter for two of the spare scuba rigs in Grantville that Sam and Al Morton had left behind to vanish.

Where, and by whose hands? No one knew. But Jesse was certain that enemy agents had been responsible. Probably French agents, but . . . it could have been almost any one. Perhaps simply one of the many independent espionage outfits that worked on a free-lance basis for anyone willing to pay their price. Like mercenaries in general, they seemed to be crawling all over Europe—and nowhere in greater concentration than in Grantville. For good or ill—and Jesse could feel either way about it, depending on his mood of the moment—Grantville's ingrained traditions and customs didn't allow the CoCs there the same latitude when it came to "proactive security" that they had in Magdeburg.

So . . .

Jesse would be very surprised if there weren't already French or Danish top secret projects working around the clock to duplicate American capabilities with underwater demolitions. Or both, and he wouldn't rule out the Spaniards either, especially the ones in the Low Countries, which had probably the highest concentration of skilled craftsmen anywhere in the world outside of Grantville itself. For sure and certain—Mike's head of espionage Francisco Nasi had been able to determine this much—there were at least three enemy efforts underway to build submarines.

Primitive ones, surely, just as whatever they came up with in the way of diving equipment would be primitive. Not to mention dangerous as all hell for the men operating them, with sky-high fatality rates. But there was no more of a shortage of bravery in Europe than there was a shortage of ingenuity. Soon enough, some of that stuff would be put into action—and not all of it would fail.

But there was no point in fretting over that now. Especially since whatever energy and time Jesse had to spare for fretting, he'd spend fretting on the subject that would impact him immediately and directly. Nasi had also been able to determine that there were at least *eighteen* separate projects underway somewhere in Europe to build aircraft. Most of them in enemy territories, but not all. Many of them harebrained, but not all.

And if all of them were risky, so what? In the world they'd left behind, the early pioneers of flying had been willing to accept ghastly casualties. Why would anyone in their right mind think that seventeenth-century aviation pioneers would be any less bold?

These were the same people who didn't think twice about undertaking voyages around the globe on ships that were practically rowboats, by late twentieth-century standards. Something like thirty percent—nobody knew the exact figure—of the commercial seamen in the seventeenth century wound up dying at one point or another, just in the course of doing what was considered a routine job. Probably an equal percentage wound up maimed or crippled or at least seriously injured in the course of their working lives. So far as Jesse was concerned, anybody who thought down-timers would shy away from still higher casualty rates for the sake of mastering aviation or underwater demolitions was just a plain and simple idiot.

Unfortunately, whatever his many virtues, Gustav Adolf shared in full what was perhaps the most common vice of seventeenth-century monarchs and princes. He liked to boast. So, boast he had, to his enemies, and damn the price his people would wind up paying for it downstream.

But Jesse tore his mind away from those gloomy thoughts. Mike was coming back to the subject.

"So it's doable, then?" he asked.

"Yes."

"How soon?"

Jesse shrugged. "The weather's fine. We could leave this afternoon, if you're ready to go. Well . . . at least once we hear back from Luebeck that that field is clear. But the radio connection is good enough now that we shouldn't have to wait for the evening window to get word back."

Mike shook his head. "There's not *that* much of a rush. And I need to spend this afternoon"—he made a little sweeping gesture with his head toward the other officers in the room—"dealing with some other matters. Let's figure on tomorrow morning; how's that?"

Jessed nodded. "Fine. Do you need me to stay for that discussion?"

Mike looked at Jackson and then Simpson. "Gentlemen?"

Jackson grinned again. "Not unless Colonel Wood's changed his mind about fitting machine guns onto his planes."

Jesse grimaced. There were times he felt like a man under siege himself, the way enthusiasts—down-timers worse than up-timers—would deluge him with eager questions on the subject of when the USE's warplanes would be able to start riddling the enemy with machine-gun fire. "When," measured in terms of this week or next week. Alas, among the many American terms that had made its way into the down-time German lexicon, some damn fool had included the verb "to strafe."

"No," Jesse growled. "I haven't. We're still at least two generations of aircraft away from mounting machine guns. Any that are worth mounting, anyway—which those antique contraptions you're talking about aren't."

"Okay, then," said Stearns. "In that case, there's no reason you need to stick around for the wrangle. Unless you want to, of course."

Jesse shook his head. "No, I've got plenty of other things to attend to. And participating in another argument over machine guns ranks somewhere below getting a colonoscopy, in my book."

Torstensson perked right up. "What is a colonoscopy?" he asked. "And how soon could we have one deployed against the Ostenders?"

✧   ✧   ✧

After Jesse left—and Frank clarified the nature of a colonoscopy—Mike decided to cut right to the chase. He had a faint hope that Simpson wouldn't argue the matter for more than an hour, if Mike made clear from the outset that he'd made up his mind.

"Gentlemen. After long and careful consideration, I've decided that the army's claim to the volley guns has to take first priority."

"Blast it, Mike!" exploded Simpson, jettisoning his beloved protocol. "We need volley guns for the timberclads, if we're to have any hope at all of suppressing cavalry raids on our river shipping."

A faint hope got fainter.

"And who cares about that if we can't win the battles?" demanded Jackson. "The best way to suppress cavalry raids is to smash up enemy cavalry before they can go out on raids in the first place."

"Yes, I agree completely," said Torstensson. "With all due respect, Admiral—"

Fainter and fainter.

It took closer to two hours, but in the end Simpson gave up the fight. Looked at from one angle, it was absurd for him to persist so stubbornly in the matter. With both his prime minister and the top commander of the USE's military arrayed against him, he was bound to lose the dispute and was perfectly smart enough to have been aware of that five minutes from the outset.

Mike knew full well, of course, that what Simpson was really doing was storing up negotiating points. He'd eventually conceded the Requa volley guns—and within two days, at the outside, would be using that to twist Mike's arm for something else he wanted.

So it went. Mike was no stranger to negotiating tactics himself. He'd probably agree to whatever Simpson wanted, if it was within reason. But, push came to shove, he'd never been a stranger to the magic word "no."

After Simpson left, Mike gave Frank Jackson a sly little smile. "I take it from the vehemence of your arguments that you lost the debate you'd been having with Lennart here."

Jackson gave Torstensson a look that was unkind enough to be right on the edge of insubordination.

"Well. Yeah, I did."

Torstensson sniffed. "As if we down-timers are so stupid that it never occured to us that skirmishing tactics are a lot safer than standing up in plain sight, all of us in a row. Ha! Until a good cavalry charge—even good pikemen, with good officers—shows us the folly involved."

The jibe made and properly scored, Torstensson relented. "Frank, when your mechanics can start providing us with a sufficient quantity of reliable breechloaders, we will rediscuss the matter. But, for now, even with the new SRGs, we simply do not have a good enough rate of fire to be able to risk dispersing our troops too much."

Jackson didn't say anything. He just stared out of the window gloomily.

"C'mon, Frank, fill me in," Mike said. "What happened in the exercises?"

Frank took a deep breath and let it out in a sigh. "Pretty much what this cold-blooded damn Swede said would happen. The skirmishers did just fine—until the OPFOR's cavalry commanders decided they'd accept the casualties to get in close. After that, it was all over. Even the best riflemen we've got need twenty seconds to reload those SRGs. They're still muzzle-loaders, Minié ball or no Minié ball. Cavalry can come a long ways in twenty seconds."

He gave Torstensson another unkind look. "As he so cheerfully rubbed salt into my wounds, so can a good line of pikemen, if their officers are decisive enough. Which his were."

Jackson sighed again. "After that, it's just no contest. The skirmishers are scattered, not in a solid line with their mates to brace them and their officers right there to hold them steady. And a cavalry charge is scary as all hell. Most of them just took off running. The ones who did try to stand their ground got chopped up piecemeal. Bruised up, anyway." Another unkind look was bestowed on the Swedish general. "They weren't any too gentle with those poles and clubs they were using instead of lances and sabers, let me tell you."

"Spare the rod and spoil the recruit," Torstensson said cheerfully.

Mike nodded. He wasn't really surprised, though. One of the things he'd come to learn since the Ring of Fire, all the way down to the marrow of his bones, was that if the ancestors of twentieth-century human beings didn't do something that seemed logical, it was probably because it wasn't actually logical at all, once you understood everything involved. So it turned out that such notorious military numbskulls as Ulysses S. Grant, Robert E. Lee, Phil Sheridan, Stonewall Jackson, William Tecumsch Sherman and all the rest of them hadn't actually been idiots after all. It was easy for twentieth-century professors to proclaim loftily that Civil War generals had insisted on continuing with line formations despite the advent of the Minić ball-armed rifled musket because the dimwits simply hadn't noticed that the guns were accurate for several hundred yards. When—cluck; cluck—they should obviously have adopted the skirmishing tactics of twentieth-century infantry.

But it turned out, when put to a ruthless seventeenth-century Swedish general's test in his very rigorous notion of field exercises, that those professors of a later era had apparently never tried to stand their ground when cavalry came at them. *After* they fired their shot, and needed one-third of a minute—if they were adept at the business, and didn't get rattled—to have a second shot ready. In that bloody world where real soldiers lived and died, skirmishing tactics without breechloading rifles or automatic weapons were just a way to commit suicide. If the opponent had large enough forces and was willing to lose some men, at least.

Seventeenth-century armies did use skirmishers, to be sure, but they were literally just that—skirmishers, usually called "light companies" attached to the regiments and battalions. When two heavy formations closed for battle, the respective skirmishers who'd often started the fighting withdrew back into the safety of the main formations when the two sides closed within long gun shot.

"So be it," he muttered. That meant high casualty rates, of course. But it was also the reason he'd come down on the army's side over the issue of the new volley guns. True enough, the navy could put them to

good use. But for the army, they could be a Godsend.
If enough volley guns could be provided for the army
in time for the spring campaign, Torstensson could
put together heavy-weapons units for all of his regiments and incorporate their capabilities into his plans.
That still wouldn't allow for real skirmishing tactics,
but it would go a fair distance in that direction. At
least the infantry could spread out a little, instead of
having to stand shoulder to shoulder and make the
world's easiest target.

"How'd the two volley gun batteries do against the
cavalry?" he asked.

Finally, both of the generals smiled in unison.

"Oh, splendidly," said Torstensson. "It was almost
as humiliating an experience for my arrogant cavalry
captains as a colonoscopy would have been. By the
way, are there enough of those devices in Grantville
that I could get one for the army? I'm thinking it
would do wonders for discipline."

Chapter 6

After the waitress brought them steins of beer, Eric Krenz started drinking right away. But Thorsten Engler just stared at his stein for half a minute before, almost desultorily, beginning to sip from it. After setting down the stein, he let his eyes wander about the tavern for another half minute. Seeing, but not really thinking about what he saw. No matter what he looked at, the image that kept flashing back into his mind was that of Robert Stiteler having the life swatted out of him as if he'd been nothing but an insect. He'd had a nightmare about it the night before, too.

Eric's voice startled him. "If you can't get it out of your head, you should go see those American women. The ones I told you about. The 'social workers,' they call them."

Engler stared at him, for a moment, trying to bring his mind to bear on what his friend was saying.

"What are 'social workers'?" he asked.

Eric shrugged and drained some more of his beer. "I'm not sure, really. I think—"

A voice coming over Thorsten's shoulder interrupted him. "They're a variety of what the up-timers call 'psychologists.' Except real psychologists—so I'm told, anyway, I don't think the Americans actually have any here—only handle customers one at a time and they charge a small fortune for it. These 'social workers' are apparently the type that get assigned to the unwashed masses."

Grinning in his vulpine sort of way, Gunther Achterhof pulled out a chair and sat down at the table. "Like you and me," he finished.

He leaned back in his chair, turned half around, and waggled a hand at a nearby waitress. When she came over, he ordered a beer for himself. Then he turned back to look at Thorsten. "And I agree with Eric. Especially if you find you're having regular nightmares about it."

Thorsten winced a little.

"Thought so," Gunther said, nodding. "They have a name for it, even. They call it PTSD. The letters stand for 'post-traumatic stress disorder.'"

He used the actual English terms rather than trying to translate. Engler and Krenz had been in Magdeburg long enough to have a good grasp of the peculiar new German dialect that was emerging in the city—as it was in Grantville and many other towns in the USE. People were starting to call the dialect "Amideutsch." It was a blend of Hochdeutsch and Plattdeutsch, essentially, but with a very large number of American loan words and a more stripped down grammar than that of most German dialects. The new dialect had adopted the simplified English system of verb conjugations, for instance. Newcomers to Amideutsch found it a bit peculiar to say *Ich denk* instead of *Ich denke*, but they soon got used to it.

Although Engler and Krenz didn't have any difficulty with the fact that the terms were English, they still didn't really understand what they meant. So Achterhof spent a minute or so clarifying the matter.

As best he could, anyway.

"Stupid, you ask me," was Krenz's conclusion. "So bad things that happen to you are upsetting. What else is new? For this we need fancy up-time words?"

Achterhof shook his head. "For you, Eric, it's maybe that simple. Crude and coarse blockhead that you are. But for sensitive and poetic types like me and Thorsten, things are different. It's more complicated than you think."

Krenz snorted in his beer. "You! 'Poetic'!"

But Engler found himself wondering. "These 'social workers.' Have you been to see them?"

Achterhof nodded. "The prince himself suggested I go to them, when I told him once about the nightmares. So I did. They were quite helpful. I still have the nightmares, but not as bad and not as often. And there are . . . other things, that are not so bad."

He didn't seem inclined to elaborate, and Achterhof was not a man whom one would lightly press on such a matter. Engler knew enough of his personal history to know that he'd had plenty of things to have nightmares about. Quite a bit more than Thorsten himself, for certain. A terrible accident was one thing. What Achterhof had lived through . . .

A little shudder went through Thorsten's shoulders.

"How much do they charge?" he asked. "I can't afford much, now. I got fired this morning. Because of the accident."

"Assholes," said Krenz. "It wasn't Thorsten's fault."

Gunther shrugged. "No, it wasn't. But the coal gas plant was owned by Underwood and Hartmann. The biggest American prick in partnership with the biggest German prick. What do you expect? 'Shit rolls downhill,' as the up-timers say—and any company owned by Underwood and Hartmann might as well have that for its official motto."

He took a long pull on his beer. "They probably would have fired you too, Eric—every man working the shift—except the rest of you were in the union." He tipped the stein in Thorsten's direction. "Engler wasn't, since he was officially part of management."

Eric shook his head. "I still say that's silly. In the guilds—"

"Fuck the guilds," said Achterhof harshly. "Yes, I know. In the guilds, a foreman like Engler would have been a member. Which is one of the many things wrong with the guilds. It's the guildmasters and top journeymen who run them, and fuck everybody else. The American union system is better for the common man. Much better—even if, now and then, something shitty happens like this. Just the way it is."

Engler agreed with Achterhof, actually. Krenz came from a family of long-established gunsmiths. Even though he'd joined the Committee of Correspondence soon after he arrived in Magdeburg, in some ways he still had the attitudes of a town guildsman. Thorsten's family, on the other hand, had been farmers from a small village. Prosperous enough ones, until the war ruined them and forced the survivors into the towns—where they got no help or friendship from the haughty guilds.

"Yeah, fuck the guilds," he murmured. "I understand the situation, Gunther, but it still leaves me in a bad place. I've got enough money saved to get me through for maybe a month. After that . . ."

He shrugged. "There's always plenty of work here. But it won't pay very well. Unlike Eric, I don't really have any skills. I was lucky to get that foreman job."

"Luck, bullshit," said Krenz. He used the English term. No American loan words except purely technical ones were adopted wholesale the way their delightful profanity was. "You were a good foreman, Thorsten. That's why they promoted you in the first place. They're shitheads, but they're not stupid."

Achterhof drained his stein and called for another one. "Eric's right, Thorsten," he said, after the waitress left. "I asked around. All the men thought well of you. Being a foreman is a skill too, you know."

"Sure is," agreed Krenz. "I know. I've had plenty of bad ones. Either they didn't know the work or they were afraid to make a decision—usually both—or they knew what they were doing but were rude and unpleasant bastards to work for. It's not that common to find a foreman who doesn't have either vice."

Engler made a face. "I *didn't* really know what I was doing."

A sudden flashing image of Stiteler came, and he paused while he desperately tried to fend it off. It was the same image as most of them. There'd been a moment there, after Robert had been slammed into a stanchion, when his body seemed to be glued in place by the force of the blow. His face had been untouched, but the back of his head had been completely crushed. Eyes still open but empty, the man already dead, with blood and bits of his skull and pieces of his brain starting to ooze down the metal column.

Thorsten closed his eyes and shook his head. That seemed to help, sometimes.

When he opened his eyes, he saw Achterhof gazing at him. Sympathetically—and knowingly.

"Go talk to the up-time women, Thorsten," the CoC organizer said softly. "If you can't pay right away, they'll make arrangements."

Engler took a slow, deep breath. "All right, I will. Where is their business?"

"It's actually a government enterprise. Part of what they call the 'Department of Social Services.'" The waitress arrived with Achterhof's beer, and he paused long enough to pay her. Then, with the stein, gestured in the direction of Government House. "They're in the corner next to the river, on the third floor. Just ask for the social workers."

Thorsten nodded, drained what was left of his own stein, and then contemplated the empty vessel. More to the point, contemplated whether he could afford to order another. The very fact that he even had to think about whether he could do so drove home to him just how quickly his financial situation would become desperate.

Well . . . "desperate," in a sense. Finding a job that would pay enough to keep him fed and sheltered and even reasonably clothed wasn't the issue. Magdeburg was what the Americans called a boom town. If he started looking early the next morning, Thorsten could have a new job by the end of the day. Maybe even by noon. But it would be unskilled labor, almost for sure.

The problem wasn't even the work itself, as hard as it would most likely be. Thorsten was not lazy and, though he was no taller than the average man, was stocky and very strong for his size. In particular, like most people raised to farm work, he had a lot of endurance.

It was the *boredom* that would slowly—no, not so slowly, not any more—drive him half-mad. Now that Thorsten had had the experience of a job that was interesting and challenging, the idea of going back to spending all day wielding a pick or a shovel was far more distasteful than it would have been a few months earlier. He'd been spoiled, really.

"I'll have to make arrangements," he said, almost sighing the words. "Even though I hate being in debt."

He noticed, suddenly, that Achterhof's earlier sympathetic expression had been replaced by something else. There was now a look on his face that wasn't exactly what you could call predatory. But it reminded him of the way hunting dogs fixed their gaze on something that *might* be prey.

"Join the army," Gunther said. He nodded toward Krenz. "Like he's going to do."

Surprised, Engler looked at Eric. Krenz shrugged, smiling perhaps a bit ruefully. "Hey, look, Thorsten. They didn't *fire* me, true enough. But there's not going to be any work for me there until they rebuild the whole factory. Which will take months—and Underwood and Hartmann are not the old-style type of masters who'll pay a man when he's not actually working."

The young repairman looked a bit uncomfortable, for a moment. "Besides. I'd been thinking about it anyway. It's also a matter of patriotic duty."

Patriotic. That was another up-time loan word in

Amideutsch. The notions involved in the term weren't completely foreign, not by any means. Any German who had citizenship rights in a town—which many didn't, of course—understood perfectly well that the rights also carried obligations. Including the obligation to serve in the militia when and if the town was threatened. But the Americans gave a sweeping connotation to the notion that was quite different from the traditional one. Almost mystical, in a way. As if such a nebulous thing as a "nation" was as real as an actual town or village, and could make the same claims on its citizens.

Now suspicious, Thorsten looked back and forth between Eric and Gunther. "You set this up," he accused. "The two of you."

Achterhof snorted. "Don't be stupid. Of course we did. The minute Eric told me you were moping around—that was halfway through the morning—I told him to get you down here this afternoon and I'd recruit you into the army. Both of you. That'll solve all your practical problems at one stroke—and you can stop feeling like a worthless parasite feeding on your nation like a louse."

"I *wasn't* feeling like a worthless parasite," Thorsten said stiffly.

Gunther's eyes widened, almost histrionically. "You *weren't*? A man as smart as you?"

Thorsten was starting to get a little angry, but Eric's sudden burst of laughter punctured that. His friend had a cheerful outlook on life that was often surprisingly contagious.

"He's only smart about things that he's actually thinking about, Gunther," Krenz said, "and he concentrates his attention to the point of being oblivious about everything else. That can make him as stupid as a mule about something he hasn't really considered."

He took a swallow of beer, then raised the half-empty mug in a saluting gesture. As if he were making an unspoken toast. "Like the war."

A bit defensively, now, Thorsten said: "Keeping the factory going was part of that."

Achterhof nodded. "Yes, it was. That's why nobody from the CoC came by to urge you—pester you, if you prefer—to volunteer. But the factory blew up, and even after they get it rebuilt there's no job for you there. And while I'll admit that if you squint real hard, you can claim that digging a sewer ditch is also a contribution to the war effort, it's pushing it. Not to mention being a complete waste of your skills."

Engler made a derisive sound, just blowing air through his lips. "Ha! As opposed to carrying a musket? At least digging a ditch, I don't have to work shoulder to shoulder with some smelly Saxon like Krenz here."

Eric grinned, and so did Gunther. But that expression on Achterhof's face *was* predatory now. He might as well have been a fox in human clothing, sitting at a table and drinking beer.

"Who said anything about carrying a musket?" He issued his own derisive puff of air. "And you can forget that 'shoulder-to-shoulder' nonsense."

Eric leaned forward. "They're forming up new units, Thorsten," he said eagerly. "'Heavy weapons squads,' they're called. Gunther told me he could get us into one of them."

Thorsten eyed Achterhof skeptically. Granted, the

man was one of the top organizers for the CoC in Magdeburg, and granted also the CoCs had a lot of influence in the new regiments. But one of the things that made those regiments "new" in the first place—even the most ignorant farmboy knew this much—was that recruitment wasn't based on the same who-you-know methods that were standard for most mercenary regiments. Instead, it was done—depending on who you talked to—in a manner that could be described as "fair" or "nonsensical" or "as stupid as you can imagine."

Red tape, after all, was another up-time loan word in Amideutsch. At least the old-style mercenary recruiters could generally be depended upon to deliver on whatever promises they made. No such thing could be said about recruitment into the new regiments. Thorsten personally knew a man—he'd been working at the plant when Engler first hired on—who'd signed up for the army thinking he'd become a cavalryman because the recruiter had told him his horsemanship skills were useful and would be prized. Instead, he'd wound up in the Marines—spending all day on his feet standing at attention while guarding the navy yard, bored half to death. Not even the fancy uniform had consoled him.

And why? Apparently because some careless clerk had jotted down something wrong in his papers. But try getting it changed, after the fact! In the real world, often enough, *we play no favorites* was a gleaming phrase whose immediate and tarnished successor was *and we don't pay any attention to what we're doing, either*, followed by the downright sullen *no, that's too much of a bother to fix now that it's done.*

"It's true," Eric insisted.

Thorsten was still squinting at Achterhof. Gunther smiled, took another drink from his beer, and then shrugged.

"No, I can't guarantee anything. But I know General Jackson and he's an easy man to talk to. More to the point, the Swede Torstensson put Jackson in charge of the new units. And why did he do so? Because the reason they're called 'heavy weapon' squads is because they'll be using gadgets that only the Americans really understand that well yet. And the Americans—you know *this* to be true, Thorsten, from your own experience—prize nothing so much as a down-timer who seems to have an aptitude for mechanical things."

He pointed at Eric with his beer stein. "That's him. And they also prize down-timers who seem to know how to manage men with mechanical skills. Which is you."

Another flashing image of Stiteler came. And went, thank God, faster than most.

"Oh, yes," Thorsten said gloomily. "I can just imagine how enthusiastic your Jackson fellow will be, Gunther, when you tell him that—O happy occasion!—the fore-man who managed to oversee several men getting killed and the whole coal gas plant getting destroyed is now available to be a sergeant—that's the rank they use, am I correct?—in his new units."

Eric grimaced. But Gunther's smile actually widened.

"It'll be the easiest thing in the world, Thorsten," he said. "After I tell the general that Quentin Underwood owned the factory which he knows already—and that he blamed you because he didn't take the time and spend the money to have you trained properly. Jackson will have you sworn in ten minutes later."

Engler squinted at him. "Why?"

"Ha! You don't know anything about Frank Jackson, do you? Well, he wasn't a general up-time, I can tell you that. He—and the prince himself, you know—were both coal miners. Leaders of their union. And Quentin Underwood was the mine manager. And if you think *you* have a low opinion of Underwood, ask Jackson about him someday. Make sure you stand back a few paces, though. Your skin will likely blister if you don't."

Thorsten pondered the matter. He'd had so little direct contact with up-timers that he'd never really given any thought at all to what they'd done or who they'd been in the world they came from. To him, as to most Germans he knew, all the Americans seemed somehow *Adel.* True, they didn't fit any of the existing categories of the nobility, but what difference did that make? They'd simply added another one of their own, which they enforced either by simple prestige or the still simpler method of beating naysayers into a pulp on a battlefield.

A coal miner.

Thorsten came from a village not far from Amberg in the Upper Palatinate. There were iron mines all over that area. For generations, men in his family had often supplemented their income by doing a stint of work in the mines. Thorsten himself had done so for a few months, when he was seventeen.

A former miner, for a commander. That might be . . . pleasant. Even in a war.

Perhaps *especially* in a war. Anger that had been

simmering for a day and half, under the grief and the guilt, fed by the nightmares and the horrible sudden images, began to surface.

The accident *hadn't* been Thorsten's fault. Being fair, it hadn't even been the fault of Underwood or the plant manager. Everyone was being pushed, by the demands of the war. Which was just another way of saying, by the aggression of Richelieu and Christian IV of Denmark and Charles of England and the Habsburg king of Spain.

"So fuck them," Thorsten growled softly. He *liked* the way things were happening in Magdeburg, and everywhere else that he knew of in the Germanies that the up-timers had an effect upon. One of his uncles and three of his cousins had moved to Bamberg after their village had been destroyed. Thorsten had gotten some letters from them since. Part of what they talked about in those letters was their good opinion of the new up-timer administration of Franconia. And part of the letters seemed very veiled, which meant that something explosive was brewing down there. Something which the Americans might not be leading or even really know about, but also something that his uncle and cousins didn't expect the up-timers to oppose, either.

A prince of Germany—the *only* prince that all Germans had, commoners for sure; that much Thorsten had already concluded—who had once been a coal miner. That was also . . . pleasant to think about.

"Okay," he said, unthinkingly using the one American loan word that had swept over Germany faster than any plague and bid fair to do the same across all of Europe. "Where do I sign up?"

Achterhof hoisted his stein in another half-salute. "Right here. In about"—he glanced at the big clock hanging over the bar—"forty-five minutes. I told Frank to meet us here."

Both Engler and Krenz stared at him.

That vulpine smile that fit so easily came back to Gunther's face. "I told you. I know him. Quite well, in fact. And he's partial to the beer in this tavern, and doesn't mind getting his general's hands dirty doing lowly recruitment work. He's very enthusiastic about the new squads, too."

He looked down at his stein, which he'd set back on the table. It was almost empty. "Speaking of which— another round? Oh, stop looking like a fretful housewife, Thorsten. I'll buy."

Achterhof did know Jackson quite well, as it turned out. The first sentences out of the American general's mouth after Gunther finished his summary of the way Thorsten had been singled out for blame with regard to the accident was:

"Quentin Underwood is the biggest fuckwad asshole who ever disgraced the state of West Virginia. Yeah, fine, he's a competent mine manager. He's also a complete prick and a miserable shithead and if the cocksucker was lying in the gutter dying of thirst the only thing I'd do is walk over there to piss all over the worthless motherfucker."

He took a long pull on his beer. "So forget that bullshit. What matters is that after Gunther raised this with me, I went and talked to Mike about it. He was right there next to the two of you all the way through that nightmare. He told me if I didn't sign you up, assuming you volunteered, I'd be an idiot. Not to mention a bigger asshole than Underwood, which probably isn't possible anyway given the laws of nature."

Another long pull. "So. Thorsten, I can start you right off as a sergeant. We promote from the ranks, so anything after that is up to you. Eric, you'll be what in my old army we would have called—ah, never mind—but what it amounts to is a technical specialist. The thing is, these volley guns aren't that complicated all by themselves. They're really just a fancier version of organ guns. But what I'm looking toward is replacing them as soon as we can with *real* machine guns. That'll most likely be Gatlings, first off, but who knows? So I need as many men as I can get who've got the knack for this stuff. Especially someone like you—this is what Gunther tells me—who comes from a gunsmith's background."

When Engler and Krenz reported to the army headquarters the next morning, so it proved. The papers were already prepared and ready for their signatures, enlisting both of them in one of the new heavy weapons units. As promised, Engler with the rank of sergeant and Krenz with a specialist rating.

No clerk had made an error.

Given Jackson's command of the more salient features of Amideutsch, Thorsten was not surprised. Paper was flammable, after all. So were clerks, when you got right down to it.

Chapter 7

Luebeck

Two hours later that same morning, Jesse Wood and Mike Stearns were at eight thousand feet, flying toward Wismar. The air was cold and clear, albeit choppy and turbulent. Jesse noted the course as best he could on the bouncing compass, confirmed it with familiar ground references, and put in a large chunk of drift correction. The wintry earth below appeared lifeless, blotched with large white patches of snow-covered fields and some dark woods here and there. The aircraft bucked, pitched, and shuddered in the uneven bottom edge of the low winter jet stream. Jesse looked at an obviously uncomfortable Mike Stearns in the right seat and chuckled.

Stearns shot him a look. "Something funny?"

Jesse realized that Stearns had misunderstood his attitude and held up a placating palm.

"No, well, yeah, a little. Do you remember last summer when that group wanted us to concentrate on ultralights? 'They're cheaper, they burn less fuel, they're easier to fly.' All that horsepucky? Well, every time I get up here where it's a little bumpy or cloudy, I remember how Hal Smith stood up in front of the resource board and said, 'I build aircraft, not toys.' He reminded me of that German engineer in that old movie, *Flight of the Phoenix*." Jesse grinned.

Stearns mustered a small smile of his own. "I remember. You don't look much like Jimmy Stewart, though."

Wood was about to reply when a stiff gust swatted the aircraft, forcing him to take a moment to wrestle the plane roughly back on course.

"Well, anyway, don't worry about this bird. She flies just fine. I would've liked to use a Gustav, but I'm still learning about them myself." He passed Stearns a thermos full of tea. "Here, warm up a bit. But take it easy, we've got maybe three hours to go with this headwind. We're lucky Hal figured out a way to get a little heat in this version of the Belle. It's probably twenty below out there."

Stearns took the thermos and nodded his thanks. Jesse let him alone and concentrated on flying. The cold and the constant juddering of the aircraft discouraged talk as they flew over the seventeenth-century landscape.

When they finally reached Wismar, Jesse flew low over the town, which looked almost deserted on this cold December day, save for the curls of smoke from nearly every chimney. The few townsfolk in the streets looked up at the sound of the aircraft and watched it for a bit, but there were none of the gawking little crowds there would have been just a few weeks earlier. Jesse reflected again on how quickly the people of this time became used to the wondrous American machines. He turned towards the airfield as Stearns took in the sights.

Jesse flew over Richter Field, checking the wind and surveying the light snow covering on the grass. He noted many improvements made since his last visit, over a month ago. No need for a tower, as yet, but already there was a shed big enough for two air-craft and the shack that had been the sole building in October had been replaced by a big, solid-looking structure with new plank walls. He reckoned that another low building, surrounded by a berm near the field, must be the armory *cum* fuel storage. The new construction showed the importance placed on this small spot of turf near the frigid Baltic.

As he took in the scene, it was as if Stearns read his mind.

"Shame it takes a war to get things done quickly, eh, Jesse?"

Jesse glanced over at his passenger and nodded. Looking down again, he noticed two figures, hands jammed in coat pockets, standing next to the wind sock, faces turned upward. He hooked a thumb towards his window.

"It's also those boys down there. Nothing very important gets done without the 'Sons of Martha.'"

After he spoke, Jesse realized that Mike might not understand the reference. The man had had something of a haphazard education, with just three years of college. But you never knew. He also read extensively and had a wife who was a genuine intellectual.

So, Jesse wasn't really surprised by Mike's nodding reply. "Yeah. Kipling knew a thing or two, didn't he?"

"Yes, he did. Or will. Or something."

Jesse checked the windsock again and turned down-wind for landing.

"Might as well get this beast on the ground."

Later that afternoon, two aircraft moved through the North German sky at five thousand feet, headed toward Luebeck. "Snarled through the sky," Jesse often thought of it. There was that one advantage to propeller aircraft compared to the jets that he'd mostly flown up-time. Damnation, they *sounded* like warplanes.

Jesse flew as wingman, in a rather loose formation off Lieutenant Woodsill's left wing. He'd decided to let Woody lead, since he knew the way. In any case, he realized that Woody and his copilot Ernst Weissenbach had not had any recent formation practice.

Best keep 'em where I can see 'em, Jesse thought.

Otherwise, he had absolutely no complaints about the two young officers. Having been left in charge of the airfield at Wismar and with the original Belle, once a third had been built, the two young pilots had performed superbly. They'd made good use of the shipments of fuel and rockets sent to them overland. According to accounts from Luebeck, their observation and harassment of the League of Ostend's armies besieging the city had been instrumental in holding off several assaults.

As a result, Colonel Wood had listened carefully to Woodsill as the lieutenant had described what they could expect around Luebeck. Though the enemy had crossed the river and nearly cut off the city, they had not yet gotten any artillery across, apparently content, for the time being, to keep all of their field pieces on the west side of the river. That would probably change, especially if the rivers froze solid, but it meant that, for now, the area near the city's eastern walls was reasonably unmolested. Unless very unlucky, they could probably land fairly close and reach safety under the city guns before the enemy pickets could even give warning.

"Aside from scattered pickets and some small cavalry units, the Ostenders aren't very much of a bother there, sir," Woody had said. "Naturally, we've been concentrating our attacks on the main encampment of the Dennies on the other bank."

"Dennies?" Jesse had interrupted.

Woody hesitated. "Uh, yes sir, that's what folks have taken to calling them."

Jesse was mildly amused. It seemed to be an iron law of nature that soldiers immediately found pejorative terms to refer to the enemy. All very politically incorrect, no doubt, but he figured it was fair and square. He was quite sure the enemy reciprocated in full. Going way back, for that matter. A friend of his who was a military history buff had once told him that Napoleon's soldiers referred to Austrian troops as "Kaiserlicks" and English troops as either "the grasshoppers" or—Mike's own favorite—"the goddams." Jesse didn't doubt at all that the ancient Assyrians and Hittites had done the same.

"Anyway," Woody continued, "we've mainly been concentrating on the Frogs, since they constitute most of the enemy troops who crossed the Trave and are threatening Luebeck from the south."

"How many are there now?" Jesse asked.

The Air Force lieutenant pursed his lips. "Hard to know exactly, sir. Most of them arrived early on in the siege, transported by ship, but there have continued to be smaller units arriving by overland march. The Spanish are apparently letting them though the Low Countries as long as they don't send too many at a time. We figure by now there are about twenty-five thousand French troops, to add to the Danes' twenty thousand. Then figure maybe two thousand Spanish—they're mostly cavalry—and one thousand English."

Jesse frowned. It said something for Gustav Adolf's gambling spirit—and his confidence in Luebeck's garrison and fortifications—that he'd been willing to withstand a siege waged by almost fifty thousand men with a defending force of not more than twelve thousand. Even taking into account the fact that he was favored by winter conditions—disease in the besieging forces had to be getting terrible by now—and a large civilian population that would be desperately supporting him because if he failed the city was sure to be sacked. As it had so many times since, the savage destruction of Magdeburg and the slaughter of most of its inhabitants by Tilly's army in 1631 had backfired on the imperials. Cities under siege that might have contemplated surrender in earlier times rarely did so any longer.

"I didn't realize the English had sent anybody."

"It's really a token force, sir, is the way we figure it. When I said 'one thousand' I was probably being generous."

Woody went back to the map. "We've mixed up

the timing and direction of our attacks, trying to keep
the enemy off balance. It's been working pretty well,
but if you see a block of soldiers standing motionless
while everyone else is running, break off your attack
run. They know by now that our rockets aren't all
that accurate and any group standing still is probably
under the command of a steady officer. It's pretty
clear they're hoping for a lucky shot from massed
fire to bring us down, the way they got Hans. We
try to discourage that little trick by carrying a couple
of black powder grenades. Ernst here, has gotten
damn—uh, quite good at chucking grenades. They're
actually more accurate than the rockets, though they
don't have as much punch, of course."

Woody paused and pointed to a spot on the map
he had made of the Luebeck area.

"One other thing, Colonel. During our last reconnaissance a couple of days ago, we noticed some
activity in this grove to the south of this one Dennie
encampment. Right about here. We'd already expended
our rockets and we didn't get too close. Don't know
what it is, but it looked like tents and buildings of
some sort. I recommend we give it another look this
afternoon. Maybe one of us can make a low pass,
while the other flies cover. No telling when we'll have
two aircraft here, again."

The idea was tempting, but . . .

Jesse hesitated, glancing at Mike. This was already
a somewhat risky enterprise, flying the USE's prime
minister into a city under siege. Adding into the
bargain getting him involved in an actual combat
operation . . .

But Mike just grinned. "Sure, Jesse, go ahead. Don't

mind me. Actually, I'd like to see how it works. Give me a much better sense of what 'air power' does or doesn't mean in the here and now."

There was always that about Stearns. He was a politician, sure enough, and had most if not all the vices of the breed. But you couldn't ever accuse the man of lacking balls. Even brass ones, in his case.

Jesse finished replaying the briefing in his mind. The flight from Wismar to Luebeck hadn't taken more than twenty-five minutes and he could see they were nearing the city. The radio crackled and Woody's steady voice came out of the speaker.

"Two, this is Lead. Approaching Luebeck and descending to one thousand feet. Luebeck Radio should be listening." A pause, then: "Luebeck, Luebeck, this is the Richter Express, five minutes out."

Whoever was manning the radio for Gustav Adolf was on the ball.

"*Guten Tag*, Richter Express, Luebeck here. Have you brought presents for the enemy, today? They've been getting lonely this past day or so."

"Roger that, Luebeck," Woodsill confirmed. He sounded amused. "And some visitors. Better send for His Majesty."

"Roger, Express. *Ein moment, bitte.*"

The Swedish king must have been nearby. The sound of someone fumbling with a microphone and a muffled, "Closer to your mouth, Your Majesty" was followed by the unmistakable voice of command.

"*Hallå där*, Lieutenant Woodsill. Do you have Colonel Wood with you?"

"Yes, sir. Stand by, please. Go ahead, Two."

Jesse was ready. "Good afternoon sir. Colonel Wood here. As promised, we have your mail and will deliver it shortly."

They didn't think anyone had sold the Ostenders a radio yet, but communications security was always a good idea. The enemy would soon know there were two aircraft in the area, but there was no sense in letting anyone, even the radio operator, know who Jesse's passenger was. Word had already been passed to Gustav Adolf by coded message the day before.

"Very good, Colonel," the bemused sounding monarch replied. "All is in waiting for you."

"Yes, sir, thank you. But first, we must deliver some gifts to your neighbors. We will call again in fifteen minutes."

"We will be ready for you, Colonel."

Jesse clicked the mike. He looked over to see Mike Stearns give a thumbs up and gave one in return. Time to get to work.

"Lead, this is Two."

"Two, Lead."

"It's your show, Lieutenant. Call the shots."

The Richter Express, flight of two, flew low over the besieged battlements of Luebeck. As they passed, Jesse paid close attention to the flat green just outside the city's east wall. Thousands of faces craned upward, mouths open, cheering wildly. Most of those cheering people, whether noblemen, soldiers, or peasants, had never seen an aircraft until two months ago. Waggling their wings, the aircraft flew the length of the city and then turned westward towards a decidedly less friendly audience.

As had been briefed, the aircraft overflew the

enemy encampment, the pilots taking careful note of potential targets. From high above, the camp looked like a disturbed ants' nest, as men scattered or ran to their posts. Jesse could see no tent city, no large horse herd, no grouping of flags and standards—which would seem to indicate that air power had already made an impact on this bit of seventeenth-century warfare. Siege cannon facing the city were thoroughly dug in, even from the rear and, all around, men were jumping in holes dug into the frozen earth. A large train of wagons was hurriedly pulling off the road leading into the camp from the west. By now, traders and camp followers knew the danger as well as any soldier. As the aircraft passed the camp, Woody gave his first order.

"Two, maintain orbit at one thousand feet just south of camp. Rejoin on command."

Jesse merely clicked the mike and banked left, turning back over the French camp. Blocks of men had begun to form on the ground below. Woodsill and Weissenbach continued westward, passing from view of the enemy. Jesse continued to circle, just over the southern edge of the camp. Once, smoke erupted from a regiment formed up in a square below. Though no sound reached him, Jesse unconsciously edged upward two hundred feet.

Come on, come on, Jesse thought. *Let's get going, Woody.*

As if reading his mind, Woodsill called. "Two, Lead has you in sight, beginning run. We'll take a left climb out."

Jesse wracked the aircraft around and immediately spotted the other Belle, which, having circled well to the south, was now at no more than three hundred feet, hurtling at full power. The lower aircraft passed directly over the trees where the suspected enemy activity had been spotted. Just as he reached the edge of the trees, Woody turned energy into altitude, zoom climbing to the left. A group of soldiers sent a futile volley into the sky, far behind the climbing aircraft.

Keeping the lead aircraft in sight, Jesse put the stick over and pushed left rudder, putting his nose inside of Woodsill's turn. Performing a three dimensional aerial ballet, the two Belles continued turning, with Jesse sliding his aircraft "up the line" until the two were once again a rejoined flight.

The Richter Express once again flew over the enemy camp. People on the ground a thousand feet below hugged the dirt in their holes, fearing what might come. Woody reported what they had found.

"Two, target is a hidden gun park under trees. Tents, wagons, guns, and what appear to be unfinished bunkers. Lots of people down there. We might catch a loaded caisson or two."

Jesse's jaw tightened into a hunter's grin as Woodsill rapidly went on.

"We'll racetrack north and south, right-hand turns, ten second spacing. Aimpoint is just inside the tree line. Fire at six hundred feet, four rockets per pass, and watch for secondaries. Copy, Two?"

Jesse replied. "Roger. Two copies all. Right race-track, ten seconds."

Woody gave the signal. "Lead's in the pitch . . . now!" His aircraft turned sharply right, rolling out just as sharply when aligned with the target. Jesse continued north, counting to ten, and then copied the other aircraft's steep turn and rolled out precisely behind it. Focusing entirely on lead, he waited, waited.

Suddenly, the aircraft ahead changed aspect, beginning a dive. Jesse again counted to ten and followed in a dive of his own. For the first time, he could focus on the target. From a slant range of no more than half a mile, Jesse could pick out shapes among the trees. Conforming to Woody's dive angle, he displaced slightly left of Woody's path and waited for him to fire.

Suddenly, smoke and fire burst from under Woody's wings, as four rockets came off their rails and streaked downward. Woody's aircraft pulled up into a climbing right turn and then it was Jesse's turn. He'd begun counting when Woody fired, but when he reached ten, he held fire for a couple more seconds. Woody's rockets had already impacted in the trees, four explosions throwing dirt, branches and smoke skyward. Just as Jesse fired his rockets, he saw a small figure running out of the woods, chased by a larger one in skirts. A woman following a child. He didn't have time to look longer, pulling hard and banking into his turn. He could hear his rockets explode in the trees beneath him as Stearns craned his neck, looking behind.

"Christ, Jesse, there are women and kids in there!" Stearns shouted.

Busy following the first aircraft, Jesse did not turn his head or answer immediately. As he reached a trail position behind Woody, he turned toward Stearns and asked, "Mike, did you see any secondary explosions?"

His face pale, Stearns replied, "Uh, no. Not that I could tell."

"Okay," Jesse said. "Maybe we'll get lucky next pass."

He didn't say anything further. With Stearns—in this respect, he was different from most politicians Jesse had known—you didn't have to waste time with stolid and antiseptic little speeches about the "unfortunate but inevitable side effects that come with war." Mike detested the phrase *collateral damage* as much as Jesse did himself, and he was perfectly aware that given the nature of seventeenth-century armies, almost all of them had lots of camp followers mixed in with the soldiery.

You simply *couldn't* fight against such an army without accidentally killing or wounding some women and children. Mike's protest had been the simple horror of the moment, that he'd just swallow and let go. Unlike—some very sour memories got stirred up here—any number of politicians Jesse could remember from back up-time. Men who had no hesitation ordering something done—nor any hesitation thereafter washing their hands of the consequences that had been guaranteed by those same orders.

The second pass was performed like the first, except that they now had smoke and dust as an aimpoint. Woody aimed to the right side of the smoke and Jesse slightly more left. Once again, Jesse and Mike watched as rockets hurled from Woody's aircraft. This time, as they impacted, there was a huge secondary as one of the rockets found something very explosive. Fire and smoke belched upward with a gigantic sound. Without thinking, Jesse fired his rockets and stomped left rudder, turning to avoid the still climbing smoke and debris. The blast's concussive force shoved them sideways. Stearns stared out the window on his side, peering intently downward until the turn took the scene from his view. As he regained control and rolled out, Jesse could see where his rockets had struck. He saw no secondaries, but there were several fires burning down there and he could see people prone on the ground. Where Woody's rockets had struck, there was nothing but a large smoke-filled gap, the trees blown flat, flames and smaller explosions hiding the ground itself.

The rockets had done better than they usually did. Quite a bit better, in fact. But that was part of war, also. You got good luck as well as bad. More of the former than the latter, if you were aggressive but kept just this side of recklessness.

Once the two aircraft had rejoined, Jesse could smell his own acrid sweat and tried not to consider what might have happened if he had flown directly behind Woody on that pass. He'd crossed that line some, he knew. This really had been too risky, after all, with Mike on board. There'd probably be hell to pay after Admiral Simpson found out.

So be it. Jesse wiped his brow and grasped the radio mike.

"Lead, Two. Good show, gentlemen. Well done. I suggest you revisit that spot in a day or two. That secondary was no caisson. It was probably a hidden magazine. Keep hitting the tree line all around their camp. They're sure to have more such stores around the perimeter. Oh, one more thing. Should we ever do that again, I suggest that a thirty second spacing between aircraft might be more suitable."

Woody replied crisply, "Yes, sir. That might be more comfortable."

Jesse felt almost calm, now. "Excellent work, Woody.

By the way, you are now a captain and Ernst is now a first lieutenant. Now let's complete this mission and the two of you can go home and wet down your promotions. I'll be sending you some help before very long."

The rest of the flight went smoothly enough. While Woody and Ernst distracted the French pickets by overflying their positions, Jesse slipped in behind, flying slow and low. Lined up on the grassy sward just outside the city wall, Jesse carefully picked his aim point and flew his approach only a few knots above stall speed. Power up and nose abnormally high, he firmly dropped the Belle onto the turf, rolling to a stop in only a short distance. He actually had to add power to taxi toward the outlying bastion where Swedish soldiers waited to aid them. After Jesse had shut down, the soldiers pushed the aircraft into dead space next to the bastion and surrounded the machine with fascines readied for the purpose. It would be well guarded for their overnight stay.

Chapter 8

Mike found Gustav Adolf waiting for him in one of
the many rooms of Luebeck's Rathaus, which he'd
turned into his central headquarters for the siege. He
had only one aide with him, Colonel Nils Ekstrom. He
and his brother Sigvard were among the small circle
of Swedish officers that Gustav used for the most
delicate matters. That was a signal, in itself, that the
emperor wanted to be able to speak freely—which, with
Gustav, usually meant bluntly. If he'd had his usual
coterie of officers, he'd be quite a bit more discreet.
But Ekstrom was his closest adviser in Luebeck, and
Mike knew the emperor had complete faith in him.

Mike had to struggle a little to keep his expression
solemn. There was something about the bearing of the
emperor and the colonel—perhaps they were breathing
a bit too heavily, it was hard to know exactly—that
made it clear to Mike that they'd just gotten here
themselves. Having walked there very quickly, so they
wouldn't have to admit to Mike that they'd actually
been standing on the city walls watching his plane
land, just as if they were one of the city's bumpkins,
instead of awaiting his presence in royal serenity.

103

As was his way, Gustav went right past the usual formalities.

"So!" he half-bellowed. "Deny it if you will! It was *you* who gave the order to pass our medical secrets to the damned Spaniards outside Amsterdam." The sneer that followed was as royal as you could ask for. "Or will you try to claim—I believe you scheming up-timers call it 'plausible deniability'—that the fault was entirely that of the nurse. Anne—Anne—"

He cocked an eye at Ekstrom.

"Anne Jefferson," the colonel supplied. "Although it might be Anne Olearius, now. She was to be married to that Holstein diplomat, I'm told, and she may insist on that peculiar American custom of women changing their last names to their husbands'."

"It's actually an English custom in its origins, I believe," Mike said mildly. "They're not married yet, anyway. As for the other, Your Majesty, the answer is yes. Of course I'm the one who gave the order. Leaving aside the fact that she's no more careless than any good nurse, why would Anne have been carrying the formula with her in the first place—when she was simply posing for Rubens?"

"Ha! You admit it, then!"

That was . . .

About a three-quarter bellow. Between the volume, the tone, and various subtleties in the emperor's expression lurking under the bull walrus ferocity on the surface, Mike decided Gustav Adolf was in negotiating mode. He did have a temper, and he was perfectly capable of throwing a genuine royal tantrum at whatever subordinate had roused his ire. But he was very shrewd, too, and knew that his famous temper could also serve as a useful bargaining ploy.

It was all old hat, for Mike. In times past, when he'd been the president of his mine workers local having a confrontation with management, Quentin Underwood had used exactly the same tactic. Granted, Gustav was much better at it—not to mention having the status of an emperor instead of a mere mine manager, to give weight to the thing. But a bargaining tactic is a tactic, no matter how different the circumstances of the negotiation.

So, he responded with his usual riposte. Calm, forebearing reason. Not *quite* suggesting that the emperor was a five-year-old having a childish fit, but bordering on it.

"'Admit' is hardly the correct term, Your Majesty. The ploy was obviously to our benefit and could not possibly do us any harm."

"Do us no harm! You may well have saved the lives of thousands of enemy soldiers—the same ones baying at our allies in Amsterdam like a great pack of wolves."

"Oh, hardly that, Your Majesty. To begin with, chloramphenicol is so hard to make in any quantities—even for us, much less the Spaniards—that providing them with the formula was almost entirely a symbolic gesture. I doubt if more than a dozen Spanish soldiers will benefit from it, over the next year—and they will be entirely top officers, not the men who would be storming the ramparts. As for the rest—"

He shrugged. "My wife tells me that after the first week, the Spanish have not been pressing the siege. And pressed it even less, after we passed them the formula. They're behaving like watchdogs, not wolves. Which makes perfect sense, since the cardinal-infante is really aiming at a settlement, and would far rather keep Amsterdam and its productive population intact than see it all destroyed in a sack."

Gustav glowered at him, for a moment. "Still. Michael, you are trying to *maneuver* me. Do not deny it!"

Mike decided it was time to show a little of the bull walrus himself. So he almost sneered. Not quite. "Oh, for the love of—"

Now, a sigh, almost histrionic. Not quite.

"Gustav II Adolf, you've been a king for over twenty years—and a smart one, to boot. You know perfectly well that *every* adviser you have is trying to 'maneuver' you—if you insist on that term—practically every time they talk to you."

"Not me," said Ekstrom mildly.

Mike glanced at the colonel, and gave him an acknowledging nod. "No, Nils, not you. Not directly, at least. But—don't deny it, since we seem to be demanding that all cards be placed up on the table—your whole stance toward the emperor is a maneuver, in one sense. Yes, I know you simply try to help him determine what his own wishes really are. That's part of what a monarch needs."

Mike smiled. "Let's say that the emperor is using you as a tool to maneuver himself, if you prefer."

Ekstrom smiled back. "Yes, I would prefer it. And it's not a bad description of my duties"—he glanced apologetically at the emperor—"if Your Majesty will allow me the liberty of saying so."

Gustav puffed out his thick blond mustache. "And

why not? Since my prime minister takes far greater liberties."

He began pacing a little, half-stomping in the heavy cavalry boots he favored. That was a familiar sign to Mike—to Nils also, judging from the slight look of relief on the colonel's face. It meant the sumo wrestler preliminaries were over, for the most part, and the serious negotiations were about to begin.

"And you think we should do everything in our power to move that along," the emperor said. Almost growling the words, but not quite.

"Yes, Your Majesty, I do."

"Why? Michael, I am quite certain that when I launch our counteroffensive in the spring that I will crush the Danes and beat the French bloody. That stinking traitor Bernhard also, if he lets his arrogance rule him instead of his brain, and gets in my way. The Spaniards too, if they come out into the field."

"But they won't," said Mike firmly. "I don't care what they promised the French. The Spanish shed most of the blood in the naval war, and they are in no mood to do the same on land. Don Fernando has never sent more than a token force to the siege here. And when the fighting starts in the spring, he'll only move his main forces out just far enough to look like he's doing something—but will make sure he can get back behind his fortifications if your offensive succeeds."

He gauged that the time was right to adopt informality. "Gustav, on *that* subject we have—being blunt, the Committee of Correspondence in Amsterdam has superb intelligence. Partly, by the way, as a side effect of the medical assistance we've been providing the army outside the walls of the city. Gretchen's made sure that at least half of those medical advisers are CoC members."

That roused the emperor's temper again, as Mike had known it would. But since it would happen in any event, best to get it out of the way now.

"That damned Richter! All we need in the mix is that she-devil in Amsterdam! And that was your doing, too! Deny it!"

"Well, in this instance, I will deny it," said Mike patiently. "None of us had any idea the NUS embassy to the Netherlands would wind up getting trapped in a siege in Amsterdam. Or"—he arched an eyebrow—"are you now suggesting I somehow manipulated Richelieu and Christian IV and Charles I and Philip IV into forming the League of Ostend and launching a sneak attack on the Dutch? If so, that makes me the devil himself."

Gustav waved a meaty hand impatiently. "Fine, fine. You did *not* plot and scheme to plant Richter in Amsterdam. She's still there, stirring up trouble."

Mike maintained the same patient tone. "By all accounts the city's population is not restive at all. Gretchen's people are actually helping to maintain morale and discipline. Becky tells me that Fredrik Hendrik has now had three meetings with her, all of which went quite cordially."

Gustav stopped his pacing and frowned. "Is that true?"

"Yes, it is. Even Gretchen is now willing to admit that a good settlement in the Low Countries would be preferable to a deepening of the conflict. So Becky tells me, anyway." Mike smiled. "Mind you,

Gretchen's definition of a 'good settlement' is pretty astringent."

"Ha! I can imagine! Not only complete freedom of religion but sheer anarchy of expression and belief!" The emperor's mustache was practically quivering.

Mike responded a bit stiffly. "I simply think of it as freedom of speech, freedom of the press, and the freedom to assemble. We have the same principles encoded in the constitution of Thuringia, as you well know, and—as you well know, also—I am doing my level best to incorporate them in the new constitution of the USE. I probably won't be able to pull it off—yet—because I think Wilhelm will win the election. But those are my beliefs, and I will not waver from them."

The emperor got a distracted look on his face. "Speaking of which, when do you propose to hold the elections?" He gave Mike a look through those bright blue eyes that reminded Stearns that the emperor was a very shrewd man, beneath the sometimes blustery exterior. "You know—if you were a proper schemer and plotter—you would hold the elections right in the middle of the campaign. Most Germans would be more comfortable with Wilhelm Wettin as their prime minister, I think also. But . . . in time of war? I'm not so sure, Michael. You might get reelected."

Mike shrugged. "And so what? The war would be over, soon enough, and then I would face a reluctant electorate when it came time to implement the policies I want. Better, I think, to let things unfold at their own pace. Once Germany has the experience of Wettin in power, people may feel differently about things."

Ekstrom had been following the discussion closely,

and by now had become an astute observer of the politics of the USE. "You think he will insist on restricting the franchise? That will be the explosive issue, you know, not the religious business. I wouldn't think Wilhelm would be that stubborn."

Gustav Adolf was now listening intently also, but not saying anything. There was more in his stance and expression of an interested and curious observer than that of a ruler who had to make a decision any time soon. Mike wasn't positive, but he didn't think Gustav had any definite opinion on the subject of who should—and should not—be a citizen of the United States of Europe.

There was no reason he needed to have one, after all. Not yet, at least. His title of Emperor of the USE might be abstractly more prestigious than his title of the King of Sweden, but Gustav's real power stemmed from the latter, not the former. In Sweden, he ruled as a monarch, with few of the constitutional restrictions he faced as emperor of the new German nation. And as thorny and potentially volcanic as the problem of defining citizenship was for Germans, it was simply not an issue in Sweden.

"Left to his own devices, Nils," Mike said, "I think Wilhelm would prefer to just let the controversy over citizenship die a natural death. He knows that my party will introduce a proposal for complete and universal adult suffrage, whether I'm still the prime minister or simply the leader of the opposition. And no matter what, I can't see any realistic outcome of any election held within the next year or two that didn't produce a legislature at least one-third of whose members belonged to my party. In the lower house, we might even wind up with a majority. So all Wilhelm would have to do is quietly see to it that enough of his supporters agreed to it. And since the prime minister has no say-so over measures adopted in a special constitutional convention, he couldn't even be blamed for not vetoing it."

"But . . ." The emperor cocked his head.

Mike shrugged again. "He owes too many favors, Gustav. Way too many. He made the mistake—this is my opinion, anyway—of going for a quick victory instead of taking the time to solidify his position. Those 'Crown Loyalists' of his are not really a political party so much as a coalition of several different parties, first of all. Second, they don't have anything you could properly call a program. What they have is basically just a pastiche." He grinned, rather sarcastically. " 'What we don't like about Mike Stearns,' is really all it amounts to—which is not the same thing as 'what we believe.' And finally—"

He started scratching his jaw, in an old mannerism, before remembering Francisco Nasi's insistence that it was a bad habit for a political leader. Before she left, Becky had told him the same thing.

"And finally"—he dropped his hand—"the only real cement that holds that ramshackle 'party' of his together is a complicated crosshatch of favors exchanged between Wettin and a large number of people, most of whom—almost all of whom, except for Quentin Underwood and a few other up-timers— are noblemen of one sort or another. There are a few of them, like the landgrave and landgravine of Hesse-Kassel, who are smart enough and secure enough that I think they'd just as soon see the citizenship issue buried.

Ironically, I think Wilhelm's brother Ernst feels the same way about it."

That last sentence was as much of a question aimed at the emperor, as it was a statement. Ernst Wettin had decided to let his brother Albrecht assume the position of Duke of Saxe-Weimar after Wilhelm abdicated in order to run for office in the Commons. Instead, Ernst had accepted Gustav Adolf's offer to become the imperial administrator for the Upper Palatinate. Officially, he still retained his title as one of the dukes of Saxe-Weimar, but that no longer really meant very much.

Gustav nodded. "Yes, I think you are right. Judging from what I hear from General Banér, at least. Ernst is too fussy for Banér's taste—of course, almost anyone is too fussy for that man—but he never issues the sort of complaints about stupid petty aristocrats that he normally bestows on German noblemen."

Mike decided to let the matter drop, for the moment. He was tempted to probe a little further, to see if he could get the emperor to take a definite stance on the citizenship issue. But . . .

One thing at a time. He had an immediately pressing issue to deal with. And one that he could no longer handle by—he'd admit to himself the charge had been true enough—maneuvering Gustav Adolf. To do what needed to be done now, he had to have the emperor's full agreement, or it would all unravel come next spring.

Gustav, as perceptive as he normally was, spotted the moment also. "You want to keep driving the negotiations with the Spaniards. Or rather—since what you obviously have in mind is splitting the Spaniards—with the cardinal-infante."

"Yes."

Gustav, cheerfully defying all counsels concerning the proper mannerisms for august political leaders, began tugging at his mustache. "It's tempting, Michael. Yes, it is. As God is my witness, I can think of few things that would delight me more than seeing those stinking Habsburgs divided and quarreling among themselves as much as possible."

He left off the mustache-tugging and held up an admonishing finger. "But! Two things concern me. The first—the simplest—is that I am also sure I can overrun the Netherlands myself."

Catching sight of Colonel Ekstrom's slight wince, the emperor barked a laugh. "You too! Another skeptic!"

He went back to his mustache-tugging. "Well. I should have said, the three northern provinces. None of them have any great allegiance to the United Provinces, being mostly Catholics I agree it would be unwise to try to push further, into the Dutch heartland."

Mike took a deep breath. They had now entered very perilous territory. For all that he basically liked and admired Gustav Adolf, he never let himself forget that at bottom the king of Sweden was not that much different from any monarch of the time. He was an imperialist, at heart. For seventeenth-century rulers, grabbing as much land as possible was second nature. The nationalist sentiments that would dominate Europe before too long were still nascent in most places, although you could easily see them emerging if you looked and knew what to look for.

But no monarch did, not even Gustav Adolf. They thought in dynastic terms, not national terms—even those of them who, like Richelieu or Gustav himself, had carefully studied the histories brought back in time through the Ring of Fire. There was simply that deep-seated part of them that didn't quite *believe* that any ramshackle dynastic territory they built up would surely come to pieces, sooner or later, if it didn't have firm roots in popular sentiment.

Again, however, Mike decided to let it slide. He was pretty sure that Gustav's desire to add three small Dutch provinces to his dynasty wasn't really important to him. Assuming Gustav won the war, Mike intended to keep just enough to allow the USE Navy to dominate the Zuider Zee, if need be. His own motives were mostly as a way of throttling the life out of the slave trade while it was still in its infancy. But he was fairly certain that Gustav would settle for that, over time, simply as a token of his triumph.

The emperor's real territorial ambitions were toward the east. First, once the war with the Ostenders was over, Mike knew that Gustav was determined to punish the electors of Brandenburg and Saxony for their treacherous behavior by expropriating their territories outright. He'd do what he'd already done with Mecklenburg and Pomerania, simply add them to the USE as provinces.

So much, Mike had no quarrel with. In fact, he was for it. Saxony—even Brandenburg in this day and age, which hadn't yet undergone its metamorphosis into Prussia—were both German lands. But the problem was that any war with Saxony and Brandenburg was almost sure to bring in the Poles, and Gustav would then use that as a pretext to try to conquer Poland. Or a good chunk of it, at least. From his point of view, why not? Poland and Sweden had been fighting for decades, and it wasn't as if the king of Poland didn't claim that *he* should rightfully be the king of Sweden. Serve the bastard right.

Except, if that happened, Mike knew full well that the USE would simply be tying an albatross to its neck. Giving itself the same grief with Poland that, in a different universe, the Russians had done—more than once, and it had never worked.

But . . .

Let it slide, just let it slide. That was going to be quite literally a battle royal, when it happened. But it was a problem that wouldn't arise for about a year—and Mike had the situation in the Low Countries on his plate right now.

It was better, for the moment, to deal with Gustav's other objection. Mike was pretty sure he knew what it was going to be—and, if so, he thought he could persuade the emperor to follow his advice.

"And your second reservation, Your Majesty?"

Gustav dropped his hand from the mustache and spread both arms wide. "Oh, come, Michael! Surely it's obvious. The inevitable result of your plotting and scheming—your wife's, too! even worse than yours!—will be a powerful realm in the Low Countries. More than that. A united Netherlands is bound to sweep into it any number of the surrounding small principalities. What you propose is nothing less than the recreation of old Burgundy. And is that—"

Gustav went right back to his mustache-pulling. A bit enviously, Mike reflected that there were some advantages to being a king. To hell with advisers nattering you about perfectly comfortable habits. *L'État, c'est moi*—and that includes the damn mustache.

"Is that really in the interests of the United States of Europe?" Gustav concluded. "Or Sweden, for that matter, especially since—I will brook no arguments on this, Michael—you know I have every intention of recreating the Union of Kalmar. Once I've finished pounding that drunken Danish bastard Christian into a pulp."

There was no way Mike was going to stick his thumb into *that* issue. Not now, anyway. Personally, he had reservations concerning the emperor's plan to forge the first united Scandinavian realm since the Middle Ages. Maybe it would work, maybe it wouldn't—but, either way, it was not an issue that directly confronted the USE.

"Look at the problem the other way, Gustav. You read the histories. Half the grief suffered by Europe— the western part, anyway—came from that endless back-and-forth between the Germans and the French over the territory in the middle. In the here and now, and all the way through the next two centuries, mostly as a result of French aggression. Thereafter, usually, because the Germans got strong enough to respond in kind. And to what purpose, in the end?"

The emperor scowled slightly, but said nothing.

"No purpose at all—but tens of millions of people lost their lives in the process. So I think it would be wise to do what we can to forestall the mess altogether. And I can think of no better way to do it than to create a nation in the middle which is powerful enough—unlike the Holland and Belgium of my old universe—that both the French and the Germans have to think twice before they decide to pick a fight.

"Besides that," he pressed on, "having a commercially

prosperous and industrious Netherlands will be to our benefit economically. And they can't ever pose a real military threat, because even a recreated Burgundy simply can't have a large enough population to field big armies."

"They could certainly become a major naval power," Ekstrom pointed out. "The Dutch have managed that much on their own, even today."

There wasn't much vehemence to his statement, though. It was more in the way of an observation than an argument.

Mike didn't even have to answer that himself, in the event, since Gustav Adolf did.

"I am not much concerned about that, Nils," he said. "Without Denmark, they can't bottle us up in the Baltic. And"—here, a heavy shrug—"I do not foresee us having to squabble with them much with regard to the world beyond."

He was eyeing Mike by the time he finished, but didn't add anything. Mike was almost certain that Gustav knew how unyielding Mike intended to be over the slave trade—an issue that would certainly produce clashes with the Dutch, no matter what political entity emerged in the Low Countries. True, the Dutch weren't involved much in the slave trade yet—but "yet" was the operative term. They almost surely would be, within a decade at the latest. The same powerful commercial dynamics that had led them to become one of the leading nations in the slave trade in Mike's former universe applied just as fully in this one.

But, as with the issue of USE citizenship, the slave trade was simply not an issue that a king of Sweden cared much about. Not directly, at least. Neither Sweden nor any of the Scandinavian countries had been significant players in the slave trade, in the world Mike came from, and there was not much likelihood they would be in this one either.

Like Mike himself, the emperor had enough sense to let issues slide for a time, that didn't need to be dealt with immediately. His gaze was very keen, now, his eyes seeming to be as blue as blue could get.

"All right, Michael. Let's get down to the heart of things. You did not undertake such a flamboyant and somewhat risky venture as flying into Luebeck—I admit, it was splendid for the morale of my soldiers—simply to chat with me. You have something specific in mind. Something you suspect—ha!—I would dismiss out of hand if it came to me in the form of a radio message."

"Yes, I do. Here's what I propose . . ."

Gustav didn't explode, when Mike finished. Not in a temper tantrum, at least. He did, however, erupt into a truly imperial spasm of uproarious laughter.

"Ha! Ha!" he finally managed to exclaim. "Never since Menelaus has a husband displayed such an obsession for a wife! But that pitiful Greek wench simply launched a thousand ships and destroyed a city, so her husband could bed her again. To do the same to your wife, you propose to launch an entire nation!"

Mike could have argued that, of course, any which way from Sunday. It was actually not true at all that a crude desire to see his wife again after an absence of many months—fine, *copulate* with his wife again—was the motive impelling him forward.

Well, not the first one, anyway. Not even the second. The third, he'd grant.

But he said nothing. Partly because that third motive was pressing so closely on the first two that he wasn't quite sure he could pull it off with a straight face. And partly because the ribaldry had put Gustav in such a good mood.

"The cardinal-infante would have to agree to a cease-fire, though," Ekstrom cautioned. "I don't see any way you could land the plane in the city itself."

Mike nodded. "Well, yes. That would have to be part of the deal—and as good a way as any to test his trustworthiness."

Finally done with his laughing, Gustav peered at Mike. "And you are willing to be the bait? Well, I can see that. She is a very beautiful woman. And not unfaithful, like that wretched Helen. What was Menelaus thinking, the idiot?"

Chapter 9

Magdeburg

Thorsten found the office easily enough. After he entered Government House, for the first time since he'd settled in Magdeburg, he discovered a big plaque posted right next to the entrance that listed every office in the building and specified which floor they were on and even gave the room they were using a number. Then, once he reached the third floor, there was another plaque facing the stairwell that listed the offices on that floor—with arrows pointing either to the left or right, along with the name and number of the office. Only a village idiot could not have managed to find their way.

He found it all rather amusing. The term *Amerikanisch* had many connotations in Amideutsch, most of them quite positive. But one of the prominent connotations was "fussy, obsessed with detail, precise to the point of absurdity." Those neat plaques and arrows were a perfect illustration of the trait. *Everything must be in order!*

What was amusing about it was that Gunther

Achterhof had told Engler that in the universe the Americans came from, they perceived themselves as "rugged individualists"—whatever that might mean, exactly—and it was their accepted mythology that *Germans* were the world's natural bureaucrats.

Germans! Who squabbled about everything, including even the language they spoke, and were notorious throughout Europe for the production of religious sects, mass rebellions, mercenary soldiers—everything *except* order.

So, getting to the right office was easy. And, sure enough, there was another precise plaque on the door:

ROOM 322
UNITED STATES OF EUROPE
DEPARTMENT OF SOCIAL SERVICES

When it came time to enter, though, he found himself hesitating. Unlike Gunther, he'd had very little contact with up-timers—and that, only with male Americans. But this office was reputedly run by Americanesses, and the stories about them were enough to make any sane man pause.

Incredible women, by all accounts—although the stories Thorsten had heard rarely agreed with each other from that point forward. Some legends claimed they were the most lascivious creatures in the world, practically outright *succubi*. Others claimed they could find an issue concerning sex over which to take offense that no one else could possibly discern. The deadliest females in the world, and the most fragile females in the world. Sorceresses and fools at the same time, who could undertake chemic wonders but had no more sense than a chicken when it came to a multitude of practical matters.

Thorsten didn't know what to think—and was not at all sure he wanted to find out.

He paused with his hand on the door handle for a while. Finally, he decided to open it. They couldn't possibly be any more peculiar than his great-aunt Mathilde, after all. So, fortifying himself with the image of Mathilde's fierce eyes—badly crossed and nearsighted, but always fierce—and her constantly disheveled hair and the bizarre utterances that issued from a mouth whose teeth were about the worst anyone had ever seen, he entered the office.

And found himself staring at a young woman seated behind a desk, looking up at him with a smile.

About his age, he thought, somewhere in her mid-twenties. Hard to be sure, though. One of the things Americanesses had a reputation for—most accounts agreed on this—was that they seemed to have a peculiar resistance to aging. Some pointed to that as a sign of witchcraft, but most people ascribed it to their well-known chemic skills.

It was certainly impossible to imagine this woman as a witch, whatever her age. If someone had set Thorsten to the task of picturing a woman who was the exact opposite of his great-aunt Mathilde, he didn't think he could have come up with anything better.

To begin with, where Mathilde had always been very short and became shorter as she grew old—shorter and hunched—this woman was tall. That much was obvious, even seated as she was. Secondly, every hair was in place. True, the style of the hair was perhaps a bit strange, cut short the way it was, but not really all that much. More important, the hair was colored a rich brown, almost chestnut, and very healthy looking, where his great-aunt's hair had gone from an ugly black to a still uglier gray without ever once losing its most distinguishing characteristic, which was looking like a sheep that had gone unshorn since it was a lamb—but had had many an encounter with briars and thorns. Family legend had it that small animals and birds were occasionally spotted nesting in Great-Aunt Mathilde's hair. Even as boy, Thorsten had had his doubts, but . . . you never knew.

The eyes were completely different, too. Straight, not crossed; a bright and clear greenish color that went superbly with the hair, where Mathilde's eyes had wavered from a sort of muddy blue to a still muddier gray, depending on her mood of the moment. More striking still was that the green eyes studying him seemed friendly. Mathilde's mood of the moment had either been frenzied or angry or simply crotchety—but never friendly.

But all of that Thorsten noticed almost as an aside. From the moment he set eyes on the woman, his gaze was riveted on one feature alone.

So. At least one legend proved to be true, in every particular. The woman's teeth were *perfect.*

Perfect, and . . .

Also stunning. Because the teeth came as part of a wide mouth that had a smile on it that was the most beautiful smile Thorsten had ever seen. It would have been a little scary, if it hadn't been for the friendly green eyes floating somewhere above.

"Well, you sure took your time about it," the woman

said, somehow managing to smile more widely still. "I was starting to wonder if I'd need to get help, come nightfall, prying your hand off the handle so we could leave for the day. Or if I could do it myself, with a crowbar."

Startled, Thorsten glanced behind him. Only then realizing that he'd turned down the handle *before* he'd paused for a while.

"Ah," was all he could think of to say.

The smile stayed on her face, but at least the mouth closed. Thorsten thought if a man stared at those teeth for too long, it might turn him to stone. Or something.

"Never mind," she said cheerily. "You managed to get in. I'm Caroline Platzer, by the way. I'm the receptionist here, three mornings a week. What's your name, and what can I do for you?"

Thorsten cleared his throat. "My name is Thorsten Engler. A pleasure to make your acquaintance, Fraulein."

He thought he was safe enough, using that last appellation. So far as he could see, the Platzer woman wasn't wearing one of those gold rings that Americanesses used—so legend had it, at least—to signal their status as married women. He couldn't be positive, though, because even while speaking to him her hands continued to fly about the desk, doing . . . whatever it was a "receptionist" did. He might have missed one of the fingers.

She startled him with a soft laugh. "Oh, relax, will you? Herr Engler, I promise you I won't bite. Even if you do use one of the—how many are there supposed to be, by now?—eighty-three thousand, six hundred and forty-two Absolutely Forbidden Words in my presence. That includes any one of the five hundred and six Absolutely Prohibited Forms of Address, except three."

Warily, Thorsten eyed her. "And those three . . . are which?"

"If you call me a bitch or a cunt or a twat, I'll knock your head off." Her right hand came up, waggling a little. "A broad or a dame . . . depends."

He stared at her. He was familiar with the terms "bitch" and "cunt," since the words had been absorbed into Amideutsch. He had no idea what "twat" meant, but in context, he could guess. "Dame" was obvious, although he suspected he'd encountered a different connotation than the usual one.

"I would never do such a thing anyway," he said. The words came out automatically, not even a protest so much as a simple statement of fact. Most of his mind was still trying to make sense of "broad." He understood the approximate meaning of the term, but could see no connection to women.

Her eyes crinkled. "Y'know, I believe you. Would you like some tea?"

Without waiting for the answer, she rose from her seat and went over to a counter where a pot waited, simmering on a peculiar little mechanical candle of some sort. On her way, Thorsten saw one guess confirmed. She was indeed tall. Slightly taller that he was, he thought, though not by much. Less than an inch.

Then she bent over to reach the jar of tea nestled on a shelf below, and the sense of the term "broad" became instantly clear to Thorsten. Just as instantly as the stirrings of an erection.

Dear God in Heaven. None of the legends had prepared him for *this.*

Yes, certainly, she was a bit exotic and a bit startling with that direct manner she had, and she was a bit of this and a bit of that and it was all silly nonsense. She wasn't even beautiful, although she came awfully close. What she was, was something Thorsten had felt and understood since he was fourteen years old and had first laid eyes on one of his second cousins.

Desirable. Sheer and unalloyed, it was as simple as that.

Poor Brigida, that had been, who had died in the first epidemic that swept the village. She'd only been sixteen years old, a little older than Thorsten at the time. But for every day that had passed in the two years since the glorious moment he first met her and the horrid time they took her body away to be burned, he had desired her. He'd been completely smitten, in the way boys often were and young men were never supposed to be, once they entered adulthood and had to be practical about such things.

Thorsten had never expected to encounter that sensation again. Certainly not under these circumstances.

Fortunately, while those thoughts and emotions roiled through him, the Platzer woman was looking elsewhere as she went about the business of preparing the tea. By the time she turned around to face him and, still smiling, handed him a mug of tea, he was reasonably composed again.

"Reasonably composed," that is to say, in the way that a twenty-six year old man will be when raw desire is sweeping through him, back and forth, like great waves washing over a ship's deck in a storm. Not more than one-fourth of his brain was able to concentrate on anything besides the woman herself. Fortunately again, the heavy workman's clothing he was wearing to fend off the December cold kept the half-erection from showing. He did manage, as casually as he could, to wipe his mouth with his hand. He was afraid there might be drool showing. He had no idea at all how a man went about courting an Americaness, but he was quite sure that starting off by acting the uncouth boor would not be helpful at all.

"You still haven't answered my question, Herr Engler," she said, resuming her seat behind the desk. "What can we do for you? And would you please sit down?" She pointed at a chair behind him and a little to his left.

A bit clumsily, Thorsten sat down. Clumsy, because three-quarters of his attention was elsewhere. Her *fingers* were gorgeous. He could imagine them—

That way lay disaster. Hastily, he broke off the surging reverie and wracked his brain to think of something appropriate and intelligent to say.

Informality. That little piece of the many legends got jostled loose and rose to the surface. Almost all of them agreed on that, too, so it was probably true.

"Please, call me Thorsten." That came out much more stiffly than he'd intended. But he was afraid to smile. His mouth open that far, drool was sure to come.

"Thorsten it is, then. And please call me Caroline." She leaned forward a bit and waved a finger at him, playing the scold. "But I warn you, sir! It's 'Caroline,' not 'Carol.' Cross that line at your peril."

The same finger, alas. Was there *any* part of the

woman that was plain, at least, since he couldn't imagine anything actually ugly. Something he could focus on to keep from sliding into the behavior of a village idiot or—worse yet—a schoolboy.

The best he could come up with was: "I would not dream of it. Caroline it shall always be."

He said it too intently. Too . . . roughly, almost. She would think he was coarse.

And, indeed, the smile that seemed permanently fixed now faded some. And, suddenly, she had a different look in her eyes. But it didn't seem to be one of irritation or revulsion. Simply . . .

Startled, perhaps?

Who could say, with an Americaness?

Luckily, he still had enough of his wits to remember that she'd now asked him the same question twice. Or maybe it was even three times.

"Friends told me I should come here. Today, because I just enlisted in the army and I will soon be leaving for the training camp. I was involved in the accident at the coal gas plant. Very closely involved. And . . . well, I am having nightmares. And I keep seeing images of what happened. Very vivid images. They told me I might be suffering from some sort of—of—what is it called?"

Caroline was not smiling at all, now. "Post-traumatic stress disorder. We heard about the accident, of course. That must have been horrible."

He took a breath. "Yes. It was. Does this mean I might be . . . ah, going insane?"

She shook her head, very forcefully. "Oh, no, nothing like that. In fact, you may not have PTSD at all. Thorsten, all the reactions you're having are perfectly normal, after people go through an experience like that. We don't define it as PTSD until quite a bit of time has passed. It's only if the symptoms such as nightmares, flashbacks, hypervigilance—there a lot of them and they vary from one person to another, but those are the most common—don't fade, that we conclude something abnormal is happening. But 'abnormal' does not mean insane. There's nothing at all wrong with your mind."

She leaned forward still further, lowering her head and pointing to the back of her skull. Which, of course, was also shapely. Thorsten was racked by a sort of thrilled despair.

"Back here is what we call the limbic part of the brain. To simplify some, you can think of it as the most primitive—and most basic—part of the brain. It's where automatic responses and our animal instincts are centered. But it's not where thoughts are formed and emerge. That happens here"—she raised her head and pointed to her forehead, using both forefingers this time—"in what's called the cortex."

She paused briefly, gathering her own thoughts. "What seems to happen with PTSD is that the traumatic memories get stored in the limbic part of the brain, instead of the parts where they would normally get stored. We don't know why it happens, really. Or rather, why it happens to some people and not to others. But once it does happen, the problem is that the memories are now locked into a part of the brain that doesn't think rationally and doesn't respond to reason. That's why traditional talk therapy doesn't usually work all that well, with PTSD. In fact, a lot of specialists—Maureen Grady, who set up and runs this department, being one of them—think talk therapy by itself is more likely to be harmful than helpful. They think all it does is keep stirring up the traumatic memories without doing anything to alleviate them."

Thorsten tried to sort through what she was telling him. Relieved, finally, to have something interesting to think about other than Caroline Platzer herself. That would help him . . . he thought the American expression was "keep his cool."

It *was* interesting, too, even fascinating. It had never occurred to him to think of the brain as something with different parts that did different things.

"So—perhaps I do not understand something—what you are saying is that there is not much that can be done for me. Yes?"

"No, not exactly. There are some techniques for dealing with PTSD that seem to be successful much of the time, or at least helpful. Using mental imagery as a way of soothing your limbic system before you engage in talk therapy often helps. There's even"—here she chuckled softly, and shook her head a little—"don't ask me how it works, because it's always seemed like magic to me. Maureen could explain it to you. It's a peculiar method of getting a person's eyes to move rapidly back and forth while they're undergoing therapy—a lot of times the therapist just has them follow their finger—which seems to decouple the limbic responses. Like I said, it seems like magic. But, however it works, it does seem to work a lot of the time."

She leaned back in her seat and half-turned, glancing first at a clock on the back wall and then at one of the doors behind her. "Maureen's seeing a client right now, but she should be free, in a moment. I'll talk to her about giving you the finger therapy. It's also useful even for people just suffering from temporary symptoms."

She turned back to face him, lacing her fingers together. Caroline was the sort of person who gestured a lot when speaking, so her fingers had been fluttering about. Now, for the first time, all of them were still and visible. He'd been almost certain already but now he could definitely see that while she was wearing three rings, not one of them fit the description of an up-time wedding band. And none of the three rings was on the finger that, if he remembered correctly, was supposed to hold the wedding band.

He could only hope that *that* legend was true, at least. Any number of the others had already fallen like pigs at slaughtering time.

"But the main thing," she continued, "is simply that it's much too soon to determine if you have PTSD in the first place. You may very well not be suffering from it at all, Thorsten."

The door behind her opened, and a middle-aged woman emerged, followed by another. From various subtleties of dress and manner—mostly the latter—Thorsten knew that the second woman was the up-timer.

His assessment was confirmed an instant later.

"Thank you, Maureen," said the first woman. "I shall see you next week, then."

"Yes—but at noon, not the usual time, Cleopha."

While the German woman passed through the outer room, nodding in a friendly way to Caroline and a polite way to Thorsten, Maureen held her door open.

Once Cleopha had left, she glanced at Thorsten and then looked at Caroline.

"Can I speak to you for a moment, Maureen?"

"Of course, Caroline. Come in."

Once Thorsten was alone in the room, he was finally able to relax a bit. "Relax," at least, in the way that a twenty-six year old man will relax while his mind seems to have dozens of ideas ricocheting about at random—all of them involving a plot or scheme or ploy or maneuver to figure out how he could possibly manage to see this woman again, each and every one of which he is almost certain is completely harebrained.

After Caroline finished her quick summary of the Engler case, Maureen Grady shook her head. "God, that accident was horrible. Dennis got there toward the end, you know. There were still pieces of people lying all over. One corpse he saw hadn't even been decapitated. The head was simply disintegrated. Dennis almost vomited."

Caroline grimaced. Maureen's husband Dennis was a cop, and as hard-boiled as most cops are. It took a lot to penetrate his hide.

Maureen was now consulting her calendar. "Did he tell you when he'd be leaving for boot camp?"

"No. I don't think he knows himself."

"Damn army!" Maureen said, half-chuckling. "Whatever else is different between this universe and the one we left behind, one thing for sure and certain stayed the same. The army's motto is still 'hurry up and wait.'"

She pushed the calendar aside. "I can see him tomorrow, at two o'clock. After that . . ."

She shrugged slightly. "We'd have to wait anyway, even if he weren't going into the service. But it might still be helpful for him to have a counselor to talk to. Do you want to handle it yourself? It doesn't need to be here, since you're mostly at the settlement house. You could set it up to see him over there, in one of the spare rooms."

Caroline issued the same sort of half-chuckle. "'Spare rooms'! A broom closet, maybe."

She hesitated, then looked at the door beyond which an unseen Thorsten Engler was waiting. Then, still hesitating, looked out of Maureen's window.

"Oh, don't tell me," Maureen said. The chuckle that came out this time was a full one.

Caroline made a face. "For Pete's sake, Maureen, I just met the man. Still . . ."

She gave Maureen a look that tried and failed to be aloof. "Seeing as how you insist on maintaining the social workers' professional ethics code, in every jot and tittle . . ."

"You're damn right I do, young lady. I don't care if we'd been planted back in the Stone Age. If you take someone on as a client, that will be your one and only relationship with that person. Ever. I don't care if it's twenty years later."

Caroline nodded, and looked back out the window. She hadn't expected a different response—and, for that matter, didn't disagree with Maureen anyway. There was a very good reason for that tight-laced code of ethics.

Mostly, she realized, she was just startled twice, today, and by the same man. That . . . certain sort of startlement. The one that suddenly, unexpectedly, makes you *focus* on a person. She hadn't felt that since the Ring of Fire, which had torn from her the man she'd loved since she was seventeen and had been planning to marry in six weeks. Hadn't really expected she ever would again.

"In that case, no," she said. "I think it might be better if someone else took him on as a client."

"Fine." Maureen was all business, now, back to checking her calendar. "If he wants to see someone before he leaves, tell him I can set something up. Lutgardis would do fine. So would Maria Magdalena or Rosina. Maybe Gertrud, too, although I'd be happier if she had a little more experience. We'll manage, one way or another."

Maureen made sure to get a good look at the Engler fellow, as she ushered Caroline out the door. Nothing too long or rude, of course. Just enough to get a sense of things.

She was quite satisfied by the brief study. Engler had that certain unmistakable look about him. Caroline wouldn't really grasp it, of course, since she was too close to the matter. But to Maureen it was obvious.

Rather a good-looking man, too, even if you couldn't really call him handsome. Dark-haired, blue-eyed, quite a nice mouth and a perfectly acceptable nose. A bit on the stocky side, maybe—but to make up for it he seemed to have better teeth than usual.

But all that was trivial. What mattered was the look on his face, that Maureen had seen but Caroline hadn't because she'd been too busy looking somewhere else while Engler tried and failed miserably to keep from ogling her.

Okay, "ogling" wasn't really fair. He seemed a perfectly polite man. But it was still The Look. The one—perhaps the only one—that made men really, really cute. She could remember the same look on her husband's face, years back, when he'd spent two hours skittering all over before he finally asked her out on a date. By the end, she'd thought he might have a complete meltdown before he managed to get the words out.

It was the look on an ox's face, she imagined, when the hammer comes down. She'd never worked in a slaughterhouse, so she wasn't positive. But if it wasn't, it *ought* to be.

She checked to make sure the door was closed. It was a nice thick heavy seventeenth-century door, too. Not quite soundproof, but close enough. Then, started hopping up and down and pumping her fist in a cheerleader's gesture of victory.

"Yes! Yes! Yes! About fucking time!"

"No, you wouldn't be seeing me, Thorsten. I only work here part of the time, anyway. Just in the mornings on Mondays, Tuesdays, and Thursdays. Most of the time I work at the settlement house. Are you familiar with it? It's almost on the river, not far south of the navy yard."

"Oh. Yes, I've seen it. Never went in, though."

She gave him her best smile. "You should drop by some time, then."

"I would not wish to intrude."

"Oh, don't be silly. It'd be nice to see you again. Really, it would."

Chapter 10

*The siege lines of the Spanish army in the
Low Countries, outside the walls of Amsterdam*

"This would be an irrevocable step, Your Highness. I
do not say you should refuse, simply . . ."

Pieter Paul Rubens shrugged. "Simply be aware,
from the beginning, of the likely consequences. They
will most probably be severe."

Don Fernando turned his eyes away from their
examination of Amsterdam's walls to look at Rubens.
The Habsburg prince most people called the cardinal-
infante—he was the younger brother of Philip IV,
king of Spain—knew from his reading of the up-time
texts that as the centuries passed, Rubens would be
remembered almost entirely for his art. But in the
world he lived in, he was just as well-known for being
one of Europe's premier diplomats.

And not by accident. In the weeks—months, now—
since the siege began, Don Fernando had come to
have the same confidence in the artist that most
members of the Habsburg dynasty did. Members of
other dynasties, for that matter. Whatever his private

opinions, which he generally kept to himself, Rubens invariably gave counsel designed to help the person asking for it determine what they actually wanted in the first place. He did not ever seem to have—to use the American expression the prince had learned from the nurse, Anne Jefferson—"an ax to grind."

A charming expression, as were several others the prince had learned from Jefferson in her various visits to the Spanish camp. Visits that she'd officially made as a model for Rubens, but which had actually been disguised diplomatic maneuvers of one sort or another. Both the cardinal-infante and his opponents on the other side of Amsterdam's walls, the prince of Orange and the Abrabanel wife of the USE's prime minister, had found the young and innocent-looking nurse a most handy instrument for conducting what amounted to negotiations while officially fighting a bitter siege.

But he was not thinking of those charming expressions, explained to him by a very charming woman. It was something else she'd said to him, in her last visit, that had been gnawing at him for days, now. Especially coming on top of many months of growing doubts and uncertainties. To use another one of her expressions, *the straw that broke the camel's back.*

"I asked her," he said abruptly, "what she—an educated woman, quite intelligent—knew about the Habsburgs. Not today, but when she still lived in that . . ."

He waved his hand, vaguely. "Future world she came from."

He would leave it at that. The prince knew of the speculations and arguments that had been roiling

Europe's theologians and philosophers—not to mention kings and princes and their advisers—since the Ring of Fire. They ranged from crude and simple accusations of demonism and witchcraft to logical arguments that were so convoluted they were impossible to follow at all. Inevitably—God knows how they managed it, but they did—a number of the theologians had even tied the debate back to the dispute over transubstantiation versus consubstantiation.

One bishop in southern Italy had gone so far as to suggest that the Ring of Fire somehow called into question the Nicene Creed. Of course, the man was obviously a lunatic—the proof of it being that he'd advanced the argument within reach of the Spanish Inquisition. A reach which had grasped him as quickly and surely as a snake seizing a mouse.

Rubens inclined his head. "And her response was . . ."

Don Fernando could feel his jaws tightening. "She was quite startled, you understand. And I pressed the matter—perhaps rudely—because I really wanted to see what her answer would be."

He took a deep breath and let it out. "Worse than I'd feared. Far worse." He could still remember, quite vividly, the nervous way the nurse's eyes had shifted about. As she so obviously tried to think of something pleasant she could say. Inoffensive, at least.

She'd failed, because the prince had not given her time. He had been rather rude, he could see now. Still, the rudeness had served its purpose.

"What she said—her exact words, Pieter—was: 'Well, you suffered from a lot of hereditary illness. And you all had that famous lower lip.'"

Rubens smiled faintly, as did the prince himself.

Hard not to—since Don Fernando himself had the famous lip.

"Perhaps . . ." said Rubens. "Please remember that—yes, the woman is quite intelligent, but still—she had a limited education. Tightly focused, it would be better to say."

"And what does that matter?" demanded the prince, with some exasperation. "It makes it all the worse, in fact. She's certainly no more poorly educated than most people of her time. Which means that her unstudied response is a good reflection of what posterity will remember about us. What the *world* will remember. Who cares what a few scholars in that future might think?"

He waved his hand again, not vaguely but firmly. "And what they think is not much different, anyway. Don't play the diplomat here, Pieter. I've read some of the scholarly accounts."

Don Fernando had to force himself to loosen his jaws. He'd almost snarled the last few sentences. It wouldn't do to have Rubens think he was angry at him. He wasn't, at all. He needed the man's sage advice, now more than ever.

"We were—are, damnation—the greatest dynasty ever produced by humanity. If that sounds arrogant, so be it. Who compares to us? The Plantagenet dynasty of England that those up-time accounts romanticize so grotesquely? They were limited to part of an island and part of France, and they only lasted three centuries. We've already lasted longer than that, and according to those same up-time accounts, will—would—ah! how does one express it grammatically?—better those idiot logicians should concentrate on that practical problem—last well over half a millennium. And we dominated the entire continent almost throughout. As we do today. As we have since at least Charles V. And not just Europe! Half the world, for the past century."

Now he waved—again, firmly—toward the east. "I even examined what I could find about the Chinese and the Persians and the Hindus. None of them, so far as I can determine, ever produced a dynasty that lasted longer than the Plantagenets. Nor did anyone in the ancient world. The famous Roman Antonines didn't even last two centuries."

He looked at Rubens, almost glaring. "You've read more of the texts than I have, I imagine. Did *you* encounter anything different?"

After a pause, Rubens shook his head. "No, Your Highness. I did not."

"Thought so! No, Pieter, I am not mistaken about this. Let things continue as they did—as they will, if nothing is done—and our posterity in this universe will be the same. Some sort of horrid diseases, and"—he flicked his fleshy lower lip with a finger—"this stupid thing. Not even a nose!"

He lowered the hand and clasped the other behind his back. Then, began rocking on his feet a little. "Will you keep our discussions privy, Pieter? I mean, from my brother as well."

Rubens nodded. "Yes, Your Highness. I do that with all such discussions, in any event. But in this case . . ."

The artist and diplomat gazed at Amsterdam. "In this case, I have been coming to many of the same conclusions myself. And being a Catholic and not a blithering Calvinist, I know that God gave us free will."

Now he looked at the prince directly. "And that good works will receive their reward in the afterlife."

The prince smiled. "Of course, the trick is defining 'good works' in the first place, isn't it? And then, only being able to hope that the saints and the angels and the Lord Himself will agree with your definition. Which, alas, you won't discover until it's too late to correct whatever errors you made."

Rubens smiled back. "Yes, indeed. That is the difficulty. Inevitable, of course. Without that uncertainty, 'free will' would be meaningless."

There was silence, for a time, as the prince and his adviser both went back to their study of Amsterdam's fortifications. It was a pointless study, really, just a means for the prince to finally steel his will. By this time, he knew every foot of those walls. And knew, as well, just how terrible the cost would be of passing through them. The heady and triumphal glory of the first weeks of the reconquest of the United Provinces had long gone. Ages past, it seemed, even though it had only been a few months.

"Enough," he said quietly. "Let my family rot in Spain, as they certainly will so long as they listen to Olivares and his ilk. With my brother and the count-duke demanding from me every week more and more treasure from the Low Countries. They insist I must despoil and ruin the Netherlands—and for what? So they can piss it away down a bottomless toilet, as they have done for a century with the New World's silver. Let my cousins in Austria do the same, if they choose, as they did in another world. I will start here, anew. My dynasty had six centuries in that other world. In this one . . ."

He laughed softly. "What do you think, Pieter? If I claim a full millennium as my goal, would that constitute the sin of pride?"

"I couldn't say, Your Highness. I'm not a theologian. But I am an artist, and I can promise you some splendid portraits."

He eyed the prince's costume, which was a purely martial one. "I assume you will not wish to pose in your cardinal's robes."

Don Fernando grinned. "Be a bit awkward, wouldn't it? Since the most important portraits will be of me and my future wife—whoever she might turn out to be—surrounded by our children. That *is*, after all, the first thing you need for a successful dynasty."

"Indeed." The diplomat pursed his lips, for a moment, thinking. "Dispensing with the title of cardinal should not be too difficult, I think. You could simply resign unilaterally, although that would cause a stir. But the pope is generally quite practical about these things, and I know—I've spoken to him—that Urban is none too pleased with the endless war."

"I've come to the same conclusion," the prince said. "As God Himself knows, it's not as if I ever wanted a cardinal's robes in the first place. My father and his advisers insisted on it. That leaves . . ."

His eyes became slightly unfocused, for a moment. "A wife. It will have to be someone acceptable to the haughtiest monarch or nobleman in Europe. That's essential."

Rubens inclined his head. "Yes, of course. Under the circumstances, a morganatic marriage—anything that even had a whiff of it—would be out of the question." He went back to pursing his lips. "I can begin some discreet inquiries. There are not really all that many options, you understand?"

Don Fernando gave him a quick, stoic nod of the head. "Yes, Pieter, I know. Do your best to find someone reasonably pleasant and not too ugly, if you can. But what matters is that she be fertile and young enough to bear a number of children. The rest I can—will have to—just live with."

His expression brightened. "But what I am saying? *First* I have to win this war—or get a good enough settlement, at least. A wife can wait. *Must* wait, in fact. No suitable bride will be found for a king who doesn't have a realm to show for the title. Even the Germans would laugh at such a one."

Rubens was a little amused to see the way the prince—a man still in his early twenties—so obviously found the demands of war more congenial than the demands of marriage. Of course, for royalty, that attitude was not so unusual, even in much older men. Very rarely was congeniality, much less affection, a significant factor when it came to choosing spouses. As it would not be in this instance, either.

Within seconds, after a polite but brief dismissal, Don Fernando was consulting with his officers over the best place to prepare what the Americans called a "landing field." Before too long, Rubens was sure, the prince would come to the inevitable conclusion that—since neither he nor any of his officers had ever seen an airplane—they would need to send an envoy to Amsterdam to discreetly inquire if the up-timers residing in the city could provide them with some advice.

Rubens himself would probably be the envoy chosen, in fact.

❖   ❖   ❖

As he walked back to his quarters, picking his way carefully through the trenches and earthworks that had turned the land around Amsterdam into something that reminded him of nightmarish paintings by the elder Brueghel, Rubens mused over which up-timer would be sent as a consultant.

Not Anne, unfortunately, as much as Pieter liked the woman. The young nurse had several times commented jokingly on her complete ineptitude with up-time mechanical devices. "Outside of nursing and medical equipment, I'm hopeless. I can change a light bulb and that's about it. Ask me to tell a spark plug from an alternator, and I'd have to go *eeny-meeny-miny-mo*."

The terms themselves had all been meaningless to Rubens, but the gist of the statement was clear enough.

Who, then?

Probably the big one, who was married to the agitator woman, Gretchen. Jeff, his name was, if Pieter remembered correctly. The artist had gathered, from various comments he'd heard, that the young man was considered a "geek." So far as Rubens could determine, that referred to a person who was obsessed with up-time devices and mechanical skills—something called "electronics," especially. Like some astrologers and alchemists of his own time, it seemed, about whom similar jokes were made.

Odd, really. From the man Jeff's appearance, Pieter would have assumed he was a simple soldier—and perhaps a brutish one, at that.

He paused for a moment, after negotiating his way through a particularly tortuous set of trenches, and gazed back at Amsterdam.

But that was the key to it all, he thought. In a small way, that contradiction between a young up-timer's appearance and the lurking truth behind it was a good symbol.

How else describe that titan who stood behind the boy? Who had in some way, even been responsible for creating him. A brute on the outside, but underneath . . .

Rubens resumed his walk. Very slowly now, because his thoughts were mostly elsewhere.

The cardinal-infante's confidences had come as no surprise. Rubens had been expecting them, before too long. The enemy's proposal to allow their prime minister to fly to Amsterdam and land safely beyond the walls right in front of the Spanish guns had simply been the immediate trigger. Had the proposal not been made, the prince would still have done the same a bit later.

Rubens had seen it coming, for weeks. Partly because, from his long experience as a diplomat, he could see the logic and sense the way it was unfolding in the mind of the prince who sought his advice and counsel. But mostly for the simplest reason of all.

Pieter Paul Rubens, a man who had been faithful to the Habsburgs all his life—and he was now fifty-six years old—had come to the edge of treason. To call things by the name that almost everyone would soon be calling it. Granted, the difference between a "traitor" and a "loyalist" being something that only history could finally pass verdict upon. If Don Fernando's scheme succeeded, the world would only remember the success. All but a sullen few would forget that the triumph began with treason, for treason it surely was—just as surely as Rubens would be executed for it, if the prince's plans failed and Rubens fell into the hands of the Spanish crown.

For, even before the prince spoke, Rubens had already decided he would support the plot and do everything in his power to make it succeed.

And why? Because a titan had been set loose in the world, and the monster had a mind more cold and savage and ruthless than any king or prince of the day. Not since Constantine, Rubens thought, had such a terrible soul walked the earth. Perhaps not since Alexander.

And there, of course, lay the quandary. For had not Constantine created the basis for the triumph of the true church? Had not Alexander, before him, created the world in which that church could arise?

Let the churchmen and the theologians insist that Constantine was a saint who had been impelled by his own faith. What difference did it make? Suppose the opposite were true, and the Roman emperor had been motivated by nothing beyond his own ambition. The result was the same, no?

Rubens had reached his quarters, now. He could hear his wife chatting with a servant in the kitchen, but he passed by the entrance and went to the room set aside for his work. There, as if driven by compulsion, he opened a drawer and drew out the document. He still had the original papers the nurse had left behind. Acting, he was quite certain, on another's orders.

HOW TO MAKE CHLORAMPHENICOL

The pages that followed that title gave precise instructions for how to manufacture the world's most potent medicine.

The monster's stiletto, that the creature had driven into the heart of the world's greatest dynasty, his aim guided by a dragon's cunning and the force of the thrust by a titan's thews.

Who else could have conceived such an assassin's stroke?

For a moment, he had to fight not to crush the papers in his hands. Those papers that had opened the door to treason.

A sudden burst of laughter from the kitchen drew him there, again as if under compulsion.

When he entered, his wife looked up at him, smiling. Helena Fourment, only nineteen years old, of whom he was very fond. He would have five children by her, the first of whom was now sitting on her lap. The last child would be born eight months after his death at the age of sixty-three. Which would seem to indicate that he never lost that affection, even at the end—nor the ability to express it.

Seven years from now.

Perhaps. That was his biography in another world. Who could say, in this one?

But he wasn't really looking at Helena. He was seeing another face there. That of his first wife, Isabella Brant, whom he had also loved.

But that was the past, fixed, certain. Not something even the monster and his minions could change.

Isabella had died five years before the Ring of Fire. Taken from him by disease, at the age of thirty-five, in the prime of her life.

He looked now at his new daughter. Barely one year old. He had named her Clara Johanna, in memory of his first daughter by Isabella, Clara Serena.

Who had also been taken from him by disease, at the age of twelve. One of many struck down by another epidemic.

"Is something wrong, husband?"

"No, dearest. I'm . . . simply preoccupied."

And he was, suddenly. With a glorious burst of inspiration, such as he had not felt in years. Not since he first saw the up-time book that depicted his life and work—much of which he still hadn't done, or even conceived of—and sensed a great emptiness yawning beneath him.

How does an artist paint something he has already painted? Without the master becoming his own apprentice? Ending a life full of triumphs as if he were nothing more than an understudy?

Another of those impossible quandaries the monster brought with him into the world. But Rubens could resolve it now, using the monster himself.

He came into the room and wiggled fingers at his daughter, who was staring up at him with the wondering eyes of a child barely one year into a life that, for half the children in the world—including some of his—would never be much longer than that.

Then he smiled at Helena to reassure her, while he gently stroked the hair sprouting on Clara Johanna. "You will live, girl," he said, so softly that he didn't think Helena could hear the words. He hoped not, certainly, since she would insist on an explanation later, and what could he say? If nothing else, he would carefully shield Helena from any charges of treason.

"But I must go to work now," he said abruptly, and left.

❖   ❖   ❖

By the end of the day, he already knew it would be one of his best paintings. He had that sure sense of the thing, that always came with the very finest ones.

A painting that existed in no up-time book, because he had never conceived such a portrait in that other world. Could *not* have conceived it. He didn't think Brueghel's fevered mind could have dreamed of it—nor even the mad brain of Hieronymus Bosch, for all that the structure of the image shared the logic of Bosch's triptychs.

"The Titan's Choice," he thought he would call it. Or, better still, simply "The Titan." The choice being obvious in the painting itself. Cities wracked by flame and destruction issuing from the right hand, clad in mail and armor. The right hand that any man could resist, with sufficient will and courage. While the left hand, unarmored—the assassin's hand, with the main gauche—delivered the fatal blow. Children spilling out like fruit from a cornucopia. The blow that passed beneath any armor, any defense, any will or steadfastness or courage, because it did not strike at kings and princes and soldiers at all. It struck the fathers and husbands hidden beneath.

Of course, he would not be able to show it in public, but that didn't really matter. The joy of finally recapturing his own creation was enough.

Who could he show it to, after all? Even if Don Fernando triumphed, Rubens would have to conceal it from the prince become a king. Rubens liked the young Habsburg scion, a great deal, and he wished him all the best. A long reign over a prosperous realm, with many children to carry on his line, sired upon a convivial and comely wife he actually loved. Had affection for, at least.

For that matter, Rubens was partial to the Habsburgs taken as a whole, and hoped that Don Fernando would be able to revitalize that great family. But he also knew that Don Fernando's dreams of future Habsburg glory were already doomed. The best the prince and his heirs would manage—no small thing, of course—would be to protect and nurture one corner of the world.

The world itself no longer belonged to them. A titan had come, and shaken it loose. For good or ill, it would be his name that the future would bestow upon this time, just as it had in ages past upon Alexander. And would, in the future of the titan's world, bestow upon a man named Napoleon.

His enemies could assassinate him tomorrow, and it wouldn't matter. The deadliest blows had already been delivered. Alexander died in Babylon at the age of thirty-three—but the Persian world was already gone, swept aside by the Greek torrent brought by its conqueror. Just as surely as the world Rubens and Don Fernando had been born in was already gone.

So be it. Rubens had made the father's decision, the husband's decision. In the end, dynasties were a small thing.

He decided he would leave the face till the last. True, he could request a portrait of some sort—they might have one of those "photographs" in their possession, in Amsterdam—but why bother? That would require awkward explanations, and he would have several days to study the titan himself after he arrived, with no one being the wiser.

❖   ❖   ❖

He came. He went. For days, that fair but plain face fascinated Rubens. He'd thought he would have to idealize it—or demonize it, perhaps—but in the end decided the face was perfect as it was. Inscrutable in its simplicity, just as were the titan's deeds themselves.

A week later, the painting was done. It was the best work Rubens had done in years. A pity it would have to remain hidden, of course. But whatever else, the work had shattered the artist's paralysis. Everything he'd done since the Ring of Fire, except this, had been a copy of something, in one way or another. If not a copy of his own works, those of another—like that portrait he'd done of the Gretchen woman and her magnificent bosom, mimicking an artist of the future named Delacroix.

Well, not some of the Jefferson portraits, perhaps. But those had been so closely tied to a public purpose that he'd felt tightly constrained.

He thought he probably still only had seven years left, himself, regardless of what happened. He'd died of gout, in that world that would have been. From what Anne had told him, there didn't seem to be any magical medical cure for that condition, not even for the up-timers. Only a dreary list of things he shouldn't eat, and a still drearier list of things he shouldn't do. It hardly seemed worth it, just to gain a few extra years. Sixty-three wasn't so bad, better than most.

He didn't care much, really. They would be seven productive years, perhaps the most productive of his life. And he always had the consolation—given to precious few men since Adam—of knowing that almost the last act of his life would be to impregnate a wife whom he would leave behind in comfort and good health.

✧　　✧　　✧

Still, as weeks passed, he felt increasingly dissatisfied. He hadn't even dared show the painting to Helena. *Somebody* should see it, before his death.

Finally, he realized that there was one witness possible. Who better, really? And she could certainly be relied upon to hold the confidence, for a multitude of reasons.

So, in one of the many visits across the lines into Amsterdam—those had practically become a regular traffic, by then—he passed the word along. And, two days later, his witness arrived at his home.

He ushered her into the small room where he kept the painting tucked away in a closet. He'd chosen that room because, small and awkwardly designed as it was, it had the only closet in the house that was big enough. It was a very large painting.

After setting it up on an easel for viewing, he unwrapped the cloth that hid it. Then, waited while she studied his work.

By the time she was done, Rebecca Abrabanel's brown eyes were watery. "Oh, Pieter," she whispered. "It's magnificent. But it's so . . . *wrong*."

She turned the eyes to him, her gaze almost—not quite—an accusing one. "He is not a cruel man. I can assure you of that. Very kind and gentle, actually, most of the time."

So, Rubens knew he had succeeded.

"Of course not. I never imagined he was cruel." Finally satisfied, and in full, he gazed upon his work. "Nothing but grace can wreak such havoc and destruction, Rebecca. Nothing else can even come close. Had Lucifer understood that, we would never have needed for the Christ to be sent at all."

Part Two

Frenzies bewilder, reveries perturb the mind

Chapter 11

The Tower of London

January 1634

"I think I'm going to tear my hair out," Melissa Mailey announced, to no one in particular. She was looking through one of the windows in St. Thomas' Tower that overlooked the Water Lane that separated it from the Inner Ward and the rest of the Tower of London. Glaring through it, more precisely.

Sitting next to each other on an ornate divan, not far away in the big central room of their quarters, Tom and Rita Simpson looked at each other. Then, back at Melissa.

Tom cleared his throat. "I think it's an attractive shade of gray, myself." His wife winced.

Melissa swiveled her head, bringing the glare onto Tom. "I am not *that* vain, thank you."

She was fudging a bit. Outside of being clean, well-groomed and reasonably well-dressed, in a school-teacher's sort of way, one of the few things about her appearance that Melissa was sensitive about was her

hair color. Perhaps it was because she was a natural
dark-blonde who'd spent too many years being belligerent about blonde jokes. Whatever the reason, as she'd
gotten into middle age she'd found herself dismayed
by the gray creeping into her hair, where the wrinkles
creeping into her face and the various little sags in
her body hadn't bothered her in the least.

So, for years, she'd dyed her hair. Subtly, of course.
Melissa Mailey would just as soon commit hara-kiri as
become a peroxide blonde. In her lexicon of personal
sins, being garish ranked just barely below being
reactionary or bigoted.

Alas, while the seventeenth century had plenty of
methods for coloring hair, "garish" pretty well defined
the end result for any of them. So, since the Ring
of Fire, Melissa had rationed the supply of up-time
hair-coloring that existed in Grantville which suited
her needs. But she'd only brought a small amount
when they came to England on a diplomatic mission,
the past summer. That had long since vanished in the
months since they'd found themselves imprisoned in
the Tower of London.

She looked back out the window. "I propose to tear
my hair out not because of its coloring—which suits me
well, enough, I assure you—but because of the activities
and behavior of a certain Darryl McCarthy. One of *your*
soldiers, let me remind you, Captain Simpson."

Tom settled his massive frame a bit further into
the divan. "Oh. That."

"Yes. Oh. *That.* If he gets that girl pregnant . . ."

Tom cleared his throat again. "That'd be a neat
trick, Melissa. Seeing as how—being crude about
it—he hasn't managed to get into her pants yet. Well,

not pants, ladies' garments being what they are in this day and age. Lift her skirts and undo . . . whatever she's got on underneath."

Rita Simpson winced again.

So did Melissa. "The operative phrase being 'yet,' I take it. You admit he's *trying*."

"Well, yeah, sure. Of course he is. He's a dyed-in-the-wool hillbilly, Melissa. Might as well ask him to give up his pickup and Cat cap for a VW and a beret, as ask him not to put the make on a girl. He's got his self-respect, y'know. On the other hand, he's not being crude about it and he's not even really pushing all that hard. Just enough for form's sake. Being as how—miracles do happen, from time to time—he's actually got the serious hots for the girl, he's not just trying to get laid."

Melissa looked back at him, squinting a little. "And exactly how do you know all this?"

"He talks to me about it, how else?" Tom spread his huge hands. "Who else would he talk to, concerning this subject? He's a *hillbilly*, Melissa. He certainly isn't going to discuss something like this with—you know—"

His wife chuckled. "A girl. And he defines anything female as a 'girl.'"

"Well, not Melissa. He pretty much still defines her as the Schoolmarm From Hell. Her gender comes a long way second to her innately demonic essence. But, yeah, a girl. It wouldn't even occur to Darryl to talk to anyone except a guy about it."

Melissa tossed her head a little, indicating one of the rooms to the side. "There's Friedrich."

Tom shrugged. "Friedrich's a down-timer. Darryl gets

along fine with down-timers, but this isn't a subject he'd feel comfortable discussing with one of them. Even a male down-timer. So that leaves me—even if I am his commanding officer."

Sitting a bit further off in a chair, Gayle Mason issued a soft, half-grunted chuckle. "Especially since rank sits very lightly on Darryl McCarthy's consciousness. It's a good thing you don't have a General MacArthur sort of temperament, Tom, or he'd have been court-martialed by now."

"Ten times over," Tom Simpson agreed placidly.

"You're *sure* about this?" Melissa demanded.

Rita spoke up. "Melissa, I really do think you're worrying too much. I spend a lot more time than you do in the Tower's residential quarters, because of my medical rounds. It's not simply a matter of Darryl's intentions. Or the girl's, for that matter. As cramped as everything is in the Tower—and as good-looking as Victoria Short is—I can guarantee you there isn't more than five minutes at a time when she's out of somebody's sight."

"The 'somebodies' involved usually being her own family," Tom added. "Who include her brother Andrew, who's a Yeoman Warder; her mother Isabel, who is definitely in the 'no sparrow shall fall' camp of parenthood; her brothers, motivated to watch her by honor, and her sisters, motivated by envy; several cousins; and, last but not least, her uncle Stephen Hamilton—"

"Eek," issued from Gayle.

"—whom nobody this side of an insane asylum, and sure as hell no level-headed hillbilly like Darryl, is even going to *think* of pissing off. Relax, willya? Yes, it's true that Darryl has the serious hots for

Victoria Short. No doubt about it. But I can tell you, Melissa, that the hots are serious enough that he's even—twice, no less—uttered the young male hillbilly's ultimate curse."

Melissa lifted her eyebrows. "Which is?"

Gayle snorted again. "Can't you guess?" Her voice dropped an octave, roughened, and got a heavier West Virginia accent. "Damn, I think I'm gonna have to get married."

"Yup," said Tom. "Except the prologue was a tad stronger than a mere 'damn.' The first time it was 'I'm fucked, aren't I?' The second time it was just a simple declarative 'I'm fucked.'"

Melissa couldn't help but laugh. "O brave new world, that hath such miracles in it! Well, I hope you're right. The only thing that's made our captivity here fairly tolerable—well, I'll admit the earl of Strafford has been civilized—is that the Warders have been so friendly to us."

She gave Rita an acknowledging nod. "Mostly because they think—and rightly so—that she's kept their kids alive and in good health."

Rita's face darkened a little. "Mostly. There've still been a few deaths, and it was touch and go with some others. Still is, with poor little Cecily."

Her husband laid a hand on hers. "That's way better than they expected, love, child mortality rates being what they are in the here and now. You know it—and so do they."

Melissa looked back out the window. "Speak of the devil, here he comes."

In the alley below, Darryl McCarthy was heading for the stairs leading up to St. Thomas' Tower. The young American soldier barely returned the friendly nod the Warder on duty gave him. Not surprising, that, given the expression on his face.

It was a mix of emotions. Gloom. Frustration. Yearning. Despair.

Melissa laughed again.

Not far away, in that section of the Tower of London known as the Lieutenant's Lodging, Thomas Wentworth, the earl of Strafford, was fending off questions raised by his daughter. No easy task, that. Nan was precocious, not in the least bit bashful, and had the normal lack of tact possessed by any six-year-old child.

"But why don't you have them standing guard outside the dungeons? A prisoner might escape!"

"There *are* guards watching the dungeons, Nan," her father explained patiently.

She waved her hand, the gesture accompanied by a derisive noise. "They're just standing on the wall, here and there. And not too alert, at that. They're lazy, those Warders. You should have at least four of them outside of every dungeon entrance."

He smiled wryly. "I can just imagine how well the Warders would take to *that* idea."

"Just tell them!" his daughter insisted. "You're the king's minister! They have to do what you tell them!"

Wentworth briefly considered trying to explain to the child that formal authority and real power were not synonyms, and that any official who routinely abused his authority would soon find that authority undermined. In practice, at least, if not in theory. In this instance, if he infuriated the Yeoman Warders by constraining them to tasks they considered irksome, pointless and annoying, they would soon retaliate by slacking off at every occasion. Be a man never so powerful, he still only possessed two eyes, neither of them at the back of his head.

As it was, whatever their sometimes informal manner, the Warders made a superb guard force for the Tower. They were elite soldiers and considered themselves such, and did so with good reason.

But, after a moment, he discarded the notion. Bright as she no doubt was, Nan was still six years old. There'd be time enough, as the years passed, for her to learn that the world was mostly composed of shades of gray, with precious little in the way of black or white.

So, all he did was pick her up playfully and exclaim to his wife Elizabeth: "I have it! We'll betroth her to the tsar of Russia! What a natural match!"

That was a joke twice over, actually. The current tsar was no Ivan the Terrible. Russia's so-called "Time of Troubles" had ended with the ascension to the throne of Mikhail Romanov twenty years earlier. But the new dynasty's hold on power was still fragile and depended at least as much on the authority of the new tsar's father, the Patriarch Filaret, as it did on the tsar himself.

"What's a Zar?" Nan demanded. "And who's Russia?"

Later, early in the afternoon, Strafford made his farewells to his wife and children.

"I really wish you would spend more nights here, Thomas," Elizabeth said wistfully. "I miss you, often."

The words pleased the earl. He was under no illusion that his nineteen-year-old wife was really consumed with passion for his forty-year-old self. Theirs had been essentially a marriage of convenience, made the year before. He'd needed a mother for his children after the sudden death of his wife Arabella; and Elizabeth—more her father, Sir Godfrey Rodes, really—had seen in the newly appointed Lord Deputy of Ireland a splendid match for his daughter and a way of advancing his own prospects.

Still, Thomas had become very fond of his new wife, and he knew the affection was reciprocated. He missed her, too, often enough, in his solitary bed in the royal palace at Whitehall.

"I simply can't, dearest, except on rare occasions." Wentworth hesitated, glancing around to make sure that the children were out of hearing range, then said quietly: "Things are a bit tense at the palace, Elizabeth. It's all I can do to persuade His Majesty to remain in London, during this unsettled period, instead of haring off to Oxford as he wants to do. If I slept outside Whitehall myself that often, it would just encourage him in . . ."

He left off the rest. Using the word "folly" in reference to the king's state of mind would be unseemly, even to his wife in private.

Elizabeth frowned. "Is he *still* fretting over the danger of epidemic? I thought he'd gotten over that."

"He did, for a time. But there is a lot of disease in the city, since we brought over so many mercenary soldiers from the continent. It flares up constantly, you know. And the queen—"

Again, he left the rest unsaid. *And if the king's a fool, half the time, his wife is an hysteric three-fourths of the time . . .*

Would be even more unseemly, said aloud. Even to his wife. Even in private. Even given that it was true.

Elizabeth shook her head. "Why don't His Majesty and the queen come to reside here at the Tower, then? You were quite right, you know, I've become convinced of it. Since you allowed the Americans held pris—ah, staying in St. Thomas' Tower—to oversee the castle's sanitary and medical affairs, there's been very little disease of any sort here. And that, almost all children."

Wentworth sighed. "I tried, Elizabeth. I pointed out that within a week I could have Wakefield Tower completely refurbished as a royal residence. It was used as such by Henry III, after all. But the king refused. He said it would seem as if he were afraid of the city's unsteady population."

Which he is, the earl left unsaid also, *despite the fact that the new mercenary companies have a firm grip on London.*

Daughter of a country squire she might be, but Elizabeth was not dull-witted. Her mouth twisted into something halfway to a derisive sneer. "And racing off to Oxford *wouldn't*?"

Wentworth rolled his eyes. "Exactly what I said to him. But—ah, come, dearest, let's not squabble. It's the way it must be."

"Of course, husband. Whatever you say."

Once outside the Lieutenant's Lodging, Thomas headed for the gate next to Wakefield Tower that gave onto the Outer Ward and, from there, the gate at Byward Tower that allowed egress from the fortress entirely. But he paused, for a time, realizing that he hadn't spoken to Oliver Cromwell in weeks. Had rarely even thought about him, in fact. As the months passed with no incidents since Oliver's arrest, Thomas had come to the conclusion that while he still thought it would be wiser to have Oliver executed, there was really no pressing need to do so. And . . .

He liked the man, when all was said and done.

"Oh, why not?" he murmured to himself. Even in London in midwinter, he still had plenty of daylight left to reach Whitehall. And it was an unseasonably warm and sunny day, to begin with.

There were Warders standing guard at *this* door, of course. The only door to the dungeons of which that was true, in the whole castle.

Only two of them, however, not four. Oliver Cromwell was not an ogre, after all. Even if, in another universe, he'd overthrown the English monarchy, executed the king, and set himself as what amounted to a dictator under the benign title "Lord Protector."

Not a particularly brutal or capricious dictator, granted, judging from the up-timers' history books. But a dictator nonetheless; certainly a regicide.

After the Warders unlocked the bolts and chains and let him in—which they had to do twice; once at the entrance and once at the actual dungeon—Thomas found himself in the same small cell he remembered from his early visits. But it was much cleaner, and while it was still definitely a dungeon it was no longer a place of sheer misery and squalor.

Oliver even had a small table now, with a chair, along with his sleeping pallet. Unwise, that, looked at from a certain viewpoint. A desperate prisoner could provide himself with a club by dismantling either piece of furniture. Quite easily, in fact, as rickety as they looked to be.

Wentworth decided the judgment of the Warders was sound enough, in this case. Oliver was rather well-built, true enough, but he was no giant. Against two trained Warders equipped with bladed weapons, he'd have no chance at all armed with a mere club.

Probably more important was simply the man's temperament. There was an innate sureness to Oliver Cromwell—the term "dignity" came to Thomas, and he couldn't deny it—which would not allow him to ever descend that far into despair. Did the worst come, and he be summoned to lose his head, Oliver would not put up a pointless and futile struggle, like a common criminal might do. He'd simply march to the execution ground with no resistance. He'd sneer when the sentence was pronounced, spit on the ground at the king's name, kneel calmly to lay his neck upon the block—and tell the headsman, jokingly, not to fumble the business.

Cromwell had set aside the book he was reading before Thomas entered. He'd heard them coming, of course, for well over a minute.

It was the Bible, Wentworth saw. "Which book?" he asked.

"The Lamentations of Jeremiah, at the moment. You're looking well, Thomas. But you've aged, I think."

Thomas smiled thinly. "What man doesn't, as each day passes? But, yes, I suppose I've aged more than I might have otherwise."

"He must be a horror of a king to serve. Craven and stupid in big things; petty, spiteful and stubborn in small ones. No, you needn't respond to that. I hope your wife and children are well."

"Yes, quite well." Wentworth nodded toward the west. "They're living here now, in fact. There's disease in the city—not quite an epidemic, but too close for my comfort—and I thought they'd be safest here."

Cromwell's smile was thin, but not unkind. "You too, eh? Well, you're right. I have an American visit me from time to time, cleansing my cell of pests. 'Fumigating,' he calls it, which seems to be the word they use for killing pests you can't see."

He glanced at the pallet. "Barely an occasional bedbug, any more. Mind you, it's a bit of a mixed blessing, since the same man who sees to my bodily health hates me with a passion, and spends all his time here leveling curses upon me."

Wentworth frowned. "Why?"

"He's of Irish stock. And it seems—in that other universe, you know—that I butchered half the world's Irishmen. So he says, at any rate. I can't really see why I'd bother, myself."

"Neither can I. Beat them about a bit—which is not hard, since you can always find one Irish clan chief who'll beat another for you, at a small price—and they're manageable enough."

Now that he thought upon the matter, Wentworth did remember that among the many things he'd read about Cromwell in the American books that had made their way to England—copies of them, usually—he'd read something about Cromwell's ferocious reputation among the Irish. But he couldn't remember the details, since he hadn't cared about that.

A thought came to him. "Does he speak of me, at all? If I recall correctly, in that other universe I served for years as the Lord Deputy of Ireland, instead of being summoned back almost immediately to London."

Oliver's smile wasn't thin at all, now. "Oh, yes. 'Bloody Tom Tyrant,' you are. Or were, I suppose I should say. The grammar's tricky, dealing with that business. Quite a notorious fellow, it seems, in the Irish scheme of things."

Wentworth returned the smile. "Well. That's a cheery thought."

Cromwell cocked his head slightly. "Why did you come, Thomas?"

Wentworth had his dignity also. He'd lie, readily enough, for purposes of state. But not here, not to this man. "I don't really know, Oliver, to be honest. I just felt an urge to see you again."

There was silence for a moment, as both men remembered a time years earlier when they'd served together as young members of Parliament. They'd been on quite good terms, then.

"But there's really nothing much to say, is there?" said Oliver Cromwell.

Thomas Wentworth—the earl of Strafford, now— canted his head in agreement. "No. There really isn't. Goodbye, Oliver."

He left, and Cromwell went back to his perusal of the Bible.

"Fucking bastard," muttered Darryl McCarthy, as he watched the earl of Strafford passing below the windows in St. Thomas' Tower, on his way to the outer gate of the fortress. "Bloody Tom Tyrant."

But there wasn't any heat to the words. In fact, Tom Simpson could barely hear them at all, even standing at the window right next to Darryl. They didn't really sound so much like a curse, as a simple mantra a stalwart Irish-American lad might speak aloud. As he steeled himself for a moment of great spiritual crisis and peril.

"Yeah, there it is, Tom. I've thought about it until my brain's just spinning in circles. No way around it. I am well and truly screwed, blued and royally tattooed."

"That bad, huh?"

"Yeah. Maybe if Harry Lefferts was here—bracing me, so to speak—but—"

"It's not really the end of the world, y'know? Hell, I did it myself."

Darryl gave him a glance that was none too friendly. "Yeah. So? You ain't no hillbilly."

"Oh, come off it, Darryl. Even hillbillies do it, more often than not. Can't be more than twenty percent of you that are outright bastards. Legally speaking, I mean. Figuratively, of course, the percentage rises a lot."

"Fucking rich kid."

Tom chuckled. "Poor old Doug MacArthur's got to be spinning in his grave, right now."

"Huh? What's that supposed to mean?"

"Never mind. You sure about this?"

"Well." Darryl took a deep breath. "Well." Another deep breath. "Yeah."

"I mean, *really* sure? As in: steps will now be taken. You've been making people kind of nervous, you know."

That required perhaps half a dozen deep breaths. But, eventually, Darryl said: "Yeah. I'm sure."

"Okay, then." Tom turned his head, looking toward

his wife and Melissa and Gayle Mason, who were politely sitting some distance away. Thereby, of course, allowing The Guys to conduct their affairs in the necessary privacy.

But Tom didn't give those three women more than a glance. All up-timers, all Americans, they'd have only the barest knowledge of how to handle the situation.

No, he needed Friedrich Bruch's wife, Nelly. She was not only a down-timer, but she'd been born and raised in London.

He was about to call out her name when he saw her emerge from the small room she shared with Friedrich.

"Nelly! Just the person I was looking for." He hooked a thumb at Darryl. "Our young swain here wants to know how a fellow goes about proposing to a girl, in the here and now."

Nelly smiled. Rita and Gayle grinned. Melissa looked to the heavens.

"Well, praise the Lord," she said.

Darryl scowled at her. "Melissa, you're a damn atheist."

Still looking at the ceiling, Melissa wagged her head back and forth. "True, been one since I was twelve. But maybe I should reconsider. Seeing as how I think I'm witnessing an act of divine intervention."

Several hours later, after Gayle took down all the radio messages relayed from Amsterdam that had come in during the evening window, she came into the main room with a big grin on her face.

"Speaking of divine intervention, you're all going to

love *this*. Especially you, Rita." She held up a message in her hand, one of the little notepad sheets she used to record radio transmissions.

"What is it?" demanded Rita, rising from the divan and extending her hand.

"Tut, tut! It's not for you, dear, it's for your husband." Still grinning, Gayle came over and handed the message to Tom, who'd remained sitting.

Tom read it. Then read it again. Then, read it again.

"Well," Rita asked impatiently. "What?"

"It's from Mrs. Riddle." He reached up and started scratching his hair. "'Bout the last thing I ever expected."

"The wife of the chief justice?" Melissa asked. "Why would she be sending you a radio message?"

"No, not her. Chuck Riddle's mother."

Rita nodded. "Mary Kat's grandma. She was a year ahead of me in high school. Mary Kat, that is. Not Veleda. What does she want?"

"Here, read it yourself. Better read it out loud, while you're at it."

Rita took the message and began reciting it so everyone could hear. By the time she got to the last few sentences, she was rushing.

TOM. WHILE YOU'RE THERE. EPISCOPALIANS
IN GRANTVILLE HAVE NO PRIEST. SHOULD
HAVE A BISHOP TOO BUT THAT GETS COMPLI-
CATED. ARRANGE TO SEE ARCHBISHOP LAUD.
BE ORDAINED. AS A PRIEST IF NOTHING ELSE
BUT SHOOT FOR BISHOP. AM SURE HE CAN
MAKE AN EXCEPTION TO THE RULES. BEST
WISHES. V RIDDLE

"Ordained?" Rita's voice rose to a shriek. "Over my dead body!"

Melissa Mailey looked concerned. "Tom, you've never said anything about having a religious vocation."

"Well, I didn't have one." He cleared his throat. "Until now."

"You don't have one now!" Rita protested.

Tom settled back in the divan. He seemed to be struggling against a smile—or a grin as wide as the one still on Gayle's face.

"Yes, I do, dear. You read it yourself. I didn't have one two minutes ago, but I do now." He looked up at his very non-Episcopalian wife; the grin started to show around the edges of his still-solemn face. "You can't think of it—a vocation, I mean—as being something that's all inside you. It's like those bishops and things back in the early church, who wrapped their arms around a pillar of the church yelling, 'No. Not me!' while the congregation dragged them out to be promoted."

Melissa nodded, apparently quite solemnly. Rita just looked blank.

Tom continued, "Or, maybe like the prophets in the Old Testament who were just sitting there when the voice of God mucked up all their plans. Jonah, for instance. God said, 'Go there,' and he said, 'I don't think so, thank you very much,' so it took some persuading. A calling can come from outside, too."

There was no smile on Rita's face, for sure. "I wasn't born to be a preacher's wife," she hissed. "No. Tell her no. That's easy enough."

Tom went back to scratching his hair, lowering his face in the process. In that pose, the grin that was now spreading openly on his face made him look a bit like a weight-lifter shark, coming to the surface. "She does have a point, you know. That is, the Episcopalians in Grantville do need a priest, for sure, and we should really have a bishop."

He pointed to the message still in Rita's hand. "The reason it gets complicated is because none of the national churches in the Anglican Polity—that's what we called all right-thinking Episcopalians all over the world, back where we came from—actually had any authority over each other. But they all recognized the archbishop of Canterbury as sort of the first among equals, so it makes sense to see if he'd be willing to get the ball rolling."

He looked over at Melissa, still grinning. "Maybe I should just ask Laud for an appointment? Talk to him about it? What could it hurt?"

"What could it hurt?" Rita's fists were clenched. "I could end up chairing Ladies' Aid meetings at a church I don't even belong to!"

Gayle and Tom started laughing. Even Melissa was smiling, now. "I agree, Rita. Fate worse than death—and I've chaired a lot of godawful meetings in my day."

Eventually, Rita's glare stifled her husband's laughter. "Look, sweetheart, I've actually got no intention of proposing myself. I have no idea why Mrs. Riddle came up with the idea. But if you strip that aside, she *does* have a point. We've got some Episcopalians in Grantville, with no structure—and no clear idea how to set one up with legitimate authority. Like she says, we'd be bending the rules—so would Laud, although he doesn't know the rules have been set up yet—but

I'm pretty sure she's right. If I could get the archbishop of Canterbury to ordain somebody—or send somebody himself—we'd be off and running."

Tom shook his head. "It wouldn't have to be me, or anybody in Grantville. Maybe the archbishop could find someone else to send, from England. Someone who wants to be a missionary in foreign parts, or just someone he'd like to get rid of."

"He'd like to get rid of us, I expect," Darryl McCarthy interjected.

"Yes, he would," said Melissa. She looked at the message. "Especially after I pass this along."

Chapter 12

The English Channel

"Well, that's a pisser," said Harry Lefferts, lowering his eyeglass.

Standing next to him at the small ship's rail, Donald Ohde scowled at the vessel in the distance. "Doesn't anybody have any imagination? They tried this once before, and it didn't work."

"The Channel *is* notorious for pirates," Harry pointed out mildly. "I really don't think we got spotted making our way through France. Especially as fast as we moved."

Paul Maczka was standing at the same rail, to Harry's left. "No ambush, you're saying."

"Can't see it, Paul. I mean, why would the French bother with a complicated ambush? They had to do it with Becky's ship, because she was a diplomat and they couldn't let their hand show. Us? We were just thugs sitting in a tavern in Dieppe, dickering to buy a boat. The guy who sold it to us probably figured we wanted it to turn pirates ourselves. Send in a platoon of infantry, that's all."

Both Paul and Donald were scowling now. Harry smiled. "Yeah, well, so that platoon gets shot up. They send in a whole company. We're still fried, guys, before we even set foot on our new boat."

He looked back at the ship pursuing them. "No, this is just garden-variety piracy. We still got to deal with it, though."

Donald shrugged. "Easy enough."

Harry shook his head. "Not so easy as all that. Oh, sure, ole Jeff could just send them packing with a few grenades. But he didn't care if there were any witnesses left. We can't afford that."

He'd said "ole Jeff" with that certain note of approbation that one righteous hillbilly refers to another member of the clan. A few years back, he'd have done no such thing, of course. Harry had never been one of those high school jocks who harassed geeks, but that was simply because such behavior was beneath his dignity. Does a lion harass mice? Still, his attitude toward geeks like Jeff Higgins hadn't been any different, really.

However, that was then, and this was now. Jeff still wasn't a hillbilly, properly speaking, and never would be, but Harry was quite willing to extend him honorary membership. He'd landed one of the best-looking girls around and blown close to a dozen Croat cavalrymen into pieces, hadn't he? What more could you ask for?

"No . . ." Harry mused. "We can't do it Jeff's way."

He glanced to the northeast, checking to see that they weren't too close yet to entering the Strait of Dover. Then he turned his head and looked at the helmsman. That was Matija Grabnar. Like many of the commandos in Lefferts' unit, his ethnic background was a mix; in his case, German, Slovene and Lithuanian. For whatever reason, Harry seemed to attract hybrids. He claimed it was because his charismatic personality and proven leadership qualities just naturally drew the cream of the crop from every nation.

Mike Stearns had once commented that it might even be true—if you defined "cream of the crop" the way Harry did, and nobody else would except Ba'alzebub.

"Hey, Matt! Get us out into the middle of the channel, will you? I don't want any witnesses."

Felix Kasza, who'd been sprawled comfortably on the deck, lounging against the mainmast, rose to his feet. Then, ambling over, he said: "We do it like *Guns of Navarone*, eh?"

"Yeah, what I figured." Harry gave the three men around him a sly little grin. "Good thing I overruled you male chauvinist pigs and let the girls come along, ain't it? This'll work a lot easier with Sherrilyn and Juliet to dangle like bait."

"I heard that, Lefferts!" One of the two women in the unit, both of them sitting on the deck next to the opposite rail, lifted her head. "Talk about male chauvinist pigs. You got your nerve. What're we? The designated rapees?"

Harry shrugged. "Well, yeah—except it'll never get that far."

"Sure won't," she half-snarled. It wasn't a particularly cold day, for this time of year, but it *was* late January, in the English channel. So, sitting on the deck, Sherrilyn Maddox and Juliet Sutherland had covered themselves with a couple of wool blankets. Sherrilyn flipped part of the blankets aside and rummaged somewhere beneath for a moment. Her hand emerged holding a very lethal-looking .40 caliber automatic.

"They'll have to fuck my dead body—but I guarantee you, Harry, if you aren't dead by then already, I'll make sure of it. You and your stupid movies!"

All of Harry's male commandos, including Harry, were addicted to action movies. The down-timers, though not Harry himself, were also addicted to action novels. It was their commonly held and firm belief that, when it came to fiction, there was no God but Matt Helm and Donald Hamilton was his prophet. Admittedly, the Sacketts and Louis L'Amour came a close second.

The woman sitting next to Sherrilyn was the female half of the only married couple in the unit. She took the pipe out of her mouth, did her—very feeble—best to look prim and proper, and said: "My husband will have to agree. He's crazy jealous, you know. His wife being gang-raped by dozens of pirates is likely to set him off."

Her husband, as it happened, emerged from the hold just in time to hear that. Frowning, he lifted his head and peered over the rail. "Didn't realize they were getting that close," he said. "*Guns of Navarone?*"

"Yeah, that's the plan."

George Sutherland planted his hands on either side of the hatch and heaved himself onto the deck. As big and heavy as he was, that took quite a heave, but he had the muscle for it. It wasn't actually true that he was particularly jealous. An easygoing and phlegmatic personality combined with nineteen inch biceps made him one of the most placid husbands Harry had ever met.

George and his wife were both English, which was the reason Harry had selected them for this expedition. Better still, they'd both been active in London's theater before a byproduct of a brawl George had gotten into forced them to flee to the continent. The byproduct in question had been the broken neck owned by the brother of one of Southwark's more notorious criminal gang leaders. Unfortunately, between his drunkenness and the chaos of the melee, George had gotten confused. He'd thought the neck he was breaking belonged to the gang leader himself, which he'd figured would settle the business well enough.

Once they arrived in London, Harry planned to set up their base of operations in the sprawling slums on the south bank of the Thames across from the Tower, where the theater district was located. That might get a tad awkward, if they happened to accidentally stumble across the same gang leader in their comings and goings. But Harry wasn't particularly concerned about that problem. There was an easy solution to it, after all.

Juliet claimed to have become an actress, once she got to the continent where women were permitted to play roles on stage, although she allowed that her parts had been minor. That most likely meant she'd started off as a young woman in London as a whore working the theater district, before she got hooked up with George, who'd been a stagehand. But Harry had never pried into the matter. None of his concern, first of all; and, second, having a husband the size of George would have made even a Nosy Parker shy away from the business.

"You'd better stay below, George," said Harry. "Big

as you are, you're likely to make them nervous. Give Gerd a hand with the fireworks."

Sutherland sucked his yellow crooked teeth, pondering the problem. "Grenades?"

"I'd rather save the grenades, if y'all don't mind." The last phrase was said in English, drawled with a heavy Appalachian accent, tacked onto the Amideutsch that was their standard lingo.

George smiled, and began lowering himself back into the hold. "Tightwad. But we'll manage."

By now, Grabnar had the small ship heading into the center of the Channel, miles from either shore. Anyone on land who observed the unfolding little drama wouldn't really be able to make out any of the details, even with an eyeglass. Two ships meet; one leaves; one doesn't. Who can say what actually happened?

Matija was also, cleverly, making sure the ship lost headway while he was at it. The pirates pursuing them would notice, probably, but they'd just write it off to panic and lousy seamanship. Harry didn't think there was much chance they'd get suspicious at all.

Why should they? The English Channel had been infested with pirates for centuries, going back into medieval times. For the past few decades, piracy in the Channel had been dominated by so-called "Sallee rovers," because they operated from the port of Salé in northwest Africa, not far from Rabat. They were usually referred to as Algerines, although the members of the crews came from all over Europe as well as the Moslem world.

A few rare occasions aside, neither the English nor the French crown had ever made much of an effort to eliminate the vermin—not even after the Sallee rovers, early in the seventeenth century, became bold enough to raid towns and villages in Cornwall as well as attack ships. Partly, that was because neither nation had a powerful navy, and partly it was because the usual victims of the pirates were poor fishermen. The Algerine pirates were more interested in capturing slaves than cargo.

So, they'd grown arrogant, which was fine with Harry Lefferts. He'd been dismantling overconfident bullies since he was eight years old. Six years old, if you counted Fatso Binghampton.

He looked around the deck, and then pointed to a tarpaulin piled up untidily toward the bow. "Paul, you set up with a shotgun. You can hide in there until the business starts. Donald, you go back with Matt at the helm, and figure on using rifles when the shit hits the fan. Felix, you stay with me. You're the best shot with a pistol. You got a backup?"

Kasza sniffed. "Do I have a backup?"

"Sorry, didn't mean to offend you."

"Yes, of course I have a backup. Two, if you count the little ankle gun."

"Ought to do. Blow 'em off the rail, scare the shit out of them, George and Gerd will do the rest."

"What about me?" demanded Sherrilyn. "If you think I'm just going to sit here looking terrified, you can—"

"Easy, girl, easy." Harry glanced at the oncoming pirates. They were still three hundred yards away, too far to really see anything. "Holler down to Gerd to pass you up his ten-gauge. Now's your chance to prove you can handle a man-sized gun."

Sherrilyn's sniff was on a par with Kasza's. "He'll

whine at me. He loves that ten-gauge. There's something unnatural about that relationship, if you ask me. Even for you gun nuts, it's over the top."

Harry chuckled. It was invariably Sherrilyn's habit to ascribe to the male members of the unit all of the macho sins to which she was even more prone herself.

Gun nut? She owned at least twenty that she'd admit to. And when it came to the Ultimate Macho hang-up, Harry was convinced there was no greater practitioner in the world than Sherrilyn Maddox. The woman simply *could not* resist a challenge. Evel Knievel with tits. Before the Ring of Fire, she'd been one of the high school's P.E. teachers. She'd been a rock-climber, sky-diver—you name it; if the sport was dangerous and within the pocketbook of a West Virginia schoolteacher, she'd done it.

She'd also been an avid hunter, and while she wasn't in Julie Mackay's league—nobody was—she was undoubtedly one of the best shots in Grantville. She'd brought home her deer every year, never later than the second day of hunting season. Her second deer, rather, because she'd already gotten one during bow-hunting season.

Needless to say, the charge of lesbianism had followed her like a trailing mist for years, despite the fact that Sherrilyn had been no slouch at proving otherwise. With Harry himself once, in fact, in a fling that had only lasted three weeks but was still a fond memory. Very fond memory, indeed, the way that a man who'd been only twenty himself at the time will remember an affair with a woman eight years older than he was.

Sherrilyn was a lot of fun and somebody you could

always count on, even if part of that was counting on her to blow you off sooner or later. The truth was, outside of a purely formal bow in the direction of male chauvinist protocol, Harry hadn't hesitated at all when she'd volunteered to transfer from the Thuringian Rifles to his unit. Leaving aside the fact that he knew Sherrilyn could cut the mustard, guts and mayhem-wise, her being a woman might come in handy for the unit someday.

Every man in the unit had raised a fuss at the idea, of course. And then, of course, every one of them had hit on her as soon as she joined. Fat lot of good it did them. They would have bounced anyway, even if Sherrilyn hadn't heard about the ruckus they'd raised over her transfer—which she didn't hesitate to rub in the faces of the would-be Casanovas once she arrived.

Harry could have told them, but hadn't bothered. Good ole boys, sure, but they just weren't suave and debonair enough to have profited from his advice anyway. The only way you hit on Sherrilyn Maddox was to get her intrigued by a challenge. Standard issue lines were a pure waste of time. The way Harry had pulled it off was to ignore her altogether until he ran across her one day in a bar over in Clarksburg, where he was drinking with a fake license, and she'd started making suggestions herself.

"I dunno," Harry had said, looking at her dubiously. "Word is you're a rock-climber. Is that true?"

After she confessed to an enthusiasm for the sport, a little shudder had swept his shoulders. "Jeez, Sherrilyn. Your hands must be like sandpaper. Strip the skin right off a man's back."

Worked like a charm.

He smiled at the memory, as he watched the ten-gauge getting hoisted out of the hold and into Sherrilyn's hands. He could hear Gerd's voice coming from below, although he couldn't quite make out the words themselves. From the tone, though, Gerd was sure enough whining and grousing. There *was* something a little kinky about his love affair with that monster, even if Harry didn't think it quite crossed the line into outright perversion.

He looked at the pirate ship. Two hundred yards away.

"Hey, Paul! We ought to be starting to get drunk around now."

Maczka frowned at him. Harry's unit had a capacity for prodigious alcohol consumption, when they relaxed. But they were stone sober any time they were on duty. Then, realizing what Harry was getting at, his frown deepened.

"I don't think we got any empty bottles. Hate to waste good liquor, pouring it out."

Sherrilyn looked up from checking the loads in the shotgun. "Pour it into one of Juliet's bowls. We'll make a punch for the celebration afterward."

Paul nodded and lowered himself down the hatch.

"Bring up my second-best hat, while you're at it!" Harry hollered at him. Then, went over to Sherrilyn and sat down beside her.

"You'll need the hat to keep your face hidden. Mostly covered by a blanket, lady weight-lifter or not, and even pushing forty like you are, ain't no way anybody's going to mistake you for a guy, up close."

"Harry, have I ever told you that you have the worst come-on lines of anybody I know?"

"Sure. The morning after we spent the first night in bed together. I couldn't tell if you were really pissed, though, the way you were laughing."

She chuckled, softly. "Walked into that one, didn't I? Okay, genius boss, what's the plan?"

"You open it up. That ten-gauge will deafen 'em, even if you miss—which you hardly can't, at this range, as short as Gerd sawed down the barrels."

"I'll bust my shoulder if I try to fire this thing without—"

"I ain't stupid," Harry cut her off. "Don't bother getting up. You don't really gotta aim it anyway, just point it in the general direction." He nodded at the blankets covering her and Juliet. "You don't need both of them now. Roll one of 'em up tight and use it as a brace for the butt."

Sherrilyn thought about it for a moment, and then nodded. "Okay, that'll work. Well enough, anyway. But the blanket—the one that'll still be on us, I mean—"

"Way ahead of you, Sherrilyn. I should have said you'll open up the shooting. I'll start the whole business by yanking the blanket off you and waving it at the foe. Works for matadors, and these guys are way dumber than any bull."

Paul emerged from the hold with Harry's hat perched on his head. He was climbing the ladder a bit awkwardly since he held a bottle in each hand. Both were filled with clear liquid. Water, presumably, taken from the supply they boiled for drinking purposes.

"You hear that, Paul?"

"You start it, Sherrilyn shoots first, the rest of us pitch in afterward."

"Right. Pass it on to everybody else, will you?"

Paul leaned over and handed Harry one of the bottles and the hat. Then, moving more easily with one hand free, came the rest of the way out of the hatch and headed toward the stern where Donald Ohde was talking to Matija Grabnar. He still had time to pass along the plan to them and get back to the tarp in the bow before the pirates got close enough to make an accurate count of the crew members of their prospective victim.

Not that it really mattered if the count was a little off. By now, realizing that escape was impossible and resistance even more so, the ship's crew would be in semi-chaos. A man might be on deck one minute and cowering somewhere in the hold, the next.

Speaking of cowering . . .

Harry leaned over Sherrilyn and looked at Juliet. Sutherland was still sucking away on her pipe, looking as placid as a cow.

"Can you *really* act?" he asked.

She took the pipe out of her mouth. "The audience adored me. I've told you before—I would've been a star, except jealous rivals kept me down."

"Right. So you did." He looked at the pirate ship. One hundred and fifty yards. "Well, here's your chance to prove it, Lady Sutherland. I'll give the signal."

She nodded, still as placid as ever, and put the pipe back in place.

"Okay, then," Harry said. "We got a few minutes to relax. Contemplate philosophical thoughts. Whatever does the trick."

He settled back comfortably against the rail and tilted his head toward Sherrilyn.

"Whaddaya say we get laid afterward?"

"I never screw the boss."

"Okay. I'll resign my commission. Become one of the guys."

"I never screw guys in my unit."

"Damn, you're a hardass, Sherrilyn. Fine. I'll quit the army. Become a civilian. How's that?"

"Like I said, Harry. You've got the worst come-on lines I ever heard. Three complete losers in a row."

"Oh, hell, that's nothing. I can come up with way worse come-on lines than that."

She gave him a skeptical glance. "Prove it."

"Look, Sherrilyn, you gotta face facts. You're a natural dyke, all there is to it. Your desperate efforts to go straight are just distorting your soul. Spend a night with me in the sack and the experience will be so repulsive that you'll finally be able to see your way to dykedom and sexual freedom."

Maddox burst into laughter. Loud enough and long enough that Harry started worrying. Even with the wind blowing, the pirates were getting close enough to hear.

"Hey, cool it, willya? Or at least make it sound hysterical."

That shut Sherrilyn up instantly. "I don't do hysterical," she said, scowling.

Harry looked at the Algerine ship. One hundred yards off, now. From the looks of the figures crowding in its bow, he estimated a crew of somewhere around thirty men.

"Any minute, Juliet."

She removed the pipe from her mouth and spent a few seconds making sure the tobacco wasn't still

burning. There wasn't really much chance that smoldering tobacco could set a ship on fire, but anyone
familiar with wooden sailing ships wasn't going to take
any chances. That done, she stowed it somewhere in
her skirts.

"Just say the word."

Harry saw that Donald and Matt were starting to
pass their bottle back and forth, and decided it was
time to emulate them. So, he took a swig from the
bottle Paul had handed him.

Water, sure enough, with the flat taste of boiled
water that hadn't been any too good to begin with.
There was a reason that people in the seventeenth
century didn't usually drink the stuff.

He passed it over to Sherrilyn. By now, she had
the hat on, tilted forward to cover most of her face.
She took a swig from the bottle, careful not to tilt
her head too far back in the doing.

They passed the bottle back and forth a couple of
times. Just taking sips, really. The only purpose of the
exercise was to make the oncoming pirates think the
despairing crew had decided to indulge themselves
in one last hurried drunk before entering years of
enslavement and hard labor at the hands of Moslems
who weren't supposed to drink liquor at all.

True, the Moslems on that ship were probably none
too faithful about the business, especially since at least
half of them would be Europeans whose conversion
was pretty much a formality. Algerines treated their
Christian slaves harshly in order to goad their relatives
into ransoming them. But if the goad failed, after a
few years they were usually fairly lenient about letting
a slave convert to Islam and get out of servitude. A

fair number of the pirates on that ship would have once been slaves themselves.

That didn't make Harry any more inclined to show them mercy. A man got his ticket punched on the wrong train, that was his problem. In the Lefferts' school of theology, being stupid was the eighth mortal sin. If he'd been the guy bringing the stone tablets down the mountain, he'd have added *Thou shalt not be a cocksure dumbass* to the other ten. He couldn't see where God would have objected, being no dummy Himself according to all accounts.

"Okay, Juliet," he said. "Showtime."

Chapter 13

"Give me the bottle," she said.

Harry passed it over, still half full. Juliet rolled out from under the blanket and surged to her feet. It was an ungainly motion, due to her own chunky build and the need to use one hand to hold the bottle. But there was plenty of muscle under the Englishwoman's heft, and she was up in less than two seconds.

Once erect, she staggered over to the rail and flung the bottle at the Algerine ship. It was thirty yards off now, coming alongside and preparing to board.

It was a vigorous heave, but her aim was off—or wasn't, more likely. Instead of hitting any of the pirates, the bottle smashed into the side of the ship itself. A product of the stout German school of bottle-making, it didn't shatter but simply bounced off into the waters of the Channel.

One of the pirates whooped. Just about all of them were grinning. Leering, it would be better to say.

Juliet flung her hands wide, rolled back her head, and emitted a truly ear-splitting shriek. It was loud enough and piercing enough that several of the pirates winced. But most of them were too preoccupied

189

examining her figure. In that pose, even with her
heavy winter garments, Juliet Sutherland's female
identity was blindingly obvious. The woman was rather
homely, in point of fact. Not ugly, just having the
kind of a heavy, bluff-featured face that would suit
her as a matron once she was fifty instead of thirty.
But her figure was the sort that Rubens favored for
his paintings.

Some of the pirates started yelling at her. Harry
couldn't make out the words. They weren't from any
European language he was familiar with, and by now
he was familiar with a lot of them. But they didn't
sound particularly Arabic, either. If he remembered
right, a lot of the Sallee rovers were Berbers. Back
before the Ring of Fire, like any hillbilly, Harry had
pretty much lumped all ragheads together. But he'd
gotten a lot more sophisticated since then, especially
from the months he'd spent traveling with the very
cosmopolitan Catholic diplomat Giulio Mazarini.

Whatever the exact meaning of the words, however,
the general drift was obvious. The ogles and the grins
were clear enough. Just in case there was any doubt
at all, one of the pirates unlaced his trousers, pulled
out his penis, and waved it at Juliet.

That drew a *really* ear-piercing shriek. Juliet clapped
both hands to the sides of her head, in a gesture of
horror and despair that would have made any actress
in the silent-film era look like a devotee of the method
school of acting. Then she flung her arms apart again,
issued another shriek, and began racing up and down
the deck.

"Racing," at least, in spirit. Her actual progress
was more of an unsteady stagger. The seas weren't

especially heavy this day, but the deck was rolling noticeably. That was something Harry had already taken into consideration in his own plans, as he was sure the other members of the unit would have also. This would have to be done up close and personal. The footing just wasn't good enough for fancy marksmanship.

On her way, Juliet shook her fist at Harry and Sherrilyn. Then, when she neared the stern, shook her fist at Donald and Matija.

"Fucking cowards!" That was more of a bellow than what you'd call a shriek. As you might expect from a woman with that bosom, Sutherland had a splendid pair of lungs.

She came back toward the bow, staggering worse than ever now that she had both hands pressed to the sides of her head again. She almost fell, at one point. Probably would have, except she regained her balance by throwing both arms wide and emitting another shriek.

"I am fucking impressed," Harry murmured.

"Yeah, me too," came Sherrilyn's voice from under the brim of the hat. "Does it look as good as it sounds?"

"Even better. All this time, I thought she was bullshitting about the jealous rivals."

To be sure, in the world somewhere on the other side of the Ring of Fire, Juliet Sutherland would have been laughed off the stage. Any stage, even that belonging to an amateur theater group in West Nowhere. But patrons of the theater in the here and now would have had an equally derisive opinion of the understated and subdued thespianism of the late twentieth century. They would have thought even silent-film era stars were pale imitations of True Actors.

Juliet certainly had the Algerines mesmerized. The pirate ship was now completely alongside, with less than ten yards separating the two vessels. Four of the pirates had grappling hooks ready. Harry estimated the length of the poles at no more than twelve feet.

Five yards, then. He wanted them as close as possible without the two ships actually being linked together. Whatever concoction Gerd had come up with in the hold, it was sure to be hellish. Quite literally, incendiary—and having his own ship burn up was no part of Harry's plan.

In the end, he got nervous enough about that possibility that he decided six yards would do the trick. He surged to his feet, far more athletically than Juliet had done, and yanked the blanket off of Maddox.

Juliet had been watching for it, of course. The moment she saw him move, she issued the loudest shriek she'd managed yet. Then—she must have undone the lacings while Harry hadn't noticed—she clawed aside her upper garments and exposed her bosom.

A very impressive bosom, indeed. Between the shriek and the breasts, the pirates barely noticed Harry at all until he snapped the blanket wide open and hurled it into the air at them.

There was no chance the blanket could make it across the space, even if there hadn't been any wind, but that didn't matter. As a visual distraction, it worked almost as well as Juliet's tits. The incredible thunder clap of the ten-gauge going off came as a complete surprise to the Algerines.

One of the pirates holding a grappling hook caught

most of the pellets, which pretty well shredded his upper body. Even with a sawed-off ten-gauge, the range was just too short for the spread to be very wide. Still, one or two stray pellets hit the men on either side, causing both of them to flinch violently—and their swords, added to the one the slain man dropped as he went down, caused more injuries to the men bunched next to them. None of the injuries were really major, leaving aside the pirate who'd been slain outright, but as a distraction and a source of confusion—especially coupled with the noise the shotgun made as it went off—you couldn't ask for anything better.

Harry waited until the second barrel went off before he sprang to the rail. As good a shot as she was, and as much as he trusted Sherrilyn, nobody in their right mind is going to get anywhere near the possible line of fire of a sawed-off ten-gauge loaded with buckshot.

Maddox's second shot took out another grappling hook holder. Harry was at the side an instant later, bracing his left hip against the rail and firing half-sideways with a two-handed grip. He favored a nine-millimeter himself, which he could easily fire one-handed. But that was on dry land, not a ship's deck at sea. Even at a range of six yards, he had to concentrate.

He double-tapped the pirate right across from him in the chest. Then he shifted his aim from left to right, double-tapping each target as he came to it. Following right behind him, Felix had taken position toward the stern and was doing the same. A better and faster shot with a pistol than Harry, even starting a bit later, Kasza had taken down his fourth man by the time Harry killed three—and he'd managed to shoot another one of the pirates holding a grappling hook, while he was at it.

That left one grappling hook holder still to worry about, but Harry didn't bother looking for him. Speed was everything in this situation, and he just concentrated on killing the nearest targets, whatever they had in their hands.

Swords and other hand weapons only, so far as he could see. That was what he had expected. No sensible pirate captain would arm his men with firearms just to capture an unresisting merchant vessel with a crew less than a third the size of his own. Leaving aside the ever-present risk of accidentally shooting one of your own in the excitement of the moment, loaded guns on a ship—and they'd all be matchlocks, to make it worse—posed too great a danger of starting a fire.

The pirates were shrieking themselves now, but Harry blocked that out of his mind. There was just a row of targets, that's all. The only sounds that registered at all clearly were the sharp and unmistakable cracks of a semi-automatic rifle going into action from the stern.

One rifle only, from the sound. That meant Matt, who could see everything unfolding from his position far better than Harry could, had gauged that the situation was well enough under control that he needn't take the risk of releasing the helm and adding his own rifle to the mix. And it also meant Harry didn't have to worry about that last grappling hook. Donald would have targeted that man first, and he was a superb marksman with any kind of rifle.

Not in Julie's class, of course, but Julie was a freak of nature. What difference did it make? The range here was measured in yards, not hundreds of yards.

When his pistol ran out of ammunition, Harry just dropped it onto the deck, pulled out his backup, and kept firing. There weren't any scuppers nearby in the ship's bulwarks, so there wasn't much danger of the valuable gun slipping overboard.

Maddox had joined Harry and Felix at the rail with her own pistol, and, not more than two seconds later, Paul Maczka was out from under the tarpaulin he'd hidden under and weighed in with his shotgun at the bow. Like all seventeenth-century soldiers Harry knew, Paul positively adored pump-action shotguns. *Clickety-BOOM, clickety-BOOM, clickety-BOOM, clickety-BOOM.* By the time he started reloading, the bow of the enemy's ship was a charnelhouse.

Harry decided he could afford to pause himself. Not to reload—he still had four rounds left—but to take stock of the overall situation.

Good enough, he decided, after a quick scrutiny. They'd killed or wounded close to half of the Algerine crew already. More than a third, for sure. And while the pirates still outnumbered them, they were obviously so stunned by the incredible mayhem that had been visited upon with no warning that they posed no immediate danger at all. Whatever rumors they might have heard about the rate of fire of the witch-weapons brought from the future, they'd dismissed as nonsense.

They wouldn't any longer, of course. But, for them, "any longer" was a time span that had shrunk down to minutes.

"Front and center, Gerd!" Harry shouted.

Gerd popped out of the hatch. Literally popped. George must have been standing in the hold below with Gerd's feet in his hands and just heaved him up.

Gerd rolled when he reached the deck, not even trying to find his feet right away. He was simply concentrating on keeping the large canvas package in his hands from getting damaged.

Once he got to his knees, he leaned back over the hatch and held the package out. A very large hand came up holding a slowmatch and lit the fuse sticking out from the canvas.

It was a very short fuse. Gerd surged to his feet, raced to the rail, and pitched the package onto the deck of the pirate ship.

"Get us the fuck out of here, Matt!" he yelled, half-sprawled over the rail. Then he just flung himself down onto the deck.

Matt already had their ship veering aside. Harry and the other shooters sprawled to the deck also, as fast as they could while making sure their guns didn't go off by accident. The package went off not more than a second later.

The blast wasn't so bad, but Harry could feel the heat through his heavy coat, even sheltered where he was. Whatever Gerd had put in that makeshift bomb, it was mostly designed to set the enemy ship on fire. Harry could only hope it wouldn't ignite one of their own sails before they got far enough away.

"Cut it a little fine there, didn't you?" Paul hissed at Gerd.

Harry was tempted to add his own admonishment, but manfully resisted. What could you expect? "Cutting it fine" and "let Gerd handle the fireworks" were pretty much a given. Which, of course, was the reason Harry had given him the assignment in the first place. As hair-raising as the results might be.

He levered himself up and peered over the rail. The Algerine vessel was already an inferno. Several more pirates had been killed outright by the blast, at least as many injured—and the intact members of the crew were paying no attention to anything except getting their two dinghies overboard. They didn't have a prayer of stopping that blaze, and they knew it.

By now, Grabnar had them far enough away that there was no danger of the fire spreading to Harry's own ship. He rose to his feet and took a few seconds to study the pirates working at the dinghies. By the time he was done, Sherrilyn was on her feet also and standing next to him, reloading her pistol. Harry picked up his own gun from the deck but didn't reload it. There'd be time later to do so, as well as scavenge the brass.

"You're the best rifle shot we got except maybe Ohde," he said to her. "Go to the stern and get Paul's rifle. Between you and Don, you ought to be able to keep them from launching either of those dinghies."

The pirates did manage to get one of the dinghies into the water. Or Sherrilyn did, if you believed her later boast that one of her rounds had cut the last remaining line and dumped the dinghy before any pirate could get into it. Either way, it didn't matter. That dinghy drifted off, unoccupied, while Donald and Sherrilyn systematically slaughtered any pirate who tried to lower the other one.

At the end, not more than half a dozen pirates threw themselves into the sea to get away from the holocaust that their ship had become.

"Get us closer and we can pick 'em off!" Ohde hollered.

198   Eric Flint & David Weber

Harry shook his head. "Waste of ammo, Don. Just let 'em be. They'll all be dead anyway, in less than ten minutes."

People had swum across the English Channel from time to time, Harry knew, in the world he'd left behind. But they hadn't been Algerine pirates picked at random, they'd been people who'd trained for it for years. And he was pretty sure they'd done it at the narrowest stretch of the Strait of Dover, which was still many miles away. And he was dead sure they hadn't done it in January. Maybe if he were wearing a wet suit—and assuming he was a good enough swimmer in the first place—a man could make it to the French shore, well over ten miles away.

But these pirates didn't stand a chance. The first dinghy had drifted too far away for any of them to get to it in time. Hypothermia would take them under in a few short minutes.

No, there'd be no inconvenient witnesses to make awkward comments about the little group of disreputable-looking travelers who'd be arriving in London soon. Disreputable didn't matter, certainly not in Southwark. Dangerous as demons did, until the demons finally bared their fangs at the Tower.

George came up out of the hold. "You all right, love?"

"It was horrible. Look at this!" She'd never relaced her vest, having concentrated entirely on just getting out of the way once the shooting started. Her breasts were more impressive than ever, now that she hauled them out in her hands. "They're frostbitten!"

George ambled over. "Not to worry. Come down below and I'll take care of the problem. Between me and some rum—especially me—they'll be as good as ever in no time."

"Right." She stuffed the medical objects in question back where they'd come from. Then, gave Harry a very haughty look. The sort that would have fit a real dame far better than did her face.

"See? Didn't I tell you? It was jealous rivals did me in."

"I never doubted you once," said Harry. Proving, despite his flamboyant reputation, that he followed the eleventh commandment with devout scruple even if he was none too diligent about the other ten.

Chapter 14

Magdeburg

"Well, go in, why don't you?" Eric Krenz had his arms crossed and his hands tucked into the folds of his heavy coat. "It's *cold,* Thorsten. I always hated January even before an up-timer told me we're in the middle of what they call 'the Little Ice Age.'"

Thorsten was very cold himself, it being one of those clear-skied days in midwinter when everything seemed to turn to ice. But he still wasn't ready to take the last few steps to reach the entrance to the settlement house. Mostly—so he told himself, anyway—because the settlement house was actually a large and impressive-looking monastery. The oldest surviving structure in the city, in fact, founded centuries ago.

The *Kloster Unser Lieben Frauen,* as it had formerly been known. The literal translation into English was "the Monastery of Our Loving Women," but it was actually a convent dedicated to the Virgin Mary—and it was still referred to as such by Magdeburg's more devout inhabitants, who cast a skeptical eye on the new activities to which the ancient building was being put today. The Lutherans, perhaps oddly, even more than the Catholics from whom the monastery had been seized after Gustav Adolf established his control of the city and began rebuilding it from the devastation left by Tilly's army in 1631.

But perhaps that was not so odd. There weren't that many Catholics in Magdeburg, which had been the center of Lutheranism in Germany since the previous century. Or, at least, not many who made a point of it. Feelings could still run high about the horrible massacre, which had happened less than three years earlier. Since the emperor had allowed the Catholics to retain the small cathedral of San Sebastian not far from the huge Lutheran Dom, and his soldiery—the CoC, still more so—kept the religious peace in the city, Thorsten imagined the city's Catholics were inclined not to make a fuss about the former *Kloster*.

"Thorsten, I'm *freezing*. And we've only got a one-day leave. Either shit or get off the pot. If you can't work up the nerve to see the Americaness again, then"—Eric snatched a hand from beneath his coat and pointed to the north; then stuck it right back—"there's a nice warm tavern not two blocks away."

A tavern sounded . . . very tempting. Warm, good beer—and most of all, a familiar and comfortable situation. As opposed to marching into a monastery-become-peculiar-charity-project, where lurked a young female who intimidated Thorsten almost as much as she attracted him.

In the end, the decision was made for him. The big door to the settlement house opened and Caroline herself emerged. With the same incredible smile on her face that Thorsten vividly remembered.

Did more than remember, actually. In the weeks since he'd last seen her, he'd used the memory of that smile to fend off the image of Robert Stiteler being slaughtered. That worked very well, he'd found. He was having fewer and fewer nightmares and flashbacks as time went on.

"Do you *always* make a habit of this?" she asked him cheerfully.

Peering out the same frosted window through which Caroline had first spotted Thorsten Engler standing outside, Maureen Grady smiled almost as widely as Caroline. "Well, this is shaping up nicely. I am *so* fond of men who aren't always cocksure about everything."

Anna Sophia, the dowager countess of Schwarzburg-Rudolstadt, half-rose from her seat near the window and looked out also. "Is that the young man you mentioned to me last week?"

Her nineteen-year-old sister-in-law Emelie, born a countess of Oldenberg-Delmenhorst but the new countess of Schwarzburg-Rudolstadt since her marriage the previous summer, rose from her chair and came to the window also. "Nice-enough looking fellow, I will say that. But are you sure he's suitable for our precious Caroline?"

Maureen started to say something, but broke off in a half-choked laugh when she spotted the expression on the face of the older countess. Anna Sophia was looking very prim and proper indeed. Much the way a middle-aged and eminently respectable lady reacts to something unmentionable being spoken aloud in public. Silence, that somehow still manages to exude wordless disapproval.

"Yes, I'm sure," Maureen said, when she recovered. "The dowager countess is none too pleased about it, mind you. But I checked with my contacts in the Committee of Correspondence."

Emelie glanced at Anna Sophia and smiled. "Your very *extensive* contacts in the CoC."

"Well, yes. In this instance, I checked with Gunther himself. Then, after hearing his story, I had my husband ask around in the navy yard. If anyone has anything bad to say about Thorsten Engler, they're keeping very quiet about it."

"As if anyone could hide anything from those people, with their spies in every house," the dowager countess said stiffly. "I do not approve, Maureen. I say it again. No good will come of this."

She didn't add *mark my words,* but she might as well have.

Her sister-in-law resumed her seat. "Oh, stop it, Anna Sophia. We've had no trouble with the CoC at all. What really upsets you is that our work depends so heavily on them."

"We should be relying on the churches," the older countess insisted. She and her sister-in-law shared the same birthday, June 15, but they were thirty years apart in age—and at least that far removed in some of their social attitudes.

Maureen slouched back in her chair with her elbows on the armrests, and steepled her fingers. Then, gazing at Anna Sophia over the fingertips, said: "I will be glad to, Countess—as soon as you can find me more than three churches in the city whose pastors or priests don't insist on imposing doctrinal qualifications on our clients. I will add that the only one of those

three churches which carries any weight is—brace
yourself—the Catholic church."

Anna Sophia's lips tightened but she said nothing. If
she had, Maureen suspected, the words she'd have said
would also have been: *Those people*. With perhaps even
more disapproval in her tone than when she used *those
people* to refer to the Committees of Correspondence.
Like most upper-class Lutherans in the USE—young
Emelie being one of the exceptions—the dowager
countess of Schwarzburg-Rudolstadt viewed the recent
upsurge of the Catholic church in Magdeburg with
great alarm.

By what insidious devices had the miserable papists
come to wield so much influence over the masses in
central Germany? Until very recently, a bastion of
Lutheran orthodoxy?

In public, they usually ascribed the phenomenon
to the well-known deviousness and cunning of the
Jesuits, "the damned Jesuits" being a handy catch-
all explanation for Lutherans of their class. Or they
ascribed it to the supposedly massive immigration of
uneducated Catholics into the burgeoning capital city.
But Maureen wondered how much they really believed
that themselves. The great majority of immigrants
into Magdeburg came from Protestant areas of Germany and Europe, not Catholic ones. And while the
reputation of the Jesuits was well-deserved in some
respects, the near-magical powers ascribed to them
by their enemies was just plain silly.

No, the explanation was far simpler, and required
no formula to explain beyond the well-tried and
ancient one. As usually happens with powers-that-be,
the Lutheran establishment in central and northern

Germany—laity and clergy alike—had gotten fat, self-centered and complacent. And more than a little selfish. The headway made by the Catholic church was no more mysterious than the headway Protestant churches had made against Catholicism in the Latin America of the world Maureen had left behind in the Ring of Fire.

But there was no point in raking this old argument over the coals again. Anna Sophia was one of a dozen important figures in the Lutheran establishment in Germany—which, in this area, was essentially identical with the political establishment—who'd been willing to serve as public sponsors for the settlement house. With no lesser a person than the queen of Sweden herself as the figurehead—and her very energetic seven-year-old daughter as a frequent and enthusiastic visitor.

For Maureen Grady's purposes, that was plenty good enough. Emelie was the only one of the "Elles," as Caroline called them—"Eminent Lutheran Ladies"— who had a get-your-hands-dirty involvement in the daily work of the settlement house, anyway. Whether as a matter of personal temperament or simply because she was by far the youngest of the Elles, being still a teenager, Emelie had no trouble working with either the CoC or the Catholic church in Magdeburg.

In any event, it was time to break off the gossip session. The door was opening and Caroline was ushering the Engler fellow into the room.

Thorsten's relaxation at Caroline's obviously friendly attitude vanished the moment he went through the door she'd led him to. Other than Maureen Grady, he knew neither of the women in the room beyond. But everything about them, from the obviously expensive clothing they wore to their hair styles to subtleties about their expressions and mannerisms made it clear as day that they were noblewomen. Probably *Hochadel,* to boot, not lesser nobility.

Thorsten didn't share the automatic hostility toward the German aristocracy that many CoC members possessed. But he was certainly not partial to them, either—and, more to the point in this situation, had had so little personal contact with any real ones that he didn't know how to conduct himself properly. The one *reichsritter* who'd lived near Engler's village had been a very small landowner without much more in the way of pretensions—and certainly not refined manners—than any prosperous farmer in the area.

Fortunately, the younger of the two noblewomen smiled and extended her hand for an American-style informal handshake. That much, Thorsten had long since mastered.

"A pleasure, ma'am," he said, managing to get the words out smoothly and evenly.

"I am Emelie, the countess of Schwarzburg-Rudolstadt," she said. Then, gesturing toward the older noblewoman sitting by the window: "And this is my husband's sister-in-law Anna Sophia, the dowager countess."

There being no offer of a handshake coming from that quarter, Thorsten simply bowed. "A pleasure, ma'am." The elderly countess nodded in return but said nothing.

"This is the inner sanctum, Thorsten," said Caroline. "I figured I'd bring you in here first, so you wouldn't think this place was being run according to principles of anarchy. Appearances to the contrary. But we can go now, and leave the ladies to their machinations. See you later, Maureen. Emelie. Countess."

And off she went, taking Thorsten by the hand and leading him out. He made no protest. Leaving aside his own desire to escape, this was the first time they'd had any physical contact. He was quite thrilled.

After the door closed, the dowager countess of Schwarzburg-Rudolstadt emitted a sniff. "I find myself wondering if your precious CoC fellow made any recommendations about *her*. She's quite shocking at times, you know."

"Don't be silly, Anna Sophia. I find Caroline immensely refreshing."

Maureen looked from one to the other. "For what it's worth, I share Emelie's enthusiasm for Caroline— and, yes, Anna Sophia, sometimes the girl practically defines the term 'bluntness.' But what I mostly care about, seeing as how I really know very little about Thorsten Engler, is that I'm seeing a human being's emotional paralysis finally coming unraveled."

Now simply interested, the older countess raised her head. Maureen nodded toward Emelie. "She knows the story, but I don't think I've ever told you. Caroline's not a native of Grantville like most of us here. The only reason she was in town when the Ring of Fire hit is because she was one of Rita Stearns' college friends attending her wedding to Tom Simpson. Part of the reason she came is because she thought she might pick up some good tips—seeing as how she was supposed to get married to her own fiancé six weeks later. In Philadelphia, where he lived—and where the Ring of Fire left him."

"Ah." Anna Sophia looked out the window again. "I wonder if we will ever understand God's purpose there. I don't think so, myself, whatever the parsons say. The learned arguments they advance today to explain the Ring of Fire are no more learned, after all, than the arguments I can remember them advancing not so many years ago—which sagely explained why the age of miracles is long past and will never return until the Christ himself."

Maureen was startled by the words, as she always was whenever someone spoke of the Ring of Fire that way. She shouldn't be, really, since this was hardly the first time she'd heard a similar sentiment expressed. Looked at from that viewpoint . . .

True enough, the Ring of Fire was a palpable, physical miracle, like something right out of the Bible. The parting of the Red Sea might have been more spectacular, perhaps. But those waters had returned, after Moses and his people passed. Whereas all anyone in Europe had to do—as untold thousands had done, by now—was travel to within three miles of Grantville to see the modern miracle with their own eyes. Nine-hundred-foot-tall cliffs that had not existed an eyeblink before God made them to be; rivers running in new courses; lakes drained and lakes created. Perhaps most of all, if a bit more subtle, thousands of sometimes peculiar people set loose in the world, who had in less than three years been the human equivalent of an earthquake.

The problem was that, despite her own sincere Catholicism, Maureen Grady simply couldn't think that way. She *knew* Grantville, having lived there for years since she'd left Chicago to take a better job at the big Veterans Administration center in Clarksburg. The idea that she and her neighbors—her cop husband, too, with his mania for baseball? their two sons, with a worse mania? their three dogs, with their mania for stealing the best seats in the house and shedding fur all over them?—were all part of a miracle just seemed completely absurd to her. Miracles were like *Star Wars*. They happened long, long ago in places that were far, far way—and had names that were hard to pronounce. They did not happen in dog-food-out-of-a-can plain old West Virginia.

They just *didn't*, unless God was a lot more like an American Indian style prankster deity than the one Maureen had grown up with and worshipped. So, Maureen had long since plunked herself down on the "unknown natural causes" side of that debate. She could accept that blind nature might pick West Virginia for the Ring of Fire.

Why not, since nature had given them the seemingly immortal Senator Robert Byrd? Nobody ever explained *him* as being due to any sort of miracle. The occasional Republican whispers that he'd sold his soul to the devil could be discounted, she thought.

"This is the day-care center," Caroline said, as they entered a section of the settlement house that was a newly constructed extension from the medieval monastery.

Thornton looked around carefully. The great one room wooden structure was really just a huge barn, with what amounted to big stalls for children instead of horses or cattle. True, the floor was wood instead of dirt, and was amazingly clean given the swarms of children everywhere. But the design and craftsmanship of the extension itself was just about exactly what you'd get with a well-made barn. Very sturdy and solid, to be sure, but with no frills whatsoever.

The one thing that puzzled him at first was how they managed to keep such a big wooden structure warm enough in the winter. He saw no signs that the walls were insulated by anything except a double layer of planking. But then he spotted one of the peculiar-looking new American stoves that were becoming quite popular in the city. "Franklin stoves," they were called. Thorsten's own landlord had been talking lately about getting some for their apartment building.

He looked around again, and spotted two more. Apparently, they had such a stove in almost every one of the stalls for children.

"Well, what do you think?" Caroline asked. Glancing at her, Thorsten realized that he'd been silent for quite some time, as he'd given the day-care center much more than a casual examination. His friend Eric teased him about that characteristic quite often. Thorsten supposed it was probably true that he tended to concentrate on something to the point of being half-oblivious to the world around him.

"It's very sturdy," he said. "Former farmers built it, I am thinking."

"Well . . . yes, I suppose it could have been. It was done by a crew sent from two of the construction workers' unions. Most of those men are from rural areas, true enough. I don't know if they were farmers, though. Why do you say that?"

Thorsten waved his hand about. "It's designed like a big barn, Caroline. Better made than usual, but that's what it is."

She looked a little startled. "A *barn*? I wouldn't have said so!"

Fearing that she was on the verge of becoming offended, Thorsten chose his next words carefully.

"Ah . . . I don't mean to be impertinent, but I take it you were not born and raised in a country village?"

Caroline's burst of laughter reassured Thorsten, as well as intrigued him. She had a raucous, almost harsh-sounding laugh, quite at odds with her actual voice. Everything about the woman was fascinating.

"Hell, no! I'm the o-riginal city girl, Thorsten. Born and raised in and around Washington, D.C. When I was growing up, going on a 'country outing' meant finding an Eritrean restaurant instead of the run-of-the-mill Ethiopian ones. The first time I saw a cow was when I transferred to WVU my junior year because I didn't like—well, never mind. Let's just say it took Rita Stearns fifteen minutes to walk me through the differences between a cow and a horse so I could tell them apart." She frowned rather dramatically. "And she's never let me forget it even though the truth is I could have managed it in two minutes if she hadn't been laughing her head off the other thirteen."

Thorsten tried to imagine not being able to tell the difference between a cow and horse at a glance. Finally! Something about the woman that was clearly far from perfect. It came as a great relief.

"For someone like me, Caroline, a good and well-made barn is nothing to sneer at. Many people live their whole lives in much worse. I meant no offense."

She turned her head and looked at him for a long moment, without a trace of her usual smile. "I believe you," she said eventually. "I think you're one of the nicest men I've ever met. And none of it's phony."

He didn't know what to say to that. But the smile returned, and she took him by the hand again and led him elsewhere. The "soup kitchen," she called it, even though they were serving no form of soup at all, so far as Thorsten could determine.

"So how was the food?" Eric asked him that evening, over beers in the tavern. He'd left the settlement house much sooner than Engler, of course.

"Who cares?" was Thorsten's reply.

"That silly smile has no business on your plain German farmer's face," declared Krenz. He turned to Gunther Achterhof, who was sitting at the table with them. "Don't you agree?"

"No." Gunther studied Thorsten for a bit. He really did seem quite distracted.

"Still having dreams?"

"Oh, yes."

Gunther drained his beer. "I changed my mind. You're right, Krenz. That is the silliest smile I've ever seen, on anybody's face. Better he should have kept suffering, like a farmer should."

Chapter 15

The more he saw in the workshop that his father had built in a new wing of Frederiksborg Castle, the more appalled Prince Ulrik became. By the time he got to the worktable at the end, with its dully gleaming centerpiece, Ulrik felt as if his stomach was residing somewhere below . . .

Best not to think about that.

He turned his head to examine his guide. More precisely, to gauge how much he could confide in him.

Oddly, there was something about Baldur Norddahl's piratical appearance that was reassuring. Perhaps it was because Ulrik had concluded the appearance was by no means skin deep. He'd spent enough time with Norddahl, since he'd returned to Denmark from Schwerin a few days earlier at the king's command, to get a sense of the man. Even that portion of the Norwegian's history that he'd been willing to divulge— and that usually took several mugs of good strong beer to wheedle out of him—made Baldur Norddahl an

213

adventurer with few equals. Ulrik wouldn't be surprised at all to discover that some of those adventures *had* included piracy. Where else would the Norwegian have learned Arabic but from the Algerine corsairs? He was rather fluent in the outlandish tongue, although he claimed he couldn't read it except bits and pieces of the aljamiado script.

Spain, Norddahl claimed, was where he first learned Arabic, along with several dialects of Spanish itself. His proficiency in the Muslim tongue he'd gained in parts beyond, when he spent some time with Morisco traders—plunderers and slavers, too, one got the sense—in caravans crossing the great desert to the fabled city of Timbuktu.

If there were a camel in Denmark, Ulrik would be interested to put the matter to a test, and see if Norddahl could ride one of the grotesque animals. On the other hand, he probably could, even if the rest of his stories were false. To use one of the many American expressions that were spreading all over Europe, Baldur Norddahl was a man of many parts.

True, most of those parts wouldn't bear close examination, taken one at a time. Even his name was suspect. To begin with, Ulrik had never heard of a Norwegian with the first name of "Baldur." An Icelander, maybe, since some of the old pagan names still survived on the island—but Norddahl spoke with a Norwegian accent. "Norddahl" was almost as suspect, to the prince. The word simply meant "of the north valley"—which could be just about anywhere. Norway had a thousand little valleys in its northern parts. Most Norwegians didn't use farm or location surnames, in the first place, they used patronymics.

But a father could be traced a lot easier than a valley somewhere "to the north," should someone go looking.

Nonetheless, that there *were* a lot of parts to the rogue, the prince didn't doubt at all.

"This strikes me as madness, Baldur, now that I've finally been able to see it myself. Tell me the truth."

The Norwegian took a few seconds to look around the immense workroom. It was deserted now, except for the two of them. Norddahl had ordered all of the workmen to take a break from their labors while he guided the prince about.

"It depends how you define 'madness,' prince. All of these devices—their descendants, at least—will work. Even the submarine."

"Even *this*?" Ulrik picked up the huge bronze helmet with its bizarre glass visor. With considerable strain, since the thing was very heavy. He tried to imagine himself fitting the ghastly device onto his head, and then lowering himself into water with it.

"Oh, yes. Actually, the problem with this particular enthusiasm of your father's isn't the diving helmet. I'd be quite willing to trust my life to that. It's the hose"—he swept his hand down the long table, indicating the canvas and wire contraption that lay sprawled across it in great coils—"and the pump and the rest of it that makes the project so close to suicide that I told His Majesty I refused to test it myself."

Ulrik winced. Given the risks Norddahl was usually prepared to take—for enough money—the fact that he considered this one almost suicidal made it suicidal indeed.

"Did you ask the American lieutenant?"

Baldur smiled. "Does a bear shit in the woods? As God is my witness, I would forgive the up-timers just for their delightful sayings alone, even if they hadn't brought such wonderful gadgets with them. Yes, Prince, of course I asked him. Pried him rather, over the many beers I bought the lad." The smile expanded a bit. "Which I charged to your father's account, you understand. Being, as it was, clearly a research expense."

The prince smiled back. He couldn't help it, even if one of the things about his father that aggravated him was the king of Denmark's ability to shed money like rainwater. But he was unable to get angry over Baldur's amoral cheeriness. Ulrik had come to realize that the Norwegian adventurer lied about very little, except his past. That was something of a relief, for a prince who'd been acquainted with courtiers all his life.

"And what did Eddie say?"

The smiled left Norddahl's face. "He said it was very dangerous—all of this—although he claimed that he couldn't provide me with many details beyond depicting what he called 'the bends.'"

Ulrik grunted skeptically. "I'm surprised you got anything out of him—or that he didn't regale you with the outlandish claims he tells my father."

"Oh, it's not hard. You simply have to know the trick of it."

The prince cocked an eyebrow. "Which is?"

"The lad's squeamish. You wouldn't think it, of a man who drove what the up-timers call a 'speedboat'—and isn't that an appropriate name!—into a Danish warship.

But he is. Eddie Cantrell will lie through his teeth without hesitation, if he thinks he's deceiving his enemies." Norddahl shook his head. "Meaning no disrespect, Prince, but your father is far too gullible when his enthusiasms get the best of him."

Ulrik chuckled. "To say the least. Yes, I know. But you still haven't explained 'the trick.'"

The Norwegian shrugged. "Eddie's not a cold-blooded killer. If you make it clear that someone's *life* depends on what he tells you—depends directly; immediately; soon, not as vague later possibility—he simply can't bring himself to keep lying. He'll get vague, evasive. If you press him—beer helps—you can eventually pry some honest warnings from him. Even details, if he knows them."

"But he doesn't, I take it?"

Baldur shook his head. "No, not really. Not about this business, at least." The last, he said with another sweep of the hand at the contents of the workshop. "He came from a mountainous province, far inland. I think the only time he started learning anything about ships and the sea was after he came here through the Ring of Fire. So most of what he knows is what he calls 'book-learning,' and spotty at that."

"What are these 'bends' he warns about?"

"I'm not entirely sure, Prince. Eddie couldn't really explain it—and much of what he said didn't make a great deal of sense to me to begin with. But if he's right—I'm sure he's not lying here, he simply may be wrong himself—it seems that if a man goes deep enough into the water various parts of the air enter his actual blood. One of them is supposed to be particularly dangerous. Niter . . . something."

Ulrik had been feeling slightly dizzy ever since he arrived in Denmark and his ebullient giant of a father had immediately placed him in charge of what the king was pleased to call "our secret navy projects." The dizziness increased slightly, as he tried to wrack his brain to pull up what he'd managed to learn in hasty perusals of up-time texts.

"Yes, I remember. Nitrogen, they call it. The up-timers claim that air"—the hand-wave the prince now made took in everything about them—"is not really 'air' at all, but a mixture of several airs. What they call gases. Oxygen is the one we actually use to breathe. Most of it is nitrogen. Four parts in five, if I remember correctly."

He frowned. "But they also claim that nitrogen is harmless. 'Inert,' is the word they use."

"Most of the time, maybe. But Eddie insists it's dangerous underwater. At least, if you go far enough down. He says what happens is that the—'gas,' you call it?—saturates the blood. Then, when a man rises back to the surface—if he rises too quickly, that is—the gas boils back out of his blood. That's what they call 'the bends.' Does terrible things, apparently, especially to the joints. It can even kill you."

Ulrik grimaced at the image. As if there weren't already enough sickening ways to maim or kill a man!

"And what else is dangerous?"

Norddahl shrugged again. "That was the only thing he could tell me specifically. But all of the dangers, including the bends, seem to come from the same general peril. What he calls the pressure of the water itself. That's another way of saying—"

"Yes, I understand." That much of the up-time texts,

at least, had been easy enough to comprehend. The idea that even the air had weight, pressing down on a body, had seemed peculiar at first. But once Ulrik remembered his experience trying to breathe, the one time he'd ventured into the high Alps, the concept had come into focus. And he'd swum and dove often enough—and deep enough, now and then—to understand full well that water got . . . thicker, the farther down you went. "Pressure" was not a bad term at all to describe it, since his ears had felt as if a soft-handed giant had been squeezing them.

On the other hand . . .

"There's something I still don't understand." He set down the helmet. "Not even my ebullient sire proposes to send a man or a machine very far beneath the surface." He turned slightly and pointed to the submarine being built. "Even that preposterous device is not intended to go much deeper than thirty feet."

"Nor"—he rapped the helmet with a knuckle—"is this. Fifty feet perhaps. Sixty or seventy, at most. Am I right?"

"Yes, Your Highness."

Ha! Apparently Ulrik was making an impression on the rascal. Norddahl was finally using the proper appellation, instead of the "prince" business that bordered on disrespect.

"And I understand what you're questioning," the Norwegian continued. "Many men dive that deep, or even deeper. I've been thirty feet down myself, more than once, and there are sponge fishermen who go much deeper than that. Do it for a living, day after day, and suffer none of the consequences Eddie warns about."

"And what do you conclude? Since you don't believe he's lying."

Baldur paused, scratching his chin while he examined the helmet himself. Then, with a very dubious look in his eyes, studied the coils of the hose. "I posed that very problem to him, as it happens. He was obviously puzzled for a moment. I really *don't* think he knows very much about all this. But he finally said I was overlooking what he called 'the differential.' What he meant by that is that—this is what he says—when a diver without all this complicated gadgetry goes deep, somehow the pressure of his body is enough to resist the pressure of the water."

Ulrik's eyes almost crossed. "That's . . . hard to make sense of."

"Isn't it?" The cheery smile returned. "But I think I understand what he's talking about, Your Highness. When a diver goes deep, what he does is breathe very heavily—but then he expels all the air before he dives. If you didn't—I learned this myself—you simply can't get very deep to begin with."

Comprehension began to come again. Even at the age of twenty-two, Ulrik had quite of bit of military experience. He'd seen a human body—more than one—torn to pieces.

"Yes, I see. If you picture the lungs as empty sacks, not full of air . . ."

He turned his head and squinted at the bizarre-looking boat being constructed at the far end. "But that shouldn't affect men in a submarine."

"No, I don't believe it does—unless the hull shatters. But what about a man in this contraption?" Again, Norddahl wrapped the diving helmet with a knuckle. "So long as the pump above is keeping him supplied with air, he should be fine. But what if the pump fails—or the hose ruptures?"

The prince tried to imagine the consequences. "Well, he'd drown very quickly, if you didn't pull him up in time."

Baldur shook his head. "No, Your Highness, I don't think he would. I think something much worse would happen to him."

"What?"

"I don't know. Neither does Eddie. He says he read about it once, but can't remember any of the details. What he did remember was that, whatever it was, it was quite horrible."

"And you believe him?"

"Oh, yes. That's why I told His Majesty I wouldn't go down in it myself, once we got it finished. The submarine, I'd be willing to try—but not this devilish device. Of course, no one will be able to test it for a few months anyway, even if we had the pump ready. The water would be much too cold during the winter, assuming you could find a spot without ice cover. But, come spring, by which time everything should be done, I still won't do it."

Ulrik didn't blame him. Courage was one thing. This was just lunacy, and it got worse the more he learned. Devoting any effort to this particular project was completely pointless. It had no possible military application at all, that Ulrik could see. How was a man laboring under the weight of a huge bronze helmet and a heavy diving suit—even assuming you could make a long enough hose to provide him with air, which was impossible—supposed to pose a threat to a warship?

He suspected that not even his father thought it could. The king had simply . . . gotten interested. Christian IV was also a man of many parts. He read relatively little, unfortunately, but he was very intelligent and was fascinated by a wide range of things. In particular, he adored mechanical contrivances and would have made quite a good artisan himself.

"So let us return to the beginning, Baldur. I said this seemed all madness, and you disagreed. Why?"

"I disagreed only in general, Your Highness. Eventually, I think all of these contraptions can be made to work. I'm quite partial to the submarine, in fact. But I think it's . . . well, not wise—not for me to label your august royal father a madman!—to believe they can be made to work in time to fend off the American ironclads. They'll be here by May, I'm thinking, at the latest."

Ulrik looked back to the submarine, then at the helmet. "You don't share the opinion of my father's courtiers, I take it? Most of them insist that the up-timers are not magicians, simply artisans—and that there is no way to get such ungainly boats down the Elbe and through the North Sea and the Kattegat and Skagerrak. Even leaving aside the political problem of passing Hamburg and the likelihood—the near-certainty, to hear those very martial fellows talk—that heroic units of our army—perhaps even the miserable French—will destroy them before they ever smell a whiff of saltwater."

Baldur chuckled. There was a bit of a sneer in the sound. "Oh, the Americans are certainly not magicians. On that much, I quite agree. But I'm wondering how many of those courtiers were there, at the battle of Wismar?"

"Not one," said Ulrik flatly. "I asked."

"What I thought. Well, I *was* there, Your Highness. I was aboard the *Lossen*. Fortunately for me, after the airplane crashed into us, I was one of the officers detailed to command the boats we lowered. So I wasn't aboard when the magazine finally exploded, a few minutes later."

There wasn't a trace of the usual humor in Norddahl's face, now. In that moment, Ulrik thought he was finally seeing the man beneath the rogue. A burly Norwegian, somewhere around the age of forty, with ash-blond hair and very light blue eyes—and an impressive collections of scars even on that small part of his body that was visible. The prince didn't doubt for a minute that there were plenty more beneath the heavy clothes Baldur wore in the workshop. This was a man who had seen more of danger than most any ten other men. Without the sheen of humor on the surface, he was like a grim ancient who'd gone a-viking every summer of his life since he was a boy.

The prince sighed. "What I feared."

Ulrik's eyes moved around the workshop again. Slowly, because there was so much to be seen. His father was nothing if not an enthusiast, once something took his fancy. Where another monarch might have ordered one or two such dubious naval projects set underway, the king of Denmark had ordered a dozen.

"Is there *anything* in here that isn't harebrained?"

The smile came back. "Oh, yes! Two of the projects, in fact. Alas, I've not been able to generate much interest in them on the part of His Majesty. Too simple for his taste, you understand. But I think they have quite splendid possibilities. Here, let me show you."

✧   ✧   ✧

After he finished his study of the first project Baldur had led him to, Ulrik straightened up. His spirits, even more than his back.

"A 'spar-torpedo,' you call it? Nothing more than a big simple bomb, really, stuck out on the end of a pole. Taken into battle by a sturdy boat, such as we've known how to make for centuries."

"Your Highness has penetrated to the heart of the matter splendidly," agreed Baldur, his customary cheer back in place. "Better still, a device that's been tested recently and shown to work quite well, even using down-time equipment almost throughout. This was how the up-timers in Amsterdam sank a Spanish ship, you know. There is one problem, though."

Here he pointed to the one and only exotic part of the whole project. "The up-timers in Amsterdam had to row the whole way. Whereas we lowly Danes will have an American engine to propel one of our boats. What they call an 'outboard motor.' I obtained it through . . . well, let's just say informal methods, and leave it at that. Luckily for us, that Americans are definitely people and not devils is proven by the fact that they share all of the usual human vices. Greed and carelessness being prominent among them."

A bit skeptically, Ulrik eyed the gadget. "Are you sure . . ."

"Oh, yes, Your Highness. I've tested this myself, many times, on boats I've taken out onto the Castle Lake. So long as you have the fuel for it—and that's not really so hard to buy on the black market in the Germanies, certainly not the little we'd need—this thing is just about as reliable as oars. That's because it's what the Americans—have I told you how much I enjoy their little saws and turns of phrase?—call 'store-bought.' This isn't something they cobbled together here themselves, from whatever bits and pieces of their old world they brought with them. This is something that was made—in great huge lots of thousands, they say, like a shop making nails—in one of those giant factories they had up-time."

The dizzy feeling returned, for a moment. Ulrik tried to imagine a world whose cities housed millions and whose landscapes—he'd seen many of the pictures himself, when he'd visited Grantville—were dotted by giant manufactories as if they were dairy farms.

He shook it off. Thankfully, the kingdom of Denmark in the coming year would not have to fend off such an incredibly powerful world. Simply a fragment of it. Insofar as the term "simply" could be applied to a task that even such a fellow as the Norwegian with him viewed grimly.

Ulrik was quite fond of up-time expressions, himself, as it happened. He'd picked up quite a few while he'd visited the Germanies where the Americans had spread their influence.

"Hard-boiled," the Americans would have labeled Baldur Norddahl. Very hard-boiled, indeed.

"You said there was a problem with it, though."

Baldur ran fingers through his hair. "Yes, there is. Once I finally got my hands on the contraption and tested it, I discovered that with a boat that has any weight at all—and we need something fairly sturdy to support a heavy bomb on the end of a long pole—the outboard motor isn't really any faster than just using oars. The big advantage it has is that it doesn't wear out the crew the way pulling oars does. But any attack we launch on those American ironclads will have to be quick, anyway, so the advantage disappears. And the engine makes an incredible racket. A very distinctive sound that the Americans will certainly recognize."

Ulrik thought about it. "Perhaps we should plan on using the thing as a decoy, then. Draw their attention with the outboard motor, but plan the real strike with oared boats."

Baldur looked surprised. Then, quite respectful. "That's an intriguing idea, Your Highness. I hadn't thought of it. Be awfully rough on the men on the decoy ship, though."

"Yes, it would. Unless we can figure out another way of confusing the enemy at the same time. But let's leave that be, for moment. What was the other project you thought had promise?"

"That's even better—or would be," he said, half-sighing, "had I been able to interest His Majesty in it. That's over there."

Five minutes later, Prince Ulrik was struggling not to curse his own father.

"*This* would have been sensible!"

Norddahl shook his head, his expression unnaturally lugubrious. "It certainly would have. Almost no risk involved at all. And the up-time texts say that it's the most effective anti-ship device ever designed by the hand of man. Beautiful in its simplicity, isn't it? It's not even very different from things we down-timers have done before, although never on such a scale."

Ulrik looked first at the device itself—Baldur called it the "prototype," using yet another American term—and then spent some seconds admiring the clever way the Norwegian had shown how it would work in practice. He called that the "scale model."

As simple as you could ask for. Just litter the narrow confines of the Danish straits with mines. Straightforward bombs, whose design posed no insurmountable problem, each big enough to sink even an ironclad. Devices that could be set in place by boats such as the Danes already had in profusion, rather than one or two intricate and exotic ships to be designed and built in a hurry—with who could say what result in practice?

With enough of them, they could possibly do more than close the Straits. If they closed the Kattegat, they could keep the ironclads from even getting near to Copenhagen. Granted, that would take an enormous number of mines and was probably impractical.

"We could still . . ."

But Norddahl was shaking his head, his expression more lugubrious still. "I'm afraid not, Your Highness. There simply isn't enough time left. I did my best to persuade the king—right from the beginning—that we should abandon everything else in favor of this alone. But . . ."

He spread his hands. "Your father, you understand."

Ulrik had to suppress a sudden spike of nearhysterical laughter.

"Yes, I understand. My father."

The up-time texts and records didn't really have very much concerning the history of Denmark, taken as a whole. It had been a small and unimportant country in their time, and not close to their own. But there was a fair amount in the libraries in Grantville—the woman with the huge and eccentric personal library had had even more, which she'd been kind enough to let Ulrik examine—concerning King Christian IV himself. A very flamboyant and long-lived monarch he'd been, it seemed, who'd been quite popular with his people despite his seemingly endless excesses. Ulrik's father had made such an impression on his land that he would be one of the few monarchs of the era still vividly remembered centuries in the future.

Remembered for many things. One of them being the fact that he'd produced over two dozen children, a goodly number of them illegitimate.

Such was Ulrik's father, for good or ill. You could hardly expect such a man to satisfy himself with one or two special projects for his navy—when he could conceive a dozen.

"You're certain?"

"Yes, Your Highness. I did the calculations. If we'd started earlier, things would be different. Starting now . . ."

Norddahl's eyes went to the prototype. "Even now, if you could persuade your father to drop everything else, I think I could get enough made and put in place to close the Øresund. That would protect Copenhagen, at least. But there's no chance any longer that we could make and place enough to close off even the Little Belt, much less the Great Belt."

"Either of which would allow Admiral Simpson access to the Baltic—and our fleet blockading Luebeck."

"Yes, Your Highness."

"Let's assume—for the moment—that I could keep the king pried off your back enough to allow you to devote . . . oh, let's say one-half of your efforts to the mines."

Norddahl's eyes narrowed and grew a bit unfocused, while he did his calculations.

"I couldn't close off the Øresund. But I could certainly make and put in place enough mines to make it dangerous for the enemy's ships."

"And you're certain that one of these mines would be enough to sink an American ironclad? I've *seen* them, Baldur. At something of a distance, of course. They were friendly enough, when I passed through Magdeburg, very respectful of my diplomatic status, but they obviously weren't going to let me into the shipyards. But even under construction, seen from afar, they are formidable looking things."

Norddahl chuckled again. "Oh, yes, Your Highness. I've never been able to get my hands on a copy of the actual plans, but there's really no great mystery about the ironclads. Give me the wherewithal and enough time—"

He waved at one of the projects looming darkly in a corner. "—and I could build one myself. Though even the king agrees that would take far too long, so I've never done much but fiddle with it. But one thing is known for sure. However much armor the ironclads may carry above the water, the hulls themselves are just wooden hulls. These mines are powerful enough they'd probably even hole an iron hull. They'll certainly shatter a wooden one."

Ulrik nodded, and then looked back toward the area where the spar torpedo project was underway.

"And how many of those could you have ready by May? Assuming—for the moment—that I could give you enough breathing space to devote . . . oh, half the time that's left, after the mines. I'm afraid there's no way around the fact that you'll have to keep at least a quarter of your effort devoted to these other ridiculous schemes. I can keep my father at a distance, to a point. But I'd have as much chance of fending off a great bear with my hands as I would keeping my illustrious sire from meddling at all."

He was a bit startled to realize how far he'd allowed himself to discard circumlocutions in the presence of a man who was, technically, nothing but a servant. His instincts had led him there, though, and Ulrik trusted his instincts about people. He'd come to have a great deal of confidence in Baldur Norddahl, and needed to make sure the reverse was true as well. This was going to be a desperate enough business, under the best of circumstances. If anything was to work at all, it would require a close bond between a prince of Denmark and a Norwegian adventurer, rascally as he might be.

Baldur had been pondering the question. "It's not quite as simple as that, Your Highness. I could have a number of boats built and ready with spar torpedoes, by May. But I have a bad feeling they won't do much good."

Ulrik frowned. "You just told me yourself that's how the up-timers sank a Spanish ship in Amsterdam."

"Not the same thing at all, Your Highness. In Amsterdam, the Americans had the advantage of complete surprise. In the Øresund, we won't. You can be as sure as anything in the world that the American admiral knows all about the danger of mines and . . . they'd call them 'torpedo boats,' I think. They'll be alert at all times, even in a storm, and they have more than enough weaponry on board those ships, even leaving aside the main guns, to destroy any rowboat before it got close enough to pose a danger."

He grimaced. "I'll be willing to lead the thing, when the time comes. But only because it's not *completely* suicidal, and I have a taste for adventure."

"More than a taste!" exclaimed Ulrik, half-laughing. "But I see your point. All right, then. There's no point in throwing away the lives of our sailors to no purpose. Spend enough time to make sure you have the torpedo boats ready, in case we can figure out a way to make them effective. The rest, devote as much as you possibly can to the mines."

"And you'll keep your father as far off as you can."

"Yes. And when the time comes, you and I will both see what a torpedo boat can do."

Norddahl's eyes widened. "Ah . . . you're a prince, Your Highness. I'm not sure your father   "

"Damn my father. As many children as he sires, what difference does it make? I have two older brothers anyway, not even counting the morganatic line."

He gave the Norwegian the best royal stare he had. He knew it was quite good, too. He'd learned it from watching Gustav Adolf, the king of Sweden, in the time he'd spent with him as a youngster. A man he liked and generally admired—and was now his enemy. But such was the life of a prince.

Finally, Ulrik got what he needed. There was nothing but respect in Baldur Norddahl's gaze, any longer. No trace of the rogue or the rascal. Just that of the grim ancient that the prince of Denmark would need at his side come a desperate moment in the spring, when they both went a-viking.

Chapter 16

When he emerged from the workshop, Prince Ulrik discovered that the overcast skies of the morning had turned into an afternoon's snowfall. He was just as glad, though. First, because the really bitter cold days in January were the days with clear skies; second, because he liked snow anyway. When he was a boy, he and his brothers had greeted a heavy snowfall with great enthusiasm. It meant days of marvelous play in the castle gardens, digging tunnels through the snow and erecting what they were pleased to call fortresses.

The big workshop the king had had built for Baldur Norddahl was on the southernmost of the three islands in the lake that Frederiksborg Castle was built upon. It was located almost adjacent to the two round towers erected by the castle's original founder, Ulrik's grandfather Frederik II. Giving those familiar sights a mere glance, the prince headed for the S-bridge that would take him to the middle island.

He took a shortcut through the royal stables. That was quicker, warmer—and he liked horses even more than he did snow. As he passed through, he exchanged greetings with the stablehands he encountered, but did not, as he usually would, take the time to chat with them. He was preoccupied today, lost in thoughts that were dark and foreboding.

Once across the S-bridge and onto the middle island, Ulrik stopped in the square to gaze at the Neptune Fountain.

There'd been snowball fights also, of course, many of them in this very square. Lots of those. Ulrik liked to fancy that he first learned military tactics in those melees.

Melees they'd been, too. One of the advantages of being a boy prince—perhaps simply one of the realities, advantageous or not—was that you always had a coterie of other boys around you. Sons of courtiers or sons of stablehands, either way or both. At that age, people did not make the fine distinctions they would grow into as time passed. That was one of the things about his childhood that Ulrik found himself missing a great deal, especially after he visited Grantville and came to realize how very differently the up-timers calculated rank and station in life.

Sadly, the main lesson Ulrik had learned from those mass snowball fights was that the surest of all military tactics was simply to outnumber the foe. "Sadly," because his illustrious father, for all his erratic but undoubted brilliance, seemed to be unable or unwilling to accept that reality and everything that flowed from it.

Slowly, ignoring the snowfall that was covering his hat and the shoulders of his heavy coat, Ulrik walked most of the way around the Neptune Fountain in the middle of the square, examining, as he passed, the edifices around him.

His father had ordered this castle built, transforming Frederik II's rather modest hunting manor into one of the great royal palaces of Europe. No idle boast, that, either. Ulrik had traveled enough to have seen many of them. Christian IV had had Frederiksborg designed in the Dutch Renaissance style, with its copper-covered roofs and spires, sweeping gables, sandstone decorations. The end result, completed in 1615, was quite magnificent.

Having completed his round of the fountain, the prince continued to the north, to the island that held the royal palace and his own quarters.

Easy to forget, when you lived in such a palace, that the kingdom which had been wealthy enough to afford it was still a small kingdom. Easy to forget, when you woke up every morning in a bedroom as magnificent as that of any monarch in Europe, that great bedrooms and halls and gardens and fountains did not translate into great armies and navies.

Easy to forget, staring up at ceilings as splendid as any in the world, that they were still ceilings and not endless open skies. Easy to forget the most important lesson that Ulrik thought any king or prince had to learn down to the marrow of his bones.

For all beings except the Almighty, there were limits. No matter who you were, there were limits. And you had to develop as keen an eye for them—as acute a taste, if you would—as you did for good architecture and fine paintings and music. Or you would soon enough find that you had lost everything within those limits. A great deal, at least.

Ulrik himself had always been good at seeing limits. Perhaps that was because he was an average-sized man, in all respects, where his father was not at all. Christian IV was tall, immense in girth, and possessed a capacity for procreation that was only exceeded by his imagination and his capacity for drink. Had he not possessed a reasonably kind disposition—certainly by royal standards—he would have been a veritable ogre.

This war was madness. Ulrik's father had been well-nigh insane to believe that by allying himself with the two of the three great Catholic powers in Europe he could somehow displace the Swede as the preeminent monarch in the Protestant lands. Even that wretched King Charles of England had been thinking more clearly. Richelieu and the Spaniards would use Denmark like a man squeezes all the juice out of an orange, and then cast the husk aside. And it would be that husk—not France, not Spain, certainly not England—upon which the full fury of the Germans fell.

And it was their fury that Ulrik feared, not that of the Swedes. Sweden was not so big a kingdom itself, when all was said and done. Larger in size but smaller in population than Denmark. It was that reality that always grated on his father. Why Sweden, and not Denmark?

They were all idiots. In the end, Ulrik thought, Gustav Adolf as much as Christian IV. Unable to see that the role played by Sweden and Denmark over the past century or two was solely due to the fact that the Germanies had been disunited and, to make the blessing of Scandinavia complete, ruled by as sorry a lot of squabbling and incompetent princes as you could ask for.

Ulrik was now passing over the second bridge, and into a crosswind. He shivered, from the sudden cold.

So he tried to tell himself, knowing that was an excuse. With these thoughts running through his head, he would have shivered on the warmest day of summer.

He could remember shivering exactly so, in fact, on a warm summer day in Magdeburg.

Grantville had been exhilarating. Magdeburg had been . . .

Terrifying. All the energy and ingenuity brought by the up-timers through the Ring of Fire, that Ulrik had seen in Grantville also. But Grantville was a place of limits. Tightly circumscribed, first, by its surrounding hills; even more, circumscribed as well by the customs and traditions of its inhabitants.

By and large, Ulrik had discovered that he liked most of the Americans. Not all, of course. But they were a decent and unassuming folk, for all their mechanical wizardry.

Magdeburg seemed limitless. A new city arising like a phoenix from the ashes and ruins that Tilly and his butchers had left behind, on a vast and open plain. But now, with that same American ingenuity coupled to a people who outnumbered all other people in Europe and had a great rage coiled within their souls.

And who could blame them—when, for fifteen years, every other land of Europe had used theirs for a battlefield? Taking advantage of Germany's disunity and the fecklessness of its princes to turn Europe's center into a wasteland. Destroying their towns and cities and villages, slaughtering their men, ravishing their women, starving their children and old folk.

And for what? So this prince over here could claim a bit more land than he had before, and that king over there could add a new title to a list that was already preposterously long.

Well, it was over, whether or not those bickering kings and princes were able or willing to recognize it. The Germanies had become Germany—call it whatever you will—and it had produced a prince like no other before him. And this one cared not in the least for the trappings of royalty. He cared only for the substance of the power those titles claimed to embody—and did so, to make it worse for the princes with the fancy titles, on behalf of the commoners who had suffered the most from the war.

Ulrik had met him, twice. Very briefly, on both occasions. He certainly couldn't claim to know him, but he didn't need to. He'd spent considerable time in Magdeburg just walking through the new industrial districts, drinking in the taverns of the men who worked there, and idling many hours in the Freedom Arches which dotted most of the city. And, everywhere he went in that most plebeian of all great cities in Europe, hearing over and over the term *Prince of Germany*. The prince who would, they all seemed as certain as the tides, lead them to victory come winter's end.

The phrase was a shell, depicting a man. The confidence and determination that his people poured into that term, no shell at all. Any monarch or chancellor in Europe who believed so was either blind or mad or both.

The Swedish king, to give him credit, had held off the alliance Richelieu formed to destroy him. The alliance Ulrik's father had been fool enough to join.

Whatever delusions Christian IV might still have, buttressed by the flattery of a pack of worthless courtiers, Ulrik had spoken to enough Danish officers to know that no one seriously expected to be able to take Luebeck this winter.

By summer, they'd say. But that summer would never arrive, because spring would come before it. The spring of the year of our lord 1634, when the fury of Germany finally fell upon its torturers. Ulrik could only hope—and he'd do what he could for the purpose—that Denmark itself might survive that storm.

He'd reached the northern island, and the royal palace. By now, his mood was far darker than the leaden skies.

So . . .

He was finally able to laugh, a bit. So he'd do what he'd found himself doing quite often, these past three months.

Go visit an American, what else?

Eddie Cantrell stared up at the canopy over his bed, feeling like an idiot.

Four times over, to make everything perfect.

To start with the smallest idiocy, what was a country boy from a small town in West Virginia doing in a bed—no, a whole bedroom—that he didn't think the fanciest up-time hotel in the world could boast?

Just *look* at it, fer chrissake.

Okay, the bed was a bed. Big, sure, but not actually as big as a king-size bed you could have bought up-time for a few hundred dollars. In that small respect, at least, there was still a trace of sanity in the world.

From there, all reason fled. The bed coverings would have cost a small fortune, and God only knows what you'd have had to pay for the four-poster bed frame and the canopy hanging from it. The thing was a no-fooling fricking *tapestry*. Eddie was dead certain that its like back up-time could be found only in museums.

His eyes dropped from the canopy to scan the bedroom. Of course, why not?—since the whole damn room belonged in a museum. There wasn't a square inch of the ceiling that wasn't decorated; not a square foot of the walls that didn't have a painting or some sort of art work on it. Any of which, Eddie was just as certain, museum curators and art thieves back up-time would have drooled over. Nor was there a square yard of the floor—a beautiful parquet floor, naturally, that would have probably bankrupted your average American millionaire back home—that didn't have a piece of furniture on it, or statuary, or just huge vases, any one of which would probably have bankrupted your average up-time multimillionaire.

Eddie's eyes went to the big window across the room from the bed. Not to mention, of course, that if he hauled his sorry ass out of bed and hobbled over to the window, he'd be looking out at a vista that these crazy Danish royals chose to call "gardens" but didn't look like any gardens Eddie had ever seen. Sure as hell not the vegetable gardens his mother or any of their neighbors had had. Even leaving aside the fact that they were bigger than a football field.

And that was only the smallest of the idiocies.

Move on to the next. What was a proper West Virginia country boy doing in bed in the first place, now that it was afternoon? Lolling about like that crazy French writer he'd read about once, who not only spent half his life in bed but wrote books—famous books, even—about a man who spent most of his life in bed.

Eddie didn't even have the excuse of being bored. How could he be bored, when he was a captive of a medieval king who had dungeons to spare and torturers on his payroll?

Fine. "Early Modern Era" king, if that'd make the scholars happy.

Swell. What that meant in the real world, as far as Eddie was concerned, was that he was in transition from brutal illiterate kings whose powers were actually limited in practice to the Brave New World of absolute monarchies, whose torturers and executioners were literate so they could stay up on the latest innovations. Thank you very much.

No, he was just in a funk. The sort of funk that might be respectable enough somewhere in Greenwich Village or the lower east side of Manhattan, but any solid hillbilly would sneer at. *Go fix the suspension on your car or something, you dummy.*

And why was he in a funk? Oh, let's move on to Idiocy Number Three.

Secret Agent Man. James Bond, 007. Mike Stearns had entrusted him with the task, in captivity, of ferreting out the secrets of the enemy and foiling their plans with fiendishly clever countermoves. Like fucking Houdini.

Right. That made Mike Stearns an even bigger idiot than Eddie, sure, but Stearns wasn't sleeping three floors over a dungeon.

Well, maybe he was, actually—given that Gustav Adolf had insisted on having his architects draw up the plans for Hans Richter Palace and oversee its construction. The Good Old Swedes, in this day and age, weren't exactly what you'd call good ole boys. A lot closer to their troll roots, still, than they were to Ingrid Bergman.

But so what? They were *Mike's* dungeons, whose tongs and pincers and God knows what else *he* didn't have to worry about.

Well. At least not until he lost the election. After that—this day and age being what it was—who could say?

Big deal. The election Mike had to worry about was at least a year away. Eddie could lose his election any time that damn drunken Danish king who kept him up half the nights till the wee hours drinking along with him chose to punch his ticket.

Did I mention I have absolute power? No? Well, not to worry—here's the proof of it. Lads, take this fellow downstairs and pluck off another part of his body.

Eddie heard the door opening. All thought of the Three Lesser Idiocies were swept from his mind. The Great One had arrived.

"Still in bed! Eddie, you should be ashamed of yourself! And don't pretend you have a hangover because my father let you go long before the carousing was over last night. I know, Ulrik told me. Oh, he's here, too."

Eddie sat up to look. Sure enough, the youngest of the king's three sons in the royal line was coming in right behind.

Perfect. The outrigger, so to speak, to the Greatest of All Idiocies.

On the other hand—they had bestsellers in this day and age, too, he'd discovered—maybe if Eddie survived it all he could write a book and become rich and famous. Okay, rich and the laughingstock of an entire continent, but what the hell.

The Life of a Secret Agent. No, that'd be fudging. *The Secrets of a Secret Agent; or, How to Turn 007 Into a Seven Percent Solution.*

Chapter One. Get captured in a naval battle. Make sure you lose a foot while you're at it.

Chapter Two. Get some moron of a president to make you his secret agent while in captivity.

Chapter Three. Ingratiate yourself to an alcoholic enemy king by drinking as much as you possibly can in his company, when you don't like liquor to begin with and the stuff scares you to death because your dad was a souse.

Chapter Four. Feed him a pack of silly lies and just hope that he's not sober enough to catch you at it.

Chapter Five. Make friends with his son the prince.

Chapter Six. Fall in love with his daughter the princess. Fine. The "king's daughter"—as if that's going to make any difference when they figure it out, seeing as how James Bondaged .07 was clever enough to pick a girl who's jail-bait back up-time and dungeon-bait in this one, so it wouldn't matter if she was a butcher's daughter.

Chapter Seven . . .

But Eddie flinched from that still-unwritten one. He could only hope the red-hot tongs would cauterize the wound at the same time they rendered him unconscious from agony, when they removed the offending body part in question. Sometimes he found himself wondering if, in this day and age, they made wooden peg-dicks to match wooden peglegs.

The scariest thing was, they probably did.

"Why are you staring at me like that?" Anne Cathrine demanded. "You'd think I was a ghost or something."

Ulrik pulled up a chair next to the bed, blithely ignoring the cost of the chair or whatever damage it might do to the floor. Eddie was afraid to sit in most of the furniture, himself, and whenever he couldn't walk barefoot on the floor he practically tiptoed.

Of course, Ulrik could confidently expect to *inherit* the dungeons and the tongs and the what-not. He had a chance of it, at least. Danes still had the custom that the nobility got to elect the king, choosing from whoever was eligible in the royal family. They'd already elected the oldest prince Christian as the successor, but if he died before his father did, Ulrik might still wind up on the throne even though he was the youngest of the three princes. Even if he didn't, he'd surely come out of it with a dungeon or two, along with a reasonable share of the torturers and tongs and pincers and what-not.

"It can't be you, Sister," said Ulrik cheerfully. "Look! He's giving me the same stare."

Anne Cathrine planted her hands on her hips. Very shapely hips. She was fully past puberty now, but still had a completely teenage female figure. Fifteen going on *Eddie-if-you-ever-lay-a-finger-on-her-your-ass-is-grass.*

Fortunately, he'd managed—so far—to avoid that

one and only idiocy. But unless Admiral Simpson steamed into the Øresund with an icebreaker before the winter was over, Eddie wasn't sure how long he could hold out.

The problem was that Anne Cathrine wasn't exuding any of the well-known signals from Eddie's past that informed him in no uncertain terms that *this girl ain't interested, buddy, so forget it*. If she had, his course would have been easy. Miserable, sure, and pining away with unrequited love—but he was used to *that*. His high school experience had been four almost solid years of pining away after girls whose titles might as well have been *You-Gotta-Be-Kidding* or *In-Your-Dreams, Buster*.

What he wasn't used to was a princess—fine, "king's daughter"—who planted those same very shapely hips on the bed right next to him, leaned over, spilling her gorgeous red-gold hair, took his cheeks in her hands and gave them a little shake. "Stop looking at me like that, I tell you."

Ulrik laughed. "Sister, you're being forward. If I tell Father, he'll scold you."

"No, he won't," she said serenely.

"Yes, Princess," Eddie said, not serenely at all.

That got him another cheek-shaking. "How many times must I tell you! 'King's daughter.' Not 'princess.' My mother's marriage to my father was morganatic." She twitched her head toward her half-brother. "Ulrik is a prince because he is in the royal line. I am not. Just a 'king's daughter.'"

Eddie nodded, simply thankful that he'd escaped disaster. He'd almost said "Yes, dear."

He wondered what might have resulted from that.

Would they just satisfy themselves by removing his cheeks with hot tongs, or would they add all his teeth into the bargain?

Ulrik laughed again. "Eddie, you always cheer me up. I'm not sure why. Maybe it's because you can do melancholy better than any Dane."

"Well, sure. I read the book. I don't know if it's been translated into Danish yet."

"What book?" the king's daughter asked.

"It's the one I told you about," her half-brother explained. "I read it in English. The play that English-man wrote about a Danish prince in Helsingør—he called it 'Elsinore'—who finds out his father was murdered and can't decide what to do."

"Oh, that one." She released Eddie's cheeks and waved a dismissive hand. "I don't want to read it, even when my English gets better. What a silly fantasy. Any Danish prince—princess, too, even a king's daughter—who found out that someone had committed such a crime would have his head by the morning."

Chapter Eight. Did I mention the jailbait will inherit the jail? Well, at least one or two cells in it. With a share of the tongs and the pincers and the what-not.

Chapter 17

February 1634

"Three more!" shouted King Charles, holding up the middle three fingers of his left hand. With his right, he pointed accusingly in the direction of the palace's servants' quarters. "A cook and two cleaning women. That's quite enough! The city has become a pesthole. The queen and I depart for Oxford on the morrow."

Sitting in his chair, the king lowered his head, gazing up at the earl of Strafford in the way that a stubborn child will make clear to his parent that he is most displeased. The royal expression combined sullenness, petulance, anger and resentment—and was about as unregal as anything Thomas Wentworth could imagine.

He took a breath, but before he could speak Charles snapped: "That is all, I say! There will be no further discussion on this matter. Simply see to the arrangements. I want a full escort out of the city, mind. London has become as infested with unruly apprentices as it has with vermin and disease."

Thomas bowed his head, bowing to the inevitable at the same time, and left the royal chamber. Outside, in the corridor, he took several deep breaths. Partly to control his anger; partly to give himself time to decide what steps he might still be able to take to alleviate some of the political damage that would be caused by the king leaving the capital for Oxford.

He considered, for a moment, simply biding his time and approaching the king with a proposal to reconsider later that day, or in the evening. That had worked twice before, after all.

Almost instantly, he discarded the notion. On the two previous occasions, the king hadn't been as set in his course. And, what was more important, his wife hadn't been involved. But Thomas has already learned from one of his assistants that Queen Henrietta Maria had been in hysterics this morning, after she heard about the latest outbreak of disease in the palace. With the queen in that state of mind, there was simply no chance any longer of persuading Charles to remain in the capital. The king doted on his wife. It was a personal characteristic that Thomas might have respected and even found attractive, had the king's doting not been so excessive and the wife herself such a blithering fool.

The fact that disease continued to crop up in a huge palace in the middle of winter, especially in the cramped servants' quarters, was a given. Thomas' assistant had told him that none of the cases involved plague. They were simply the sort of illnesses that were inevitable under the circumstances, and posed no real danger to the king and queen, living where they did elsewhere in the palace—in conditions that were anything but cramped.

For that matter, they weren't even inevitable—if the king had been willing to either move to the Tower or allow Thomas to bring the American nurse Rita Simpson into Whitehall to oversee the reorganization of the sanitary and medical practices in the royal residence. But the king had refused, to the second proposal even more vehemently than the first. As the months had passed, Charles had developed a detestation and fear of the captive Americans that was simply not rational. Even for him, it was not rational.

Thomas wasn't certain yet, but he was coming to the conclusion that a cabal against him had formed among the queen's courtiers. More precisely, a *competent* cabal. Even more than disease in winter, it was a certainty that a cabal would be formed against the most powerful minister in the government, by one or another of the cliques that made up the not-so-small horde of courtiers who infested the palace even worse than vermin did. The queen, with her love of flattery and lack of common sense, provided them with a natural center. And the long nights and slow months of winter provided them with the time and idleness to engage in their schemes and plots.

A given, in short, and not something Thomas was normally given to fretting about overmuch. Every powerful chief minister in English history had faced the same, after all.

But, lately, some new faces had been showing up at the queen's masques. Men of real substance, like

Sir Francis Windebank and Sir Paul Pindar, Endymion Porter, or noblemen such as the earl of Rutland, Francis Manners. The most dangerous of them was probably Richard Boyle, the earl of Cork. He was one of the kingdom's richest men, very astute, given to malevolence, and as ambitious as anyone Wentworth had ever met.

Thomas began pacing slowly down the hall, his hands clasped behind his back. He'd been incautious, he realized. The severe and unprecedented measures he'd taken to secure the king's rule and forestall any possibility of the English revolution that the up-timers' books depicted had enraged much of the populace. Especially those inclined toward Puritanism, of course.

So much, he'd expected and planned for. What he hadn't considered was that the same measures would stir up the ambitions of men who were inclined to support them. In a sense, by breaking the rules under which England had managed its affairs for so long, Thomas himself had inspired others to do the same. If he could do it, why couldn't they? The fact that his own motives, allowing for a reasonable amount of personal ambition, had been primarily political, was neither here nor there. Men like the earl of Cork wouldn't care. Such men were simply too self-centered to see any distinction at all between what they wanted and what the nation needed.

So be it. Thomas was confident enough that he could outmaneuver his rivals. Their great advantage was equally their disadvantage. Seeing—correctly—in the queen, the softest target in the court, they set their aim there. It was not hard to gain her confidence and support, after all, if you were prepared to ladle flattery and fawning with neither shame nor restraint. But once it was gained, the confidence always proved to be as soft as the target itself. Henrietta Maria was a superb complainer, whiner, critic and naysayer. But Thomas had never once seen her throw her influence with the king behind a project or person for any motive beyond petty and usually personal ones. She was simply not cut from the same cloth as Marie de Medici, the French king's mother who had been an incorrigible meddler in political affairs for years, and was still continuing her intrigues from her exile in Brussels.

Whitehall was possibly the largest palace in the world—certainly in Europe—and it was more in the nature of a small town with buildings all jammed together than a palace as such. All told, it had more than a thousand rooms and a multitude of corridors. So, long before Thomas reached the quarters he'd set aside for himself, he'd settled his nerves over the king's foolish decision. There was nothing for it except to make sure the foolishness went smoothly.

Encountering two guards at a corridor intersection, both of them in the colors of the mercenary company he'd decided to use for the purpose, he instructed one of them to find Captain Leebrick and have him report to the earl's quarters. Anthony Leebrick was one of the steadiest of the mercenary captains, with a well-trained company and good lieutenants. He also had a phlegmatic personality, which he'd need dealing with Charles and Henrietta Maria in the course of a long journey to Oxford in midwinter. Their complaints would be incessant, especially the queen's.

✧   ✧   ✧

Leebrick arrived not long after Thomas reached his quarters. Once Wentworth had explained the situation, and what was needed, the captain quickly left to make the arrangements. Even with as well-trained and disciplined a company as his, Leebrick was still dealing with mercenary soldiers—who were not prone to do anything "on the morrow" except sleep off a bout of drunkenness, unless they were actively on campaign in the field.

That done, and remembering that his friend William Laud was still in London, Thomas decided to pay him a visit. The archbishop had decided to postpone his visit to Canterbury for a few more days, in order to deal with a few problems that had come up lately. Having only recently been elevated from bishop of London, he was a bit overwhelmed by the demands of his new station.

That probably meant Thomas would have to put up with at least half an hour's worth of listening to William's querulous complaints, until he settled down his nerves. But it was a small price to pay. One of the drawbacks to becoming England's most powerful minister was that Wentworth had found he had very few friends left. More precisely, friends whose motives he didn't have to scrutinize carefully at every turn. He had plenty of the other sort, most of them men who'd never indicated the slightest fondness for him in times past—and a fair number who'd been actively hostile.

For all his many faults, William Laud was one of the few left whom the earl of Strafford could accept at face value. Perhaps the only one, really, except . . .

And there was an odd thought. Except a prisoner sitting in a dungeon in the Tower named Oliver Cromwell. Who, to be sure, had played a major role in separating Thomas Wentworth's head from his body a few years from now in another universe. But who also, Thomas was quite sure—in that world as much as this one—had never lied to him or told him anything except what he thought.

There was an irony there, of course. It seemed the more powerful a man became, the more limited became his pleasures. To the point where, reaching the pinnacle, it sometimes seemed that the only pleasure left to him was simply knowing that a statement made was the truth and not a lie or a ploy. Even if the statement was "let me out of here, and I'll try to slit your throat."

He even laughed then, in a very dry sort of way.

"And now this!" the archbishop exclaimed, throwing both his hands in the air. When they landed back on the armrests of his chair, Laud had them clenched into fists. Then, after taking a couple of deep breaths, he gave Wentworth something of an apologetic grimace.

"Yes, yes, I realize it must seem like a small matter to you, this business of the Americans asking me to appoint a bishop for them. Certainly compared to the problem you're having to deal with." He sniffed, disdainfully. "Our beloved monarch decamping from his own capital in the middle of a crisis."

"I wouldn't call it a 'crisis,'" Thomas said evenly. "More in the way of a tense time. But you're actually wrong about the rest. I don't think the matter you're wrestling with is a small one, at all. In fact, I wouldn't be surprised if—"

He broke off abruptly, realizing the precipice he was nearing.

Unfortunately, he'd forgotten just how perspicacious his friend could be, at times. The Archbishop of Canterbury's faults were so pronounced that it was easy to underestimate the man. William Laud hadn't fought his way up from very humble beginnings to become the primate of the Anglican church without there being a keen brain there, beneath the mulishness and the peeves and the personal quirks and foibles.

"You're thinking about it, aren't you?" said Laud, peering at him intently.

Frowning in as innocent a manner as he could manage, and being careful not to clench his own fists, Wentworth said: "Thinking about what?"

"Don't play the innocent with me, Thomas—and for sure and certain, don't try to play me for a fool. You know perfectly well what I'm talking about. It's not as if we haven't danced about the subject for weeks, now. You're thinking about the Glorious Revolution, that's what."

Wentworth sighed, and turned his gaze from the archbishop to the window looking out over London. Slowly, his hands curled on the armrests of his own chair. Not quite into fists; more like a man might try to seize something intangible in midair.

"Oh, yes, it's been quite obvious to me for some time," continued Laud. "Even if you do manage to stymie the revolution of 1640, then what? You can't continue this way, you know it as well as I do. This is *England,* not—not—the Ottoman empire."

Wentworth said nothing. He just continued to gaze out over the city. There really wasn't much to see, beyond a gray sunset lowering over a city that was grayer still. Gray everywhere he looked, nowadays, it seemed to him.

"Come, come, Thomas, speak up. I shall not betray you. You must know that, if nothing else."

There was that, after all. One of the few certainties in a world that grew less certain by the day.

"Very well, William. Yes, I am thinking about it—and, yes, of course you're right. Everything I've done since the king brought me to London has been a stopgap. Just a temporary measure—often enough, a ramshackle one—to keep a situation from spiraling out of control. But that's all it is. The king may be under the delusion that he can rule this way for a lifetime, and his successor after him, but that's all it is. A delusion. A ruler needs legitimacy before all else, and legitimacy in the end must have its base in the consent of the governed. Their acquiescence and acceptance, at the very least. When all is said and done, that's as true for the Turk as it is for the Englishman."

Laud made a face. Wentworth chuckled. "Granted, the Turk is more acquiescent to begin with. But read the histories, William. Even the Ottomans fell. Even the tsars fell. All of them fell—or they accommodated to survive. How is England to be the sole exception? Even allowing for God's special favor."

He planted his hand on the armrests and pushed himself erect, feeling far wearier than any forty-year-old man should be, who hadn't done anything more physically strenuous that day than walk corridors and sign documents. He went to the window, hoping, perhaps, that the city might look less gray if he could peer at it directly.

No, it didn't. He wasn't surprised.

"He was an excellent ruler, you know," he said softly. "I've pored over the records that we've been able to obtain. All of them, twice over and more. And the more I read, the more I found myself wishing that I'd been his chief minister. All that Charles isn't—nor his father before him, nor any of the Stuarts—Oliver Cromwell was. Firm, steady, decisive. Yet not given to harshness for no purpose. He'd be labeled a tyrant after his death—they even dug up his corpse to decapitate it—but it wasn't true. Compared to Henry VIII? Or Elizabeth? Any of the Tudors? To say nothing of the Plantagenets. Ridiculous."

"He was a rebel and a regicide," Laud said stiffly. "Graciously, I will leave aside that he had the two of us executed, as well."

"Yes, he did, and so he was. But much more to the point, William, he was a rebel who never found the path to legitimacy. That's what did him in, in the end. His regime, rather, since"—Wentworth barked a harsh laugh—"no one tried to beard the lion while he was still alive. But after he died, it all fell apart. And there's really the lesson, I think. If a supremely capable and successful rebel can have his regime undone by a lack of legitimacy, what chance does a legitimate monarch who is not capable and successful at anything beyond petulance and caprice have of not squandering it away?"

He turned from the window to face the archbishop squarely. "That was not a rhetorical question, William. I need an answer to it. Quite desperately."

It was Laud's turn to look away. He glanced at the various portraits on the wall—men and women once famous, now half-forgotten—before spending a minute or so staring at a vase. A very attractive vase, and a very fragile one.

"No chance at all," he said finally, the words almost sighing from his mouth. "No more chance than I have, in the end, in what I had hoped to do. Damned Scotsmen."

Wentworth laughed again, rather gaily this time. "Oh, please, William! It was hardly just the Scotsmen!"

"They started it," Laud growled. "But . . . no, it wasn't just them."

He looked up at Wentworth, the expression on his face a half-pleading one. "I've been pondering the matter a great deal myself. Always managing to evade the collision, until . . ."

"Until Tom Simpson and Lady Mailey asked you to appoint a bishop for Grantville."

There'd been a time when William Laud would have objected to the term "Lady," applied to a commoner like Melissa Mailey. But, like many things, that time had passed. Seemed very ancient, in fact.

"Yes. A simple and straightforward request, on the face of it. Underneath, something vastly different. If I refuse, I undermine the true church of which I am the primate. But if I accept, I must limit that same church. I must agree—acquiesce, at least—to limits I have never heretofore accepted."

"And?"

"And . . . I don't know yet, not for sure. But I think I will finally agree. Because, in the end, I don't believe I really have any choice. Whether I like it or not."

Wentworth nodded. "No, I don't believe you do. Any more than I do."

Silence, again, for another minute. Then Laud asked: "What do you propose to do, then?"

"I have no idea, at the moment. My thoughts have gone everywhere for the past weeks—and come back as if they'd never gone. I even contemplated for a time releasing Oliver from the Tower and helping him overthrow the dynasty."

Laud's eyes were practically protruding. "You *must* be joking."

"Oh, no. I gave it quite serious thought. But what would be the point? He failed once; why would he succeed now? The goal was unobtainable in the first place, insofar as he ever had a clear goal in mind."

For a moment, his gaze grew unfocused. "It would be quite fascinating, you know, to be able to speak to that man. Not the man in his early thirties named Oliver Cromwell who sits this moment in a dungeon, but the man he became in that other universe, a quarter of a century from now. The lord protector of England, in his late fifties. What had he learned? What did he regret? What would he do otherwise, could it do it over again?"

The gaze came back into focus; a very keen one, in fact. "A fancy, you'll say. But is it? Are we not—you and I—in a position every bit as fanciful? Two *dead men*—my head rolling off a block on Tower Hill on May the twelfth of 1641, and yours in the same place on the tenth of January, not four years later—who are even this moment speaking to each other nonetheless. As if two severed heads on a mantelpiece were to be having a conversation."

"Oh, that's . . ."

"Yes, I know. Fanciful."

"I was going to say, 'silly.'"

"That, too, I suppose. But the substance remains. We are not in much different a position than two men who have a chance to relive their lives. What we chose once, we do not need to choose again."

"Yes, true enough—but it doesn't make our current choices any easier or less uncertain. And, for me at least, what shakes my resolve is not my knowledge of errors made in another universe, or a life that might have been. What shakes my resolve—all my certainties, except that I believe in Him—is what God did in *this* world."

Laud rose from his chair. Almost sprang from it. "It's none of that, Thomas! It's the Ring of Fire itself that my brain cannot wrap itself around. Let the papists prattle about 'God's hidden purpose' all they want. Let the Calvinists do the same. The *fact* remains. For the first time since the Resurrection, the Lord moved His hand so powerfully and so visibly that any man can *see* it. The first undoubted miracle in sixteen hundred years. *Why?*"

"I don't know."

"Of course you don't. None of us do. But He *did.* That, whatever else, can neither be questioned nor denied."

He fell back into the chair, collapsing as quickly as he came out of it. "We ignore the deed at our great peril. I am uncertain of most things, now. But of that, I am not uncertain at all."

Again, silence.

"So. What will you do?" the archbishop asked the minister.

"I don't know. I simply know that it cannot go on like this."

Wentworth glanced at the window, and saw that the sun had set. He hadn't noticed earlier, because of the grayness of the day outside and the light cast by the lamps in Laud's chamber.

"I must be off. The captain I entrusted with the task is a capable one, but I'd best make sure there any no unforeseen problems."

Laud nodded heavily, but said nothing.

When he reached the door, a thought came to Wentworth. Half-smiling, he turned back. "You, on the other hand, should have—just now—answered your own question."

The archbishop looked up. "Eh?"

"The question of the bishop. As you said yourself, God moved His hand. That being so, how can you refuse to send a bishop to that very place He did the deed, when his presence is requested from there?"

For a moment, Laud looked alarmed. Then, smiled—and quite cheerfully. "Why, yes. That's very nicely put, Thomas. My thanks, indeed. It *would* seem to border on apostasy, wouldn't it? Can't have that."

Chapter 18

Between the nature of his assignment and the day's weather, Captain Anthony Leebrick was in a foul mood. With his usual imperturbability, he hadn't let any of it show; certainly not to his own soldiers and not even to any of the royal party, not even the coachmen. But when he saw the first elements of a Trained Band moving out of a side street to block Tyburn Hill Road, he finally lost his temper.

"Oh, God's blood!" he snarled. "Not *today,* lads. I'm in no mood for it!"

He wouldn't have been, even if the sun was shining. Under these conditions, with a sleet coming on top of the past few days' thaw turning every road in the city into a mess of half-frozen mud, he had more than enough to worry about.

The horses were skittish already, as large animals always are when the footing is treacherous. That was even true—especially true, perhaps—of the horses hauling the royal carriages. Where a sensible and level-headed farmer or tradesman who needed to haul a heavy wagon would have selected horses for the purpose who were sturdy and placid beasts, kings and queens and high noblemen were far more likely to select them for their appearance. And, indeed, the eight steeds pulling the king and queen's conveyance were a fine-looking group, and even matched for color. So were the ones pulling the carriage behind it, which held the royal children and their nursemaids and nannies. But they were very far from the sort of animals Leebrick wanted to rely on to carry the royal party to Oxford under bad weather conditions in the middle of winter.

He'd made an attempt this morning to persuade King Charles to postpone the journey until the weather cleared. But the king had been adamant, and the queen even more so. They were convinced that London was so infested with disease that the risk of remaining for another day or two was unacceptable. Henrietta Maria had even started shrieking at Leebrick.

Fine for her, of course, to ride through sleet in a sheltered carriage. Fine, at least, in terms of her immediate comfort. Leebrick was quite certain it had never once occurred to Her Majesty that the driver and coachmen—and the horses—were going to be miserable and doing their jobs under terrible conditions. More to the point, that their ability to do their jobs in the first place might very well affect her own well-being.

So be it. The queen of England was well known for many things. Good sense had never been one of them.

About the only consolation the weather was giving him was that the sleet wasn't so heavy that everyone on the road couldn't look over and see the gallows alongside Tyburn Hill. Great heavy things, too, they were—a three-beam affair on three legs, for when they had a batch to hang at once. Leebrick glared at the Trained Band taking up positions across the road ahead of him, imagining several of their commanders swinging from the scaffold.

His anger was due to the moment, not the general situation. Ever since the earl of Strafford had brought a large number of mercenary companies from the continent to impose iron royal rule over England, there had been frequent clashes between the mercenary companies and London's long-established militia. For the most part, however, aside from the initial period, it had been a reasonably good-natured business. The earl had been careful to give the assignment of controlling London to companies like Leebrick's own, whose soldiers were almost all Englishmen—many of them from the same plebeian neighborhoods in London that were the stronghold of the Trained Bands. A fair number of Leebrick's men, in fact, had once belonged to one of the Trained Bands themselves.

As long as no one got too rambunctious, the confrontations and scuffles these days were more in the way of a very rough sport than anything a hardened soldier like Leebrick would call "combat." A lot of bruises, the occasional broken bone or gash from a pike, but almost no fatalities and not even many serious wounds. Mostly, once they accepted the verdict of the first few weeks of serious clashes, the Trained Bands were simply determined to demonstrate their stout London spirit and their unwillingness to capitulate to royal tyranny like so many curs.

"Not *today*, lads," Leebrick repeated, now growling softly instead of snarling.

His two lieutenants, Richard Towson and Patrick Welch, had drawn their horses alongside his. "How do you want to handle it, Captain?" asked Towson.

Before Leebrick could respond, Welch added: "There's another group coming down the side road we just passed. Not as big, but enough to require more than a handful of men."

Leebrick frowned. The Trained Bands didn't normally do anything as complex as a flanking maneuver. For the first time, he wondered if this encounter was more than the simple bad coincidence he'd assumed it was. Could the Bands have gotten word that the king was leaving the city? They'd have had precious little notice, even if they did, since the royal decision to go to Oxford had been made impulsively. The servants had had to scramble madly to get everything ready by the morning.

It wasn't impossible, by any means. Servants talk, after all. The reason Leebrick still thought it unlikely that this was a planned encounter was that the Trained Bands were a militia, mostly made up of the city's artisans and their apprentices. He'd had a hard enough time himself, getting his own company of professional soldiers ready on such short notice. What was the likelihood that the Trained Bands could so as well?

Not very. But whether planned or not, he still had a bad situation on his hands. The problem wasn't the Trained Bands, in themselves. He and his men could handle those perfectly easily, even if it came to a real fracas. The real problem—

A piercing female shriek from behind let him know that "the real problem" had just surfaced. Apparently, the queen had spotted the Trained Band advancing toward them down that side road. Glancing back, he could see that the royal carriage had come to a stop right at the intersection of that road and the Tyburn Hill Road.

More bad luck, piling on top of other. As that playwright whose work Anthony's paramour Liz was so fond of quoting had put it in one of his plays, when troubles come they come not single spies but in battalions.

"Nothing for it," he muttered. "I'll have to go back there and seen if I can calm down the stupid bit—ah, Their Majesties. Richard, you keep the main body of the company here. Move into formation in case the Band ahead of us thinks of doing something foolish, but don't do anything else unless you're attacked. Patrick, take your men onto that side road and do the same."

He turned his horse and headed back for the carriage, moving as quickly as he dared given the icy footing. Which wasn't quickly at all, since he could sense the nervousness of his mount. Like any good horseman, Leebrick knew full well how much horses hated bad footing—and how easy it was to panic even an experienced warhorse if his rider seemed agitated or unsteady.

From their vantage point atop Tyburn Hill, three men could see the situation unfolding below them quite well, despite the sleet. The hill wasn't especially tall but it had a good view of the gallows. In fact, it was the popular spot for the mob to gather for entertainment when a hanging was in progress.

"Oh, this is shaping up very nicely, indeed," chortled

Richard Boyle, the earl of Cork. His good humor completely overrode the discomfort that, until just a minute or two ago, had kept him shivering in his coat and made him wish he'd never agreed to this affair—or, at least, hadn't been foolish enough to come watch it himself. "My congratulations, Endymion."

One of his two companions shrugged, the motion barely visible under the heavy outerwear he had on himself. "Won't come to much, of course, Your Lordship. Not with Leebrick commanding the force."

"A steady man, I take it."

"Oh, yes, very steady. That's why Wentworth uses him for these things."

"Any chance—"

"No, I'm afraid not. Leebrick's just a mercenary, that's all. The man has neither interest in politics nor any desire to get involved in them. I made two attempts—my agents, rather—before I wrote him off."

The third man grunted, a bit humorously. "Even with my money to wave under his nose. The captains of the Trained Bands weren't so particular, I can tell you that, when I put them on notice last week that the king might be leaving for Oxford some time soon. Of course, it helped that the agent I used as my go-between was a known Puritan."

The earl frowned. "Paul, that seems a bit unwise."

Sir Paul Pindar pulled his hand out from his coat where he was keeping it from the chill, and made a little deprecating motion. "The man's not *actually* a Non-Conformist, Your Lordship, he just keeps up the pretense. I find it useful, from time to time."

"Ah." The earl peered down at the scene below, squinting to shield his eyes from the sleet. "Well, let's wait a bit longer to see how it unfolds. Even just as it is, that damned Wentworth will find another stain added to his reputation with the king. All we could hope for, of course."

Boyle glanced back at their horses, being held by servants a little ways down the hill. He was tempted to simply leave. They'd already accomplished their aim, and the conditions were truly miserable. There was nothing quite like a sleet to chill a man down to his bones, even if the temperature wasn't nearly as cold as a bright sunny day in winter. Especially at the age of sixty-six.

As he drew closer, Captain Leebrick could see that the eight horses pulling the royal carriage were considerably more nervous than his own, even though they weren't moving at all any longer. The queen's shrieks—half fear; half fury—were stirring them up. The coachman riding the near lead horse was doing his best to keep the beast steady, but his efforts were continually undermined by the queen's outbursts. When she was agitated, Henrietta Maria's voice had a particular shrill tone that would put a stone's nerves on edge. It didn't help any that she also tended to lapse into her native French, which confused her servants—and probably added to the horses' agitation. Anthony couldn't prove it, but he was certain that horses grew familiar with a certain language, even if they couldn't understand the actual words.

He pulled up alongside the carriage window, after glancing down the side road where a new Trained Band was advancing. Just a glance was all it took, to his experienced eye. That group posed no danger at all, even now, much less once Patrick got his men in position. From the queen's squeals of panic you would have thought those apprentices moving up the icy road were a veritable horde of Barbary pirates, already clambering aboard. In fact, they were still at least fifty yards distant and were moving across the treacherous footing in a very careful and gingerly manner. He could see two of the lads sprawled on their buttocks, where they must have slipped and fell. One of them was still clutching his club, but the second had two other Bandsmen yelling angrily down at him. He'd probably been carrying the pike that Anthony could see lying on the road a few yards away, and had come close to injuring them when he lost his grip on it.

Leebrick had chosen to approach the carriage window on that side in the hopes that because he and his horse would block the sight of the Bandsmen, he might thereby steady the royal nerves. Unfortunately, that also put him on the queen's side, instead of the king's. Dealing with Charles himself under these circumstances would have been difficult, but manageable. Leebrick had no high opinion of England's monarch, any more than most people he knew did. Still, being fair, Charles was not really given to hysteria. He was simply unpleasant to deal with because of his unreasoning mulishness and petulance. Now, alas, he had to try to talk to the king by shouting across the queen—shouting, because her French gibberish was so loud that speaking in a normal tone was impossible.

Luckily, Anthony didn't speak French, never having served under French colors. His German was fluent, his Spanish near fluent, and his Italian was passable. But he didn't comprehend French at all—certainly not spewed at him in an angry stream—and the king knew it. So, later, if need be, Anthony could claim he'd certainly never intended to offend Her Majesty, he'd simply not grasped what she'd been saying to him. Which probably didn't amount to anything more than curses and condemnation anyway.

"Your Majesty," he began, leaning over from the saddle, "I can assure you the situation is quite under control. Give me ten minutes—no more—and I'll have these rascals out of here."

"I need to get to Oxford!" the king shouted.

"Yes, I understand, Your Majesty. As I say—"

He broke off, unable to keep from wincing. The queen had stuck her face in the window and shouted something at him.

"As I say—"

She shouted again.

"Just allow me—"

She shouted again. The king waved his hand in a gesture of dismissal, and moved to comfort his wife. Even in a royal carriage, that meant pushing aside some blankets to reach her. English coaches were still primitive compared to continental ones, with the passengers resting on trunks covered with cushions and blankets instead of real seats.

But the hand gesture was enough to satisfy protocol. Heaving a sigh of relief after he turned his horse away, Anthony took a moment to gauge the situation on the side road before returning to the front of the column.

No danger there at all, now. Leebrick had chosen Patrick to cover that flank because the Irishman's men were more lightly equipped than most of the company and could move very quickly. In battle, he usually used them as skirmishers.

Lightly equipped or not, even just the thirty of them, they were more than a match for the Trained Band on the side road. They were outnumbered perhaps two-to-one, but that made no difference. Welch's skirmishers were mostly armed with rifled muskets and swords, with just enough pikemen to form a shield. One volley—if needed at all, which Leebrick doubted—would take down the front rank of the Bandsmen and send the rest scampering.

He still hoped nothing of the sort would be necessary, though. Wentworth had given him clear instructions to handle the Trained Bands firmly but avoid, if at all possible, the sort of mayhem that would stir up the whole populace. It was a sensible policy, in Anthony's judgment—and, by temperament, he wasn't a man given to pointless bloodshed himself.

"Well, that seems to be it," said Boyle, looking down from the hill at the company commander of the royal escort making his way back to the front. The earl of Cork peered for a moment at the larger of the Trained Bands that was positioned across the Tyburn Hill Road. There were at most a hundred and fifty of them. They didn't even outnumber the soldiers Leebrick had under his command, and there was no comparison in terms of fighting ability. Even from the distance, it was obvious that the Trained Bandsmen were edgy. The ones in the front rank still seemed steady, but there was already a small trickle of Bandsmen in the rear ranks who were starting to sidle away.

One charge—not even that; just a lowering of pikes and a steady advance—would send them all packing. In the first few weeks after Wentworth brought over the mercenary companies, some of the Bands had made a serious effort to fight in the streets. But they'd soon learned, at bloody cost, that they were no match for professional soldiers who were veterans of the great war that had been raging across much of the continent since the Battle of the White Mountain fifteen years earlier.

"Enough," said Boyle, drawing his coat around him tightly. "I'm freezing. Let's be off, gentlemen."

He turned—carefully, because of the icy ground—and began walking down the hill. His steps were almost mincing ones. Endymion Porter came with him. Paul Pindar stayed atop the hill for a few seconds longer, and then started to follow.

"Wait!" he suddenly cried out.

"All right, Richard," said Leebrick, after he rejoined his lieutenant. Towson already had the front ranks of the company drawn up, ready to begin a pike charge. A pike advance, rather, since "charging" was quite out of the question in the condition the road was in today. "Before we do anything, I'm going to cross over there myself and see if I can speak to the lads. Explain to them that today's no day for tomfoolery, and if they bloody well aren't out of my sight in three minutes there will be—"

A sudden ruckus brought his head around, looking to the rear. Shouts and the sounds of gear clattering. The royal carriage was being turned around to head back into London. The second carriage holding the royal children was preparing to do the same thing. For a moment, Leebrick could only gape at the sight. By the time he clamped his mouth shut, the first carriage was already on its way—and moving far more rapidly than any sane driver would push any sort of vehicle on the road today, much less a carriage as big and heavy and ungainly as the one carrying the royal couple.

"What are they *doing*?" demanded Towson.

Leebrick had no idea himself. Until a moment ago, the king and queen had been in no danger at all. Nothing worse than perhaps a ten minute delay in making their way to Oxford. Now, not only had they left their military escort behind and were completely unprotected, but—far, far worse—they ran the serious risk of having a bad accident.

The queen's panic must have finally unsettled the king, was all he could imagine. A king, unfortunately, who was none too steady himself.

"God only knows," he said, between gritted teeth. "Richard, clear this bloody damned road. If they won't give way, then kill all of the bastards if you have to. I'll see to the king."

He sent his horse after the fleeing carriage, moving as rapidly as he dared. It didn't take him long to overtake the carriage holding the children, which had just completed the turn-around. The driver of that carriage, clearly unhappy at the situation, was keeping his team to a slow pace. But to Anthony's growing horror, he saw that the carriage holding the king and queen was actually outdistancing him. There was no way in Heaven that an experienced and capable driver—which that carriage certainly had—would be pushing his mounts like that, under these conditions. It didn't matter how many threats the king shouted at him. That meant the driver was already losing control of the team. He could see the coachman riding the near lead horse staring back at the driver. Even at the distance, Anthony could sense the panic in the man's expression.

"After me!" he shouted at Patrick and his men, when he reached the side road. "To perdition with those lads!"

He didn't care any longer about the small Trained Band on the side road. If need be, Towson would handle them also. Anthony and Patrick and his skirmishers needed to catch up with the king's carriage. It wouldn't even take Patrick that much longer than it took Anthony himself. Welch was the only one with a horse, but with this sort of footing a man could move as fast as a horse anyway. Faster, if the horse wasn't being pushed beyond its natural inclination.

So, alone for the moment, Leebrick continued his pursuit of the carriage. By now, it had passed around a bend in the road and he couldn't see it any longer. All he could hope was that the driver could bring the team under control again.

"Oh, marvelous!" exclaimed the earl of Cork, who was now back on top of the hill. He watched the royal carriage disappear around the same bend in the road. "Wentworth may even be dismissed, on account of this affair!"

He turned eagerly to his horse. After taking two steps, one foot flew out from under him and he landed on his buttocks, then slid down the slope for a good fifteen feet before he stopped. The fact that he slid that far on a gentle slope was a sharp reminder of just how bad the footing was. Sleet mixed with the mud from a long thaw made for truly treacherous ground.

His two companions hurried to reach him, as best they could, and help him to his feet. By the time they got there, Richard Boyle was grinning cheerfully. "I'm fine, I'm fine. Just a moment's embarrassment. Oh, what a splendid day! Is there a patron saint for sleet?"

Saints weren't exactly frowned on by the Church of England, although they weren't anywhere nearly as prominent as they were for the Catholic church. But neither of the earl's companions was surprised by the remark. For all his Protestant Irish harshness toward Catholics, the earl of Cork didn't feel himself bound personally by any fussy doctrinal obligations.

"I'm not sure, Your Lordship," said Pindar, helping him to his feet and brushing off the mud from the earl's coat.

"Well, if there isn't, by God, there damn well should be! And I'll see to it!"

Chapter 19

Coming around the bend, Leebrick saw one of the coachmen lying on the side of the road, holding his head in both hands. Thrown off, apparently. Or perhaps he'd simply jumped, figuring he could claim he was thrown. Under the circumstances, Anthony couldn't blame the man.

There was another bend, perhaps seventy yards farther. To Leebrick's dismay, it looked to be a much sharper one. That matched his memory, also.

His own horse almost went out from under him as he neared the bend. He spent a minute standing still, simply calming the poor beast. He'd been transmitting some of his own anxiety, he realized. Under these conditions, that was utterly perilous. As heavy an animal as it was, with this sort of icy and unsteady surface, all four of a horse's legs would tend to go in separate directions. Left to its own devices, in fact, the horse wouldn't willingly move at all.

The problem was that horses simply weren't very smart; they were herd animals—and they considered their human masters to be the leaders of the herd. So, once let panic seize them, they'd go from unmoving

stolidity to a blind and bolting runaway pace. That was
dangerous enough on a good dry road in midsummer.
On this road on this day in midwinter, it was—

Leebrick's head came up from speaking soothingly
to his mount. He thought he'd heard a scream, coming from around the bend.

He set his horse back into motion, not trying for
anything faster than a walk. As imperative as it was
to find out what had happened, there was no point in
adding himself to whatever havoc had occurred.

Before he got to the bend, he hear the sound again,
and it was definitely a scream. Not a scream of fear,
either, for it came from no human throat. That was
the sound of a badly injured horse.

When he came around the bend and could finally
see down the next stretch of road, his worst fears
materialized. Some thirty yards beyond, the royal
carriage was a shattered wreck. He could see a deep
rut in the road ten yards ahead of him, and what was
left of one of the carriage's wheels.

He was aghast, but not surprised. Having a wheel
or axle break on a carriage, especially a heavy one,
was a frequent occurrence. Adventuresome young men
in taverns would make bets that they could make it
from one city to the next without a broken wheel or
axle—and the house odds were against them.

That was in midsummer. Nobody laid bets on the
matter in wintertime, not even drunken young carousers.

To make things worse, the royal carriage was of
the new Cinderella design. They were fancy looking
things, but their suspension was even more fragile
than that of most carriages. They were particularly
prone to having the rear axles break.

Leebrick had no trouble figuring out what had happened. Coming around the bend as fast as it had been going, the carriage must have started to slide on the slick surface. Then, either from panicky movements of the team, or too sharp a correction by the driver, or simply a minor obstruction in the surface—any or all three put together—the axle had broken. That, in turn, had simply splintered the wheel.

Within a few yards, the carriage had spilled on its side—and then, on this surface, it had slid right into the wall of a building. One of the horses had been killed outright, and at least one—the one screaming in agony—had suffered a shattered leg. Two others were lying on the road. One appeared to be just stunned but the other was clearly dead. A great jagged piece of wood had been driven into the creature's belly.

They were the only horses in sight. The harness had come to pieces in the accident. The pole holding the doubletrees must have shattered—that would be the source of the wood that had killed the one horse—and the four lead horses must have continued their panicked race around the next bend in the road. At a distance, Leebrick could see the body of the coachman who'd been riding the near lead horse. He, too, might either be dead or simply stunned.

But he'd have to wait. Anthony needed to find out what had happened to the king and queen. He still had hopes they might have remained uninjured—or simply bruised, at least. They'd had the protection of the carriage body and all the cushions and blankets within.

But as he came nearer, Anthony's hopes started fading. He'd thought at first that the carriage had struck the side of the building and then been upended from the impact. But now he saw that the situation was far worse. There was apparently a sunken stair into which the carriage had plunged. Instead of the weight of the carriage's body protecting the occupants, the body had caved in on them.

He brought the horse to a halt, got off, and clambered onto the carriage. The first thing he saw was the driver. His body, rather, for there was no question whether this man was dead or stunned. He'd been thrown into the stairwell and part of the carriage had landed on top of him. The front axle had crushed the poor man's chest like a great blunt spear. His sightless eyes staring up at the sky were already half-covered with sleet.

Almost frantic now, Anthony reached the carriage's door and tried to pry it open. Finding it jammed, he drew his sword and used it as a lever. Thankfully, it was one of his everyday swords, not the expensive one he kept at Liz's lodgings for ceremonial occasions. He was quite likely to break it, since swords were not designed to be tools for such use.

Indeed, it did break—but not before it finally snapped whatever obstruction was keeping the door jammed. Anthony tossed the hilt onto the ground and, using both hands, pried the door the rest of the way open.

Peering in, he couldn't determine anything at first. It was a dark day because of the overcast and very little of what light there was made its way into the carriage. To make thing worse, the interior was in a state of sheer chaos. The trunks must have been flung open and had scattered their contents everywhere. At first glance, the inside of the carriage looked like nothing so much as a huge, half-filled laundry basket.

Then something pale moved, coming up from under the blanket that had been covering it. A face, Anthony realized.

The king's face.

"Help me," Charles whispered. "My leg . . ."

Hearing a call, Anthony looked back. To his relief, he saw that Patrick had arrived with his Irish skirmishers.

"Just a moment, Your Majesty, I'll be right there," Anthony said hurriedly. Then, to Patrick: "I need three of your men up here. Have the rest tend to whatever else they can—but *don't* shift the carriage about yet."

Hearing the horse scream again, Leebrick winced. "And put that animal out of its misery, would you?"

That done, he lowered himself into the carriage, being careful not to step on the king's body. Wherever that body was, since all he could see was still just the royal face, staring up. He had no idea at all where the queen had wound up.

Once he got to the king, he slid his arm down into the tangle of blankets and cushions to cradle the man's shoulders and lift him. But the moment he did so, the king started to shriek. "My legs! My legs! Stop, damn you!"

Anthony left off immediately. He'd thought from the king's first plaint that he'd suffered a broken or wounded leg. But "legs" probably meant something worse. He didn't dare move Charles at all until he could see what the problem was.

One of the Irish soldiers was at the window, now.

"Come down," Leebrick ordered. "But make sure you put your feet over there." He pointed behind him, to a part of the carriage that seemed safe enough. He still didn't know where the queen was.

While the skirmisher lowered himself into the interior, Anthony shifted himself a bit and began carefully removing the items that covered the king's body.

"Where's my wife?" Charles asked. He seemed more puzzled than anything else.

Leebrick decided to ignore the question, for the moment. He had no answer, and that was more likely to panic the king than anything else. He just kept at his labor.

"Where's Henrietta Maria? Where is she? Why isn't she here?"

Thankfully, it was clear from Charles' tone of voice that the king was in a daze. He wasn't really asking a question aimed at a specific person, he was simply uttering a confused query to the world. He sounded more like a child than a grown man.

Finally, Anthony cleared enough away to see most of the king's body. By then, he knew the situation was a very bad one. The last blanket he'd removed had been blood-stained.

Charles' hip was shattered. Anthony could see a piece of bone sticking up through the flesh and the heavy royal garments.

He tried to restrain himself from hissing, but couldn't.

"What's wrong?" asked the king, still in that confused little boy's voice.

"Everything's fine, Your Majesty. It'll just take us a moment to get you out of there."

Leebrick wondered if he even dared move the

king at all, until his men had cut away most of the
carriage. If Charles' hip was shattered, there was a
good chance he had a broken back also.

But he decided he didn't have any choice. If the
only problem had been the king, he'd just wait. But
even after spending several minutes in the carriage,
he'd still seen no sign of the queen. He had to find
her, and probably very soon—if it wasn't too late
already. The carriage had landed on her side, not the
king's. If the impact had caused this much damage to
Charles, it was likely to have caused worse to her.

A second skirmisher had made his way into the
carriage.

"All right, lads. Here's the way we'll do it. Tell
Patrick to have two men—no, it'll likely take four—to
start cutting away the side of the carriage. And tell
him, for the love of God, to do it carefully. This carriage is half-shattered already. We just need enough
space to lift His Majesty out using a sling of some
sort. A big one, that'll cup his whole body. We can
make it out of these blankets and what's left of the
harness. Understood?"

Gravely, both men nodded.

"All right, be about it. I've got to find out what
happened to the queen."

The last he said very softly, not to alarm the king.
But when he turned back, he saw that his caution had
been unnecessary. Charles was no longer conscious.

Under the circumstances, that was a blessing. Moving as fast as he could in the cramped space, Anthony
used a blanket and the aid of one of the skirmishers
to shift the king's body far enough to the side to be
able to see what might be lying under him. That

took some time, despite the urgency of the situation, because he had to be as careful as he could not to twist the king's back in the process.

But, finally, it was done. Feeling like a miner digging through expensive clothing and blanketry—practically tapestries, some of them—Anthony worked his way toward the side of the carriage that now served as its floor.

The first thing he spotted were the queen's eyes, staring at him. He couldn't see the rest of her face, because it was covered by some sort of heavy garment.

"Your Majesty! Just a moment and I'll have you out of there." Hurriedly, he shoved more things aside to clear her shoulders.

"Your pardon, please." He took her shoulders and tried to lift her up. But after shifting perhaps two inches, her torso seemed to hit some sort of obstruction. A very sudden one, in fact.

To his surprise, he realized that the queen still hadn't said anything to him. Very unusual, for her.

He looked down at her face and instantly understood the reason. Her eyes were still looking at him, but that was sheer chance. Those weren't eyes, any longer. They were just pieces of a human body. Henrietta Maria, sister of King Louis XIII of France and wife of King Charles of England, would no longer be saying anything to anybody, in any language, except whatever tongue might be spoken in the afterlife.

Below, the mouth gaped open. What had once been a torrent of blood was starting to dry on her chin and her neck and what he could see of her chest. Roughly, he shoved the rest of the material down to her waist, trying to spot the obstruction.

Nothing, oddly. But there was certainly no question the woman was dead. Even if she could have survived that much loss of blood, the fact that there was no further blood coming was proof enough.

He closed his own eyes, and took the time for a quick prayer for the woman's soul. Then, moving much more quickly because he needn't fear any longer the queen's displeasure at having her body groped, he pried his hand under her back looking for the obstruction.

It didn't take him long to find it. Her torso hadn't been kept from moving by something on top, it had been hooked from beneath. From what he could sense with his fingers, a large piece of the carriage's frame had been smashed up just as the queen's body came down. As ragged-edged as a barbed spear, the huge splinter had pierced her heart and jammed somewhere in her ribs, or perhaps against her spine.

He'd seen very much the same thing happen as a young man, when he'd spent some time serving on a warship. After two naval battles, he'd decided to make his fortune as a soldier rather than a seaman. A soldier had to fear metal in many shapes and varieties, but at least simple pieces of wood weren't likely to tear him to shreds. For a boy whose father had been a cabinetmaker and for whom wood had been a comfort, that seemed somehow grotesque.

He heard Patrick's voice. "We're ready, Captain."

Looking up, Anthony was surprised to see that Welch and his men had already cut away most of the carriage's side. Roof, now, the way it was lying. He must have spent more time working to find the queen than he'd realized, and he'd been so focused on the task that he hadn't even heard the noise they'd been making.

That meant there was also more light coming into the interior, thank God. Looking over, Anthony saw that the king was still unconscious. Thank God, again.

"All right," he said, standing up. A bit carefully, because although his footing wasn't as bad as icy mud, it was still nothing much more than soft rubble. "Let's get the sling under him and get him out of here."

"The queen?"

Leebrick shook his head. "I found her, but there's no hurry there. No hurry at all."

Patrick winced, understanding. "There's going to be hell to pay, Anthony."

Gloomily, Leebrick nodded. Hell to pay, for sure and certain—and the devil was most likely to present the bill to the officer in charge. Given that he had neither friends in high places nor fortune of his own.

In fact, when he emerged from the carriage after the king's body was lifted out, Anthony saw that the devil's bookkeeper had already arrived.

The earl of Cork himself, no less.

But, to his astonishment, Richard Boyle was both friendly and considerate.

"Yes, yes, Captain—Leebrick, is it?—I understand completely," said Boyle, waving down Anthony's attempt at an explanation. The earl jabbed a thumb at his two companions. Anthony recognized them also, although he couldn't say he really knew either of them. Sir Paul Pindar and Sir Endymion Porter, both prominent figures in court. In his few encounters with the men, he'd found Porter to be aloof but Pindar to be a civil enough fellow. Perhaps that was because Pindar's influence was due to the wealth he'd amassed as a major figure in the Levant Company and a moneylender to the crown, rather than pure and simple favoritism from the high and mighty.

Porter was considerably younger than the other two men, being in his late forties where the earl and Sir Pindar were well into their sixties.

"We happened by chance to be in the vicinity and saw the whole thing unfold," the earl continued. "No fault of yours or your men, it was obvious. The king—"

Boyle shook his head lugubriously. "Well, who's to say what motivated him? Most unfortunate. Had he simply stayed in place, the whole affair would have ended with no trouble. A splendid company you have, by the way."

Endymion Porter was frowning at the carriage. "The queen . . . ?"

"She perished in the accident, I am most aggrieved to report. Must have died instantly, however, so she didn't suffer."

The earl's head-shaking speeded up. "How terrible. His Majesty will be beside himself."

So he would—and *beside himself* did not bode well for one Anthony Leebrick, captain of the royal escort.

As much as he disliked asking for favors, Anthony saw no choice. He cleared his throat. "Begging your pardon, my lord, but . . ."

The head-shake turned into a nod faster than anything Leebrick would have imagined. "Oh, yes, certainly.

You needn't fear, Captain, I shall be glad to give the same testimony to the king himself." He looked a bit startled. "Well . . ."

"The king won't want to hear it, Richard," said Pindar quietly. "You know he won't, whether it's true or not. Not from you, not from anyone."

The merchant looked at Leebrick. "If you'll take my advice, Captain, I strongly recommend that you"—he glanced at Welch—"as well as your lieutenants, make yourselves hard to find for a few days. Once he recovers consciousness and discovers his wife is dead, I'm afraid His Majesty is likely to simply lash out at the most obvious and convenient target."

That was exactly what Anthony figured himself. "Yes, Sir Paul. But if I do that, I'm just likely to bring further suspicion on myself."

Boyle went back to head-shaking. "Only if you do it the wrong way, Captain. Go into hiding somewhere unknown . . . then, yes, certainly you'd draw suspicion."

The head-shake came to an abrupt stop, and a big smile appeared on the earl's face.

"But not if you place yourself in the custody of a respected public figure, and await His Majesty's pleasure at a well-known location. I'd recommend, in fact—"

"Richard!" said Porter.

The earl waved his hand impatiently. "Be done with your constant caution, Endymion. Be done, I say! Captain Leebrick, I recommend that you simply return with me to London— you and your lieutenants; Paul's quite right about that —and plan on spending a week or so at my residence there."

Anthony stared at him. The offer made him suspicious, simply because Richard Boyle, the earl of Cork, had no reputation at all for being a man given to goodwill toward his lesser fellows. Quite the opposite, in fact.

Apparently sensing the hesitation, the earl's smile became something vaguely predatory. "Oh, please, Captain. Surely it's no secret to you—is it to anyone in England, other than village idiots?—that I'm on no friendly terms with Thomas Wentworth." His mouth pursed, as if he'd tasted a lemon. "The earl of Strafford, as he likes to call himself now—but he's only an earl due to the king's favor. Which I daresay—"

There was nothing at all vague about the predation in that smile, now. "—is about to be abruptly removed. Indeed, I shall do my very best to see that it is."

Put that way . . .

Anthony felt his suspicions ebbing, at the same time as he felt his distaste for the earl of Cork rising. Given a choice, he'd far rather serve a man like Thomas Wentworth than Richard Boyle.

But he probably didn't have a choice, any longer. And when it came down to it, although he'd found Wentworth a good master, he was hardly what you'd call a personal friend of the man. It was likely true that the kingdom was about to be swept by another royal storm, and that Boyle would surge to the fore as Wentworth was cast out. Better to be in Boyle's good graces, then, than stranded as he now was with no friends at all in court.

He glanced at Patrick, who'd overheard the whole discussion. The Irishman gave him a slight nod. He'd come to the same conclusion, obviously. So would Richard, most likely, had he been present.

"Very well, my lord. I accept your offer, and with

thanks. I'd need to bring Patrick here with me, and one other man." He pointed up the road. "That's Richard Towson, the lieutenant I left in charge—"

"Oh, yes. Splendid man. He sent those Trained Band louts scampering smartly. I saw a bit of it before I raced off to see what had become of His Majesty."

That very moment, Anthony heard the sound of a military force approaching. A few seconds later, the first ranks of his company appeared around the bend. At the fore was Richard himself, on his horse. Still better, the carriage holding the children came right after him, with soldiers helping the driver and coachmen to steady its team. Whatever else had happened, at least the heirs to the throne were still safe.

"I'll need to see to my men first," Anthony said.

"Don't tarry, Captain," said Porter. "Haven't you a good sergeant or two, who can take charge of the rest of this business and then get your company back to their quarters?" He pointed at the carriage. "We still need to extract the queen's corpse, you know. And get the king himself back to the palace where he can get proper medical attention."

Before Anthony could say anything, Pindar spoke up. "Yes, Captain, that will also stir Wentworth into motion—and he's a man who can move quite well, under most circumstances. But not these. I'm afraid the so-called earl of Strafford is about to discover that turning most of the court into enemies is a tactic that only works so long as you have the royal favor."

The merchant glanced at the king. Charles was now resting in the same sling that had gotten him out of the carriage, but two poles had been added to create a litter held by four of Patrick's skirmishers. Welch must have ordered that done. Wisely, he'd decided that on the road today, a litter would be safer carried by men than horses.

"A royal favor which is not conscious at the moment," Pindar continued, "and will almost certainly vanish when consciousness is regained. Time presses, Captain. If you intend to take up the earl of Cork on his gracious offer, you'd best do it very quickly. We weren't the only witnesses, be sure of that. It won't be long before word of the disaster reaches Whitehall. By midafternoon, if you and your lieutenants aren't in the earl's custody, Wentworth will have you arrested. He'll have no choice, you understand."

No, he wouldn't. *Somebody* would have to take the blame for this. Were there any justice, the blame would be accepted by the man actually responsible, who was the man lying unconscious in the litter. But there was less chance of Charles doing that than there was of the sun stopping in its tracks.

For a moment, Anthony found himself desperately wishing he'd joined his friend Christopher Fey and enlisted in the new regiments that Gustavus Adolphus was forming in the Germanies. True, Kit complained bitterly in the letters he occasionally sent Leebrick about the riotous conditions in the ranks of those regiments. But Kit was a complaining man at all times—and the one complaint that had been noticeably absent in those letters were any complaints about the monarch he served. The Swede wouldn't have panicked in the first place, at the sight of a ragged militia. And, if he had, would have taken the responsibility for whatever happened on his own shoulders.

But, Leebrick had turned down the offer. The

money Wentworth had offered was better, first of all. Even more important was that Liz was in London, not Magdeburg. Ten years ago, that wouldn't have weighed much with Anthony. But now that the age of forty was nearer than the age of thirty, he'd found the pleasures of a purely bachelor mercenary's life were waning. Rather quickly, in fact. There was a lot to be said for the regular company of a woman he liked and trusted, even if her history didn't bear close examination. It wasn't as if Anthony Leebrick came from the sort of family that had to worry about such matters.

"Yes, you're right," he said. He gave Richard Boyle a little bow. "If you'll just give me a moment or two to speak to the sergeants."

"Of course, Captain. There's not *that* much of a hurry, never mind what Paul says."

The smile hadn't left the man's face, although it wasn't that of a predator any longer. Not, at least, a predator in pursuit of prey. It was simply confident. As a lion's might be, after a meal.

"I *am* the earl of Cork, after all. Hardly likely that anyone—including Wentworth—is going to pester me when I'm about my lawful affairs, now is it?"

Chapter 20

Amsterdam, Holland

"He was only here for a short time, woman," Gretchen Richter said accusingly. "Not even a month!"

Rebecca Abrabanel looked serene.

Sitting on a divan in the USE embassy's salon next to her fiancé Adam Olearius, Anne Jefferson laughed softly. "God, she does that better than anyone I've ever known."

Rebecca looked toward her. "Are you referring to me? Does what?"

Anne laughed again, louder. "Oh, sure, play the innocent. That Mona Lisa look. Serene. Inscrutable."

"What nonsense," said Rebecca. "I am simply not given to pointless passions"—she stuck a finger at Gretchen—"like this one here."

Gretchen's eyes widened, her expression going from accusatory to outraged. "Pointless passions? *Pointless passions?* You—you—have the nerve to accuse *me* of such?"

She clapped a hand on the broad shoulder of her husband Jeff, sitting next to her on another divan. "I remind you that he and I have shared the same bed here for months now—and used it to good purpose, rest assured! But you do not see me"—here she slapped her midriff, which was surprisingly slim given her impressive bust and hips—"pregnant again, do you? Whereas—*you!* He was here less than a month!"

Rebecca shrugged, somehow managing to do it without losing a trace of the serene expression on her face. "You are more disciplined than I am, Gretchen. Besides, fine for you to preach the virtues of the rhythm method, rigorously and ruthlessly applied as only you could manage the miserable business. But I remind you—as you pointed out yourself—that you have had your husband available the remaining three weeks of every month. I did not. I was supposed to tell him, poor fellow, that he chose the wrong time of the month to fly into Amsterdam? Ha."

She looked out the window at the snow-covered streets. "I say it again. Ha. Besides, what does it matter? I enjoy having children. If it had not been for Baruch I think I might have gone mad here, so much do I miss my little Sepharad."

Jeff Higgins glanced over into a corner of the salon, where Baby Spinoza—as everyone called him except his adoptive mother—was sleeping in a crib. "He's a cute kid, Becky, I'll give him that. Even if he is a genius."

But Gretchen was not to be so easily diverted. "All kids are cute, it's in the nature of the creatures," she said dismissively. "How else could they survive? But two are quite enough for any reasonable woman, if she plans to spend her life engaged in worthwhile work beyond using her tits. I leave aside the small matter that this irresponsible vixen chose to get herself pregnant in the middle of a bitter siege."

Rebecca looked at her.

"Fine. Not-so-bitter siege. It's still a siege. And who knows how long it will last? If your new baby is not born in rubble, so he—worse yet, she—will be born into starvation and disease."

Rebecca was still looking at her. Gretchen threw up her hands.

"Damn Mona Lisa! Fine, Becky. Tell us how long the siege will last."

Rebecca's serene smile returned. "Do not be silly, Gretchen. How could I possibly do that? But what I can say, based on my meeting with the prince of Orange yesterday, is that—"

"Hold it, hold it, hold it!" Anne Jefferson rose to her feet and extended her hand to Adam. "I think it's time for us to be out of here. Seeing as how my fiancé is officially the agent of a foreign and possibly hostile power. Which for some damn reason y'all seem to keep forgetting."

"Hardly that, dearest," Adam said, rising. "The hostile part, I mean. I will allow a foreign power, but it's absurd to think my employer is going to be engaging in hostilities with anyone. Alas for him, the duke of Holstein-Gottorp is in the position of a mouse surrounded by cats. Hungry cats, to make it worse. His strategy these days is entirely that of the sensible small rodent caught in the open. Hold completely still and hope no predator notices you."

Jeff waved his hand. "Oh, hell, Adam, sit down. By this time"—he glanced around the room—"I don't think any of us is worried that you'll spill our beans on anybody's else plate. And if you did, who cares? Who would you tell? The cardinal-infante already knows what the beans look like."

"Not the point," replied Adam, shaking his head. "You may not care, but I do. Much as I'd personally prefer making my living as a mathematician, I do not live—neither do you, any longer—in that magical up-time world where great universities paid people simply to teach and research mathematics. No, alas, here I need a *job*. And since my existing credentials are as a diplomat, I think it best that I not—how would you say it?—tarnish my resumé, I believe."

Jeff squinted at him. "I'm not following you."

"Jeff, of one thing you may be completely assured. If Rebecca's scheme works even remotely the way she plans—yes, of course, I know what it is even if no one ever told me in so many words—then this episode will go down in the long annals of European diplomacy as one of the art's true masterpieces. Which means, in turn, that the deeds of everyone involved—and that includes me, as mouselike as my role may have been—will be subjected to long and careful scrutiny, by a very large number of minds. Some of which are exceedingly acute—and would be my most likely future employers. Now do you understand?"

"Oh."

"Yes. Oh. Whatever other lines may exist on an unemployed diplomat's resumé, the one that absolutely *cannot* be there is: 'not to be trusted; plays both sides of the fence.'"

He went over to the rack beside the door and removed his coat as well as Anne's. "And now, we shall be off."

✧   ✧   ✧

Once they were outside, Anne tucked her hand into the crook of his elbow. "Is that going to be that bad? 'Unemployed,' I mean."

Olearius pursed his lips. "Mostly likely, I'm afraid. No matter what happens, I can see very few alternatives that would produce a still-independent duchy of Holstein-Gottorp at the end of it. Neither can my employer. My instructions from Duke Frederik are no longer to strive to maintain his independence. Simply to get him the best possible deal when he gives it up."

Anne nodded, sighing. "Well, I was afraid of that, not that I'm really surprised. It means we'll have to move around a lot, I suppose. Damn it all. I like Amsterdam, and now I've got a practice of my own. I was hoping we could stay."

"I . . . wouldn't be so sure of that, Anne." Olearius stopped at a corner, gently disengaged her hand from his elbow, and turned to face her squarely. "Perhaps it is best for me to say this as bluntly as possible. Lay all the cards on the table, as you might put it."

Anne looked up at him, tucking her hands into her pockets. "Okay."

"It's not complicated. We both want children, and children require a good income. No matter what employer I wind up with, however, it will almost surely be the case that your income as a medical practitioner—let's call it doctor, rather, since neither one of us is a guild idiot—will exceed my own."

He smiled, a little ruefully. "By a great margin, most likely. Much as it grieves my proper seventeenth-century masculine spirit to say it."

Anne chuckled. "Honey, relax. You do one hell of a lot better job of keeping the testosterone to a reasonable level than most up-time men I ever knew. Sure as hell West Virginia hillbillies. I'm not complaining."

He gave her a little appreciative bow. "Well, then. It seems quite obvious. By all means, let us stay in Amsterdam. Within a year—two, at the outside—you will have a medical practice here that dwarfs that of all other so-called doctors in the city. And since your clientele—your extremely loyal, even devoted—I will not say fanatical clientele, although I could—consists mostly of CoC members, it's not as if you'll have any worries that the medical or apothecary guilds will be able to shut you down. Much less threaten you with physical reprisals."

Anne chuckled again, quite a bit more loudly. "Ah . . . no. That's not likely. As in snowball's chance of hell likely." She cocked her head slightly. "Do they really do that in most places?"

"Oh, yes," Adam said solemnly. "Believe it that they do, dearest. The guilds will not tolerate even a man who officially and publicly practices medicine or dispenses medications without their license. A woman, except as a midwife? Unheard of."

"Jesus." Anne looked around, as if finding reassurance from the familiar sights of Amsterdam. Which, in fact, she did. After months of the siege—more to the point, months of Gretchen Richter—the largest Dutch city was a CoC stronghold. Not even the prince of Orange tried to pretend otherwise, any longer. Not after, a few weeks since, the CoC had simply disbanded the former city council—most of whose patrician members were in exile to begin with, having been wealthy enough to flee the city before the Spanish army invested it—and replaced it with a new one of their own creation. To which eight out of ten members elected had run openly on a CoC platform.

Two days later, they'd done the same to the city's militia, most of whose officers had also fled into exile. Nine out of ten of the officers who'd replaced them had been CoC members. To be sure—Gretchen Richter had gotten far more sophisticated, with experience—they'd been quite careful to elect the prince of Orange's seven-year-old son William as the official commander of the city's military forces. No one except possibly the boy himself was fooled by the formality; certainly not Fredrik Hendrik. Still, it allowed the prince of Orange to maintain the necessary public image.

Gretchen would be gone some day, of course. Probably, Anne thought, with as many regrets as Anne would feel, if she had to leave. Amsterdam was the place where Gretchen Richter had finally come into her own. The place where she'd learned to make herself and her skills match her reputation; where she went from a famous but uncertain firebrand and orator to a superbly capable organizer and revolutionary political leader.

Which meant, in turn, that it wouldn't really matter to Anne whether Gretchen was still here in the flesh or not. Firebrands are very visible, but they leave few traces behind. Gretchen's footprints would stamp Amsterdam for at least two generations, and probably forever. Deep enough, certainly, that if any guild doctor or apothecary returning from exile was foolish enough to protest Anne's medical practice, he'd be lucky if he just got out of it with his shop turned into a wreck. The journeymen and apprentices who were the backbone of the city's CoC were in no mood to tolerate any presumptions by returning guildmasters. Not any longer; not after they withstood the might of Spain, while their former masters fled into exile.

Anne took Adam by the arm again and resumed walking. "But what will you do? Adam, I *really* don't like the idea of you leaving for long stretches on diplomatic missions."

He grimaced. "Neither do I. But I probably won't have any choice, dearest."

Anne took a deep breath. "Uh . . . How's your testosterone level doing, at the moment?"

He looked down at her, curious. "No worse than ever, I'd say. Why?"

This time it was she who stopped, disengaged her hand, and turned to face him squarely. "Okay, fine. Then let's cut through all of it. Here's the truth. If I put my mind to it—yes, even with children—I can turn this half-assed medical practice I started on the side, more to keep from getting bored stiff than anything else, into a serious money-maker. I wouldn't even have to gouge anybody. I've already got such a long line every time I open my door that what I really need to do anyway—I'll ask Mary Pat if she thinks Beulah MacDonald is up to leaving Jena for a couple of months to come here and walk me through it—is set up a real medical clinic. Eventually, maybe, the city's first hospital worth calling by the name. You follow my drift?"

He frowned. "I'm not sure I even follow your idiom."

"Oh. Sorry. I forgot we were speaking English instead of German. Easy for me to lapse into American slang when we do that. What I meant was, do you understand what I'm proposing? We *both* stay here. You only take diplomatic missions that won't keep you from home for . . . what's reasonable? Two months?"

He shook his head. "You have to allow at least four, Anne, for anything serious. Even if I'm going no farther than a hundred miles."

She thought about it. "Okay. I can live with four months. Six, tops. But that's it."

"That would mean I'd be unemployed most of the time."

"Don't be silly. You just do the work you really want to do, anyway. Your mathematics. And—pardon my English—fuck whether or not you're getting paid for it. Who cares? I'll make enough for both of us."

He looked away. "Let me think about it."

"Sure. How long?"

"Um. Two days?"

"Make it four."

He laughed, and they went back to walking. After a few minutes of companionable silence, Adam cleared his throat.

"Do you think that was really true? What Rebecca said, I mean, concerning Gretchen's—ah, what was the phrase?—rigorous and ruthless methods for preventing pregnancy. Granted that Gretchen is the dominant one of the couple, but I wouldn't have thought she could keep her husband that much under her thumb." He looked a bit alarmed. "I trust that you have no such plans?"

Anne grinned. "You haven't seen any signs of it so far, have you? Relax. I'm a doctor, remember? Well, nurse—but that makes me one of the few doctors worth calling by the name, in the here and now. I've got other ways of handling that little problem. Which I've been using since the first time you finagled your way into my bed, not that you'd ever notice. Men. So would Gretchen, if she'd follow my advice. But you know what she's like. Politics aside, she's almost a reactionary. The old methods work, so why mess with them?"

Adam had the grace to look a little embarrassed. "I had wondered, actually. But . . . ah . . . since you didn't seem concerned . . ."

"Ha! Men, like I said. And besides, you're wrong about the rest of it, anyway. The part about Gretchen and Jeff, that is."

"How so?"

"She's the flamboyant one of the two, no doubt about it. And since she also knows what she wants to do with her life and has the determination of a glacier—and Jeff really doesn't care otherwise and is willing to go along for the ride—you make the mistake of thinking there's dominance involved. There really isn't, Adam. I think Gretchen would be quite lost without him. He's her anchor, you could say."

"You know them much better than I do, so I shan't question your judgment. Still, it seems odd. He's such an unassuming young man."

Her eyes narrowed. "And this became a problem for women . . . when, exactly?"

He laughed. "I surrender!"

"Best you do, buddy. Or the next time Rubens asks me to pose for him, I'll do it in leather and spike-heeled boots."

❖   ❖   ❖

After Rebecca finished her report of the outcome of her last meeting with the prince of Orange, Gretchen rose and went to the window.

Jeff, from the couch where he'd remained, said: "I don't get it. Why doesn't Don Fernando just cut the deal now? I mean, what's there left to squabble about? Nothing but a bunch of third rate issues that neither he nor Fredrik Hendrik cares that much about anyway."

His wife shook her head. "You're thinking like a commoner, husband. A level-headed and unassuming one, at that."

"Well, sure. Any geek who isn't a moron learns to do that by the time he's in tenth grade. Or he's just a great big bruise. Your average high school jock could give any prince in Europe lessons on being a cocksure, stupid and arrogant bully."

Gretchen turned her head to look at him, smiled, and then looked into the corner where the arms were kept in a cabinet. Prominent among them, Jeff's shotgun. "Not any more."

"Well. No. Not any more. Any of 'em tried it now, they'd be hamburger. But it's still the way I think. The only difference, nowadays, is I know how to handle it if I have to."

Gretchen stifled a sigh. Alas, it was the wrong time of the month. There were times she was tempted to take up Anne's offer, for sure and certain, as much as she distrusted fancy methods to do what simple methods could. Tonight would certainly be one of them. Jeff had so many ways to trigger her passion. The fact that he almost never realized he was doing so, being perhaps the greatest of them all.

So be it. Discipline!

She turned her back to the window, leaning on the sill with her hands. "His mind is full of wickedness, Jeff. Ancient royal evil pretensions. So he cannot—yet—bring himself to the simple recognition that the good he would do for an entire nation is not outweighed by a medieval sense of honor."

"To put it another way," Rebecca added, "for Gretchen is surely right, Don Fernando cannot betray his brother in cold blood. No matter how sensible doing so would be."

Jeff frowned. "I still don't get it. He's *already* betrayed the king of Spain. Not that I give a shit, since I can't think of anybody who deserves it more, except that asshole Charles in England. I mean, what else would you call the secret negotiations he's been having with the Dutch?"

"No, he has not," said Rebecca, shaking her head. "Not in his own mind. What he has been doing—never forget that he was born, bred and trained a prince in Europe's greatest dynasty—is simply preparing an alternative course of action, should the results of the valiant test of arms be unfortunate."

"Huh?"

Gretchen burst out laughing. "You are my beloved, for sure, but you would make a truly wretched prince."

"Hey, look, I flunked out of Royalty 101. Didn't need it for my math and sciences track."

"You must have been inattentive in the introductory course on royalty, also," said Rebecca. "Until the *war* is settled, Jeff, the cardinal-infante of Spain is paralyzed. Not by external reality, but by his inner

self. He can make plans, yes; negotiate to see to it
that those plans can be set in motion, yes. But act
until he can claim he had no choice? No, that he
cannot do. You could. I could. Gretchen could. My
husband—him!—would have done it last month. But
the Habsburg prince cannot."

Jeff looked over at the gun cabinet. "Fine, then.
We'll do it his way—and you watch Fredrik Hendrik
carve another great piece of his flesh, when Mr.
Habsburg and his fine Spanish army come tumbling
back in rags."

"Oh, hardly a great piece," said Rebecca. "He's a
very *cunning* sort of Habsburg, and they're a cunning
family to begin with. His army won't come tumbling
back in rags. They'll simply turn around, take two
steps, and find themselves right back in their fortifications. But that'll be enough to save the royal face
and salve the royal conscience."

"Jesus. Stupid fucking kings. Who needs them,
anyway?"

"Not I," said his wife serenely.

Rebecca smiled. "You say that better than anyone
I've ever known."

Chapter 21

London, England

"Sorry, fellows," said Captain Anthony Leebrick. His hands clasped behind his back, he was looking out the window in a room on the second floor of the earl of Cork's mansion. There was nothing much to see beyond an occasional pedestrian on the street below, slipping and sliding as they made their way. Here in Westminster, it had been a slushy snowfall rather than a sleet. The precipitation had stopped for the moment, although it looked as if it might resume at any moment. Even without precipitation, it was still a very gray day, between the heavy overcast and the approaching sunset.

"I should have known better," he added.

"Or supped with a longer spoon," said Richard Towson ruefully. "Need a longer one with Richard Boyle than you do with the Devil himself, I suspect."

The third man in the room, Patrick Welch, turned away from one of the portraits on the far wall. "Stop flagellating yourself, Anthony. It's not as if Richard or I made any objections. It seemed the best thing to do, under the circumstances. We all agreed on that."

Leebrick's jaws tightened. "Still. The earl of Cork. Given his reputation, I should have had more sense."

There were no bars on the windows, but aside from that the room they were locked into made as good a gaol as almost any in England. Given the dimensions of the mansion, it was impossible to simply jump down to the street below, from the second floor. Impossible, at any rate, without breaking at least one major bone in the process.

And that was after you'd smashed the windows, since the earl had seen to it that the room was one that had sealed instead of latched windows. That would be easy enough, yes. A dirk pommel would suffice to smash the windows—or they could simply use any of the heavy pieces of furniture in the room. Unfortunately, these were heavy and well-built windows, with solid glass. No way to do it without alerting the two guards standing in the corridor outside. Who, unlike Anthony and his mates, had guns and swords in their possession.

They no longer had their swords, because the earl had politely but firmly insisted that they give them up once they came into the mansion. They *were* technically "in custody," he explained, even if it was just a formality—but a formality that would be completely threadbare if it was discovered the earl had allowed them to remain armed.

That had been the first thing to arouse Anthony's suspicion. Still, the explanation had been plausible enough, and he'd not seen any clear alternative to obeying. It hadn't been until they heard the door locked behind them that he'd finally realized they were cat's paws in some game of Richard Boyle's. Disarming an officer in custody was reasonable enough; locking him into a room was not. Criminals needed bars and locks to keep them in, not gentlemen who'd given their word they'd make no attempt to escape.

Foolishly, however, the earl had not had them searched. Either out of lingering politeness or simply because, not having any military experience, he hadn't realized that mercenaries often carried hidden weapons. Anthony and Patrick still had their dirks. Anthony's in his boot and Patrick's in a sheath concealed under the back of his coat. Only Richard had carried his in plain sight.

So, breaking the windows was a simple enough proposition. But then what? Had this been a bedroom, they could have torn up the bedding to make a substitute for a rope. But it was simply a small salon. The one tapestry hanging on a wall wasn't nearly big enough to suit the purpose, even leaving aside that cutting the thing into strips would be an incredible chore.

Without a rope of some sort, Anthony didn't think there was any way for them to lower themselves safely to the street. With the windows locked, he couldn't actually see the side of the building. But from what he'd seen on their way in, the exterior had been rather plain, with none of the ornamentation some buildings featured that might have given them handholds.

In short, they were in a trap, and the fact that it was an impromptu one didn't make it any the less difficult to escape. The truth was, the only way out was to fight their way out—with two armed mercenaries standing guard outside the door, and who knew how many more somewhere in the great building? There could easily be a small company of soldiers. Richard Boyle was not only one of the wealthiest men in England, he had no hesitation when it came to displaying those riches. His mansion was huge. And he certainly had enough money to pay for as many mercenaries as he needed, short of an actual army.

"What should we do?" asked Patrick.

"I don't know," replied Leebrick. He turned away from the window, tired of staring pointlessly at the street below. "I suppose we'll simply have to wait to see what the earl has in mind for us."

"And if what he had in mind doesn't suit us?" Towson's expression was dark. "I mean, *really* not suit us, Anthony?"

Leebrick considered the problem, but not for long. Ten years worth of fighting in the Germanies hadn't left much in the way of timidity in his soul. Precious little charity or mercy, either.

"We'll fight our way out. Try to, at any rate."

Patrick nodded. "Fine with me," said Richard. "What signal? It can't be anything obvious."

Anthony paused, considering again. Welch suddenly grinned. "I have it. Just refer to me as 'Paddy,' why don't you? That'll get my blood up in an instant."

Leebrick and Towson chuckled. Patrick was a common first name in Ireland, used by Protestants as well as Catholics. But "Paddy" was a Catholic nickname— and Welch came from a sturdy Presbyterian family, even if he wasn't much given to piety himself.

"'Paddy' it is, then," said Leebrick.

Not far away, Whitehall was a scene of confusion. Word had reached the royal palace of the accident, although the details were contradictory. The king was dead; the king was fine but the queen was dead; they were both dead; they were both injured; the queen, three months' pregnant, had had a miscarriage—who knew?

Officials and ministers raced about, trying to find the earl of Strafford to get clear directions. As much as many of them disliked the man, Thomas Wentworth was nothing if not decisive.

But Wentworth was nowhere to be found. Eventually, several guards were found who explained that he'd left the palace an hour earlier—because he'd been brought an early warning that the king's carriage had suffered a bad accident on the West Road near Chiswick. The earl of Strafford had hurried off to see to the matter himself.

The West Road? Why in the world would the king have decided to go that way?

Fortunately, the earl of Cork arrived soon thereafter, bringing order into the chaos. Even a measure of calm.

"Yes, it's true. A terrible accident on Tyburn Hill Road. My companions and I happened upon the scene shortly afterward. His Majesty is badly injured and I'm afraid the queen is dead. The children are fine, fortunately, since their carriage was not involved. Where's Strafford?"

Babbled explanations came.

"What's he doing haring off to Chiswick? It's a miserable little fishing village. The royal party wasn't within miles of there. And he shouldn't have left the palace himself, even if he had managed to get the right location. What was he thinking? With the city on the edge of revolt?"

After heaving an exasperated sigh and composing his features into firm and steady resolve, Cork continued. "Well, we can't wait for him to return, wherever he got himself off to. The situation is far too perilous. There was clearly treason involved. There's no way Trained Bands would have known the king's route fast enough to have laid that ambush without forewarning from right here in the palace."

More official babblement.

"Oh, yes, be sure of it. Treason, I say. Get moving, all of you! I'm having His Majesty brought here to Whitehall, under military escort, along with the heirs. And Her Majesty's body, lest rumors begin to fly about. Get moving, I say! Find the king's doctors and make sure they're here when he arrives. Shouldn't be more than an hour, at most. And have the companies mustered and summon their captains here as well. We *must* keep the mob from even thinking of rebellion. Until Strafford returns, I'll take charge of things."

He had absolutely no authority to do so, and some of the officials and ministers were a bit taken aback. But instantly, it seemed, there were well-placed and prestigious figures supporting Cork's course of action. And not just Sir Paul Pindar and Sir Endymion Porter, either, who'd accompanied him. Men like the secretary of state, Sir Francis Windebank, threw their support to Cork also.

The flock of ministers charged off, leaving Boyle alone for the moment with Pindar and Porter.

"Very nicely done, Paul," he murmured. "My apologies for doubting you."

"I thought it would work. Wentworth's headstrong, and not good at delegating authority. I was almost certain he'd race off himself if I had word sent ahead."

Porter smiled thinly. "And sent him off the wrong way, to boot. Masterful, Sir Paul."

The elderly merchant made a face. "Let's not get overconfident. Cork, you have perhaps three hours to seize the reins before Wentworth gets back. Might be as little as two. And if the man is headstrong, don't forget that's a compound term—and the second word is 'strong.' He knows how to command men also."

The earl just smiled. "So he does—but who'll listen to a traitor? Endymion, I believe it's time to bring our dear captain into play. See to it, would you?"

"Yes, milord. Shouldn't take me more than an hour to get back with his testimony. Leebrick's nothing but a mercenary, so he'll see reason soon enough. And your mansion is just down the street."

"Remember, I want no loose ends."

After Porter left, Cork started rubbing his hands. It wasn't actually the gesture of glee it appeared to be. His hands were simply still cold.

"I think it's going quite well, myself. Amazingly well, in fact, given that we had to put it all together on the fly."

Pindar, on the other hand, was starting to get overheated in the palace. He looked around for a servant to help him with his heavy coat. "That's actually what works most in our favor, Richard. It was always hard to get a plot going against Strafford, because he maintains so many spies and informers. He really is quite a competent man."

Seeing his imperious gesture, one of the servants

standing nervously some distance away came over and got the heavy coat off, then took it away to be hung up to dry somewhere. "Unfortunately for him," Pindar continued, "Wentworth confuses efficiency with results. He's like a horseman who thinks he's getting to his destination because his mount is trotting along smartly. And he's never understood—not well enough—the difference between having subordinates and friends. He's feared at court, but not liked at all. Not by any of the factions, since he's run roughshod over all of them."

Cork scowled. His faction included. The truth was, he'd come to purely detest Wentworth. "There's Laud," he pointed out.

"Yes, we'll have to do something about him. A pity, really. Laud's a good enough man and his theology suits me. But . . ." Pindar shrugged. "His well-known ties to Wentworth make him an easy target, under these circumstances, and he's too stubborn to know when to give way."

"True. But the Tower's a big place. Plenty of room for him, too." Now the earl's hand-rubbing was definitely gleeful. "And whether you think well of him or not, Paul, I detest the man."

Cork was good at detesting people. Almost as good as he was at hiding the fact, when he needed to, until it was too late for his prey.

"So that's how it'll be, Captain." Endymion Porter tapped the sheet of paper he'd set down on the small table in the salon where the three officers had been imprisoned. "Your signature here—all three of your signatures—and you're on your way." The same finger flicked the small but heavy bag he'd set down on the table alongside the document. "As you've seen, there's enough silver here to get you to the continent quickly and set you up—all three of you—for some time. More money than you'd have made in His Majesty's service in several years, and nothing to do for it beyond the few seconds it takes to sign this sheet of paper."

Anthony ignored him, still studying the document. The testimony, rather.

It didn't take much time, and most of that was simply due to the poor penmanship. The testimony wasn't long, covering less than a single page. He was quite certain Porter had scrawled it hurriedly himself, just minutes ago.

It didn't need to be long, because it was very cleverly done. Porter—and Cork and Pindar, of course, since the plot was now obvious—hadn't made the mistake of trying for anything too elaborate. The document simply testified that the earl of Strafford had instructed Captain Leebrick, in the event there was any sign of interference by Trained Bands in the king's progress out of the city, to return the royal party at once to Whitehall. Over the king's objections, if need be.

Nothing more. Leebrick wasn't being asked to confess to any treason himself. He'd simply been obeying orders.

He no longer wondered at the manner the Trained Bands had appeared on the roads, coming from two directions. Cork himself—his agents, more likely—must have had them in readiness. Not to produce the end result that had occurred, to be sure. That had been a completely unforeseen accident, brought on by the king's own folly. Cork had simply wanted to embarrass

Wentworth and undermine his position at court. Aside from being more clever than most, it was just the sort of petty political maneuver that Leebrick had seen dozens of times on the continent. One nobleman trying to jostle aside another, that's all.

But once the accident did occur, with its catastrophic consequences, Cork and his people were moving quickly to take full advantage of the situation. They'd match Leebrick's signed testimony against something similar they'd extract from whichever leaders of the Trained Bands had taken their money. Again, nothing that implicated those leaders directly in any treason—but did implicate Wentworth.

Looked at from one angle, the hastily conceived plot was completely ramshackle. Any judicious eye would start picking it apart, soon enough, and with a bit of patience could unravel the thing completely.

But it would be no patient set of eyes that looked at these documents. It would be the eyes of England's king, his body wracked with agony and his spirit wracked still worse by the death of his wife. Even if that king had been of the caliber of Henry II, he might be taken in, under these circumstances. Given that Charles wasn't fit to shine the great Plantagenet's boots, England's current monarch would swallow it whole.

So much, Anthony was almost sure of. What he was completely certain about, was that he and Patrick and Richard wouldn't survive putting down their signatures for more than a day. Probably not more than the few hours it took to get them out of London.

"And, as I said," Porter went on smoothly, gesturing at the officer standing behind him, "Captain Doncaster and his men will escort you out of the city and see you safely onto a ship at Dover."

Anthony glanced at Doncaster, and then at the two soldiers standing behind him, not far from the open door. He didn't know Doncaster personally, having only met him briefly and casually on a few occasions. But the flat look in his eyes was enough. If it hadn't been, the sight of two common soldiers armed with wheel locks would have done the trick. Those pistols were far more expensive than anything men in the ranks would be carrying. They must have been loaned by some of Doncaster's officers, or perhaps they were even his. They were an officer's or a cavalryman's weapon—and Doncaster's was an infantry company.

The great advantage of wheel locks, of course, was that they could be carried with the wheel's spring already under tension and the weapon ready to be fired. There was no need to fiddle around with matches, as there was with a matchlock. Just flip down the lever holding the pyrite—that was called either the cock or the doghead—against the wheel, and then pull the trigger. That was a great advantage to a cavalryman. Or an assassin.

But Anthony's glance had mainly been for the purpose of assessing the tactical situation. So far as he could determine, Porter must have ordered the two guards who'd been at the door earlier to leave. They'd be part of the mansion's regular guard force, and not privy to anything beyond their normal duties.

More importantly, Richard had slowly edged his way into position. And Patrick was scratching the back of his neck, the way a man pondering a difficult decision might do.

"Very well, I'll sign it." Anthony took the quill pen and dipped it into the ink well, taking a moment to gauge the modest thing. It was a sturdy pen, and recently sharpened. He leaned over to sign the testimony—which also brought him closer to Porter. "I'm sure Richard will sign also."

He paused just before signing and grimaced. "Mind you, I make no guarantee about Welch. He's a damned Irishman and like any Paddy—"

Chapter 22

Welch's hand was already coming away from his neck with the dirk in it before Anthony even got to the "Paddy." He'd been following the logic—and that wasn't actually a dirk, it was a throwing knife. It struck one of the soldiers squarely in the throat, sinking almost to the hilt.

Richard slammed into the legs of Doncaster, spilling him.

Anthony seized Porter by the back of his head and drove the quill point into his left eye. Hard and deep enough to pierce the brain. Then—he was quite strong—lifted the small table and the corpse collapsing onto it and used them as a battering ram against the soldier who'd yet been untouched.

A good man, that. He had the pistol out and even managed to get the doghead down before Leebrick could reach him. But between the shock and his haste, he had no time to aim. All he did when he pulled the trigger was shoot Porter in the back and kill him again.

The impact slammed the soldier back against the side of the door. His helmet flew off, clattering into

315

the corridor beyond. But it hadn't protected him enough to keep from being momentarily stunned—and a moment was all it took Leebrick to get his dirk from his boot and stab him under the chin.

He twisted the blade loose, letting the corpse fall into the corridor alongside the helmet. From the sounds behind him, there was still a struggle going on.

He spun around. Not a struggle, as it turned out. The sounds he'd heard had been Doncaster's boot heels drumming the floor. Richard was lying under him and had a garrote around his neck. Leebrick had forgotten that Towson carried the horrid thing, even though he and Patrick both made jokes about it.

But even with a garrote, strangling was too slow. There'd be more guards coming any moment. Glancing over, Anthony saw that Patrick was still occupied trying to pry his knife from the other soldier's throat. The throw must have gotten the blade jammed into the vertebrae.

He strode over to the two men struggling on the floor and slammed the pommel of his dirk down on Doncaster's head. Being an officer, Doncaster had been wearing a hat instead of a helmet and the hat had flown off, so there was no obstruction to the blow.

Once, twice, on the forehead. Doncaster went limp. Leebrick seized his thick mane of hair and twisted his head sideways, then brought down a ferocious strike of the pommel on his temple. For good measure, did it again. That was enough. If he wasn't dead already, he would be soon. Either way, he'd never regain consciousness.

Anthony yanked Doncaster's body off Richard, who'd already released one end of the garrote. "Let's go! Quickly! For the love of God, Patrick, just leave the knife be!"

Welch was *still* trying to pry the blade loose. But he quit the business, as soon as Anthony yelled.

"That's an expensive knife," he hissed, leaning over and scooping the dead man's unused wheel lock from the floor.

"Who cares?" said Towson. On his way off the floor, he'd scooped up the bag of silver that had wound up lying close to him. "We'll buy you another. A hundred, if you want, with what's in here."

Leebrick looked around for the document, but couldn't see it anywhere. God only knew where it had flown to, in the fracas.

There was no time to hunt for the thing, and it had no signatures on it, anyway. That wouldn't help Wentworth, of course. But so it went. The earl of Strafford was on his own.

"Now, out!" Anthony just took enough time to extract Doncaster's sword from its scabbard. He ignored the second wheel lock. It had already been fired, and he doubted very much if they'd have time to reload it.

Once in the corridor, Leebrick raced toward the main staircase with Patrick and Richard close behind. He'd have preferred to find a more obscure servants' stairwell, but he didn't dare risk the time it would take to find one. The only route he knew out of the mansion was the same one they'd taken when they were brought in.

As it turned out, he was in luck. Hearing a martial clatter from the far end of the corridor, he realized that the mansion's guards must have been stationed in the servants' area themselves. So *they* were charging up that stairwell—while he and his two fellows would take the main stairs.

Two guards did emerge from the main staircase, just as Anthony arrived, matchlocks in hand with the fuses lit. He cut one of them down. Richard booted the other back down the staircase, head over heels. The man's musket went off, sending the bullet smashing into the ceiling above.

Patrick picked up the gun that had been held by the soldier he'd sabered. Fortunately, while the blood gushing from a neck hacked halfway through had soaked the barrel—and was still soaking the carpet, as the body slid down the staircase—the grip was clean. He handed it to Welch, who checked to make sure the match was still smoldering.

Edging to the side to keep from slipping on the blood, they scurried down the stairs and into the mansion's great entrance hall. Once they reached the bottom of the stairs, Anthony pressed the tip of his sword against the throat of the man who'd been sent flying by Richard's kick. But there was no need to kill him, since he was clearly unconscious. Leebrick had made it a point to kill Doncaster because of the officer's treachery, but this was just a common soldier.

Just as he straightened up, two more guards emerged, bursting into the room from a side door. Richard shot one with the wheel lock; Patrick shot the other with the matchlock. The Irishman's shot was dead on into the chest, punching right through the breastplate. Patrick's only struck his man's arm.

It didn't matter. The guard was down and would stay down. A three-quarter-inch musket ball did terrible damage when it struck any solid part of a human body. If the man didn't bleed to death, he'd probably lose the arm. If he survived the surgeon, which he probably wouldn't. Either way or any, Leebrick didn't care at all.

There was a doorman standing at the front entrance. Standing quite still, paralyzed with shock and terror, just staring at them.

That was good enough, too.

"Open the fucking door or I'll kill you," Anthony said, speaking almost conversationally. The man was so frightened that a shout would probably just keep him paralyzed. "*Now*, damn you."

The man did as he was told. "Leave him be," Leebrick ordered, on his way through the door. There was no point in killing the doorman. It wasn't as if there was any chance of hiding their identities, after all.

In the event, the mercy was pointless. Before Leebrick and his two companions made it down the outer stairs to the street, soldiers from within the mansion started firing at them. They missed, mostly because the doorman was still standing in the doorway, gaping down at the three fleeing men. Four bullets struck him and sent him flying. His body hit the street just a split second after Leebrick and his fellows started racing off.

"Racing," at least, insofar as the term could be applied to men who were skating as much as they were running. The footing wasn't quite as bad as it had been on Tyburn Hill Road, but it was still terrible.

Anthony was glad of it, however. The same footing would slow the pursuing guards just as much. Probably more, in fact, since they were the pursuers and not the prey. The hound runs for his meal; the hare runs for his life.

Best of all, it had started snowing again and it

was now late in the afternoon. The sun set very early in London, in midwinter, even on a clear day. The visibility was bad and it would soon get worse. Within an hour, they would have the further shelter of nightfall.

One more shot was fired, just as they went around the first corner. At them, presumably, but Leebrick couldn't see where the bullet had gone. As confused and anxious as the mansion's guard force had to be, after the carnage, whoever had fired that shot might well have just hit a building across the street. Or simply fired into the air at nothing at all.

Glancing back as they went around the next corner, Leebrick saw that they'd outraced the guards completely and were now finally out of sight. He turned the next corner the other way and then came to an abrupt halt. He needed to catch his breath, before they did anything further. From the way their chests were heaving, so did Patrick and Richard.

He leaned over and planted his hands on his knees. Started to, rather, until he realized he still had the sword in his hand.

Fortunately, while Cork had taken their swords, he hadn't taken the scabbards. Fortunately also, Doncaster had favored a blade not too dissimilar from Anthony's own. It didn't fit the scabbard perfectly, and it would have to be yanked out with some effort in the event of another fight, but it would do. An officer making his way through London with a sword in a scabbard was a common sight. If he kept it in his hand, people would notice.

He saw that Patrick and Richard had already disposed of their guns somewhere along the way. "Better throw away your scabbards too," he said, still gasping a little. "Empty, they'll be noticed."

Richard complied instantly, tossing the thing into some bushes. Welch followed, after a moment's hesitation. Good scabbards were as expensive as good knives, and the Irishman was something of a miser. On the other hand, he wasn't stupid.

"Now where?" asked Richard. "Don't dally about, Anthony. The guards will be here any minute. They'll search every street."

Leebrick already had part of the answer—the end goal. What he wasn't sure of, was how to get there.

"I'm not that familiar with Westminster. Either of you?"

Towson nodded. "I know it quite well. Spent years as a lad, helping my father make deliveries in the area."

"You lead the way, then."

"Lead the way, where?"

"Southwark. Liz will hide us."

Welch and Towson stared at him, their expressions both full of doubts.

Different ones, as it turned out, as were their different temperaments. Richard inclined to the practical, being from Derbyshire; the Irishman, to the acerbic.

Richard expressed his first, as he led them down an alley. "Only way across is either London Bridge or taking a boat at Westminster Stairs, which I don't advise. It's the first place they'll look, and boatmen talk."

"It'll have to be the bridge," said Leebrick. He wasn't looking forward to a walk of two or three miles on streets in this bad a condition, but he saw no choice. Taking a boat would be madness, unless they could steal one—and finding an unguarded boat in midwinter was a dubious proposition. Any time of year, for that moment. Boats were expensive, too.

"They might close off London Bridge before we can get there," pointed out Welch.

"Not likely," said Leebrick. "This wasn't part of any well-planned conspiracy. Cork is just putting it together as he goes, taking advantage of happenstance. The ink was barely dry on that stinking document of Porter's. There's no way Cork has control of the military forces in London yet. Not all of them, for sure—which means not enough of them to seal off every exit."

"True," mused Towson. "But London Bridge is a pretty obvious one, I'd think."

Even while talking, though, he'd been leading them as quickly as the ground allowed in the direction of the Bridge. By now, they had to be far ahead of any pursuit coming from Cork's mansion.

"No, actually, it isn't," said Anthony. "Aside from the two of you, no one knows of my liaison with Elizabeth Lytle. I've kept it—"

Seeing the sour expression on Welch's face, he let that drop for the moment. "The point is, no one has any reason to think we have any connection with Southwark. So why would we try to hide there, instead of leaving the city entirely?"

"Same reason any criminal does," snorted Welch, his tone sounding as sour as his face looked.

"Not the same thing, Patrick. All a common criminal has to evade are the courts and constables. We'll be charged with treason—and Cork has enough money to offer a huge reward for us. Southwark's the worst place in England for someone to hide, if there's money being waved about to find their whereabouts, unless they can stay completely out of sight. Scratch any criminal and you'll find an informer."

Patrick came to a sudden stop, planting his hands on his hips. "Right, so you will. And here's what else is true, Anthony Leebrick—and I'll say it straight out even if Richard won't. Scratch any whore and you'll find an informer, too."

So, there it was. Towson drew in a breath, almost hissing.

But Leebrick had seen it coming, and was ready for the matter. "She stopped whoring when she took up with me, Patrick, which not even you will deny."

He paused, forcing Welch to answer.

The Irishman drew in a sharp breath of his own. "Fine. No, I'll not deny it. I'll go further and say that I've no particular animus against whores to begin with. On average—and this is based on lots of experience—I've found them no more dishonest than most and considerably less than some."

A quick smile came to his face; Patrick's saving grace was that he was acerbic about everything, himself not excepted. "Including just about every soldier I ever met, leaving aside thee and me and Richard here. But they're still no less the mercenaries, themselves, even if they use fleshy instead of iron tools in their trade. So, tell me, Captain Leebrick. Why *wouldn't* your precious Liz turn us in for the reward?"

But by the time Patrick had finished—as Anthony had expected would happen—he'd already talked himself out of his position. Halfway, at least. It was obvious just from his expression. And he'd talked Richard completely around.

"Oh, leave off, Patrick," said Towson, sounding quite acerbic himself. "The woman dotes on our dashing captain; you know it as well as I do. Even whores fall in love, you know."

Patrick did his best to rally, essaying a sneer.

"Oh, come on!" Towson jerked a thumb at Leebrick. "Why else do you think he keeps her a secret from everybody except us? Most officers brag about their kept women, especially ones as good-looking as Lytle. The reason he doesn't is because he knows he'd be the laughingstock of the companies if they found out he was keeping one he planned to marry."

"Against my advice, I remind you," said Patrick. "I want that registered on the record. This current mad scheme even more than that idiot proposal of marriage."

From Welch, that was complete capitulation. Towson set off again, leading the way to the bridge.

They got across London Bridge with no problems at all. So far as Anthony could determine, whatever pursuit had been organized still hadn't gotten out of Westminster.

"So, here we are in Southwark," said Patrick, a while later, "about to test a legend. Is there really such a thing as a whore with a heart of gold?"

From anyone else, Anthony would have taken offense. But he and Patrick went back a long way together. So he just chuckled. "And after it's all over, you'll insist the test was false, anyway."

Welch frowned. "Why would I do that?"

"You idiot," said Towson, chuckling himself. He dug

into his coat and pulled out Porter's bag. "I'll be glad to set this great heavy thing down finally, I can tell you that. Patrick, you benighted Irishman, there's enough silver in here to offset any reward of Cork's. Halfway, at least."

Welch stopped again, planting hands on hips. "You miserable bastard, Leebrick. You're cheating!"

"That's why he's the captain," said Towson, "and we but his lowly lieutenants."

"Dear God," said Richard Boyle, his face pale. "Endymion? *Murdered?*"

He looked away, his eyes ranging across the crowd that was now packed into the outer rooms of the palace. Mostly courtiers, standing about and gossiping pointlessly, with some harried officials here and there trying to make their way through the mob. The king had arrived, just minutes earlier, and Cork had had to threaten to have soldiers fire on the crowd to clear a path for the litter. Then, do the same shortly thereafter to clear a way for the royal heirs and the queen's corpse.

"Dear God," he repeated. "I can't believe it. He was alive—right here!—just—just—"

"Cork, pull yourself together," said Sir Paul Pindar sharply. "I'm as sorry as you are about poor Endymion, but Wentworth will be here any moment. Don't you understand? Porter's murder casts the final die—and it's *perfect.*"

The earl gaped at him. For all his ruthlessness, Cork was a man who'd made his way up using money, not steel. The same could be said of Pindar, of course, but the merchant's fortune had come from the often steely demands of the Levant trade, not peddling influence and making advantageous marriages.

"He's right, Richard," said Sir Francis Windebank. "A signed testimony is one thing. Might be forged, who's to say? But now there are bodies to point to, corpses anyone can look at. Brutally slain, by men whom everyone can now see must have been skilled and deadly assassins. Appointed to their posts by Strafford himself. Probably working in collusion with a foreign power."

That was sheer gibberish, from any logical viewpoint. But Boyle was starting to regain his wits. Gibberish, yes, if you pulled it all apart. But if you ran it all together quickly—past a dazed and grief-stricken monarch—and you controlled the ensuing investigation yourself . . . and had plenty of money to throw around . . .

"Yes, you're right. Poor Endymion—but he'd be the first to tell us to seize the occasion."

There was a stir at the outer entrance. A moment later, Thomas Wentworth was forcing his way through the crowd.

"Clear a path, damn you!" he shouted angrily. "Make way! I'm the earl of Strafford!"

He caught sight of Richard. "Cork!" he cried out. "Is there word of His Majesty? I could find no sign of him—"

Before Wentworth got halfway through that last sentence, Boyle had already gauged the crowd in the vicinity. Courtiers, mostly, not actual ministers except the secretary of state standing right beside him. Best of all, the soldiers were the same ones he'd used to bring in the king. And given their captains the promise of a very hefty bonus.

"Arrest that traitor!" he bellowed, pointing at Wentworth.

Chapter 23

Brussels, the Spanish Netherlands

Don Fernando was, of course, only twenty-three years old. That accounted for many of the things that he had already achieved. He did not yet know that they were impossible. His aunt Isabella and her advisers, on the other hand, did—and she was still the ruler of the Spanish Netherlands.

Isabella Clara Eugenia was certainly old enough to know better. According to the incredible encyclopedias to be found in Grantville, she should have been dead by now. More than three months ago, in fact, on the first day of December 1633.

Given how she felt this morning, that did not surprise her in the least. However, instead, she was quite alive and sitting in a wheeled chair at the conference table in her palace in Brussels, in the presence of her very closest and most trusted advisers and confidants. Wearing, as she had since she'd joined the order in 1625 a few years after her husband's death, the vestments of a nun of the Sisters of Saint Clare rather than the flashy court apparel and regalia of her younger years.

The decision that they had just placed on the table was not, perhaps, impossible. It was just . . . dangerous. Dreadfully dangerous.

"It is my will," she said.

Hers was an imperious voice, still, for all that it was beginning to quaver with age. Infanta of Spain by birth; daughter of Philip II, archduchess of Austria by marriage, joint sovereign of the Netherlands with her husband Archduke Albrecht VII of Austria, and sole sovereign since his death twelve years earlier.

"It is signed. Witnessed. Sealed. From the first, it was my father's intent that the Netherlands should be an *appanage* for us, for Albrecht and me. The lawyers have revisited all the provisions of my marriage contract in detail. For us, and for our children, to revert to Spain only if we did not have children."

A shadow of regret for three tiny, frail, babies, dead so long ago, flitted across her face. "Not that they should return to being directly ruled from Madrid after my death. I bore children, so the Netherlands became ours, no matter that they died soon after their birth. Mine, since my husband Albrecht's death. Not, of course, that it will prevent other lawyers, paid by other masters, from interpreting the clauses in other ways. So be it.

"It is my *will*," she repeated. "My nephew Fernando has earned my trust. I have bequeathed my holdings to him. Let the king of Spain react after he finds that the deed has been done. It will not be long."

Her confessor Bartolomé de los Rios y Alarcon shook his head. "Please, Your Grace! You are not dead until you are dead—and you are only sixty-seven years old."

The archduchess gave the Augustinian priest a rather cool look. Arch, it might be called.

"Only?"

De los Rios seemed discomfited, and looked away. Across from him at the table, Pieter Paul Rubens chuckled. "He's a priest, Your Grace—and Spanish, to boot. You can hardly expect him to say it out loud."

He shifted his chair forward and planted his forearms on the table. "But since I am merely an artist—and Flemish, to make it worse—I will undertake the crude business. You thought you were on your deathbed last summer, remember? And yet here you are, quite definitely alive. The only reason you know you were 'supposed' to have died at the end of last year is because you read it in a copy of a Grantville book."

She nodded. "And . . . so?"

A bit sternly, he said, "So read some of the *other* books. In the world that book was written, the average age at death of an American woman was almost eighty. And most of them were active and alert—reasonably enough—until the end. So stop predicting your imminent demise. Who knows?"

"I say it again—and so? In that same world, my three children would not have died in infancy. But they did, nonetheless."

She leaned back in her wheeled chair, sighing. "Let us not quarrel. Especially since it hardly matters anyway. Whether I live or die"—she pointed to the papers on the table—"if this transpires, it will be my great-nephew and not I who will have to defend it in a test of arms. Not even when I was twenty could I have led an army into the field as its commander, after all."

De los Rios winced, as did two of the other advisers at the table. Those were Henri de Vicq, who was Flemish, and the Walloon Gerard Courselle. Both of them were men well past middle-age. De Vicq was sixty years old and Courselle, sixty-five.

"Perhaps it will not come to that," the priest said.

"Perhaps not," said Isabella. "But who at this table can make such a promise—or claims to be able to foresee the future? Keep in mind that while King Philip IV may be reluctant to wage war against his younger brother, he has counselors also. The count-duke of Olivares is not likely to hesitate, and those around him, still less. Spain has dominated the field of battle for so long, I'm afraid, that a military solution comes immediately to mind, whenever it is challenged."

Silence fell on the room, for a moment. Then Rubens shrugged and said: "It's still not so easy as all that, Isabella. Just to begin with, how would they send troops from Spain or the Italian possessions? The Spanish Road is no longer open—and won't be, so long as Bernhard of Saxe-Weimar squats atop part of it while the Swedes squat upon much of the rest. Each for their own reasons, neither is about to allow passage to Spanish troops—and both are strong enough that any Spanish army that fought its way through them would be too weak to do anything once they reached the Netherlands. If they could fight through at all, which they might against Bernhard but I doubt very much could do against the Swedes."

He leaned forward still further, his expression intent. "That means transport by sea, and that requires a fleet—and it remains to be seen exactly where Admiral Oquendo will end up, when the time comes. He is deeply bitter over the way the Spanish navy provided Richelieu with his cannon fodder at the Battle of Dunkirk—with the consent of Philip IV and the count-duke of Olivares."

"*If* the time comes," the archduchess said. She smiled a bit wanly. "Let us not overlook the minor detail that my great-nephew has not agreed to any of this. And without Don Fernando—leading, not simply acquiescing—it will all mean nothing."

Rubens looked at her from lowered eyes. "He is much inclined that way, though. Of that, I am certain."

The old woman shrugged. "Yes, so am I. And—again—so what? You know him, Pieter, by now probably better than anyone of us here at this table. He is a prince of Spain, for good or ill, not a Flemish burgomaster. And he's very young, too, which makes it all the harder."

Rubens nodded. "Yes, I know. He will wait, until the test of arms in the spring. But I can tell you this, Isabella. He may be waiting like a very young fox, but fox he surely is. I know enough of military matters to know that his troop dispositions are not those of an impetuous commander eager to sally forth onto the field again, as soon as the season permits. There will be no repetition of Haarlem, come the spring. He will make Fabius Maximus look like a daredevil."

That brought a little round of laughter. Rather relieved laughter.

"You're sure, Pieter?" asked Alessandro Scaglia.

Rubens swiveled his head and examined the man, for a moment. Privately, Pieter still had doubts about the former Savoyard diplomat. He thought Isabella had been incautious to draw him into her very closest circle.

The problem wasn't that he disliked Scaglia—he'd quite enjoyed his company, actually, the few times he'd spent with the man—it was simply that the Savoyard's history was almost *too* cosmopolitan. Could a man who had served so many courts really be depended upon, in the end, to serve only one? Most of all, why had he left Savoy's service in the first place? Rubens had never gotten a very satisfactory explanation of that.

But, mentally, he shrugged. It was done now, for better or worse. Scaglia already knew enough, if he changed his allegiance, to have all of them executed for treason except the archduchess herself. Because of her royal blood, she'd more likely be walled up in her beloved convent of the Discalced Carmelites attached to the palace—with Spanish guards at the door of her cell, instead of nuns.

Besides, there was something downright preposterous about Pieter Paul Rubens faulting another man for an excess of cosmopolitanism. That stray thought almost made him laugh out loud.

"Yes, I'm sure, Alessandro. Partly from my own observations—alas, I've become far better educated on military affairs than I really ever wanted to be— and partly from various remarks made to me by the cardinal-infante himself. Most important of all, however—my opinion, at least—is that I've watched carefully which officers Don Fernando has made his closest subordinates, as the siege went on."

Scaglia lifted an eyebrow. "Ha. I wouldn't have thought to look there. But I don't really know any of them all that well to begin with."

"I do, by now," said Rubens. "Here is where it stands."

He lifted his forearms from the table and began counting on his fingers.

"His closest military confidant—no question about this—is Miguel de Manrique."

"Ah," said Scaglia. "That is . . . significant. I agree."

Bartolomé de los Rios y Alarcon looked from one to the other. "I'm a priest, not really a diplomat and certainly not a soldier of any kind. Please explain."

"Manrique commanded the Spanish army that surrendered to the Americans at the Wartburg," said Scaglia. He held up his hand, with thumb and forefinger almost touching. "He came this close to being executed for it, after his return to Spain. It was the worst disaster for Spanish arms in a century, at least."

"It was Don Fernando who got him out of the clutches of the Inquisition and brought him to the Low Countries," Rubens elaborated.

"The point to all this," Scaglia continued, "being that if there is any captain of Spain *least* likely to underestimate the enemy, it is Manrique—and from what Pieter tells us, he is closer to the cardinal-infante's ear than any other of his officers."

"I see. And the others?"

Rubens went back to his finger-counting. "Not one is a Spaniard, to begin with. Two Italian officers—in the Spinola mold, if you understand what I mean—and the Irishman, Owen Roe O'Neill."

Isabella frowned. "I know the two Italian officers you're referring to—and, yes, I agree. They think of themselves more as professional soldiers of a Netherlands army than agents of the king of Spain. But while I've met O'Neill twice, briefly—I don't understand why you think he's important."

Rubens lowered his hands and smiled. "I think in some ways he may be the most important of all, at least in the long run. Whatever else, he'll not want to see Don Fernando embroiled in wars on the continent. O'Neill has a cause of his own, you see. He's what you'd find called an 'Irish nationalist' in the up-time books."

The priest frowned. "Since when is Ireland a 'nation'? It's just an island, full of half-savages who quarrel even worse than Italians. Even worse than Catalans, if that's possible."

That brought another little round of laughter.

"True, true—today. But O'Neill already detested England—and any English ally—even before he got his hands on copies of Grantville's books."

Isabella gave the arms of her chair an exasperated little slap. "Does *anyone* in the world not wind up reading those things? It's absurd!"

Rubens tilted his head and gave her a sly smile. "Well, *you* did, after all."

She half-scowled at him. "I'm rich. Those books— copies, not even the originals—emptied half my treasury. Well. A tenth, at least."

Scaglia chuckled. "Your Grace, you either got cheated or you insisted on very fine copies." He, also, tilted his head. "Or perhaps it was simply that you got the very first editions."

She sniffed. "Well, of course I got the very first copies. The ink was barely dry on them. I'm the daughter of Philip II of the Spanish empire, an Austrian archduchess, and the sovereign of the Netherlands in my own right. I should wait?"

Now, both Rubens and Scaglia chuckled. "Your

Grace, I hate to tell you this," Pieter said, "but the production of replicas of up-time books has become a staple of the printers' trade everywhere in Europe. They're not *quite* out-selling the Bible yet, in most places, but I was told—just last month—by the biggest printer in Brussels, that he expects they will within a year. And I know from speaking to printers in Amsterdam that they did so there within a month after the siege began. Even in Counter-Remonstrant households, it seems."

Isabella rolled her eyes. "Marvelous. Pedro the shepherd and Hans the sausage-maker will be trying to direct their little farms and shops based on their attempts to read their fortunes. I predict disaster."

"You don't have to predict it," Rubens said solemnly. "It's already happened, right in front of our eyes—and on the scale of kings and princes, not shepherds and sausage-makers. What else was Richelieu's Ostend scheme but an attempt to read the future and force a different outcome? And"—he held up his hand, forestalling a comment from de los Rios—"let us not wax too indignant on the subject. For we, too, are attempting the same, are we not?"

He rose out of his chair, leaned over, and planted his forefinger on the papers in the middle of the table. "What else is all this, after all? But an attempt on our part to circumvent—'short-circuit,' the Americans would call it, and don't ask me to explain the precise details of what that means because I asked Anne Jefferson and *she* couldn't tell me—three and half centuries of bloodletting and misery, most of which served no purpose whatsoever. Not even, in the end, the purposes of the bloodletters."

There was no trace, any longer, of the genial humor which usually tinged Rubens' voice when he spoke. For once, the artist and diplomat was speaking in dead earnest.

"Richelieu is a madman if he thinks he can circumvent the single most obvious and overriding reality of that future world. And that is this." He half-turned and half-bowed to Isabella. "Meaning no personal offense, Your Grace, for you are indeed—I make no jest here—beloved by most of your people. Today, all nations are ruled by kings and princes. Beginning less than two centuries from now, all that will be swept aside and the common folk will come into their own. For good or ill, they *will*. You—we—anyone—has as much chance of preventing that as the legendary King Canute had of ordering back the tides. Be sure of it."

He sat down heavily. "The difference between us and Richelieu—us and the king of Spain—is that we are not looking to block the outcome. Simply to . . ." He smiled. "The Americans have another term for it. I swear, they produce the things with even greater profligacy than they produce gadgetry."

"If anyone at this table uses the word 'okay' I shall have them executed," Isabella stated firmly. She waggled her finger. "I'm serious!"

There was a burst of laughter, in which the archduchess did not participate, although she seemed to be struggling against a smile.

"I'm serious," she repeated, still wagging the finger. "The gloves will come off!"

"Ah!" Rubens exclaimed. "That's one of my *favorite* American expressions."

That brought uproarious laughter; from Isabella, also. When the humor faded, Scaglia asked: "And what is the term, Pieter?"

"Well . . . it would mean a great deal more to you if you had seen one of their airplanes come down from the sky onto the ground. I watched myself, when Stearns came to Amsterdam. For the entire last part, I was holding my breath. The term is 'soft landing.' I think it's a very good description of what we are attempting here. A soft landing for the future. Foolish to stand against that future, yes. But I see no reason we need to submissively accept every particular in it. No reason, to name just one matter, that we need French and German troops—English, too—marching back and forth across our Low Countries once every generation, it seems."

He smiled again. "We are not, after all, Calvinists with idiotic and heretical notions concerning predestination."

That brought a round of chuckles. Rubens continued. "Neither, by the way—he sees the matter from a very different viewpoint, of course—does Michael Stearns himself. From a political standpoint, I think that was the single most important thing I learned about the man from his visit. If *we* are willing to compromise, he will at least begin with that stance also. There will of course be many disputes."

De los Rios looked skeptical. "Him, maybe. But what about that Richter creature of his?"

Rubens stifled some irritation. For all the priest's undoubted kindliness, he still had much in him of Spanish insularity if not Castilian arrogance. "She is not a 'creature' to begin with, Bartolomé—and she's certainly no creature of his."

"She carries a pistol at all times, they say! What sort of woman—"

"A woman who was gang-raped at the age of sixteen by mercenaries, saw her mother abducted, her father murdered before her eyes, and spent two years as the concubine of one of her rapists in order to keep what remained of her family alive," Scaglia said bluntly; indeed, almost coldly. "I've learned her history, Father de los Rios, which I suspect you haven't."

"Oh, how ghastly." Isabella had her hand pressed to her throat. "I had no idea."

Rubens was too astonished by Scaglia's statement to speak, for a moment. He'd known Richter's history himself, but had had no idea Scaglia did. That was . . .

Very telling, he thought. He could sense a transformation—*sea-change,* an American term which ironically came from an Englishman already dead—happening in his attitude toward the Savoyard.

But, for the moment, he simply cleared his throat and added: "Yes, what Alessandro says is quite true. I learned of it from her husband, as it happens. Quite a nice young fellow, by the way, in my estimate. But what's perhaps more to the point is that he also told me she's never used the pistol except on a practice range since she participated in fending off the Croat raid on Grantville that Wallenstein launched. That was well over a year ago."

He turned toward the priest. "Do not underestimate that woman, Bartolomé. Whatever else, do *not.* She could teach Richelieu himself the meaning of ruthlessness—but she's no hothead. In fact"—he was able to smile again—"Don Fernando was quite taken by her, when they finally met last month."

"He *did*?" Isabella was back to her throat-clutching. "That reckless boy! What was he thinking? I hope—please tell me this much—that he did not permit her to bring that horrid pistol into his presence."

Rubens grinned; he couldn't help himself. "Quite the contrary. He made that stipulation in his request that she come into his camp for a visit—and invited her husband along also, with his shotgun. A weapon, I might add, that is considerably more ferocious and one which, in his case, is almost as famous as hers. He's quite an impressive fellow, actually, in his own much quieter way."

Isabella was practically gaping. "My nephew is a prince of Spain!"

"Your Grace, he did not dispense with his own bodyguards," Rubens said, in a more serious tone. "Please—you *must* stop thinking of these people as simple, unlettered rabble-rousers. To be as blunt as I can, they could also teach Europe's kings and princes and counselors"—his eyes swept the table—"I do not exempt us, either, the meaning of organization and leadership."

He leaned back in his chair. "Besides, the cardinal-infante had no real choice. By that point in his negotiations with Fredrik Hendryk, everything had been settled. But he had not reached a settlement with Rebecca Abrabanel over the issue of whether the Dutch right to retain their councils and deliberative bodies would be extended in full across the entire Netherlands, in the event the nation was reunited. Not one that she was satisfied with, at least—more precisely, one that she said would satisfy Richter and her Committee of Correspondence. So, Don Fernando decided to talk to Richter himself."

Isabella shook her head, chuckling. "Dear me. I had no idea my rambunctious great-nephew was thinking that far ahead."

"I told you, Isabella. He's a very young fox—young enough that he can't accept the inevitable without at least one clash of arms—but he's a genuine fox, nonetheless. Fredrik Hendryk once told me, rather ruefully, that Don Fernando reminds him in some ways of his father, William the Silent."

That brought a moment's respectful silence. Given the source—any knowledgeable source, really—that was high praise indeed.

"And what was the outcome of the meeting?" Scaglia asked.

"Oh, Don Fernando agreed, in the end. Richter's bargaining argument was so simple, he told me afterward, that he saw no way to refuse."

"And this argument was . . . what?"

"She told him—very pleasantly, apparently, no shouting involved at all—that she was ultimately indifferent to the matter. Don Fernando could give her the extension of democratic representation across the Netherlands that she wanted. Or she would take it. The difference, she estimated, was not more than two years. Four, at the outside."

Isabella stared at him, wide-eyed, her hand back at her throat. "She *bullied* a Spanish prince?"

"Oh, hardly that. No, no, Your Grace, you don't understand. It wasn't any implied threat that persuaded Don Fernando. It was simply that—so he told me, afterward—it was quite apparent that Richter *was* indifferent to the matter. Completely indifferent. He said it was like negotiating with a glacier whether it will reach the sea."

Isabella lowered her hand. "I *must* meet this woman. Can it be arranged, Pieter?" Impatiently, she waved her hand. "Fine, fine. She can bring the pistol, if she insists. Her husband, too, with his—whatever you call it."

Pieter was taken by surprise again. "I . . . don't know. I shall enquire, when I return to Amsterdam. Which, by the way, I must do on the morrow. Is there anything further we need to discuss? I will need most of the afternoon and evening to make preparations for the journey."

Isabella and her advisers looked at each other. Finally, seeing that no one seemed to feel any urge to speak, she said: "It seems we are finished, for the moment. Nothing more we can do, really. Everything is ready from our side for the transition, once—if, but let us pray it is simply 'once'—my great-nephew finally decides."

Chapter 24

Rubens paused, in the corridor beyond the conference room, until Scaglia emerged, then fell in beside him.

"I was thinking we should talk some more. We've really not had that much in the way of private discussion."

"Yes, I agree. I was meaning to approach you myself, Pieter. Where? I can come up to the siege camp, if that's easier for you."

Rubens smiled. "Oh, there's no need for anything so rigorous. Mind you, the house I purchased there is quite adequate. But within a week, I believe I shall have acquired a much more spacious home in Amsterdam itself."

"Dear God," Scaglia said, chuckling. "What a preposterous siege this has turned into. The chief diplomat for the besiegers setting up his domicile in the city besieged. What's that American expression? Charles V must be spinning in his grave."

"There are some precedents, actually. Not many, I admit. But that's always the advantage of being an *artist*, you know. People are willing to label my behavior as 'eccentric' when they need to look the other way."

"True enough." Scaglia sighed. "I should have thought of that, when I began my career. Of course, I doubt if even the most wretched and ignorant *reichsritter* in Germany would have paid a Swedish copper for anything I painted. Two things, Pieter."

"Yes?"

"I've been to Grantville myself, you know. The first thing is that I want your solemn assurance that you will stand shoulder-to-shoulder with me in doing everything in our power to prevent the *American* trampling of the Low Countries. They can have their Freedom Arches, fine. But no hamburgers. I want those abominations banned."

"Done. Mind you, I doubt we can do it by law. But I'm sure we can find more subtle means to the same end. If nothing else, I'll do a still-life of a hamburger that will nauseate anyone who looks at it. And the second thing?"

They'd reached an intersection at the end of the corridor. Scaglia stepped to the side, out of any traffic, drawing Rubens with him. Very quietly:

"I was taken by the expression 'soft landing,' once you explained it. And I've been thinking for some time myself—you're absolutely right about Richter—that we need our own committees of correspondence. One that is completely continental, just as they are. Call it the European Committees for a Soft Landing, if you will."

Rubens thought about it. He'd often had similar notions himself, although he'd never crystallized them the way Scaglia had.

"The membership to consist of?"

"Open to anyone, from prince to pauper, who wishes to join. I think that's essential, Pieter."

"Yes . . . I agree. Difficult to carry out in practice, you understand. Neither you nor I—not I, for certain—is really that well-suited to organizing the masses."

"No, we're not. We're diplomats, not agitators. But I have studied the CoCs very carefully, Pieter. I've read a great deal of their literature, spent time in their Freedom Arches, talked to their supporters and activists. Most of what their enemies ascribe to their supposedly demonic methods is no more intelligent than the Protestant prattle about Jesuit devils. The real key to what the CoCs do is simply that they plant their flag, out in the open, where everyone can see it. And then people come to *them*. And it is among *those* people that you find your organizers. We can do the same. Not as easily, no, and we'll certainly be drawing a much higher portion of our supporters from more prosperous classes than they do. That will give us the advantage of more money and better connections with existing powers, but shallower roots in the populace as whole. Still, it can be done. With will and energy, it *can* be done."

Rubens studied him, for a moment. "Are you willing to be—what's that American term?"

"The point man. Yes. I believe I have the skills for it, also."

Rubens continued to study him, for quite a while longer. "So do I. And I think a little mystery—for me, at least—just got cleared up. This is really why you left Savoyard service and came here, isn't it? And—ah, I will not say 'wormed' or even 'worked'—but got yourself into Isabella's graces."

"Yes. I've been thinking about it for two years, now. Ever since the full ramifications and implications of the Ring of Fire became clear to me." He made a little waving gesture with his hand. "I'm partial to the Savoyards, I admit, and probably always will be. But the Savoy is a hopeless place from which to . . . Perhaps a better way to put it is to remember Archimedes. 'Give me a lever long enough and a fulcrum, and I can move the world.'"

Rubens nodded, looking away down the corridor. Not at any of the decorations on the walls, or the guards standing at the end, but simply seeking a sense of space and perspective. "Yes, I see it. It will be up to us to construct the lever. But the Low Countries can be the fulcrum. God and Don Fernando willing, at least."

"Exactly."

"Done." He extended his hand and they exchanged a clasp. "How soon can you come up to the siege?"

"A week, you said, for the new house? How about . . . eight days from now?"

Gretchen Richter arrived in Brussels three weeks later. She came quietly, with her husband, not quite in disguise but absent her usual insistence on doing everything as visibly as possible. She brought her pistol, too, and her husband brought his shotgun. But after she came into the archducal palace and was escorted to her room, she and her husband left the weapons there.

"I only brought them in case we encountered robbers," she explained to Isabella, once they finally met in a private audience chamber. Other than two guards standing some distance away at the door, the only person who accompanied Isabella was her confessor,

Bartolomé de los Rios y Alarcon. But the priest never spoke once, throughout.

"Well, I am relieved, I will admit," said Isabella.

The Richter woman's husband smiled. It seemed a very sweet sort of smile, too, although the man was much larger and more imposing-looking than the archduchess had expected. Perhaps that was because Gretchen Richter's reputation was so much that of an ogress that Isabella had assumed any husband would seem tiny next to her.

"Ms. Isabella," the husband said, "I'm not really what you'd call a religious person. But you never know—and while I'm willing to risk the devil, I'm not willing to risk the chance that I might run into my parents in the afterlife. Anywhere in an afterlife, heaven or hell or anything in between. My mother finds out I brought a gun into the presence of a lady, I'd never hear the end of it for eternity. And my pa—this is guaranteed—would whip my ass for a good portion of it."

The meeting went quite well, to her surprise. Very pleasant, in fact, more often than not.

Partly, because they made no attempt to negotiate anything of political substance. There was no point in that, really, under the circumstances. Everyone in the room—probably half the people in all the Netherlands—understood that everything now waited until a young prince of Spain could finally make a decision.

Isabella had simply wanted to get a sense of the *woman*, beneath the reputation. And, after two hours, thought she had done so.

The key was the husband. From almost the moment

he'd come into the room, something about him had nagged at her memory. It took two hours, however, before she could finally bring it into focus—and when she did, she felt a catch in her throat.

Twelve years, now. They didn't look the least bit alike. But there was something there that reminded her of Albrecht. A quiet gentleness—say better, considerateness—beneath the massive appearance. In the young husband's case, the physical mass; in her husband's, the mass brought by titles and position. But both of them were men who would take that extra moment to consider what their actions might do, to those around them, before they shifted the mass.

She could not imagine such a man, married to an ogress. A *ruler*, yes, even a ruthless one as all rulers must be at times. And that Gretchen Richter was a ruler was no longer in doubt, to Isabella. Titles were ephemeral, in the end. The Christ had said so himself, in terms which were unmistakable to anyone not willfully blind. The young woman already wielded more in the way of real power in Europe than most princes, did she not? She'd even bullied Isabella's great-nephew!—and Pieter's attempt to put a philosophical gloss on the matter could go into a chamber pot, as far as Isabella was concerned.

The archduchess could live with that, well enough. It would be hypocrisy, if nothing else, to feel otherwise. She, too, had been what most people had considered the dominant partner in the joint sovereignty she'd exercised with her husband. By his nature, Albrecht had been too . . . considerate, to be able to do what was sometimes necessary. But he'd always been there, for her; her bulwark, when she needed it; her restraint also, when she needed that. She often thought that only his memory had enabled her to continue after his death. For sure and certain, she'd only been able to make the great and fateful decision she'd just recently made after many hours spent on her knees in the chapel, consulting his spirit as much as she prayed to the Lord they both worshipped.

There was only one ugly moment, at the very end.

"It has been most pleasant," she said, when they rose to leave. "I would ask you to visit again, but . . ." She sighed, half-caressing the arms of her wheeled chair. "It's not likely I'll be alive long enough to do so."

Richter's face turned to stone. A very pretty young woman—almost beautiful, actually, and Pieter had certainly been right about that magnificent bosom— transformed, in a instant, into something so harsh it was almost cruel.

"You are what? Sixty-five?" she demanded.

Startled, Isabella replied: "Ah . . . no. Sixty-seven."

"My grandmother is not so much younger. Do you know my history?"

"Ah . . . yes. Basically."

"Do you know *hers*?"

"Ah . . ." Isabella had never even considered the possibility that someone like Richter would have a grandmother in the first place. "No."

"When the soldiers came, she was too old to be raped. So she was able to protect my younger sister while they murdered her son in front of her eyes and raped me. In the two years that followed, she lived through torments that you have never seen outside of paintings."

Like an ancient heathen idol, that face was now.

"Many times I've heard her complain about her age. Bores everyone to tears, sometimes, going on and on about her aches and pains. But I've never once heard her sighing like a stupid sheep and whining about her inevitable imminent death. Stop it, woman. I despise cowardice—and you have no excuse at all."

With that, she turned and left. On his way out, following her, the young husband paused at the door and looked back. With that same sweet smile with which he'd entered.

"Yeah, I know, she's rougher than a cob, sometimes. Sorry 'bout that. But she's still right."

And he was gone, too. Isabella gaped at the empty doorway. No one had spoken like that to her . . .

Ever, so far as she could recall. Not even her father. And he had been the ruler of the world's mightiest empire!

"The impudence! I can't believe—!"

For a moment, she considered summoning the guards.

But . . . Well, she *had* promised safe conduct. And as quickly as she imagined the Richter creature was striding, she'd probably reach her room before the guards could catch up with her. With that horrid pistol in it, which Isabella had no doubt at all the monstrous creature would use before letting herself be arrested.

Her husband's shotgun, too, which might well be worse. Isabella had heard tales of the destruction those up-time weapons could deliver, at close quarters. Higgins himself was even famous for it, apparently. But it hardly mattered. Albrecht had been but an indifferent armsman, but had anyone ever come for Isabella they would only have reached her over her husband's corpse.

So, she let it pass. But she was livid for the rest of the day, furious for three, and sour and disgruntled for a week thereafter.

That night in the chapel, though, when he said his evening prayers, Bartolomé de los Rios y Alarcon added a prayer for the soul of Gretchen Richter. She was Catholic herself, after all, even if mostly a lapsed one. But Bartolomé would have prayed for her soul even had she been an outright heathen. He was quite sure the ogress had just added five years—three, for sure—to the lifespan of the archduchess.

Chapter 25

Southwark, England

"Well?" asked Harry Lefferts, after George and Juliet Sutherland had brushed the snow off their coats and hung them up. "Do we need to start planning how to get rid of that crime lord of yours?"

Looking even more placid than usual, George glanced around the large central room of their lodgings, where most of Harry's wrecking crew were sprawled about. The assortment of furniture that served them for the purpose could most charitably be described as "modest." Like the house itself, the furnishings were old, often ramshackle, and looked to have been assembled in a completely haphazard manner.

Not bad, though, by the standards of Southwark. Although Southwark was now legally part of London, under the formal designation of "The Ward of Bridge Without" and the more commonly used term "The Borough," it amounted to a separate city in most practical senses of the term. It dated back at least to the time of William the Conqueror and hadn't been officially incorporated into London until 1550. And, for centuries, it had been divided from the larger city just across the Thames by long established customs and traditions.

Southwark wasn't exactly the lawless part of London, but it came rather close. It was where England's capital perched its most disreputable establishments, like the theater, and was the city's largest and most active red light district. Much of the area was simply slums, but nestled here and there were any number of more prosperous dwellings. If there was a lot of poverty in Southwark, there was also quite a bit of wealth—and some of it highly concentrated.

Harry wasn't sure yet, because he hadn't moved about much himself since they'd arrived two days before. But he thought he was going to love the place. It reminded him of Las Vegas. Not the boring and oh-so-damn-proper adult amusement park that Las Vegas had become in his lifetime, once Big Respectable Money started erecting their huge theme casinos on the Strip, but the fabled city of vice and sin that his father and uncles had told him about.

It was too bad, really, that he hadn't rented one of the fancier houses in the area. He could certainly have afforded it, with the money they'd finagled out of a semi-legal art deal they'd pulled off in Amsterdam before leaving for England.

Regretfully, he'd concluded that would give them too high a profile. And there was always the possible awkwardness of having to explain to Mike Stearns exactly *why* a commando unit which was officially part of the USE's army—even if most of that army's officers would have been surprised to discover the fact, and a fair number would have been positively aghast—had found it necessary to spend money on lavish digs while in the middle of a Desp'rate Feat of Derring-do.

Well . . . he could probably razzle-dazzle Mike himself. But there was no way he'd get the explanation to fly past Don Francisco. The Sephardic nobleman who served as Mike's head of intelligence was not only very shrewd, he was so wealthy himself that simply handwaving references to the need to spend a lot of money wouldn't make him blink.

Yes, I understand that. What I fail to grasp is why you needed gold cufflinks instead of silver ones. The last time I checked the market—just yesterday—

No, not a chance. Besides, this house was suitable enough. It wasn't actually falling apart anywhere, and the furniture worked even if some of it was weird looking. Better still, the location and the design of the house made it very private, with no way for a nosy neighbor to see what they were doing by just leaning over a fence or peeking through a window. And best of all, the house was situated almost directly across the Thames from the Tower of London. With a simple eyeglass, a man could keep the Tower under close observation so long as the sun was up.

"We'll not have to be concerned about him," said George. "It turns about that Johnny Three-Fingers fell afoul of the authorities last year. And I doubt if his ghost will bother us any."

"Hung him, did they?" said Sherrilyn. She shook her head, somehow managing to combine disapproval and admiration in the same gesture. "You can't accuse the courts in this day and age of coddling criminals, I'll say that much."

"No, no." George made a dismissive motion with his hand. "Not those authorities. *The* authorities. In Southwark, I mean."

"Ah," said Harry. Seeing that Sherrilyn was looking puzzled, he added: "I think what he means is that Johnny Three-Fingers pissed off the local equivalent of Al Capone."

George knew who Al Capone was, so he'd catch the reference. In fact, the whole wrecking crew had a long-running friendly argument over which of the movie versions was the best. It was a fair split between Rod Steiger's 1959 portrayal and Robert De Niro's in the much later *The Untouchables*, with George plumping down firmly for Steiger. All of them, of course, felt that both movies were a pale imitation of the great gangster performances by Jimmy Cagney, Humphrey Bogart and Edward G. Robinson—but since none of their films had technically been about Al Capone, they were disqualified from the debate.

"Not exactly," said George. "You Yanks have a shockingly casual attitude about such things. The authorities here are more like the original Sicilian fellows that your Yank gangsters were trying to imitate. Be that as it may, Johnny Three-Fingers is in no position any longer to avenge his brother. Neither is his other brother, for that matter, since the authorities felt it wise to dispose of him at the same time." He gave Sherrilyn a reproachful glance. "And they certainly didn't hang them. Barbarous business, that is, sometimes a man lasts for minutes. The authorities are far more civilized." He illustrated his definition of civilization by drawing a finger across his throat.

That was something of a relief, if a minor one. But

by the time George had finished, Harry realized that his wife was looking rather distressed.

"What's wrong, Juliet?"

"I'm not sure if anything is wrong. But we also ran across an old friend of mine. Liz Lytle, her name. A very close friend, when I lived here. But . . ." She gave her husband an uncertain look.

"She seemed very distant," George finished for her. "As if she were distracted by something. Odd, that was. Liz was normally as cheerful a woman as you could find. 'Outgoing,' as you Yanks put it."

George had taken to calling Americans "Yanks" from watching too many of those same movies. More in the interest of precision than because he really cared, Harry had once tried to explain to him the none-too-fine distinctions between a New Englander and a West Virginian, but George had waved off the matter. "Might mean something to you Yanks, but to us Englishmen a Yank is a Yank."

Naturally, the first thing George had done once they set foot on English soil was bestow a very disapproving look upon Harry. "And, indeed—just as I was warned. Here the Yank is, himself. Overpaid, oversexed and over here."

Harry had ignored the quip. It was silly, anyway. Oversexed, he'd grant, and "over here" was a done deal. Overpaid was ridiculous.

"Not like her at all," Juliet said, looking a bit drawn. For the first time, Harry realized that the Englishwoman was actually quite upset. Juliet had a temperament that was, if anything, more placid than her husband's. For her, this amounted to a screaming fit.

"You really think something is wrong? With her personally, I mean. Keep in mind that from everything you told us last night the whole city's been in an uproar ever since the queen got killed."

Juliet sneered. "Who cares about that silly French bitch? Nobody in Southwark, I can tell you that."

Her husband smiled. "Not until the lord chamberlain finally remembers to order the theaters closed for a period of mourning, at any rate. But she's got the right of it, Harry. *Westminster* is in an uproar, sure enough. Rumors are flying all over the place, even here in Southwark. But it's not as if any of London's commoners will shed a single tear over the accident. That would have been true even if the whole royal family had been killed. They'd be more likely to throw a celebration, come to it."

Harry wasn't surprised. The Stuart dynasty had spent the three decades since it came to power steadily squandering away whatever goodwill it might have started with. Constant clashes with Parliament, the incredibly excessive favoritism showed to the duke of Buckingham by both James I and his son Charles, the son's asinine attempt to marry a Spanish infanta with that same Buckingham as his sidekick, the list went on and on. Charles I hadn't been popular even before he brought in Wentworth and imposed direct royal rule, using mercenary companies from the continent paid for with a very mysterious and suspicious source of money.

Juliet nodded. "Elizabeth and I were very close friends, Harry—and we hadn't seen each other in several years. But she acted as if she just wanted to get rid of me."

The first thought that crossed Harry's mind, of course, was to wonder if that was because this Lytle woman had figured out why they were in England. But he dismissed the notion almost instantly. None of the crew had left the house since they arrived except George and Juliet. Since they were natives and knew Southwark particularly well, Harry had sent them to cruise about to get the sense of things. There was no way Lytle could have deduced anything simply from the fact that the Sutherlands had reappeared in England.

"See what you can find out, then," he told her. Then, seeing a questioning look from Gerd, he shrugged. "Why not? We can't do anything more until we get in touch with Julie and Alex. Speaking of which—"

He glanced up the stairs, where Paul Maczka was setting up the radio in one of the upper rooms. "It's probably about time for one of us—"

"It's your turn, Harry," said Matija. He held up his hand forcefully. "Don't argue about it! I've kept the records."

Harry scowled. "Where the hell did this idiot tradition get started that everybody in the crew shares equally in the manual labor? Dammit, I'm the commanding officer."

George cleared his throat. "Well, actually, you started it. If you'd been an Englishman, you'd have more sense. But you Yanks are besotted with that silly egalitarian business." He started putting his coat back on. "Come on, Juliet. Let's see what's up with Lizzie dear."

She looked a bit startled. "Right now? It's getting dark out."

"Yes, I know. That's why right now. A man my

size creeps about better in the dark than he does in broad daylight." He gave his heftily built wife a look that was both measuring and appreciative at the same time. "So do you, for that matter."

After they left, Harry climbed the stairs. He didn't *quite* trudge the steps, but that was only because he felt he had to maintain a certain august demeanor as the commanding officer. Even if all he was going to be doing was the coolie work of cranking the pedals to fire up the blasted radio so Paul could get in touch with Amsterdam.

Luckily for him, they had a good window that evening and they got all the reports relayed sooner than usual. So, it was with light and airy steps that Harry came back down the stairs.

"Gentlemen!" Then, with a little bow to Sherrilyn: "And lady. I am pleased to announce that we've gotten in touch with Julie and Alex Mackay. Indirectly, at least—but it won't be necessary to use the Amsterdam relay any longer."

"They're *that* close to London?"

"No." Harry struggled to make his grin cheery instead of savage. "They're not 'close.' They're here." He pointed to the wall of the house that faced the west. "Apparently, they're taking in the theater tonight. Julie insisted she wanted to see the Globe Theater while she was in town. Seeing as how she probably wouldn't have the chance again."

"Harry," said Sherrilyn. "Stop grinning. You'll scare the children."

His grin widened. "Don't be silly. There aren't any kids here in the first place."

She covered her face in the peekaboo manner a child uses. "Fine. You're scaring *me.*"

"Me, too," said Felix.

Harry went alone, since he saw no reason for a large party. He spotted Julie and Alex Mackay as soon as they came out of the Globe. It wasn't hard, since they were almost the first ones out.

He angled across to intersect them. Alex spotted him coming before Julie did, and his hand moved down to the hilt of the sword at his waist. In the dark, of course, Harry would just look like any man.

"Psst!" he hissed. "Hey, lady!"

He opened one side of his Lee Van Cleef style coat. "Wanna see some feelthy pictures?"

The couple came to an abrupt half. There was silence, for a moment. Then Julie said: "Harry, you're a jackass."

"Hey, it worked, didn't it?"

On their way to the house where the crew was staying—the Mackays had rented quarters on the other side of the theater district—Julie was full of complaints.

"Jesus, that theater *stinks.* If that was Shakespeare, you can have it. The audience were pigs. And since when"—her voice got a bit shrill—"does Juliet get played by a *guy?*"

Alex cleared his throat. "I did try to warn you, love."

"I thought you were pulling my leg. Juliet—played by a *guy?* So was every so-called woman in the play—including the nun! Jesus! Why don't they just call it the Drag Queen Palace and quit pretending they're doing legitimate theater? It's disgusting!"

Thankfully, the skies were overcast and it was

quite dark. So Harry didn't think Julie could see his
smile. "Well, tell me. Did you find out the truth? Did
Balthazar have it right? Shakespeare wasn't actually
written by Shakespeare?"

"Who cares?" Julie hissed. "Whoever the hell wrote
that play, he was a fucking pervert. Juliet—played by
a *guy.*"

Once they arrived at the house, Julie quickly became
the center of attention. For a wonder, given the group
of men there, that wasn't because she was young and
pretty. Testosterone can work in mysterious ways.

"Did you bring *the rifle?*" Felix asked. He said
"the rifle" much the same way that a breathless child
speaks of a wondrous magic item.

"Sure," said Julie. She jerked her head over her
shoulders. "Got it hidden back at our place."

Harry thought for a moment that the guys were
almost going to say "ooh" and "aah." None of them
except Harry and Gerd had been there when Julie
carried out her now-legendary feats of marksmanship.
But by now they knew about them—down to every last
detail, in fact. They could be a little obsessive, that way.

"Where'd you learn to shoot like that?" asked Matija.

"My grandma, mostly. She was the best rifle shot in
the area in her day, too."

Donald looked skeptical. "One small town produced
two women who are great shots?"

Hurriedly, before Julie could get her dander up,
Harry intervened. "Hey, man, she's just telling it
just the way it is. Her grandmother was Anna Lou
Ballew, although I only knew her as Mrs. McQuade.
She was the national teenage rifle champion at Camp

Perry twice—first time when she was fourteen—and she qualified for the U.S. Olympic team." Harry gave Julie a sly smile. "They wouldn't let her go, of course, men being men in those days and her being a girl and all. But she was sure as hell good enough. She was appointed West Virginia athlete of the year, too. I can't remember which year."

"1940," said Julie. "First woman ever got the honor. And the only one who's ever done it in Marksmanship. She kept shooting on her company team until she retired, and she spent every summer traveling to Camp Perry for the nationals."

Julie paused, for a moment, her face scrunching up a little. "She's probably still doing it, in fact, wherever she is. She was still alive and in good health last time I saw her—and so was Grandpa. They were living in Florida by then, though, so they got left behind when the Ring of Fire hit us."

By now, Julie's initial ire had vanished. She even gave Harry an appreciative little nod. "Yup, that was my grandma. Anyway, she's the one who taught me. 'Course—not wanting to sound like I'm a braggart like Harry here—there was some natural talent involved. Mine, I mean."

Harry took her by the arm. "Come on, Julie. Let's go upstairs and I'll show you the shooting gallery."

Julie peered out the window in the corner room upstairs that was closest to the Tower, looking across the Thames. "Can't see a damn thing, in this light. What's the range?"

"Oh, hell, I was kidding. I didn't actually mean you'd be *shooting* from here."

"What's the *range*?" she asked again, very firmly.

He started to say *too far* but decided that was risky. With Julie, you never knew. She might insist on trying it, just to prove she could make the shot.

"Look, Julie, it doesn't matter. You might be able to make the shot—except it won't be 'the shot,' it's likely to be a lot of them. You *have* heard the term 'getaway,' haven't you? We're not exactly going to be nestled in the palm of our own army here, with the emperor himself looking over your shoulder, the way he was at the Alte Veste. Once it's done, we've gotta get out of here. Mucho pronto. And this house is hardly the best place to start from, taking it on the lam-wise."

She chewed her lip, for a moment. "Okay, that makes sense. Where do I set up, then? You *have* heard the term 'gun rest,' haven't you? Across this big a river, you can't make a good shot just standing up. Not me, not anybody."

"Relax, willya? Tomorrow we'll look around. We'll find something suitable."

Julie looked at Sherrilyn, who'd come up to the room with them. "Does this Great Commando Leader always plan his operations with such careful and deliberate precision?"

"Oh, hell no, girl. Usually Harry just wings it."

"You're ganging up on me," Harry complained.

"Sure we are," said Sherrilyn. "We're girls. You're a guy."

Julie patted her arm. "Still, we oughta ease up. At least Harry's a guy playing a guy. Now that I've seen the pervert ways of London, I figure that's gotta count for something."

❖   ❖   ❖

By the time they got back downstairs, Juliet and George Sutherland were back.

"Something *is* wrong," Juliet said. "Liz has three men staying with her."

"Ah . . ." Harry tried to find the right way to say it. This could get delicate.

"Oh, leave off!" snapped Juliet. "You and your nasty mind. Sure, in times past there might have been the odd fellow coming and going, of an evening. What was that, George?" The last question had been addressed rather sharply at her husband.

"Nothing, dearest. Just talking to myself. Thoughtless habit of mine, now and then."

What he'd actually murmured—Harry had heard it, quite clearly—was *several odd fellows, and at any time of day or night.* But he thought that remark was best left buried. Perhaps run a herd of horses back and forth across it too, to obliterate all traces, the way he'd heard the Mongols had made sure nobody could find the grave of Genghis Khan and dig him up.

Fortunately, Juliet seemed inclined to let it go. "As I was *saying*, while it's true that Liz was not exactly what you might call a proper lady, she'd never have had three strange men staying in her lodgings at once. And they look to be settled in, too."

"Especially one of them," added George. That got him another sharp look from his wife, but this one he didn't evade. "Dearest," he said, spreading his hands, "it's just a fact. You saw it as well as I did. Whoever those other two fellows were, she certainly wasn't unhappy with the presence of that one."

"How do you know?" asked Harry.

Juliet looked a bit embarrassed. George, however,

was pretty much a stranger to that sentiment. "How do you think? Once we found out where she was living—which wasn't hard, seeing as how it's the same place she was living when we left some years back—we crept up and peered through the window. The bedroom window, to be specific. Juliet, when you speak to Liz again, you should caution her that cheap curtains don't really provide much in the way of privacy. It would have helped if she and her unknown paramour had put out the lamps before they started—well, no need to get into the details."

Harry ran fingers through his hair. "All right, fine. So she's glad the one guy is there, and who knows why the other two are. But I can't see where any of this has anything to do with us. I mean, I didn't mind the two of you going out to set your minds at rest regarding your old friend—or not—but that was just because I thought we had plenty of time to kill. Now that Julie's here, we really oughta get rolling. You know. The Tower. *The Great Escape. Stalag 17. Von Ryan's Express.* That *is* why we're here, after all. Not to play Sherlock Holmes."

"Yes, of course," said George. He laid a hand on his wife's shoulder. "He is right, dearest."

Juliet looked very unhappy, but all she did was nod.

Harry offered to walk Julie and Alex back to their quarters. Insisted, in fact, after Alex told him it really wouldn't be necessary.

"I want to get a good look at the Globe. I barely had a chance, earlier, since Julie was in such an allfire hurry to get away from the place."

"Since when did you give a damn about high culture?" Julie demanded. She pronounced it *kult-cha*.

"Hey, I spent months with Giulio Mazarini. Rome, Paris, places like that. You wouldn't believe how much culture I got exposed to." He pronounced it the same way.

"Oh, bullshit! You were just checking out the red light districts, don't lie to me, Harry. And you'd be wasting your time at the Globe, for sure. Any whores hanging around there would most likely be guys pretending to be girls." The expression that now came to her face was one of Dawning Comprehension. Like Juliet Sutherland, Julie Mackay would never get any plaudits from devotees of method acting. "Unless . . ."

Neither was Harry, come down to it. His shrug exuded Shameful Confession.

"Yeah, I been corrupted." He hooked a thumb over his shoulder. "It's Sherrilyn's fault. She's been playing so hard to get lately that it's twisting me inside."

"Harry, you're a jackass," said Sherrilyn.

"Two women in one night," said Harry smugly. "Maybe there's hope for me yet."

Julie and Sherrilyn blew simultaneous raspberries.

"It's true," Harry insisted stoutly. "A real man measures his macho by the number of times women dump on him. That's why we only watch chick flicks under protest. Might screw up the readings on the wimp-o-meter."

Julie and Sherrilyn looked simultaneously cross-eyed, trying to follow the logic. "What the hell is a wimp-o-meter?" Julie demanded.

"You wouldn't understand. It's a guy thing."

Chapter 26

"She says she wants us to lock everything down, for the moment, until she can find out what's happening with Wentworth. Do nothing until she gives us the word." The expression on Paul Maczka's face was just as dubious as the tone of his voice. In some indefinable manner, so was the way he tossed the radio note onto the kitchen table.

"What the hell for?" demand Donald Ohde, sitting at the far end. "Who cares which minister they throw in the Tower this week? Give it a few days, and you'll see Wentworth out and Cork inside, staring at the walls." Irritably, he slapped the table. "You ask me, I think the woman's just losing her nerve."

Harry Lefferts wagged his fingers in a gesture of restraint. "Easy, Don, easy. I know Melissa Mailey; you don't. High school kids don't call her the Devil's Bitch for nothing. She is one tough old broad." A little reminiscent smile came to his face. "I always liked her myself, even if none of the other guys did. Even after she made me write *I will not be a smartass in front of a way smarter teacher* two hundred times on the blackboard. What the hell, I *had* been a smartass—and, more to the point here, she *is* smarter than me."

Ohde made a face. "Fine. I still say, so what? She can be the Devil's counselor as well as his bitch, what difference does it make? We're *commandos,* for Christ's sake, not monks in a cell. We don't meditate patiently, we break things."

Like all of Harry's unit, whatever seventeenth-century inhibitions against blasphemy Ohde had ever possessed, he'd long since cast aside.

Harry repeated the finger-wagging gesture. "I think she's got something in mind. And if I'm right . . ."

Slowly, a huge grin spread across his face. Amazingly huge, given that there was really not a trace of humor in the expression at all. "*Great Escape,* indeed. *Stalag 17,000. Von Ryan's* great big *long* freight train. Piss on '*Express.*'"

Ohde stared at him. So did everyone else gathered around the table. Maczka looked around for a vacant chair; finding none, he leaned back against a wall.

"Holy shit," he said. "Are you serious?"

"I told you. She is one tough broad—and don't ever let that prim and proper manner of hers fool you any. Underneath it all, she's got a temper like you wouldn't believe, even if she's the only person I ever knew who could chew you up one side and down the other in grammatically correct sentences and never use a single cuss word."

He glanced around the table. "Guys, we're talking about a sixty-year-old woman who's spent her whole life giving the finger to the establishment. And now that same establishment"—this time, he waved his whole hand, not just the fingers—"close enough, anyway, the

Devil's Bitch never saw much distinction between one establishment and another—just went and locked her up for over half a year."

The grin came back, though not as large and with some actual humor in it. "I don't remember it myself, 'cause I was just a little kid then. But she got herself tossed in jail during the big '78–'79 coal miners strike for heckling the cops too much. Soon as they let her out she went home just long enough to make up a picket sign and then—I mean, she didn't stop for a hamburger, nothing—she made a beeline right to the big police station in Fairmont and started up a one-woman picket line of her own. Sign read: *You're STILL assholes.*"

Everybody laughed. "I thought you said she never used cuss words," said Felix.

"Well . . . she never did, dealing with kids. Not even a 'damn.' But I guess she figured it was okay if she was picking on somebody bigger'n her."

"Did they arrest her again?"

"Naw. Truth is, the Fairmont cops weren't really bad guys. I think most of them thought it was pretty funny themselves. And what would be the point, anyway? They'd have to let her out sooner or later, and—given Melissa—who knows what she'd have come up with next?"

Smiling now, Ohde shook his head. "All right, I get the point. But do you really think she's seriously considering springing anybody but them?"

"Yup. I think she's mad enough she wants to get even as well as get out."

"Why not?" said George Sutherland heavily. "We were already planning to get Cromwell out. What's one more man?"

"Be more than that," his wife mused. "Wentworth's wife and kids are in the Tower, too. I can't imagine he'd leave without them."

Harry scratched his chin. "Good point." He stood up and waved at Paul, summoning him to follow. "Let's back up there and find out exactly how many people she's got in mind. I only figured on two boats. We might need another one."

The answer came back immediately. Paul didn't bother writing it down, with Harry at the receiver. He'd only written down the first one out of habit, anyway. At this close range, they were in direct verbal communication, not using Morse code.

"Don't know yet, Harry. From what we can tell, everything's up in the air. But we haven't been able to find out much, beyond the obvious fact that a coup d'etat *is in progress. The Warders aren't talking to us, but Darryl says Vicky's whole family is edgy. 'Tenser'n cats at a dog convention,' is the way he put it."*

Harry frowned. "Who's Vicky—and why's her family figure into this?"

"Oh. Forgot to tell you. Darryl got engaged. Vicky's his fiancée. Most of her family—men, that is—are members of the Yeoman Warders."

"You're shitting me!"

"Still cussing, huh? If there's a blackboard over there, write on it fifty times 'I will not use bad language in front of my ex-schoolteacher.' No, I'm not shitting you. Why is that a surprise, anyway? A lot of the men in the Tower are Warders."

"Not that! Darryl got *engaged?*"

"Sure did. Hey, we're in the seventeenth century,

Harry. Age of miracles. If Darryl were a statue, he'd probably be leaking tears of blood."

Blankly, Harry stared out the window. The Tower was quite visible in the bright winter sunlight. The weather had finally cleared up.

"We're talking about Darryl McCarthy, right? I mean, you didn't get something criss-crossed and wind up with a different Darryl?"

"Don't be silly. How many other Darryls did I ever have write on a blackboard three hundred times 'My name is Darryl McCarthy, not Redd Foxx'? And then make him correct his spelling because he kept dropping the extra d's and x's."

Harry chuckled. "All right, good point. He was pissed as hell about it. Didn't stop crabbing for two weeks afterward. Still. I had him figured for a lifelong righteous bachelor."

"Like you, I take it?"

Even though she couldn't see him, Harry twisted his face into something that was halfway between a grimace and a questioning expression.

"Not actually sure any more, Ms. Mailey. The seventeenth century makes a man think about things a lot more carefully. God, I love this time and place." A bit hurriedly, he added: "Not that I'm in any hurry to get married, y'all understand."

"You would love this time and place, you young rascal."

"Damn right I do. Back home I would've just been calculating how long I could stay in the mines before I started getting black lung and had to quit and go flip hamburgers for minimum wage. Get to look forward to retirement, sitting on a rocking chair on a beat-up old porch wheezing to my buddies about the good old days. Hell with that. This here's like being in Las Vegas—the old, real one I'm talking about—except the bouncers've got swords and guns and the cops use red hot tongs instead of handcuffs. Just makes the odds more of a thrill."

"God help us."

"He might have to—if we're supposed to spring Darryl's whole pack of new in-laws too. I mean, jeez, Ms. Mailey, I was figuring on a couple of little riverboats, not a cruise ship."

"I don't think it would be all of them. They're Yeoman Warders, don't forget. Just Vicky. In fact, I'm not even sure—hold on a minute, Harry. From the sounds outside, I think something's happening."

Paul had drifted to the window, as he listened to the conversation—Melissa's end of which he could hear clearly from the microphone.

"Something sure is happening," he said sharply. "Better come here and look at this, Harry."

Harry came over to the window. Unlike late twentieth-century cities, which didn't use wood for heating, London in the seventeenth century had very few trees. So he had an unimpeded view of the Tower across the Thames—and he'd picked this house to rent partly because it had a good view of the fortress' main entrance on its western side.

He pursed his lips, and then blew air through them slowly. "Oookay. Paul, I gotta bad feeling all our plans just flew south for the winter."

An army was marching up to the Tower. The lead elements were already beginning to pass through the Middle Tower and nearing Byward Tower. A small army, true enough. But Harry was pretty sure the guard force at the Tower had just gotten massive reinforcements. It certainly wasn't an attacking force—the gates of Byward Tower were swinging wide open to let them in.

These were professional soldiers, too, it was obvious even at the distance. Probably several of the mercenary companies the English crown had hired on when Charles threw in with the League of Ostend. As an actual guard force, Harry doubted if they were as good as the Yeoman Warders. But so what? A jailbreak had just turned into the prospect of a siege—with a handful of besiegers.

"Well, shit," he said.

"No, not in there," said Sir Francis Windebank. "I don't want Laud in communication with Wentworth. Even on separate floors, I don't want both of them in the Bloody Tower."

Stephen Hamilton, one of the captains of the Yeoman Guards, considered the problem, letting no sign of his fury show on his face. "Well, Sir Francis, that's a bit difficult—seeing as how you'll be needing the Lieutenant's Lodging and Beauchamp Tower for your officers, and you're wanting Wakefield Tower for yourself and your staff."

"And the White Tower for my men, yes, I know. How long will it take to clear that out, by the way?"

"Can I draw on the soldiers themselves for labor?" asked Hamilton, eyeing the huge central keep of the fortress. "It's mostly been used for storage for some thirty years, now. The inside's a jumble."

"I can't see why not," said Windebank impatiently.

"Yes, yes, the soldiers will complain, but that's a problem for their captains. They either clear it out or they can sleep in the open."

They'll be shitting in the open, either way, thought Hamilton. The White Tower was ancient, dating back to the time of William the Conqueror. Its sanitary facilities were scanty and primitive. Not the least of the reasons Stephen was so angry was that he knew the careful sanitary arrangements that the American nurse Rita Simpson had spent months overseeing were being shat upon along with the Warders. Give it a few weeks, with hundreds of new soldiers crammed into the Tower, and the diseases which had been mercifully almost absent the past months would come back with a vengeance.

But there was nothing he could do about it. Cork had replaced Strafford, and the earl from Ireland was determined to prove to anyone that his fist was even harder than that of his overthrown predecessor—and he'd not be bothering with gloves, thank you. Not dealing with such as the Yeoman Warders, at any rate, however gracious he might to English noblemen and wealthy merchants.

"It'll have to be the Salt Tower, then," said Hamilton. "It's not really fit for the archbishop, what with all the priests that were held there a time back—that many, they left it a mess and we've never had the funds to repair the damage—but it's the only space that remains." He set his jaw. "Unless you're prepared to place William Laud in one of the dungeons."

Sir Francis winced. For just an instant, the man's arrogant surface vanished and Hamilton got a glimpse of the fear and uncertainty that lurked beneath. He and Cork and their new ruling party were taking a fearsome gamble, here. That much was obvious to any simpleton urchin in London, much less a captain of the Yeoman Warders. Their authority was even less broadly based than Wentworth's had been. In the end, it rested on nothing more substantial than the support of King Charles, who was by all accounts now a cripple, half-out of his mind with grief over the death of his wife—and a monarch who was notorious in any event for being fickle and undependable.

The only reason their sudden coup had succeeded at all—this much was also evident to a Warder captain, if not to street urchins—was that Wentworth had amassed such a great pile of resentment against him on the part of England's upper classes. The earl of Strafford was without doubt a very capable man, but he tended to be oblivious to the personal reactions of people around him. He could and did give offense without even realizing it; often enough, without even meaning to. He was like a good blacksmith who understood every aspect of his trade—except the fact that he was trying to mold people instead of metal. Iron does not resent the strike of a hammer or the rough grip of tongs. People do, deeply.

"No, no, that's absurd," Windebank said hastily. "The archbishop of Canterbury, in a dungeon? Grotesque."

He didn't add "and most unwise as well," but that was clearly uppermost in his thinking. As well it should be. Let the king's favor turn, and Sir Francis Windebank might easily find himself in the Tower—and given the same accommodations his enemies had been given. A prisoner could survive decent lodgings in the Tower for a very long time. Kings had lived here,

in times past. Sir Walter Raleigh had lasted in the
Bloody Tower for thirteen years—and then had died,
not from ill health, but the ax-blade of the headsman.
Surviving one of the dungeons was a much different
proposition, especially for a sixty-year-old man like
Archbishop Laud. Or a man in his early fifties, like
Windebank, for that matter.

"Very well, Sir Francis, I'll see to the archbishop's
new quarters."

He turned to leave, but Windebank held him back
with a hand on the arm. "One last thing, Captain
Hamilton. In case I haven't made it clear enough.
Both Wentworth and Laud are to be well kept, and
in good comfort. But they're not to speak to anyone,
beyond the guards themselves. Is that understood?
No visitors of any kind, nor are they to be allowed
onto the grounds."

Hamilton nodded. Again, he had to fight down
an expression. Not a scowl of anger, this time, but a
sneer of contempt. Windebank's fear of allowing either
of the two new prisoners to have any outside contact
was itself a sign of the new regime's fragility. Beyond
that, it was a sign of the man's stupidity.

No, not outright stupidity, he thought, as he walked
away. Just that imitation of it that so many men fell
into, when they let their preoccupation with immediate tasks blind them to the world beyond.

Hamilton passed through the gate next to the Bloody
Tower that connected the Inner and Outer Wards.
Then he headed west down the Water Lane toward
the group of men alongside Bell Tower, who were
guarding the archbishop. Along the way, he passed
by St. Thomas' Tower, and gave it a glance.

Sheer stupidity it was, though, whatever its provenance. Sir Francis had given orders that no one was to be allowed contact with Wentworth and Laud—but had given no such orders regarding the people held prisoner in St. Thomas' Tower. Stephen Hamilton smiled, thinly. That was like a man ordering mastiffs muzzled as well as collared—while leaving bare the teeth of wolves.

And wolves they were, too, no matter how much the Warders might have come to like the beasts. Stephen Hamilton liked the Americans himself, for that matter, insofar as his cold soul had it in him to like anyone who was not of his own family. But he'd never once lost sight of the fact that he had wolves under guard.

He hadn't brought the matter to Windebank's attention, however. And now that he had a bit of time to think, Hamilton had to ask himself why he hadn't.

The answer didn't take long in coming. Nor did it surprise him. He'd given the matter some thought already, from time to time. He'd had no difficulty understanding the nature of those prisoners in St. Thomas' Tower, for the good and simple reason that he was at least half wolf himself. Not even that, really, since his wife died. He was simply a wolf who'd chosen to wear a watchdog's uniform, for the well-being of his family.

Treat me like a cur, would they?

After he finished seeing to the archbishop being placed in the Salt Tower, Hamilton returned to his own quarters. He shared rooms in the Lieutenant's Lodging with the rest of his family. Quarters which had been quite spacious, until today.

The first persons he encountered when he entered were Patricia Hayes and Victoria Short. As was true of all the members of Stephen's family, they were in-laws, not blood relations. The Warder captain had no surviving kin of his own, only those whom his wife Jane had given him before she died in childbirth. The infant had died with her, leaving Hamilton bereft of children as well as spouse.

Patricia was his wife's sister. She was a widow, now, her husband having been killed in a horsefall a few years since. Victoria and her older brother Andrew were the children of his wife's long-deceased half brother.

Both women were carrying bundles of bedding. "They're driving us out!" Patricia said angrily. "We're losing two of our rooms!"

"Better than most, at that," Stephen said. "Some of the Warders with no officers in the family are being forced out of the Lodging altogether. They'll have to find a shack out on the grounds against the wall. Or make one, more likely."

"What's happening?" asked Victoria plaintively.

Hamilton now had his anger completely under control. Iced down, it would be better to say. "The earl of Cork feels that leaving his new prisoners in the care of Yeoman Warders might be risky. It seems—this will come as a surprise to everyone, of course, including ghosts—that there might be some questions concerning our loyalties. So he's brought in three companies of mercenaries to see to the Tower's security."

"That's idiotic!" snapped Patricia.

So it was. The Yeoman Warders of the Tower answered to the king of England, whoever he might be and whatever they thought of him. No business of theirs, which ministers came and went at the king's favor. Lock one up; let another go; theirs was simply to see to it that the locks were sound.

"As it may be," was all he said, however. "Victoria, I need to speak to you. In the kitchen, as soon as you've put away that bedding."

She looked at him, blankly. "Just me?"

He considered the matter for a moment. "Is Andrew about?"

"He's next door, helping the Hardwicks," said Patricia. "Poor people. They're being forced into a single room—even losing their kitchen."

"Get him too, then." Hamilton headed for the kitchen, not waiting to see if the women would obey. He had no doubt they would. Although he was no blood relation to anyone in his family, over the years he'd come to be what amounted to their patriarch. Partly because he was the oldest, being now into his forties. Partly because . . .

He was who he was. He never bit. He never snarled. He never needed to.

Victoria came into the kitchen with her brother Andrew just behind her.

"Sit, girl." Hamilton pointed to the chair across from his at the small work table in a corner. "I've a question."

"What is it?" she asked uncertainly, pulling out the chair. There being no other in the room, her brother just stood to one side, his arms crossed over his chest.

"Your swain, the McCarthy lad. He hasn't come through the window, has he?"

She was startled. Then, flushing, she started to glance nervously over her shoulder, toward her brother.

"Well . . ."

"I want the truth, Victoria. Whatever it is. I won't care—and neither will Andrew. You're betrothed, now, so what does it matter?"

After a moment, she swallowed. "No. He hasn't."

"It's upset you."

Her nervousness at being asked such questions in the presence of her brother suddenly vanished, replaced by simple hurt. Her green eyes seemed a bit watery. "Yes. It makes me wonder . . ."

Hamilton chuckled. He glanced at Andrew and saw that the girl's brother was trying to suppress a smile.

"Oh, I shouldn't worry about *that,* Victoria," Hamilton said. "Whatever Darryl's reasons, lack of ardency is hardly the answer."

The look she gave him belonged more on the face of an eight-year-old girl, than one who'd just passed her twentieth birthday. "You're certain, Uncle?"

He had to suppress a smile himself, now. Victoria's brother wasn't bothering to do so, any longer, since he'd sidled over a bit and was now standing behind his sister where she couldn't see him. Stephen and Andrew had made jokes to each other, often enough, about the way Darryl McCarthy looked at Victoria when he thought no one was observing. Jokes about tongues hanging down to belt buckles and enough drool to drown an ox.

"Oh, yes, I'm quite certain."

"Then, why—"

Suddenly, she gave him a hard look. Almost an angry one.

"It's because he's afraid of you," she pronounced. "It's your fault. Uncle, you shouldn't scare people that much."

Hamilton knew that wasn't the reason either. Darryl McCarthy was wary of him, true enough. All men were, once they got to know Stephen Hamilton—if they had the sort of background that enabled them to gauge him in the first place.

That same background, however, was the key. Hamilton had always understood Darryl McCarthy, from the first day the young man had spent some hours in their quarters. Not too different from Hamilton himself, really—or from Andrew, rather. A tough young man from a tough background, who wasn't a fool but wasn't afraid of men, either.

Hamilton had understood McCarthy, yes—but he'd still underestimated him, and badly. So much was now clear.

"No, I don't think that's it," he said calmly. "I think the reason he hasn't come through the window is simply because he's afraid of getting you pregnant."

She almost crossed her eyes. "But—but—"

Her confusion was understandable. Once a couple was betrothed, the girl's family relaxed. By law and custom both, a betrothal was as good as wedding vows. Young couples often had to postpone the marriage, sometimes for years, until they could put together what they needed to set up their own household. It would be stupid, not to mention cruel, to force them into unnatural abstinence in the meantime. If the girl got pregnant, so be it. She'd hardly be the first one to waddle up to the altar. Likely enough, her mother and half her sisters and aunts had done the same.

But it was time to end this, before the girl's suspicions became aroused. Hamilton shook his head. "No, it's simply that I think the Americans have different customs."

He gave Andrew a quick, meaningful glance.

"I'm sure that's the reason, too," her brother said reassuringly. "I inquired with Lady Mailey, you know. They were a wealthy enough people that they got married quite young. Not like us. So they'd wait—were supposed to, at least, and Darryl's a good lad—until they were actually married."

That was twaddle, of course. Not the generalities—Hamilton had inquired himself, not from Lady Mailey but Captain Simpson—but its application to Darryl. Simpson hadn't come right out and labeled McCarthy a tomcat, but he'd said enough in the way of warning that Hamilton had made sure the girl was watched carefully until McCarthy finally betrothed her. Ironically, his only concern thereafter had been that the American might view his betrothal casually. Hamilton knew their customs were different there, also.

Ironic, indeed, in light of what he now understood.

"You really think that's all it is?" Victoria asked. She seemed aggrieved and mollified at the same time.

"Oh, yes. But now I need to talk privately with Andrew, Victoria."

She rose from the table and left immediately. More slowly, Andrew came over and took the chair she'd vacated.

He started to say something, but then, seeing the distant expression on the Warder captain's face, he fell silent.

✧   ✧   ✧

Stephen Hamilton was distant, indeed, for a time. Not dwelling on his past—it was not one he liked to think about, except for those few years after he met Jane—but simply letting its essence saturate him. He'd passed through a hell that had left nothing much of the tough young man from a tough background who'd begun the journey. Just a cold, hard predator who'd luckily managed to find a pack of his own. That was now his only lifeline to humanity.

And even that was conditional. Stephen Hamilton would accept duty, well enough. Not because he cared about leashes but simply because he found a certain personal comfort in restraints. That comfort removed, his view of the world was very stark and very simple.

There were two sorts of people. Two, and only two.

His, and everyone else.

"Good God!" Andrew suddenly exclaimed, pulling Hamilton back into the kitchen. From the look on the Warder's face, he'd finally worked his way through the puzzle.

"He's planning an escape, Stephen. *That's* why he's afraid to get Victoria pregnant."

Hamilton shook his head. "Not exactly. Yes to the second, no to the first. Yes, that why he's restrained himself. But, no, he's not planning an escape. He's *expecting* one."

Andrew's head turned, in the direction of St. Thomas' Tower. Hamilton had no difficulty following his thoughts. Who knew what devices the Americans had with them? Wentworth had never ordered a search of their quarters. Who knew if they'd been able to stay in touch with their people back on the continent? And if they had, who knew what might be coming to the Tower? Stephen and Andrew had not only heard the accounts, they'd spoken to veterans returned from the continent. Yes, it was true that Wallenstein had been struck down from a range that was not known for certain—but it was certainly longer than the Thames was wide.

"What do you want to do?" asked Andrew. He gave his older kin a look that was quite hard itself.

"Can't see where it's any of our business, any longer," said Hamilton. "Seeing as how our superiors have not seen fit to trust us."

Andrew nodded. "The way I see it too." His gaze went back to the wall of the kitchen that faced St. Thomas' Tower and, after a moment, softened a great deal.

"This speaks well of my future brother-in-law, I'm thinking."

Hamilton could feel the latch closing, and knew that he'd come to his decision. Somewhere in that bleak and savage wasteland within the Warder captain that other men would call a soul, a young American had just completed a journey. He'd passed over from *one of them* to *one of mine.*

"Oh, yes," said Hamilton softly. "It speaks very well of him indeed."

Chapter 27

Amiens
Picardy, France

March 1634

After stomping into the office that Robert du Barry and Yves Thibault maintained for their new arms manufactory, shrugging out of his winter coat and hanging it on a peg, Henri de la Tour d'Auvergne glared at his two subordinates. Or glared in their direction, at least.

"The Vicomte de Turenne seems in a foul mood today," said du Barry. The French cavalry office's tone of voice was mild.

His civilian gunsmith partner looked up from the sketches on the table. "Must be the local Picards pissed him off again, the way they butcher the French language. Or maybe he just doesn't like every building made out of dark red brick."

"Including ours."

"Very witty," growled the twenty-two-year-old French marshal, brushing a bit of snow from his trousers and

wiping his boots on a mat. "I wasn't actually thinking of you at all—though if you maintain this stupid
badinage, I may yet."

"God forbid." Du Barry pointed to the sketch. "Well,
come here, then. This should cheer you up, Henri."

His expression lightening, Turenne came over to the
table. "Do you really think you can get it to work?"

Thibault laughed. Du Barry grinned. "Better yet."
He jerked a thumb at the gunmaker. "Yves has one
already made. And, yes, it certainly does work."

Hearing that, Turenne simply glanced at the sketch.
"Show me the gun itself, then. I'm a soldier, blast it,
not an artist—of which the French army has sufficient
as it is." His scowl returned. "All of them loudly assuring Cardinal Richelieu that they are about to unveil
a military masterpiece, in two months."

Du Barry lifted an eyebrow but asked for no clarifi-
cation. It was a mark of his young commander's anger
that Turenne had said anything at all on the subject
of his clashes with the French military establishment,
in the presence of a civilian. He'd give Robert the
details later, in private.

Thibault was already heading for the door into
the workshops. "This way. Since I knew you'd be
arriving today or tomorrow, I have it set up in the
firing range."

Five minutes later, after handling the new gun
without firing it, Turenne shook his head.

"I owe you an apology, Yves. I take back every
sarcastic remark I ever made on the subject of breechloaders and gunsmiths who can't control their obsession
with the things."

Thibault smiled, then shook his own head. "You would probably have been right, if Servien's spies in Grantville hadn't found enough of a diagram of this mechanism for me to work from. I confess I was thinking only in terms of those wonderful modern American breechloaders. That would have been . . . not impossible, no, to make in small numbers. But—"

He hurried forward to cut off Turenne's certain interruption. "Yes, yes, Henri, I know! You told me once, you told me a thousand times. Better to have weapons that are good enough in numbers an army can use, than to have a few splendid ones that will only wind up hanging on the wall for a general to admire."

Turenne grinned at him, his mood obviously lightening. "My motto, indeed." He hefted the rifle. "And . . ."

Thibault wiggled his hand back and forth. "I can't possibly make enough of these—not in time for this spring's campaign, certainly—to arm every soldier of France. But I can have enough ready by the end of May to equip your force for what you need."

"Not soon enough, Yves. Things are getting darker by the day. How many can you have ready by . . . let's say, the end of April."

The gunmaker scratched his chin. Then he took a few steps to the entrance of the firing range and looked out at the big workshop beyond, in which dozens of workmen were plying their trade.

"Let's see . . ." he murmured. "If I take Francois off . . ."

Turenne turned away. From experience, he knew that Thibault would take several minutes in his muttering cogitations before he'd provide him with an answer. Might as well take the time to test the gun himself, while he waited.

He held up the rifle again, looking at du Barry. "Have you fired it, Robert?"

"Oh, yes. It's not complicated at all." He extended his hands and Turenne gave him the weapon.

"This lever here. It looks like a large trigger guard—which it is also—but it's actually what works the mechanism." He lowered the trigger guard and pulled it forward. "See how this block slides, opening the breech for loading? It's called the drop block."

Turenne leaned forward. "And the block is solid enough to withstand the powder charge?"

"More than solid enough." He closed the lever, showing how the block moved back into position, then reopened it. "There's some leakage, you understand? No way to eliminate all the backflash. The breech will wear and leak more over time, too, but it is adjustable with this screw here. That's the only adjustment on the whole rifle, so the shooters shouldn't be able to fuck it up too badly. Still, the soldiers will complain about it, so be prepared."

Turenne grunted. "Troops always complain. But they'll be so delighted at the prospect of being able to reload without standing—or reload in the saddle without dropping everything half the time—that I don't imagine the complaints will be more than what's needed to maintain soldierly self-respect."

"What I figure also. And there's this added advantage." He pointed to the face of the breechblock. "The rifle is a single-shot, you understand. Still needs to be reloaded each time it's fired. But we can used prepared cartridges—no need for messy and clumsy powder flasks—and you see this edged blade here? It will cut the linen cartridge and expose the powder, all at the same time, which makes everything very quick. All you have to do—"

He broke off while he demonstrated the steps by which the rifle was to be loaded, ending with: "And now you simply place the percussion cap on the nipple—like . . . so—and all that's left is to cock the hammer and pull the trigger."

He extended the weapon to his superior. "Go on, try it."

Turenne fit the stock against his shoulder, cocked the hammer, and took aim at the post some twenty yards down the range. "Anything I should know?"

"Prepare to have a bruised shoulder, if you fire it enough."

Turenne frowned. "I thought it was only a half-inch bore."

"It is. What the Americans would call a .50 caliber. But it's a .50 caliber *carbine,* Henri. You wanted a light gun, short enough for cavalrymen to handle easily. There isn't much weight there to absorb the recoil."

"So I did—and so it is. I forgot—well, to be honest, I didn't really expect Yves could have it done in time."

He pulled the trigger, not trying for more than an indifferent aim. Then, lowered the rifle and gave it a very respectful look. "Sure enough, it kicks like a mule."

"Something else to keep the troops happy, in their grousing. But they'll love it, they surely will. This is a real cavalryman's weapon. The first gun you could properly call that in history, I think."

"Yes, it is." Seeing that Thibault had finally concluded his self-deliberations, Turenne placed the rifle back on the bench.

"I can have two thousand ready by then, Marshal. No more, I'm afraid. But training is very important if the rifle is to be used properly. So I will have twenty guns ready in two weeks, so your sergeants and officers can start learning how to use it soon enough to train the rest."

Turenne pursed his lips, while he did his own much quicker calculations. "Two thousand should be enough, I think. It means I can arm almost half—well, no need to get into the details. Intending no offense, Yves, but the enemy has spies too."

"None of my business," the gunmaker agreed pleasantly. "And now, I'll take your leave and give Francois his new marching orders."

After he was gone, du Barry turned to Turenne. "Are you sure—"

"Robert, please! I know you want to accompany the expedition, but that's just foolish. I have enough good cavalry commanders. This—right here—is where you're indispensable. Without you to serve as my watchdog, these maniacal gunsmiths would have gone in twenty different directions. You know it as well as I do. We need a real soldier in command here."

Du Barry took a breath, and blew it out loudly. "Well, so be it. Are you still planning the same campaign?"

"Basically, yes." Turenne looked back at the rifle. "But with these . . . I think I can add a nice extra touch. Send perhaps a third of the force to threaten Hesse-Kassel while I press on to the target with the rest. I'd keep all the breechloaders—what name have you picked for them, by the way?—for the main force, since they'd make up for the fewer numbers, and the diversionary force wouldn't actually need to engage in any real fighting."

Smiling slyly—and perhaps a but ruefully—du Barry ran fingers through his hair. "Well, that's a problem, there. What to name the rifle, I mean. It depends on whether you'd prefer to taunt the enemy or instill pride in our own. If the former, then why not just call it a Sharps rifle? Let the damned Americans grind their teeth, that we have their own famous historical rifle and they have nothing but muskets."

Turenne chuckled. "Well . . . it's tempting. But not altogether wise, I think. Besides, it's not even really true. Yes, we got the design of the gun from our spies, but the key is the percussion caps. Which—"

Here, his chest swelled with genuine pride. "Resulted entirely from the genius of France."

Turenne was not a puffed-up peacock by nature, however. So, a second or two later, his chest deflated and a similar smile came to his face. Half-sly; half-rueful. "I grant you, the genius consisted mostly in hiring a German alchemy wizard, who did the actual work."

"John Rudolph Glauber." Du Barry shook his head. "It's amazing, in a way, that he could see what not even the up-timers could. They decided to abandon any quick attempt to develop percussion caps because they could only think of using fulminate of mercury." He grimaced. "Which is, indeed, very nasty stuff. We lost three men here, ourselves—and twice that many, maimed or badly injured—before Glauber came up with his alternative of using potassium chlorate, as he calls it."

Turenne shrugged. "Not so amazing as all that, Robert. The Americans are no different from anyone else. Once people get a notion firmly fixed in their heads, they usually become blind to any alternative." His early scowl started coming back. "I could show you a much worse example—not that I'd subject you to the misery—at any collection of generals back in Paris."

"They haven't budged at all?"

"Not an inch. I'm afraid I'm partly to blame for that. They're none too smart at the best of times, but this degree of mule-headedness is unusual even in their circles."

"They resent you, Henri, it's as simple as that." Du Barry clapped Turenne on the shoulder. By now, at least in private, their relationship was as much that of two friends as commanding and subordinate officer. "You're half the age of most of them, and already a marshal."

Turenne grunted softly. "Yes. I often think the cardinal made a mistake, promoting me so quickly."

"That's crap. Pure crap. I *know* those generals in Paris. And why are they still in Paris to begin with, dining in palaces—when their soldiers are shivering in trenches around Luebeck? I served under them, for more years than I want to remember, not being a sprig like you. De la Valette is probably the worst of the lot, but none of them are any prizes. It's been too long since France fought a real war, that's all, unless you count that butchery in Mantua. The officers have gotten rotten and the men are mostly undisciplined. And what good young officers do show up, like Jean de Gassion, have been coming into your service. No fools, they."

"Yes, I know. It means I have as good a cavalry force as probably any in the world—but that's still only five thousand men. Even if every last man in the ranks was armed with one of these"—he pointed to the rifle—"five thousand men simply can't withstand what's coming in the spring."

"That bad?"

"I think so, yes," said Turenne gloomily. "Fucking idiots. All they hear from the spies—all they listen to, rather—is 'volunteer regiments.' So they assure the cardinal that the Swede will be bringing nothing but a poorly trained rabble into the field. All the *rest* of what the spies tell them, they simply ignore. Have no illusions, Robert. Say what else you will about him, Gustavus Adolphus is one of the great captains of the day. He didn't sit in Luebeck for months waiting for Torstensson to present him with a shiny new army, if he thought it would collapse at the first trial of arms."

He threw up his hands. "But what does Gustavus Adolphus know? A barbarous Norseman, is he not? We shall forget that he's probably fought and won more battles—and bigger ones—than all of today's French generals put together."

The firing range was filled with a grim silence, for a moment. Then du Barry sighed and said: "So we'll be depending even more heavily on Bernhard of Saxe-Weimar and his mercenaries than ever. At least you can always count on that shithead to fight. He can move troops quickly, too. Enough that he could come up in time from Alsace, even with his fifteen thousand strong army."

Turenne made a face. "I'm not so sure about that, any longer, I'm afraid."

Robert cocked his head. "You know something?"

"I don't *know* anything. Neither does the cardinal, I don't believe. Servien told him that getting spies into Bernhard's inner circles had proven impossible, so far. I just have a bad feeling about that whole situation. Mostly"—here he smiled, thinly—"because I've noticed that Bernhard hasn't been bragging as incessantly as usual, the past two months."

"Ah." Du Barry swiveled his head and studied the target at the other end of the range. The thick wooden post was getting pretty badly shredded, by now. "Yes, that is a bad sign."

Two hours later, as Turenne was putting his coat and hat on for the long trip back to Paris, du Barry reminded him of an overlooked detail.

"The name of the rifle. You still haven't decided."

Turenne finished buttoning his coat, while he thought about it. Then, with a smile: "Let's call it the Cardinal."

Besançon,
The Franche-Comté

From Saint Etienne, a high plateau that opened onto the Jura massif and overlooked the ancient town of Besançon, Bernhard of Saxe-Weimar studied the Doubs. The river made a great loop below, which enclosed the town on three sides—more like eighty percent of its circumference, actually. The town itself was situated inside the loop, with a fortress protecting the neck and the beginnings of fortifications on the two hills which flanked it.

Only the beginnings yet, at Besançon. Bernhard's official military headquarters were much farther to the northeast, at the Abbey of St. Peter and Paul at Schwarzach on the Rhine. Though by nature a very thrifty man, Bernhard had spent a great deal of money to acquire his own copies of the *Encyclopedia Brittanica* brought by the Americans through the Ring of Fire. He'd chosen that location, to the discomfiture of the Benedictine monks residing there, on the basis of his careful reading of some of Louis XIV's Rhineland campaigns in the 1680s. That world would now not happen, of course, but the logic of the choice of location remained. Schwarzach had a convenient set of large buildings and was not far from what had once become Fort Louis. What was now becoming Fort . . . Whatever, since it didn't have a name yet. But construction was well advanced.

However, Bernhard and his handful of intimate advisers—*Das Kloster*, they called themselves since they had settled at Schwarzach, "the cloister," only half-joking—had agreed that to do more to fortify Besançon at this point would create too much suspicion. Bernhard's civil administrative headquarters were already in the town's Hotel de Ville, true enough. Cardinal Richelieu had agreed that an army the size of Bernhard's needed a civil administration to support it, or the mercenary soldiers would start looting the inhabitants they were supposed to protect. But no one really expected any military action in Besançon, or anywhere near it. Why would any army come here? The town was prosperous but not wealthy, and it was tucked against the mountains. It was certainly not the most inaccessible place in Europe, but the terrain was difficult enough to deter any of the casual plundering expeditions that the war had spilled around itself like a dog shedding water.

"Any chance the cardinal will increase your commission, Your Grace?" asked Friedrich Kanoffski von Langendorff.

Bernhard turned his head to glance back at the Bohemian mercenary officer who was perhaps the most trusted adviser he had in the Cloister. "No," he said firmly, shaking his head. "I don't dare even ask any more. Richelieu's the canniest fox of the lot, you know. I think he's already starting to ask himself questions. We'll simply have to settle with our existing commission. Ten thousand foot and six thousand cavalry. Less than we'd like, of course, but we can live with it for the moment."

Kanoffski wasn't surprised. The closer they came to the spring, and what everyone expected to be a volcanic resumption of hostilities in the field against the Swede and his Germans, the more insistently Richelieu was calling on Bernhard to move his army farther north. Saxe-Weimar had been able to forestall him so far, pointing out quite reasonably that he had to keep an eye on the Swedish general Horn's forces in Swabia. Since that was, indeed, the specific task for which the cardinal had employed Bernhard and his mercenary army—and one which Bernhard had carried out quite satisfactorily for the past two years, keeping one of the Swede's most capable generals and his army pinned to the southwest and away from the main theater of the war—Richelieu had accepted the excuse. Thus far.

But Richelieu's intendants ran a very extensive

and capable network of spies. They had no one in or near Bernhard's inner circles, the Cloister was quite certain of that, but they were hardly deaf or blind. By now, if nothing else, Richelieu would be wondering why Bernhard was keeping so many of his troops this far into the Franche-Comté instead of closer to the Rhine.

"Yes, we can live with it, Your Grace," Kanoffski said, "but let me take this occasion to make clear that I am a most unhappy soldier. More precisely, a most unhappy payroll officer."

A little smile came to Saxe-Weimar's face. "Don't tell me. You're going to desert."

They both chuckled, softly. Kanoffski could remember a time when the same remark would have triggered off one of Bernhard's rages, instead of a jest. The man was as notorious for abusing his officers as he was for his arrogance toward almost everyone. Kanoffski had gotten his share of that, in the beginning, and still got some today, from time to time. But he'd found that once Bernhard of Saxe-Weimar did let someone into his confidence, he could be as charming and witty—and generous—as he normally was not at all.

Granted, he was still not an easy man to work for, as a close subordinate. But Kanoffski was thick-skinned by temperament, and had had plenty of experience as a mercenary officer since he left Bohemia. He'd served under commanders every bit as arrogant and harsh as Bernhard—some, more so—but who had not one-tenth of the Saxe-Weimar duke's intelligence and ability. Bernhard was frugal without being stupidly stingy; he was a truly excellent administrator; bold in battle and shrewd on campaign. Overall, in Kanoffski's estimate, one of the very best commanders in all of Europe.

He was even, in his own way, a pious man. His ordinances for the conduct of chaplains in his mercenary army demonstrated both his concern for the spiritual well-being of his soldiery—and his usual canny sense of the abuses to which chaplains were prone. Well, not abuses, precisely. "Limitations" might be a better word. The ordinances made plain that although the chaplains, like Bernhard himself, were all Lutheran, they were to avoid doctrinal fine points in their sermons and stick to the basics, as the duke saw them. "Lead us not into temptation and deliver us from evil" worked well, right along with, "Thou shalt not take the name of the Lord thy God in vain." The duke disapproved of blasphemy. That might be the only thing he had in common with his brother Ernst. Plus, they made it clear that any chaplain who wanted to collect his pay was going to provide spiritual consolation to every man in the regiment, no matter what his own official religion might be. Catholic or Calvinist, sectarian or heretic, a dying soldier was to be given words of comfort.

Kanoffski didn't think it was even hard to understand Bernhard's sometimes outrageous behavior. He was the youngest of four brothers. Four living brothers. Six other sons of his parents had died as infants or children, or been killed in the war—or, in one case, gone mad and committed suicide. That didn't count the one, William's twin, who had been stillborn. All four of the surviving brothers had inherited the duchy of Saxe-Weimar, and Bernhard quite obviously nursed a certain sense of grievance at not having gotten his just due. As the youngest of the four, he could never realistically expect enough of an income from the inheritance to live on it in the manner of a *Hochadel*.

So, from the moment he became his own agent as an adult, his consuming passion was to find a place for himself in the world, one that suited his sense of his own stature. Which was perhaps grandiose, but certainly not absurd. In Kanoffski's estimate—being in many ways, not so different a man himself—it was that ambition as much as any admiration for Gustav Adolf or commitment to the Protestant cause that had led Bernhard to seek his fame and fortune as a soldier under the Swedish king's banner.

But that lurking sense of grievance had exploded when Gustav Adolf, for all practical purposes, handed over Saxe-Weimar's lands to the American upstarts. The fact that Bernhard had not really lost very much from the decision, in cold-bloodedly calculated material terms, simply didn't matter. What mattered was that a man trying to gain in stature had just had what little he started with cut out from under him. The fact that the three older brothers had acquiesced in the outrage, arguing political and military necessity, had simply incensed Bernhard further.

He'd given his oath of allegiance to Gustav Adolf— and the treacherous Swede had repaid him with a stab in the back. And an insult, to rub salt into the wound. Not directly to the duke's face, of course, but various people—several of them—had made it their business to ensure that he heard what the king had said to Oxenstierna at Mainz. In the hearing of others.

No, no, no. In this, the dukes of Saxe-Weimar are

proving to be as petty as any German noblemen. In their absence—protracted absence, let me remind you—the people of their principality have seen fit to organize themselves to survive the winter and the depredations of the war. What were they supposed to do, Axel? Starve quietly, lest the tranquility of the dukes be disturbed?

As if the reason for their "protracted absence" had not been that they were serving in the king's own army! As if they had been luxuriating at some mineral hot springs rather than fighting in his campaigns!

Kanoffski had heard it often enough. From Bernhard's point of view, the common perception that *he* had "betrayed" Gustav Adolf stood reality on its head. The truth was the other way around. He'd simply repaid the Swede's infidelity with its just reward.

They were quite a quartet, those brothers, Friedrich mused. Saxe-Weimar had never been a very important principality in Germany, even before the Americans overran it with their rebellion. Yet, even though dispossessed from what little they'd had, at least three of the four brothers looked to be emerging as major players in the great game of the continent, almost entirely due to their own capabilities. They were an exception—not the only exception, to be sure, but perhaps the most startling one—from the usual run of German princelings, whose pretensions were generally in inverse proportion to their measly land-holdings and still measlier talents.

The day might even come when the oldest of the brothers, Wilhelm, faced the youngest across the field of battle. Not as two generals, but as two heads of state.

Who could say, any longer? The war that had begun

at the White Mountain in Bohemia fifteen years earlier had steadily pulled more and more of Europe into its maelstrom. And then God had thrown the Ring of Fire into the very center of it. For what purpose, neither Friedrich nor Bernhard had any idea at all.

But to what *effect*?—oh, to that question, they had found an answer, with Bernhard leading the way.

When the youngest duke of Saxe-Weimar broke his oath to Gustav Adolf, he also broke all his ties to established custom. Whether you viewed him as a traitor or—as Bernhard did himself—the one betrayed, the end result was the same. He was now a man on his own, with no limit to his ambition and no restraints beyond whatever objective reality might pose.

In their smaller and less ambitious ways, all of the Cloister shared the same view. They were new men, in a new world.

Altogether a new world, even if most of Europe's powerful and mighty persisted in closing their eyes to the reality. Bernhard and his intimates thought most of the American prattle about equality and liberty was just that—prattle—but they'd all come to accept what they saw as the heart of the thing. Which Bernhard himself, something of a patron of the arts like all the Saxe-Weimars, said he'd found best expressed in an up-time book of poetry he'd run across in Grantville. A line penned by an English poet of the future.

A man's reach should exceed his grasp, or what's a Heaven for?

So, *Das Kloster*. As Bernhard had put it to them, in what Friedrich had whimsically come to think of as their own—very different—version of a constitutional convention, held four months earlier at Schwarzach:

"If Wallenstein can do it, why can't we?"

That really meant *me,* not "we," since Bernhard was not proposing any sort of constitutional monarchy, much less a republic. But none of the seven officers in the room had objected to that aspect of the matter. That there would be a first among equals—and quite a long ways first, at that—was a given. They remained monarchists, at bottom; they'd simply shed the false and illusory notions concerning so-called legitimacy with which the powers-that-be cloaked themselves. Legitimacy, to a new man with eyes to see, was simply what you made of it. Nothing more—and nothing less.

Friedrich Kanoffski had been the first to speak. Verbally if not in writing—of course not in writing, since they weren't fools—putting down what the Americans would call his John Hancock.

"Wallenstein is Bohemian, you know. So am I."

That brought a circle of grins. They probably should have called it the Wolfpack rather than the Cloister.

Bernhard turned away from the view below. "I think it would be prudent for the time being, Friedrich, for me to take quite a few companies into the Breisgau. Put the cardinal's mind at rest. Send Caldenbach and Ohm, maybe Rosen as well, toward Mainz. All three of those units can move very fast when they need to."

"Yes, your Grace. Anything else?"

Bernhard looked down at the ground beneath his boots. "Here," he said, stamping his foot on Saint Etienne, "We'll put the big fortress here. Tell Bodendorf to have his military architect start working on the plans while I'm away."

Chapter 28

Magdeburg

"I'd recommend we include Nils Krak's men, too," said Frank Jackson. "They're all dragoons as well as sharpshooters, and with their rifled muskets they should give the Thuringian Rifles whatever extra support they might need. We can only send one squad of the Rifles with the combat team."

John Chandler Simpson was half-amused and half-irritated at Jackson's stubborn insistence on using the up-time phrase "combat team" to refer to the special combined arms force they'd be sending as an escort for the ironclads as they made their way downriver to Hamburg. They'd all agreed that sending the ironclads without a land escort would be foolish. As powerful as the war machines were, there were just too many ways in the narrow confines of a river for the enemy to set traps. It could be something as simple as obstructions in the river bed that required the ironclads' accompanying service craft to pause for a bit, while the crews removed the obstacle—easy targets for snipers firing from the river banks. In much the same way that a main battle tank working its way through the narrow streets of a city needed infantry support, so long as they were on the river the ironclads did as well.

The problem—tiny, tiny problem—was that the down-timers had no fixed terminology to use for most such military purposes, just as they tended to use terms like "lieutenant" and "captain" in a very loose and fluid manner. That didn't bother Simpson much, but it drove a former sergeant like Frank Jackson half-crazy. So, once he got on Torstensson's staff, Jackson had insisted on developing precise terminology.

The Swedish general had been willing enough to accommodate him, in principle. But, alas for Jackson, Torstensson insisted on picking the actual terms. And after Simpson had casually mentioned that the sort of combined arms land force they were putting together, as a temporary unit for a specific task, had a different term in the up-time German tradition than the American "combat team" appellation Jackson proposed, Torstensson had chosen it instead. He thought it sounded better.

So, "battle group" it was to be—but Jackson wouldn't budge from using combat team instead. Granted, no one who knew the man could accuse Frank Jackson of being xenophobic, especially after they met his Vietnamese wife Diane. But in many ways, the former coal miner's American chauvinism was so unthinking and deeply ingrained that it was impossible to uproot. In that respect, he was very unlike his long-time close friend and former union associate Mike Stearns, who was generally quite cosmopolitan.

Fortunately, the Swedish general whom Gustav Adolf had placed in overall command of the USE's military seemed more amused than anything else by his American adjutant's recalcitrance.

"Of the two other squads," Jackson continued, "one of them is in Luebeck and I'm assuming"—he cocked his head toward General Torstensson—"that you'll want to keep the third squad in reserve, for whatever you might need them for."

"Whatever Gustav Adolf might need them for," Torstensson grunted. He smiled thinly. "Or are you foolish enough to think the king will let me remain in command after he's broken the siege?"

Admiral Simpson half-scowled. "He certainly *should*."

The young Swedish general shrugged. "Yes, perhaps. But there is not much chance of it, John, as you well know. I *will* do my best to restrain him from personally leading any cavalry charges. Even there, I can make no promises."

Simpson was tempted to pursue the matter, but it would be pointless. For good or ill—and it was sheer irresponsibility on his part, as far as John was concerned—Gustav Adolf was one of those monarchs who insisted on leading his men on the battlefield. Perhaps the only such monarch left, in this day and age, although there were several princes who'd do the same. Quite capably, in some cases, as the Spanish cardinal-infante had so graphically demonstrated in the Low Countries over the past six months.

He decided he'd do better to save whatever few bargaining points he had left—he'd already used up most of them, he figured—to try to get Colonel Christopher Fey's force beefed up a little.

"Frank," he said, clearing his throat, "please don't take this as any sort of implied criticism of either Krak's people or the Thuringian Rifles. But the fact remains that I don't think they're enough, by themselves."

Jackson frowned. "They *aren't* by themselves. I'm assigning two volley gun batteries to the combat team."

"Yes, I know. But that's still not enough, if they run into a large cavalry force that's willing to accept some casualties. Don't forget that the only unit that'll have repeating breechloaders will be the one Thuringian Rifles squad commanded by Sergeant Wilson. That's not more than—what?—a dozen men?"

"Ten men and two women, to be precise," said Jackson. His expression made it clear that he wasn't too happy about the last part of that equation.

Neither was Simpson, for that matter. On this subject, if not many others, he and Frank Jackson were generally in agreement. Fortunately, it was not a problem Simpson had to deal with much himself. Since the navy had been formed later than the army and drew most of its personnel from the Magdeburg area, John had been able to resist—sidestep, at least—letting any women into the combat units. The pressure for that had come almost entirely from up-time women in Grantville, and had naturally focused on the army and the air force.

Out of the corner of his eye, he could see Colonel Wood smiling a little. There was just a hint of derision in that expression. Oddly, given that he was such a dinosaur in so many other ways, Jesse Wood didn't seem to have any reservations about including females in combat positions in the air force.

The smile was a bit irritating, but Simpson didn't rise to it. He was certain that if Wood had to command people who'd spend months at sea together instead of a few hours in a plane, he'd change his tune quickly enough. John's reservations about having women in combat units didn't stem from the same simple paternalistic traditionalism—call it male chauvinism, if you insisted—that lay behind Jackson's opposition. Nor did it result from Simpson's assessment of the martial capabilities of women. Except for units—mostly infantry—whose job required a considerable degree of muscular strength, he thought women were just as capable of killing as men were. More capable, in some instances. If he'd had any doubts, all he had to do was examine Julie Sims' track record.

No, the problem was that they got *pregnant*. Something that couldn't be managed without incredible acrobatics in the two-seat cockpit of a small airplane could be managed quite easily on a ship. And a state of pregnancy that posed nothing more than a minor nuisance on an army or air force base could be a real headache on a ship that couldn't return to port for months on end. True, that wasn't a problem he'd face in his ironclads, since the things were only marginally seaworthy. But Simpson was already looking ahead to the next generation of warships for the USE Navy. Those ships would be faster than any sailing ship of the time, but they would still wind up spending a year or more away from their home ports. Months at a time, at sea.

One of Torstensson's colonels spoke up. Bryan Thorpe, that was, one of the many mercenaries from the British Isles who served under Swedish colors. A bit unusually, an Englishman instead of a Scotsman.

"Frank, that will not be enough," he said, "if they run into real opposition." He spread his hands in a vaguely apologetic gesture. "Unfortunately, we do not have time to put the matter to a test in field exercises. But I can assure you that if they run into a regiment of good cavalry they are likely to get ripped to pieces unless they have some units who can defend them."

Jackson was starting to get exasperated. Enough so that he lapsed into the sort of casual blasphemy that Americans took for granted but rubbed seventeenth-century people the wrong way. "For God's sake, Bryan! We're only talking about an expedition from here to Hamburg—almost all of it in our own territory. Where the hell is a whole regiment of enemy cavalry going to come from in the first place?"

Perhaps because the blasphemy annoyed him—he was something of a Puritan—Thorpe's rejoinder was even sharper in its tone. "Where would they come from? I have no idea, General Jackson. The enemy is not in the habit of confiding his plans to me. That's why he's called the *enemy*, you understand?"

Torstensson intervened, to keep the issue from escalating into an outright quarrel. "I have to say I agree with Bryan, Frank," he said mildly. "USE 'territory' is a bland phrase, you know. Very mushy, like oatmeal. Let us be more precise. We are not talking about the vastnesses of the Russian forests or the great steppes. We are talking about a stretch of land between here and Hamburg that is not more than two hundred and fifty miles following the river. None of which beyond the bend of the Elbe is patrolled by anything other than local militias, except in the vicinity of Lauenburg and Dömitz. And those are garrison troops, not likely to react swiftly and sally out to deal with a passing cavalry raid."

He raised his voice a little, overriding Jackson's beginning of a protest. "*More to the point*, as the ironclads and their accompanying land escort approach Hamburg, they are not more than fifty miles from the French and Danish lines around Luebeck—and the emperor's forces are hemmed in the city, on the *other* side of those lines. They certainly won't be available to come to the admiral's rescue, will they?"

Fortunately, Jackson had enough sense to yield the point, seeing that the army's top commander had come down on the other side. Simpson was sure that Frank's opposition hadn't been all that deeply rooted, anyway. He had no specific objections, he was simply reacting automatically. Guarding his pieces against the plundering damn squids.

Still, when he wanted to be, the man could be more mulish than a mule. "Fine. But I don't see how you expect pikemen to keep up with dragoons. They're certainly not going to be able to handle those eighteen-foot spears on horseback. Assuming they could ride a horse in the first place, which a good half of them can't."

Torstensson took a deep breath, settling his temper. "Frank, please do not be more pigheaded than necessary, would you? We have hardly any pike units left in the USE's army, in any event. Obviously I do not propose to send pikemen. We will simply use . . ." He turned his head and cocked an eye at Thorpe. "Bryan?"

Thorpe was the adjutant Torstensson generally used for such matters. What, in the U.S. Army back up-time would have been called the G-1, assistant chief of staff, personnel. The English colonel mused for a moment, then said:

"Mavrinac's company, I think. Erik has them trained to serve as dragoons, if need be. They won't ride as well as the Thuringians and Krak's people, but well enough to keep up with the ironclads. We've already agreed that the volley guns can't make better than thirty miles a day. Mavrinac and his men can certainly manage that. We'll have to provide them with the horses, though. They won't have enough of their own, not for a company of two hundred men."

Torstensson nodded and looked around at the other officers in the conference room. "Gentlemen? Any further objections or considerations you wish to raise?"

Frank was still looking skeptical, but didn't say anything. For his part, Simpson went over the matter in his head, to see if he agreed with Thorpe's assessment.

He didn't know the unit in question, and to the best of his recollection had never met the commanding officer. But Thorpe wouldn't have picked a green unit, and by now most of the volunteer regiments had gone through enough training that just about any of their companies could handle the relatively straightforward task of forming a line or square to defend against a cavalry charge. Two hundred well-disciplined men armed with rifled muskets and bayonets would provide enough of a shield for the volley guns and the sharpshooters to defeat any cavalry force no bigger than a regiment. The likelihood of encountering anything larger than that was remote.

John was more concerned about the ability of Mavrinac's company to keep up on the march, actually, than he was with their fighting capabilities. The problem was their horsemanship, not their marksmanship. Strip away Thorpe's politesse and the gist of what he'd said was that Mavrinac's men were half-assed dragoons. Men who could ride a horse, but most of them not particularly well.

He looked out of the window onto the training ground below. From the second story vantage point, he could see one of the volley gun batteries going through some exercises. Quite nicely, so much was obvious even at a distance. But most of the men in those batteries had been selected, in part, because they were experienced riders.

John brought his gaze back into the conference room, still gauging. He'd only reluctantly agreed to the thirty-mile-a-day estimate in the first place. Unless they had mechanical trouble, he thought his ironclads would manage quite a bit better than that, at least forty and perhaps fifty miles in a day. He hadn't pressed the point too far, however, because he'd also been confident that the volley guns could match whatever his ironclads would do. Certainly the Thuringians and Krak's men could. They were officially dragoons, but all of them were excellent horsemen. As good if not better than most cavalry units.

After a moment, he decided Mavrinac's people could probably manage well enough. The Elbe was flanked by roads all the way down to Hamburg, so it wasn't a matter of riding cross-country. And the whole force simply wasn't big enough to pose the usual problem of a march, which was simply that no one road could possibly handle a sizeable army. More often than not, the real problem wasn't the ability of the grunts to stay on their feet or in the saddle. It was the ability of their officers to coordinate a march that required using multiple roads.

That simply wouldn't be an issue here. John did the arithmetic quickly. Two hundred dragoons added to a dozen Thuringians and Krak's three dozen sharpshooters, then figure two heavy weapons batteries with a total of . . .

He searched his memory, and found the figures easily. That briefing had been recent. There were six volley guns in a battery, and each gun was served by a three-man crew. The crews themselves handled the six horses who drew the limber. They'd ride the three near horses unless one or more of the horses fell by the wayside, at which point some of them would either walk or ride the limber. Add an ammunition wagon for each battery, each with two men, and a battery wagon carrying the repair equipment and gear needed for the whole force. Another two men. Add a sergeant in command of each battery and a captain and a lieutenant in command of the whole unit . . .

Forty-six men. Added to the others, a total force of about three hundred. Even with all of them on horseback, the roads along the river were sufficient to handle the traffic without having to break up into separate columns, which was where the grief usually came in.

Unless they ran into a lot of mud. And things *would* get muddy, the farther they got into April. Leaving at the beginning of the month, the way they were, they were catching the spring flood just as it started really rolling. Within a week . . . on the other hand, the roads were mostly at least fifty yards from the river itself, usually farther . . .

"Admiral?" Torstensson's voice snapped John out of his brown study. He saw that everyone was peering at him. A bit embarrassed, he realized that they'd all been waiting for him to finish whatever he was pondering over.

He still had some reservations, but none of them were really that severe. And, in any event, he was pretty sure he'd just used up all his bargaining leverage. Torstensson was looking a bit impatient.

"Yes, fine," he said. "That should do nicely."

"Excellent," said the Swedish commander. "Now I propose to move on to the issue of refueling. John tells me that there is now sufficient diesel stocked at Lauenberg to provide enough fuel to get the ironclads through Hamburg—patience, patience, Bryan, I'll get to the political situation in a moment—and well into the Frisian islands. But that still leaves the problem of bringing enough diesel down the river so that the ironclads can get the *rest* of the way." He smiled around the room. "Which is essential, of course. I've seen the Frisian islands. I wouldn't wish my worst enemy stranded on those miserable things, much less our splendid navy."

That got a little laugh.

They spent a few minutes resolving the fuel issue. That really didn't take long, because the key problem was the political one of getting passage through Hamburg, not supplying the ironclads once they did.

Torstensson cleared his throat. "Now. As for the politics involved—"

That seemed to take forever. John was puzzled by the fact that Torstensson was giving such a detailed recitation of the political situation involving Hamburg. There was nothing new in what he was saying. It was almost as if he were deliberately using up the time left for the meeting.

The gist of the problem was quite simple, and could be easily summarized in two or three short paragraphs.

There was no way to get the ironclads into the North Sea except by using the Elbe, and Hamburg stood astride the Elbe and Hamburg was an independent imperial city. Alas, the Hamburg authorities were still dancing about, unwilling to make any commitment. They wouldn't say yes; they wouldn't say no.

Alas again, with the emperor locked in Luebeck, there was no real possibility of bringing military pressure to bear. Needless to say, once the emperor broke out and began his counterattack, his ability to snarl at the Hamburgers would escalate with incredible speed—and he snarled very nicely, thank you. But the delay involved would be enough to scramble the timing needed to get the ironclads in place for the breakout itself.

It was all very tangled. A thorny problem, indeed.

Jackson and Thorpe began to speak simultaneously, but Torstensson raised his hand. "Gentlemen, please." He consulted his up-time wristwatch. "I'm afraid I used up too much time. Admiral Simpson still has a great deal of work ahead of him, if the ironclads are to—slip their moorings, I believe is the correct nautical expression?—the day after tomorrow."

"At dawn, day after tomorrow," Simpson half-growled.

"Yes. And most of the rest of you will need what's left of the afternoon to get Mayrinac and his men ready to go. And all the rest of the preparations. So let's not waste any more time."

He shrugged heavily "And a waste of time is what it would be. We've thrashed out the mess in Hamburg half a dozen times already. In the end, it's a political problem, not a military one. That'll be the emperor's business—and decision—not ours."

Torstensson clapped his hands on his knees. "So that's it, then. Let's all get about our business. Admiral, I'd appreciate it if you would remain behind."

The cue being obvious, everyone else rose and filed out of the conference room. When they were gone, and the door had closed behind the last officer to leave, Torstensson rose and went over to the same window John had looked through before.

"The situation in Hamburg hasn't changed a bit in months, John. And we can't postpone deciding on a policy any longer. So—it *is* his decision to make—I had a long radio exchange on the matter with the emperor last night. As it happens, he's been reading a history of the United States—the one you used to have, I mean, the one up-time—in his spare moments. He instructed me to tell you one thing and ask you two questions."

"Yes, sir?"

"What he wanted me to tell you is that he is prepared to make the decision himself. But, for a variety of reasons, would much prefer it if he did not have to. The diplomatic repercussions, you understand."

Simpson nodded. "Yes, I understand. And the questions were?"

"The first question. Are you familiar with the history of your country? Especially its military history."

Simpson nodded again. "Fairly well, to the first. Very well, to the second."

"Good. The emperor told me that you needed to

be able to answer 'yes' to that question, or the next one would be meaningless."

By now, John was intrigued. It was quite unlike Gustav Adolf to play games like this. The fact that he was doing so made it clear just how severe the "diplomatic repercussions" might be. He was not a man to shilly-shally and dance around a subject.

"And that question?"

Torstensson turned his head to look John. "The question makes no sense at all to me. But it's quite simple. The emperor wanted me to ask you if you were willing to take Florida for him?"

After a couple of seconds, Simpson began laughing softly. He even slipped into informality. "I have to tell you, Lennart, that's *got* to be the first time anyone ever compared me to that no-good class-baiting rabble-rousing bank-busting son of a bitch. But, yes. You can tell Gustav Adolf that I will be his Andy Jackson. I'll give him Florida on a plate, and if he needs to he can wash his hands of the whole thing and swear up and down he had no idea I was going to do it. Of course, just like Monroe did, he'll keep Florida. A *fait accompli* is what it is."

"Oh, splendid. No, no, please!" Torstensson held up both hands, and then brought them together as if in prayer. "Do not explain the specifics."

"I wasn't about to. You might very well be called upon to do some public hand-washing yourself."

"So I might. It's shocking, really, the sort of outrages that headstrong subordinate officers can commit when they take it upon themselves to act on their own initiative instead of remaining within the limits of sober official policy."

He lowered his hands and then gave Simpson a quick, stiff nod. Not quite a bow, but close.

"Should I not have the chance again, John, let me say that it has been a great pleasure to work with you."

Simpson rose and returned the nod. "Thank you, sir. One favor, though."

"Yes?"

"Whatever happens, please don't tell my wife about this conversation. My opinion of Andy Jackson is pallid compared to Mary's. On this subject, her blood runs as blue as the Danube is supposed to and doesn't."

"Ah. This Andy Jackson fellow was not favored by proper folk, I take it?"

"To put it mildly."

Quizzically, Torstensson cocked his head. "Yet . . . your own opinion of him is not so severe. Why is that?"

Simpson smiled. "The son of a bitch got us Florida, didn't he?"

Chapter 29

Thorsten hadn't hesitated in front of the door to the settlement house since the first time he'd visited, back in January. In the two months since then, he'd come to see Caroline Platzer every time he'd been able to get leave from the army's training camp outside the city. Six times, now, all told. Half of which he'd been able to spend a full day in her company; none of them, less than three hours. His friends in the volley gun batteries had taken to ribbing him mercilessly about it, with Eric Krenz leading the charge. Complete with every conceivable variation of a joke on the subject of brainless moths being drawn helplessly, with no willpower of their own, into the scorching flames of a lamp or a fire.

All that, Thorsten had ignored with no difficulty. To hell with them. He hadn't let the opinions of others deter him from pursuing a goal since, at the age of seven, he'd let one of his more timid cousins persuade him not to swipe an apple from the orchard of a neighboring village that everyone knew produced the best apples in the area.

Twenty years later, almost, and Thorsten could

still taste what that apple probably would have tasted like. The very next day, he'd made a solemn vow to himself, in the way small boys will, that whatever else happened in his life he would not find himself on his deathbed passing into the afterworld with a cart-load's worth of regrets. He'd added a great many curlicues to that vow since, with the increase of wisdom that the years brought and a better recognition of what was realistically possible and what wasn't—but he'd never relinquished the heart of it.

Nowadays, of course, he could pass up a stolen apple without a second thought. But that was just a piddly fruit. Figuratively speaking, Caroline Platzer was the biggest and juiciest apple he'd ever seen in his life. Bigger and juicier than he'd ever *imagined* in his life.

Still, he hesitated. Not because the step he was about to take was irrevocable, but from a much deeper worry. Irrevocable steps came quite easily to Thorsten Engler. He was not in any way a man prone to indecision—nor was he a man who'd second-guess himself once he did make a decision.

The problem was far simpler, and perhaps intractable. Would the blasted Americaness *understand* what he was doing?

He'd wracked his brains for a month over the problem. He'd gone so far as to ask the advice and opinions of Eric and the rest of his soldier friends—and gotten nothing in return except more stupid jokes. He'd even gotten up the nerve to ask Gunther Achterhof, who, when the mood took him, could be the most savagely caustic humorist in the world.

❖   ❖   ❖

Alas, while Gunther had been sympathetic, he'd been no help either.

"Sorry, Thorsten, I've got no idea. I'm afraid"—here the vulpine grin—"my relations with the Americans, although close in many respects, have never extended into this little area. What the up-timers would call a 'minefield,' by the way. They also talk about 'walking on eggshells.' What the first means—"

"I *know* what a minefield is," Thorsten growled. "We're starting to train on laying them as well as digging them out. The up-timers didn't even invent them, although—damn complicated people; too gnarly-brained to understand, half the time—I'll grant you they developed some fiendish elaborations. And why would any sane person be walking on eggshells to begin with? Stupid. Waste of good eggs, trampling them into the dirt—not to mention the pain of cleaning your shoes afterward. Crack them and put them in a pan. Only Americans would even think of such a silly expression."

"Oh, my. Disgruntled, aren't we?"

"I don't know what to *do,*" Thurston said, between gritted teeth. "I'm certain she likes me. As a man, too, not just . . . you know. A friend. I'm certain of that, by now. But—but—"

"Yes, I understand. Where do you go from here? I take it you've gotten no indication from the lady herself?"

"*Who knows?*" Thorsten threw up his hands with exasperation. Fortunately, he remembered to relinquish the tightly gripped full mug of beer before he did so, or he'd have flung the contents onto the men at the next table. That would have produced a fight as well as waste of good beer. The fight, Thorsten wouldn't have minded at all, the mood he was in. But he was saving up all the money he possibly could from his sergeant's salary, and he could ill afford to throw away the beer.

"Who *knows*," he repeated, hissing a statement rather than a question. He took a draught from the beer. "Gunther, for all I know she might have been giving me signals every five minutes of every hour I've spent with her—and that's a lot of hours by now. But if she has, they're Americaness signals—and from three and a half centuries in the future, to make it still worse. Who can tell what she wants me to do? Or not do."

"Why don't you just ask her?"

Thorsten glared at him. Not because the proposal was insane—he'd considered it himself, at least a hundred times—but because . . .

He couldn't. It was as simple as that.

Could. Not.

Achterhof understood, of course. "Can't, ha? Well, no, I suppose not. Even for me, the way they sometimes come right out and blurt things in the open makes me feel like I'm dealing with village idiots." He slapped his chest. "We're proper Germans, after all. And you, a farmer, to make it still worse."

Silence followed. Then Achterhof drained his beer. "Another?"

"No." Thorsten held up his own. "All I can afford, for today."

Gunther studied him for a moment, then chuckled. "Yes, I can see that. Not for Thorsten Engler to settle for a good pair of socks."

Thorsten *had* considered a good pair of socks, in fact. It hadn't taken him two seconds to discard the idea as preposterous. For a German village woman, maybe. For an Americaness from the future, who knew how the different parts of the brain worked? God only knows what she'd think.

"Oh, I'll buy you one. But just one! Not that I'm stingy, Thorsten, but you clearly need to keep your wits about you."

They finished the next round of beers more or less in silence. Chatting a bit about the weather, that's all. When Achterhof finished his beer, Thorsten followed his lead. He suspected the CoC organizer was probably good for another round, regardless of what he said, but Thorsten didn't like to impose. Besides, the bastard was right. He *did* need to keep his wits about him. The few that the damn woman had left him.

He rose. Achterhof looked up at him, and shrugged. "You'll just have to do it like an impetuous cavalry charge, that's all. And hope you don't suffer the all-too-common result."

And now, it was time for the charge—and Thorsten was hesitating again.

Fortunately—or not—Caroline emerged from the door. Smiling the way only she could.

"You haven't done this in ages! What's the matter, Thorsten?"

Before he could think of an answer, there was some sort of commotion behind her. Caroline turned her head.

"Oh, God, she's impossible sometimes!" She began to hurry back in, but paused quickly to wave an invitation at Thorsten to follow.

A bit hesitantly, he followed—and found himself,

once he entered the big outer room of the settlement house, looking at a small girl in very expensive clothing standing at bay, surrounded by four women in clothing that was just barely less expensive. Put together, at a guess, there was enough valuable finery there to set up a butcher shop.

Caroline was in the midst of it, looking like a plain sparrow among peacocks—except she was taller than any of them and, leaving aside her utilitarian working clothes, much better looking.

Much better for Thorsten, at least. But even an observer as judiciously impartial as Solomon would have allowed him half of that. Three-quarters, more likely, since Solomon had been male himself with a reputation for having an eye for women.

"Kristina, you *can't;* it's as simple as that." Unlike the others, who were trying to use the advantage of their height to overawe the child, Caroline had squatted—she did that *so* easily, with her athletic figure, and the end result had the usual effect on Thorsten—to bring her eyes level with the girl. "Your father would have a fit if he found out."

"So don't tell him. He's in Luebeck. And he does it himself! All the time!"

One of the other women—all down-timers, Thorsten now recognized—tried to intervene.

"Be still, girl! Your father is the *king,* and you are not. And there's an end to it."

Thorsten had none of Caroline's psychological expertise, much less Maureen Grady's, but no villager he knew—certainly no village woman—would be so obtuse as to think that such an obviously headstrong child could be reined in with a mere admonition. In a situation like this, you either reasoned with a child or simply beat them into obedience.

In a village, of course, the second option would already be in play by now, nine times out of ten. Thorsten wasn't sure, however, if the same rules applied to royalty. He'd had even less contact with such than he'd had with Americans.

The girl's reply led him to believe the rules were otherwise.

"Will be someday!" came her very spirited response. She seemed as unabashed as a small wolf being chastised by large lambs. She even—Thorsten almost laughed—shook her finger in the face of the woman who had admonished her. As high up as she could reach, at least. She wasn't more than seven years old, eight at the most. The finger was actually being shaken at the woman's midriff.

"And you watch what happens to you then! I've got a good memory!"

The woman seemed to flinch, a bit. But Caroline's response was quite different. She took the girl's finger-shaking hand and brought it down. Then, spoke to her quietly but very sternly.

"That is *enough*, Kristina. And don't you *ever* let me hear you threaten someone again." When the girl—by now, Thorsten had deduced this must be the famous daughter of Gustav Adolf—avoided Caroline's eyes, the Americaness seized her cheeks with her other hand and forced her to look at her.

"Look at me. You can't do that, Kristina. It's not fair, it's not right—and it's bad for you too. You know it is, and you know why. We've talked about it, plenty of times. Haven't we?"

Kristina was trying to glare at Caroline now. Not . . . very successfully.

"Haven't we?"

By now, Caroline's grip on the girl's face had loosened into something closer to a caress than the initial vise.

"Yes," said the princess, in the half-whine of a child agreeing—very grudgingly—to an adult's wisdom.

"And why is that?"

Thorsten glanced at the four down-time women. Noblewomen, he assumed, assigned to watch over the princess. Fortunately, this time, they seemed far more inclined to let the much younger American woman handle the situation. In fact, they seemed downright relieved. There were also two soldiers standing against the very far wall. The princess' bodyguards, those would be. From the expressions on their faces, it was quite obvious they intended to continue their splendid imitation of wooden soldiers, too.

He looked back at Caroline and the princess. The girl was looking away again, trying evade the question. But Caroline didn't repeat the stern cheek-grabbing maneuver. Instead, she lowered her hand from the girl's face altogether, and shifted it to her left shoulder. That was definitely a caress, now.

"And why is that?" she repeated. Softly, gently, not in the same stern tone she'd used earlier.

Kristina wiped her nose. "Because all the studies show that kids"—the English term slid easily, in and out of the German—"who are mean to animals grow up to be nasty people. Monsters, some of them."

"And?"

The nose got wiped again, more vigorously. "And it's much too easy for a kid whose father has a lot of power, and will herself someday, to start thinking of people as animals. Which is even worse."

That seemed to open the floodgates. Every trace of the royal fled from Kristina's face, leaving only the greatly distressed child. She flung herself into Caroline's arms, sobbing in the unrestrained and chaotic way that a seven-year-old will.

"But I'm such a good rider, Caroline! I can do it! I know I can!"

"Yes, dear, I know. You're a wonderful horsewoman. Everyone says that, and I don't doubt it. Even if—"

Sudden shrieks of laughter burst through the sobs. "You! You can't hardly tell a horse from a cow!"

They were both laughing, now. Thorsten, on the other hand, almost felt like crying from despair. The biggest apple he'd ever seen in his life had just gotten so big he could barely see the edges. He'd wondered, often, what sort of mother she would make.

To his surprise, Caroline suddenly turned her head and gave him a strange look. A very considering one, it seemed, as if she were gauging something.

What? His clothes? But he was just wearing the same uniform he always wore. He managed to keep himself from raising his hand to stroke his own cheeks. Silly, that. He *knew* he'd shaved this morning. He'd checked several times. Eric had made jokes about that too.

Caroline looked back at the noblewomen, giving them a subtle but unmistakable glance. *Leave, please. I'll handle this.*

Not being fools, they obeyed, sidling quickly toward a distant corner of the room.

Caroline rose and took the princess by the hand. "Come here, Kristina. I want you to meet a . . . good friend of mine. He can explain to you better than I can. He's a sergeant in the new volley gun batteries. Almost a cavalryman himself."

That perked up the girl's interest immediately. Thorsten had the sense of a very bright child who was interested in a great many things. No dullard, for sure. Hardly surprising, of course, given her sire.

Before Thorsten quite understood what was happening, Caroline had ushered him and the princess into the office nearby that she used for consultations. She even closed the door behind her, which she'd never done the times Thorsten had visited her alone.

"Please sit, Thorsten. You too, Kristina." Both obeyed, and Caroline went around behind her desk and took her own seat. "Thorsten, the princess—"

"What's that big package you've got?" Kristina demanded, staring at the large cloth-wrapped bundle Thorsten had awkwardly perched on his knees.

"Ah . . ."

"Kristina!" Caroline half-barked, half-laughed. "Can't you keep your attention focused on one thing for one minute?"

The girl looked at her a bit guiltily. With that inimitable smile on her face, Caroline shook her head and pointed to the closed door. "Wasn't but a minute ago you were throwing a fit, remember? Forget Thorsten's package, whatever it is. Ask him to tell you why you can't participate in the army's field maneuvers."

Lightning-quick, all thoughts of anything else left the girl's mind. She looked at Thorsten, with a half-pleading and half-eager expression on her face.

"I can *really* ride a horse! Really, really, really. Ask anybody!"

Thorsten stared at her. How in the name of all that was holy had a mere obsession with a most-likely-unobtainable woman led him to *this* state of affairs? If Krenz ever found out about it, he'd be teasing Thorsten all the way into the grave. Maybe beyond, who could say?

Not knowing what else to do, he fell back on his sturdy village background. Forget that she was the daughter of Gustav Adolf, king of Sweden and emperor of the United States of Europe, perhaps the premier captain of the day. Thorsten couldn't begin to deal with that.

What he *could* deal with, however—had, in fact, many times—was explaining to an overly confident child why it wasn't a good idea for them to try helping with the heavy farm work. No sensible farmer would beat his boys for pressing him on such a matter. The heart of it, in fact, was something he needed to encourage. So, it was a time for calm explanations. Not talking down to the boy—avoid that at all costs—but simply taking him into your confidence and trying to get the child to look at the problem from the standpoint of what would best help the farm.

That wasn't so bad, he discovered. True, he was dealing with a girl instead of a boy, but so what? The phenomenon that Americans called a "tomboy" was hardly unknown in German villages.

"—and that's really the biggest problem, Your Highness. It's not riding the horses, it's—"

"Call me Kristina!" she commanded. "I like you. I'll tell my father to make you a count or something. At least an officer."

"Ah . . ." Best to ignore that altogether, he decided.

The girl really did seem extremely intelligent, but she was only seven years old. Still too young, even for someone raised in a royal court, to be able to follow the tricky issues involved in whether or not the emperor of the USE—but technically only the captain-general in Magdeburg province, as he was in Thuringia, not the king of Sweden—could override the normal procedures for advancement in the very prickly and often radical regiments. Technically, he could, of course. But it would be very unwise, with a few possible exceptions—and this was certainly not one of them. Thorsten could just imagine the reaction of his fellow soldiers if he got promoted because he'd ingratiated himself to a child princess. Not even Krenz would be friendly about it.

"Kristina, then. What I was saying is that the real problem is that handling the guns in action has to be done very, very carefully. What everyone will be worrying about is hurting your own people. The American term—we've adopted it—is 'friendly fire.' It's a really big problem in a battle, you know. Lots of times as many men get hurt or even killed by their own as they do by the enemy. Not as bad, it's true, on training maneuvers, but you still have to be very careful."

"I won't get in the way! And I certainly won't get thrown. I'm a *really* wonderful rider!"

"Yes, but . . . you're not understanding me. No, it's probably that I'm not explaining it well. The problem isn't so much what you might do, it's that the men will all be *worrying* about you. They won't be able to concentrate on what they should be concentrating on, because all of them—trust me, please, because I certainly would—will be devoting half their attention to looking around to see where the princess is. Kristina, please. It is *so* easy for a man to hurt or kill himself—or his buddies—when you're dealing with firearms. Any kind of firearms, much less the kind we work with."

There was silence, for a moment. Then, deflating like a little balloon, Kristina said: "Oh."

Then, a bit later, in a very small voice. "I wouldn't want that to happen. I'd feel really bad about that."

She looked up at Caroline. "This is part of not being mean to people, isn't it?"

Caroline gave her a gentle smile, not the gleaming one. "Not exactly. There's nothing mean involved here. But, yes, it's the same principle. You have to be careful, Kristina. Being a princess has disadvantages as well as advantages; it's just the way it is. It's much easier for you to hurt someone, even when you don't mean to. So you have to learn to be more careful than most girls your age need to be. I know it's upsetting, sometimes. But—"

She held up and waved that same humorously-scolding finger that Thorsten remembered so vividly from his first encounter with her. "Don't complain. If you weren't a princess, you'd never have gotten your own horse by now. Certainly not the one you got." The finger was now pointed at Thorsten. "Ask him. He comes from a farm family."

In that lightning-interest way she had, Kristina was now peering at him. "Really? Where is your family's estate?"

"Ah . . . it was destroyed in the war, I'm afraid." His innate honesty made him add: "But it was a very small estate."

Not *that* honest, but . . . He pressed forward. "At this age, you'd maybe be riding a pony. But probably not. Probably one of the really old horses, that aren't able to do much work any longer."

"Oh." She made a little face. "That doesn't sound like fun."

Thorsten almost blurted out: *To the contrary, the farm girls love it. What is it about girls and horses anyway? They're just dumb beasts, and they'll break your foot in an instant.*

But he said nothing. After a moment, the girl's eyes got fixed on the bundle again.

"What's in the package? You *still* haven't told me!"

"Ah . . ."

Fortunately, Caroline diverted her again.

Excruciatingly, Thorsten couldn't tell if that was because she'd already guessed what was probably in it.

He squirmed inside that Iron Maiden for five minutes, until Caroline finally shepherded Kristina out of the room and back into the clutches of the four down-time ladies.

Then she came back and returned to her desk, smiling.

"All right, Thorsten, I'm curious myself. What *is* in that bundle?"

He rose, unfolded the cloth, and laid the contents on her desk. "I would like you to take these. From me."

He had no idea what to do next. In his growing panic, all he could think of was to race to the rear.

"But I must be off, Caroline. We're leaving tomorrow morning—very, very early, the admiral insists—on our expedition."

Out the door he went. Not quite running.

❖   ❖   ❖

Once in the street, striding as quickly as he could toward the army depot where he could get a seat on a wagon returning to the base, his stern sergeant's training came back.

He'd just violated security, he realized—and grossly at that. The expedition was supposed to be kept a secret.

But as stern as it might be, his sergeant's training was a patina over a young man in a state of emotional chaos—and a practical German farmer, at that.

Fuck it. The up-timers were lunatic on the subject of security. What difference did it make if a civilian in Magdeburg knew what several hundred enemy spies certainly knew by now anyway? No one doubted there *were* that many spies in the city. Not even Gunther Achterhof thought the CoC security apparatus could do more than keep the bastards from anything direct or ambitious. But there was no way to keep them out of Magdeburg altogether, since it was a city full of immigrants and more coming every day.

All a man needed was half a brain and a decent eyeglass—which were hardly rare—and a good patch of woods. There were woods all over. From there, he could watch the regiments in their training. If he had any military experience at all, which he certainly would, he'd know the battle group was getting ready to march. There were apartments all over, too. The city was full of modest windows—but plenty big enough for an eyeglass. From one of them, he could watch Simpson's ironclads getting ready also.

Fuck secrets. All the more so, this day, when the only secret in the world that Thorsten Engler cared about was the secret heart of a woman he could only half-understand.

Chapter 30

Caroline sat at her desk for two hours. Part of the time, staring at the objects on it. Part of the time, staring at a photograph which she pulled out of her desk drawer. Most of the time, staring out the window. To the northwest, where the army camp lay, so she had to crane her head a little. Finally, seeing the sun lowering itself into the window, she realized what time it was. And how little time remained.

She snatched up the objects—rebundled them, actually, since Thorsten had left the cloth too—and hurried into Maureen's office. To her great relief, the Schwarzburg-Rudolstadt countesses hadn't left yet. They were usually in Maureen's office, this time of the afternoon, having a leisurely chat over the affairs of the settlement house.

That was good, because she didn't think Maureen would know the answer any more than she did. Not for sure, anyway—and this was one of those times you had to be *sure*.

Ignoring their startled greetings—she'd pretty much just burst in—she laid the half-wrapped bundle on the table.

"Do these mean what I think they mean? I need an answer, ladies. No fooling, down and dirty, and *now.*"

Frowning, Anna Sophia rose and came over. But her nineteen-year-old counterpart was there first, already unfolding the cloth.

"Oh, Caroline, how splendid. Thorsten gave them to you, I assume?"

Emelie held up the salt cellar and pepper grinder. "Nice enough, if not fancy. These would be an heirloom, you understand. Something—probably his mother's—that he was able to save from the farm."

She put them down and held up the other pair of objects. "These now . . . Very good shoes, they are. He must have saved half his salary to buy these."

"Emelie!"

The young countess of Schwarzburg-Rudolstadt handed the shoes to her. "Don't be silly," she said, smiling. "Yes, they mean exactly what you think they mean, Caroline. What else would they be?"

The older countess was at the table, now, frowning at the things.

"Yes, of course. He is asking you to betroth him. But—Caroline . . . You can do better than a former farmer and an army sergeant. I'm quite sure. Much better, in fact."

Caroline looked around, saw an empty chair, and sat down. Then, quickly, she took off her shoes and began trying on the new ones. As always when she was under tremendous emotional stress, she grasped at practicality.

"No, Anna Sophia, I don't think I can. I really don't—and believe me, I've thought about it a lot, the last few weeks. More to the point—way, way more to the point—I don't want to."

Her foot got jammed halfway into the shoe. "Three years is too long, isn't it, Maureen?"

"Don't be stupid. If we were still back up-time, with what you've learned, you'd be a licensed clinical social worker by now. If it was up to me, excessive and self-indulgent grief would be listed in the *Diagnostic and Statistical Manual* as a no-kidding mental disorder. Of course it's too long. Way too long."

"Yeah, I know. It's just—oh, damn the man! Why didn't he *ask*? They're at least a size too small!"

"Same reason you didn't, I imagine. Didn't know what to ask or how to ask it in the first place."

Caroline put back on her own shoes, her shoulders slumped. "I'm an idiot. And now it's too late because—"

Her shoulders unslumped and her head came back up. "Is Kristina still here?"

"Should be. Last I saw she and the four-headed Cerberus were—"

Caroline didn't hear the rest. She snatched up the shoes Thorsten had left and raced out the door. Once in the hall beyond, she located the princess by the simple, direct—and incredibly improper—expedient of just bellowing: *"Kristina! Where are you? I need you right here, right now!"*

Kristina popped out of a doorway not three seconds later.

"Okay, girl, you keep telling me what a great horsewoman you are. I need to get to the army camp before they close the gates at sundown. No way there's enough time to get a carriage—too slow, anyway—and if I tried to ride a horse I'd fall off before I got to the end of the street."

"Oh, I can take you! Just ride behind me and hold on tight!"

It didn't strike either one of them that the notion of a full-grown woman—bigger than most, at that—"holding on" to a seven-year-old girl—smaller than most, at that—while cantering on a horse was perhaps not a good idea.

Of course, it *did* occur to the four-headed Cerberus. "You can't do that!" they shrilled as one.

"Watch me!" came the imperious reply, and off they went. Kristina only paused long enough once they reached the stable to tell Caroline, "You'd probably better put those shoes in the saddlebag. So you can hold on with both hands."

The four noblewomen almost got trampled as they came into the stable, just at the moment the horse and its two riders went out. Fortunately, they were spryer than they looked. The two soldiers had been lagging so far behind they only needed to take two steps aside to clear the street.

"This is so much *fun*!" Kristina shrieked.

Caroline was far too scared to think it was "fun." Kristina had—what a surprise—a truly superb horse, and she did in fact know how to use it. Her notion of a "canter," however, was nothing Caroline would have called by the name. Not, admittedly, that Caroline could tell the difference between a trot and a canter and a gallop much better than she could the difference between a horse and a cow. But it did seem to her that they were racing along faster than she could remember driving on a freeway.

All things are relative, though, and at the moment Caroline's fear of their speed was pretty much drowned beneath her fear at the speed with which the sun was setting.

However, they got to the gates before sundown. The question now became . . .

How does a civilian female holding a pair of shoes get herself admitted into an army base?

Luckily, Kristina had the answer. "Open the gates! I'm Princess Kristina, daughter of the king and emperor! My friend Caroline, the countess of Oz, needs to see Thorsten"—there might have been just the tiniest hesitation here—"the count of Narnia!"

The four guards stared at her. The princess stamped her foot. "Now! Or I'll—well, you won't like it."

She cocked an eye up at Caroline. "Is that okay?" she half-whispered.

"I'm not about to give you a hard time over it, that's for sure. But where in the world did you learn to tell fibs like that?"

Kristina sniffed. "How silly. Watching my father and Uncle Axel. And all the others. They're frightful fibbers, you know."

An officer emerged. "What's this all about?" he demanded, half-sternly and half-worriedly. Whether or not his soldiers knew who the girl was, he certainly did.

It took another two minutes, but in the end he let them through. In fact, he even offered to guide Caroline and Kristina to the right barracks. Surprisingly, perhaps, Caroline was almost sure it was more the silent appeal in her own eyes than Kristina's royal proclamations that turned the tide.

Or perhaps it was simply that he knew Thorsten Engler. And, like everyone Caroline had met, liked the man. That didn't surprise her at all.

"There," he said, pointing to one of the barracks, once they were fifteen yards away.

Kristina surged to the fore again. "Thorsten Engler! Come out!"

A few seconds later, he did. Stared at Caroline, then at the shoes in her hand. Then, turned his head away slightly. A subtle but unmistakable look of great sadness came over his face.

She'd done something wrong. In God's name, *what?*

So, it was over. Thorsten realized—he should have listened to Eric and the others—that he'd not only been foolish, but had even insulted the woman. So greatly that she'd come out here, the same day, to return the gifts in person. Lest he be under any misapprehension at all.

Suddenly, she started striding toward him. That same very athletic stride that could still arouse him so. But he only watched from the corner of his eyes, since he couldn't really bear to look at her directly.

Until she was standing just three feet way, and extended the shoes. The gesture was oddly tentative, not the firm thrust he'd expected.

"Thorsten . . . Oh, damnation. Look, I can't help it. It's just the way I am, take it or leave it. I'm a practical girl. And I've got big feet for a woman. The shoes are too small. But . . ."

Hope surged, where he'd thought there was none. His eyes went to hers.

There was no anger at all, in those green orbs. No

smile on the face below, either. But the eyes were simply . . .

Appealing? Uncertain?

"Can I—or you?—I don't care—trade them in? I'd love to have a pair that fits." Her eyes started watering. "I can't tell how much I would. But . . ."

Her voice was barely above a whisper. "I don't know what to do, either. And I don't want to do anything wrong. Not now. God, not now."

Perhaps he smiled. He never remembered. Whatever. Finally—for sure—he did *something* right.

Caroline's full smile erupted. She dropped the shoes. "Oh, fuck it," she said. "And fuck whatever horse anybody rode in on."

The next thing he knew she had him in a fierce embrace, and was kissing him more fiercely still.

So. At least *that* legend was true. Americanesses *did* use the Austrian kiss. Her tongue felt like it was halfway down his throat. Good thing he came from sturdy farmer stock, with stout hearts on both side of the family. Or he would have died, right then and there.

Eventually—who could say when? who cared?—she broke off the kiss and nuzzled his ear. "I'll write to you, but I don't know if the letters will get delivered. Please write to me, whenever you can."

"They might," he murmured back. "Hard to know. Damn army. But whether they ever get to you or not, I will write them."

The bugle blew. "Oh, damn," Caroline said. "Does that mean what I think it means?"

Kristina managed to extort another five minutes for them. She'd inherited her father's ability to throw a

truly majestic temper tantrum along with his prominent nose. But, eventually, the officers insisted. Push
comes to shove, officers with combat experience are
less susceptible to the menace of a shaking seven-
year-old finger than noble ladies.

But, by then, it really didn't matter. Enough had
been said—enough finally understood—that Caroline
and Thorsten would either have all the time in the
world, or Thorsten would be dead before she saw
him again.

Grief she could handle, if need be. Hopefully, this
time, she'd handle it better. But at least uncertainty
was gone.

Oh, so very very very gone. He had a wonderful
kiss, too. And she already knew he'd make a wonderful
father, just from watching him with Kristina.

After she was out of sight, Thorsten turned back
and reentered the barracks. There, in the middle
of the room, he planted hands on hips and looked
about at the pitiful inhabitants. They'd all watched, of
course, half of them crammed into the doorway and
the other half crowded at the windows.

"Go ahead," he said. "Make a joke. Any joke . . ."

Eric Krenz covered his eyes. "He's going to be
insufferable, fellows. Absolutely insufferable. How
did it come to this, anyway? This is absurd. It's not
in *any* of the legends."

Part Three

A glittering sword out of the east

April 1634

Chapter 31

The next morning, Thorsten Engler was trying hard not to laugh at his friend Eric Krenz. Eric was in a foul enough mood as it was. Fortunately, since Eric was riding behind him and to his right, Krenz couldn't see the grin on Thorsten's face.

"Where did they get these fucking nags, anyway?" he heard Krenz complain.

After making sure he'd suppressed the grin, Thorsten turned his head and looked back. As he'd expected, Eric wasn't even looking at the horses drawing the battery wagon at all. Instead, his gaze was fixed, like a paralyzed rabbit's on a snake, at the limber pole swaying back and forth very close to his right leg. The "tongue," as it was often called, would inevitably wind up slamming against that leg from time to time, when the limber's wheels struck an obstruction or rut of some sort. Of which there were bound to be some, especially this time of year, even in a road as well designed and graded as the road that followed the Elbe north of Magdeburg.

The blow could easily cause bruises, and possibly even break a bone. That was the reason that the right legs of the volley gunners riding the three near horses of each gun crew had an iron guard encased in leather. So did those of the riders on the ammunition wagon and the battery wagon. The devices worked perfectly well, even if it was a bit startling to have the tongue suddenly slam against you.

The problem was twofold. The first aspect was that Eric simply wasn't accustomed to it. By now, Thorsten had plenty of experience riding the near horses on a gun team, even if—as was true today—he would normally ride his own horse on campaign. That being one of the chief perquisites of his august status as the sergeant in command of a battery, not assigned to any specific team.

Eric, however, being none too fond of horses to begin with, had used every opportunity during their training to avoid riding the blasted beasts. He'd been able to get away with it because he wasn't assigned to one of the crews in Engler's B Battery either. Instead, he'd accompany the battery wagon with its load of tools and equipment to repair whatever needed to be repaired on campaign.

The second part of the problem was even simpler. Krenz was a mediocre horseman, at best. He invariably referred to horses as "surly brutes"—even though, in point of fact, Captain Witty and Lieutenant Reschly had selected the most placid animals they could find. Eric's stubborn insistence on indulging his dislike for horses meant that his rudimentary skills in a saddle had not improved much throughout the course of their training. By no means all of the volley gunners came from backgrounds, like Thorsten's own farming, that gave them experience with horses. But, by now, all of them—except Krenz—were at least passable riders. Thorsten's own horsemanship was quite good, as good as that of most cavalrymen.

Engler had warned Krenz several times that eventually Eric would have to get on a horse. But Krenz had cheerfully insisted that what he called "proper military doctrine"—and there was a laugh, since Eric missed as many of the formal classes as he could, too—meant that he'd always either be on foot or, at worst, riding on the limber.

"Artillery officers want their men on foot, Thorsten," he'd said stoutly, a few weeks back. "I read that in the manual."

"Not our manual, you didn't," replied Engler, a bit irritated. "That's the general manual you're talking about, which is mostly addressed at heavy artillery. Eric, we're the lightest artillery there is. What they call 'flying artillery' or—brace yourself—'horse artillery.' We're supposed to be able to keep up with cavalry, on anything except an actual charge or a fast reconnaissance."

Krenz just looked stubborn. He could do that superbly well, when he was of a mind. "I *read* it," he persisted.

"No, what you read was that in the *regular* artillery, they only use one or two riders on the near horses. Yes, fine, you could get around that, *if* you were assigned to something like a six-pounder or twelve-pounder battery. As bad a horseman as you are, no sergeant in his right mind wants you guiding a horse team. The manual's insistence that the gunners who aren't riding must stay on foot except under special circumstances like fast maneuvers is because they don't want lazy gunners riding on the limbers, like so many of them will do if the officers or sergeants aren't watching. That's because they're likely to get injured if the limber hits a hole or a rock and jostles them hard enough."

He might as well have been talking to a brick wall, from the expression on Krenz's face.

Thorsten sighed. "Still don't get it, do you? When we actually go out on a campaign—especially the one we're training for, where we have to keep up with the ironclads—you *will* be riding a horse. Everybody will. There's no way we could keep up otherwise."

Alas, when he wanted it to be, Eric's capacity for self-justification was an endless cornucopia.

"Oh, that's nonsense, Thorsten. I heard one of the up-timer sergeants in the infantry—not more than two weeks ago—saying that a properly conditioned man on foot can travel longer and faster than a horse over long distances. He said they even had some tribe of savages in their old country—'Apashoes,' or something like that—who could make a hundred miles a day on foot."

Thorsten silently cursed Paul David Willcocks. Though now in his mid-forties, with no excuse for the childish habit, the up-time sergeant who served the volunteer regiments as a special trainer had the incorrigible practice of regaling his soldiers with tales from his former universe, many of which Engler thought were probably what the up-timers called "tall tales." But whether true or not, Willcocks never seemed to give any thought at all to whether the stories were appropriate for a training sergeant to be blathering to his men.

"Apaches," he corrected. "Yes, I know, I've heard the story. Here's what else is true. Since you now seem besotted—and when did this magical transformation take place?—with proper military doctrine. Apaches were light infantry—as light as it gets—detached into small units. A dozen men, perhaps. They didn't have to worry about keeping hundreds of men moving on a single road, and they weren't carrying any equipment worth talking about. You, on the other hand, unless you used horses, would have to carry several hundred pounds of gear, powder and shot. You couldn't even pick up your share and take one step, much less outrun a horse. You couldn't outrun a tortoise. Even in the infantry, the average soldier in the regiments has to be able to tote fifty pounds on campaign."

Since Krenz was obviously still willing to argue, Thorsten had broken it off. "Never mind," he'd said, waving his hand. "Be as stupid as you want. But if you fall off your team horse a few weeks from now and get turned into sausage by the wheels of the limber and the wagon, don't claim I didn't warn you."

Now that the joyous day of *I-told-you-so* had finally come, Thorsten wasn't actually worried that Eric would fall off his mount. Given the white-knuckled way he was grasping the pommel, Krenz would probably manage to stay in the saddle even if he and his horse were both swept up by a tornado. In any event, Thorsten had made sure the least skilled horseman in his battery was riding the third of the near horses, the one closest to the limber. The "wheelers," as they were called—the other two on each side would be the "swing" and the "lead" horse—were the biggest and steadiest horses on each team. Even if Eric did fall off he'd manage to land on the limber instead of under it.

Of course, Engler knew he probably wouldn't be able to bask in the sunshine of just retribution for more than a few weeks. They were setting off on the expedition with six horses assigned to each gun or wagon, when four would be plenty and, in a pinch, the volley guns were so light they could be hauled by two. That was because it was inevitable that some of the horses would fall by the wayside as time went on. Lamed, ill, killed or wounded in action. So, sooner or later, Eric probably would be able to start walking or riding on the limber.

Captain Witty had told Thorsten that they could expect, at best, to lose one horse in ten over the course of the expedition—and that was assuming they didn't fight any major actions. That was the average for a good cavalry unit. In reality, Witty thought their losses would be closer to one horse in four. Most of the men in the volley gun batteries were only passable horsemen, and the price for their inexperience and clumsiness would mostly be paid by the horses themselves.

As it happened, Captain Carl Witty was thinking about the matter himself, that very moment. And his thoughts were every bit as acerbic as that of his master sergeant.

"Let's hope they get better as time goes by," he grumbled to his second-in-command.

Lieutenant Markus Reschly—"Mark," now, since he'd adopted the up-time abbreviation of his name—was a more cheerful man by nature than his commander.

Smiling, he said, "Oh, they're bound to. Training exercises are one thing; a real campaign, quite a different matter. They'll learn."

"Yes, I know. But how many horses will they grind up while they do? Horses are not cheap."

From the blank look on the young lieutenant's face, it was clear as day that he'd never once thought about that aspect of the problem. That was a bit odd, actually. Had Reschly been one of the usual volunteers, Witty wouldn't have expected him to understand that whatever else war was, it was also an economic enterprise. But Reschly was one of the traditional sort of mercenaries, of whom there were plenty in the USE's new army, especially in the officer corps. Witty himself was another, from Switzerland.

Reschly came from the Moselle valley, a region that produced both horses and mercenaries. Plenty of the former and, if not as many as Switzerland, a fair number of the latter. Mercenaries usually understood the economics of war quite well, especially mercenary officers who had to bear a lot of the cost out of their own pockets. And Markus came from a traditional mercenary family, too.

On the other hand, Reschly was still very young. And although he was officially a "mercenary" it had become quite obvious that he'd used the family tradition, along with a decent amount of training in the skill of arms, to wrangle himself a position in the USE's Army for primarily ideological reasons. If most of the volunteers came from the German lands heavily influenced by the pestiferous Committees of Correspondence, the new USE Army was drawing enthusiasts from all over Europe.

Which was a damned nuisance, as far as Witty was concerned. Not even in the most ill-disciplined mercenary company he'd ever served in had he encountered such a disputatious lot of soldiery. True, the men maintained a tight discipline over themselves when it came to the usual problems of drunkenness and thievery. Much better than mercenaries would. But they were quite prepared to argue about almost anything else. Gloomily, Witty foresaw the day when these idiot "democrats," as they liked to style themselves, would insist on the right to vote whether or not to have a battle—or even a charge.

He consoled himself with the thought that the pay was as good as that of most armies in Europe, and there was that one great benefit on the side. Among the many peculiar ramifications of the up-timers' notion of "democracy" was that they considered it outrageous to expect soldiers—even officers—to pay for their own military equipment. That was to be provided by the state, it seemed.

An idiot notion, of course. If Witty were the emperor, he'd damn well see to it that his soldiers bore as much of the financial burden of war as possible. Let them make up for it by looting.

Which the up-timers *also* considered outrageous—to the point where they'd even persuaded General Torstensson to ban looting altogether, under pain of draconian punishments. There seemed to be no end to the silliness they could generate out of their heads. Perhaps the absurdly lavish care they devoted to their teeth made their brains rot instead.

Ah, well. Witty had calculated everything carefully, before he agreed to take a commission, and decided it was still worth doing. The pay was decent, after all, and he figured that whatever he'd lose by not getting a captain's share of the loot, he'd make up for by also not having to pay a captain's share of the expenses.

Still, old habits died hard. Every time he saw one of the inexperienced gunners misusing a horse, he couldn't stop calculating what that was likely to cost a few weeks down the road, even if he wasn't the one who'd be paying for it.

On the positive side, the road was good. Very good. However fantastically impractical the up-timers might be in their politics, there was no question they designed good roads. The best roads Europe had seen since Roman times were now those in the Germanies. Well, some of the Germanies, at least. Pomeranian roads were still said to be as bad as ever.

But Pomerania was the armpit of the continent anyway. Witty had been there once. Hopefully, he'd never go again. He was thirty-three years old now. A few more years and he'd be able to return to Switzerland with enough money to set himself up nicely.

Who knows? He might even have enough to pay a dentist before he retired. Not likely, of course.

The river was unpleasantly cold in the bright morning light.

Well, of course it was. It was only late March, and the Elbe River was never exactly what one might have called toasty warm, Admiral John Simpson reflected as he stood with hopefully impressive calm in the conning tower of SSIM *Constitution*. He'd been a bit surprised that the river hadn't frozen, although intellectually he'd understood that the past winter hadn't *really* been as cold as it had sometimes felt, Little Ice Age or not.

It was still cold enough to offer the very real threat of hypothermia to anyone who found himself immersed in it, though. A thought which John Chandler Simpson found rather reassuring as he contemplated the intelligence reports about possible threats his command might face. Not that there weren't entirely enough purely physical problems, without any need for enemy action behind them, to make his current task sufficiently daunting.

Captain Franz Halberstat maneuvered *Constitution* cautiously away from her dockside mooring. "Give me ten degrees of starboard rudder, reverse thrust on the starboard jet, and increase to ten percent power on the port jet," he said.

"Ten degree starboard rudder, ten percent power on the port jet, aye, aye, sir!" his helmsman repeated crisply, and the engine-room telegraph jangled as the quartermaster transmitted the orders.

The ironclad's twin rudders moved, and a curved section of pipe lowered itself over the nozzle of the starboard pump as a pair of engineers spun the geared wheel that controlled it. The pipe clamped tight, capturing the output from the pump and directing it forward, underneath the ship's hull, while the port jet continued to push forward. The combination turned the vessel sharply, and *Constitution*'s five-hundred-ton bulk seemed to quiver slightly underfoot.

That was probably his imagination, Admiral Simpson told himself. On the other hand, maybe it wasn't.

The ironclad moved slowly but smoothly towards midstream and away from her mooring, and Halberstat's quiet orders returned the starboard jet to normal operation. Simpson nodded in satisfaction, and then stepped out onto the bridge wing, looking astern as the other six ships began to move as well.

He wasn't the only person watching them. The navy yard's entire work force was out in strength, standing on the river banks, bobbing about in every rowboat they could lay hands on, shouting and cheering and stamping their feet. The sound of their voices would probably have been deafening, if the raucous sound of the ironclads' sirens (actually, horns purloined from diesel trucks that weren't going to require them any longer), the timberclads' whistles, and the ringing of Magdeburg's bells hadn't drowned out any purely human sounds.

So much for operational security, Simpson thought dryly.

Of course, there'd never been much chance of maintaining any sort of security, even if Mike Stearns—or John Chandler Simpson—had wanted to in the first place. Everyone in Magdeburg, which undoubtedly included literally hordes of spies for everyone from Richelieu to Christian of Denmark to Emperor Ferdinand of Austria to the Wizard of Oz, had known the navy would be moving out as soon as possible for its spring showdown in the Baltic. There'd been no possible way to conceal that. Nor was Simpson particularly averse to letting the other side know what was coming.

There's damn-all they're going to be able to do about it, anyway, he thought with a certain grim satisfaction. It wasn't a thought which someone with his own profound respect for the Demon Murphy was prepared to express out loud, but Simpson was well aware of the potency of the weapon he had forged.

Standing there and simply watching the ships of his squadron was one of the more difficult things Simpson had ever done. Every nerve ending in his body cried out to take the con himself, at least for his flagship. Certainly, even ten or twelve months ago, the mere thought of allowing seventeenth-century officers to command vessels like this would have been a guaranteed source of permanent insomnia. After the exhausting weeks and months he'd spent working with and training the officers in question, that problem at least no longer applied.

Well, he thought, *let's be honest with ourselves here, John. It doesn't apply very* much, *anymore.*

He snorted with humor carefully concealed behind his impassive "the admiral is on duty" expression as he admitted the real reason his entire epidermis itched with the need to give the helm and power orders himself. These ships were very much his babies. Building them, and the navy to employ them, had been probably the most satisfying task he'd ever undertaken in a life filled with substantial accomplishments. He wasn't prepared to admit that to anyone except, possibly, his wife Mary, but *he* knew it was true, and he simply hated the thought of delegating responsibility for what happened to *his* ships in any way to someone else.

At least the skippers he'd appointed to command the ironclads had all been given the opportunity to practice with the slower, clumsier, smaller river steamers already in commission. In fact, Simpson had used those practice and training sessions to wash out several prospective watch-standing officers. The transition from sail or oar power to paddlewheel steamers had required greater mental flexibility than most up-timers would have expected, for a lot of reasons, and some people—whether up-timer or seventeenth-century—simply lacked that flexibility.

One problem that had caused quite a bit of confusion for the down-timers, at least initially, was the fact that Simpson had insisted upon providing all of his new vessels with wheels, rather than the simple tillers virtually all seventeenth-century ships utilized. There were several reasons for that particular decision, and the opinion which he knew some people had expressed—that it was simply the system with which *he* was familiar—wasn't actually one of them. The use of a geared quadrant system to shift the rudder not only permitted him to build in a much greater mechanical advantage for the helmsman, but also offered a substantially greater amount of maneuverability.

All contemporary vessels used a tiller. For all intents and purposes, it was simply a stout bar attached to the head of the rudder stock and used to steer much as the tiller was used in a modern sailing dinghy or outboard motorboat. Unfortunately, the length of the tiller had to be in direct proportion to the forces required to shift the rudder, and its maximum length was restricted by the width of the ship itself. In larger ships, a "whipstaff" was required simply to control the rudder, and that made things even worse. The whipstaff was essentially a vertical lever, mounted on a pivoting center and extending from the ship's quarterdeck down to the level of the tiller, where it was attached to the end of the bar. It provided the helmsmen with a powerful mechanical advantage, but meant that the rudder's range of movement was even more sharply restricted. As a result, a large sailing ship (although "large" was a relative term) found it impossible to apply more than five or six degrees of rudder.

That Simpson's ships, on the other hand, could apply up to *eighty* degrees of rudder, would have made them immensely more maneuverable even without the fact that they weren't solely reliant on wind power or oars. It had taken his seventeenth-century officers a while to make that mental adjustment, and then to make the necessary *counter*-adjustment and learn to respect the limitations that still existed. Actually, the second adjustment had been rather more harrowing for Simpson to observe. For a while, it had reminded him forcefully of Hans Richter's adventures behind the wheels of up-timer vehicles.

After that, they'd settled down, and Simpson felt reasonably confident of their ability to handle the paddle-wheel timberclads. The *ironclads*, though, were a different kettle of fish entirely. Crude as they might still appear to up-timer eyes, they were far more advanced in both concept and execution than the steam kettle timberclads. For all their greater size, they actually accelerated faster and had a tighter turning radius (proportionately) and a higher sustained speed than any of the steamboats that had yet been produced here in the United States of Europe.

And they were lots, lots bigger.

"Meet her," Captain Halberstat said.

The captain's voice came faintly but clearly through the open armored door. Simpson couldn't hear the helmsman's response, but *Constitution* steadied on her new heading, steaming directly down the center of the river. Well, not *"steaming,"* precisely.

The pair of pumps around which each of the

four ironclads had been built turned them into what
Simpson sometimes thought of as the world's biggest
jet skis. They'd allowed him to avoid all sorts of
problems in building the things, and they offered significant tactical advantages. They didn't come without
drawbacks of their own, of course. For one thing,
they were big, and designing their intakes and flow
lines had presented quite a few headaches. Foreign
object damage was also a consideration, and designing screens to protect the intakes against objects
large enough to inflict damage without thoroughly
obstructing water flow had provided another set of
headaches.

On the other hand, they'd kept Simpson from
having to figure out how to design truly efficient
propellers—something he was going to have to do by
the time they started laying down the proposed screw-
frigates. They were also far less vulnerable (and far
more mechanically reliable) than the paddle wheels
he'd used for the supporting steamers. And they were
immensely more efficient at moving water . . . which,
after all, was what any mechanical propulsion system
had to do.

He stepped to the front of the open bridgework
wrapped around the armored conning tower and looked
ahead down the river. The pair of up-time power
boats leading the ponderous line of gunboats downstream looked particularly anachronistic this morning.
The fact that they were stuffed with Marines armed
with flintlock rifles only added to their incongruity,
but Simpson couldn't have cared less. Each of those
boats, like each of his ironclads, mounted one of the
precious up-time fishing fathometers and carried one

of the experienced Elbe River barge pilots. Over the last several weeks, those boats and pilots had scoured the upper reaches of the Elbe, familiarizing themselves with its waters in order to pick practicable channels for Simpson's vessels.

The fact that the river was running springtime deep and that the ironclads' draft could be reduced to as little as five feet by pumping out their trim tanks had helped immeasurably with that task, but there were still a few problem areas waiting for them. Most of those had been addressed by building *staustufen*, or temporary holding dams, on the shallow bits. Like the more permanent *wehrleucken*, the *staustufen*'s function was to raise the water level in a given section of river to something which would float the gunboats. *Unlike* the *wehrleucken*, *staustufen* were intended from the beginning to be temporary structures. Once the water had risen sufficiently, they were simply breached and the vessels upstream of them rode down with the released wave. *Wehrleucken*, on the other hand, were permanent dams with central spillways that were supposed to be broad enough for barges and other river traffic to pass through.

Unfortunately, none of the existing *wehrleucken* had been built to handle anything like the size of the USE's steamboats and gunboats. In the long run, a more formal and efficient system of locks was going to be necessary, and its construction was already underway. But for now, Simpson was stuck with what was already in place.

And what's already in place is stuck with me, *too,* he thought with a certain grim satisfaction. *You should have listened to Matthias, Freiherr. He was trying to be* much *more reasonable than* I'm *going to be.*

One thing about Mike Stearns, the admiral reflected. The man had nerves of steel and an *intelligent* ruthlessness whose depth Simpson, for once, had been woefully slow to recognize. In his own way, Stearns was every bit as ruthless and willing to resort to bare knuckles at need as Gustav Adolf himself . . . and just as pragmatic.

The prefix for the ships themselves, in fact, was a reflection of that characteristic of the man. SSIM stood for *Schiff seiner imperialen Majestät*—"His Imperial Majesty's Ship," in English. The CoCs had raised a ruckus, wanting USES instead. But since there'd been no substance to the matter beyond pure symbolism, and the issue was raising the emperor's hackles—more because he saw the CoCs as challenging him than because he really cared himself—Stearns had squelched the CoCs and settled the issue to Gustav Adolf's preference. Figuring, Simpson had no doubt, that he'd save his bargaining leverage for issues that really mattered. When the time came to fish or cut bait, Prime Minister Stearns, unlike certain other up-time political leaders Simpson could have named, never waffled.

Careful, John, he told himself. *You're actually starting to* like *the man!*

Chapter 32

"Are you *sure* about this, Darryl?" asked Melissa. Both she and Tom Simpson were practically squinting at McCarthy, with pretty much the same expression on their faces they might have had if Darryl McCarthy had just announced he was going to become a monk. Or, perhaps more to the point under these circumstances, he'd announced that he knew a batch of Las Vegas showgirls who'd decided to take holy vows.

"Yeah, I'm sure. Why is it so goddam hard to understand?"

"They're *Yeoman Warders*, Darryl," said Tom patiently. "You know. The Tower of London's Beefeaters—even if they won't be called that for another half century or so. Renowned for their unswerving loyalty to the king. That sort of thing."

"Oh, piss on that," snapped Darryl. He gave Melissa a wary eye. "Meaning no offense."

"Good thing for you there's no blackboard around," she said, half-smiling. "As I believe I've mentioned about twenty times since we got stuck in here. But Tom's question still stands, Darryl. I'll grant you that the Beefeater reputation got overlaid with a lot of

sentiment by our time. But it's still true enough—and
nothing we've seen since we got here has indicated
otherwise. Yes, they've been very pleasant to deal
with. Far more pleasant, God knows, than this bunch
of thugs who've been running the Tower for the last
few weeks. But I've never doubted for a moment
that the Warders would do their best to stop us
from trying to escape."

"I ain't talking about 'the Warders,'" Darryl pointed
out, trying for the same patient and level tone of
voice that his commander Captain Simpson always
did so well. "I'm just talking about one family among
them. More to the point, Stephen Hamilton's family.
You think *you're* pissed about these new mercenaries
who've been running roughshod over everybody in
the Tower? You don't know what the word 'pissed'
even means, to somebody like him. And it's a double
whammy. Just being angry wouldn't have given Stephen
Hamilton a way to do anything about it. But now, me
being part of the family and him having figured out
we're planning to escape . . . I think from his point of
view, that settled the question."

Tom rubbed his heavy jaw. "I think Darryl's probably right, Melissa. All the Yeoman Warders are quietly
furious about the situation, not just Hamilton and his
kin. I haven't spent much time out and about in the
Tower since the lid came down, because we all agreed
we'd be wise to keep a low profile. Darryl and Nelly
are the only ones who go out regularly any more,
because they've both got legitimate excuses that not
even that prick Windebank questions. A sweetheart in
Darryl's case—betrothed, to boot—and simply shopping
for food in Nelly's. But I've been out there a couple

of times, for an hour or so, and all it takes is a few minutes to figure out how mad they are. If word came down from Whitehall that King Charles had tired of Windebank and the Warders could do with him as they chose, they'd have the arrogant bastard staked out naked on the Tower green and be laying bets on which ravens would pluck out his eyes."

When Melissa had visited the Tower of London as a tourist, back in the late twentieth century, she'd thought the ancient custom of having ravens as pets of a sort in the Tower was charming. Even then, she'd known the historical origins of the custom. But it had all seemed very far removed, as harmless as a medieval sword displayed in a museum case. Now that she'd been imprisoned in the Tower during its "operational period," so to speak, she'd developed a different attitude. The ravens were indeed there to pluck out eyes—the eyes of men beheaded on the orders of the English crown.

Tom was still rubbing his chin thoughtfully. "And Darryl's also right about Stephen Hamilton. You haven't met him, not really. I have. That is one scary human being. Not somebody I'd want mad at me, for damn sure."

Melissa grimaced. "Tom, I have to tell you that 'one scary human being' is not actually a recommendation on a resumé. Not for me, anyway."

Tom gave her a thin, rather cold, smile. "We're in different lines of work, so to speak. From my point of view—being the commander of a military force that you couldn't call a 'squad' without breaking into hysterical laughter—'scary human being' looks pretty damn good, unless we're dealing with an actual sociopath. Which I don't think is true of Hamilton."

Darryl frowned. "Hey, take it easy. He's really a pretty good guy, you know. Hell of a nice grandpa for all the kids. I know him a lot better than either of you. He's just . . . Well, he never talks about it—nobody does in the family—but I think he's been in some very bad places in his life. The one thing for sure is that he's nobody you want to cross unless you've got a really good reason. 'Really good reason' like in: 'I'll die if I don't, so I may as well, even though he'll probably kill me.' I could tell that the first day I met the guy. Even Harry would walk carefully around him."

He cleared his throat. "Which, uh, kinda brings us back to the point. Is it gonna be 'would' or 'will'?"

"A miracle," stated Melissa. "God, they seem to happen every other day in this time and place. Darryl McCarthy just made a clear and correct grammatical distinction."

Darryl looked vaguely alarmed, the way a righteous hillbilly will when his credentials are challenged. She might as well have suggested he liked Brie and crackers with dry white wine.

"Hey!"

"Oh, relax, Darryl," said Tom. "I'm sure it was just a momentary lapse. My lips are sealed." Then, to Melissa: "But, yeah, you're right. It is a clear grammatical distinction. So what's going to be our correct response?"

Now it was Melissa's turn to look vaguely alarmed. "Oh, dear. Tom, I'm really not good at this sort of thing. Gauging violent people, I mean. I thought my college boyfriend was really cute until he turned out to be a screwball, fiddling with explosives that he had no idea how to make and even less idea of where and why and how he'd use them. I think it just made him feel like a dangerous anarchist."

Darryl sneered. "Ain't the same thing, Melissa. Stephen Hamilton is the real deal. For that matter, so's Andrew and the other guys in the family, even if none of 'em are in the same great gray wolf league that Stephen is."

"Got to tell you I agree with him, Melissa," said Tom. "If Darryl's right and the veiled remarks Stephen and Andrew have made to him mean that they're offering to switch sides, we'd be crazy not to accept." The army captain twitched his head, using it to point across the Thames that ran below one set of the windows in their quarters. "I can tell you for sure and certain that Harry'll be tickled pink. Even as brash as he is, Harry's been scratching his head for weeks trying to figure out how to pull off Jailbreak, Version Two, Super-sized. Having half a dozen Warders to work with would make a huge difference."

He smiled wryly. "'Course, he'll also have conniptions when we tell him he's got to plan for springing another couple of dozen people—all the way down to toddlers."

Melissa winced. So did Darryl. Harry's last remarks on the subject of jailbreakees who kept adding more jailbreakees to the list had started with sarcastic and gone downhill from there.

In the event, however, Harry Lefferts' reaction was quite otherwise.

"Hot diggedy damn!" he exclaimed, after switching off the walkie-talkie. "Guys, scrap plan—whatever number we're up to. Things are looking up. Way, way up."

He'd been using the walkie-talkie in the kitchen, instead of the room upstairs that they'd set up as their radio room. Over the weeks they'd now been in Southwark, once their initial plans for a quick jailbreak had gotten scrapped after the earl of Cork's coup d'etat, Harry had soon realized that the radio room was pointless for the walkie-talkies. Just a relic from old habits, when they'd had to rely on fancy communications equipment with tricky antennas and, even then, relaying everything through Amsterdam. The walkie-talkies worked just fine in the kitchen, and that way he didn't have to repeat everything to the rest of the team.

Felix didn't share his enthusiasm. "For Christ's sake, Harry, twenty or so more people? Three of them babies?"

"None of them babies," said Juliet, sniffing disdainfully. "You've got to understand the distinctions here. Good thing you have women with you."

She began counting off on her fingers. "If I've followed all this properly, we've got one infant, two toddlers, and five other children. I don't count the teenagers. They're not a problem."

Sherrilyn Maddox rolled her eyes. "I'd love to hear you say that to my mother."

Juliet sniffed again. "I doubt if your mother ever participated in a mass jailbreak. Not a problem, I say. Unless the two boys got too eager and we have to haul them away by the short hairs."

"They'll get too eager and we'll have to haul them away by their short hairs," predicted her husband calmly. "But, yes, not a problem." He opened a huge hand and closed it. "See? Easy."

That brought a little ripple of laughter around the table, from everyone except Felix. As usual, he was the self-designated Cassandra of the team. "Maybe not in the escape out of the Tower—but what *then*?"

It was his turn to start counting on his fingers. "Let's add it all up. Start with our own people in St. Thomas' Tower." He did a quick count. "Mailey, the Simpsons, Darryl, Gayle, and Friedrich and Nellie Bruch. That's seven." He started over again with a new finger count. "Cromwell. Wentworth. Add in Wentworth's wife and his three children. How old are they, by the way?"

"The son Will's the oldest," said Juliet. "He's almost eight, I think. The oldest daughter Nan is about six and a half years old. The youngest daughter Arabella is only four and a half."

Felix rolled his eyes. "Marvelous. More kids. Just what we need. But let's keep going. So far, we're up to thirteen, three of them children. No teenagers, either; we're speaking of real children. Then we add Laud to bring us up to fourteen."

He broke off the finger count and spread his hands wide, encompassing everyone in the kitchen. It was a large kitchen, but it was still very crowded. "And that's just the escapees. Since I assume our fearless leader wasn't planning to have us surrender ourselves into the king's custody, we've also got to plan for our own escape. And there are nine of us—eleven, counting Julie and Alex."

Mackay and his wife were in a corner, Alex perched on a stool and Julie perched on his lap. She shook her head. "I don't know if you should figure us in it. We gotta get out of London, sure—but then we're headed back to Scotland, where we left our daughter with my father-in-law."

"I imagine Cromwell will want to come with us, too," added her husband. "He's still got his own children hiding out in the Fens somewhere, don't forget. I doubt very much if he'd agree to leave England without them."

Seeing the gathering storm on Kasza's brow, Alex barked a laugh. "Oh, leave it be, Felix! You needn't plan a *second* escape. It'd have to be weeks or months later, anyway. Let us worry about it. Or Cromwell, if he decides to go on his own after he finds his kids. By all accounts, y'know, he's a full-grown man and quite capable of handling his own affairs. He *did* manage to become lord protector of England, in whatever other universe his duplicate self is in."

Harry coughed. "Ah . . . I think it's a little more complicated. I know Darryl is planning to stick with Cromwell—dunno about whether his squeeze Vicky will go with him, though—and I'm pretty sure Gayle is too."

Everyone stared at him. "You never said anything about that," complained Ohde.

"Yeah, Don, I know I didn't. Darryl asked me to koop it to myself, until we got closer to *Der Tag.* Seems he's gotten to be friends with Cromwell—you gotta know Darryl like I do to understand how completely weird *that* is, but I'll skip over it now—and he also thinks he's got to keep an eye on him."

The stares didn't waver. Harry sighed.

"Look, guys, this'll mean a little bit to Julie and Sherrilyn but it won't mean squat to the rest of you. Darryl's family are Irish, and they get real fruitcake on the subject. Give money to Noraid, the whole bit. For reasons I am *not* going into now, Oliver Cromwell ranks right up there with Satan's top demons, in their book—and here Darryl's gone and made friends with him. But I guess Darryl figures the guy's probably still a demon, even if he likes him, so he isn't letting him out of his sight."

Maczka shook his head. "Never mind. Politics in this century are bad enough. And Gayle? Is she one of these fruitcakes too?"

"Ah . . . no. Seems she's gotten interested in Cromwell. Personally, I mean. Which is a neat trick, seeing as she's never even met the guy. Just talks to him on the radio they snuck into his cell."

Kasza threw up his hands again. "This is sheer lunacy!"

Harry grinned. "It's like Melissa says. We're in an age of miracles. But you oughta keep going, Felix. I'm finding it actually helpful."

Felix scowled a little, but went back to the finger counting. "Fine. So we had *already* reached the preposterous figure of twenty-five people, for what we laughingly call a 'jailbreak.'" He gave Julie and Alex a sharp glance. "For the moment, we've got to include the two of you also. Regardless of how many parties wind up going in separate directions, we've got to get everybody in the Tower out of there and them and the rest of us out of London."

He looked at Harry from lowered brows. "And now,

how many Warders are we talking about? Keeping in
mind that if they're the berserk clansmen they sound
like, they won't agree to leave without bringing every
single one in the clan."

"I'm not sure, exactly. I'll have to get Darryl to give
me an exact count. Somewhere around twenty is all
I know, including all the women and kids."

By now, even George Sutherland was starting to
look aghast. "Ah . . . Harry. You're talking about almost
fifty people. Just exactly how many boats did you
figure on using?"

Throughout, Harry had been standing up, leaning
back against one of the kitchen walls. Now, he pushed
himself off the wall with a little heave of his shoulders
and came up to the table.

"The way I figure it, we get one big boat for all of
us except the people heading for the Fens."

Matija grimaced. "For the love of God, Harry. A
boat big enough to hold something like forty people,
even packed like sardines? You're talking about one
of those Thames barges. We'll be lucky if we make
three miles an hour over whatever the current's doing,
unless we've got a good wind—and who knows if we
will?"

"Yeah—and so what? I figure there'll be enough
confusion that we can get out of London without any
trouble. After that, it won't actually be all that easy
for cavalry—much less infantry—to catch up with
us. We're on the river, doing at least five miles an
hour with the current. They've got to follow country
roads, most of which don't parallel the river hardly
at all. Brit road-makers in the here and now aren't
any crazier than they are up-time. You don't build

roads right next to rivers, especially not a river like the Thames. The soil's too crappy."

"There are tow paths all along the Thames," pointed out Paul. "Stretches of them, anyway."

Harry shrugged again. "Sure. And would you want to take a cavalry horse down one of them? With us on the boat with up-time weapons and plenty of ammunition? And we've got enough ordnance here that we can give most of the Warders up-time guns."

"They've never used them," protested Gerd. Feebly.

Harry laughed. "Yeah. I know. They're also Warders. How long did it take any of *you* to figure out how to operate a pump-action shotgun? Being delicate and all, I won't mention the sicko kinky love affairs that followed."

That drew a laugh, even from Kasza.

"I'm not actually worried about any of that," said George. "The Thames is a wide river, even here in London. By the time you get down to Tilbury, where it narrows a bit, it's almost a thousand yards wide. Even at Tilbury, it only 'narrows' to something like seven hundred yards. Cavalrymen—even infantrymen—standing on the banks and shooting at us with matchlocks and wheel locks stand almost no chance of hitting us. We'll stay in the center of the river, of course, just to avoid the shoals if nothing else."

He held up a big forefinger in the way of warning. "There's the fort at Tilbury to get past, too, don't forget."

He didn't say it with any great alarm, just more in the way of a reminder. Harry and his crew had made it a point to visit the fort on their way up the Thames when they arrived in England. That hadn't been hard, since they'd sold their boat in Tilbury and therefore had an excuse to be lounging about for a time. Harry and Don-Ohde had taken the opportunity to visit the fort while the others handled the commercial transaction. The soldiers manning the fort had been so delighted to have visitors that they'd shown them all about. For their part, Harry and Don had been polite, letting no sign of their professional contempt show visibly. Henry VIII had had the fort built, in the previous century, and it had fallen into a state of almost complete desuetude. The entire garrison wasn't more than thirty men, and none of the fort's few cannons looked to have been fired for years.

Felix being Felix, he rallied and went back to his Cassandra routine. "Fine. So we make it down to the mouth of the Thames. And *then* what, Harry? I'll grant you, especially with some initial confusion, that even a barge can probably make it down to the sea before a cavalry force can intercept them. But nobody's ever accused the earl of Cork or the men around him of being morons. Greedy assholes, yes; imbeciles, no. They'll certainly have enough sense to send couriers down to the royal dockyard at Sheerness. And there'll be at least one or two warships stationed there. Once they move into the Thames, we're fucked. Or do you propose that a shallow-draft barge spilling over with women and children and armed with a few rifles and shotguns can take on a Royal Navy warship? Even one of those converted merchant ships."

"No, of course not," said Harry. "But I doubt very much if those warships are going to be in any position to intercept us. In fact, I'll be surprised if they still exist at all."

Everybody was staring at him again. Harry planted his hands on his hips and gave them a look of exasperation. "Give me a break, willya? I treasure my reputation more than anybody—but I'm not actually a loose cannon on the deck. Wildass cowboy, sure; rebel without a cause, no. *Obviously* I'm not going to do something like this unless we get backup. Like in real serious, Admiral Simpson type backup."

"Those ironclads aren't really seaworthy," protested Matija.

"No? Then why is Simpson proposing to sail them out into the North Sea, around the Skaw, and into the Baltic?"

"Risky. And he's got four. I'll bet you—good odds—that at least one of them breaks down and doesn't make it."

"Maybe you're right," said Harry, "and maybe you're not. But I figure that's the admiral's business. And what I know for sure, is that this decision is way over my pay grade. In fact, Melissa told me yesterday it was way over her pay grade. So she relayed the whole thing to Magdeburg."

That brought a moment's silence. Then Felix said: "And the answer was . . ."

Harry gave him a very cheerful grin. "What do you think? We're talking about the prince, guys. Of course he told us to go for it. He said he'll make sure we've got the backup we need, when the time comes."

It was almost comical, the way everyone at the table seemed to simultaneously relax and perk up at the same time. They almost never discussed the subject, simply because it was something taken completely for granted amongst them. But, like Harry Lefferts himself, all of his team had become dyed-in-the-wool partisans of Mike Stearns. It wasn't really even a political matter for them, or if it was, only tangentially so. True, they all accepted the basic principles of Stearns' political view, but that was simply a veneer. What lay underneath was simple, rather savage, and completely medieval. He was the prince and they were the prince's men. And—once again—he had not failed them.

Felix clapped his hands together, all traces of Cassandra gone. "Well, then. Now that we don't have to worry about the women and children—"

He broke off, his peripheral vision having spotted the Rapidly Rising Backs of Sherrilyn and Julie Mackay—even Juliet's was coming up—and hastily said:

"The noncombatants, rather. But let's move on to the rest. Now it gets *interesting*."

Later that evening, in the kitchen that was used by the small clan of Warders, Darryl spoke quietly to Stephen Hamilton and Andrew Short.

"So there it is, guys. Up front, and all cards on the table. You're in or you're out."

He could have added, *or you turn me over to the authorities*, but didn't. Partly because he knew it was no longer necessary, but mostly because he knew that saying any such thing would enrage Stephen Hamilton. Now that he'd become part of the clan himself—so much, Hamilton himself had made quite clear—any suggestion that the clan would turn on him would be deeply offensive.

"We're in," said Stephen immediately. Andrew's nod came not more than a split-second later.

With someone else, Darryl might have asked if they were really sure. But, again, that was both unnecessary and might quite possibly trigger off Hamilton's anger. The Warder captain was not a hot-tempered man—quite the opposite, in fact—but if you made the mistake of treading on areas that meant a great deal to him, you ran the risk of stirring up that hidden, incredibly cold and ruthless capacity for fury. Darryl would no more have considered stepping on a cobra, just to see if it was awake.

"Good. Now, first thing. Since they're still letting the Warders guard our quarters in St. Thomas—fucking idiots, but there it is—we need to start sending the men over there, one at a time. Whenever nobody looks to be watching."

"That's not a problem," said Andrew. "We've often come into St. Thomas' Tower, helping Nellie with the groceries. Can't stay inside for more than half an hour, though, or suspicions might get aroused."

Darryl smiled thinly. "With you guys, half an hour will be plenty. Biggest problem will be just tearing you away from your newfound loves."

Both Warders frowned at him, puzzled.

"Won't be able to fire them, of course. But the noise of working the slides ain't much, and we'll only do it when one of your kin is standing guard at the door anyway."

Darryl's smile wasn't thin at all, now. "Gentlemen. I will shortly be introducing you to a couple of very sleek dames. Lady Pump-Action Shotgun and Lady Automatic Pistol. Several sisters there, actually. I'm personally partial to Ms. Nine Millimeter. You'll even like their papa, Mr. Dynamite."

Chapter 33

"There's something very peculiar going on over there, I tell you." Elizabeth Lytle finished pouring the broth and started passing out the cups to the three men sitting at her kitchen table.

"What? Followed her, did you?" asked Richard Towson, nodding his thanks.

"Good idea, that," said Patrick Welch, blowing on his broth to cool it off. "Just in case this friend Juliet of hers might turn out to be an informer of some sort."

Liz gave him a disdainful look. "Not likely! If you knew her the way I do . . ." After setting down the kettle, she gave her short dark hair a little toss. "I was just curious, really. There's something . . . mysterious about her, now. Not like she used to be."

"It's been years since you saw her, love," pointed out Anthony Leebrick calmly. "While she was on the continent."

"Not that many years. And what difference does it make, anyway? George is still with her, so nothing fundamental's changed. I met him too, on one of my lunch encounters with Juliet. He hasn't changed a bit, from what I can tell."

475

"Are those wise in the first place?" asked Richard, a bit carefully, since Liz had something of a temper.

"I suggested she do so," said Anthony. "Avoiding an old friend completely when there was no obvious reason to do so was more likely to cause suspicion."

"Let's get back to the point," said Welch. "Since you followed her, what did you discover?"

Liz sat down and stared pensively at her own cup of broth. "The first thing I discovered was that I couldn't get near the house she's living at. Not without being spotted by several pairs of eyes. Very keen ones, too, let me tell you. There are men in that house, several of them, and at least one other woman. And two other men lounging about the tavern nearby, that don't belong there."

Welch looked dubious. "And how could you tell if they belonged there or not? People come in and out of Southwark all the time. It's hardly what you'd call a stodgy little village."

"They didn't look right," Liz insisted. "Too alert. Too fit-looking. At least, too fit-looking for men who weren't swaggering about bullying people and looking for a fight. They made me edgy. They spotted me as soon as I entered the street and their eyes kept following me the whole time I was there. I felt like a plump mouse being watched by cats."

Towson hid his smile behind his cup. Leebrick cleared his throat, a bit smugly. Patrick, undiplomatic as usual, barked a harsh little laugh. "For the love of all that's holy, Liz. Men *do* have a habit of eyeing you, y'know?"

"Excluding our couth selves," added Richard. "But he's got a point, Liz."

She gave both him and Welch an exasperated look. "Let me see if I understand this. Your suggesting to me—a woman whose past bears no close scrutiny—that some men are lecherous. Oh, dear. I never would have guessed."

Towson chuckled. Welch tipped his cup a little, in a gesture that acknowledged a hit had been scored.

Elizabeth Lytle had inherited a number of things from her Portuguese mother, along with her dark eyes, slender frame, and attractive appearance. Among them was a wide mouth that lent itself very nicely to a derisive expression. "Tell a former whore about the salacious nature of the male sex, will you? I believe I am quite familiar with *that* phenomenon, Patrick Welch, thank you very much. And I'm telling you those two men weren't thinking of bedding me. They were contemplating—not seriously, simply as a possible measure—whether they might have to slit my throat."

Her slim shoulders shivered slightly. "Scary, they were, in a quiet sort of way. I'm telling you, they didn't belong there. They're up to something. Some sort of criminal enterprise."

"That hardly makes them out of place in Southwark," said Leebrick. "They might have no connection to Juliet and George at all, you know?"

Liz sipped slowly at her tea, thinking about it, then shook her head. "I can't prove it, Anthony, but I think they do. The tavern they were sitting outside of—with the table they'd chosen—allowed them to keep Juliet's house under observation. Along with the rest of the street leading to it. Well, part of the house, at least. It's set back a ways from the street, right close to the river."

Leebrick looked at his two companions. After a moment, Towson shrugged. "The hunt for us has died down. As many weeks as it's been since we escaped Cork, by now they must think we're out of England entirely. They certainly don't think we're anywhere in London. And I, for one, am sick to death of never seeing anything except the inside of Liz's lodgings. Meaning no offense, you understand."

Patrick scowled, slightly. But the expression was more a matter of habit than anything concrete and specific to the moment. Perhaps because he was Irish, Welch was the sort of man who just naturally looked for the trap, the moment he spotted a juicy morsel. That made him occasionally annoying, in casual circumstances, but it also made him a superb officer to lead reconnaissance missions.

"I've got no objections," he announced, after a few seconds. Again, he made that little tip-of-the-cup acknowledging gesture, this time at Leebrick. "I will admit—not that I'll sign anything to that effect, mind—that our gallant commander has proven to be right. Hiding in London was a stroke of genius. The hunt passed right over our heads, and they'll never think of looking for us here now. So why not move about some, finally?"

His sneer was even better than Elizabeth's. "We have the added protection, after all, of the portraits they circulated everywhere on reward notices. A man could have those posters in his hand, be staring right at us—and he'd swear there was no resemblance at all."

Leebrick chuckled. "They were wretched, weren't they? I was quite offended, actually. The only thing they got right was our beards."

Smiling, Towson tugged at the goatee of his Vandyck. "So they did. Doesn't help much, though, does it? Seeing as how every other man in England—half the continent, too—shares the same style. They showed us wearing clothing, too. Thereby clearly distinguishing us from all the traitors running about the island stark naked."

Leebrick finished his cup. "Fine, then. Liz, draw us up a little map, would you? We'll go tonight, and see what your friend is about."

She frowned. "Why don't I just guide you?"

Welch shook his head. "Not a good idea. You said yourself those two men watched you closely. Even in the dark, they'll recognize you."

"Oh, nonsense. I'll wear a bonnet."

Patrick scratched his head and said nothing. For a wonder, a spasm of diplomacy seemed to have seized him.

Leebrick smiled. Towson chuckled outright. "Won't matter if they see your face, girl. They'll recognize your walk."

"My *walk*?"

"Yes. You have a certain way of . . . well, you're not prancing, exactly. But it's quite distinctive."

She gave her paramour a sharp, suspicious glance. Anthony's smile widened. "I'm afraid he's right, love. First thing I noticed about you, when we met. Well. More precisely, when I first spotted you on the street and began following you. We hadn't actually met yet. Quite entrancing, it was."

She sniffed disdainfully. "Men. It's a wonder you get anything done."

Since everyone had finished, she gathered up the

cups. "All right, but be careful. They really are rather frightening-looking people."

At least, they'd allowed him paper and a pen. So Thomas Wentworth was able to communicate with his wife in some manner, even if it was ridiculous to be writing letters to a woman to whom he could have spoken in person by simply taking a two-minute walk from the Bloody Tower to the Lieutenant's Lodging. But Sir Francis Windebank refused to allow Thomas to leave the Bloody Tower, for any reason, and he refused to allow him visitors of any sort. Not even his wife and children.

Naturally, they wouldn't allow him to seal the letters he wrote. Windebank's men would read every line before they passed the letters on to Elizabeth—and the same, with any of her replies.

Once the shock of those first days had passed, Thomas had been able to gauge the near-maniacal manner of his imprisonment for what it was. A sign of fear on Cork's part, not confidence. Richard Boyle had come to power by seizing on a fluke, not by dint of anything more substantial. True, he'd had a powerful faction following him already, but so had several other men. It had only been the terrible nature of the completely unforeseen accident combined with Cork's sheer luck in being in the right place at the right time—and his own decisiveness, of course; Thomas would give him that much credit—that had allowed the earl to seize power in a single day.

Wentworth wondered again, as he had so many times since he'd been overthrown, whether Cork's presence at the scene of the accident *had* simply been fortuitous. The coincidence reeked, after all. But, no matter from what angle he examined the problem, he simply couldn't see any way that Boyle could have manipulated the situation. Not the accident itself, at any rate. He'd certainly manipulated the aftermath. It was blindingly obvious, in retrospect, that the warning brought to Thomas that the king had suffered a mishap on the West Road was a ploy of Boyle's—and, for perhaps the hundredth time since that day, Wentworth cursed himself for having been a fool. If he'd simply stayed at Whitehall and sent a lieutenant to investigate, he'd have been able to forestall Cork's later machinations.

But he was well-nigh certain, after weeks of thinking upon the matter, that the horrible accident that had taken the queen's life was simply that. An accident, unforeseen by anyone. True enough, the sudden appearance of the Trained Bands at that particular time and place might have been the work of Cork, or one of his accomplices. But the Bands hadn't caused the accident. Leebrick and his mercenary company could have dispersed them in a few minutes. Something else had caused the carriage to race off, and there could only be two explanations. Either the king had panicked—the queen, more likely, with the king acquiescing—or the commander of the escort had somehow caused it to happen.

Again, as he had dozens of times before over the past weeks, Thomas reviewed his knowledge of the king's character, and that of Captain Leebrick—and again, as he had dozens of times before, came to the same conclusion. That Charles or Henrietta Maria would panic in such a situation was not difficult to believe at all. That Leebrick was a traitor was not impossible, but Wentworth thought it extremely unlikely. All the more so since one of the guards keeping him captive in the Bloody Tower had let slip that there was a giant manhunt on for Leebrick and two of his lieutenants. They'd been taken for questioning by Cork, it seemed, and had then made a daring—and quite bloody—escape from his mansion.

That same bloody escape, of course, was being pointed to by Cork and his party as proof of Leebrick's complicity in a treasonous plot masterminded by Wentworth himself. But Thomas knew that was nonsense, and nonsense thrice over.

First, because as the supposed mastermind of the plot, he knew for a certainty it had never existed.

Second, because the supposed plot was preposterous to begin with—which was exactly the reason, he was quite certain, that Cork had not as yet pressed any formal charges against him. The charge was simply incoherent, looked at from the standpoint of logic.

What was he accused of trying to do? Take power? Thomas Wentworth had already *had* the power. As much as any minister of any king in English history had ever had. The only step up he could have taken would have been to depose the dynasty and replace it with one of his own—which was so ludicrous a proposition that he wondered if anyone even in that den of fools that called itself Parliament could say it publicly and keep a straight face.

In the end, he imagined, they'd accuse of him of having plotted to make himself "Lord Protector of England," using the known history of that other world as his guide. They might even go so far—probably would, in fact, since Thomas had never made a secret of his visits to the dungeon—accuse him of plotting with Cromwell himself.

Finally, it was nonsense because of the business with Leebrick. If he'd been working for Cork, why not simply pay him his thirty pieces of silver? Richard Boyle could certainly afford it. And even if one presupposed that Boyle had wanted to silence Leebrick and his men, surely—with a prepared plot and a cabal in place—he could have managed it without there having been the possibility of such a flamboyant escape by his intended victims.

No, none of it made sense. Happenstance alone had given Cork his opening, and he'd taken it.

Bleakly, Thomas stared out the window. His weeks of captivity had forced honesty upon him. Well, not that, exactly. Thomas thought he'd always been an honest man. But he'd now allow that he'd also been a man who was so intent on the rightness of his own course that he'd been oblivious—indifferent, certainly—to what other people around him might think of that course. Especially those who purported to be its supporters.

He'd made enemies, many of them, and many of them unnecessary ones. Cork had seized upon that, too.

Thomas could also have made the walk to Tower Green in two minutes, and someday he might very well do so. Walk to the same spot on the Green where William, Lord Hastings, had lost his head in 1483. The same spot where Henry VIII had beheaded two of his wives, and Queen Mary had beheaded Lady Jane Grey.

Not likely, though. The Tower Green was only used for executions that the crown wanted to be kept reasonably private. Most men lost their heads on Tower Hill, in front of the cheering mob—the London mob that detested Wentworth, because he'd stifled them. Cork would surely want to pander to that same mob.

So be it. Thomas knew now, with the advantage of hindsight, that Cork was repeating many of his own mistakes—and adding ones of his own into the bargain. Richard Boyle would find that the mob was fickle, and the king's favor more fickle still. He'd seized the power. Now, let him try to keep it.

A clatter at the door announced the arrival of the cleaning woman. The guards who accompanied her, rather. Left to her own devices, the woman would have knocked before she entered. The guards simply slammed the door aside. It was just one of the many petty little arrogances they indulged themselves in, not realizing that their effect was the exact opposite of what they intended. The earl of Strafford knew the ways of power far better than his captors. It was not true, of course, that all bullies were cowards. Many of them were not. But it was true that all bullies were insecure. Fearful of the world, if not the man they confronted at the moment.

She was a new one, he saw, but obviously a Warder's kin like the former one. Perhaps his regular cleaning woman had taken sick. That would hardly be surprising, given the cavalier way the new mercenaries had ignored Rita Simpson's sanitary arrangements. Wentworth worried now about the health of his own wife and children.

The woman placed the basket of foodstuffs upon the table and then went about her business quickly and efficiently, while the guards waited at the door, lounging against it in boredom and chatting idly. Wentworth himself simply remained at the window, ignoring them all.

To his surprise, the cleaning woman spoke to him briefly on her way out. Very softly, in words the guards couldn't hear.

"Make sure you try the new bread, my lord. It's quite tasty."

He stared at her for a moment, as she hurried toward the door, then looked back at the window. A few seconds later, he heard the guards closing the door and bolting it from the outside. That took a few seconds, since the original bolt was a heavy one and they'd added two more.

Even if they decided to re-enter, they couldn't do so quickly. Now intently curious, Thomas went over to the table and picked up the loaf of bread. When he broke it open, he discovered that a note had been tucked inside. He extracted the little piece of paper and went over to the fireplace. This early in spring, there was a fire going. Not a big one, but big enough to consume any small piece of paper that got tossed into it, within a few seconds.

It was a short note, with no signature. But Thomas was fairly certain that he recognized the handwriting. Lady Mailey's, he thought. He and the American ambassadress had exchanged a fair amount of correspondence over the months since he'd had her and her party sequestered in St. Thomas' Tower—which he could have reached from here with a walk of less than a minute. He'd been struck by the combination of her excellent penmanship and the complete absence of any of the flourishes that people in his time who had good penmanship normally added as a matter of course.

A very short note. *King James. Jeremiah 51, Verse 44.*

The one book they'd allowed him—no way to refuse, not that book—was the Bible. And it was the King James version, of course.

He found the passage quickly.

> *And I will punish Bel in Babylon, and I will bring forth out of his mouth that which he hath swallowed up: and the nations shall not flow together any more unto him: yea, the wall of Babylon shall fall.*

Slowly, he set the Bible aside and stared at the fire. Then, placed the note into the flames. Then, went back to staring at those same flames, as they consumed the wood that had once been solid and hard.

Chapter 34

By midnight, Elizabeth Lytle was anxious. Anthony and the others should have returned by now. Quite some time earlier, in fact. It didn't take but twenty minutes to walk to the house where Juliet was staying. They'd been gone for over two hours.

She put on her outerwear and opened the door, then hesitated. Walking the streets of Southwark in the middle of the night was not safe for a woman. Not for a man, either, come down to it, unless he was armed and capable with weapons.

For a moment, her lips twisted into a grimace. There was one sort of woman who did it as a matter of course, without normally being bothered. Attacked, at least. But in her whoring days, Liz had never worked the streets. She'd worked the theaters, with a far more select clientele—and one that invariably carried swords. She applied the term "whore" to herself simply because she was blunt by nature, but she'd actually been more in the way of a courtesan for gentlemen.

Still, although she'd never done it, she knew the way it was done. So, after a moment, she took off the outerwear and spent a few minutes changing into more flamboyant costume. Fortunately, with the early spring chill, she'd still cause no notice if she wore the outerwear. But any footpad would spot the underlying garments and assume she was a streetwalker plying her trade. More to the point, he'd also assume that whatever money she was carrying from her night's work wouldn't be enough to warrant the risk. Whores could be dangerous in their own right; their pimps, even more so.

She went out the door and hurried into the night. She was actually far more worried that she'd encounter a pimp who, not recognizing her, would assume she was attempting to operate on her own, and would take it upon himself to explain to her—with a beating—that such was not the way her business was properly done.

This late at night, though, the pimps would mostly be in the taverns. There really wasn't much trouble with whores in Southwark, neither from footpads nor the whores themselves. The rules were far too well established and understood. The biggest problem was usually just a too-drunk customer, but most whores could handle that difficulty on their own. All of them carried knives, if the need arose.

Liz had a knife herself, even though she'd never carried it in the course of her own assignations, in times past. Perhaps ironically, though, she probably knew how to use it better than any but the coarsest streetwalkers. Anthony had taught her—and she was carrying it tonight.

Luckily, she encountered no pimps, and only one would-be customer. He'd accepted her refusal readily enough, without pressing the matter. A youngster, some-where from the country west of London. A village lad, probably, in London for whatever reason, who'd decided to sample the wares in famed and sinful Southwark—and was far more nervous than she was. He'd practically scampered off when she declined. The biggest problem Liz had faced was not bursting into laughter at the look of confusion on the face of the poor boy. Nowhere in the legends he'd heard about Southwark was there a place for a harlot who said *no*.

Soon enough, she was near the house that Juliet and George occupied. Deliberately, she avoided the obvious approach using the street. Those same two men who had observed her earlier might still be there. Whether or not Anthony and his friends were right about her distinctive walk, and even wearing a bonnet, Liz didn't want to risk it.

So, reluctantly, she made her approach through the backways and alleys. Reluctantly, because she'd made the mistake of wearing one of her two good pairs of shoes—and Southwark's backways and alleys were even filthier than London's. She'd have to spend at least an hour getting them clean. Two, more likely, judging from the stench.

But, eventually, she made it to the house that was closest to the one she sought. Carefully peering around the corner of the house, she found herself staring right into the barrel of what she thought was a gun. A pistol of some sort, although it seemed much smaller than the wheel lock Anthony had owned.

"Not bad for an amateur," said a soft male voice. "Didn't trip even once, the last stretch. All right, Elizabeth Lytle, just step around quietly. No fuss, no ruckus. I'm not going to hurt you, I'm not going to rob you, and I'm not going to rape you. But if you give me any trouble, I will shoot you dead on the spot. Don't think I won't."

She didn't doubt it for a moment. There was something very deadly in the casual and relaxed way the man said the words, whoever he was.

She couldn't see much of him, even after she came around the corner and he was standing in front of her. On the big side, though not especially massive. But something in his easy stance made it clear to her that he would be a formidable opponent in any sort of physical confrontation. Whatever vague thoughts she'd had about the little knife tucked into her garments vanished on the spot.

His face wasn't discernible, though, between the darkness and the hat he was wearing.

"All right," he said, still speaking softly. "Now let's just go into the house."

She obeyed, moving ahead of him. She did summon up the courage to ask him: "How did you know my name?"

"What other woman would be creeping about tonight? I didn't get the name by torturing your handsome captain, if that's what you're worrying about. Just pure deductive logic. Sherlock Lefferts, that's me."

The first thing she saw when she went through the door was Anthony. He and Richard and Patrick were sitting close together on three chairs toward the back of the main room. Sitting very, very still, with their hands placed visibly on their knees.

She didn't wonder at the stillness, once she looked around the room. It seemed packed full of men, all of whom were holding peculiar weapons. Guns of some sort, although none she'd ever seen before.

There was a woman, too—not Juliet; someone Liz didn't know—holding a gun of her own. She didn't look any less dangerous than the men.

Thankfully, Juliet and George were in the room also. George looked placid; Juliet seemed distressed.

"Sorry, love," said Anthony. "I'd hoped you wouldn't come. I'm afraid they caught us as soon as we got here. It was as neat an ambush as I've ever seen."

"Wouldn't call it an 'ambush,' exactly," said the man who'd captured Liz and had just come in behind her. She heard him close the door. "I imagine you're good soldiers, Captain Leebrick, but you've got a lot to learn about our line of work."

Anthony cleared his throat. "Which is what, exactly, if I might ask? And I'd be curious—just idly, so to speak—as to how you learned my name. You've asked us no questions at all since you caught us, and we certainly didn't volunteer anything."

The man who'd captured Liz moved around her into the center of the room, so she could finally get a look at him. He'd already removed his outerwear.

Quite a handsome fellow, actually. And once she saw the grin that spread across his face, she didn't think he'd ever lack for female company. Unless he was very shy, which seemed about as likely as the Thames running backward.

"We call it commando work," he said. "As for the other, it's like I told your sweetheart. Sherlock Lefferts, they call me."

"Oh, bullshit," said the woman Liz didn't recognize. There was something quite odd about her accent. Liz was familiar with most of the accents and dialects of English in the islands, but she didn't recognize this one at all. She realized now that she'd detected the same accent in the voice of the Sherlock fellow, but it had been far more subdued. Much the same way as the accents of Anthony and Richard, if not Patrick. They'd traveled enough that they more or less automatically adapted their speech to whichever native inhabitants they found themselves among.

"Harry, stop bragging," she continued, sounding exasperated. "You got as much resemblance to Sherlock Holmes as I do to Mata Hari." She gave Liz a look that was even more exasperated. Not quite unfriendly, but close. "The only reason any of you are still alive is because you're friends of Juliet and George—well, you are, anyway. Juliet says she doesn't know these three characters from Adam. Harry figured out who the captain was just by using plain horse sense. We've known for weeks that you had three men in your house. Three men who never left it. Why? Once we got curious, Juliet asked around. Nobody knew your name, but plenty of people knew that Elizabeth Lytle had become the kept woman of an officer. A captain, not that that rank means anything in this day and age."

She turned to one of the men standing next to a side table. "Hand me that stupid thing, Don."

She held up what he passed her, and Liz saw that it was the reward poster that had been passed around all over the city. "Good thing for you the crown of England apparently is too broke to afford anyone who can draw," the woman said sarcastically. "Like idiots, we took this for good coin. I say, 'like idiots,' because we'd already figured out who those three men had to be—until we saw this stupid thing, and figured we had to be wrong. But after they tried to creep up on us tonight, the lightbulb went off."

Liz had no idea what a "lightbulb" was, but the gist of the remark was clear enough. "They might have been simple criminals," she protested. Pointlessly, of course, now that Anthony himself had already confirmed his identity.

The woman tossed the poster on the floor. "Oh, sure. Three footpads who decided it was a really bright idea to break into a house full of men. Lady, even though we've made sure none of them ever got a glimpse of our up-time weaponry, we saw to it within the first week we got here that no ambitious cutpurse would bother us. The local hoods are scared to death of us. They must figure we're a new gang of criminals setting up shop. Biggest thing we've been worried about lately is that one of Southwark's self-proclaimed 'crime lords' would hear about us and decide to lower the boom. At which point, of course, the boom turns into splinters and Ye Great Crime Boss gets turned into mincemeat, but we don't want the publicity."

"Oh, Lord in Heaven," muttered Patrick. He glanced about at the peculiar-looking guns. "You're Americans, aren't you? Come here to break into the Tower and get your people out."

"Bingo," said the Harry fellow. "Sherlock, meet Nero Wolfe. Except there's actually only two Americans in this room, properly speaking." He pointed at the woman who'd been talking. "Sherrilyn over there, and me. The rest are a bunch of down-time thugs and hoodlums I picked up along the way, being as my life's work is the rehabilitation of the criminally inclined."

Every face in the room suddenly displayed a grin, even Juliet's. Liz didn't find the sight at all reassuring, however. They looked more like a pack of wolves than ever.

The Harry fellow studied Anthony and his two companions for a few seconds. "All right, now that identities are established and everything's out in the open, let's get down to business. Captain Leebrick, the way I see it, you've only got two choices. If you choose the first option, I'd appreciate it if you'd move into the kitchen so's I can slit your throat over the washbasin. Be a lot less cleaning up to do."

"I believe I can safely state that I shall not choose that option," said Anthony. "I shan't even bother inquiring as to the opinions of my two mates. Seeing as how, come down to it, they're my subordinates."

"Didn't think you would. The alternative, then, should be obvious to you."

"Indeed it is." He was sitting between Welch and Towson, and gave them each a quick glance. "Our former employer having proven to be an unreliable fellow, we are in need of a new one. Rather desperately, in fact, especially one who has the wherewithal to get us over to the continent."

"For Christ's sake, Harry!" Sherrilyn exploded. "Are you out of your mind?"

For the first time since Liz had met him, the Harry fellow didn't seem even slightly amused. "No, Sherrilyn, I'm not," he said forcefully. "And don't push it, or I'll actually go so far as to pull rank on you. Much as I hate the idea in general. What the hell else do you want to do? Those *are* the only two options we've got, under the circumstances."

He jerked a thumb at Liz. "And if we kill them, we've got to kill Lytle too."

A little noise came from Juliet. Something halfway between a growl and a snarl.

The Harry fellow didn't even look at her. "Right. And then we've got what I will delicately call 'dissension in the ranks,' which is the last goddam thing we need. Screw it, Sherrilyn. We can always use a few more men handy with weapons, right?"

"We don't know a fucking thing about them! They could turn us in tomorrow!"

Harry stared at her. After a moment, she looked aside. "Well . . ."

"Yeah, 'well.'" He took two steps, leaned over with easy grace, and plucked the reward poster off the floor. "Yeah, well. Turn us in to the same jolly fellows who had this printed up and passed all over London. Hoping, I guess, that the picture's so crappy they wouldn't be recognized."

"Ah, not possible," said Anthony, clearing his throat. "The portraits are a travesty, true enough. But any reward for American assassins would certainly be large enough that Richard Boyle's purse would have been tapped—and I'm afraid the good earl spent some time in our company. So did Sir Paul, for that matter, and he's the other moneybags of the group."

"We'd be utter fools to even think of it, anyway," added Towson. "They'd have our own throats slit before we could start counting the money. What else could they do? We know enough to be a major embarrassment— at the very least—once they finally bring charges against Wentworth."

"Charges which they'd have to press before Parliament," Anthony picked up smoothly, "and if Parliament discovers we've surfaced—and there'd be no way to hide the fact—they'd demand our testimony."

The Sherrilyn woman's face was pinched, but she wasn't putting up any argument. Her expression was that of someone forced to eat something she didn't like, but knowing she had no way to refuse.

After a moment, she gave something in the way of an appealing look to one of the men who hadn't spoken yet. He was a tall, spare fellow standing in one of the corners of the room. There was something saturnine about his face; not sluggish, but certainly skeptical.

"Don't look at me, Sherrilyn," he said. "I think it's a splendid idea, myself."

"*Et tu*, Felix?" the woman muttered.

He smiled, the expression making him seem much less gloomy, then moved into the center of the room and took the poster from Harry and held it up in front of her.

"What more do you want, Sherrilyn? You, especially, being an American and thus obsessed with forms and documents and paperwork."

"And just what is the point of that wisecrack?" she demanded.

"I'd think it was obvious. First thing any proper bureaucratic American wants when someone applies for a job is a resumé. And here it is—complete with the best character references you could ask for. Three officers, feared enough by the earl of Cork that he wants them dead."

"Doesn't say that," she protested.

Felix waited.

"Well, not exactly," she added. Then, after glancing again at the poster held up in front of her: "All right, all right, fine. Sure, and any moron knows the truth. It's easier to bring in somebody dead than alive, anyway."

She gave the three officers a sour look, and then transferred it to Liz herself. "I withdraw my objections. But I still don't like the idea."

"Right," said Harry, clapping his hands. "Captain Leebrick, we'll discuss your pay later. Don't worry, we're not misers. And you certainly don't have to worry about getting out of England. For the moment, though, I'd like your opinion. You *have* been inside the Tower of London, I hope?"

"Oh, yes, many times. So have Richard and Patrick."

"Once had the assignment of transferring old ordnance into the keep, in fact," added Richard. "Spent a week and a half in the Tower. Went all over the place."

"I knew this was a great idea. Juliet, would you be so kind as to haul out the diagram we've been fumbling with? We can move the kitchen table out here and finally get that damn thing up to snuff."

Juliet headed for one of the rooms. Two of the men moved toward the kitchen. Harry bestowed that quite amazing grin on everyone in general and no one in particular.

"I'll think I'll retire the Sherlock monicker," he announced. "Fu Manchu Lefferts, that's me. You know, the guy that was Sherlock's enemy."

Sherrilyn squinted, painfully. "God save us. Harry, Sherlock Holmes' archenemy was Professor Moriarty."

"Oh. Well, can't have that. I ain't got a tweed jacket with elbow patches."

"How about Harry the Merciless?" suggested Felix.

"Got a nice little ring to it, doesn't it?" mused Harry.

"God save us," repeated Sherrilyn. "God save us all."

Liz thought it was probably a good sentiment. But whether it was or not, the glance Sherrilyn gave her now was more of an appealing one than a hostile one. *Us all*, clearly enough, was a term that had just been expanded to include four more people.

Chapter 35

The Elbe, near Dömitz

"You can't do this! You're destroying my property! It's illegal!"

Admiral John Simpson stood on the foredeck of the SSIM *Constitution*, his back to the closed port stoppers of the wing ten-inch guns, and glanced at his wristwatch while Freiherr von Bleckede frothed.

"Unfortunately, Freiherr," Matthias Schaubach said reasonably, "Time is no longer—"

"Be *silent*!" Bleckede literally stamped his foot, glaring at the ex-salt merchant who had inherited the thoroughly unpleasant task of negotiating with the scores of people—like Bleckede—who controlled the existing means of navigation along the Elbe.

Or, rather, Simpson thought coldly, *the scores of people who* used to *control the means of navigation*.

"I refuse to permit this!" Bleckede snapped. "If you dare to—"

"Excuse me, Freiherr von Bleckede," Simpson said, looking up from his watch, "but I'm afraid this entire conversation is rather pointless. Unless, of course, you are prepared to resort to force."

Schaubach hid a smile behind a suddenly raised hand as Simpson quirked one eyebrow. The admiral simply gazed attentively at Bleckede, without once so much as glancing at the escorting cavalry and volley gun crews watching with interest as Simpson's Marine combat engineers placed the charges.

Bleckede seemed to swell to even greater dimensions, and his face turned a remarkable shade of puce. For a moment, Schaubach entertained the hope that apoplexy was about to carry the man off—*and leave the world a better place, afterward*, the Magdeburger thought tartly. But he was disappointed. Instead, the baron drew a deep breath and clenched his jaw.

"Of course I can't 'resort to force,' Admiral!" he said after a moment. "But that doesn't change the fact that—"

"Freiherr," Simpson said, "Herr Schaubach has been attempting for months to negotiate a mutually satisfactory solution to our problem. You, unfortunately, have declined to cooperate with that effort. Well, we've run out of time, and we *are* going to move these ships down this river. Which, unfortunately, means that unless you wish to come with us, it's time for you to go ashore."

"But . . . but . . . !"

"I'm afraid this conversation is over, Freiherr," Simpson said coolly. "If you have any further points to make, I invite you to make them directly to Emperor Gustav. In the meantime, I have a schedule to keep. Lieutenant," he glanced at the uniformed, stonefaced

Marine standing at Bleckede's elbow, "would you be kind enough to escort the baron ashore?"

"Of course, sir!" the Marine replied crisply in a broad, lower-class Saxon accent. It would, perhaps, have been untactful to have dwelt upon the undeniable gleam of pleasure in the lieutenant's eyes as he turned and bowed with exquisite courtesy to Bleckede.

"If you'll come this way, Freiherr," he invited. The baron glared at him, then started to turn back to Simpson, and the lieutenant, who was at least three inches taller than the dyspeptic, overweight, middle-aged aristocrat, took him politely but firmly—*very* firmly—by the elbow.

"I'm afraid I'll have to insist, Freiherr."

The Marine's tone was still polite, but just a bit more frigid than it had been a moment before, and Bleckede winced as the lieutenant's fingertips dug into the nerves of his elbow.

"I have friends close to the emperor!" the baron said, rather less forcefully. "I assure you, you haven't heard the last of this, *Admiral.*"

"No doubt, Freiherr," Simpson agreed. "And now, good day."

He nodded to the lieutenant, and Bleckede was escorted courteously across to the rowboat moored alongside *Constitution.* He climbed down into it, still spluttering like eggs frying in bacon grease, and the grinning navy sailors at the oars promptly cast off and began pulling strongly towards the shore.

"Admiral," Schaubach said as the boat moved away, "did you enjoy that conversation as much as I did?"

"Probably," Simpson said judiciously. "At any rate, I've been looking forward to it for quite some time."

"As have I." Schaubach's profound satisfaction was evident, and Simpson chuckled.

"I must confess," the ex-salt merchant continued after a moment, "that I expected him to . . . see reason in the end."

"Some people are just too deeply committed to the way they *think* the world works to recognize the way it really does work," Simpson replied. In fact, as he was unhappily well aware, he had occasionally found himself in that particular group. "Usually, they discover their error rather . . . painfully," he added. And that, too, was something John Chandler Simpson knew about from personal experience.

"Well, it may be petty of me, but I can't deny that I feel a certain satisfaction that the good baron's refusal to cooperate means he won't be compensated for his losses," Schaubach admitted, and this time Simpson's chuckle of agreement was harder and harsher.

Freiherr von Bleckede was the owner of one of the *wehrleucken*. Unlike the majority of his counterparts, he had flatly refused to cooperate with the effort to get Simpson's squadron down the river. Work crews had labored through the wet and miserable winter to build temporary *staustufen* atop most of the existing *wehrleucken*. In some cases, where the owners had signed on enthusiastically to the original plan to improve navigation on the Elbe, the modifications were permanent, not temporary. In those instances, the *wehrleucken* themselves had been raised to the new, higher level, with much wider spillways—effectively, locks controlled by movable wooden cofferdams. Those *wehrleucken* were now large enough—and deep enough—to allow the gunboats passage, and their owners could anticipate substantial future revenues from the increasing trade moving up and down the river.

Others, who had initially resisted, had capitulated when Schaubach mentioned that the emperor would be personally very grateful if they could only see their way to assisting his American allies and subjects at this particularly crucial moment. Since there had usually been at least a hundred or so of the emperor's Finnish cavalry standing rather prominently about and looking as disreputable as possible, even the most recalcitrant had generally found it within themselves to cooperate with their emperor in his time of need.

Those individuals had watched as their *wehrleucken* were raised by additional *staustufen*. In most instances, breaking the *staustufen* to allow the gunboats to surf through on the resultant wave had resulted in fairly moderate, repairable damage to the *wehrleucken* involved. In some instances, unfortunately, the damage had been much more severe. But because their owners had cooperated, they could expect reasonable compensation for their losses. Of course, "reasonable" as defined by Gustav Adolf might not be precisely the same amount *they* had in mind, but it was certainly going to be better than nothing.

And then there was that handful of individuals, like Freiherr von Bleckede, who had obstinately refused to see reason. There were no *staustufen* in their cases. Instead, they could anticipate visits from Simpson's demolition engineers.

And, unfortunately, Gustav Adolf, who was a firm believer in the stick, as well as the carrot, was about to prove remarkably resistant to *their* demands for compensation.

Too bad, John Chandler Simpson thought cheerfully as he turned and started up the steep ladder to *Constitution*'s bridge once more while Captain Halberstat carefully maneuvered his command into position. He could see spectators lining the banks, and every crewman who could had come topside to watch the show, as well. Although Halberstat and the other gunboat skippers had already done it several times, shooting the gap in the dam through the flurry of rushing water and foam was going to be exciting, for both spectators and participants, and Simpson grinned at the thought. He wasn't about to admit it, but he found the experience just as exhilarating as his most junior seaman did.

And this time, he reflected as the last of the engineers finished placing their charges and scampered for cover, it was going to be even more enjoyable than usual.

The Øresund, near Helsingør

"I'm none too happy with these things, Ulrik," said Baldur Norddahl. He was bestowing a very dubious look on the mine they were about to lower off the stern of the little ship into the Øresund. More precisely, a dubious look at the five flimsy-looking contact fuses that protruded from it, all of which were tied together by a thin cord. Once the mine's anchor was resting on the bottom somewhere between thirty and sixty feet below the surface, and the mine's depth was properly adjusted, Baldur would yank on the cord. That would remove the little pins that kept the fuses from being armed prematurely.

In practice, Baldur had told the prince, the act of yanking the cord itself would set off the mine one time in six. That could produce a dangerous situation for the mine-laying ship, of course. But it was not nearly as dangerous as taking the risk of fuses that were too sensitive.

"Don't blame you," said Ulrik. He would have added—for perhaps the thousandth time—*my father and his damned enthusiasms*, but in this instance that wouldn't have been fair. The king of Denmark had allowed his son to determine how to detonate the devices, since he wasn't very partial to them anyway. Ulrik had been the one to finally order this method, since it was the only one feasible in the time they had.

A pity, that. Ulrik had wanted to use the sort of manually controlled detonations by wire that Baldur had found in one of the copies of up-time texts. The Øresund was narrow enough here between Helsingør and Helsingborg—only three miles—that that had seemed feasible. But . . .

There just hadn't been enough time. By now, Baldur's artisans understood the basic methods for generating electricity, well enough. Getting a good enough current to pass through a long wire immersed in salt water, however, had proven to be a lot more difficult than they'd anticipated.

So, in the end, Ulrik had opted for the contact fuses. With the new percussion caps supplied to them by the French, those had been workable. Tricky—not to mention risky—but workable.

The men handling the mine slid it into the water. Ulrik straightened up and looked across the sound at Helsingborg, on the Scandinavian mainland. The town and its fortress belonged to Denmark in this era, as it had for a very long time. At some point in the middle of this century, however, it was "scheduled" to be taken by Sweden. The prince's father was determined to see that wouldn't happen, but as time passed Ulrik himself was becoming increasingly gloomier. He wouldn't be surprised if the Swedes held it by the end of the year.

Or the end of the summer. The young Danish prince knew that his father had been both foolish and reckless to throw his lot in with the League of Ostend. Richelieu and his assurances, bah!

There was simply not enough *time*. At best, even at the relentless pace Baldur and his men had been working, they'd only have perhaps a third of this narrowest part of the Øresund protected by mines before the ironclads arrived.

If they arrived at all, that is. Christian IV's courtiers were still assuring the king of Denmark that the foolhardy American admiral would come to ruin long before he could even reach the Skagerrak. That was possible, of course, but Ulrik had his doubts. He thought Simpson *would* come—but might very well avoid the mines altogether. The American admiral certainly had to be aware of the possible danger, and he'd also have figured out that the Øresund was the only one of the straits that his enemy could possibly have laid with mines. All he had to do was simply approach Copenhagen through the Great Belt. That would add many miles to his voyage, true enough— but what would that matter, if he could make the much longer voyage from the mouth of the Elbe through the North Sea, the Skagerrak and the Kattegat?

At which point, of course, he might ignore Copenhagen altogether. At least initially. Once he exited the Great Belt, he would be closer to Luebeck than to the Danish capital. He'd probably go after the Danish fleet in the bay outside the besieged city before he came to threaten the Danish capital.

But come he would, sooner or later; of that Ulrik had become almost certain. And if he came from the south, all the labor of planting these mines would have been useless. In the end, all they'd have would be the spar torpedoes.

Ulrik saw that Baldur seemed satisfied with the placement of the mine. The Norwegian planted a foot on the gunwale and took a tighter grip on the arming cord.

"Brace yourselves!" he hollered. "This is the joyous moment, boys."

Seeing the Danish sailors around him flexing their knees—the "minelayer's stance," they called it—and grasping whatever supports stood nearby, Ulrik did the same.

After glancing around to see that everyone was ready, Baldur gave the cord a heroic yank.

The prince held his breath. There was . . .

Nothing. Not a trace of the water column Baldur had warned him about, that could snap a ship caught by it right in half and break the legs of a man if he was standing stiffly. The fuses had been armed without being detonated.

"And wasn't that fun?" said Baldur cheerily, coiling the lanyard as he reeled it out of the water.

"We'd best return," said Ulrik. "My father insists that I attend the diving demonstration."

"Another joyous occasion," said Baldur. "I wouldn't miss it for all the world."

Ulrik could have said those sentences dripped sarcasm, but that would be inaccurate. They were saturated with sarcasm. Oozed it from every pore.

"Yes," said Ulrik. "Not for all the world."

He could have added *my father and his enthusiasms,* but there was no point. By now, as closely as they had worked together for the past few months, Ulrik and Baldur had exhausted all possible variations on that theme.

The man being fitted into the diving suit had very pale skin to begin with, so it was hard to tell if his pallor was due in any part to fear. If that had been Eddie himself, he was sure he'd have been as white as a ghost.

"You look very pale," Anne Cathrine said. "Are you ill again?"

Damn the girl, Eddie would have thought, except he was long past the point where he could bring himself to curse this particular female, even to himself. How in the name of God had a sensible—well, within reason—twenty-year-old naval officer developed a crush on a fifteen-year-old? The worst crush he'd ever had in his life, to boot, even worse than the one he'd had when he was her age for Casey Stevenson, the head cheerleader at the high school.

Maybe he just had an attraction for unobtainable women, he thought gloomily. Casey had been three years older than he, which, in the social context of a rural high school, made her no less out of his league than the princess standing next to him.

Fine. "King's daughter." What was the difference, in this day and age? Even leaving aside the fact that she was the offspring of his sworn enemy?

"Are you ill?" Anne Cathrine repeated, this time with more concern in her voice. "You are still weak, Eddie. And you are a bit frail to begin with."

Oh, swell. Frail to begin with. Any moment now, Eddie, you'll be sweeping her off her feet.

"No, I'm fine," he muttered.

Actually, he was, relatively speaking. His stump didn't ache much anymore, he'd gotten fairly accustomed to the wooden pegleg, and he'd recovered from the illness he'd come down with for a week in February, whatever it had been. Eddie just labeled it "the medieval crud" and left it at that. If *he* were the king of Denmark, he'd be throwing every spare coin he had at the plumbing industry, not wasting it on a dozen grandiose military schemes—at least half of which had no serious application to warfare anyway. Not for a decade, at least.

Like this one. Leaving aside the incredible risk to the men involved, what in God's name did Christian IV think he could do against Simpson's ironclads with a man in an old-fashioned diving suit?

Scuba equipped divers, now, that might be a different story. Eddie knew that the French had somehow managed to get their hands on some of that equipment. The king had let that slip in one of his drunken confidences—along with his bitter resentment that the French refused to let him have any of it.

Eddie and Ulrik had once teamed up to try to talk the king out of the diving suit nonsense. Eddie had felt a little guilty about that, since from a cold-blooded

Agent 007 standpoint, he should probably have been encouraging Christian to continue with the foolish business. But . . .

The problem there was that, over the months of his captivity, he'd come to be almost as fond of Ulrik as he was of the prince's half-sister Anne Cathrine. And, as bold as the prince was, Eddie was worried he might test the crazy diving suit himself.

Damnation. He was reminded of a quip that he'd once read in a book, made by one of the great particle physicists up-time when they'd discovered a particle nobody had expected or predicted. He wasn't sure which one had made the wisecrack—Fermi, maybe, or Murray Gell-Mann—but he'd been charmed enough by the comment itself to remember it.

Who ordered this?

Exactly the plaint Eddie had been making silently for some time now. If Fate were to have him be captured by the enemy, what idiot ordered captors that he *liked*? Even had the hots for, in the case of one.

Eddie half-glared down at the king. Eddie and Anne Cathrine were standing by the stone ledge that served as a safety barrier for the road running alongside the Øresund a few miles north of Copenhagen. Christian IV, besotted as always with mechanical contraptions, was standing below them on the wharf right next to the pump, overseeing the whole process. Or driving the artisans nuts, take your pick.

The truth was, Eddie even liked the Danish monarch. Except when he was drunk, at least, which was half the time. Even then, Christian was a friendly and jovial souse, not at all like the nasty bastard Eddie's father had been when he was pickled. But having grown up with

an alcoholic parent, Eddie didn't drink much himself
and had a low tolerance for drunkards.

Anne Cathrine tugged on his sleeve. "You should
be wearing a better coat, Eddie. It's still cold, in the
beginning of April."

He almost grit his teeth. The princess—fine, "king's
daughter"—was wearing nothing more than her usual
apparel. The same sort of garments she wore in the
castle.

She wasn't frail, of course. Oh, hell no. A cross
between a Valkyrie and a Danish dairy maid. With
the looks of the former and the constitution of the
latter. All she needed was breast plates.

Best not to think about that, though. They'd probably have to be whatever the Valkyrie equivalent of
D-cups were—C-cups, for sure—and Eddie was *trying*
to maintain his sanity and not do anything incredibly
stupid and suicidal like—

Really best not to think about that.

Fortunately, he had a distraction. The diver was
finally entering the water, carefully lowering himself
into the Øresund with the help of two other men
holding ropes. Even leaving aside the risk, Eddie didn't
envy the poor man. That suit had to weigh a ton, and
the water would be frigid. Hopefully, the first misery
would offset the latter, at least to a degree.

The man wasn't supposed to spend all that long
underwater, at least. Even the king had allowed that
it wouldn't make much of a test if the testee froze
to death halfway through.

"He's a brave man," Eddie said, shaking his head.

Anne Cathrine shrugged. "Not so brave as all that.
He was supposed to be executed next week. Tortured

first, too, I think. Killed a man and his wife in a robbery. Our father promised him a pardon if he survived the test."

The matter-of-fact way she said that reminded Eddie forcefully—it was easy to forget, often, around her and her half-brother—that he was not only a captive, but a captive in the miserable benighted seventeenth century, to boot. "The Early Modern Era," historians called it.

What a laugh. *Ripe Medieval* would have been Eddie's pick. Complete with dungeons and heated tongs and outdoor sewage.

Hearing a commotion behind him on the road, he turned his head. A carriage was pulling up and coming to stop. Prince Ulrik and his tame Norwegian half-tech-whiz and half-cutthroat had finally arrived.

"About time!" boomed the king, once his son emerged from the vehicle. "You almost missed it!" He pointed at the water, where the diver's helmet was disappearing beneath the surface.

Ulrik gave his father a half-apologetic wave of the hand and came to stand next to Eddie and Anne Cathrine. His Norwegian sidekick, on the other hand, climbed down the ladder to the wharf and went over to the pump. Baldur was almost as bad as the king, when it came to being obsessed with gadgetry, even gadgetry that he didn't approve of. Eddie knew that Norddahl was no more in favor of working on diving suits than Ulrik was.

But the king had decreed, and so it would be—and Baldur wasn't about to miss the chance to fiddle with his gear.

Hopefully, he wouldn't be fiddling much, if at all.

Ever since Ulrik and Baldur had raised this project with Eddie, he'd been trying to remember what he'd read about it years earlier. There'd been a brief stretch there, back when he was fourteen, where Eddie had developed the ambition to become an oceanographer. He'd dropped the idea, soon enough, once he got a better sense of how much tedium the apparently glamorous profession actually had in practice. In that respect, it was much like being an archaeologist or an astronomer. They were all professions that looked really cool in the movies, but in the real world mostly involved tedious and repetitive work recording data. The intellectual equivalent of being a ditch-digger, it seemed to him. By then, he'd veered off into his *I'll-be-a-NASCAR-race-driver* phase, anyway.

The problem was that Eddie couldn't remember much about whatever he'd read concerning this sort of diving. Or scuba diving, for that matter. Like any proper fourteen-year-old enthusiast, Eddie had been interested in *deep* sea diving. The sort of enterprise that you couldn't possibly do in any kind of personal diving gear. For that you needed the really nifty stuff like bathyspheres or bathyscapes—and if something went wrong at those depths, there wasn't anything to worry about.

Poof—or maybe *crunch*—and it was all over.

The only thing he did recall was that something he'd read had made him solemnly vow he'd never get into this sort of diving suit. But he couldn't for the life of him remember what it was. Just . . . something, that went beyond the usual perils of drowning or the bends. Something really grisly.

The diver had now apparently reached the bottom.

Eddie didn't know what sort of surface he was walking on. Nothing too rocky, he hoped. But he did know that the depth here was almost sixty feet, because the king had remarked that he'd picked this spot because it was the deepest place his workmen had been able to find in the Øresund that wouldn't require doing the test from the back of a boat. At least Christian had had enough sense not to add that complication on top of everything else—although it was typical of the man to have chosen the deepest possible place for a first test. God forbid anything should be done by halves in Denmark, the way they were in more sensible lands ruled by dullard but thankfully unimaginative kings.

There being nothing to see beyond a hose entering the water and moving slowly about, Eddie dredged up his memory and did some calculations. Water pressure increased by one atmosphere every thirty-three feet, with sea level pressure being 14.7 pounds per square inch. Call it thirty pounds per square inch at a depth of thirty-five feet, and forty-five pounds at a depth of sixty-five feet. That meant the diver, at a depth of approximately sixty feet, had about forty pounds per square inch pressing on every square inch of his body surface.

The suit's surface, rather. How many square inches did that suit have?

Eddie had no idea. The only answer he could come up with was *lots*. He lifted his forearm and looked down on it, trying to estimate how many square inches there were just on that small part of his body alone. The coat sleeve wasn't as thick and bulky as a diving suit, of course, but . . .

Close enough. He figured there were somewhere

between sixteen and twenty-four square inches of surface just on the upper side of his forearm. Call it twenty square inches. Then multiply by . . . he figured three times would give a reasonable estimate of the total surface area of his entire forearm. Sixty square inches, then.

Each and every one of which, for that diver down there, had an extra twenty-five pounds squeezing down on them. That was three-quarters of a ton's worth of pressure just on one forearm alone. For his whole body, who knew? Ten tons, at least. Maybe fifteen.

To be sure, he wouldn't be feeling it, since the pump was maintaining a higher air pressure in the suit to compensate. But if anything went wrong . . .

Eddie suddenly remembered what he'd forgotten. *No wonder he'd forgotten it!*

"Eddie, you should go inside," Anne Cathrine said forcefully. "You're looking more pale than ever."

He ignored her, turning to Ulrik. "Do you have a—a—? Ah! I can't remember what they're called. A safety valve. On the hose, near the pump."

He made vague, groping gestures with his hands, trying to delineate something he could only vaguely describe. "It's like a check-valve. What it does, if the pump suddenly fails, is automatically lock—so the higher-air pressure in the suit can't escape."

Ulrik frowned. "I don't know. I don't believe so. But I'd have to ask Baldur."

As always, they'd been speaking the German which served the royal Danes and Eddie alike as a common tongue. The prince raised his voice and started jabbering some Danish at the Norwegian standing next to the king below. Eddie could now understand some of the language, but these quickly shouted words he could only guess at.

Baldur looked up. After a moment, he shook his head and jabbered something back. It was clear enough to Eddie from the expression on Baldur's face that the answer wasn't even *no, we don't*. It was more along the lines of *what are you talking about?*

"Get him out of there, Ulrik," Eddie hissed. "The diver, I mean. Pull him out. *Now*."

Ulrik frowned. That would require overriding—trying to, anyway—his father. Which was no small chore, to put it mildly, whenever Christian IV had his heart set on something.

He shrugged. "I'll try."

But before he could even speak a word, there was a sudden hubbub among the men working the pump.

One of them jabbered something at the king. Eddie had gotten familiar enough with Danish to grasp that the gist of what he was saying was that something seemed to be wrong.

Eddie looked at the hose. Sure enough. There were *so* many ways to get killed doing this. The hose was now thrashing about, in a sluggish sort of way. Eddie was sure it had ruptured somewhere along the line.

"Pull him out! Now!" Ulrik shouted. Those simple Danish terms, at least, Eddie understood.

The king didn't seem inclined to argue the matter. The diver had two ropes attached to him as well as the hose. The workmen standing by started hauling on them. Meanwhile, the men at the pump continued their useless labor.

Baldur took off his boots and his coat and jumped into the water, disappearing below the surface.

"What's wrong, Eddie?" asked Anne Cathrine. "And you look really sick, now. You should go inside."

He grasped at that straw. He knew what was coming up out of the water—he remembered it all, now, too late for it to do any good—and he had no desire to let the king's daughter see it. She was only fifteen years old.

For that matter, Eddie didn't want to see it himself. He could remember being sick to his stomach, just reading about it.

"You're right, I'm not feeling well. Perhaps I should return."

"Into my brother's carriage, at least. We'll have to wait for Ulrik before we can go back to Rosenborg Castle. But it'll be warmer in the carriage than it is out here, with the wind. Here, let me help you."

She took him around the waist with her right arm and began propelling him toward the carriage some twenty yards away. Then, not satisfied with the arrangement, pulled his left arm over her shoulder so she could carry more of his weight, while he used his cane with his other arm. By now, Eddie was getting around well enough on his wooden leg that he'd been able to dispense with the crutches.

The contact was intimate enough to distract Eddie quite nicely from more unpleasant matters. Of course, it also made him very nervous. Even after the months he'd spent in Danish captivity, he still hadn't been able to figure out the social parameters involved. Christian IV seemed oddly oblivious to the relationship that was developing—so to speak, since Eddie didn't really know what it was himself—between his American captive and his oldest surviving daughter.

Fine, she wasn't technically a "princess" because her mother, Kirsten Munk, hadn't been highly enough ranked in the nobility for anything but a morganatic marriage. Big deal. The oldest daughter was still the oldest daughter—and the father was a no-fooling seventeenth-century goddamit king. One hell of a lot closer in time and spirit to Henry VIII than he was to the harmless royals that Eddie had grown up with. Queen Elizabeth II waving at crowds from an open car, looking sweet and just a bit insipid; Princess Diana, who couldn't harm anything except the reputation of the British royal family and who cared anyway; and a whole passel of silly idiots losing money in the casinos in Monte Carlo.

Eddie never quite knew what might or might not get him hauled to the chopping block. What made it all the more odd was that Anne Cathrine seemed just as oblivious to the matter as her father. From one day to the next, Eddie couldn't tell if she was in any way attracted to him as a man. One day, he'd swear she was. The next . . .

Who ordered this?

Granted, Eddie had never been what anyone in their right mind would call a ladies' man, bowling over the girls right and left. But at least in his comfortable and familiar world back up time, he'd known when he was pining away hopelessly.

Okay, pretty much all of the time, that had been. But he'd *known*.

"Will that man be all right?" Anne Cathrine asked, as they came up to the carriage. A coachman held the door open for them.

There was no point in lying. "No, he won't," Eddie

said harshly. "He's already dead. He was dead before Baldur went down after him."

Frowning, the king's daughter more or less hoisted him up into the carriage without waiting for the coachman's assistance. The combination of that pretty teenage frown and the Valkyrie strength almost made Eddie laugh, despite the circumstances. His new world seemed full of contradictions.

"That can't be right," she said firmly, climbing in after him. "Drowning isn't that quick."

Eddie eased himself into the bench, and the king's daughter sat next to him. He was about to say, "He didn't drown, Anne Cathrine," but caught himself in time. The girl was nothing if not inquisitive. She'd want an explanation, and that was the last thing Eddie wanted to provide her. He didn't even want to think about it himself.

Especially not after, thirty seconds later, she gave him a mischievous smile. "You are too much the gentleman," she proclaimed. "I've given up."

Then, kissed him. Then, did it again, for a lot longer.

So, at least one question was answered. There remained only the petty details of which form of execution the king would select, once he got wind of the situation. But Eddie, in the middle of the hottest necking session he'd ever had in his life, gave that piddly problem no thought at all.

Some time later, they heard people approaching the carriage and resumed more decorous positions. Anne Cathrine looked a bit flushed, immensely pleased, and fifteen going on thirty. Eddie had no idea what he looked like. Twenty going on thirteen, he suspected.

Not that he cared. Bring on the headsman; he'd greet him with a sneer. The world has no greater armor than a flood of hormones.

Ulrik came in first, with his sidekick right behind. As he clambered in, Norddahl called out something to the coachmen. As soon as he closed the door, the coach set off for Copenhagen.

"Ghastly," the prince proclaimed. "Never seen anything like it."

He was sitting on the bench opposite Eddie and Anne Cathrine. Norddahl slid onto the same bench. "You, Baldur?" the prince asked. "Have you?"

The Norwegian shook his head. "No, Your Highness. And I'd have thought by now I'd seen just about any way a man could get killed."

Alas, Anne Cathrine was now intrigued. "What happened? I thought he drowned."

"Oh, no. Lucky for him, I suppose," said her half-brother. "Drowning's slow. People say it's a good way to go, though I have my doubts. But this one died instantly."

"Couldn't have even known it was happening," Baldur said, "it had to have been so quick. Judging from the results."

The king's daughter's eyes were wide. She didn't look fifteen-going-on-thirty, any more. She looked fifteen-and-no-kitten-is-more-curious.

"What *happened*?"

Ulrik grimaced and held up his hands, as if holding a big globe. "Most of his body was in the helmet. All mashed up like you wouldn't believe. Every bone in pieces, all crushed together with flesh and blood. You couldn't really recognize most of the organs."

"Never seen anything like it," Baldur repeated. "The first fifteen feet of the hose attached to the helmet were full of him, too. Like a bloody meat paste."

The king's daughter clapped her hand over her mouth. "Oh! That's horrible!"

Norddahl shrugged. "He died a lot quicker than he would have, a week from now, in the executioner's hands. But it was the most gruesome thing I've ever seen."

Ulrik was peering at Eddie. "Can you explain what happened?"

Since Eddie's attempt to shield the girl was now pointless, he heaved a little sigh. "Yeah. There was probably something like twelve tons of pressure on his body, that all caved in at once. Like a giant squeezing a toothpaste tube. His body had nowhere to go except into the helmet and the hose. I think they call it 'excarnation.'"

He had to say the last word in English, of course. But what everyone really wanted was an explanation of the other American term. And once he explained what a toothpaste tube was, even Norddahl grimaced.

"Oh, that's icky!" said Anne Cathrine. She frowned at her half-brother. "Ulrik, you have to *promise* you won't try that yourself. You either, Baldur."

"No fear of that!" Ulrik exclaimed. "Even our sainted father is now persuaded that it's a hopeless way to wage war."

The Norwegian wasn't looking as cheerful, though. "He'll still want me to keep working on it. Not much, of course, since I've already provided him with what he needs."

Eddie squinted at him. "Huh? I thought you said—"

"Hopeless for *war*," explained Ulrik. "On the other

hand, it struck my father that it would make a splendid form of execution. Too expensive, of course, for common crimes. But for high treason—gross outrages against the monarchy—that sort of thing—the king thinks it would serve nicely."

That sort of thing. Eddie wondered if necking with the king's daughter fell into that category. It might. You never really knew until it was too late. Fucking goddam seventeenth century.

Anne Cathrine's hand slid into his and seemed bound and determined to stay there. Her half-brother gave the clasp a glance, then smiled slightly, but said nothing.

On the other hand, you really *didn't* know. It might all work out very nicely, too.

Who the hell ordered this, anyway? I'm just a West Virginia country boy.

Chapter 36

Magdeburg

"But no bombing?" Jesse asked.

Mike Stearns shook his head. "No. John's got his ironclads parked—moored, anchored, whatever the right term is for boats on a river—not more than three miles from Hamburg. If he has to make the run, he tells me that any bombs you could drop would just be a drop in the bucket." Mike grinned. "He also added that you shouldn't take offense at any implied sneer coming from a squid."

Jesse sniffed. "Give it a few more years and let's hear him say that." But he didn't argue the point. Right now—probably for a fair number of years—the destruction Simpson could bring down on Hamburg with four ironclads and their ten-inch main guns simply dwarfed anything Jesse could do with two airplanes. Even the Gustavs were still small warcraft. While they could carry far more weight than a Belle, they weren't exactly B-17s. They were armed with a mixture of rockets and bombs, though the rockets were still inaccurate and the few bombs no more than one-hundred-pounders.

Not that they didn't pack a punch. Unlike the Belle, the Gustav had been designed from the start with hardpoints under its low wings and fuselage and had the power to lift a solid war load. Up to eight twenty-five-pound rockets could be carried under the wings, plus either two fifty-pound bombs or one hundred-pounder under the fuselage. At need, two rockets could be replaced with an additional fifty-pounder on each wing.

But the bombs were black powder packed into aerodynamic wooden casings. An inner lining of rifle balls made them deadly against soft targets, but they couldn't penetrate squat all. Hal Smith was working on an incendiary version, but they hadn't tested it, yet.

"Besides," Mike continued, "I want to avoid that anyway. I know you don't want to hear this from a politician covered in muck, but the fact is that I want to avoid as much as possible anything that neither you nor I likes to call 'collateral damage' but there it is. Meaning no offense, again, but you're also a long ways away from what anyone would call precision bombing. And you don't have a so-called 'smart bomb' to your name."

Jesse sniffed again. "I always thought those terms were oxymorons, anyway. A bomb's only as smart as the person aiming it. War's war. People get killed, and plenty of them are noncombatants. Way it is."

He gave the prime minister a skeptical look. "Although why you think that Simpson's guns are going to do any better is a mystery to me. Dive-bombing, I can pretty much promise a circular error probable of one hundred feet. That can't be any worse than his ten-inch guns will do, firing into Hamburg from the river."

Mike shrugged. "They won't do any better. At least

some of those shells are bound to miss the fortifications and go sailing into the city. But down-timers are plenty familiar with cannons and what they do and don't do. If John misses, people will assume he missed. If you missed, who knows that they'll think?"

Jesse thought about it and decided Mike was probably right. Whether he was or not, however, he was certainly the boss so that was that. And Jesse didn't really care anyway. For all the back-and-forth ribbing and needling between him and Simpson, there wasn't any real heat to it. The few genuine arguments they got into at least involved genuine issues. Thankfully, they were also a long ways from being in a situation where they had to squabble over contracts for the sake of guarding budgetary turf. If Jesse was lucky, he'd be dead before that became a problem.

"And they'll have an airfield ready?"

Mike nodded. "John already has his army escort working on it. Doesn't take much, he said, since they found a nice field close to the river. It's actually on a big island formed by the confluence of the Elbe and one of its tributaries, so it's well protected even if it's not a huge area. Meaning no offense from a squid, he added, suggesting that your splendid fighting machines didn't exactly require a landing field suitable for a B-52."

"Guy's a smart-ass, Mike, beneath that oh-so-proper upper crust exterior. But I'll take his word for it. How soon?"

"He said you could land by tomorrow, midafternoon. Then do the overflights the next day. He needs that time anyway to do maintenance on the boats and get their fuel tanks topped off. If the Hamburg establishment doesn't come to their senses, he'll do the run the following morning."

"He'll do it in daylight?"

"That's his plan—unless you spot something that requires him to rethink it."

"Like what?"

"Who knows?" Mike said, shrugging. "A fourteen-inch gun that might actually threaten his armor, instead of the cannons he's pretty sure they have. Failing that, he'd rather have the advantage of daylight."

"If the Hamburgers were smart they'd have a big chain across the river—and a mine field. I might spot the chain, but I'm not likely to spot any mines unless they're badly placed."

"They've got a chain, all right. But no mines."

"You're sure about that?"

Mike smiled coolly. "Oh, yes. There *are* advantages, you know, to being a disreputable rabble-rouser."

"Don't tell me. Gretchen's got people in Hamburg."

"Be better to say the CoC does. They've become quite powerful there, in fact, But I don't think Gretchen herself had anything to do with it. That she-devil reputation she's gotten—all across Europe, seems like—is more than a little inflated."

Jesse chuckled. "Handy, though, isn't it?"

"Yup. For me even more than her, as often as not. But the point is—yes, we have excellent intelligence in Hamburg. More than that, in fact. The CoC is prepared to cut the chain for us. I don't know the details, but Simpson's been in touch with them and seems confident they can manage it."

Jesse grimaced. "That's likely to get tough on them, after the ironclads pass through."

The expression on the prime minister's face lost any trace of humor. "No, it won't, Jesse. The CoC has a lot of people in Hamburg by now, enough to hold off the garrison for a day or two. And that's all it'll take. Torstensson's personally leading eight regiments to Hamburg. They started marching five days ago—they'd already been pre-positioned at Lauenburg—and by tomorrow evening should have reached the airfield. They'll set up camp there. At which point you'll fly back here and be ready to fly me to Hamburg."

"Ha. The negotiator with a big gun. Walk softly and carry a Sequoia. You're not fooling around, I take it."

"Nope. And Gustav Adolf sure as hell isn't. If Simpson has to blow his way through Hamburg, that city's authorities just lost whatever trace of goodwill they still had in the emperor's account. Which wasn't much to begin with. They'll register a flaming protest to him, and the gist of his answer will be: 'If you think that was bad, *heeeere*'s Torstensson. Or you can cut a deal with Mike Stearns.' And I'm going to be a real hard-ass."

"I'm not sure eight regiments are enough to storm the city, Mike, if they balk. Hamburg's got pretty damn good fortifications, by all accounts."

Mike's cool smile came back. "Not after the admiral goes through them, it won't."

The Elbe, near Hamburg

"That's the final readiness report, sir," Lieutenant Chomse said.

"Good." Admiral Simpson nodded in satisfaction. Franz-Leo Chomse was as conscientious and efficient an aide as he could have asked for. In fact, in most ways, he was far more satisfactory than Eddie Cantrell had ever been. He was certainly more attentive, and he carried around none of Eddie's impossible to eradicate "smartass attitude," for want of a better word. And yet, however little he was prepared to admit it to most people, Simpson found himself deeply regretting Eddie's absence.

It wasn't the first time that had happened. Simpson often wondered if Eddie was as surprised by the turn their relationship had taken as he himself was. Or, for that matter, if Eddie was actually fully aware of that turn. It didn't really matter one way or the other, of course, but as the inspiration behind the squadron's construction, Eddie should have been here to see it go into action for the first time at last.

And if he were here, he'd undoubtedly be busy comparing this to running the batteries at Vicksburg, or possibly Farragut's attack on New Orleans. Simpson shook his head. *Unbelievable. I'm actually* missing *the chance to hear him rattling on about it!*

"Admiral?" Chomse said, and Simpson realized he'd allowed his smile to surface for at least a moment.

"Nothing, Lieutenant." He shook his head again. "Just a passing thought."

He accepted the folded message slip from Chomse and glanced over it. It contained no surprises. Commander Wolfgang Mülbers, commanding the timberclad *Ajax*, was a stickler for detail. Simpson had expected his readiness report to come in last, given Mülbers' attention to every little thing, just as he'd expected that report to announce *Ajax*'s complete preparation for battle.

Not that Ajax *should have all that much to do*, the admiral reminded himself.

Ajax and her fellow timberclads had turned out to be even more resistant to seventeenth-century artillery than he had anticipated. He'd known the weight of shot and muzzle velocity of contemporary artillery was substantially below that of even the eighteenth century, far less the nineteenth-century Civil War artillery the progenitors of his current ironclads had faced. As a result, he'd anticipated that the forty-eight-inch wooden bulwarks he'd used to "armor" the timberclads would be effectively impenetrable by the sort of relatively lightweight field artillery which was likely to be deployed against them along river banks.

Instead, he'd discovered that that much timber was invulnerable even to heavy shipboard guns—or what passed for them in 1634, at any rate—at any range beyond sixty or seventy yards. It simply absorbed the impact of the hurtling shot—when the shot in question didn't just bounce off, that was—while the ships it protected got on about their business. Their decks were completely unprotected, of course, which meant they would always be vulnerable to plunging fire, delivered from above, but other than that, they had turned out to be remarkably capable of standing up to any weapons that might be employed against them.

Unfortunately, their armaments were far less powerful than those of his ironclads. Wooden hulls were much more massive and heavier, strength for strength, than iron hulls, and the same was true of wooden armor, when compared to iron armor. A timberclad simply could not mount as many or as large guns as an equally well protected ironclad of the same displacement, and their reliance on bulkier, less fuel-efficient steam power plants only put an even tighter squeeze on their internal volume. That was why the timberclads like Mülbers' ship carried only carronades, not the massive, long-ranged ten-inch muzzleloaders which were the ironclads' true teeth.

Ironically, that was going to make the timberclads even more effective than the ironclads in ship-to-ship engagements. Their weapons were fully adequate to deal with any down-time warship, and they were also much more rapid-firing. *Constitution* and her sisters mounted three carronades in each broadside, themselves, but the timberclads mounted six, plus two of the mitrailleuse-derived navy version of the army's volley guns. They were designed for close-range, rapidly firing engagements that would usually be over, one way or the other, quickly.

The *ironclads*, on the other hand, were designed for sustained slugging matches against the heaviest prepared defenses and fortifications here-and-now could produce. That was the true reason for those enormous ten-inch guns. They were far heavier than anything that would ever be required against a wooden seventeenth-century warship . . . but just the thing for drilling straight through little things like the fortress walls protecting Hamburg.

As the good, cautious, pigheaded, ass-covering burghers of Hamburg were about to discover.

At noon, Thorsten Engler did a final walk-through down the whole length of the field, using every man in his battery to check for any small stones or other obstructions that might have been missed. The four military engineers attached to Fey's company went with him.

He didn't expect to find much. Between the farming equipment they'd "borrowed" from two of the nearby villages and the equipment the engineers had brought themselves, they'd been able to prepare quite a good landing field. So, at least, the engineers assured him—and all of them had experience at the work. That was to a large degree why they'd been selected.

"Should do fine," one of them said, once they reached the far end of the landing strip.

"It's better than the one they started with in Wismar," added one of his partners. He pointed off to the side, where soldiers had erected large, crude sheds to provide shelter for the two planes. They'd demolished two nearby barns for the materials. The farmers hadn't even objected too strenuously, since they'd gotten paid more than the structures had really been worth.

"Even that's a better hangar than they had in Wismar, at the beginning."

Thorsten had no idea if they were right. He'd seen the airplanes, any number of times, but only up in the air and at a great distance. But since they seemed so confident on the matter, he saw no reason to worry much about it.

His only real concern had been the soil itself. The spring melt was underway, and everything was a bit soggy. Not too bad here, though. They were a half mile from the river and the engineers had picked a field that was slightly elevated to begin with. By the time they were done preparing the field, the strip was still a bit on the moist side but nothing you could actually call muddy. And by the time the planes arrived, several hours later in the afternoon, the sun would have dried everything still further.

"We're ready, then," he said. The engineers all nodded.

"Fine. I'll tell Captain Witty and he'll tell the admiral."

Something in the engineers' expressions made Thorsten smile, as he walked off. Clearly enough, they didn't much care what any miserable squid thought or didn't think. The engineers had brought their own radio equipment and they'd be the ones guiding the planes as they approached Hamburg.

That gave the two batteries a full day and a half to get ready themselves. They wouldn't be going with the admiral, if he had to make "the run." There was simply no room for them, even if they left the horses behind. Instead, Colonel Fey would lead the rest of the battle group in a fast march around Hamburg the day before, and would meet back up with the ironclads downstream from the city.

It was quite interesting, in a way. Good soldiering presented all sorts of mental challenges that Thorsten had never considered as a civilian. Eric Krenz was even making noises that he might take up the military as a career.

Thorsten wouldn't, though. He'd serve through to see the war finished. But after that . . .

He'd decided to become a psychologist. Since the up-timers hadn't brought one with them through the Ring of Fire—so Caroline and Maureen Grady insisted, at least—the career prospects seemed quite good. There'd be a great deal to learn, of course. Years of study ahead of him, while he scraped together the wherewithal to get by in the meantime. He was sure Caroline would be supportive, which was really all that mattered. And he had the great advantage, he'd come to realize, of not being burdened ahead of time with all those silly up-time superstitions.

Such as "the dangers of corporal punishment applied to children." *Gott in Himmel.* It was amazing what foolish notions the Americans had in their heads, rubbing right up against brilliant ones. They even had a term for it, which they'd stolen from the French: *idiot savant.*

The French would know, of course.

Jesse was determined to make the flyover of Hamburg to be something for the kiddies to remember. Having returned to Grantville, he had left the Belle and taken two Gustavs—the only two that were airworthy—back to Magdeburg. Now he was leading the two ships towards Hamburg. Emil Castner occupied the rear seat, while Lieutenants Enterprise and Endeavor Martin flew the second aircraft. He'd chosen Ent and Dev because they'd shown a promising aptitude for formation flying.

That aptitude had already come in handy, since the weather thus far hadn't been the best, layers of thin stuff that suddenly thickened and thinned with little warning. The Martin brothers had hung in there just fine, but it had put a strain on Jesse's navigation skills until they picked up the signal from the airfield at Ochsen Werder. He wouldn't care to fly an instrument approach with the crude direction finder in his cockpit, but it was just fine for providing an area vector.

Naturally, with the perverseness of all flying weather, the sky was beginning to clear now that they were "on the beam."

Jesse keyed his mike, "Two, this is Lead, loosen it up, Ent." He looked over to the aircraft on his right.

Ent confirmed the order with two mike clicks and slid his aircraft "down the line" until he was about thirty yards off and behind Jesse's wing.

Jesse nodded in the exaggerated manner pilots used in the air.

"Check fuel, Lead has fifty percent."

Ent replied, "Two has forty percent."

That's about right, Jesse reflected. It normally took more fuel to fly on somebody's wing than to lead. Forty percent gave them over ninety minutes of flying. Plenty for the job.

Descending to five thousand feet, the two aircraft neared the makeshift airfield south of Hamburg. Jesse noted the direction needle drop to the bottom of the case as they passed the radio signal and turned left to enter "holding," a racetrack around the field with one-minute legs. They were waiting for the third aircraft assigned to this mission, the Belle from Wismar.

In the meantime, Jesse called the field. "Ochsen Werder, this is Gustav Flight entering holding overhead."

The reply was immediate. "Good afternoon, Colonel. All is ready for you."

"Ah, roger that, Ochsen," Jesse paused. "Stand by."

Scanning the sky to the north as he turned back to the field on their second turn in holding, Jesse picked out a dot that could only be an aircraft.

"Wismar Belle, Wismar Belle, this is Gustav Flight. Over."

Lieutenant Ernst Weissenbach was flying the Belle. "Gustav Flight, this is Wismar Belle, we have you in sight."

"Good, Ernst," Jesse said. "We are at five thousand feet in left turns, speed ninety knots. Join on my left wing."

While he waited for Ernst and Woody Woodsill to join them, Jesse wondered if those on the ground realized what a miracle was taking place over their heads. *Miracle on top of miracles*, Jesse mused. *Real aircraft, meeting over seventeenth-century Germany, with seventeenth-century Germans in them. And all done with the precision of the proverbial Swiss watch.*

He looked down at the river, where he could see smoke coming from the stacks of Simpson's timber-clads.

"You watching this, Admiral?" he whispered to himself.

Within minutes, the Belle was flying off his wing opposite the other Gustav. Jesse nodded to Woodsill who held up an instant camera—their reason for being here. They had used it before over Luebeck and it was supposed to have four or five unexposed negatives in it. Jesse figured there was no better time than now to use them. If they were still good, that is.

"Okay, Woody, Ernst," Jesse began. "While Gustav Flight entertains the good burghers of Hamburg, you're to take pictures of the river channels. Make sure you get high enough to get good coverage. Try to get a good shot of the chain barrier that's supposed to be across the main channel. Make sketches as backup. Go no lower than one thousand feet and one of you keep your eye on us at all times. Stay well clear of us. As soon as you're finished, call out and then RTB here. Understood?"

Ernst replied, "Copy, *mein Herr*. Stay clear, call, and return to base here at Ochsen Werder."

Jesse looked over and saw Woody give a thumbs up. Turning to his right, he saw Ent do the same.

"Roger, gentlemen, let's do this. Wismar Belle, break off and proceed independently. Gustav Two, close it up."

As the Belle angled off, Gustav Flight climbed towards Hamburg. Jesse detected a slight unsteadiness in the other aircraft that probably meant Ent was a bit nervous. He keyed the mike.

"Okay, boys, just as we briefed it. Weather's clear, fuel's fine, this is gonna be fun. You ready, Ent?"

Ent gave two clicks in reply.

They were almost at ten thousand feet as they reached Hamburg. Holding the aircraft's nose high, Jesse reduced throttle and bled off airspeed until nearing stall.

"Speedbrakes . . . now!"

In the rear cockpits, Emil and Dev spun the wheels that forced a perforated metal plate into the windstream under each aircraft. As the brakes bit in, the aircraft pitched over into a steep dive. Jesse pushed the stick forward until he could have sworn they were going straight down, though a quick check of the reference lines on the canopy told him they were only in a seventy-degree dive. As the aircraft sharply nosed over, sirens on the left gear of each flipped open and began to howl, dopplering higher and higher as their speed increased. Jesse, a wide, toothy grin plastered on his face, fought the tendency of the nose to rise, pushing hard on the stick. An incongruous thought crossed his mind.

Thank you, Ernst Udet. This was another one of the many ironies created by the Ring of Fire. Jesse was introducing to Germans the Stuka dive-bombing tactics developed by one of their own in another universe. The roofs of Hamburg grew rapidly closer as they dove, howling madly now. The high-pitched scream of the sirens was every bit as attention-grabbing in 1634 as it was—had been, would be, whatever—for Udet's beloved Ju-87 Stuka of 1940, and as they flashed past four thousand feet with the airspeed at 160 knots, Jesse began to see crowds in the streets below, all looking up. Passing 3500 feet, he made the call.

"Speedbrakes . . . in!"

While Jesse and Ent pushed their throttles forward and pulled hard, hard, sucking the sticks back into their laps, Emil and Dev hit the releases that allowed the metal plates to streamline along the fuselage. Jesse grunted against the force of a five "G" recovery, tightening his stomach muscles to trap the blood there. Despite that effort, his vision narrowed as blood drained from his head. The sirens stopped their racket as the noses came up and Jesse squinted to see. Noting a positive climb more by feel than anything else, he released back pressure and could see again as he held the zoom climb, rocketing skyward, trading airspeed for altitude. As he leveled off high above the city, Jesse loudly expressed the exhilaration of every pilot since the first dive recovery.

"Hot damn, that was fun!"

Grinning like a kid, Jesse looked into the small mirror at the top of the windscreen and saw Emil grinning back at him. Jesse nodded, sharing the feeling that only airmen felt, a feeling that, for the moment, erased all differences between them. Jesse glanced over at his wingman and saw two more grins. Nodding again, he was suddenly glad they had brought no weapons.

Nobody should get killed on a day this fine.

He keyed the mike. "Gustav Two, go trail."

As Ent slid out of fingertip and lined up a hundred yards behind, Jesse spoke again. "Okay, Ent, just like in training, stay on my six and don't let go."

Getting two clicks, Jesse slowly rolled to his left and began another dive back toward the rooftops of Hamburg. What followed was a thirty minute aerial tango, a whirling, diving, turning, roaring, howling dance that took the aircraft high, high above the city and down low, dashing just clear of the rooftops and steeples. As they continued, Jesse made his maneuvers more abrupt, more unexpected, testing the limits of Ent's ability. At one point, snapping down out of a vertical climb, he looked through the top of the canopy and saw Ent, still going up, looking at him through his canopy. As he tried to shake the young pilot off his tail, he almost forgot why they were there. Leveling off for a moment over the city, he saw he needn't have worried. The streets were full of people, all staring upward, waving their arms and shouting unheard cheers. Clearly enough, however recalcitrant Hamburg's authorities were being toward Gustav Adolf's proposal—demand, really—that the city join the USE, a large number of its citizens had no problem with the notion at all.

I always did like an airshow, Jesse thought. He

suddenly realized he was tired, wrung out by the strain and the work of heavy aerobatics. Calling Ent back into fingertip, he was preparing for a slow pass around the city walls when Ernst called from the Belle.

"Wismar Belle is RTB to Ochsen."

"Uh, roger, Belle, RTB approved. Gustav Flight is ten minutes behind."

Jesse led his flight around the walls, absorbing the views of the ancient city. Finally, waggling farewell, he turned away, back to land, back to war.

Chapter 37

Hamburg

"All stations report closed up and ready for action, sir!"

"Very good."

Captain Halberstat acknowledged the report from the signalman manning the voice pipes, then glanced around SSIM *Constitution*'s conning tower one more time, letting his eyes sweep across the uniformed officers and sailors of the USE Navy. The conning tower about him was very, very different from anything he had ever seen in his previous career, and not simply because of its gleaming efficiency and up-timer lighting.

The notion of providing *sailors* with actual uniforms had struck him as incredibly outlandish when he first volunteered for Admiral Simpson's newborn navy. Not even armies bothered with that sort of thing, and *they* had to worry about identifying one another in the midst of confused melees on a field of battle. But Simpson had insisted, and like so many other of his initially preposterous seeming ideas, it had repaid his efforts enormously. The navy-provided uniforms (and Simpson's draconian notions of diet and hygiene . . . and discipline) created a powerful sense of identity. Not to mention the healthiest ships' companies Halberstat had ever seen.

Franz Halberstat was a highly intelligent man. One who had served at sea his entire life, starting on his father's North Sea fishing boat and working his way up to the command of his own coastal lugger, with temporary diversions as a deck officer on French and Danish naval vessels. Yet he knew now that he'd been slow to recognize just how different John Simpson's navy truly was. This world had never seen anything like it, for it was the first truly *professional* navy in history. And that, Halberstat had come to realize, was an even more fundamental change than the marvelous ships the up-timers had been able to build.

"Ready to proceed, Admiral," *Constitution's* captain said, turning to his commanding officer with a crisp salute. "All hands are closed up to action stations and the ship is flooded down to fighting draft."

"Very well, Captain," John Chandler Simpson said formally. "Carry out your orders."

"Aye, aye, sir!"

Thorsten Engler looked up as the flagship's horn gave a single raucous burst of sound. Having ridden around the city, he and the other members of his battery, along with the rest of the cavalry escort, were dug in around and on a slight rise that lay just down the river from Hamburg. Now, from a distance they watched the ponderous-looking ironclads getting slowly underway in the morning light those of them, at least, who had access to an eyeglass. Simpson's flotilla was barely visible to the naked eye. Fortunately,

Lieutenant Reschly was willing to share his eyeglass with Thorsten.

They'd been supposed to begin their attack at dawn, Thorsten knew. He wasn't certain why they hadn't, but he suspected it had something to do with the heavy mist that had cloaked the river. Camp rumor said that Prime Minister Stearns had "suggested" to Admiral Simpson that he underscore the emperor's unhappiness with Hamburg's refusal to grant his navy free passage to the North Sea. Thorsten hadn't yet seen the navy's big guns in action against a real target, but like most people who'd lived in and around Magdeburg for the last six months or so, he'd heard—and seen—their crews training with them. No one in Hamburg had done that, but unless Thorsten was sadly mistaken, Admiral Simpson had decided to wait for the visibility to clear expressly so that he could give the good citizens of Hamburg the best possible opportunity to observe the consequences of that training.

This would be their last assignment, as part of Simpson's expedition. Assuming the ironclads made it through Hamburg with no significant problems, the battle group would be dissolved. Once past Hamburg, the Elbe became wide enough that there was simply no point to keeping an escort of cavalrymen and volley guns. Engler and the rest of Colonel Fey's men would be rejoining the rest of the army under General Torstensson.

Captain Rolf Hempel felt himself swallowing hard as the squat-looking American warships came slowly, steadily towards him through the morning light. Only the four iron-plated monsters were underway; apparently the wooden ships with the smoking chimneys were going to let their bigger sisters deal with Hamburg. And, Hempel thought unhappily, those bigger sisters seemed ominously confident of their ability to do just that.

They were huge, far bigger than anything anyone in Hamburg had ever seen moving up and down the Elbe, and they looked more like looming fortresses—or perhaps enormous floating barns—than ships. There was something profoundly unnatural about watching them move with no apparent regard for wind or current. There was no visible, outward sign of whatever semi-magical marvel the intruders from the Ring of Fire used to move the things. Instead, they simply glided smoothly, silently, effortlessly down the river.

Hempel didn't know which was worse: the endless winter-long rumors about the deadly weapons Gustav Adolf's unnatural allies were building for him, or actually seeing those monstrous constructs moving towards him. The second, he decided after a moment. There was a certain . . . *immediacy* to it, after all.

According to all the reports that had reached Hamburg, the heavy gunships moving into position were supposed to be capable of preposterously high rates of speed, as well, which made their slow, deliberate approach even more ominous. It was as if they were emphasizing the fact that the Wallanlagen's heavy batteries, which had been even further reinforced over the last several months, concerned them not at all. The city had spent an enormous sum building that massive addition to its medieval defenses over the past seventeen years, secure in the well-proven axiom that no ship could fight a well-sited shore battery. The heavier guns and steadier firing platforms of a fortress were simply more than any wooden-hulled ship could face and survive, especially when they fired heated shot to set the ship's timbers on fire. Which didn't even consider the fact that a battery could be protected by enormous masonry walls and thick, shot-absorbing earthen berms, invulnerable to any ship's fire.

The fact that no one aboard those slab-sided iron behemoths appeared ever to have heard of that axiom— or to care about it, if they had—was enough to make Hempel's bowels feel distinctly watery.

John Simpson stood gazing out of one of *Constitution*'s conning tower vision slits. Somewhat to his surprise, he actually felt almost as confident as he appeared. Which wasn't precisely the same as feeling calm.

He'd invested far too much sweat, thought, discipline, and emotion in these ships and the men who crewed them to feel *calm* as the moment to commit them to action approached at last. Unlike the majority of his fellow up-timers, Simpson had seen and known the reality of combat before the Ring of Fire snatched them all back to the Thirty Years' War. He wasn't precisely looking forward to seeing it again, or to the casualties he was about to inflict upon Hamburg's defenders. But there was an undeniable sense of . . . anticipation. And there was an additional strand of satisfaction which he would have felt uncomfortable explaining to most people.

Whatever doubts he might have felt—might continue to feel, for that matter—about many of Michael Stearns' policies, John Simpson was now a citizen of the United States of Europe. Despite the opposite sides of the political divide upon which he and Stearns would have found themselves in the future from which they came, they agreed with one another far more deeply and completely than either of them agreed with the seventeenth-century establishment. And even if that hadn't been true, Simpson had served in the United States of *America's* navy. He had thoroughly internalized the belief that the navy's function was to obey the orders of the duly constituted civilian government and to defend *all* of its society, not just the parts of it that might happen to enjoy the personal approval of individual members of that navy.

Besides, the USE was his *home* now, and the city of Hamburg had decided—for reasons which undoubtedly seemed good to it—to support his home's enemies. The city fathers might not see it quite that way, but John Chandler Simpson did, and it was time to teach them that giving aid and comfort to the enemies whose sworn purpose was the utter destruction of the home and people he cared about was . . . unwise.

The American ships seemed to be moving even more slowly as they entered the effective range of the Wallenlagen's batteries, Hempel noted. That was undoubtedly a bad sign. Clearly, the Americans weren't interested in simply getting *past* the Wallenlagen's guns as quickly as possible, which suggested they had some other purpose in mind.

A purpose Rolf Hempel felt unhappily certain no one in Hamburg was going to much care for.

"Stand ready," he said, as calmly as he could, to Jurgen Esch.

"We *are* ready," his second-in-command replied, and

Hempel snorted. Esch was not a particularly imaginative man, and whatever he might *think*, Hempel was grimly certain that no one in Hamburg was truly "ready" for what was about to happen.

He started to say something more, then closed his mouth as the first of the city's artillery opened fire at last.

Simpson clasped his hands behind him as the first jets of smoke erupted from the nearest bastions.

The range was short—less than a hundred and fifty yards. He'd made that decision weeks ago, and he was a bit surprised to discover that he felt absolutely no temptation to second-guess himself at this point as he gazed through the vision slit.

On the other hand, "short range" was a relative term, he reminded himself as half a dozen heavy round shot plunged into the river without scoring a single hit. They kicked up white plumes of foam around *Constitution*, leading the squadron's steady advance, but none of them came closer than a good twenty yards.

No one in the conning tower said a word, he noted with approval. Whether they were really that calm or not was another matter, of course.

"I see the CoC did cut the chain, sir," Captain Halberstat observed as they passed the point at which the chain boom had been supposed to stop them.

"Yes," Simpson agreed.

The admiral was relieved that the Committee of Correspondence's members had managed to disable the boom. He'd been confident of his ironclads' ability to break that chain, if they'd had to, but he hadn't exactly looked forward to the possibility of the underwater damage it might have inflicted.

"Pass the word to the rest of the squadron that the boom is definitely cut," he said.

"Aye, aye, sir," Halberstat said, and Simpson heard him passing the order down to the radio room located in its well protected, central position.

All of the ironclads—and, for that matter, their three accompanying timberclads—had radio capability. Not all of the navy's ships did; the supply of radios remained strictly limited, after all. That was why all of Simpson's ships, including his ironclads, also had masts from which signal flags could be flown. And all of them (so far, at least) had signal "searchlights" converted from mining truck headlamps, as well. Flags and lights were visibility-limited systems, but they still provided a flexibility of communication which no other present-day navy could possibly match.

Yet, at least, Simpson reminded himself.

"Time the intervals between salvos, please, Captain," he said. "Let's get a feel for just how good their guns' crews are."

"Aye, aye, sir."

"What happened to the chain!" Esch demanded as the lead ironclad sailed imperturbably past the point at which the massive boom should have halted it.

"Obviously, someone cut it for them," Hempel observed with massive restraint.

"Those goddamned 'Committees of Correspondence!'" Esch swore, and Hempel shrugged.

"Probably," he agreed. "Not that it matters too much who did it at this moment."

✧　　✧　　✧

CLAAAANNNG!

Constitution's armor rang like the world's biggest bell as the defenders finally managed to hit her, and this time most of the people aboard her did flinch. The sheer volume of the sound would have been enough to ensure that reaction under any circumstances.

That was *all* that happened, however.

The round shot struck brilliant sparks as it skipped off of the sloped casement, and it left a noticeable dent behind. That was the total extent of its damage, and Simpson heard a loud cheer rippling through *Constitution's* gundeck as their ship's armor performed as promised.

"Return fire, Admiral?" Halberstat asked. There was an undeniably eager note in the captain's voice, Simpson noticed, and he smiled slightly.

"Let's not get carried away by our own enthusiasm, Franz," he suggested.

"Yes, sir," Halberstat acknowledged in a moderately chastened tone.

Simpson's smile broadened. He shook his head slightly and stepped to the rear of the conning tower, looking back across the top of the casement to where *President* followed in *Constitution's* wake.

All of the ironclads' gun ports remained closed by their heavily armored shutters, and they would remain that way until Simpson's ships reached the precise positions he had selected for them. That, too, was part of the message for Hamburg. The USE Navy would proceed methodically about its own plans, totally unconcerned by—and contemptuous of—any way in which the defenders might attempt to inconvenience it.

✧   ✧   ✧

Rolf Hempel had better eyes than most. He actually saw the black dot of the forty-two-pound round shot bouncing off of the lead ship's armor like a pea bouncing off the head of a drum. Some of the gunners were cheering at the evidence of their fellows' accuracy. Hempel wasn't. As far as he could tell, it hadn't even marked the American vessel's paint!

Constitution took six more hits before she reached her preselected position opposite the Wallenlagen's exact center. That was actually pretty fair shooting by seventeenth-century standards, Simpson reflected.

"Coming up on our position now, Captain."

"Very well," Halberstat acknowledged the report, then nodded to the conning tower signalman.

"Pass the word to Ensign Gaebler to release the anchor."

"Release the anchor, aye, aye, sir!" the signalman repeated, making certain that he'd understood the order correctly, then bent over the voice pipes.

"Both pumps to zero power," Halberstat continued.

"Zero power, aye, aye, sir."

Constitution's stern anchor plunged into the mud of the Elbe, and the ironclad came to a complete stop. The river's current was sufficient to keep her headed in the proper direction, and the defenders' fire redoubled as their target stopped moving entirely. Several more round shot clanged deafeningly off of her stout armor, and Simpson nodded in satisfaction.

"Very well, Captain Halberstat," he said formally. "You may"—his lips twitched ever so slightly—"fire at will."

Chapter 38

Rolf Hempel found the lead ironclad anchored little more than a hundred yards in front of his battery. So far, the Wallenlagen's guns had been thundering away for almost half an hour. Hempel's battery had joined in ten minutes ago, and the defenders had scored several hits in that time . . . for all the good it had done. The USE ships, on the other hand, had yet to fire a single shot in reply. Now, as he watched, two ports opened on the ironclad's side, and the snout of a massive cannon slid smoothly out of each of them.

There were three more gun ports between the two opening ones, a corner of his brain noted. For some reason, *they* weren't opening. Two more round shot from his battery ricocheted off of the ship's impenetrable armor, and he grimaced. Those closed gun ports were like yet another mocking assertion of Hamburg's impotence. Despite the scores of heavy artillery pieces firing upon them, each of those ships was prepared to reply with only two guns. It was as if the enemy was saying "Look—we don't even need to use all of our guns!"

✧   ✧   ✧

Simpson watched through the view slit as fresh, denser clouds of gunsmoke enveloped the Wallenlagen's batteries. The thunder of the city's guns was certainly impressive, and the clangor of cast-iron round shot rebounding from the ship's steel armor was deafening. Fortunately, the one aspect of the ironclads' construction which had most worried him didn't seem to be being a problem after all.

The greatest weakness of the ships' design, in many respects, was that their "armor" consisted of individual steel "planks" made by running up-time railroad rails through a rolling mill. It wasn't a single, contiguous piece of armor, and the only way they'd been able to secure it to the ironclads' wooden structure was with hand-forged bolts. He'd been concerned that those bolts might shatter as the armor took hits, and they still might, under hits that came in directly on top of one of them. But they seemed to be holding up well to the more general battering the casement was taking.

From his current position, he couldn't see *Constitution*'s ten-inch guns running out into firing position. The conning tower was located at the front of the casement, raised enough to make it possible to see back across the casement top, and faced with its own armored protection. It was also located on the centerline of the ship, which meant that he couldn't see the actual sides of the ship. But he could see *President* just fine, and his lips drew back in something only distantly related to a smile as the massive barrels of *President*'s wire-wound guns slid smoothly out of their ports. It was easy for him to imagine that he could actually hear the hiss of the guns' hydraulics—adapted from more salvaged mining equipment.

Those guns were the ironclads' true reason for being. Each ship mounted three of the short, stubby, ugly carronades between the ten-inchers, but they were much less suitable for bombarding powerful fortifications. Like the carronades mounted by the timberclads, they were the product of the new sandcasting techniques that had been introduced in Magdeburg. The biggest single weakness of cast-iron seventeenth-century artillery was that even English and Swedish gun founders—universally acknowledged to be the best makers of iron artillery in the here-and-now world—used clay molds. Clay had a very low porosity, which meant that air bubbles in the molten iron were often unable to escape when the guns were cast and, instead, formed dangerous cavities and weak points in the finished guns. Sand was far more porous, which made for much stronger, tougher artillery pieces.

Carronades were also far shorter than regular artillery pieces of their caliber. The original carronade, cast in Scotland during the time of the American Revolution—the *original* American Revolution, that was—had thrown a 68-pound round shot, but it had weighed less than the contemporary *12-pounder*. That had permitted ships to mount far heavier weights of broadside, although the new gun's shorter barrel had given it a shorter effective range. On the other hand, the greater care taken when boring it out had made it more accurate over its available range, and *these* carronades were rifled, which made them even more accurate and also permitted them to fire something besides simple spherical projectiles.

The fact that their barrels were barely four feet long, as compared to the ten-inch guns' twelve-foot barrels, meant they had a much lower muzzle velocity and a correspondingly shorter absolute range, and shell weight went up as the cube of the increase in shell diameter. Since the carronades had only an eight-inch bore, that equated to a tremendous difference between its penetrating power and bursting charge and those of the heavier, faster-moving ten-inch shell.

Of course, all of the shells in question were cast-iron, with a filling of black powder, not the steel-cased, high-explosive-packed shells of Simpson's first navy. Compared to twentieth-century artillery, they were positively anemic. But, then, what they had to contend with was *seventeenth-century* artillery . . . and fortifications.

The enemy fired at last.

Despite his own career as an artillerist, Rolf Hempel had never heard anything quite like it. The ironclads fired in succession, starting with the ship farthest downstream—the one opposite Hempel's own position—and running back along their line. The stupendous concussion of the American guns was stunning, and the ships disappeared entirely behind an incredible gush of choking, flame-cored smoke.

That was bad enough; what happened to the Wallenlagen was even worse.

Explosive shells per se were no great surprise. Mortar bombs had come into use in the Low Countries at least fifty years ago. But any mortar bombs Hempel ever heard of were far smaller than these shells. They were also lobbed at their targets so that they descended almost vertically, and they were inaccurate, low-velocity weapons, fired by crudely timed fuses.

These shells came in on a deadly accurate, flat, high-speed trajectory, and they were much, much heavier. Unlike solid shot, they didn't bury themselves harmlessly in earthen berms or ricochet off of masonry, either. They drilled into their targets like white-hot awls into butter . . . and then they exploded.

Hempel staggered as a single ten-inch shell crashed into the Wallenlagen no more than forty yards from where he himself stood.

The base-mounted fuse—crudity itself, by twentieth-century standards—was no more than an iron ball, coated in an incendiary compound and supported by a thin wire that was sheared off by the sudden acceleration when it was fired. When it struck, the released ball flew forward in the cylindrical fuse's firing chamber, against still more incendiary compound, and the resultant flash detonated the shell.

The explosion blew a crater deep enough for two men Hempel's height to stand upright in out of the Wallenlagen's face . . . and it was only one of eight.

None of the American shells seemed to have missed their targets, and bellows of stunned, shocked surprise mingled with the screams of the wounded.

Simpson raised his binoculars. He didn't really need them at this short range, but it was part of the image he'd very deliberately cultivated.

He had to wait the better part of a minute before the gunsmoke dispersed on the brisk breeze and cleared the range, but that was perfectly all right. Even with power assistance to move the shells from the magazine to the gun mounts, a ten-inch muzzleloader wasn't about to set any speed records for rate of fire.

He was glad the first guns had been available well before the ironclads could be launched. He'd had them placed in shoreside duplicates of the ironclads' mounts, and his gun crews had at least been able to practice and perfect their drill before they actually had to perform afloat. Still, this was the first time that *Constitution* had fired both guns simultaneously in anger, and the shock of their recoil seemed to jar straight up his spine from his heels to the base of his brain.

Then the smoke cleared, and his mouth tightened in satisfaction.

He'd read plenty of accounts of how rifled Civil War artillery had reduced the walls of masonry forts like Sumter and Fort Pulaski to Swiss cheese. Apparently, Hamburg's Wallenlagen wasn't any tougher than they'd been.

Rolf Hempel clawed his way back to his feet. His ears rang, his left shoulder was badly bruised by a hurtling chunk of masonry, and at least three of his gunners were down, unconscious or dead. Two more clutched at bleeding wounds, and Jurgen Esch was on his hands and knees, shaking his head dazedly.

Hempel looked at the sudden gap that had appeared in the parapet, then turned back to his gun crews.

"Don't just stand there like fucking idiots!" he bellowed. "Get back on those guns—now!"

One or two of them simply stared at him for an instant, but his noncoms were experienced, tough-minded sorts, who didn't hesitate for a moment to crack skulls with rammers' staffs when required. Hempel was confident that most of them realized as well as he did how futile their fire was going to be, but—like him—they had their duty.

And doing it may at least distract us from panicking about what's about to happen, he thought grimly.

The ten-inchers recoiled with vicious power. The articulated drive rods automatically closed the gun ports behind them, and the high-powered blowers sucked the choking, incredibly foul-smelling black powder smoke out of the casement. Shell hoists raised follow-up rounds and bagged powder charges from the magazine, and the flanged wheels of the shell carts carried them down the tram line to the gun mounts. The tapered charges, tied with cloth tape around central wooden spindles to retain their shape, went down the swabbed-out bores and were rammed home. Then the gun crew tailed onto the chain hoist that lifted the enormous ten-inch shell, and the gun captain and his assistant adjusted it carefully so that its four rows of soft metal studs indexed into the gun's rifling grooves. As the shell slid home, it rode the rifling, rotating slowly until it settled against the waiting charge.

"Clear the mount!"

The gun captains waited to be certain everyone was clear, then tripped the release, and the hydraulics opened the gun port shutters and returned the guns to battery.

Unlike most seventeenth-century guns, the weapons of Simpson's navy had sights. They were enormously simple—little more than a crude ring-and-post arrangement—but they were far better than anyone else had. Moreover, Simpson had actually test-fired his weapons with carefully measured charges, determining impact points at specific ranges from direct observation. His gunners knew exactly how much to allow for projectile drop, and they'd trained thoroughly with their pieces in the Magdeburg shoreside mounts for months.

"Fire!"

The second wave of thunderbolts arrived in a more staggered sequence . . . not that that made it any better.

The ear-shattering, earth-shaking, masonry-shredding chain of explosions seemed to go on and on. Hempel found himself back on his knees, spitting out a gritty mouthful of stone-dust and dirt, as the squat, unmoving ironclads flashed smoky lightning yet again.

They were firing independently, a strangely calm corner of his brain informed him. Firing as rapidly as each ship's gun crews could reload their demonic weapons, and every single shell was slamming directly into its target with literally pinpoint accuracy. Follow-up rounds were landing within as little as ten feet of the first craters, smashing even deeper into the fortifications, ripping out their guts in chunks of broken rock and flying dirt. The defenders continued to fire back, but much more raggedly, without the rapid, disciplined fire with which they'd begun the engagement. And his cringing ears told him there were fewer and fewer guns firing.

Another salvo of heavy shells slammed into the Wallenlagen, and a section of wall fifty feet across toppled wearily forward amid the screams of the men manning the guns enveloped in its collapse.

Hempel clawed back to his feet, clinging to the parapet. His thick brown hair was white, frosted with rock dust and pulverized mortar, and he stared out at that mercilessly firing line of ships.

John Simpson watched the breaches appearing in Hamburg's fortifications. If anything, his guns were proving even more effective than he'd hoped they would, and his jaw clenched as he tried to visualize what it must be like in those artillery bastions as shell after shell ripped into them. In many ways, it was even worse than what had happened to the Spaniards at the Wartburg. Napalm had been horrifying, and it must have seemed like a visitation from Hell itself, but the very fact that it was so alien to their victims' experience had provided at least some insulation. The Spaniards had possessed no yardstick against which to measure and evaluate the technology which lay behind that new weapon.

But his ironclads' guns, for all their size and relative sophistication, were something the Hamburgers could grasp. They were developments of weapons the defenders had seen before, used before, themselves. And that made their effectiveness and lethality even more stunning.

The Wallenlagen's fire was beginning to slacken. Two of the defensive batteries had already been thoroughly wrecked, and even through the smoke, he could see that at least one other battery had been abandoned by its panicked gun crews. But others continued to fire defiantly back, and he still heard—and felt—the occasional clang as round shot ricocheted off the casement.

Part of him was tempted to send in a message, demanding the fortification's surrender. His gunners were killing dozens, possibly even hundreds, of defenders who had absolutely no hope of beating off the attack. That much surely had to be apparent even to Hamburg by now, and Simpson took no pleasure in the slaughter of helpless enemies.

But Gustav Adolf wants Florida, he thought grimly, *and Stearns wants Hamburg to reflect on the . . . unwisdom of defying the emperor.*

Rolf Hempel had lost count.

He had absolutely no idea how many of those demonic shells had ripped into the fortifications in his vicinity. A part of him knew the number couldn't have been as high as he thought it was, but it had been high enough.

He didn't know how long this nightmare had been going on, either. It seemed like an eternity, and he cursed his superiors for letting it continue. Surely these horrible ironclads had amply demonstrated their ability to turn the entire city into a smoking heap of wreckage! How many more of Hempel's men had to die before they were allowed to capitulate and save their lives?

He was still asking himself that question when a ten-inch shell exploded three feet away from him and the point, for Rolf Hempel, became forever moot.

"Order to all units." Simpson had to raise his voice to a half-shout to make himself heard by eardrums stunned and battered by a sixty-minute bombardment. "Cease fire."

"All units cease fire, aye, aye, sir!" the signalman replied, and started shouting down the voice pipe to the radio room.

The thunderous explosions tapered off quickly as the order was passed, and Simpson opened the armored door and stepped out onto the bridge wing. He leaned out, looking down at the side of *Constitution*'s casement and saw at least a couple of dozen shallow dents. There were a few places where individual steel planks were dished in more deeply, but there was no evidence of any significant damage, and he turned to look at Hamburg.

The city, he reflected, could not say the same thing.

The Wallenlagen was torn and ripped, half-invisible under a pall of smoke and dust. The good news was that the range was so short, and the trajectory of his weapons so straight, that it looked as if none of his fire had overshot the fortifications and landed in the city proper.

And the other "good news," he thought harshly, *is that Stearns' demonstration of Gustav Adolf's . . . displeasure has just been made abundantly clear.*

He surveyed the wreckage one more time, then stepped back into the conning tower.

"Instruct all units to secure their guns, then raise anchor," he said. "I believe we have an appointment in Luebeck Bay."

Chapter 39

This was the first time in the post-Ring of Fire universe that Mike Stearns had ever flown in a plane that wasn't piloted by Jesse Wood. That made him more nervous than he would have been otherwise, and he would have been nervous to begin with. Mike didn't have a fear of heights, as such, but he'd never enjoyed flying. That had been true even in up-time commercial aircraft, with their gleaming construction and much-touted safety record.

Woody must have noticed his tension, because at one point about halfway through the flight he gave Mike a grin and said, "I want you to know that we have the best safety record of anybody flying on this side of the Ring of Fire. Ain't no commercial airline comes even close."

Mike parsed the logic. "How reassuring. Of course, the Wright brothers could have made the same claim after their first flight at Kitty Hawk."

"Well, yeah. But it's still a statistical fact."

"There's no such thing as a statistical fact, Woody. What there is, is just the odds." The plane jolted around for a bit and Mike paused, stiff-faced and solemn in the manner of a man doing his level best to appear stoic in the face of mindless danger. "As I am just being reminded, thank you very much."

But the turbulence passed, soon enough. The truth was, it was a nice day for flying, with a mostly clear sky and not really very much in the way of turbulence. Blind good luck, given that Mike's mission was urgent and he would have flown in any weather short of near-suicidal.

"Damnation," he grumbled. "I'm not a gambling man."

Woody gave him a look that Mike's mother would have called "old-fashioned."

Mike couldn't help but smile a little. "All right, fine. Outside of politics."

"I was gonna say." Woody looked down, checking the Elbe to make sure he was still on course. "Way I look at it, trotting into a city in the middle of a civil war is a lot riskier than"—he patted the console of the aircraft—"flying in an old bus like this."

"I'm not going to be trotting, and it's not what I'd call a 'civil war.'"

Woody gave him another old-fashioned look. "I'll buy the trotting. The civil war part, now . . . Have the CoC guys won? What I heard just before takeoff, the situation in Hamburg was still what you'd call a free-for-all." He leaned forward a little, peering through the cockpit windscreen. "Speaking of which, there it is."

Mike leaned forward and peered also, but couldn't really see anything on the horizon beyond a splotch in what looked like a small sea of splotches.

"You can't really see the city yet," Woody said. "But it's there."

Mike was quite happy to take his word for it. He leaned back in his seat. "Oh, it's still a free-for-all. But it's more along the lines of a high-impact civil dispute than a real civil war. The CoC has a good chunk of the city under their control and Hamburg's authorities and the official militia aren't willing to launch a full-blown offensive to pry them out."

"Why not?"

Mike was a little amused to see the way a junior air force officer was questioning the prime minister of his nation on High Matters of State without so much as a by-your-leave—indeed, quite obviously without even having considered that he might be out of line. That wouldn't have happened in Simpson's by-the-book navy, for sure. Interservice rivalry in their new world, as such, was far milder than it had been back up-time—thankfully, as far as Mike was concerned. But what you might call the cultural differences between the various services were a lot more pronounced, to make up for it. If Mike were to make an analogy with his days as a student, the navy was the in-crowd fraternities and student government types; the army was the hairy radicals; and the air force was more or less the bikers.

But he didn't care, actually. Mike had gotten along well enough with everybody, in high school and college. He'd never heard Thorsten Engler's sarcastic opinion on the subject of up-timer security mania, but if he had he would've mostly agreed with him. Mike had concluded long before the Ring of Fire that at least ninety-five percent of all the "security necessities" he'd heard about up-time were just some bigshot's way of either covering something up or trying to make himself look like a bigger shot, or both.

"Well, I can't read their minds," Mike explained. "But, at a guess, I'd say the reason Hamburg's authorities are shying away from an all-out attack on the CoC stronghold in the city is because part of that stronghold includes one of the city's gates. Just outside of which, Torstensson's parked with eight full regiments."

"Ah." Woody frowned. "Then why doesn't the CoC just open the gate and be done with it?"

Mike clucked his tongue. "Flyboys. Trained by Colonel Jesse I-don't-need-no-steenkeeng-politics Wood, to make it worse. Let's just say that political turbulence is a lot more complicated than anything you'll run into up here—and the phrase Hamburg Committee of Correspondence has more than one noun."

Woody's frown had deepened. "To put it another way," Mike elaborated, "just because they're a CoC doesn't mean they're no longer citizens of Hamburg. They'll look at it from a different angle than the city's authorities, of course, but they're also looking to cut the best deal Hamburg can get out of this."

"Oh. All right, I can see that." Most of his attention was now focused on his flying, though, since he was getting ready to land. So all he said was, "And you're the deal-maker."

Torstensson was all business. "Till midafternoon, Michael." He glanced at his up-time watch. "Call it fifteen hundred, on the nose."

"Can we make it four o'clock? Sixteen hundred, rather."

The Swedish general shook his head, glancing at the western horizon. "No, sorry. This early in April, it will be dark by nineteen hundred. I want a minimum of four hours of daylight if I wind up fighting once we get into the city. Even going in at fifteen hundred is pushing it."

Mike accepted the inevitable. "Fine. How am I getting in?"

Torstensson waved forward another officer. "Cavalry escort." He gave Mike a sideways glance. "You *can* ride a horse?"

"Oh, yeah. Long as I'm not making any cavalry charges, anyway."

"No fear of that. You'll either be trotting in on a nice city road, or it's an ambush and you'll be dead."

"You could have maybe put that a little more delicately, Lennart," Mike groused.

An easy trot, it turned out to be, with no ambushes at all. In fact, by the time Mike got to the first CoC checkpoint, there was an official Hamburg delegation to meet him, along with the designated spokesmen for the city's CoC. Clearly enough, both sides in the dispute had seen his plane land, had their own sources of information that let them know who'd been coming in the plane—and neither one was about to let the other get the inside track on the ensuing negotiations.

Again, he found himself a little amused. Dinosaur-reactionary or wild-eyed-radical, or anywhere in between, Hamburg's citizenry had certain well-defined and long-established customs and attitudes that permeated all of them. Two stood out in particular:

They were devoted to their cussed independence, and every proper Hamburger from two-year-old toddlers on up was a natural-born businessman. Except for possibly Venetians, there were no people in Europe more addicted to mercantile deal-making and money-making schemes.

According to city legend, Emperor Barbarossa had declared Hamburg a city for free trading on May 11, 1189. It had been one of the major cities in the Hanseatic League during the Middle Ages, and had had its own navy since the fourteenth century. Although Hamburg had been occupied by the Danes twice during that time, it had managed to maintain effective independence by skillfully playing off Denmark against the Holy Roman Empire. The Wallenlagen, the massive fortifications that enhanced the city's defenses, had been constructed recently, starting in 1616, just to drive home the point to anyone who might object.

Independence was gone, now, and Mike was pretty sure even the most stubborn official on Hamburg's city council understood that. If they didn't, Mike would urge them to take a tour of their much-prized Wallenlagen. As much of the fortifications, that was to say, as Simpson's ten-inch guns had left intact as he passed through the city. Judging from what Mike had seen from the plane on his way in—he'd ordered Woody to overfly the city at low altitude twice before landing—that wasn't a whole lot. Not intact, anyway. There was plenty of rubble.

But that left the matter of Hamburg's commercial and trading rights and privileges still to be determined. The Hamburgers—both sides—were clearly hoping Mike had plenty of leeway for negotiation on that subject.

Which he did, in point of fact. In his radio exchanges with Gustav Adolf, the emperor had made it clear that while Hamburg's independence was to be eliminated—and no wiggling—he didn't care much about anything else. Neither did Mike, for that matter. His principal concern—which the emperor had expressed no opinion on, one way or the other—was to see to it that the power of the city's council was either broken altogether or so severely compromised and undermined that it could never regain its former control over the city.

Naturally—Mike almost felt like breaking into a rendition of "Tradition" from *Fiddler on the Roof*—the quarrels began over the shape of the table.

Figuratively speaking, anyway. The CoC delegates were adamant that the negotiations had to take place right there on the street just beyond the open gate—and Torstensson's eight regiments. They even had CoC members hauling chairs and a few tables from nearby taverns, for the purpose. The city council's delegates were just as adamant that the negotiations should take place in the Grossneumarkt, a large square on the city's western side which, just coincidentally, happened to be the location where the city's official militia assembled and practiced.

Mike let it go on for a few minutes, simply to establish the façade that he was a thoughtful fellow who considered all matters judiciously and ponderously. He might have even broken into "Tradition," except he really couldn't carry a tune that well.

Façade, though, is what it was. He'd already decided where he'd hold court—to call "negotiations" by their right name—before he'd passed through the gate. Torstensson had recommended the place to him.

"Enough," he said eventually. "We'll continue this in St. Jakobi church."

The city councilmen and CoC members squinted

at him. Despite the age difference—the former, all middle-aged; the latter, mostly in their twenties—their expressions were almost identical. A painter might have called it "Owls, Suspicious."

"I'm not going to argue about this, people," Mike said mildly. "St. Jakobi's, it is." He turned toward his horse, giving loud orders to his cavalry escort. Soon thereafter, he set off, with the city's various negotiators trotting on foot in his wake.

He figured the church would make a suitable compromise for a meeting location. On the one hand—the key, critical hand—it was located within striking distance of Torstensson's regiments. On the other hand, it *was* a church. For all the incredible bloodshed that had engulfed Europe since the great war began in 1618, churches were still, more often than not, respected as sanctuaries. Even in the war's worst massacre, the sack of Magdeburg, those residents who had managed to find refuge in the city's *Dom* had had their lives spared.

So, he kept the substance of power while giving the city councilmen some reason to assume he wasn't actually out for their blood.

Once they reached the church, it took a bit of time for the wherewithal for a negotiation to be assembled. But, eventually, it was done. And by then it was two o'clock in the afternoon.

Right about when Mike had planned.

He looked at his watch, ignoring the keen-eyed interest of all the negotiators. Copies of up-time books were practically flooding Europe by now, but few people had ever actually seen in person one of the fabled up-time watches.

"Ah, blast it. We're running out of time. General Torstensson told me in no uncertain terms that if I didn't have a settlement by three o'clock—that's just one hour, and twenty of minutes of it will be needed to send him word—he'd storm the city."

Mike lowered the watch. "Generals, you know—and he's a stubborn Swede, to make it worse. Refused to give me any leeway at all."

Five minutes were wasted with indignant protests. Most of them, but by no means all, coming from the city councilmen. Mike waited patiently enough, since from his standpoint the more time they wasted, the stronger his bargaining position became. This was just another of life's many illustrations of Dr. Johnson's remark on the subject of a short time span concentrating the mind wonderfully.

Eventually, that thought seemed to occur to the city councilmen also. Silence fell over the ramshackle collection of tables around which everyone was sitting in the church's nave.

"Here's where we start," Mike said. "Hamburg's days as an independent city are over. Done. Finished. Don't even bother raising that issue, because the answer is 'absolutely not.' Emperor Gustav Adolf's patience was used up by you folks over the past few months, and there's nothing left. Perhaps more to the point, I can assure you that Torstensson's regiments outside the walls have no patience at all. I either go out there in a little over half an hour and tell them that they can march into the city as its legal protectors—they'll maintain discipline; you can rest assured of that—or they'll come in and sack it."

Silence. Mike waited a minute or so.

"Splendid. Now, let's move on to other matters. First, the emperor wishes me to assure Hamburg's representatives that he has no intention of abrogating or limiting their traditional and well-established rights as merchants. In fact, he plans to encourage Hamburg's prosperity by establishing it as the chief port for the United States of Europe."

That stirred up a pleased hubbub that lasted for quite a while, until Mike added: "You do understand, I trust, that will require a major naval base in the city."

That brought very sour looks from the city councilmen. Even some of the CoC delegates didn't look entirely enthusiastic at the prospect.

Hard to blame them, of course—seeing as how the ships that would be stationed there would presumably be commanded by the same man who'd just turned the Wallenlagen into a stone-and-brick equivalent of the city's traditional pounded meat patties that would someday, in a New York that didn't exist yet, be sold as "steak in the Hamburg style" and eventually add the word *hamburger* to the English language after Jewish immigrants started substituting ground beef for pounded beef.

Mike had learned that little tidbit from Morris Roth, before the jeweler left for Prague. He'd added it to the accumulating pile of evidence that the world was an interesting place, no matter what anybody said.

The councilmen's expressions were still very . . . pickled, you might say.

Mike shrugged heavily. "Look, people, face facts. The USE will need a naval outlet onto the North Sea just as much as it needs a commercial one. If we don't put the main naval base in Hamburg"—here, he added a weary sigh—"we'll have no choice but to develop another town. Most likely Bremerhaven."

That did the trick. Simpson himself, they would prefer to do without. But they were no dummies, and knew full well that a major naval base in Bremerhaven ran the risk of spilling over into an expansion of Bremerhaven's commercial significance. The ghastly prospect loomed that Hamburg might find itself with a serious rival for the North Sea trade.

It wouldn't be quite accurate to say that they spilled all over themselves agreeing, but it was pretty close.

Mike looked at his watch again. "We're running out of time. The next point. The emperor proposes that Hamburg and its environs be incorporated as a separate province within the USE, with its own autonomous provincial authorities."

It was almost comical to see the wave of relief that washed over every face at the table, including that of the most intransigent CoC negotiator. Although the process hadn't yet been constitutionally formalized the way it had been in Mike's old United States, there had developed a fairly clear delineation of the different ways in which territories could become part of the USE.

First—and way best—you could join as an autonomous province, with the right to select your own provincial authorities. Essentially, that is, enjoy the same status that a state like Wyoming or Virginia did in Mike's former United States. Examples of existing provinces in the USE which enjoyed that exalted status were Thuringia, Magdeburg, and Hesse-Kassel.

Or, you would be incorporated under imperial

authority. That could take one of several forms, the two
most common being either direct military administration by someone selected by Gustav Adolf himself—an
example here being Ernst Wettin's administration of
the Upper Palatinate, with General Banér's troops to
give him muscle—or you could be turned over to one
of the existing provinces for administration.

The best-known example of the latter was Franconia. Gustav Adolf had originally turned it over to the
New United States to administer under the former
Confederated Principalities of Europe. After the formation of the USE in October of the previous year,
the NUS had become the State of Thuringia and had
assumed the same authority.

For all the heavy-handedness of direct Swedish
military administration compared to that of Thuringians,
Mike was pretty sure that by now just about any
established authority in the Germanies would prefer
the Swedes. The problem with the Thuringians—which
more often than not meant Americans—was that they
had this unfortunate habit of bringing mass unrest
with them. By now, just about everywhere in central
Europe, people had heard tales of the Ram movement
that had emerged in Franconia and was starting to
shake the existing political set-up into pieces.

God forbid. Coming in as a full province meant
they would retain quite a bit of control over their
own internal affairs.

One of the city councilmen started quibbling over
the exact meaning of the term "and environs," but
Mike waved him down.

"We can negotiate those details later. In fact, we
have to wait. For two reasons." He raised his watch.

"First, we're almost out of time, and those 'details' will be time-consuming. Second, we pretty have much to wait, anyway, until Gustav Adolf finishes pounding the Danes into meat patties and we see how much extra land there is to spread around."

Oh, what a cheery thought. The city councilman shut up.

"We've got very little time left. The way I see it, the only major issue that remains is what form of city government will oversee the formation of the new province of Hamburg and the elections to the constituent assembly that will determine the final structure and legal constitution of the new province. You have to have one, you know—it's in the rules—and in a situation like this, with the city teetering on the edge of civil war, we need a compromise temporary ruling body to carry out the task."

He gave them the same cheery smile. "Obviously, it can't be the city council, since you're one side in the dispute. Just as obviously, it can't be the Committee of Correspondence, because it's the other side."

"Perhaps a joint committee . . ." one of the city councilmen said tentatively.

Mike shook his head. "Sadly, that's no longer possible."

He held up the watch, turning it to face them, and tapped the glass. "Less than three minutes left, if I'm to make it to the gates in time to forestall the regiments from storming into the city. So I'm afraid I'll just have to impose a temporary one-man regime, for the moment."

They were all back to squinting at him. "Who?" demanded the head of the city council.

"Me. Who else?"

Seeing the astonished looks, he added breezily. "Oh, did I fail to mention that? Hamburg's to be the main staging area for the entire USE Army. Within a week, most of the regiments will be here, to join Torstensson's eight."

He rose to his feet. "I've got to be off. I might add that Colonel Wood plans to expand that temporary airfield outside into the major base for the air force."

He managed not to laugh, seeing the expressions around the table. He did so by turning the humor of the moment into yet another breezy assurance as he headed for the street. "Look on the bright side. Hamburg's likely to be in a neck-and-neck race with Magdeburg for getting the world's first *commercial* airport."

"That went quite well, I thought," he said to Torstensson a bit later, after summarizing the settlement.

The Swedish general extended his forearm and looked at his watch.

Mike frowned. "Is there some deadline I don't know about?"

"Oh, it's not that. I just wanted to make sure you hadn't somehow swindled me out of my timepiece while we were talking."

Chapter 40

"What's wrong, Caroline?" asked the young countess of Schwarzburg-Rudolstadt, after she came into the door of Caroline Platzer's office in the settlement house.

There being no answer from that quarter, Emelie turned to the third occupant of the room. That was Princess Kristina, perched on a chair next to Caroline's desk. "Why is Caroline gripping that sheet of paper as if it were the devil's work, and glaring at it so?"

"It's a letter from Count Thorsten," Kristina piped. The princess having decreed Thorsten Engler a count, she was not about to relinquish the claim. Here as in so many instances, the daughter could teach the royal father lessons in stubbornness.

Kristina pointed to the offending letter in question. "The censors blocked out so much of what he said that she can't make much sense of it."

The seven-year-old's ensuing shrug was a gesture far beyond her years. "I don't really see what she's so upset about, myself. Practically everything they left is an endearment of one sort or another. So it's not as if she's wondering if he still wants to be betrothed."

As she'd been talking, the older dowager countess

of Schwarzburg-Rudolstadt had come into the room also. Anna Sophia took a chair; then, with a loud and disdainful sniff:

"As if he could anyway! The offer of betrothal was made in front of witnesses. Well, more or less. But her acceptance of the offer certainly was. Scandalous, that business. The whole town's still talking about it."

Taking her own seat, Emelie almost laughed. There were times she found her middle-aged sister-in-law's definition of "the whole town" quite amusing. What Anna Sophia really meant was proper society—and solely the Lutheran portion of it, at that.

Emelie didn't doubt at all that the regiments of the army had been talking about the betrothal, also. But the dowager countess wouldn't know about that, and wouldn't care if she did. Her concern, and that of her intimate circles, was that Caroline Platzer had made a *most unsuitable* match for a husband—and, alas, there was now very little that could be done about it. Seeing as how the impetuous and foolish young woman had made such an incredible public display of the business.

"I have no idea what's happening to him!" Caroline wailed, slamming the letter onto the desk under her hands.

Thankfully, Anna Sophia said nothing—and Caroline wasn't looking at her. Thankfully, because it was clear from the expression on the dowager countess' face that her thoughts were running along the lines of: *Well, you know he's still alive. More's the pity.*

The problem wasn't even so much a clash of cultural attitudes as it was a clash of expectations that were shaped and colored by those very different attitudes.

Perhaps because of her youth, or perhaps simply because she'd spent so much time with Caroline and Maureen Grady and other Americans, Emelie could see both sides of the issue where neither Caroline nor Anna Sophia could see any but theirs.

For Caroline, as for all the up-timers, the issue was simply and solely one of a prospective marriage. And since issues of class didn't matter to them, Thorsten Engler made a perfectly suitable match for Caroline. End of discussion.

There were subtleties there, of course. As she'd gotten to know them better, Emelie had come to realize that the American indifference to class was not so much indifference as it was a very different assessment of how class was defined in the first place. Unless issues of race complicated the matter—and she'd found up-timer attitudes on that subject both varied and often contradictory—then the "blood" of the prospective marital partners was simply irrelevant, especially in this instance. The Americans were a hybrid stock, whose second-largest national component after the Anglo-Saxons was German to begin with. That was certainly true of Caroline Platzer, as her surname alone indicated.

What *did* matter was, first, a person's economic status; and second and still more important, a person's prospects for economic advancement.

And there was an enormous cultural weight thrown onto the latter, reinforced over and over again in every aspect of American society. It was one of the standard themes of their popular literature, whether in the form of books or those moving visual depictions that Emelie found so fascinating. Show any American a story where a lively young woman's "hand in marriage," as they put it, was being sought by two rivals, one poor but industrious and the other wealthy and indolent, and the audience automatically knew which rival they favored.

From the standpoint of down-timer nobility, exactly the wrong one.

Everything about Thorsten Engler fit that model image. Poor, yes—but his poverty was no fault of his own. Born a farmer, an occupation which American popular culture romanticized, and then stripped of his farm by soldiers employed by that same class of idle rich whom up-timers were predisposed to detest in the first place.

A virgin birth, you might say, untainted and unsoiled in any particular. Then, he went forward "from his bootstraps," to use the up-timer expression. Something else which they found admirable. And advanced himself quite well, not letting his patriotic duty slide in the process. Two more plus marks to add to his column, as they would think of it.

Finally—no one argued this, not even the sourest Elle—he was a very nice man. There was nothing about his personality that anyone could point an accusing finger at.

From Caroline's standpoint—and Maureen Grady's, and her husband Dennis', and that of every up-timer Emelie knew—what more could you ask for?

Throughout, and this was perhaps where the cultural divergence was greatest, there was not a trace of consideration given to the blindingly obvious political aspects of the problem. Indeed, Emelie was quite sure that the political side of it had never even occurred to them.

"Caroline, you've glared at the letter long enough!"

proclaimed the princess. "You promised you'd let me take you riding!"

Emelie glanced at her sister-in-law and saw that the dowager countess was restraining a quite visible grimace.

That political problem. So obvious that Emelie was still amazed the up-timers didn't even seem to recognize it at all. But also understanding that it was that very blindness on their part that made the issue so explosive.

Kristina Vasa, only child and heir of Gustav II Adolf, king of Sweden and emperor of the United States of Europe. Arguably already—they'd know in just a few more months—the most powerful ruler in Europe. Seven years old or not, she was herself one of the most politically important figures in the continent.

And the headstrong child had chosen for her principal lady-in-waiting one Caroline Platzer. The fact that neither the princess nor the lady-in-waiting herself used the term—didn't even occur to them, in fact—made the situation all the worse. There were none of the usual accepted limitations of the post to contain the potential damage being done.

Or the potential benefits, for that matter, which Emelie herself thought far outweighed the drawbacks. But she was almost alone among the Elles—or their spouses, or their relatives, or their advisers—in her view of the matter.

To say that proper Lutheran noble society was appalled by the situation—nay, aghast and flabbergasted—would be to put it mildly.

All the worse, that the situation had snuck upon them like the proverbial thief in the night. The German nobility and their Swedish counterparts had been so concerned with the potential damage that might be done by the rambunctious princess' regular outings into the disreputable Freedom Arches and her associations with the detestable Committees of Correspondence that they'd been quite oblivious, in the beginning, to Kristina's growing attachment to the Platzer woman. Indeed, they'd even seen it as a useful counterbalance. While Caroline shared all of the usual attitudes of up-timers, she was not particularly inclined toward political radicalism. Indeed, she seemed generally not very interested in politics at all, being preoccupied entirely by social matters.

Such is the folly of mankind. Watch for the wolves, and let the weasel slide in the door. That most bloodthirsty of all predators, size be damned.

"Yes, I promised. Fine." The weasel rose and headed for the door, taking by the hand the future ruler of central Europe. The innocent chicklet, to the slaughter.

Seeing the sour look on Anna Sophia's face, it was all Emelie could do to keep from laughing.

"But no galloping, this time!" she heard Caroline's voice coming from the hall outside.

"We didn't gallop last time. That was just a canter. Well. A fast canter."

"I was scared to death."

"You didn't fall off, did you?"

Beneath the banter, the mutual affection was so thick it practically dripped like honey.

"What are we going to do?" Emelie heard her sister-in-law mutter.

The words had been spoken loudly enough that Emelie decided a response was called for.

"Live with it, that's all."

"And now she's to be married to a peasant! I had hoped—we'd found any of several suitable matches—that a proper husband might ameliorate the situation."

As if Caroline would have been impressed by a string of young counts trotted before her. But Emelie left that unspoken. She also left unspoken the fact that her own marriage to a much older nobleman—her husband Ludwig Guenther, count of Schwarzburg-Rudolstadt, would be celebrating his fifty-third birthday in less than two months—had not particularly "ameliorated" her own attitudes, had they?

Fortunately, there had been no clashes between her and her husband, over the subject of Emelie's growing attachment to the up-timers and her subtly-expressed but growing political radicalization. It might be better to say, cultural radicalization. Like Caroline Platzer herself, Emelie was not particularly interested in politics, in the narrow sense of the term. But she too, like the princess, had found herself powerfully influenced by the attitudes toward people and social relations that, in many ways, were more deeply rooted in Caroline and—especially—Maureen Grady than they were in the most flamboyant CoC agitator.

Emelie and Ludwig Guenther might have clashed, had circumstances been different. But her husband, much to his surprise, had found himself at the center of the growing storm in Lutheran theological circles, ever since he'd sponsored the now-famous Rudolstadt Colloquy, the year before. The continuing controversies over that colloquy and the decisions the count had made at it had become so contentious for the continent's Lutheran clergy that an exasperated emperor Gustav Adolf had ordered another colloquy be held to adjudicate *all* the issues under dispute—and had appointed Emelie's husband to oversee it. That, because whatever their other quarrels, all theologians involved had expressed no animosity toward Ludwig Guenther as a person. Indeed, they'd all agreed that he'd been quite even-handed and judicious—even if, to many of them, astonishingly wrong-headed.

So, Emelie and Ludwig Guenther had come to Magdeburg a few months earlier. Since her husband spent practically every waking hour attending to the Lutheran dispute, she'd found herself with a great deal of time on her hands. At her sister-in-law's invitation, she'd spent those many free hours at the settlement house. And, as the months passed, felt a subtle but sweeping transformation come over her, in terms of attitudes that she'd inherited unthinkingly from her background and upbringing.

Maureen Grady had been more influential in that respect—at least, for Emelie if not a seven-year-old princess—than Caroline Platzer. Maureen was in her late forties, in the prime of her life, with both an extensive education and an administrative practice "under her belt," as the Americans put it. The fact that she was married to an up-time policeman, with the usual conservative views of such men—conservative, at least, by American standards—gave Maureen's own attitudes that much more impact. This was no flighty girl whose opinions could be easily dismissed. This was an extremely capable and very level-headed woman, able to retain the affections of a tough-minded cop, whose views on most important social questions placed her in opposition to the standards of seventeenth-century society. Noble society, certainly.

You could start with Maureen's feminism, so deeply ingrained that she didn't even consider it "feminism" to begin with. Just . . . self-evident.

It would be interesting to see where it all wound up, in the end. And since Emelie was still only nineteen years old—and given the impact that the up-timers were starting to have on medicine and life expectancy—she had good reason to believe she'd see a great deal of whatever transformations happened to Europe, in her lifetime.

She was looking forward to it, even if—

"And now the princess seems to be developing an attachment to the *peasant*. What are we going to *do*?" demanded Anna Sophia, almost wailing the words.

—some others were not.

Fortunately, Kristina did not put up a fuss about attending the concert that night. She might have, except that the concert was supposed to include ballads from the Brillo saga, for which she'd become a devoted enthusiast and afficionado.

"Praise be," the princess' governess and official lady-in-waiting, Lady Ulrike, murmured to Caroline as they set off for the royal palace.

Unlike most of the German establishment—and most of the Swedish, for that matter—Lady Ulrike had few if any reservations about Caroline's relationship with Kristina. It might be better to say that whatever reservations the Swedish noblewoman had were simply overwhelmed by her relief at having someone who was far better suited than she was to keeping the princess under control. And if the young American's methods of "control" upset the established order, so much the worse for the establishment. They could cluck their tongues all they wanted. *They* didn't have the responsibility of keeping a girl who might be the world's smartest seven-year-old and was certainly its most self-confident and willful one—not to mention a truly superb horse rider—from running wild at every turn.

To make the situation still better for Lady Ulrike, Mary Simpson was at the concert also. She was surprised, since she'd thought Mary had left already on her trip to the Upper Palatinate.

"No, I'm not leaving for two more days," Mary explained. "Ronnie had some last minute things she needed to attend to."

That was a reference to Veronica Richter—or Veronica Dreeson, now, if you went by American custom, since she'd married Grantville's mayor. To just about everyone's surprise, including theirs, she and Mary Simpson had become quite good friends since the Ring of Fire. Veronica was determined to return to the Upper Palatinate and see what she could recover of the family's property that had been left behind when she and the survivors of her family had been forced to become camp followers of Tilly's army.

Lady Ulrike smiled. "Two more days for the rumors to keep mounting."

Mary rolled her eyes. "Tell me about it. *Why* are so many people convinced that there's some Machiavellian political scheme involved in this? It's a purely personal matter for Veronica, and I agreed to accompany her simply because she's a friend of mine, she asked me to come—and I won't be seeing my husband until the war's over, anyway."

If I ever see him again at all, she could have added, but didn't. The ironclads had passed through Hamburg, according to the radio reports, with not much in the way of casualties. The admiral hadn't been one of them, or that would certainly have been reported also. Still, there were months of fighting ahead, and Mary's husband would be in the thick of it. She might very well not hear from him again until the summer, even if he survived.

Lady Ulrike was sure that was the underlying reason behind Mary's willingness to go to the Upper Palatinate with Veronica Dreeson. It was either that or spend the next few weeks in Magdeburg, fretting with worry.

She shrugged. "Don't be naïve, Mary. You are John Simpson's wife and Veronica is Gretchen Richter's grandmother. No competent spymaster in Europe would presume that a joint trip you take—now of all times—would simply be an innocent personal matter. Especially not going to the Oberpfalz, where General Banér is locking horns with the Bavarians."

She used the German term for the Upper Palatinate, slipping it effortlessly into the English they'd been speaking. Lady Ulrike used every possible opportunity to improve her English—or her American, as she thought of it. Regardless of what happened, she was likely to continue being Princess Kristina's official lady-in-waiting. That meant she'd be dealing with the girl's new American friends and mentors for a long time to come. Understanding their language would be a help in the task. Lady Ulrike had started with a good grasp of the English of her day, but she'd soon come to appreciate the quip someone had once made about the relationship between Americans and Britons: *Divided by a common language.*

The princess came up that very moment. "Barreled up," to use American idiom. With her usual heedlessness, she flung herself into an embrace with Mary Simpson.

"Aunt Mary! I want the Brillo stuff first!"

Lady Ulrike sidled off. Let Mary deal with *that.*

It was the general opinion of the Lutheran establishment that dominated both Sweden and, to a lesser degree, the USE, that it was most fortunate that the royal child had taken a liking to Mary Simpson as well as to Caroline Platzer, the dame of Magdeburg being who and what she was.

Personally, Lady Ulrike thought that general opinion was shortsighted, as the commonly accepted wisdom so often was. True, Mary Simpson had her own version of an upper-crust view of the world. But, beneath the surface, it was really not so much different from the attitudes of someone like Caroline Platzer. In the long run, she was pretty sure, the reinforcing aspects of their mutual influence on the child would greatly outweigh whatever conservative opinions Mary Simpson might bring to the mix.

But she really didn't care. It was *so* much easier, these days, to deal with Kristina.

The concert went well, in everyone's opinion. Whatever dubious attitudes anyone in the audience might have had over the content of the Brillo ballads were more than offset by their satisfaction that the formidable dame of Magdeburg had quite successfully squelched the rambunctious princess' demand to rearrange the program. Thank God, *somebody* could discipline the child.

They were less pleased the next day, those of them who attended—not many, but all of them heard about it afterward—when the regiments of the army marched through Magdeburg on their way to the front. The war, quiescent during the winter except for the sieges of Luebeck and Amsterdam, was erupting again.

Alas, General Torstensson had sent orders to march the entire army right through the middle of the capital before sending them into battle. To boost the morale of the soldiers, was his public explanation.

And . . . it was true enough, so far as it went. The main streets of the city were lined with civilians, wildly cheering on their army as it passed.

But nobody misunderstood the other message contained in those tramping boots, accompanied by music. Certainly not anyone who was present in Hans Richter Square and witnessed the reaction of the army when it passed the reviewing stand spilling from the portico of Hans Richter Palace.

Princess Kristina was the centerpiece of that little drama. Her seven-year-old enthusiasm for the regiments passing below her was fully reciprocated. Whatever political opinions might exist in the minds of those soldiers, so heavily influenced as they were by the CoCs, the Vasa dynasty retained its popularity with them. Indeed, had increased its popularity over the course of the winter. Gustav Adolf might still be something of a Swedish foreigner, to those mostly-German troops. But his heir belonged to *them*.

They knew of the girl's frequent visits to the city's

Freedom Arches. They knew that she'd spent time, as required by the rules, learning to bake in their kitchens. They knew that she'd spent still more time in the settlement house, which had come to spread its influence through more and more of the city's workingmen's quarters.

And, by now, they'd all heard the story of Thorsten Engler and Caroline Platzer. It had become something of a legend of its own, in fact—especially the part that involved their future empress demanding that a commoner from the future be allowed to pass through the gates to betroth one of their own.

The USE's noble and merchant establishment was in a vise, in short, with its lower jaw taking the form of the regiments, and its upper jaw symbolized in the person of a seven-year-old girl. The closer those jaws closed, the smaller became their room to maneuver.

Such was the general opinion of the establishment, at least. Not all of its members shared in it, however.

A bit to her surprise—certainly to her relief—Emelie discovered that her husband was one of those dissenters. "Mavericks," as the up-timers put it.

"Well, that was certainly delightful," said the count of Schwarzburg-Rudolstadt as he and Emelie walked away from the square after the regiments passed.

Emelie, whose hand was tucked into his elbow, gave Ludwig Guenther a considering glance. She could detect no trace of sarcasm in his expression, nor had there been one in his tone of voice.

"You have no . . ."

"Reservations?" he said, chuckling softly. He stopped, placed an affectionate hand on his wife's nestled on his arm, and turned toward her. "No, dearest, I do not. Half a year ago, I probably would have. But today? After months of overseeing churchmen wrangling over doctrine?"

He chuckled again, more loudly. "Mind you, I find the theology itself and the disputes quite engrossing. But I've also come to conclude that the mentality— what's that American term—?"

"Mindset," Emelie provided.

"Yes. Splendid expression. The mindset involved in being a leading theologian stands in almost direct opposition to the mindset required for successful governance. More than once, I've found myself thinking: *Thank God for the separation of church and state.*"

Emelie smiled, and they resumed walking. After a moment, Ludwig Guenther added, "I haven't had the time to discuss the matter with you, but you should know that Wilhelm Wettin and his Crown Loyalists have been after me a great deal lately."

She nodded. "Yes, that's to be expected. Have you come to any conclusions?"

"Oh, yes. I intend to keep it to myself for the moment—except with you, that is—but I've decided that I would far rather be a moderating influence in Mike Stearns' camp than try to be a reforming influence in the Crown Loyalists."

Emelie was surprised. Quite surprised, in fact. She was fond of her husband, no question about it. But she sometimes found him judicious to the point of sheer boredom. For someone like the count of Schwarzburg-Rudolstadt, this verged on outright radicalism.

"I had the impression you thought very well of Wilhelm."

"Oh, I do. Less so today than I did a year ago, however—and the problem isn't really him in the first place." He sighed. "I fear Wilhelm has been quite incautious, in his anxiety to supplant Mike Stearns. I could live with Wilhelm, well enough. Probably better than I could Stearns, really. But I simply can't stomach so many of the people Wilhelm has become attached to. They are blind men, at best."

They'd reached the end of the square. From here, they could turn one way to return to their mansion. Or, the other, to go toward the workingmen's districts.

"You've never been to the settlement house," Emelie said, a bit hesitantly. "Would you . . ."

"Yes, by all means. I should most enjoy a visit. Finally."

Princess Kristina arrived not long after they did. With Caroline Platzer in tow.

"Blind men," Ludwig Guenther repeated.

Chapter 41

The mouth of the Elbe

"Here they come!"

Anatole du Bouvard looked up sharply at the lookout's shout, and his stomach tightened. Despite everything, he'd rather hoped this moment would never come. Of course, what he'd hoped and what he'd *expected* had been two quite different things.

He dumped the cup of hot broth he'd been drinking onto the ground beside the fire, tossed the cup to the cook, and headed for the lookout's position on the river bank.

"There," the lookout said, pointing upstream, and du Bouvard grimaced.

"I see them," he acknowledged.

He gazed at the oncoming shapes for several seconds, then inhaled deeply and looked over his shoulder.

"Get them ready, Léandre," he called gruffly.

Léandre Olier, du Bouvard's second-in-command, waved in acknowledgment and turned his attention to the two men who had "volunteered" for their part in this mission.

For several seconds, du Bouvard watched those volunteers donning the equipment from the future for which the cardinal's agents had paid so dearly. Then he turned back to the river and shook his head.

Madness, he thought. *This entire idea is madness.*

Not that he'd felt any particular inclination to point that out when he received his orders. The fact that they'd come directly from Richelieu himself had been more than sufficient to depress any foolish temptation in that direction. Still . . .

It wasn't the concept itself he objected to. *That* had an undeniable elegance, especially given what the Americans had done to the League of Ostend's fleet off Luebeck. And using equipment purchased from some of the arrogant "up-timers" themselves only added to the notion's appeal. But however du Bouvard might feel about that, there were certain practical objections which the cardinal appeared to have failed to consider.

More likely, he considered them and simply decided to go ahead, anyway. After all, what does he lose if we fail? The cardinal's calculations were seldom encumbered by any preoccupation with the survival of his tools. On the other hand, the rewards for those tools could be substantial when—and if—they succeeded.

He refocused his attention on his targets. The big ships, the "ironclads" and the "timberclads," moved steadily downstream towards him, following behind two much smaller vessels. Those would be the "motorboats" the spies had reported, and he frowned at the way they wove back and forth, sweeping their bigger consorts' line of advance. There were several musket-armed infantry (at least, he *hoped* they were musketeers and not equipped with some of the deadly up-time firearms) in each of them, and they appeared to be unpleasantly alert.

Well, there was nothing he could do about that, and he returned his attention to the rest of the American fleet.

The "ironclads" were impressive. They moved smoothly, without any fuss or bother, and despite their slab-sided appearance, they possessed a certain low-slung elegance. The three stubbier vessels following behind them—the "timberclads"—were another matter. They were much higher in proportion to their length, with massive superstructures dominating their after ends, and they looked undeniably clumsier.

That would be the "paddle wheels," he thought, looking at the high, straight-sided housings. The spies' reports had made it abundantly clear that the timberclads and ironclads had different means of movement. Personally, du Bouvard found it much easier to visualize how the "paddle wheels" must work. After all, he'd seen plenty of waterwheels in his time, and the principle was obviously the same, even if the mechanics were reversed. This notion of ships that moved by squirting water out of their asses, though . . . *that* he found difficult to wrap his mind around.

Also unlike the ironclads, the timberclads' tall smokestacks belched dense, black smoke that was visible for miles. It should have made them look even more threatening, like some sort of smoke- and fire-breathing dragons, but it didn't work that way. Instead, the very lack of any visible, dramatic signs of what made them move only made the ironclads more ominous by comparison.

Someone stepped up beside him, and he glanced to his right.

"Well?" he said.

"They're ready," Olier told him with a grunt. The taciturn Breton's eyes were on the oncoming vessels, and he shook his head. "Not that I think it's going to do much good," he added.

"Only one way to find out," du Bouvard replied.

"They're moving faster than we expected," Olier observed, and du Bouvard chuckled sourly.

"In that case, we'd better get them started," he said.

"I'll see to it."

Olier started back, and du Bouvard returned his attention to the river.

Léandre had a point, he thought. Those ships were moving at least twice as rapidly as they'd anticipated, which only made this entire operation even more problematical. As du Bouvard had attempted to point out to his superiors, when the Americans attacked the League fleet in the Trave River below Luebeck, its ships had been anchored, motionless. And they'd launched the attack under cover of night. And the Trave was a much *smaller* river than the Elbe.

None of those conditions, unfortunately, applied at the moment.

The odds of any swimmer, even one equipped with the Americans' "scuba gear," managing to place an explosive charge on a vessel moving through the water at a substantial rate of speed, in daylight, struck du Bouvard as remote, to say the very least. Adding in the frigid temperature of the water, and its inevitable effect on those same swimmers, didn't improve them. But the cavalry forces that had accompanied the American vessels as far as Hamburg had precluded any possibility of getting close enough to attempt an attack above the city. And now that the ironclads and timberclads were *past* Hamburg, it was extraordinarily unlikely that they were going to obligingly anchor anywhere else in the river. So, if du Bouvard was going to attempt this lunacy at all, this was the best chance he was going to be able to arrange.

Piss-poor as it might be.

Olier and the two divers made their way down to the river bank, and du Bouvard shook his head as he watched. The cardinal's agents had been unable to acquire one of the "wetsuits" the Americans apparently used. Du Bouvard wasn't entirely clear on exactly how a "wetsuit" worked, but he knew it was designed to protect a swimmer from the numbing effect of cold water. In the absence of whatever it was and however it worked, he and Olier had done their best by coating the swimmers' bodies thickly in insulating grease. He expected it to help; he didn't expect it to help *enough*.

The "volunteers," who—in the event of their survival—would find their sentences commuted, in addition to receiving a substantial monetary reward, pulled on their frogfootlike flippers and slipped gingerly into the water. They adjusted their equipment carefully, moving methodically through the series of checks du Bouvard and Olier had put together from their reading of the books acquired from the same source that had provided the scuba gear itself. They'd been able to make a handful of practice dives in warmer water, but the difficulty in recharging the scuba tanks had limited the amount of time they could spend actually underwater. And, while du Bouvard had chosen not to mention it to his swimmers, the books had made it clear that there were problems using normal air to fill the tanks.

They completed their adjustments, nodded to Olier, and disappeared into the Elbe.

Someone knocked on the cabin door, and John Simpson looked up from the sandwich and glass of beer of the lunch he'd been anticipating for the last couple of hours. Especially the beer. Good seventeenth-century German beer was among the best in the world, and one difference between the USE Navy and the U.S. Navy in which he'd once served was that there'd been no point at all in attempting to enforce Gideon Welles' ban on shipboard alcohol. Simpson couldn't really say he regretted that, but however he'd felt about it, no down-time German would have stood for it. So he'd settled for truly ferocious punishments for drunkenness, instead, although, to be fair, that seemed to be no worse a common problem among seventeenth-century Germans than it had been among twentieth-century Americans.

Whoever it was knocked again, and he shook his head.

"Enter!" he called, and one of *Constitution*'s assistant signalmen opened the door and stepped into the cabin.

"Message from *Achates,* sir. I'm afraid it's marked 'Urgent.'"

"Very well." Simpson sighed, pushing the beer aside, and took the radio room message slip. He unfolded it and scanned the few, terse sentences, and his jaw tightened.

"Thank you," he told the messenger, and climbed out of his chair. He started for the compartment door, then paused, scooped up the sandwich, and continued on his way.

Captain Halberstat was waiting on the port bridge wing, gazing aft through a pair of up-time binoculars, when he arrived.

The bridge lookouts came to attention as Simpson stepped out of the conning tower door, still chewing on ham and cheese, but he waved them back to their duties as he moved up beside Halberstat.

Achates was dropping out of formation, emitting a thick plume of steam as she angled towards the river's southern bank. The rest of the squadron had slowed to stay in company with her, and Simpson grunted.

"I suppose we've done better than we had any right to expect to get this far without a significant engineering casualty," he said.

"I don't imagine Commander Baumgartner feels that way at the moment, Admiral," Halberstat replied, and Simpson chuckled harshly.

"No, I don't imagine he does," he agreed. Commander C.H. Baumgartner was a dour fellow even in his sunniest moments—which this certainly was not. Simpson himself was one of the few people who even knew what the initials stood for. Most of the sailors in the navy who'd dealt with the officer just used the monicker an up-timer had given him; "Clod Hopper." Not to his face, of course.

Simpson looked at Halberstat. "Any more details on his problem?"

"He did send a follow-up message, sir." Halberstat extracted another folded message slip from the breast pocket of his uniform tunic and passed it across. "According to his engineer, it's a fractured steampipe. And he's got at least three badly injured men."

"Wonderful."

Simpson unfolded the second message and scanned it quickly. Actually, it wasn't a steam*pipe*, he saw; it was the fitting where the steampipe in question joined the boiler itself, which made the injury reports understandable enough. Indeed, they were lucky the sailors in question appeared to have escaped with relatively minor burns, given the amount of live steam that must have escaped. He didn't *feel* especially lucky, however, and he suppressed a sudden temptation to swear out loud and turned to the signalman who had followed him out onto the bridge wing, instead.

"Message to *Achilles*, copied to *Achates*," he said. The signalman's pencil poised itself above his message pad, and he continued. "Stand by to assist *Achates*. Prepare to pass a tow, if required."

"Aye, sir." The signalman read back the message, and then headed for the radio room voice pipe when Simpson nodded.

"May I ask what you intend to do, sir?" Halberstat asked.

"Unless Commander Baumgartner's initial assessment is wrong, it's going to take at least thirty-six to forty-eight hours for him to make repairs—assuming he *can* make them out of shipboard resources," Simpson replied. "We can't afford to wait that long. The emperor is expecting us at Luebeck and General Torstensson's already moving. What's the closest town?"

"That would be Ritsenbuttel, I believe," Halberstat said, pointing downstream and to the southern bank.

"All right." Simpson nodded. "In that case, let's get a message sent back to Hamburg. We're going to need some sort of security force down here, if it turns out Baumgartner's estimate is overly optimistic. Until they can get here, I think his own Marines should be able to provide any base security he requires."

Du Bouvard swore inventively and with feeling as the Americans' steady approach suddenly slowed. He had no idea why it had happened. One of the timberclads was turning out of line, and as he watched, a second timberclad moved towards it, as if to render assistance. There was also a lot of white smoke—or possibly steam—streaming up.

Why the devil couldn't they have had whatever problem they're having fifteen minutes earlier? he demanded.

No one answered, and he shook his head in disgust. If he'd only known this was coming, he would never have put his swimmers into the water so soon! And if the Americans *were* having mechanical problems, it was entirely possible they would have no choice but to anchor somewhere after all while they made repairs. An *anchored* warship would have been far more vulnerable.

Lieutenant Leberecht Probst, USE Marine Corps, stood beside the bass boat's wheel and shaded his eyes with one hand as he looked philosophically back upriver.

Probst was better educated than the majority of his

fellow Marines. Like Hans and Gretchen Richter, he was the son of a small printer. Unlike the Richters' father, however, Anton Probst was alive and well . . . and an enthusiastic supporter of the Committees of Correspondence whose political tracts had brought him so much business of late. Young Leberecht had read those same tracts while helping to set type, and one thing had led to another.

Now he watched the ironclads reducing their speed to little more than a crawl while *Achilles* went alongside *Achates*.

"What do you think, Leberecht?" Ensign Kjell Halvorsen asked, and he shrugged.

"I think somebody broke down. From the looks of things, it was *Achates*."

"Commander Baumgartner's going to be pissed," Halvorsen said with a certain satisfaction. The tall young Swede wasn't especially fond of Commander Baumgartner, since Commander Baumgartner's attractive younger daughter was *quite* fond of Ensign Halvorsen and the commander did not approve. Of course, Baumgartner didn't approve of much of anything.

"I imagine he is," Probst agreed with a slight smile. Then he looked around the boat and cleared his throat.

"I don't believe I recall suggesting that it was no longer necessary to keep an eye out," he remarked to the air in general, and his detachment's attention returned magically to scanning the riverbanks and the water around them.

"It's definitely the fitting, sir," Lieutenant Hafner, Commander Baumgartner's senior engineer, said as he climbed up the internal ladder to the timberclad's bridge. He shrugged in disgust. "We've got a crack clear through the casting."

"Damn," Baumgartner said, far more mildly than he felt. Then he shook his head. "And what about those burns?"

"Ugly," Hoffner said. "Gunther's arm, especially. Lothar is doing what he can, but—"

The lieutenant shrugged again, and Baumgartner nodded. They were lucky that Admiral Simpson had insisted that each of the navy's major combatants had to have at least one trained sick bay attendant from the up-timers' training classes aboard. Even though the SBAs like Chief Lothar Tümmel weren't considered full-fledged "doctors" by their up-time instructors, they were so much better than most seventeenth-century physicians that it was almost miraculous. Still, there were limits in all things.

"Repairs?" Baumgartner asked, shifting mental gears once more as he watched his deck crew making fast the towline *Achilles* had passed across.

"Not out of our own resources," Haffner said grimly. "A steam pipe we probably could have fixed, but this is going to have to be torched off and replaced, and we don't have the gear aboard for that. It's going to have to be sent forward to us from Magdeburg."

"The admiral isn't going to want to hear that."

"Oh, I'm well aware of that, sir. Unfortunately—"

The lieutenant shrugged yet again, and Baumgartner snorted. Haffner's apparent insouciance undoubtedly owed a great deal to who was going to actually have to tell Admiral Simpson that two-thirds of his timber-clads had just become nothing more than a floating battery on a raft. On the other hand, the admiral wasn't in the habit of blaming people for things that clearly weren't their fault.

Which was quite a bit more than Baumgartner could have said for other military officers he'd served under.

"All right, Crispus," he sighed, "I'll tell him. When you go back below, ask Nikolaus to come up here. He and I are going to have to discuss port security with Rüdiger."

"Yes, Sir," Hoffner said. Nikolaus Schimmel was *Achates'* executive officer, and Lieutenant Rüdiger Kirsch was the timberclad's gunnery officer.

The engineer saluted and disappeared back down the ladder, and Baumgartner turned to his bridge signalman.

"Message for the admiral," he said.

John Simpson grunted as he read the new message slip. It was a sound of unhappy confirmation, not surprise.

"What I was afraid of from the beginning," he said, looking up at Captain Halberstat. "It looks like we don't have any choice but to send them into this Ritsenbuttel. I'm half-tempted to detach one of the other timberclads to help keep an eye on her, too."

Halberstat looked surprised, and Simpson grimaced.

"I'm worried about those intelligence reports about the scuba rigs that may have . . . fallen into enemy hands, let's say. I don't like the thought of leaving one of our ships all alone when we don't know where that scuba gear is. Especially when the ship in question can't move under its own power."

Halberstat's surprise disappeared, and he nodded.

But he also cocked his head to one side, one eyebrow arched.

"Would leaving a second timberclad really help that
much, sir? Is there anything she could do for *Achates'*
security that Baumgartner couldn't do by keeping a
couple of his cutters rowing around the ship?"

"Probably not. That's why I'm only *half*-tempted.
And why I'm not going to do it in the end."

"What's that?" one of Leberecht Probst's Marines
said suddenly.

It wasn't the most militarily correct sighting report
in even the USE Marine Corps' brief history, but it
got the job done. Probst followed the pointing index
finger, and his eyes narrowed. The Elbe was still flowing high, wide, and muddy with springtime runoff, and
there was more than a little debris still drifting down
it. But all of that debris was drifting *down* it. Probst
couldn't think of the last time he'd seen something
moving *against* the current.

"What *is* that?" Halvorsen said as his eyes found
the same object.

"Unless I'm mistaken," the Marine said, reaching
for the up-time revolver he'd been issued when he
was assigned to *Constitution*'s Marine detachment,
"it's a head."

Du Bouvard swore again, with more feeling than
ever, as the sharp, distant pop of gunfire came to him.
The American motor boats were too far away for him
to see details very well, but he could clearly see one
of the uniformed Marines firing at something in the
water with one of the up-time pistols.

Laguia, he thought. During their practice dives, the Spaniard had demonstrated an unfortunate tendency to become disoriented and come to the surface and look around in order to check his bearings. But even Laguia should have known better than to poke his head up *that* close to one of the American patrol boats!

Be fair, Anatole, he told himself harshly as the Marine fired again and again. *The poor bastard's got to be half-frozen, despite all the grease you could slather onto him. No wonder his brain isn't working very well.*

Unlike quite a few of his contemporaries, Leberecht Probst had discovered that he was actually an excellent shot with a pistol. The revolver, a .38 Smith & Wesson Model 15 with a four-inch barrel, wasn't the most powerful of weapons to have come back through the Ring of Fire, but it was comfortable in his hand, and his target jerked up out of the water with the third shot.

It was definitely a human head, he noted, amazed by the steadiness of his own hand as the fact that he was shooting at another human being was confirmed. In fact, the head was attached to the rest of a human body, and he saw a sudden blossom of crimson on the side of the swimmer's neck as he fired a fourth time.

His target rolled over, and the glassy plate of the diver's swimming mask turned towards him like a Cyclops' accusing eye. Then the man he'd just shot submerged once again.

It didn't look like an intentional dive.

"Take us over there, Kjell," Probst heard his own preposterously calm voice saying to Halvorsen. "And report to the flagship that we've definitely sighted at least one scuba diver."

Du Bouvard's jaw tightened as the pistol fire stopped and the boat from which it had come swept around in a sharp turn. Whether it had been Laguia or not, the combination of no more shooting and purposeful movement suggested that something unpleasant had happened to the Marine's target. And the fact that one of his divers had been sighted had just reduced the other swimmer's already minute chances of success to virtually nothing.

"What do we do now?" Olier asked.

"There's damn-all we *can* do," du Bouvard replied flatly. "Except get the hell out of here before they get around to sending parties ashore to find out just where those divers came from."

"That sounds like an excellent idea to me," Olier said fervently, and started barking orders at the rest of their party.

"Is there any confirmation?" Simpson asked.

"No, sir." Halberstat shook his head. "If it was a diver, he either dove again or just sank, and the water's so muddy you can't see anything two feet below the surface. But young Probst's a reliable man. If he says he saw someone in the water, I believe him."

"So do I," Simpson admitted. "And *Achates'* problems may actually let the lunatics succeed. Mind you," he smiled thinly, "I wouldn't be willing to risk any money betting on the probability, but Murphy doesn't play favorites."

Halberstat nodded. Before joining the navy, he'd

never heard of the "Murphy" so many of the up-timers invoked, but he'd been eminently familiar with the concept Murphy enshrined.

"What are your orders, sir?" he asked.

Simpson thought for a moment, gazing down from the bridge wing at one of the mitrailleuses as the weapon poked out of its firing port and swung restlessly back and forth. He knew that some of the army's officers—like Frank Jackson—thought that his insistence on the more sophisticated and expensive mitrailleuses instead of the simpler Requa-style volley guns the army had adopted was simply one more example of his mania for "bells and whistles." And, he knew, they deeply resented the priority he'd gotten for allocations from the primers various up-time firearm reloaders had brought back with them.

But there were sound reasons for the successful, bitter campaign he'd waged in favor of the navy's mitrailleuses. The army's volley guns were an all-or-nothing proposition. Their cartridge cases had no individual primers, only touch holes, and were set off in a rapid-fire chain by a single powder train. In twentieth-century terms, they weren't "selective fire" weapons; when one shot was fired, *every* shot was fired. Even worse, in many ways, they were mounted as artillery pieces. The weapons were cumbersome, large, and impossible to traverse. When they fired, they delivered all of their rounds virtually simultaneously into a very small, relatively speaking, target area.

The navy's mitrailleuses were based on the Reffye, the most successful of the mitrailleuses used by the French during the Franco-Prussian War. They used individually primed cartridge cases, constructed very

much like shotgun shells, fired in succession by turning
a side-mounted crank. Each round was expensive, but
they could be collected, reloaded, and reused. More
importantly, the man on the crank could fire all of
them as quickly as he could turn the crank, or only
a few rounds at a time, or even single shots, and he
could vary the rate of fire to suit a specific tactical
need instead of blazing through the entire magazine
in a single eruption.

Simpson's mitrailleuse consisted of twenty barrels
arranged in five rows of four, mounted in a cylindrical sleeve, which was actually five fewer barrels than
the Reffye had had, but it produced a lighter weapon
with a slimmer profile, better suited to pivot mounts
aboard the navy's warships. It was a .50-caliber weapon,
with a crew of five, three of whom were responsible
solely for clearing expended cartridge cases from the
removable steel breechblocks and replacing them with
fresh rounds. Each gun came with four breechblocks
and a special extractor. When the block was pressed
down onto the extractor, its fingers removed the empty
cases while one of the other loaders opened a specially
prepackaged twenty-round box that worked like a huge
speed loader. A well-trained crew (and all of Simpson's
crews were well trained) could sustain a rate of fire
of sixty aimed rounds per minute, and reach up to
a hundred rounds per minute in emergencies. That
was more than sufficient to turn any small craft into
a splintered colander, and a single hit from one of its
enormous rounds could be counted upon to stop any
human-sized target dead.

If any other divers were foolish enough to show
themselves anywhere in the field of fire of one of

those mitrailleuses, he would never be a problem again. Unfortunately, Simpson couldn't count on their doing anything of the sort.

"The ironclads and *Ajax* will increase speed and continue downriver to clear the threat zone," he said. "*Achilles* will tow *Achates* clear. I want at least one of the bass boats running a perimeter around them. And instruct all units to begin dropping anti-diver charges."

"Yes, sir!" Halberstat saluted sharply and turned to begin issuing the necessary orders.

The first underwater explosions kicked up clouds of spray and dead fish less than four minutes later. The "anti-diver charges" were nothing more than somewhat heavier hand grenades, designed to be used as mini-depth charges. They were light enough that they could be used fairly close to a vessel's hull without threat of damage, but heavy enough to kill or at least incapacitate any diver in the vicinity.

Simpson listened to the muffled explosions and watched the brown river water heave up, then watched the rings of foam drift away. He grimaced. It reminded him of accounts he'd read of depth charge attacks from both world wars. Half the time, the people dropping those charges hadn't known whether there was really a submarine in the vicinity, or not—just as *he* didn't know whether or not there were really scuba divers stalking his gunboats. But, like those long-ago (or far in the future) escort ship commanders, he had no choice but to make certain.

And in the process, he thought glumly, *give anyone on the other side who's watching a quick course in the best way to deal with* our *scuba divers in the future.*

He hadn't wanted to do that . . . but he wanted even less to discover that someone had actually managed to successfully attach an explosive charge to one of his precious ships.

Anatole du Bouvard listened to the explosions coming from the river as he climbed up into his horse's saddle. There was no sign of any American landing parties coming after his shore party, but he had no intention of waiting around until they changed their mind about that.

He watched the ironclads accelerating, obviously to move clear of this stretch of river, and shrugged philosophically. He'd never really expected anything to come of the attempt, after all, and he'd clearly given it his best effort. Surely the cardinal would understand that, especially if du Bouvard and Olier showed a certain . . . constructive creativity in their reports.

Besides, he thought, pressing with his heels and urging his horse to a trot, *we have something new to offer him, as well. I suppose we should have realized that the Americans would have worked out their own ways to deal with divers before they ever used them against us.*

He led the rest of his men rapidly away from the river bank, still listening to the explosions, and considered how best to make that point in his report. He didn't give the least bit of thought to what might have happened to the second diver. Just a convict, after all, and not one of *his* men.

It was only later that day that it occurred to him that Cardinal Richelieu might want to know what had happened to the second diver's *equipment*—which, after all, had cost the French crown a fair sum of money to obtain.

What to do? Du Bouvard was certainly not about to return. In the end, after pondering the problem for a while, he decided he'd include in the report that they'd thought the diver was slain by one of those grenades the enemy flotilla had tossed in the water. Alas, under the circumstances, his body—and the equipment—had not been recoverable.

Awkward, of course, if the diver ever showed up anywhere. But du Bouvard was willing to take that chance. It was a slim one, anyway. The last thing a convict was likely to do was report back to the same authorities who had essentially forced him into that insanely dangerous position in the first place. Especially when there was still a death sentence on his head.

In the event, du Bouvard's concern was quite unnecessary. One of the grenades *had* killed the second diver. Or rather, had stunned him unconscious and blown the mask off his face. He'd drowned within minutes, and his corpse—with the equipment still attached—was slowly settling into the mud in the Elbe's estuary. Within two years, at most, the silt brought down the river would bury it completely.

Chapter 42

Düsseldorf
Duchy of Berg

"It's definite, then?" Turenne asked as soon as he came into the tavern in Düsseldorf that his cavalry officers had established as their unofficial headquarters in the city.

Brigadier Jean de Gassion rose from a table just by the door. "Yes, Marshal. We've been maintaining couriers all along the lower Elbe. The first of them arrived last night. Admiral Simpson and his ironclads passed through Hamburg four days ago. Well, five days, now."

Turenne grunted. "Good couriers. Make sure they get a bonus. And Torstensson?"

"That's still not clear," Gassion replied. He took the map on the table and turned it around, facing Turenne, then pointed with his forefinger. "From what we can tell, he's massing an army here, just east of Hamburg. He brought eight regiments with him, but there are indications that more are coming. Hard to know, though—at least in time to do us any good."

After studying the map for a moment, Turenne shook his head. "We'll simply have to make our best guess. The most sensible thing for the Swedes to do is mass the largest possible army at Hamburg and then march straight north. They'll be looking to trap our army and the Danes besieging Luebeck."

Gassion pursed his lips. "That seems . . . a bit dubious to me, sir. By now, our army up there has very well developed lines of contravallation around Luebeck. Even if Torstensson brings the entire USE army stationed at Magdeburg, he won't have more than twenty thousand men. They'd be trying to attack a superior force protected behind defensive lines."

"It won't matter, Jean. The Swede's strategy keys off the naval force Simpson is taking into the Baltic. I'm sure of it, and damn those stupid generals in Paris. Once he gets there, he'll destroy the blockading fleet—and you can be sure there'll be more troops coming from Stockholm, to reinforce Gustav Adolf in Luebeck. Our army will be trapped, with no means of getting supplied. Torstensson won't go after them directly. He'll sweep around to the west and march into Schleswig and Holstein, cutting them off completely. That will force de Valois to bring the army out of the trenches to meet him on the open field."

One of the other cavalry officers spoke up. Francois Lefebvre, one of Gassion's lieutenants. "You're assuming that Simpson will succeed."

"Yes, I am. I think any other assumption is foolish." The young marshal cocked an eye at Gassion. "Did the courier say how long it took Simpson to get through Hamburg's defenses?"

The cavalry brigadier got a sardonic expression

on his face. "About as long as it takes a knife to go through cheese. He's got some incredibly ferocious guns on those ironclads, firing some sort of explosive shells."

"What I figured. No, gentlemen, it's time for us to accept reality, even if the king's advisers won't. The USE wouldn't have spent so many months getting those ironclads ready if they weren't confident they could manage the task. Given what they've already accomplished with their American airplanes and speedboats, I think it would be pure foolishness on our part to assume they won't do the same again."

He leaned over and tapped the location on the map that indicated Luebeck's bay. "That fleet is doomed, if Simpson can get through the North Sea and into the Kattegat. About all that could stop him now would be bad weather and severe seas. From what we've learned from our spies, the one great weakness of the ironclads is that they're not especially seaworthy."

"What about—"

"Our ambush, at the mouth of the Elbe?" Turenne shrugged. "We can hope for the best, but I can't say I have any great expectations. Unlike their divers last year, ours won't have the advantage of surprise."

He straightened up from the map. "Right or wrong, that's my assessment—and we'll operate accordingly."

There was a quick round of nods from the officers gathered around the table. Whatever reservations any of them might have, Turenne was not only their commander in name but one who had won their confidence.

"When, then?" asked Gassion. "The sooner the better, from a political standpoint."

Turenne smiled thinly. "Don't tell me. The duke of Jülich-Berg is getting nervous."

Lefebvre laughed. "'Nervous' is hardly the word. By now, he's like a cat on a hot tin roof."

Several of the officers grinned. Oddly enough, given their fierce French patriotism, Turenne's new elite cavalry force had adopted American idiom with equally fierce enthusiasm. Perhaps it was their way of thumbing their collective nose at the French military establishment which most of them had come to detest as much as their commander did.

Turenne rubbed his jaw. Ideally, he'd prefer to wait a few more days before launching his expedition. The great danger he faced, from a purely military standpoint, was that if he moved prematurely Torstensson would still have a large enough army at Hamburg to send a sizeable force down to meet him. Better to wait until he was sure Torstensson had started marching toward Luebeck.

But . . . perfection was a more unobtainable goal in war than it was anywhere else in life. And whatever sarcastic remarks anyone might make about Wolfgang Wilhelm, the duke who ruled the area, it remained a political necessity to keep him from severing his ties with France altogether.

Turenne couldn't blame the duke, really. For even the boldest prince, having five thousand foreign troops quartered in or near his capital city was a very uncertain proposition. Wolfgang Wilhelm had only agreed under a certain amount of duress—and had then insisted that Turenne's force remain as inconspicuous as possible and pass through his lands with the utmost speed.

"Inconspicuous" was an absurd term, of course, applied to five thousand armed men and their horses. The fact that Turenne's officers had only set up an unofficial headquarters in the city fooled exactly no one. Certainly not the innkeeper, as happy as he might be to get the flood of business—and he'd surely have been talking to his relations and friends, over the past few days. So would the farmers outside the city, on whose land most of Turenne's troops were camped. They'd be well-compensated, to be sure—which simply meant they had the money to provide them with idle time in which to gossip.

So. Turenne agreed with Gassion. It was best to leave the city as soon as possible, and just hope that the speed of their attack—and Gassion's diversion—would keep the enemy off balance.

"We'll leave tomorrow morning," he said. "At first light."

Seeing a few frowns around the table, the marshal grinned. "Excuse me. 'Crack of dawn,' I should have said."

The siege lines of the Spanish army in the Low Countries, outside the walls of Amsterdam

"And this is definite?" the cardinal-infante asked, looking down at the message he'd been handed. "No chance of error?"

Miguel de Manrique considered the question, for a moment, before answering. "I don't think so, Your Highness. Not in this instance, anyway. The couriers who sent this report were stationed several miles downstream from Hamburg. They've seen the ironclads for themselves, after—"

"*After* having passed through the city. Yes, I understand." Don Fernando carefully folded the message, being meticulous simply for the sake of giving himself time to make the decision.

The decision, he knew, in substance if not in form. In all likelihood, at least. There was still a possibility that problems of one sort or another—mechanical, perhaps, or inclement weather, or both—might stymie or at least delay Admiral Simpson. But it would be foolish to depend on such happenstances. Judging from the report, the American admiral's flotilla had passed through Hamburg's formidable fortifications with no significant casualties. Even the three timberclads that accompanied the four ironclads had come through largely unscathed. Whatever casualties they'd suffered had apparently been minor.

The cardinal-infante was fairly certain that the French were planning to ambush the flotilla at the mouth of the Elbe. But he would be very surprised if that came to much. No, if Simpson could get through Hamburg that easily, there was nothing in the way of hostile action that was likely to stop him until he reached the Baltic. The Kattegat, for sure.

Having finished his precise folding of the message, Don Fernando tucked it away and took a few slow steps to reach the top of the berm that gave him a good view of Amsterdam. Manrique remained below, allowing his commander some distance to ruminate in peace.

Once into the Baltic, Simpson might bombard Copenhagen, but Don Fernando thought it far more likely that he'd press on to Luebeck Bay and attack the big Danish and French fleet stationed there. If he could drive them off—and assuming, which the prince thought it would be wise to do—that Gustav Adolf had sent orders to Stockholm for the Swedish navy to sally . . .

They'd have transports, too, bringing fresh troops from Sweden.

For a moment, silently, Don Fernando cursed the fact that his artisans had not yet been able to develop a radio capability of their own. They might have, if he'd ordered them to start soon enough. But until recently, he'd accepted the common assumption that radio operations required the sort of huge towers the enemy had erected in Grantville and Magdeburg. Or, later, the cables they'd attached to existing towers in Amsterdam and Antwerp, which had provided him with a radio connection to Antwerp and to Magdeburg. He had seen no need to do more than have a few of his artisans tinker with radio, thereafter, since building such structures would require many months and a tremendous diversion of resources.

Only a month ago had it dawned on him that the up-timers might not necessarily need great high antennas for radio communication. There were clues aplenty in the up-time books, once he looked at the problem seriously. He then realized, finally, that the diplomatic responses he'd been getting from Rebecca Abrabanel were too rapid. Even granting that she'd been given a great deal of leeway as an envoy, being the wife of the enemy prime minister, she was making decisions that were just that little bit too important, just that little bit too quickly.

Which meant the towers were probably a ruse of war. Don Fernando wasn't positive, but he had come to the tentative conclusion that the up-timers had other methods of using radio, that were neither as cumbersome nor as visible. And, if true, that meant they were able to coordinate their actions far better than the League of Ostend's armies and navies, even leaving aside their advantage of possessing interior lines.

He stared at the walls of Amsterdam, but they were really just a blur. His thoughts were focused inward.

So . . . If he was right, one of the principal axioms of the League of Ostend's military calculations was a mirage. Richelieu and Christian IV—probably Charles, as well, but it hardly mattered what that dolt thought about anything—had been certain that Gustav Adolf's strategy would come to naught in the end, defeated by the simple realities of war, since it so obviously depended on bringing together four major and widely scattered forces in precise and proper sequence: his own army at Luebeck, Torstensson's army that was now being repositioned at Hamburg, Simpson's flotilla, and the Swedish fleet at Stockholm.

Impossible, on the face of it. The Swedish king had grown arrogant and overconfident from his past success. His elaborate plans would come to pieces, each of the separate forces arriving whenever they did—if they did at all—and being defeated in detail.

But what if all four of those forces were in constant touch using radio? What then?

Suddenly, Amsterdam came into focus again. The city that was right in front of him, as it had been for the many months of the siege.

Almost half a year, that siege had lasted, far longer than Don Fernando had foreseen in the heady days right after he seized Haarlem and began his rapid reconquest of most of the rebellious Dutch provinces. Half a year—and it would require at least another half a year to take the city, if he could do it at all. And that assumed—not likely!—that if Gustav Adolf was victorious in northern Germany he would not continue onward to come to the aid of his ally the prince of Orange.

The cardinal-infante knew that he'd been lucky, at that. The diseases that normally ravaged besieging armies after a time had been thankfully mild, in this siege. But that was mainly due to the quiet assistance he'd gotten from the medical specialists in the besieged city itself. That, and the tacit agreement that the siege would not be a hard-fought one, so his soldiers could devote enough time, energy and resources to maintaining good sanitation in the trenches and fieldworks investing Amsterdam.

Enough. It was time to decide. There was Amsterdam in front him; concrete, palpable, a victory that was already within his hands. Or there was the storm coming to the east, as nebulous as it was dark.

He turned away and trotted down from the berm, where Manrique waited for him.

"Have the tercios ready to march out within three days, Miguel," he commanded. "Let's say . . . half of them. That should be enough."

"Yes, Your Highness. And their destination?"

Don Fernando tugged at his fleshy lower lip. "Grol. Since we rebuilt the fortresses there, Grol should do nicely."

The relief that announcement brought to Manrique was quite visible on his face. The town of Grol was at the eastern end of Gelderland, bordering on Munster. It had good fortifications of its own, was an easy march from Amsterdam—and would make just as easy a march to get back, if need be. Best of all, while it was close enough to the German territories that would soon be the scene of major battles to make it appear as if the cardinal-infante was attempting to intervene, it was very far from the Elbe. In fact, it was no farther north than Hannover.

"The archbishop will protest mightily, you understand."

"Oh, yes, of course. I shall naturally issue a fierce demand that he allow our forces passage through Munster. But . . ."

Don Fernando shifted his shoulders, in a very slight shrugging gesture. It was easy enough to include a phrase or two in such a stiffly worded demand that made it clear he was willing to negotiate. Archbishop Ferdinand, as one might expect from a brother of Maximilian of Bavaria, was notorious for being prickly and contentious, even toward his allies. By the time a settlement allowing passage of Spanish forces through his territory could be made, it would most likely all be over.

Manrique began to leave.

"One thing more, Miguel."

"Yes, Your Highness?"

"Have word sent across to Amsterdam, inviting Señora Abrabanel to dinner at my quarters. The night after tomorrow, let's make it."

"Rubens also, I assume?"

"Oh, yes. That Scaglia fellow who's visiting him, as well. And . . ."

He spread his hands and raised them, as if offering a sacrifice to the gods. "There's no point avoiding the matter. Not any longer. Invite Richter and her husband also."

Amsterdam

After the Spanish messenger left, Rebccca turned to the other people in the USE embassy's salon and smiled widely. "So. He's decided. I shall tell Michael tonight."

Gretchen eyed her skeptically. "We all know you're smart. Don't ruin your reputation at the last moment. What if he hasn't decided?"

Rebecca shook her head. "Oh, Gretchen, don't be silly. If he still wanted to negotiate—or simply stall for time—he certainly wouldn't have invited *you*."

Gretchen thought about it for a few seconds. "He did once before," she pointed out.

"That was curiosity—which you satisfied. This is . . . call it a statement. A subtle one, but a statement nonetheless."

Gretchen thought about it for a few more seconds, then smiled herself. "I suppose I should take the invitation as a compliment, then."

"Oh, yes. In a manner of speaking."

"I'm still taking my shotgun," Jeff insisted stoutly.

Rebecca's eyes narrowed. "Why?"

"Are you kidding? Yeah, sure, it's a compliment. One of those 'my, what big tooth you have, dear' sort of compliments. Best to make sure he doesn't decide he misgauged the length of the fangs, huh?"

Rebecca sat back down on the divan, sighing. "I can remember when you were a trusting and innocent sort of person, Jeff."

He grunted. "Yeah, sure, so can I. Wasn't all that long ago, either, if you measure it in years and months."

"As opposed to what?" his wife asked.

Jeff started counting on his fingers. "Lessee. One Battle of the Crapper. Followed by—well, never mind, even if everybody knows you did it and I covered it up for you—followed by one Battle of Jena. Complete with you shooting a pimp, just for the hell of it."

"It was not 'just for the hell of it'!" Gretchen protested.

"Yeah, fine. You had your reasons, which I can sure enough find with a microscope, not that I'd accuse you of being quick on the trigger, God forbid. But we were talking about my lost innocence, remember? Brand new wife gunning down pimp goes a long ways, when it comes to removing the dew from innocent hubby's eyes. You'd be amazed how well that works. Moving right along—"

He went back to studiously counting off on his fingers. "One Croat raid. One pirate ambush in the English Channel, that you know and I know and the man in the moon knows was set up by Cardinal Richelieu. Man of God, no less. One French and English betrayal of the Dutch fleet, requiring us to scramble like mad for Amsterdam. One—"

"Stop bragging, husband," said Gretchen.

Jeff dropped his hands. "Wasn't. Just explaining how it happens that at the tender age of twenty-one I'm more suspicious than your average retired cop."

"I said, stop bragging."

Chapter 43

London, England

"Search their quarters?" said Sir Paul Pindar. "Are you mad, Sir Francis?"

Seeing Windebank starting to bridle, Richard Boyle immediately intervened. "Please, Paul! That was uncivil."

Pindar visibly restrained his temper. By now, unfortunately, the antagonism between him and Windebank had reached the point where it was something of a constant problem for the earl of Cork. Not for the first time, he missed Endymion Porter. Although one of the youngest of Cork's party, Sir Endymion had had the knack for soothing frayed tempers.

"My apologies, Sir Francis," said Pindar. The curt manner in which he extended the apology almost vitiated it of any real content—there was certainly no sincerity in it—but the fact was enough.

"That's done, then," said Boyle. "Francis, I have to tell you that I agree with Paul, although he didn't need to be rude about it. Searching the quarters of the American embassy would be most unwise."

Windebank shifted his angry gaze from Pindar to

Cork. "Richard, they've been there for *months*. I only discovered yesterday that Wentworth never had their quarters or persons searched after they arrived. Proof of treason in itself, that."

Boyle had to fight to keep his own temper down, now. He didn't actually disagree with Pindar's assessment of Windebank. The man was an arrogant ass, who'd have been insufferable except that his influence in powerful circles made suffering him a necessity. That was the reason the earl of Cork had proposed him for Constable of the Tower in the first place. It was a prestigious position, which had led Windebank to accept—and had the great benefit of keeping him out from underfoot constantly at the real center of power in Whitehall.

Not out from underfoot enough, unfortunately. Sir Francis still spent far more time in the royal palace than he did overseeing his responsibilities in the Tower. The problem with the man wasn't simply that he was arrogant, but that he was an ass. Not technically stupid, perhaps, but the distinction didn't mean much in practice. Windebank was one of those men so sure of himself that, within a week, he was convinced that his own lies were the truth—which was dangerous, under the circumstances.

Referring to Wentworth as a traitor was absurd, and everyone in Cork's party knew it. The charge had served the purpose of giving Cork an immediate pretext for having the earl of Strafford arrested and removed from power. A plausible enough one, too, at the time. But, that done, to pursue it would be folly. The last thing Richard Boyle wanted was for Parliament—and such a charge would *have* to be presented to Parliament, given the situation—to start nosing about the events of that fateful day. Fabricated evidence was risky, and there simply wasn't any evidence that wouldn't be fabricated.

Windebank, overconfident as always, was sure that the bloody escape of the three officers who'd been detained was sufficient evidence in itself. But that probably wouldn't have been true even if they'd obtained a signed confession from Leebrick. In the absence of any such document, especially with Leebrick and his men still at large, it would be risky to pursue the matter.

For that very reason, in fact, they'd all agreed a fortnight earlier to destroy the unsigned document and quietly let the search for Leebrick lapse into dormancy. By now, the three mercenary officers were surely off the island, in any event. Best to just let the whole business die a natural death—given that it was so much easier to simply charge Wentworth with having grossly violated the laws and customs of the kingdom. The man was so widely hated in England that Parliament would accept that, and cheerfully. By following that course, even if Leebrick did someday surface, what would it matter? An accusation that they had falsely accused Wentworth of treason when no such charge was formally leveled would simply be shrugged off. Who was to say what had been involved in their bloody escape? Perhaps nothing more than a quarrel with Endymion Porter that had escalated to murder—which, if need be, could be substantiated by the officers' theft of Porter's purse.

So, among themselves—and in public, of course— Cork and his party had let the word "traitor" slide out of usage in favor of the more general "tyrant."

Or "usurper," at times, not with the implication that
Wentworth had *actually* tried to depose the king but
simply that he had taken royal prerogatives upon himself without the knowledge or consent of the king.

In short, only the ass Windebank still kept referring
to Wentworth as an outright traitor.

"We have no idea what devices they might have in
their possession, in St. Thomas' Tower, Richard," Sir
Francis pressed on. "Weapons, munitions, signaling
devices—who knows?"

Pindar started to say something, but Cork waved
him down. He'd handle this himself, since Sir Paul's
temper was obviously still up.

"And what if they do, Francis? They're in the *Tower*.
In the middle of London. Separated by the English
Channel from any aid."

"Separated by the North Sea, it would be better
to say," interjected Pindar. "They'll certainly get no
aid from France."

"But—"

"And on the other side of the coin," Cork continued,
driving over Windebank, "we stand to lose far more
if we create any further incidents with the American
embassy here. I remind you of two things."

He held up his thumb. "Included in that embassy
is the sister of their prime minister."

He raised his left hand, and that thumb came up.
"And the war on the continent is not looking well. Let
us please not forget that we didn't start this idiotic
war—this highly unpopular war, which we're placing
the blame for on Wentworth—and we have every
desire to see it end as soon as possible."

Wentworth hadn't actually been responsible for

enlisting England in the League of Ostend. That had been done before he arrived in London at the king's summons. But that fact was not generally known—and, in any event, once he did assume the post of His Majesty's chief minister Wentworth had certainly not opposed the war. Here as in many things, he made a convenient catch-all scapegoat.

"It's not the least of the reasons for our popularity in Parliament at the moment," added Pindar. "The mob will be angry enough, once they realize we have no intention of removing the mercenary companies. But many of the better sort aren't disturbed by that, because we don't carry with us any suggestive taint of being Spanish sympathizers. The populace doesn't call this the war with the United States of Europe, as you well know. They call it 'the King's Spanish War.'"

"'Wentworth's Spanish War,' more and more," said Cork, "as our influence prevails. We need to remove the king from suspicion, of course."

Windebank's expression was sour. Boyle spread his hands in a placating gesture. "Just let it be, Francis. A few months from now, there'll be some sort of peace settlement and we'll be letting the American embassy return to the continent, in any event. It would be sheer folly to do anything that might infuriate them enough to want to continue the war against England. As it stands, beyond the fact that they were held in captivity against diplomatic custom—which is hardly unheard of, after all—they were treated perfectly well and subjected to no indignities."

"Then why not just let them go now?" demanded Sir Francis petulantly.

Cork tightened his jaws with exasperation. He was really getting tired of this fellow. "Because," he explained, his own tone now bordering on incivility, "we still need a peace settlement—and having them in the Tower will be helpful for that purpose." He felt like adding, *you ass*, but manfully restrained himself.

"So far as I can tell, they haven't spied upon us at all since we made the agreement," said Patrick Welch quietly, sipping at the broth Liz had given him. "So we can still return to our original plan, Anthony. It's not as if breaking an alliance that was forced upon us under duress is dishonorable."

It was clear enough from the Irishman's tone that he wasn't advocating a course of action; he was simply laying out all the alternatives, for his commander to choose between.

Towson made a face. "It'd certainly feel like treachery, though. I've grown rather fond of those fellows over the past few weeks."

Welch shrugged. "So have I, when you come down to it. But that's neither here nor there. We have to look to our own interests. With the money we have, there's nothing that prevents us from returning to the plan we'd adopted a month ago. The hunt's died down, quite clearly. And those reward posters pose no danger at all, the portraits are so inaccurate. We simply slip away of an evening, make our way to the coast, and sail across the channel. Three men and a woman are a bit of an unusual party, but not enough to cause any real notice. Leaving aside the fact that Harry and his men would almost certainly not launch a pursuit anyway. They've got their own business here to complete."

As he'd listened, Leebrick had kept blowing on his own broth. Judging it cool enough by now, he took a deep swallow. Then, after setting down the cup, he shook his head. "And then what, Patrick? Even that fat purse of Porter's won't last forever. We'd be three mercenary officers without a company. And none of us has ever served under French colors, so we have no friends to intercede for us. I've had quite enough of serving the Spanish throne, thank you. Between the oversupply of inquisitors and the shortage of paymasters, it's a miserable experience. That leaves the Germanies—which are now mostly controlled by the king of Sweden. True, he's hiring officers without companies for that new continental army of his, but . . ."

He let the rest trail off, with a sardonic smile.

"But that might be just a tad risky," Richard finished for him. "Given that we'd have betrayed one Captain Harry Lefferts, an officer in that very same army. God help us if we should happen to run across the man, a year or two from now."

Welch was playing devil's advocate, however, a task he did quite well. He certainly did it thoroughly. "I have the distinct impression that Harry and his unit are only used for special duties. They're officially part of the USE army, but operate for all practical purposes on their own. So we'd likely not encounter them at all."

"No, not 'on their own,'" countered Towson. "Let's be a bit more precise, Patrick. It's perfectly obvious, although Lefferts never says so in that many words, that he reports directly to their prime minister. Which, the way I look at it, makes the whole thing still worse."

Welch looked back and forth from Richard to Anthony. "I'm simply laying out the options. I don't actually disagree with you. In fact, I'd put Richard's assessment in stronger language. If we abandon Lefferts, we'd be simpletons or madmen to even think of taking employment in the Germanies. Anywhere *near* the Germanies. With Bavaria or Austria, we'd be in the service of the USE's enemies—and whatever happens with the Ostenders, I think it's a given that Gustav Adolf will keep fighting the Bavarians and the Austrians. Bad for us, should we get captured in the course of it."

"And we can't get employment in Bohemia," Anthony said, "because Wallenstein would turn us over to the Americans in an instant, if they demanded it. He's too dependent on them for his survival." He took another swallow of his broth, draining most of the cup. "That leaves service with the tsar. How splendid."

Both Welch and Towson grimaced.

"No, I think we'll continue as we have been," Leebrick concluded. "It's certainly interesting work."

"True," said Towson. But his grimace deepened. "On the other hand, I'm not sure how long I can stand that American obsession with diminutives. 'Rick' Towson, can you believe it?"

"It's better than 'Pat,'" pointed out Welch.

Leebrick smiled serenely. "I can't say I mind 'Tony' all that much. Even if Liz hates it."

"Not as much as I hate 'Lizzy,'" she said, almost hissing the name. "I had a perfectly good diminutive to begin with!"

❖   ❖   ❖

After he finished studying the new map the team had put together of the environs of London near the Tower, Harry Lefferts shook his head.

"It's not enough, guys. Since we've decided we're not actually going to drop the bridge, we need to create another diversion."

George Sutherland planted a big finger on one spot on the map. "How about this? Easy enough to do, if we move quickly. Now that the lord chamberlain finally remembered to order the theaters to close down, in mourning for the queen."

Harry studied the spot, then ran his fingers through his hair. "I like it. Damned if I don't. Gerd, you and George put something together along the lines of what you made up for the pirate ship. Set it up with remote-controlled detonators."

Gerd frowned. "We don't have many of them left, Harry."

"So? What else are we going to use them for?"

"Well . . . all right. Setting them up won't be hard, that's for sure. Not there."

"They're *certain*?" Melissa demanded.

Darryl nodded. "Yeah, they're sure there's not going to be any search. Our beloved constable must have gotten slapped down by Cork. Andrew says Sir Francis was in the foulest mood he's ever seen him—and he's usually in a foul mood." He grinned. "It gets better. Windebank was so pissed off he told the Warders that they'd have complete responsibility for us, from now on. They're even pulling the mercenaries off guard duty along the outer wall, from Bell Tower to Develin Tower."

Rita Simpson burst into laughter. "Talk about putting the foxes in charge of the henhouse!"

Her husband chuckled. "Well, that's a break."

Melissa didn't even try to disguise the relief on her face. Her great fear, ever since the new regime took over, had been that they'd carry out a search of St. Thomas' Tower. With the Hamilton and Short family as their allies, the Americans had been able to smuggle all their ordnance over to the Warders' quarters, so at least they didn't have to worry about a search uncovering their weaponry. But there'd been no way to move the radio and the communication equipment. It was one thing for Warders to learn how to use shotguns and automatic pistols. Another matter entirely for them to have learned how to use the far more complex radio—and even if they had learned quickly enough, it wouldn't have served the purpose anyway. Melissa needed to stay in touch with Amsterdam, not just the commando unit across the river. That required using the elaborate antenna. The antenna could be placed in a window of St. Thomas' Tower at night, without being spotted, since the window faced directly onto the Thames. But there was nowhere suitable in the Warders' quarters. Certainly not since most of the Lieutenant's Lodging had been taken over by Windebank's mercenaries.

So, she'd been on edge for weeks. Lefferts and his people were ready to carry out the jailbreak whenever Melissa gave the word. They could have done it anytime over the past month, in fact. But what was the point of getting out of the Tower if they couldn't get out of England? The small party that would accompany Cromwell into the Fens could probably manage that task, well enough. But that was because the much larger party making its escape to the estuary of the Thames would draw most of the pursuit. Even leaving that aside, there was simply no way fifty-some-odd people could evade capture if they had to spend weeks moving through the English countryside. Perhaps in the Fens, they could—but they'd never get that far in the first place.

Willy-nilly, the escape from the Tower had to wait on the war being waged on the continent. Only at the point when Gustav Adolf and Mike Stearns could afford to divert warships across the North Sea did it become a feasible proposition.

Now, the wait had become easy. Even for Melissa, who didn't handle waiting well.

Darryl's grin had subsided into something more along the lines of a smug smile. For *him,* of course, the wait hadn't been hard at all. Since the alliance with his fiancée's family had been forged, Victoria had evidently put down her foot in light of the new circumstances. So to speak. Darryl had been through that window so many times since that Tom Simpson was starting to call him Peter Pan.

Nearby, in the Bloody Tower, Thomas Wentworth studied the ravens on the grounds below, ignoring the guards at the open door and the cleaning woman going about her duties in his chambers.

They were quite fascinating birds, actually. In a macabre sort of way.

After he heard the last of the bolts close, Wentworth went immediately to the bread and broke open the loaf.

Two passages, this time, both from Paul's Epistle to the Romans.

Chapter 14, verse 5:

One man esteemeth one day above another: another estemeeth every day alike. Let every man be fully persuaded in his own mind.

And chapter 15, verse 4:

For whatsoever things were written afore-time were written for our learning, that we through patience and comfort of the scriptures might have hope.

The meaning was clear enough. Frustrating, of course. But at least she'd stopped citing that tedious business about time and seasons. Thomas had never been partial to Ecclesiastes.

Part Four

Now days are dragon-ridden

Chapter 44

standard were put to the severe punishment of that Nazi Christian Monod had been amongst the few...

People in other lands quite conscious...

arrangements of concentration camps had been drawn to write about them. But at least Raoul Wallenberg had known, a quarter-century... an enormous crime—described by Ottoto's successors... the work... its full meaning... and the rulers had a crude but reasonably effective... finding arrangement

Chapter 44

Copenhagen

May 1634

Eddie Cantrell stared out the window, reflecting sourly that the worst part of the new accommodations was the so-called toilet. The rest, he didn't much care about. In some ways, the comparatively stark nature of his new prisoner's room in Copenhagen Castle's notorious Blue Tower was something of a relief, after the opulence of his quarters in Frederiksborg. For a young man who'd spent most of his life living in a trailer park in West Virginia, royal Danish notions of "stark" were hardly the severe punishment that King Christian IV must have thought they'd be.

Except for the damn toilet. Granted, the sanitary arrangements in Frederiksborg hadn't been anything to write home about. But at least Frederiksborg had been a modern castle—"modern," that is, for the seventeenth century—designed by Dutch Renaissance architects. It had running water, and the toilets had a crude but reasonably effective flushing arrangement.

Copenhagen Castle, on the other hand, was over two hundred years old. Practically medieval, as far as Eddie was concerned. It didn't help any that the current king of Denmark hadn't paid much attention to the castle's upkeep. Being no slouch when it came to his own comfort, Christian IV had decided that he needed something more modern and fancy for a royal residence when he stayed in Copenhagen instead of at his favored Frederiksborg, some thirty miles out of town.

So, he'd built Rosenborg Castle, in the center of the city. Also designed in the Dutch Renaissance style, and also with its elaborate gardens surrounding the palace. And also, needless to say, with modern plumbing.

Not for Eddie, such digs, however—not now that Christian was furious at him. No, no. Eddie got to stay in the old castle perched on a small island in the city's harbor. *Slotsholmen*, the Danes called it, which translated into English as "castle island." With a view from the Blue Tower that was a long step down from overlooking fancy gardens. Now, Eddie got to look out the window at Copenhagen's commercial seaport. What was worse, he had to *smell* the city's harbor.

Worst of all, in his old quarters at Frederiksborg he'd been able to sit on a toilet. Here, in the finest medieval tradition, squatting was considered *de rigeur*, and flushing was a synonym for gravity.

So be it. In retrospect, Eddie knew he was lucky that he hadn't fallen afoul of the king's temper much sooner. He'd known that Christian IV had a complete edition of the *Encyclopedia Britannica* in his possession, since the king bragged about it constantly. But

Eddie had assumed that since the king of Denmark had spent a small fortune to get his hands on a copy of the entire *Britannica*, he'd had enough sense to get the great 1911 edition, which was by far the most useful one for down-timers.

What an idiot he'd been! With Christian's obsession with gadgetry and all things modern, Eddie should have realized the Danish king would have insisted on the most recent edition in Grantville. That was the 1982 edition, if he remembered correctly.

Which, of course—once someone checked—had plenty of references to the various individuals that Eddie had mentioned in his sundry lies to the king. At the time, especially with his brain pickled in alcohol half the time since the king insisted he carouse with him, Eddie had thought he'd been very clever.

Ah, yes, Your Majesty, we have superb armaments technicians. The best are probably Walt Disney, Harpo Marx, and Clint Eastwood.

Oh, and by far the best gunsmith is Elvis Presley.

He rubbed his face. Then, to make things worse, Mike Stearns—him and his idiot Agent 007 schemes—had referred in a response to Christian's queries about exchanging Eddie for the gunsmith Elvis Presley, that unfortunately Mr. Presley had since passed away. And *then*—what in God's name had possessed him?—had casually referred to Eddie's fiancée Marilyn Monroe.

That had caused some tense days with Anne Cathrine, for sure. Until Eddie—had there been no end to his own folly? had reassured her that his engagement to Marilyn Monroe was off because he'd discovered that the faithless Marilyn had switched her affections to Eddie's longtime rival John Fitzgerald Kennedy.

He could have at least had the sense to *invent* some names!

Alas. Six days ago, Christian IV had finally let his son Ulrik take the precious encyclopedias out of the locked cabinet in the Winter Room of Rosenborg Castle and start examining them. Ulrik, whose suspicious mind had no business residing in a twenty-two-year-old brain, had started by double-checking every single one of the statements and claims Eddie had made in his months of captivity. More precisely, having his three assistants check the name references while Ulrik and his tame pirate-cum-tech-whiz Baldur had studied Eddie's more substantive claims.

At which point, the proverbial crap had hit the proverbial fan. The next day, Eddie had been bundled into a carriage—none too gently—and hauled before the king in one of the chambers of Rosenborg. Now that spring was here and the war was heating up, Christian IV had shifted his residence to the capital.

The Dark Room, that chamber was called, appropriately enough. Eddie had found out since that the name actually came from the fact that once the great new tower was erected the room had lost its previous direct sunlight. But, at the time, he hadn't wondered about the name's provenance at all. It had seemed blindingly obvious.

"So!" the king had bellowed. "The liar is here!"

He pointed to a large and elaborate looking armchair in front of the fireplace. "Place him in the chair!"

The soldiers who'd brought Eddie immediately complied. While they did so, Eddie had time to contemplate the rest of the arrangements.

There was a fire going in the fireplace. *Check.*

The remains of a fire, rather, since open flames might have imperiled the chair. But there were still plenty of glowing coals. *Check.*

There were tongs heating in the coals. *Check.*

Middle Ages, coming up. Eddie considered raising the fine points of the Geneva Convention, but figured that would be pretty pointless. Given the mood Christian IV was in.

No sooner had he been manhandled into the chair than he discovered the elaborate looks of the thing were no accident. It turned out there were restraints concealed in the armrests that did a very nice job of strapping him down.

Check. Middle Ages, if he were lucky. It was looking more like the Dark Ages every moment.

Ulrik and Anne Cathrine had been present in the room when Eddie was hauled in. The king's daughter was looking distressed. Ulrik simply looked thoughtful.

"You can't do this, Papà!" she wailed.

"Ha! Watch me!" He waved imperiously at another soldier standing in the corner. "Give him the treatment!"

Eddie braced himself. But, to his astonishment—he yelped here; he couldn't help it—what happened was that a flood of ice-cold water came pouring out of the backrest and soaked him.

"Ha! It works!" Christian was beaming, now. He gave his son a gloating look. "I told you it would. Even—well, we shall see."

He made another imperious gesture, this one to the two soldiers standing on either side of the chair. Quickly, they removed the arm restraints.

"Get up, you miserable liar!" commanded Christian.

Eddie rose, a bit shakily. Then, jumped, when a loud toot sounded below him. He jumped high enough, in fact, that he almost stumbled on his pegleg when he landed.

"Ha! Ha!" the king bellowed. "The trumpet works too!"

"Papà!" Anne Cathrine hurried over and took Eddie by the arm. "You shouldn't humiliate him so! And you know Eddie's delicate. He'll likely get sick from that cold water!"

The king bestowed a sneer on Eddie. "Delicate, is he? Another false pretense, daughter, be sure of it! If my own doctors hadn't put it on, I'd have that wooden leg removed. Just to be sure! I might do it anyway."

He strode forward and wagged a very large royal forefinger under Eddie's nose. "Liar! I say it, again! Liar!"

Between the fear and the sudden freezing from the water—and, most of all, the presence of Anne Cathrine and his grumpiness about her continual insistence he was "delicate"—Eddie lost his temper.

"Don't wag that finger at me, dammit! It was *you* who broke the Geneva Convention! All I'm supposed to tell you is my name, rank and serial number!"

"And there was another lie!" If Eddie's shouts had caused even the slightest waver in that shaking royal digit, he could see no sign of it. "007! Ha! Your prime minister lied, too!"

"Well . . ."

Eddie didn't really have a good answer to that. God damn Mike Stearns, anyway. It was all *his* fault!

Ulrik cleared his throat. "Father, let's not forget that he didn't lie about the rest. Not when someone's life was at stake. It was not Eddie who urged the diving suit on us. In fact, he tried to warn us it was dangerous."

That caused a moment's pause in the finger-wagging.

Only a moment's, alas. Proving, once again, that the female is deadlier than the male, Anne Cathrine immediately shifted from distress and concern to indignation.

"But he lied about his betrothed!"

"I did not! That was Mike Stearns!"

Anne Cathrine glared at him. Still holding him by the arm, though.

"So? It was *you* who lied about Johannes Fitz-stupid whatever his last name was!"

"Well . . ."

The royal finger-wagging went back into high gear. "So he did! So he did! Toying with my daughter's affections, too, the rogue! I see it all, now! The snake in our midst! I ought to have him strapped into that diving suit, I should! Try it out for its new purpose!"

Anne Cathrine's indignation vanished. *"Papà!"* That wail was downright piercing.

Christian finally lowered the finger. "Well, I *should*," he insisted, followed by a truly majestic harrumph, complete with quivering royal mustachios.

"But—magnanimously—I won't. Take him to his new cell! Ulrik, make sure it's done properly. I want no daredevil last-moment escapes from—"

His sneer was just as majestic.

"Mr. Secret Agent, James Bond, 007. Ha!"

And, bundled off Eddie was, by the two soldiers, with Ulrik following behind.

Anne Cathrine came with them, and stayed in the new cell for half an hour, making sure Eddie was properly dried and tucked into his new bed. So he wouldn't catch a chill, or something. She must have repeated the term *delicate* at least a dozen times, to Eddie's disgruntlement.

It didn't occur to him until several days later, to wonder why the king of Denmark had let his daughter do any such thing.

Not until Ulrik and Baldur came barreling into the room. With Anne Cathrine in tow.

Wide-eyed, from his perch in front of the window, Eddie watched Baldur spread some sort of large diagram—sketch, rather—across the small table in the center of the room.

"We must be quick, Eddie," said the prince, in a low voice. He glanced over his shoulder. "One of the guards is likely to mention something to his captain, and the captain might . . . Well, never mind."

Ulrik turned back to the sketch and pointed down at it. "This is another lie, isn't it?"

Hesitantly, Eddie came over. Once he was close enough, he recognized the sketch. It was a depiction—very good one, too—of the huge radio tower that the USE had erected in Magdeburg.

"Uh . . . Well, no, it's actually pretty accurate."

"Eddie!" Ulrik, normally as even-tempered a man as Eddie had ever met, was obviously on edge and seemed to be controlling his temper. "Stop it. I know it's accurate. It was drawn by one of our best spies. But that's not what I meant, and you know it. You don't *need* this, do you?"

Eddie glanced at Norddahl. The Norwegian's gaze seemed very icy. Of course, with his color eyes, that came fairly naturally. It was impossible to tell if he was really angry or not.

For a moment, Eddie wondered which of the two had figured it out—the prince himself, or his hireling?

Probably Baldur, if for no other reason than the natural injustice of the universe, which the past half a year had made so blindingly clear to Eddie. In a world run according to sane and rational principles, it would be a shy and bespectacled seventeenth-century geek equivalent who'd manage to deduce, just from matching various entries in an encyclopedia against each other, that radio didn't actually *require* huge towers hundreds of feet tall. Not for every purpose, at least, especially military ones.

In this universe, of course—mad universe; insane; irrational; unreasoning; worst of all, deadly dangerous to hapless peglegged West Virginia country boys—it was entirely fitting that the deduction would be made by a man who only needed maybe an earring to be the spitting image of Captain Morgan, Pirate Extraordinaire.

So Eddie imagined, at least. Of course, for all he knew, Captain Morgan had actually been spectacled and geeky-looking.

"I need to know *now*, Eddie." The prince's voice was low, but very steely and very insistent.

Eddie took a deep breath, and glanced out the window. He couldn't really see the Øresund, from here, but he hardly needed to.

"Did you mine it?" he asked.

"Yes. But I doubt it'll do any good."

Eddie looked away. "No, probably not. Whatever

else he is, John Chandler Simpson is nobody's dummy. He's probably forgotten more about mines than you or I will ever learn."

He gazed at the sketch for a moment. "I won't tell you anything that might bear on my admiral's operations. Or that of my nation's armed forces, for that matter. If you can't accept that, then you might as well haul out the tongs and the pincers."

To Eddie's surprise, Ulrik laughed softly. "I can just imagine *that*." He gave Anne Cathrine a quick, sly glance. "Do I do it over her dead body? Not likely, I think. You're so frail, you know—and she's like a she-bear on the subject."

The king's daughter sniffed. "He *is* delicate. Partly why I'm so fond of him. Not coarse and crude, like some people I know."

Norddahl smiled thinly. "You wouldn't think that, if you'd been introduced to the lad the way I was. Watching the berserker steer a speedboat into a warship and barely managing to jump off at the last minute."

Eddie had only fragmentary memories of all that. What he did remember for sure, though, was that he *hadn't* been steering the speedboat. The overpowered Outlaw had simply been running wild, after Larry was killed, and had hit the Danish warship by accident.

On the other hand, he'd never told anyone that, either. He would, when and if the time came to report to Admiral Simpson. But as long as he was in Danish captivity, he'd figured the legend worked to his advantage.

Probably, anyway. It was hard to tell, sometimes. But he thought he could detect, more often than not, that ancient Norse spirit lying under the seventeenth-century patina. Barely lying under it, in Baldur's case.

Eddie Cantrell, the Delicate Berserker. There were times he thought he might go mad, in this new world.

Then again—in his more honest moments—he'd admit that he'd never felt quite so alive in West Virginia. "Wild, Wonderful," was the proud claim on the state's license plates—but he'd never met a girl like Anne Cathrine there, now had he?

Or a prince like Ulrik, for that matter. Or an adventurer like Baldur Norddahl. Talk about wild and wonderful.

"Agreed?" he asked.

Ulrik nodded. "Yes, agreed."

Eddie looked down at the sketch again. "It's too late now for any of it to matter, anyway. Well, except—"

He gave Ulrik a sharp glance. "What do you know about our people locked in the Tower of London? I want a straight answer, Ulrik, or I'm not saying anything more."

The prince shook his head. "We know very little, Eddie. Not even my father. That's the truth. More to the point, perhaps, we don't *care,* either."

He made a little grimace, then. "Charles is hardly what you'd call a bosom friend of Denmark. About all I can tell you is that, at last report—a week ago, perhaps—your embassy was still locked in the Tower."

Before Eddie could say anything, Ulrik added, "I will not pass anything on to anyone who might pass it on further to the English. My solemn vow, on that, Lieutenant Cantrell. I care only for Denmark. The whole League of Ostend can go to hell in a handbasket, to use your charming expression. With that idiot Charles leading the rest."

"Fair enough. The answer to your question is that, no, it's not exactly a lie." Eddie tapped the sketch. "For the purpose of general broadcasting to a large audience, you really do need something like this. Especially in this day and age, when we're in the Maunder Minimum. But for a lot of military or diplomatic purposes, you don't. When all you want to do is transmit narrowly to specific locations or parties."

Ulrike sighed, his head sagging. "In other words, my father's assumption—everyone's assumption, all along—that there was no way for Gustav Adolf to coordinate his various forces was completely baseless."

"Well . . . I wouldn't say 'completely' baseless. It's still not that easy to do, you know, not even with radio. And there's a pretty tight range limit. But, yes, you're basically right. The admiral has radio capability, and he'll be able to notify the emperor in Luebeck once he's entered the Kattegat and is within range of a radio carried by one of the airplanes. Which . . ."

Eddie looked back out the window. "Should be any day now, I figure. Unless you were lying last week when you told me he'd gotten out of the Elbe. Or unless there was a huge storm in the North Sea I haven't heard about."

Norddahl chuckled. "You wouldn't *have* to 'hear about it.' You'd know, believe me, if there had been a big storm. What's to stop it from striking Copenhagen? The towering mountains of Denmark? The highest spot in the whole country is Yding Skovhøj, and that's maybe six hundred feet tall. If that."

"And I didn't lie to you," Ulrik added. "One of the

timberclads was apparently left behind, due to some problem or another. I didn't tell you that, simply because we only found out ourselves three days ago." He got a tight look on his face. "The stinking French pass as little information to us as possible. We found out from one of our own couriers."

Sighing, he began rolling up the sketch. "So once Gustav Adolf knows that Simpson has passed through the Great Belt—that's the route I'm assuming he'll take, anyway—he will be able to notify Torstensson by radio. And since he must have set up a radio link to Stockholm, he'll also be able to notify Oxenstierna and Admiral Gyllenhjelm."

He cocked an eye at Eddie. "Yes?"

Eddie hesitated, but . . . it really *didn't* matter, any more. And, who knows? Maybe King Christian might decide to sue for peace. The truth was, Eddie wasn't real happy himself at the thought of Simpson leveling Copenhagen. And wouldn't have been, even if he weren't perched in the Blue Tower, which was the most visible part of Copenhagen from the waterfront and almost sure to be a prime target for those ten-inch guns.

"No, you're right. You can tell your father—"

"I'm not telling the king anything," Ulrik said bluntly. "You think he'd listen? Don't be stupid, Eddie. We're long past that point, if it ever existed at all, which I doubt. He's a wonderful father, in many ways, believe it or not. But his pride is involved, and he's just not given to being sensible on such matters. Maybe after . . ."

The prince shrugged. "We'll see. Or you'll see, at least. I may very well not."

Eddie squinted at him. "What does that mean?"

"Never mind. Just accept that there are times a prince must act like a prince, or he'll be able to do nothing thereafter. Leave it at that."

He tucked the rolled-up sketch under his arm and scanned the room. "No place here," he muttered. Then, after sticking his head into the alcove that passed as a toilet, he shook his head. "And not here, obviously."

He came back into the center of the room. "The original plan, then. Baldur, have you seen to it?"

The Norwegian nodded. "Yes, Your Highness. They've been very well paid. And the carriage will be ready, when the time comes."

Ulrik nodded, and turned to his half-sister. "Any last hesitations?"

She shook her head, looking far more solemn than a fifteen-year-old really should.

"What are you all talking about?" Eddie asked.

Ulrik turned to face him. "Amazing, really. What *did* they teach you in those famous up-time schools, beyond mechanical matters?"

"What are you talking about?" Eddie repeated. Feeling, not for the first time since he'd fallen into captivity, like a dunce.

"I read a charming story about those schools," Baldur said. "The really dumb and inattentive ones, they'd make sit in a corner. With a tall pointed hat on his head that said 'dunce.'"

All of them laughed. To rub salt into the wounds, none more loudly than Anne Cathrine.

The North Sea

White water curled back on either side of SSIM *Constitution*'s blunt bows as the ironclad butted her way through the North Sea waves. Sea conditions were actually quite good, Simpson thought, standing on *Constitution*'s bridge wing while the chilly wind hummed around his ears. Wave height was only about three and a half or four feet, which was practically millpond-smooth compared to typical Atlantic conditions. Not that any of his ships had been *designed* for typical Atlantic conditions, of course.

Fortunately, he thought, turning to look astern to where *President* followed along in *Constitution*'s wake, he'd at least had coastal operations in mind when he designed the ironclads. Flooded down, they drew almost ten feet, and he'd built them around what was effectively a double hull. Each of the propulsive pumps—and the tunnel in which it worked—occupied its own individual "pod," separated from the rest of the hull (and from one another) in order to prevent them from being disabled by a single hit or hull breach. It was almost a catamaran effect, and he'd used the flood tanks to further subdivide the portion of both pods which was submerged at maximum draft, giving himself as many of the advantages of watertight compartmentalization as he could. The fuel tanks were nested inside the flood tanks, and the magazines and powerplant were, in turn, nested inside them.

While he'd been at it, he'd taken advantage of the "pod" configuration to incorporate a centerboard feature into the design. Forward and aft of the magazines and the huge, thundering diesel, he'd added a pair of centerboards between the pods, each of them basically a big wooden plank, fifteen feet from front edge to rear edge, which could be lowered vertically to add ten more feet to the ship's draft. That additional stability, "twin screw" maneuverability, and their much better power-to-weight ratio, made Simpson's ironclads far more stable and seaworthy than the majority of the original river ironclads . . . and several of the later Civil War monitors had even been sailed across the *Atlantic*, which was generally rougher than typical North Sea conditions. He'd known all of that, but it was still a great relief to discover that the USE's ironclads were having no trouble handling the requirements of their current voyage.

Of course, he thought dryly, looking back to where *Ajax* and *Achilles* steamed gamely along behind the larger, deeper-draft ironclads, *it's being a more pleasant experience for some than for others.*

The timberclads *hadn't* been designed for coastal waters—not really. They were typical, flat-bottomed, shoal-draft riverboats, designed to operate in shallow waters. Their bulky steam-powered plants had imposed design constraints of their own, as well. He'd had to locate the boilers as low in the limited hull volume as possible in order to protect them from hostile fire if they got close enough to something with guns heavy enough to penetrate their thick timbers. One of the greatest dangers to the original ironclads' crews had been the threat of fatal scalding when their boilers were breached, and he'd done everything he could to minimize that particular risk. Then he'd had to squeeze in their magazines around the boilers, for the same protective considerations. And after *that*, he'd had to find a place to put their coal bunkers, although he'd actually managed to use those to strengthen the side protection of the powerplant and ammunition. But there'd been neither space, nor pumps, nor surplus power available to worry about features like flood tanks, or variable draft, and their paddle wheels were simply a less efficient means of propulsion.

Taken altogether, those considerations made the timberclads slower, less nimble, and less *stable* than their larger, more sophisticated big sisters.

Which means they're rolling their guts out, even in this chop, Simpson thought.

It wasn't really all that bad, he supposed. No doubt it looked worse to him than it actually was, since he bore the responsibility for having designed them in the first place, not just the responsibility for getting them safely to Luebeck. Still, with wind and wave coming in from almost broad on the port beam this way, they really were rolling more heavily than he—or their crews, no doubt—liked.

Well, he told himself, *they'll only have to put up with it for another ten hours or so. Then they'll get to take the seas on their port quarters, instead, and won't* that *be better?*

Louis Franchot stood on the deck of his fishing boat beside his worthless, lazy brother-in-law and watched in amazement as the long line of impossible ships sailed past them.

He'd heard rumors about the preposterous warships the Americans were supposed to be building, but he hadn't really believed them. Everybody was always talking about something new and impossible the Americans were supposed to be inventing, or building, or conjuring out of thin air, after all.

Still, when the Crown officially offered fat rewards to anyone who actually saw and reported them, it had been clear *someone* took them seriously. Now Franchot was forced to do the same thing.

They went past him, moving with total disregard for wind or weather, and they had to be making at least ten knots, probably more. In fact, he was positive it was more than that; he just didn't know how *much* more, because he'd never seen anything move that fast. Nor had he ever seen *any* ship move without sails or oars or any other visible means of propulsion. He simply had no experience to apply to estimating how fast these ships were moving.

He'd thought at first that the two in the back must be on fire, judging from all the smoke they were emitting. Obviously, though, they weren't. The smoke was coming from what were clearly purpose-built chimneys, and even if it hadn't been, the ships were continuing blithely on their way, which they would scarcely have been doing if they'd been on fire!

He estimated their course carefully, then nodded to himself. Everyone knew this so-called League of Ostend had the Swedish emperor locked up in Luebeck. From everything Franchot had heard, that was rather like a herd of belligerent sheep getting together to besiege a large, particularly hungry wolf, but that hadn't been any of his concern. It still wasn't, but it was obvious even to a simple fisherman like him, that the warships keeping watch on Luebeck were about to get a truly nasty surprise.

He shook himself as the line of ships disappeared over the horizon.

"Get the net in, Emile!" he said sharply.

His brother-in-law gaped at him, and Franchot clouted him on the ear with one gnarly fist.

"Move, imbecile! That—" he waved an arm at the plumes of smoke still visible to the northeast "—is worth a *month's* worth of fish to the first ones to report it!"

Emile blinked at him for a moment longer, then nodded in sudden understanding and bent with Franchot to haul in the net.

The Lippe River, a few miles northeast of Soest

"Remember, there's no need to get into an actual battle," said Turenne. "All you need to do is create enough of a stir to make the enemy think we're planning an attack on Hesse-Kassel."

Jean de Gassion tugged his beard. "I have to engage in *some* combat, Marshal—or all we'll be doing is alerting the Hessians that we're in the area. If I retreat too quickly, they might come far enough north pursuing me to pose difficulties for you when you return."

As Turenne considered the problem, he watched his forces—three thousand cavalrymen, of the five thousand they'd brought on the raid—starting to ford the Lippe. He'd take those northeast to the Teutoburgerwald, while Jean de Gassion would take the remaining two thousand men to the southeast, in a feint at Kassel.

The Lippe was a small river. This far upstream, it was an easy crossing. They'd probably only lose a handful of horses, if they lost any at all. That was Turenne's main worry, at the moment, not the question de Gassion was raising. Given the imperative necessity for moving as quickly as possible, he hadn't brought very many extra horses on the expedition. He'd only allowed for losing one-fifth of the mounts they'd started with. That was a good enough ratio, normally, with experienced and capable cavalrymen. But they still had to get through the low mountains of the Teutoberg Forest. Even using the gap at Bielefeld, that sort of terrain would wear on the horses.

But that die was cast already, and there was no point fretting over it. Gassion needed an immediate answer.

"I'm just not too concerned about that, Jean. Remember that I'm taking all the Cardinals and you'll be armed with nothing except muskets and pistols. Don't get involved in anything beyond a minor skirmish or two. It's more important that you get out of it with your force intact, so you can come up in time to hold the bridge over the Weser. You actually have more distance to travel than I do."

He gave his eager subordinate a smile. Like most of Turenne's lieutenants, Gassion was also a young man—in his case, less than two years older than the marshal himself. They all tended to be a bit impetuous, and none more so than Gassion. Not surprisingly, of course, since he was a Gascon.

"Please, Jean! Restrain yourself, if you would. The one thing I do *not* want to face is racing back with the enemy on my heels and finding that I have to cross the Weser at a ford." He waved at the nearby Lippe. "This is barely a stream; the Weser's a real river."

"But—"

"Oh, stop worrying. The Hessians have most of their army to the south, facing the archbishop of Cologne, and the landgrave is with them himself. All they have left in the capital, according to our reports, is a garrison. They're not likely to march more than a regiment out of the city after you, and a regiment"—now he waved toward the Cardinal rifle in a saddle holster on his horse, standing a few feet away—"three thousand of us armed with these can drive off in a few minutes."

"If you have any ammunition left," said Gassion. Like most Gascons, he was stubborn as well as headstrong.

Turenne wasn't disturbed by that, however. The same traits also made Jean de Gassion a superb cavalry commander. So, Turenne just gave him a level gaze, saying nothing. After a few seconds, Gassion smiled and threw up his hands.

"Fine, fine! I shall be obedience personified, Marshal. And I'll be at the bridge, when you get there."

"All I ask. Godspeed, Jean, and good fortune."

Chapter 45

The Wardersee, near Segeberg
thirty miles northwest of Luebeck

The march from Hamburg had been exhausting, so General Torstensson ordered a rest once the regiments reached the Wardersee. The lake north of the town of Segeberg provided all the water they needed and they'd brought their other supplies from Hamburg. Behind them, TacRail units were laying a line from Hamburg that would make resupply quite reliable, once it was finished.

By then, of course, the war might be over. Such, at least, was Eric Krenz's caustic opinion.

"And why couldn't we have billeted in Segeberg?" he groused, wrapping his blanket around him more tightly and sliding himself closer to the campfire the battery had made. This early in May, it was still chilly in the morning.

"All twenty thousand of us?" Thorsten Engler shook his head. "Don't be stupid, Eric. I was told by Mark—Lieutenant Reschly—that the emperor gave General Torstensson orders not to weigh too heavily on the local populace. Seeing as how he intends to make them his own citizens, soon enough."

Silently, he reminded himself that he needed to restore a certain formality in his references to Mark Reschly. Captain Witty had suffered a minor accident shortly after the march began from their camp below Hamburg. Nothing really serious, just one of the almost-routine casualties suffered by cavalrymen—a broken foot from his horse stepping on him. But it was a significant enough injury that he'd had to stay behind in Hamburg until the bones healed, which had made Reschly the new commander of their volley gun company. After the battle group had been dissolved and they rejoined the rest of their company in Hamburg, that put Reschly in command of six batteries instead of the two he was accustomed to. The young officer from the Moselle was a bit frantic, these days, trying to catch up on things. He didn't need Thorsten's private familiarity with him to undermine his authority, which was a bit shaky to begin with.

Eric's capacity for grousing, alas, had become something of a legend in the batteries. "*Torstensson* has a billet in the town."

"I said, don't be stupid. Of course he does—and in the town's biggest tavern, at that. Do you really want the commander of your own army to be making battle plans scratching in the mud?" He waved at the Wardersee, whose banks were only twenty yards away. "Maybe you, but not me, seeing as how I'm not an idiot Saxon."

That got a little laugh from the other men in the battery around the campfire. Most of them, like Engler himself, were from parts of the Germanies west of Saxony. Thuringians and Magdeburgers, mostly, although Engler himself was from the Oberpfalz and there were several men in the battery from Franconia.

"Ha! Should have stayed in Saxony," Eric grumbled. "I'd be sleeping in a warm bed in Dresden."

Thorsten grunted softly. "Yes. This year. Next year"—he jabbed a thumb at one of the nearby volley guns—"you'd be looking at those from the business end. With that idiot John George for a commander instead of Gustav Adolf or Torstensson."

Krenz shook his head. "Nonsense. I'd desert. Join you fellows." He gave everyone a smile. "A year from now. Maybe in the summer, when it's warmer."

That got another laugh. Everyone liked Krenz personally, and certainly didn't hold the treachery of the Saxon elector against him. Why should they? Another of the many American loan words in Amideutsch—phrase, in this case—was *equal opportunity*. The joke had long become a staple in the regiments that John George of Saxony was an equal opportunity traitor, since he'd stabbed just about everybody in the back by now.

Like Thorsten—and Krenz himself, for that matter—most of those soldiers expected to be fighting Saxony and Brandenburg next year. Those of them who survived this war, at least. Their term of enlistment ran for three years, and none of them thought the war with the Ostenders was going to last more than a few months.

Thorsten wasn't so sure, himself. Not because he had any less confidence in their army than any of the other soldiers, but simply because his twenty-six years of life thus far had convinced him that the truest and most useful of all the American saws was *shit happens.* In war, who could say for sure?

In the main room of the tavern in Segeberg, General Torstensson straightened up from the big map spread out over a table in the center, then turned to Frank Jackson. Unlike the other top officers of the army who served Torstensson as his immediate lieutenants, Frank had no clear and definite duties on his staff. As tactfully as possible—with Frank's own cooperation—Torstensson had essentially removed him from any direct authority over large bodies of soldiers. Frank's training and temperament were entirely those of a sergeant, not an officer, and he was really not well-suited to be a commander of any body of soldiers much larger than a squad. He'd only been elevated to a generalship by the now-defunct New United States because no one else in Grantville had been any more qualified.

On the other hand, with his extensive practical knowledge of up-time technology, Frank made an excellent aide for anything that involved the interplay of the new American military equipment with the army. He jokingly referred to himself, in private, as "Lennart's utility infielder."

"Do we have radio contact yet with the emperor?" Torstensson asked.

"Just got it up and running. It's a good link, too, so we don't need to wait for the evening window."

"Good. Ask him what he wants me to do. Keep moving—if so, where?—or remain here until further notice."

"On my way." Frank headed toward the stairs that

led up to the second-story room where the army's radio operators had set up their equipment.

Torstensson turned back to the table. "My guess is that the emperor will want us to remain here, until something develops. But, whether we do or not, we need to send a force north to secure the southern shore of the Plöner See." His finger indicated a large lake less than twenty miles north of the Wardersee. "It's most likely the French will come though this corridor once they begin their retreat from Luebeck. The Danes will pass to the east of the Plöner See, looking to reach their defenses at the Danewerk, but not the French. They'll pass south of the lake, trying to reach the headwaters of the Stör at Neumünster, and follow that down to the Elbe north of Hamburg. But they won't ever get there, because we'll have them trapped here."

Frowning, Colonel Bryan Thorpe leaned over the table and placed his finger on a different spot on the map, farther south.

"They might choose to take the more direct route, General. Just follow the Trave to Oldesloe, and then . . ."

His voice trailed off, as he studied the map.

"And then . . . what, Bryan?" Torstensson shook his head. "They'd find themselves in a worse trap, and one that ought to be obvious to their commanders even before they decamp. Even to that jackass Charles de Valois. Yes, the Trave would make an easy route at the beginning, but once they pass through Oldesloe"—he began moving his finger around on the map, after Thorpe removed his own—"their choices become dismal. They could reach the headwaters of the Alster easily, of course, but what good does that do them? The

Alster would take them to Hamburg, where they'd be caught between our garrison in the city and us following them. Their only other options would be just as bad. They could march directly west, trying to avoid us, but that takes them through heavily wooded terrain with few roads, few villages, and only small streams. For an army the size of theirs, a disaster in the making, even this time of year. Or they march to the northwest, trying to reach the Stör from that direction. But the only route they could take would be to continue following the Trave, which leads them . . ."

He gave the English colonel a smile. Thorpe nodded. "Yes, I see. Which leads them right to us, here at Segeberg."

Torstensson planted both hands on the table, continuing to study the map. "Still . . . Given de Valois, such stupidity can't be ruled out. But if it does happen, we can march down the Trave from here faster than the French can come up the river. Meet them somewhere around"—he finger tapped a spot on the map—"Oldesloe, at a guess."

He spent the next few minutes discussing the army's logistical situation. By the time that was done, Frank Jackson had returned.

"The emperor wants you to stay put," he said. "The Ostenders are still in their fieldworks outside of Luebeck. Either they haven't gotten the news that Simpson has passed through the Great Belt, or they don't believe it, or they're just being sluggish and stupid, take your pick. But the emperor figures it doesn't matter. Sooner or later, they'll have to begin their retreat, and he wants you to wait for them here."

"The French, at any rate," said Torstensson. "What

about the Danes? They'll take their army back on the eastern side of the Plöner See, I'm sure of that."

Frank shrugged. "Gustav Adolf didn't say anything on that subject. Just—wait here, and trap the enemy when they come. The exact identity of the enemy unspecified. You want me to get in touch with him again?"

Torstensson shook his head. "No, that's not necessary. The orders are quite clear."

He wasn't surprised, in any event. After Mike Stearns had demonstrated in December how easy it was to fly a man into Luebeck, Torstensson himself had been flown in twice—the second occasion, just three weeks earlier—to consult with the emperor. He knew that once the siege was broken, Gustav Adolf wanted to keep Danish casualties as low as possible. Their land forces, at least. He would be quite happy to see most of the Danish navy sunk or ruined, since that would give him the greatest leverage in his negotiations with Christian IV for a new Union of Kalmar. But there was no point in killing or wounding Danish soldiers who, soon enough, would be serving under Gustav's own colors. Let them escape Luebeck and take refuge in the Danewerk. They could be plucked there like ripe fruit, once the Danish king yielded and accepted the inevitable.

It was the French army that Gustav Adolf wanted destroyed. Not simply beaten, but shattered. Defeated so thoroughly that France would be knocked completely out of the war, and wouldn't be able to resume hostilities until the following year. By then, hopefully, they'd either have a peace settlement or Richelieu would be under such pressure from disgruntled elements in the French nobility that he couldn't afford to send any troops out of France even if there was no settlement.

It was a good plan, Torstensson thought. He'd marched so quickly that he was now astride the only good route the French army could take, in their retreat from the siege. His was a better army than theirs to begin with—he was quite sure of that—and the fact that he would be slightly outnumbered didn't bother him in the least. Especially since the French suffered from a serious shortage of cavalry, which was the critical arm in terms of winning battles.

"Will the emperor be joining us, do you think?" Thorpe asked.

Torstensson smiled. "With him, who knows?"

As it happened, Gustav Adolf was coming to that decision almost the same moment Torstensson asked the whimsical question.

He didn't like the answer much, though. He even lapsed into blasphemy, something he did rarely.

"God damn it, Nils," the emperor said, "I had been looking forward to that. After six months of this miserable siege! A straight clean battle, on the open field! Do wonders for me!"

Colonel Ekstrom said nothing. It was always best, in a situation like this, to let Gustav Adolf argue with himself. However impetuous he might be on the battlefield, he was as canny a ruler as any in Europe. Certainly canny enough to recognize, once he pondered the matter, that he was indispensable in the coming negotiations with the king of Denmark—and quite dispensable meeting the French. Torstensson was perfectly capable of dealing with that matter himself.

Besides, his plaintive outcry had been more in the way of habit than anything heartfelt. Truth be told, as sieges went, this one at Luebeck had been very far from "miserable." Once the American scuba divers had destroyed several Danish ships anchored in the Trave, early in the war, the Ostender fleet had moved too far down into the bay to pose any real danger to the city. The enemy had never even been able to completely invest Luebeck. There'd always been a corridor open northeast of the city through which enough in the way of supplies had been sent to keep Luebeck's citizens and garrison from being too badly strapped.

That was due, in large part, to the USE Air Force. As few planes as the air force had, and as limited as its real fighting capabilities were, Colonel Wood's people had provided the best possible reconnaissance—and were likely to scare off whatever enemy cavalry forces were sent to cut the supply line, anyway. Even if they couldn't, there was never any possibility of the Ostenders launching a surprise attack on a supply convoy. The worst that happened was that a convoy had to return to the fortified and garrisoned supply depot at Grevesmühlen, halfway between Luebeck and Wismar, and wait a day or two for the enemy's cavalry to leave.

So, Gustav Adolf had been able to spend the past six months in Luebeck without any great immediate cares or worries. He'd even spent them in a certain amount of luxury. If not so much in terms of his accommodations—he'd settled for a fairly spartan room in the Rathaus—then certainly in terms of his library. Among the items brought into Luebeck with the supply convoys had been a large number of books. Replicas, for the most part, of certain up-time titles the emperor was keenly interested in studying.

Gustav Adolf had read a great deal, over those months. And spent as much time thinking as he did reading. The first time he'd really been able to do so, since the Ring of Fire.

The conclusions he came up with were . . . often very interesting, to Colonel Nils Ekstrom. Fortunately, unlike Chancellor Axel Oxenstierna, he felt under no compulsion to try to talk the emperor out of them.

"How do you propose to get to Copenhagen?" the colonel asked. "Aboard one of the ironclads?"

"No, no. Mind you, it's tempting. Ha! The pleasure I'd take, staring at that drunken bastard Christian over the barrel of a ten-inch gun! But . . ."

Gustav Adolf shook his head in an almost comically lugubrious manner. "No, I shall forego the pleasure. Best, I think, not to arrive in quite so martial a manner. Besides, it would be a nuisance for Simpson to have to delay things just to wait for an emperor to come aboard one of his ships. A man after my own heart, there. He'd have made a superb cavalry commander, you know."

The emperor looked out the window, which gave him a view to the east. "No, I'll take one of Admiral Gyllenhjelm's ships. That should do for the purpose."

Ekstrom nodded. "And the other matter? Regarding Stearns?"

Still looking out the window, Gustav Adolf smiled. "Ah, Nils—so diplomatic, you are. If you were Axel, you know, you'd have been haranguing me on my folly."

"I don't feel that's my place, Your Majesty." In

point of fact, Ekstrom was rather dubious about the emperor's likely decision. But . . .

That simply wasn't his place. His job, as he saw it, was to help the emperor make whatever decision the emperor felt was best. Let the chancellor try to talk him out of it, once it was made. No easy task, that, of course.

"Yes, I've decided. The equipment needed to repair the *Achates* should have arrived from Magdeburg by now. Send Stearns a message instructing him to take a force from Hamburg—a good cavalry regiment should do—down to the stranded timberclad. He's to reinforce the existing guard, of course. But, most of all, I want him to take charge of the entire operation and get the *Achates* ready for action again."

Ekstrom simply nodded. "Yes, Your Majesty."

Now, Gustav grinned. "Amazing. Not a single word informing me that I am grossly violating protocol. What, Nils? Not *one*?"

Ekstrom hesitated, before deciding at the last moment that was an invitation for him to see if he could find any fallacies in the emperor's reasoning.

"They do make a fetish, Your Majesty, of the subject of separating civil from military affairs."

"So they do. But calling it a 'fetish' misses the mark, I believe. There is a logic to the whole thing, which my extensive reading has made clear to me. The problem is not simply—not even primarily—a matter of abstractions. There is a solid core of practicality that lies beneath. I will tell you what it is."

He turned away from the window. "Organization, Nils. A society so well organized—top to bottom—that clear lines of authority *can* be defined and delineated."

He chuckled heavily. "They have their own superstitions, you know. One of the greatest being their firm belief that they are individualists—'rugged,' no less, being their favorite qualifier—and deeply opposed to anything that smacks of what they call 'red tape.'"

Ekstrom chuckled also. "True. Quite amazing, really, given that they are the world's ultimate bureaucrats. I've been told they even put up signs in their buildings, giving precise instructions as to where anyone should go to reach whatever—precisely defined—office they might be seeking."

"Oh, yes, it's true. My daughter is quite charmed by the things. She got into some trouble once, when she took it upon herself to have soldiers move some of the signs around, in the palace at Magdeburg, just to see what would happen."

"I can imagine!" But the humor of the moment led to a far more serious issue, which Ekstrom wondered if he should raise.

Gustav Adolf raised it himself, however. "Yes, yes, I know. Sooner or later, I will have to decide if I wish to heed the advice of my daughter's attendants. Seeing as how they flood me with enough missives that I use them regularly to start fires in my fireplace."

He clasped his hands behind his back and began pacing, in that heavy cavalryman's way. "But I think not. No, I think those frantic noblewomen will simply have to learn to make the same accommodations that I've decided I must make myself. Now that we've let the genie out of the lamp, putting it back in is simply hopeless. Better to make a pact with the creature. Since he is not, actually, a devil. Not that, whatever else."

Ekstrom waited patiently. Sooner or later, the emperor would come to the point.

Smiling again, Gustav Adolf tugged at his mustache. "There's a soldier somewhere in Torstensson's army. A sergeant in the volley gun batteries, by the name of Thorsten Engler. My daughter insists—instructs me, no less—that I *must* make him a count, at the very least. He has become betrothed, it seems, to her favorite American attendant."

"The Platzer woman?"

"Yes. The very one that half those frantic letters are devoted to denouncing. She is undermining my daughter's spirit, they claim. Sapping her of the necessary royal will and sense of importance."

He paused in his pacing. "Fools, the lot of them. Do you know how they proposed to solve the problem of the misplaced signs? Simply ordering the soldiers to put them back properly, and there was to be an end to it."

"I take it the Platzer woman felt otherwise?"

The emperor grinned. "Not entirely. She agreed that the signs needed to be fixed—on the following day. For the rest of that day, she made Kristina stand in front of them and *personally* give directions to anyone who came into the palace and seemed confused."

Ekstrom couldn't help it. He burst into laughter and blasphemed himself. "Good God! What did she use? A whip?" To say that their princess had a reputation among Swedes for being headstrong would be much like saying Swedes thought seawater was salty.

"Amazingly, no. She seems to be the one person in the world whom my daughter will actually listen to. Even obey, most of the time. And I am supposed to have her removed? As I said, fools."

The emperor went back to his deliberate pacing. "But we're straying from the subject. Here's the point, Nils. Whatever else he may be, the one thing my prime minister is above all else is a practical man. I am quite sure that he knows just as well as I do that his beloved democracy presupposes the existence of the world's best bureaucracy."

Ekstrom frowned. As often happened, trying to follow the emperor's train of logic was not easy.

Seeing the frown, Gustav clucked his tongue. "Oh, come! It's obvious! What is the most basic principle of law-making, Nils?"

That answer, he knew by heart, since it was one of the emperor's favorite saws. Not learned from any up-timer, either, simply part of the Vasa legacy.

"Do not pass a law you can't enforce."

"Exactly. Now apply that principle to democracy."

Ekstrom was back to frowning. Gustav clucked his tongue again.

"And you're normally so smart! It's just as simple, Nils. You can't *enforce* democracy until you have the wherewithal to do so. No point in telling a man he is the equal of any other, until you have the wherewithal to make that true in fact, as well as in theory. And that means red tape. *Everyone* has to stand in line to get whatever they want or need, be that man a duke or a pauper. No special privileges. But doing that, in turn, presupposes so many other things. Just to name three—"

He lifted a thumb. "First, everybody has to be literate. And not just enough to work slowly through the Bible, either. Enough to read and comprehend, easily, instructions written by a bureaucrat—and enough literacy that you have a veritable army of bureaucrats able to write the instructions in the first place."

The forefinger came up to join the thumb. "Second, everyone has to have enough time to spare from necessary labor to exert their new privileges. Pointless to tell a farmer or blacksmith he has the same political rights as a duke, when the duke can spend every waking moment engaged in politics and the farmer and blacksmith can barely manage to lift their heads from their labors."

The middle finger came up. "And that, in turn, requires wealth. Lots of wealth, enough for everybody to live on decently enough without constant toil."

He started to raise another finger, but broke off the exercise by simply waving his head.

"Enough to make the point, I think. Be assured of it, Nils. Michael Stearns understands all of these points, just as well as I do. Probably better. And since he's not a man to mistake today for tomorrow, or tomorrow for the day after, he'll accept my command. Why? Because to get to that clear separation of powers, he has to do many other things that are not so clearly distinct. The difference between tyranny and freedom, in the end, is often nothing more than the difference between today and tomorrow. Provided, that is, that you understand the difference between the days yourself. So send him the message. It will be interesting to see his response."

Ekstrom hesitated, then braced himself with the reminder that his job *required* him to question the emperor. "I still don't understand why you want the prime minister to handle this personally, Your Majesty. Sending a cavalry regiment, certainly—but they have a commander already. And I'm quite sure the captain and crew of the *Achates* are capable of doing the repairs without oversight, once they get the needed equipment."

To his relief, Gustav Adolf simply smiled instead of responding brusquely. "For shame, Nils! Am I the only one who can think ahead?"

"Your Majesty?"

"Michael Stearns is the prime minister of the USE *today*, Nils. But he himself expects to lose the upcoming election to Wilhelm Wettin. Assume for the moment that he does. Then what?"

The colonel stared at his king. After a moment, he said, "In truth, Your Majesty, I hadn't given that matter any thought at all."

Gustav Adolf grunted. "Didn't think so. Well, I have. Quite a bit, in fact. And the conclusion that I keep coming to is that I'd be a blithering idiot to let a man with such obvious capabilities—what's that American expression? 'sit on the sidelines,' I think—while I fight another war. Not only would that be a waste, it would probably even be dangerous. So, I intend to appoint him a general and put him in the army."

"Ah . . . Your Majesty, I don't believe Stearns has had much in the way of military experience. And that, if I recall correctly, simply as an enlisted man."

"True enough. And that's why I'm sending him down to Ritsenbuttel. Let's see how he manages in a military command position, eh?"

The response came back within two hours. The extreme some might say, highly disrespectful—informality of the words being the prime minister's way of indicating he understood the game. So the emperor claimed, at least.

Sure, Gustav. I'll get back in touch when I get there. You want that warship plain, or with fries?

"What are 'fries'?" Ekstrom wondered.

"A ghastly American way of cooking potatoes, boiled in grease. My daughter says she's become quite fond of them, though, and thinks we should import them to Sweden."

"Ah." The colonel made a silent decision to give Chancellor Oxenstierna a private warning. "And the other matter your daughter raised?"

"The Engler fellow? I was thinking we could borrow the Habsburg practice. We'll make him the first imperial count of the United States of Europe. For meritorious services rendered, that sort of thing. Since the rank stands outside of the local German landholdings, the Adel shouldn't object too much."

Ekstrom had his doubts about the last. The German nobility could manage to find a way to complain about almost anything. Still, it was a rather charming idea.

"Very good, Your Majesty. How soon do you want to make the announcement?"

"Let's wait until after the big battle. Who knows? He might get killed in it, which would make the whole issue moot. Or he might run away, which would do the same, although judging from what my daughter says, that's unlikely. Best of all, he might distinguish himself a bit—at something other than courting a woman, I mean."

"What if he doesn't?"

"Oh, come, Nils! A man of your imagination? Surely you can think of something."

❖   ❖   ❖

Ekstrom spent the rest of the day, off and on, trying to think of that "something." As a help, the emperor let him read the relevant letters from the princess.

Alas, the best he could come up with was *discovered Narnia*. A claim which, he suspected, an up-timer would surely challenge. Or anyone, for that matter, with access to one of the pestiferous encyclopedias.

Chapter 46

The Elbe

Mike Stearns' entire military experience had been a three year stint in the army during peacetime, as a grunt, and over fifteen years ago at that. So he really had no idea how to organize and manage a large expedition down a major river like the Elbe to reinforce the units guarding the *Achates* at the small port of Ritsenbuttel at the mouth of the Elbe. But he didn't worry about it, because what he *did* know how to do was organize people. And since he had a plentiful supply of experts in Hamburg, why in the world should he try to substitute his own amateurism for their professional knowledge and experience?

It was pretty much a piece of cake, from his point of view.

Needed: A commander for the military forces on the expedition. Since Colonel Christopher Fey had been left behind at Hamburg as part of the new garrison, and since he had plenty of experience working with what they called combined arms, he was the obvious choice. Mike had him appointed to his new position less than twenty minutes after he sent his radio reply to Gustav Adolf.

The first thing Fey told Mike was that they'd do well to transport as many of the troops and their horses as possible by boat.

Needed: A naval officer to command the flotilla. That was a no-brainer, because by the time Mike got the message from the emperor, five more of Simpson's timber-clads had arrived in Hamburg. Their commander—the term was "commodore," apparently—was a certain Captain Richard Henderson. He was one of the many Scotsmen serving under Swedish colors, whom Admiral Simpson had persuaded to join the USE Navy.

"We canna carry those great stupid horses on t'woodclads," he'd promptly informed Mike. "Most of the soldiers, yes. Nae the ugly brutes."

Needed: Someone who could enlist—impress, to be honest about it   a large number of merchant ships from Hamburg's harbor which could be used to transport the mounts for the cavalrymen and the dragoons.

That took a bit of time, but not much. Mike immediately enlisted the assistance of the many members of Hamburg's CoC who were either sailors or stevedores. It didn't take them more than five minutes to agree that the best choice was Captain Juan Hamers. The man's credentials were three:

First, he was an experienced and able ship captain.

Second, he claimed to be from a Scots family that had settled in Seville, thereby explaining the last name and the heavy Iberian accent. Not a single person Mike talked to believed the story for a minute. Hamers was obviously a *marrano*, a Sephardic "secret Jew," of whom there were many in the merchant shipping trade. Hamers was unusual only in having risen to the post of captain and claiming to be Spanish instead of the usual "Portuguese." For the CoCs, being Sephardic was a plus mark. Not much chance he'd betray them to the Ostenders, after all.

Third, he was the meanest son of a bitch among the merchant captains currently residing in the city.

Hamers resisted the notion, for a few minutes. First, he tried to claim he couldn't understand Mike's German, and his English was worse. No problem. Mike switched to Spanish. He'd studied the language in college and, better still, had gotten a thorough seventeenth century brush-up from his wife and father-in-law; for whom, as was true of most Sephardim, it was their native tongue.

Hamers then fell back on being a mean son of a bitch. But Mike's mean son-of-a-bitch routine was way better than his—especially with half a dozen armed CoC members to back him up.

"Okay! Okay!" Hamers exclaimed, throwing up his hands. "I do it. But I make no promises about the horses. They die like flies, on boats."

The rest went smoothly. Having been thwarted by Mike in the mean-son-of-a-bitch department, Hamers proceeded to restore his reputation by bullying several other merchant captains in the city's portside taverns. In this case, with him having the advantage of half a dozen armed CoC members at his side—who did a pretty good mean-sons-of-bitches act themselves.

That left the curlicues, where Mike was on more familiar ground. The first thing he did, seeing as how they'd already provided yeoman service, was impress the half dozen CoC members who'd been serving as his enforcers. They'd come along on the expedition also, to see to the necessary political tasks.

Those same tasks, however, required a printing press and experienced printers, which none of them were.

Not a problem. If there was one single trade in Europe that the CoCs had penetrated thoroughly, it was that of the printers—already notorious in the seventeenth century for being a radical lot, even before the Ring of Fire.

Soon enough, the printers arrived. Dismantling the printing equipment and getting it loaded on one of the timberclads took more time than anything. Mostly because the work itself was time consuming, but partly because Commodore Henderson put up a fuss. The ink would spill and ruin his deck, he claimed.

There being no feasible way to just bully a commodore in the USE Navy, Mike assured him the government would finance whatever repairs might be needed—and what did he care, anyway, seeing as how it was the government's ship, not his?

It took half an hour to bring Henderson around to an understanding of that point, proving to Mike's satisfaction as well as that of his CoC sidekicks that Henderson, at least, was a genuine Scotsman.

They left Hamburg the next morning. A flotilla of five timberclads and seven merchant ships, carrying a full regiment of foot soldiers and one company each of cavalry and dragoons. Mike had even corralled a battery of four guns; only six-pounders, but every little bit helped.

At the last minute, remembering an overlooked detail, Mike ordered the flotilla to remain at the docks until he and his sidekicks rounded up whatever soldiers in the garrison could play a musical instrument. That didn't take too long, since it was still before dawn and the troops were mostly asleep. Finding the instruments themselves took quite a bit longer.

So, after stressing the imperative necessity to sail at first light, Mike delayed the whole expedition until ten o'clock in the morning. Thereby proving to both the real Scots captain and the phony one that he was a confirmed lunatic.

Most of the soldiers probably thought the same, although they were more willing to give him the benefit of the doubt. The CoC members accompanying the expedition, however, were sure that this was just another example of the prince of Germany's canny ways.

Exactly how, they had no idea. Mike wasn't talking. Partly because he thought silence helped keep what few scraps of dignity he still had left; but, mostly, because he wasn't sure himself if he was a lunatic or not.

Jesse Wood kicked a loose clod into the dirt-filled hole and stomped on it. He looked across the field at the teams of farmers from the village still filling similar holes and depressions in the new airfield at Ochsen Werder, an island between the Elbe and one of its tributaries just southeast of Hamburg. By dint of back-breaking effort with their farm tools and wagons, the men, women, and children of the village were smoothing the ground of what had been a field of winter wheat only weeks before. The field had been hurriedly prepared by the army for their first flight over Hamburg. It was now approaching something close to an installation suitable for real flying operations and was already being called, inevitably, "The Ox."

Normally, this time of year, the farmers would have been right in the middle of the spring planting. But Jesse had promised relatively lavish wages for all and sundry, including the kids, to work on the airfield. He didn't mind the expense—in his experience, the mission came first—and it wasn't his money, anyhow. He even felt a slight guilty pleasure; half gratitude at having what amounted to an unlimited budget and half satisfaction at the thought of giving Stearns the tab for this. He imagined Mike would have a hell of a fight on some future supplemental military appropriations bill, but that wasn't his problem.

His problem was to make the field ready to provide air support to the war effort in the North German and Baltic areas. The weather was finally beginning to turn and, despite spring rains, was now okay for flying nearly two out of every three days. Once the aircraft returned from Grantville, the air force could get back in the war in earnest.

Provided he hadn't forgotten something. As he walked toward the nearly finished wooden building that was to serve as base operations, he once again mentally ticked off the essentials.

Airfield. Check. Nearly three thousand feet long, because he knew that eventually some ham-fisted or tired pilot would land halfway down the landing zone. The perimeter fence was done, so they wouldn't have to worry about cows wandering about. He'd spent more money paying for the removal of half an orchard just beyond one end of the field. The mature orchard had looked like it had been there since the time of

Adam and the freehold farmer who owned it had initially refused to sell it. He had only agreed after the local Committee of Correspondence had spoken to him, rather emphatically. Jesse had ignored the sullen farmer's black eye, shaken his hand, and given him a signed voucher for payment.

Jesse had been carefully absent during the conversation, partly because the CoC in Hamburg reminded him too much of what he imagined Mao's fanatic minions must have been like. They had all the vices of Magdeburg's CoC, without the discipline and tight organization that people like Spartacus and Gunther Achterhof provided. That was a common enough problem in outlying areas where new CoCs had sprung up. If the rumors were accurate, it was even worse in parts of Franconia.

Hangars, repair shop, fuel storage, munitions bunker. Check. Other work gangs, carpenters from Hamburg, had thrown up the buildings in jig time and one of Simpson's motorized barges had delivered precious uncut gasoline and enough methanol to last until local production could begin. The same barge had also brought scores of rockets, ample black powder, mass-produced iron nose cones, and percussion cap fuses. Jesse had employed the best of the carpenters in producing the thin wooden slats and tail assemblies which, when fitted into the slots in the tapering nose cones and sealed with pitch, formed the fifty- and hundred-pound bomb bodies for the Gustavs. The stout munitions bunker, surrounded by an earthen berm, already stored dozens of inert bomb bodies. Jesse wanted his own people to fill them with powder, which could also be produced locally.

Operations, communications. Check. Once the tower

was built next to the operations building, the radios would be served by a methanol-powered generator in a separate and well-ventilated shed under the tower.

Billeting, water, food, hygiene. Check. The barracks could wait. Since they'd be shorthanded at first, the hangars and operations building would do as sleeping quarters for now. They already had two cooks, a man and his wife who, despite having been CoC members, or maybe because of it, had run afoul of the local authorities in Hamburg. There was even a crew working on a brick, stone, and mortar communal bath, to be heated Roman-style, with a hypocaust floor. The island was cold and damp. Jesse reckoned they'd have enough problems without the men coming down sick from lack of some place to get clean. Women in the village would take care of the laundry.

Equipment, spares, personnel. He'd sent word to Hal Smith for everything he could think of that might be needed to keep the aircraft operating. Crew chiefs, mechanics, munitions specialists, a trained carpenter, spare propellers, oil and filters, wiring, tires, tools, a spare engine or two, the list was near endless. Most of it would be delivered by barge and Jesse fretted about all the things that could happen to the literally irreplaceable stuff from the future. He'd kept two pilots with him, Enterprise and Endeavor Martin, who were supervising work elsewhere on the field. Initially, Ent and Dev had reacted to the non-flying duty with ill grace, but Jesse knew they would benefit from the experience. The air force needed leaders who understood that there was more to being an officer than sitting in a cockpit. More pilots would arrive today with the aircraft. Hopefully.

Security. There wasn't much. Most of the USE contingents had moved on toward the borders and Luebeck. Those that remained seemed mostly interested in securing the future cooperation of Hamburg. Which meant, of course, staying in the city, where the beer was available, the beds were soft, and one could find women who were both. Jesse was armed with his personal Smith & Wesson Model 15 and the Martin brothers carried two of their moonshining daddy's pistols, left in the family farmhouse that had made the trip through the Ring of Fire. That was it. Luckily, there wasn't much need for security just yet. Being on an island cut down on casual traffic considerably. Still, Jesse would feel better when Sergeant Krueger showed up to take the situation in hand.

"Mein Herr! Mein Herr! Das Radio!"

Jesse looked toward the operations shack. Alois, the young man he'd left on radio watch was standing in the door, waving frantically. He broke into a run, clumping over the damp earth, and in seconds was inside the shack, grabbing the microphone from the youth. The instrument had been converted from the public address system in the Grantville grade school gymnasium, while the speakers had come from some teenager's bedroom, but the Americans were used to such jury-rigging by now. It still must have seemed like magic to the German boy who watched from the side. Jesse waited for the next incoming transmission.

"Ox, Ox, this is Eagle Leader with a flight of four. Do you read, Ox? Over."

The sound was faint and full of static. Jesse uselessly fiddled with the receiver volume and squelch switch before answering.

"Ah, Eagle Leader, this is Ox. We have you about three by three. Over."

"Roger, Ox, I have you five by five. Eagle Flight is ten minutes out. Three Gustavs and one Belle. Over."

Jesse could recognize Eagle Leader's voice now. It was Captain Woodsill.

"Roger, Woody, we'll be waiting." He glanced at the windsock outside the unglazed window. "The wind is from the southwest at about ten knots." Another glance at the barometer on the counter. "Set altimeter at three zero zero two. Give us a couple of minutes to clear the field."

Jesse was about to send Alois to find Dev and Ent, when the two brothers burst into the door. Jesse wasted no time.

"Go out there and get those people and wagons off the field. The aircraft are arriving in about eight minutes." The two spun about and raced back outside, yelling as they went.

Minutes later, the field was cleared and Jesse stood in the door of the operations shack, holding the mike and listening to the growing hum of engines.

"Ox, this is Eagle Flight, one minute out. Request permission to land."

Jess took one last look around before answering. "Roger, Eagle Flight is cleared to land."

The four aircraft approached from the south in a tight finger four formation, with the Gustavs in the first three positions and the Belle in four. The formation rapidly grew in size and the sound rose to a powerful multipitched growl as Woodsill brought them overhead and past at about two hundred feet. Alois stared in fascination at the aircraft, mouth agape.

Jesse noted the tightness of the formation with professional approval. The three Gustavs looked very impressive with the thin wooden skin of their low wings and fuselages painted a rich gray-blue with the red, black and gold USE flag toward the tail and large red numbers, 1, 2, 3, painted on their vertical stabilizers. Sun glinted off their greenhouse-style canopies and Jesse suddenly grinned at the ferocious red and white shark mouths painted on the Gustavs' noses. The Belle in the formation looked positively dowdy by comparison.

Jesse murmured, "It's okay, old girl. Don't pay any attention to the youngsters, you still look beautiful to me."

At the end of the field, Woody shook out the formation into line astern and climbed up into a comfortable downwind, still moving north. Trailing fifteen seconds apart, the aircraft followed him into the distance, finally turning one by one back to the field. The machines glided over the demolished orchard, crossed the perimeter fence, set down neatly spaced across the landing zone, and began to taxi toward the hangars.

Jesse let out a breath he hadn't known he'd been holding. By God, they had an airfield.

Chapter 47

Copenhagen

Prince Ulrik stared dubiously at the two dozen or so small vessels lined up next to each other in Copenhagen's harbor. They were typical galley gunboats of the sort called shallops: low-slung, open craft, with a single eighteen-pounder gun pivot-mounted in the bows and ten sweeps on a side. They were no more than fifty or fifty-five feet long, at a guess, with a beam of perhaps fifteen feet, and they looked undeniably . . . fragile.

"I suppose they'll do."

The rising inflection at the end of that sentence turned it into a question. Baldur Norddahl shook his head. "For our purposes here, at any rate. Look at it this way, Your Highness. We only need to go a short distance. Then, either way, it won't matter."

"It *would* be nice to have enough of a boat to make an escape, Baldur."

The Norwegian hesitated, for a moment, then said, "Ulrik, I doubt very much if we'll have a boat left to make an escape in the first place. I hope you're a good swimmer." For good measure, he added with a grin, "I swim like a seal, myself."

"You would," grunted Ulrik. But he didn't return the grin. The fact that Norddahl had used a personal form of address meant that he was dead serious.

"I read some up-time accounts of spar torpedoes," he half-protested. "I had them obtained after we agreed on this scheme."

"That must have cost a small fortune, getting them that quickly."

"It certainly did." Ulrik attempted a grin himself, although he suspected it was a sickly affair. "But I'm a prince, you know. I *have* a small fortune."

Actually, he didn't, since Christian IV kept his sons on a tight leash, financially. But it hadn't mattered, in this instance. The king had also informed his money-keepers that Prince Ulrik was to be given a free rein with spending on the new naval weapons.

"It's true that the *Hunley* sank, after using a spar torpedo, but it was a submarine. Most of the surface boats that used spar torpedoes seem to have survived the impact, well enough. For certain, the one that Richter's husband used in Amsterdam survived."

Baldur gave him a skeptical look. "I read the same accounts. First, the accounts are spotty, since the biggest use of spar torpedoes was by the Russians against the Turks and the American texts had no details. Secondly, the *Hunley* was not operating submerged when it destroyed the *Housatonic*—yet it sank anyway."

"But nobody knows *why* it sank," the prince pointed out. He wasn't really arguing the matter, though, just trying to draw out Baldur's logic. "And there's still the example of the Amsterdam attack."

The Norwegian adventurer shrugged. "Ulrik, there's simply no way to know. What I can tell you is this: From the reports, Higgins and his men were using a heavy boat. They had to, really, in that bad weather. We, on the other hand—"

He jerked a thumb toward the slim galleys tethered nearby. "—at your orders, I remind you, are using light boats. The damn things are just barely big enough to hold a crew of rowers and either an eighteen-pounder cannon or a one hundred pound keg of explosives at the end of a thirty-foot spar."

"We need to move as quickly as possible," Ulrik pointed out. "And I didn't see any reason to risk the lives of any more of our men than necessary."

"I'm not arguing that. I agree with you, myself. But the fact remains that once one of those charges goes off, five or ten feet below the surface, we'll get as big a water column as anything a mine produces—and we'll be sitting not thirty feet away in what amounts to a cockle-shell. Maybe the boat will survive, who knows? But I'm pretty sure it'll be upended, if not shattered outright, and we'll be dumped into the water. Like I said"—the grin came back—"I hope you're a good swimmer."

Ulrik stroked his beard for a moment. "Well, yes, I am. Not as good as you, I'm sure, since I'm not a crazy Norwegian. But I can make it to shore, if I'm still conscious. Better wear light clothing, though—even though the water will still be very cold."

Baldur glanced down. "Yes. And I do not recommend those cavalry boots. Barefoot would be best."

"A prince, going to war in his bare feet? That's ridiculous, Baldur. However, I do have a pair of sturdy slippers that I can kick off easily."

His half-sister Anne Cathrine had given those to him as a gift, as it happened. Ulrik made a note to have a servant blacken them with boot polish and remove the tassels. Their current color—bright green, with red trimmings and lemon-yellow tassels—would look just about as stupid on a prince going to war as bare feet would.

"Do you have any cheerier things to tell me?" Ulrik asked a bit grumpily.

"I certainly do. Come here and look at these."

Two minutes later, Ulrik was looking just as dubious. "That's *all*? Just these ugly-looking—I won't tell you what they remind me of—things?"

Baldur chuckled. "I know what they look like. Shit stuffed into a wooden tube with a fuse sticking out of them. But they'll work. I tested them out in the woods, a few miles north of the city. As God is my witness, I love those up-time texts. It's just sugar and saltpeter, you know, in the proper proportions. The only tricky part is that you have to melt them together carefully, not letting the stuff get too hot or stirring too hard."

Ulrik didn't ask what would happen if you didn't do it properly. From experience, he knew that Baldur would regale him with grisly details. The Norwegian took a peculiar pleasure in mishaps and disasters.

"Do we have enough smoke rafts?" he asked.

"Yes, we've got a dozen. Half the galleys will tow those into action, while the rest tow the floating mines. In the end, I won't be surprised if those mines do more damage to the enemy than anything else we've got."

"Do you really think Simpson will be fooled?"

Baldur raised his hands, in a gesture that was halfway between uncertainty and devout hope. "Who knows? But I think so, Ulrik, yes. You've been in battles. You know how chaotic and confusing they are. A man's natural tendency is to react to any threat immediately, without taking the time to wonder if there might be a bigger threat coming after them, that the initial assault is partly designed to disguise. Even generals and admirals do it. Them, most of all, perhaps, since they have entire armies and fleets to lose if they react sluggishly."

He'd lowered his hands by then. "So, yes. I think Simpson will concentrate on destroying the ships, not wondering until it's too late whether they're distracting him from something else. Coming like a spear through the smoke, seen too late to parry."

Ulrik smiled. "It's a nice image, I admit. Let's hope it turns out that way."

"I'm sure it will," Baldur said stoutly. "And I'm willing to wager that if I studied Snorri's sagas I could find exactly such a successful maneuver."

"Those take place in Iceland. Anything can happen in Iceland. Those people are crazier than Norwegians."

Norddahl scowled. "Your Highness, I am deeply offended. They most certainly are *not*."

Minden, on the Weser river

"We'll leave two hundred men with you; that's all I can spare," said Turenne.

"Should be enough," said Philippe de la Mothe-Houdancourt. The young French nobleman stroked his nose, a habitual gesture of his that Turenne thought was most unfortunate. Philippe had the sort of very prominent nose that invited ridicule.

Not from soldiers, though. The *mestre de camp*,

as France referred to its regimental commanders, was a very capable officer and well thought of in the cavalry.

"Should be enough," he repeated. Then, dropping his hand, Philippe glanced at the stone bridge that spanned the Weser. More than a century old, it was still in good shape despite being over two hundred yards long. "That'll be easy enough to defend against anything but an army, and we hardly need to worry that the bishop's garrison will challenge us."

Turenne chuckled. "No, that's not likely, is it?"

Minden was an independent principality under the authority of a bishop—but the exact identity of the bishop was in dispute. The Lutheran bishop who had ruled Minden, Christian von Braunschweig-Lüneburg, had died the year before. While his Brunswick cousins debated over which one of them should inherit the seat, a Catholic counterclaimant named Franz Wilhelm von Wartenberg laid claim to it himself. He was a morganatic relative of Maximilian, duke of Bavaria, and his younger brother Ferdinand, who controlled the archbishopric of Cologne as well as nearby Munster.

In short, the political situation was another example of the reason the Germanies were generally considered a political laughingstock by powerful European dynasties like the Habsburgs and the French Bourbons—or had been, at least, until Gustav Adolf and Mike Stearns began unifying the Germans. However, for Turenne's immediate purposes, the political uncertainty in Minden was a blessing. It meant the town's garrison was not in the least inclined to fight a desperate and ultimately hopeless battle against an invading force ten times as strong. As soon as Turenne had appeared at the town's outskirts and demanded an immediate surrender, the garrison had complied.

It was still a bit risky, leaving behind only a force of two hundred men to hold the town and its critical bridge across the Weser. But Turenne thought it would be enough. Philippe was certainly a better commander than the Swabian drunk who was the nominal head of the garrison; his troops were far better trained than those of the garrison, who were the typical mercenary dregs you usually found in such units; and, of course, they were far better armed. Having every cavalryman in his force equipped with a Cardinal rifle was a tremendous force multiplier.

Besides, there was a danger in leaving too many soldiers in Minden. The complicated patchwork quilt of principalities in the northwestern Germanies had been a major theater of the war in its early years, and had been badly ravaged by all armies passing through. It still hadn't recovered much, which meant that the pickings would be slim for any large body of soldiers who stayed in Minden. Philippe's unit would get badly frayed, quickly, if they needed to send out plundering expeditions—and the inevitable outrages committed by a sizeable force so engaged might stir up the population. Whatever else, Turenne could not afford to leave behind enough men to simply squelch any resistance. So, he deemed it best to leave a minimum. There was enough in the way of provisions stored in Minden itself that they could get by for a few days.

"Two hundred, then," the marshal repeated. "If all goes as planned, we'll be back very soon anyway."

De la Mothé-Houdancourt grinned. "With a large army in pursuit, thank you very much."

Turenne returned the grin with a smile. "Perhaps— and perhaps not. It's hard to say without knowing Torstensson's exact dispositions. The pursuing force would almost have to be USE troops. It's not likely that either the duke of Calenburg or the duke of Brunswick-Lüneburg would send an army after us. And by the time we get back, Jean de Gassion should have arrived to reinforce you."

De la Mothe-Houdancourt's grin never wavered. "If all goes as planned . . . I believe that's covered by the American expression 'famous last words.'"

Turenne shrugged. "Yes, but who's to say? I see no reason that Murphy's Law itself isn't subject to Murphy's Law. Now and then, you know, things *do* go the right way."

He turned toward his horse, and swung into the saddle. "Look for us in three days, Philippe. Four, at the most. We'll take Neustadt tonight, and the target on the morrow. Two days should be enough to gather up the plunder and get back, but let's allow an additional day just in case. If we're gone more than four days, we've had a disaster. If there's no sign of us on the morning of the fifth day, just get back to France. You can tell de Gassion those were my orders."

The mouth of the Elbe

When Mike got to Ritsenbuttel, he found a very tense situation. The crew of the *Achates* hadn't been able to do much to get the boat working again, since the critical repair couldn't be done until Mike arrived with the needed equipment—which had had to be brought all the way from Magdeburg.

Instead, they'd spent most of their time and energy getting the *Achates* ready to be scuttled and helping the Marines man the jury-rigged fortifications on the docks that gave the disabled warship what little protection it had.

Protection from whom? Commander Baumgartner didn't really know, but he seemed to be one of those people who invariably expect the worst. Perhaps a mob of outraged townspeople, although that didn't seem too likely. Being as how most of the townsfolk were huddling in their homes, far more frightened by the warship and its crew than vice versa. An enemy cavalry raid, perhaps. Or an enemy cutting out expedition, sent from . . . wherever.

Since Mike didn't know anything more about fixing warships than he did about commanding military operations, he left all that to the experts. Now that they had several of the timberclads and a regiment of soldiers to guard them, along with the equipment they needed, Baumgartner and the crew of the *Achates* were able to relax and get seriously to work on the repairs. Meanwhile, Mike took the first necessary steps to secure the area as a whole.

"Yeah, you heard me, Christopher. A parade. I want half the infantry and all the cavalry and dragoons turned out by midafternoon, ready to go. We'll parade right down the main street in Ritsenbuttel, with the band leading the way."

So, Colonel Fey joined the ever-growing *the-prime-minister-is-crazy* club.

By evening, however, the ranks of the club had thinned drastically. Down to only one man, in fact. Proving once again that he was a true and veritable Scotsman, Captain Richard Henderson stubbornly spent the whole evening sitting by himself at a corner table in the town's largest tavern, glaring at the ridiculous proceedings around him and muttering predictions of imminent disaster.

He didn't even have the satisfaction, any longer, of having Captain Hamers on his side. Proving to everyone's satisfaction that he was indeed no true Scotsman, Juan Hamers spent the whole evening carousing with his crew—and trying his best to serenade one of the barmaids into his bunk on the ship, by singing one love song after another to her. Unfortunately, the songs were all in Spanish, which the barmaid didn't speak at all, and he carried a tune even worse than Mike did.

So, sometime in the wee hours of the morning, Captain Hamers wound up staggering back to his ship on his own. He was not overly distressed, however. There was always the next night, after all, and by now the town was very friendly indeed. The parade and the band and—most of all—the hard Thuringian currency Mike spread around lavishly had produced a complete transformation in the attitude of the townsfolk toward the situation.

And why not? Ritsenbuttel was not an independent town, and never had been. It had been under Hamburg's authority for centuries—and still was, as it turned out. A rather startlingly transformed Hamburg, to be sure. The CoC members whom Mike solemnly assured everyone were representatives of the new city

council seemed to be a most unlikely set of burgo-
masters. They were too young; too roughly dressed;
too mean-looking but not actually mean enough.

Still, it was none of the Ritsenbuttelers' concern.
Certainly not compared to the sudden boom in business, ranging all the way from the taverns and the inns
packed to the gills with paying guests—and wasn't that
a wonder, being as they were all soldiers?—to every
craftsman and artisan in town being commissioned to
help with the repairs of the *Achates* and expanding
the piers to handle the new business the prince of
Germany assured them would soon be arriving.

Even the town's large number of fishermen were
happy. Mike sent them off to catch fish to feed the
regiment—and while they were at it, keep an eye out
for nefarious evildoers who might be creeping up on
Ritsenbuttel across the waters of the Wadden Sea or
through the island channels.

Within a day, the printing press was up and running,
and Mike began flooding the town with impromptu
propaganda. Then he hired whatever stray lads he could
find with a horse or a donkey who could spread the
good word to all the farming villages in the area.

The propaganda was simple and to the point. Three
points, actually.

Point One was that Hamburg and all its environs had
been incorporated into the United States of Europe.
Legally, legally—indeed, the Hamburg city council had
been most enthusiastic, and you could always come
into Ritsenbuttel to chat with the council's representatives yourself if you had any doubts.

Point Two was more or less a series of ferocious
snarls aimed at The Dastardly Enemy—not too precisely

defined—and boasting triumphantly of the overwhelming military might of the USE. Happily, among the printers brought from Hamburg had been an engraver who could work rapidly. By the third day, the broadsides had very nice if overlarge illustrations of the ironclads and the SRG rifle on every other page.

Point Three was an announcement that a parade, picnic and political rally would be held on Sunday, in Ritsenbuttel, following church services. With music! And, of course, the food and drink to be paid for by the new authorities.

Church services tended to be brief, that day.

So, not long after Mike arrived in Ritsenbuttel, the *Achates* was ready to go again. And it would be reasonable to say that the whole area had become a hotbed of USE sympathizers and enthusiasts for the new emperor.

Mike transmitted the gist of all that to Gustav Adolf. This time, using far more formal language.

The reply didn't particularly surprise him. For a Swede—and a king, to boot—Gustav was quite adept at American idiom himself.

Just stay put. Simpson should be arriving in Luebeck Bay any time. Expect all hell to break loose when he does. More to follow.

Chapter 48

The Bay of Kiel

"What the devil is that imbecile shouting about?" Captain Jean-Marie Grosclaud, commanding His Most Christian Majesty's thirty-two-gun ship *Railleuse*, demanded impatiently.

He stood on *Railleuse*'s tall, narrow poop deck, glaring down at the Danish fishing boat that had emerged from the morning's slightly misty visibility. The French warship had almost run down the miserable little craft, and now the boat's master (Grosclaud refused to apply the term "captain" to a Danish fisherman whose so-called vessel was scarcely larger than his own ship's second launch) was standing beside the boat's tiller shouting about *something*.

"I can't quite make it out, sir," his sailing master admitted. The master was the senior professional seaman in *Railleuse*'s company. He also had the best command of their allies' language . . . which said truly appalling things about everyone *else's* Danish, Grosclaud supposed.

"Well, tell him to stand clear," the captain said, even

more impatiently. "The fool is probably saying we've ruined one of his nets or something of the sort."

He snorted, eyeing the Dane with a mixture of disdain and irritation. The fishing boat master's fellow countrymen had been nothing but one enormous pain in the arse, as far as Grosclaud was concerned. In his fairer-minded moments, which he entertained no more frequently than necessary, Grosclaud was forced to admit that however ambitious their king might be, the majority of Danes weren't really particularly interested in helping Cardinal Richelieu's "League of Ostend" assail their fellow Protestants and never had been. Under the circumstances, he could scarcely blame them for that. If *he'd* been Danish, he certainly wouldn't have been madly enthusiastic over the notion, after all. Still, now that they were (supposedly, at least) committed, they could have been at least a *little* more efficient about doing it.

The sailing master was shouting down at the fishing boat. Even Grosclaud, whose comprehension of Danish was nonexistent, could tell that the sailing master was speaking slowly and awkwardly, with frequent pauses as he searched for the right word. He was only part way through the delivery of Grosclaud's order when the fisherman started shaking his head, waving both hands, and expostulating more loudly than ever.

"Tell him I'll drop a round shot through the bottom of his miserable boat if he doesn't stand clear!" Grosclaud snapped.

There'd never been a fisherman born, no matter what his nationality, who wouldn't claim a warship had overrun his nets and torn them to pieces. The chance of having anyone believe him might be minute, but it was worth trying. Especially when the warship belonged to someone who was playing paymaster to the fishing boat's monarch. Grosclaud, however, wasn't in the mood for it.

The sailing master waved his own hands, shouting more loudly than before as he cut off the meaningless babble of Danish. The fisherman stared up at him, shaking his head in artfully feigned disbelief, and Grosclaud snorted again. *Railleuse* was on her way home to France, and the captain had no intention of allowing a wretched fisherman's false claims of damage to delay his ship's escape.

All the fault of those damned books from the future, he fumed silently. *All that nonsense about year-round "close blockades." Madness!*

He didn't know who'd been responsible for deciding to apply that particular piece of lunatic brilliance to the present. It might even have been Richelieu himself, for all Grosclaud knew. It was the sort of convoluted, cunning notion that would have appealed to him, by all accounts. But even assuming that the books in question had told the truth (a point Grosclaud was inclined to doubt), those Englishmen of the future had never done it with ships like *Railleuse*. Nor, so far as Grosclaud had been able to discover, had they even *tried* to do it in the accursed Baltic!

He shuddered as he considered the winter just past. Ice had been a significant problem once a ship got north of Gotland, and the Gulf of Riga—as usual—had frozen over. The winter's icy winds and wet misery had turned the lot of the ships' companies assigned to the blockade into a nightmare, and the fact that Captain Admiral Overgaard had been unwilling (for reasons

Jean-Marie Grosclaud found perfectly understandable, however little he liked them) to take his ships any farther up the Trave River than he absolutely had to had only made things worse. Poor diet, inadequate clothing, poor sanitation, nonexistent hygiene, miserable, wet, unheated living quarters, and treacherous conditions aloft, had killed scores and left the ships full of sick and injured crewmen . . . as anyone but an idiot must have known would happen. The attrition rate was always high aboard ships that were forced to remain at sea for extended periods; doing so in the middle of a Baltic winter had only made it worse.

Which, of course, was the reason—or *one* of the reasons, at least—why Grosclaud had no intention of letting a Danish fisherman's spurious claims of damage interfere with his departure.

The sailing master shouted one last sentence, jabbing his pointing finger sharply westward, in the direction of the mist-blurred outlines of the island of Funen. The fisherman grimaced. Then he shook his head, shrugged his shoulders eloquently, and started shouting at his motley four-man crew instead of *Railleuse*, and Grosclaud snorted a third time—this time in satisfaction.

The fishing boat's sail filled as the crew sheeted home, and the smaller craft bore away from *Railleuse*. It was considerably faster in the current light wind conditions than *Railleuse*, and Grosclaud watched it go for several moments. Then he returned to his interrupted morning's exercise, walking up and down the leeward side of the poop deck as the mist turned the fishing boat into a fading ghost.

So much for that, he thought. *If God is good, that's*

the last Danish I'm going to be hearing this side of Hell! And even if He isn't, I don't see any—

"Sail ho!" The shout came down from aloft, and Grosclaud's head snapped around as he heard the consternation in the lookout's cry. "Sail—*ships*—on the port bow!"

John Simpson had decided against any sort of finesse as he made his way from the North Sea to the Baltic. His squadron had crossed the Skaggerak, rounded the tip of the Jutland Peninsula, swung east of the island of Laeso, then south through the Kattegat straight for the Great Belt, the passage between Zealand and Funen. It was the broadest (and most easily predicted) route he could have taken, but it was also a minimum of ten miles wide—once he got south of the east and west channels on either side of the island of Sprogo, at any rate. That was the decisive factor, as far as Simpson was concerned.

He had his doubts about the probable effectiveness of mines built with seventeenth-century technology, no matter what pointers the builders might have acquired from purloined up-timer sources. On the other hand, he'd seen sufficient proof of seventeenth-century ingenuity to prevent him from investing too much confidence in those doubts of his. He'd come to the conclusion that the contempt some up-timers—Quentin Underwood came rather forcibly to mind—felt for the inherent ability of native-born denizens of this century was . . . misplaced. Given the persistent reports of King Christian's fascination with the concept of moored mines (and the fact that, for all his fondness for alcoholic beverages and his famed bouts of excessive enthusiasm, Christian was anything but stupid), John Simpson had no intention of entering the narrow waters of the Sound until he had to.

And I'm not coming in from the north when I do enter it, he thought dryly. *If there's one place where these people could make even crappy mines effective, that's it.*

And since he'd already demonstrated that seventeenth-century artillery wasn't going to do much more than scuff the paint on his ironclads, he'd been perfectly willing to take his chances on whatever he might happen to meet as he sailed calmly through the Great Belt from the Kattegat and from there to the Bay of Kiel.

The wind was from the southeast, ideally placed for shipping headed for the North Sea *from* the Baltic, even if it wasn't very strong. He was sure the timber-clads preferred the current conditions to the awkward, corkscrew roll that had afflicted them in the Skaggerak, and although visibility was patchy (not uncommon for these waters, especially in the spring), they'd already encountered several outbound ships and fishing vessels. That was one reason he'd reduced speed to little more than three or four knots; it had turned particularly patchy over the last fifteen minutes or so, and he didn't want to run anyone down.

Of course, he thought as he watched the warship— French, from the look of her—solidifying out of the mist at a range of less than two miles, worse things could happen to a ship than a simple collision.

Grosclaud gaped in disbelief. For a second or two, he couldn't imagine what he was seeing. It was too alien, too unlike anything he'd ever seen before. It was more like some sort of slab-sided building floating toward him than any proper sort of vessel.

But it was only for a second or two. Then he knew what it had to be, and his blood ran cold as a second dark silhouette started blending out of the mist behind it.

"Clear for action! *Clear for action!*"

Even as he heard his own voice shouting the order, a part of his mind wondered what point there was to it. It had been far easier to decide the rumors about the newest American deviltry had to be grossly exaggerated when the ships those rumors swirled about were still sitting in the Elbe River at Magdeburg. It was quite a different thing, he discovered, when one saw them altering course directly toward one's ship.

Shouts, the rousing tattoo of the drum, bellowed orders, and pattering feet sounded all about him as *Railleuse's* startled crew responded to his orders, and he stared up at the set of the sails.

There was no wind, not really. The Kattegat this morning might almost have been a millpond, and *Railleuse's* canvas was scarcely even drawing. She couldn't have been making more than one or two knots, with barely a ripple around her cutwater, which meant there was no point trying to evade the oncoming monsters, and he looked at the suddenly white-faced sailing master.

"At least we know now what the fellow was trying to tell us," Grosclaud said with a smile that held no humor at all. Then he shrugged. "Come four points to starboard. We'll try to engage with the port broadside."

Simpson watched the other ship swinging to starboard, turning away from the squadron's line of advance and opening its port broadside. The range fell steadily as *Constitution* and her consorts foamed ahead, working up towards a speed of ten knots in obedience to his last maneuvering orders, and he wondered what the idiot in command of that ship thought he was doing.

"Bullhorn!" he snapped.

"Aye, aye, sir!" one of the bridge signalmen acknowledged sharply, and disappeared briefly into the conning tower. He reappeared on the bridge wing almost instantly, carrying the bullhorn that had once belonged to the Grantville Fire Department and now bore the crossed anchors of the Navy.

"Ahoy!"

Grosclaud had no idea what the single word booming impossibly across the narrowing gap of water between him and the Americans might mean. No doubt it was yet another of those "up-timer" words that were working their way into the world's proper languages.

"This is Admiral John Simpson, United States Navy," the hugely amplified voice continued, this time in recognizable German. "Lower your sails and surrender, or I will be forced to fire into you!"

"Captain?" a merely mortal voice asked closer to hand. Grosclaud turned his head and saw Leon Jouette, his second in command. Jouette's face looked like curiously mottled porridge, and Grosclaud wondered if his looked the same.

"What do you expect me to do, Leon?" he demanded harshly.

"But if the reports are accurate, what *can* we—"

"Even if they are accurate, I can't simply haul down my flag the first time someone threatens me!"

Jouette looked as if he wanted to continue to argue, but he closed his mouth with a click as Grosclaud glared at him. Then he nodded spastically and turned and hurried away, shouting orders of his own as he went.

"I repeat," the voice thundered again. "Strike your sails and surrender, or I will destroy your vessel!"

"—destroy your vessel," Simpson said the into the microphone, then lowered it and watched the other vessel.

It continued to swing to starboard, slowly under the current wind conditions, and his mouth tightened.

"Clear the bridge," he said as gun ports began to open here and there along the other ship's side. The bridge wing lookouts moved smartly past him into the conning tower's protection, and he lifted his binoculars, looking across the water at the Frenchman—now less than eight hundred yards away.

Eighteen-pounders, at best, he decided.

He looked astern to where *President* foamed along in *Constitution*'s wake. Captain Lustgarten's carronades were run out on either broadside, as were *Constitution*'s. Despite their stubby barrels, both ships' carronades would have the range to engage the French ship within the next few minutes, whatever the other captain did. When that happened, there could be only one outcome. He knew that—which didn't mean he had to *like* it.

"Captain," he said through the bullhorn, "I have no desire to destroy your ship and kill your crew, but if you do not surrender, I will have no other option. This is your final warning."

✧   ✧   ✧

"—your final warning!"

Grosclaud's jaw set tight.

The closest American was little more than five hundred yards away. The second ship followed perhaps two hundred yards astern of it, and he saw two more, identical ships beyond them. And beyond *them* was something else, something streaming smoke as it followed along behind.

A voice deep inside gibbered that Jouette had been right, that not surrendering immediately was insane. Yet he couldn't do it. He simply *couldn't* do it.

Simpson sighed, shook his head, and followed the lookouts and signalmen into the conning tower. Little though he might care for what was about to happen, he had no intention of standing heroically—and stupidly—on an open bridge while somebody fired eighteen-pounder cannon balls in his direction.

"Very well, Captain," he said to Halberstat. "If he won't stop, we'll have to encourage him to see reason. Let's try firing one shot across his bow, first, though."

"Yes, sir." Captain Halberstat looked at the signalman manning the voice pipes. "Pass the order to Lieutenant MacDougall. One shot across his bow, whenever is convenient."

"One shot across his bow, whenever is convenient, aye, sir!" the signalman repeated, and bent over the voice pipes.

Simpson was peripherally aware of one of the lookouts dogging down the clips that secured the armored bridge door, but most of his attention was for what he could see through the port vision slit. The French warship had finally gotten around on to its new heading, and the admiral shook his head.

Grosclaud's head jerked up as the forwardmost gun in the slab-sided vessel's broadside lurched back. The sound of it was hard and flat, somehow unlike any of the artillery Grosclaud had ever heard before. It spewed out a vast gush of smoke, and the round shot made a peculiar *hissing* sound before it plunged into the water twenty yards in front of *Railleuse*.

The splash was bigger than he would have expected from a gun that short. That was his first thought. Then, an instant later, his eyes flew open in shock as there was a second, much bigger—and higher—geyser of spray.

"Mother of God!" he heard Jouette exclaim. "That thing *exploded*!"

Simpson observed the explosion with a certain degree of satisfaction. The fuse he'd designed for the navy's shells was as simple as it was crude, which had suggested that it ought to function fairly reliably. On the other hand, to explode underwater, it had to be watertight, and he'd been uncertain about how well he'd managed to achieve that aspect of the design.

Now, Captain, he thought at the French ship's commander very loudly, *notice the explosion. Draw the right goddamned conclusion so I don't have to kill all your men.*

Grosclaud clutched at the bulwark, staring forward, still trying to wrap his mind around what had just happened. No one had ever fired explosive shells out of a *cannon* before! That was what *mortars* were for! It was unnatural—preposterous!

And exactly the sort of thing all the tales said he should have expected out of the accursed Americans.

"Captain? What do we do now?" Jouette demanded hoarsely.

Grosclaud turned toward him, and the fear in Jouette's eyes hit him like a fist. Mostly because he was quite certain Jouette saw exactly the same fear in his own.

"We have to at least try, Leon," he heard himself say calmly, almost reasonably. "If we don't, we'll never know."

"Know *what*, Captain?"

"Whether or not our guns can hurt *them*," Grosclaud said, and looked at the gunner.

"Open fire," he said.

"Damn," John Simpson said mildly as the Frenchman's side disappeared behind a bank of flame-swirled smoke. The range was down to no more than sixty or seventy yards, with *Constitution* following the other vessel around onto the same heading.

"Return fire, sir?" Halberstat asked, and Simpson nodded unhappily.

"You are authorized to fire, Captain. But let's not get carried away here. Give him one broadside from the carronades. Let's find out if he's willing to see reason after that."

"Yes, sir. One broadside," Halberstat repeated. "Pass the word to Lieutenant MacDougall," he told the signalman on the voice pipes. "One carronade broadside, only."

"One carronade broadside, only, aye, aye, sir."

❖　　❖　　❖

Grosclaud glared at the ugly, ponderous-looking American ship. He *knew* he'd hit it at least a half-dozen times, but as the smoke of his own broadside drifted away, the other vessel loomed up out of the water—close aboard, now—with absolutely no sign to mark the striking of his round shot.

"Well," he started to say to Jouette, "*now* we know. So let's—"

The end of the world arrived before he could complete the sentence.

Constitution's guns fired.

The range was childishly short for rifled guns, but, by the same token, both the target and the firing platform were moving through the water. And no matter how calm the Bay of Kiel might seem, or even be, compared to North Sea or normal Atlantic conditions, there *was* wave motion to take into consideration. *Railleuse* had fired a sixteen-gun broadside at *Constitution*, and (despite Grosclaud's estimate) had scored only four hits. *Constitution*'s gunners (despite their shoreside practice) had woefully little actual experience firing at sea. Despite the low range, despite the fact that they, unlike *Railleuse*'s gunners actually had sights, they scored only two hits.

The effect of those two hits was somewhat different from *Railleuse*'s four, however.

The first shell hit *Railleuse* between the fourth and fifth gun ports on her port side. It smashed through the thick planking, slammed across the tween-deck space, struck the foremast, and detonated. The mast shattered, a section of decking six feet by eight feet erupted upward in a hail of splinters, and shell fragments ripped through the crowded gunners, killing seven and wounding another twelve.

The second shell hit her aft, just below the level of the poop deck. It exploded in Grosclaud's sea cabin, blowing out the stern windows and reducing the captain's furniture to splinters. The helmsman staggered as the same explosion cut the linkage between the tiller bar and the whipstaff. The staff went abruptly loose in his hands, moving freely without affecting the rudder at all, and two seamen went down—one screaming; one already limp in death—as shell fragments and bits and pieces of deck blasted through them.

The sheared off foremast toppled, crashing down with all its weight of canvas and spars, taking the main topmast with it. *Railleuse* seemed to slow, as if she'd dropped anchor, when the wreckage thundered into the water alongside. She pivoted around the sudden drag, her stern pushing away from the wind, and there was nothing at all the helmsman could do about it.

Grosclaud felt as if someone had just hit him across the bottoms of his feet with a club. He heard the screams of maimed and wounded men, saw the wreckage of rigging trailing alongside, then stiffened as he smelled wood smoke.

"Fire!" someone shouted. *"Fire!"*

It was the greatest fear of any wooden ship, and the captain hurled himself toward the poop deck ladder as smoke came welling up out of his own sea cabin. Other men were already racing toward the flames, some with buckets of sand, others with nothing but their bare hands. They flung themselves into the smoke, treading on still more wounded crewmen in their haste. Some hurled sand at the flames; others snatched up burning wreckage, ignoring the pain in their hands when they got too close to the flames, and hurled it through the shattered stern windows into the sea. Still others ripped off shirts, or even trousers, and used them to beat at the flames, frantic to subdue them.

"Rig hoses!" Simpson snapped. "Captain Halberstat, circle around and stand by to go alongside!"

Quick responses came back, but Simpson was already tearing at the latches, hurling the bridge door open and dashing back out onto it with his bullhorn. None of the abruptly crippled *Railleuse*'s guns would bear on *Constitution*, but he was well aware that they were close enough for even a seventeenth-century matchlock musketeer to get lucky.

Just going to have to hope none of them do, John, he thought.

The corner of his brain told him he was being insane, given what he and his ships planned to do when they got to Luebeck. But they weren't at Luebeck yet. There was only one enemy warship in sight at this particular moment, and the smoke pouring out of its stern in steadily thickening clouds suggested that it might not be around a great deal longer.

"Stand by for assistance!" he heard his own amplified voice bellowing.

Here and there, someone aboard the French ship actually seemed to have noticed someone was talking to them. Some of them looked up with sudden hope; most of them simply looked blank, as if they couldn't conceive of what he might be talking about.

He looked back over his shoulder to find Halberstat standing right behind him.

"Get the hoses up on top of the casement, Captain. Then lay us across her stern."

From his expression, Halberstat would have liked nothing better than to have argued with Simpson's decision. Whatever he would have liked, however, what he actually did was to salute.

"Yes, sir," he said.

Grosclaud was vaguely aware of the same thunderous voice he'd heard earlier. He had other things on his mind at the moment, though, and he concentrated on the effort to coordinate the battle against the flames.

It was one he was losing.

There'd been no time for *Railleuse* to clear for action properly. The canvas screens and flimsy partitions, the bedding and clothing, the spirit stores, the lamps hanging from the overhead—and their oil . . . All those highly flammable items that should have been struck safely below crackled and fumed and smoked, and the ship's seasoned, painted timbers were already well alight, as well.

And then, suddenly, something loomed across the ship's stern like an iron-plated cliff, cutting off the smoky daylight. He turned, eyes widening, just in time to see the seamen standing on top of *Constitution*'s armored casement with the canvas hoses open the valves on the bronze nozzles wide.

The pumps driving the fire mains Simpson had thoughtfully provided were powerful enough to empty the ironclad's trim tanks completely in less than fifteen minutes. The pressure they could generate was sufficient to require at least two men, and preferably three, to control one of the hoses. Jean-Marie Grosclaud—and over a dozen of his men—went down, bowled head over heels, in a torrent of icy cold saltwater. *Railleuse's* captain could scarcely believe the tidal bore force of that freezing cataract, but he didn't really care. All he cared about was the instantly quenching effect it had on the flames threatening to consume his ship.

"Well, that was certainly exciting," John Simpson said mildly a couple of hours later. Captain Halberstat gave him a rather speaking glance, and the admiral chuckled.

"I don't blame you, Franz," he said, speaking with unusual informality.

"Blame me, sir?" Halberstat inquired politely.

"Blame you for wondering if I'd lost my mind," Simpson amplified. Halberstat started to shake his head, but Simpson snorted.

"Of course you did. Oh, the risk might not have been *all* that great, but we didn't know—*I* didn't know—how close all that smoke was to their powder store. *Railleuse* could have gone up any moment."

"I suppose she could have," Halberstat agreed. "On the other hand, the force of the explosion would mostly have gone straight up. I doubt it could have done significant damage to *Constitution*, even if it had gone off, sir. Not right up to the last minute, when we went hard alongside, at least."

"Well, there would have been that little matter of the exposed firefighting party," Simpson said dryly. "And, now that I think about it, that other little matter of the flag officer and captain standing out there on the bridge wing with their asses hanging out. *That* could have been rather . . . unpleasant."

"Perhaps, sir." Halberstat smiled. "On the other hand, if it had been, *we* wouldn't be the ones having to worry about explaining it to the emperor or Prime Minister Stearns, now would we?"

"That thought did cross my mind," Simpson admitted, and it was Halberstat's turn to chuckle. Then his expression sobered.

"Excuse me, Admiral, but I've come to know you, to some extent, at least. I don't think you would have broached the subject if you hadn't intended me to ask you exactly why we did it."

"No, I don't suppose I would have."

Simpson looked toward the north, where *Railleuse* had been left behind, limping steadily farther north under her mizzenmast and what remained of her mainmast. There'd really been no particular point in keeping her, and he'd needed somewhere to put her surrendered personnel, anyway, so he'd accepted Captain Grosclaud's parole with the proviso that he sail his ship directly to Copenhagen and agree to take no part in any naval actions until he and all his men had been properly exchanged for Swedish prisoners. It got them safely out of the way, and if they happened to get there before he did (unlikely, actually, in light of the ship's damages), he had absolutely no objection to their spreading all the terrifying rumors they could among Copenhagen's defenders.

On the other hand . . .

"Things are going to get messy when we reach Luebeck, Franz," he said after moment, still gazing into the north. "You saw what we did to *Railleuse* with only two hits. Well, it's going to be a lot worse than that when we engage Admiral Overgaard's squadron in the Bay of Luebeck. What happened to *Railleuse* isn't going to have much effect on what happens at Luebeck, but after this is all over, the word will get around."

" 'The word,' sir."

"The word that we blew the piss out of her with only two hits—and that as soon as we did, we went alongside and helped put out her fires. We're about to teach the world a new kind of sea warfare, Captain, one with weapons that are going to be more destructive than anything anyone's ever seen before. So, when we teach *that* to everyone else, I intend to teach them something about the Navy of the United States of Europe, as well."

"What, sir?" Halberstat asked, when the admiral paused.

"Something Winston Churchill once said. I always did admire that old dinosaur. It went, 'In war, resolution; in defeat, defiance; in victory, magnanimity.' We may have to knock them down and stomp on them, from time to time, but when it's finished, it's *finished*, and it's time to remember that they're human beings, too."

He watched Halberstat's lips move as the flagship's captain repeated the phrases to himself. Then Halberstat nodded in approval.

"I like that, sir," he said simply.

"Good. Because that's the navy we're going to build, Franz. That's the kind of navy we're going to build."

Chapter 49

The Wietze oil fields
A few miles northwest of Hannover

Like everyone at the Wietze oil facility since Quentin Underwood had arrived on an inspection tour three days earlier, the site manager was walking around on figurative tiptoes. Underwood was a hard taskmaster at any time. When he was in a bad mood because he felt production wasn't going as well as it should be, his treatment of subordinates was caustic and abrasive.

"What does he expect?" complained one of the refinery workers to the manager. "With the equipment we've got?"

The manager didn't bother to respond. By now, that was an old refrain whenever Underwood wasn't around to hear. There was no point saying it to him directly—again—because that would just elicit another hot-tempered tirade on the subject of "making do with what we've got." A tirade that was every bit as pointless, because the workers at the refinery *were* making do with what they had.

The manager straightened up from the *schlaemmbock*

they'd been examining. The extraction pipe was so badly corroded there was no longer any point in repairing it. "We'll have to—"

A shout in the distance made him break off. Looking up, he saw that one of the soldiers in the nearest watch-tower on the guard perimeter was pointing at something in the distance. The manager couldn't tell what it what was, but the guard seemed quite agitated.

There was a separating pot nearby, much closer than the watch-tower. The manager hurried over and climbed up the metal rungs welded to the side of the pot. From the top, he'd have a good view.

Two seconds after he got that view, he started shouting himself.

"All right, all right, everybody calm down," said Quentin Underwood. "They're just cavalrymen. They can't possibly do more than harass us, armed with nothing more than lances and wheel-lock pistols. We've got five hundred men in the garrison here. Plenty to drive them off if they try anything really aggressive."

A babble rose in the refinery's operations center.

"Calm down, I said!" Underwood bellowed. "Friedrich, stop prattling about 'thousands of them.' That's bullshit. How would the Ostenders get thousands of men this far south of Luebeck? The air force maintains regular reconnaissance all around the area."

Actually, that wasn't true, but Underwood figured he had to settle everyone's nerves. The USE's air force had been concentrating lately on getting a new airfield in place near Hamburg, using the planes to shuttle equipment and supplies instead of doing what they *should* be doing, which was protecting the nation's assets. Not to Underwood's surprise, Mike Stearns' regime had proven to be every bit as shortsighted and reckless when it came to war as it was with regard to everything else.

That said, Quentin still didn't think there was any chance that a large enemy force could have gotten this far south of the Elbe. Even without aerial reconnaissance, there was simply too much traffic on the river for a major crossing to have gone unreported.

One of the refinery workers started babbling about the French.

"Just shut up, will you!" Quentin hollered. "That's got to be the stupidest thing I've heard anybody say yet. How the hell would the French get all the way over here?"

He waved his hand roughly, as if shoving something aside. "Just shut up! What we've got here is just a stray Spanish cavalry unit from the Netherlands. All of you, stop panicking!"

He glared at the site's manager. "Get out there and stiffen up the garrison's officers. I'll be out myself in a minute. First, I've got to get hold of Stearns on the radio and tell the asshole that his asshole policies just resulted in another fuck-up."

It took a while to reach Stearns, since it turned out the idiot had gone haring off to the mouth of the Elbe to look at a disabled timberclad. That was typical. Stearns knew as much about delegating authority as a chipmunk. Having a man like this running an entire country was simply insane. He'd have been stretching his abilities to run a high school softball league.

But, eventually, Stearns got on the radio. And—naturally—he immediately panicked also.

"Quentin, get out of there. Now. All of you. That's got to be a French force. It's not Spanish, I'm sure of that—and there's no way French cavalry would have come that far on a whim. They've got a real raid underway, and all you've got is a small garrison unit."

"Bullshit, Stearns! This facility is valuable. No way we're giving it up without a fight."

"Forget the goddam facility! It's so primitive they can't do all that much physical damage to it anyway. The real danger is that they'll kill or capture skilled workers."

Quentin almost retorted "and good riddance," but the presence of the radio operator made him leave the sarcastic remark unspoken. "It'll never get that far. Nice talking to you, Stearns, even though it was the usual waste of my time. Just get somebody down here as soon as you can, huh? One of those fancy airplanes you waste resources on would be handy, right about now."

Hearing the sound of gunfire starting up, he realized he'd better get out on the guard perimeter. He just took enough time to snatch up his rifle, that he'd left leaning up in a corner of the operations center. Fortunately, he'd brought it with him on this trip. He normally didn't, on these inspection tours, figuring that his revolver was enough to deter any footpad. But with the war heating back up again and unsettling the situation, he'd decided that hauling the thing around was probably a wise idea.

No sooner had he taken a few steps out of the

operations center, however, than he came to an abrupt halt. The garrison whose resolve he'd intended to stiffen was no longer at the perimeter to begin with. They were already in full retreat—rout, rather—pouring away from the earthen fieldworks that protected the oilfield site. Most of them were even throwing their guns away.

"Get back there, you fucking cowards!" Quentin brandished his rifle in the air, as if it were a clumsily made sword. Then, realizing that was a little foolish, aimed it instead at one of the retreating soldiers who was running toward him.

"I'll shoot you dead, you son of a bitch—so help me I will!"

The man paid him no attention. He raced right by Quentin without so much as a glance. He'd been in such a panic that Quentin didn't think he'd even heard him at all.

The threat was empty, anyway. Quentin hadn't even come close to pulling the trigger. Hadn't really even thought about it, since he'd assumed the threat would be enough.

What in God's name was happening? Even sorry-ass garrison soldiers should have had more fight in them than this.

But apparently it was just this section that had collapsed. From the continuing gunfire, *somebody* had to be putting up a resistance.

A pretty ferocious one, too, from the sound of it. Some unit of the garrison that Quentin couldn't see from his vantage point, with a cluster of buildings blocking his sight, was laying down one hell of a good rate of fire. There was simply no way that cavalrymen armed with wheel locks could be firing that often and that continuously.

He half-ran around the nearest maintenance shed, moving a bit clumsily due to his age and weight and silently vowing—as he had dozens of times before, to no avail—that when he got back home he'd listen to his wife and start using the exercise equipment in his basement. Underwood was one of those heavyset men who tended to run to fat under the best of circumstances. In times past, the work of managing a coal mine had kept him on his feet a lot, but he'd become a lot richer since the Ring of Fire. Rich, he'd soon learned, usually meant sedentary also.

When he came around the corner of the shed, he stumbled to a halt, staring. A wave of soldiers—enemy ones, obviously—seemed to be pouring over the field-works a hundred yards away. No one was putting up any resistance at all. The few garrison soldiers still near the earthworks were already surrendering.

The gunfire he'd heard was coming entirely from the enemy. They weren't really even shooting *at* anybody, any longer. Most of them, from what Quentin could see, were just firing in the air from sheer exuberance.

How in God's name were they managing *that*? There was something odd-looking about their matchlocks, although Quentin couldn't really see them that well at the distance. His eyesight was starting to get worse, too.

But it was still good enough to aim a rifle, certainly at this distance. Underwood realized he had no choice any longer but to follow Stearns' advice and abandon the facility. No goddam way he was going to do it without firing at least two or three rounds in anger, though.

He took aim and fired. To his grim satisfaction,

the soldier who'd been his target was knocked off his feet. *Meet Lord .30-06, you bastard.*

Quentin worked the bolt, jacking another round into the chamber, and took aim again.

This time, he missed. By now, at least half a dozen enemy soldiers were aiming their guns at him, but Quentin wasn't too worried about that. They were still almost a hundred yards distant, quite a ways beyond the effective range of matchlocks. He jacked another round into the chamber and started bringing the rifle back up to his shoulder.

It never got there. Of the three .50 caliber bullets that hit him almost simultaneously, either one of two would have killed him. One wound, slowly and painfully, from the damage done to his intestines. Fortunately, the other one severed his aorta, sending a gout of blood everywhere. For all practical purposes, Quentin Underwood was dead before his body hit the ground.

"Quickly! Quickly!" Turenne waved his hand impatiently at the four soldiers ransacking the desks and cabinets in what seemed to be the oil facility's central headquarters. "We haven't much time."

He gave the stacks of documents they'd already piled up on the desks a brief examination, estimating their weight and bulk. Not too bad, in themselves—but they'd be getting added to a larger pile of what seemed to be critical small pieces of equipment.

The officer in command straightened up from the lowest drawer of a desk, with a pile of papers in his hands.

"I think we've already gotten everything critical,

Marshal," he said. Since both his hands were occupied, he used his head to point to a big stack of documents on a desk near one of the windows. "The best stuff is over there. Including what looks to be diagrams of the entire facility."

Turenne gave the man an encouraging smile. Privately, he suspected the diagrams—all the documents, for that matter—wouldn't be half as useful as the few small parts from machines they'd be taking back to France. Now that he was here and could finally see these Wietze oil works, Turenne wasn't very impressed. Overall, the technology involved was nothing that France didn't have already, although it had never been used in quite this manner.

The trick, it turned out, was building the machines that could put the oil to use. Not so easy, that. But if France could do so, they'd have no trouble providing the machines with the fuel they needed, with what Turenne had learned from this raid. He was quite sure of that, now. Even if there turned out to be no oil fields in France suitable for the purpose, there were certainly some in the New World territories that the English king had sold to Richelieu. The raw product could be shipped across the Atlantic and refined in a French coastal city.

"Five more minutes," he said. "Then load what you have on the pack horses, and set fire to the building. Let the rest of the documents burn with it."

After he went outside, he headed toward the corpse of the man who'd been in possession of the up-time rifle.

"Have you figured out who he was?" he asked the subaltern he'd left in charge.

"Yes, Marshal." The officer held up one of those elaborate leather contraptions that American men were said to use instead of simple purses. *Wallets*, they were called, if Turenne remembered correctly.

Flipping open one of the small leather sheets, the officer showed Turenne a portrait. Not a painted one, but what the up-timers called a photograph. It filled perhaps one-third of the small document it was attached to, with the rest being a simple block of text.

The marshal looked from the photograph to the body lying on the ground. The corpse had fallen face up. By some peculiar quirk, very little of the blood that had painted half the wall of the shed behind the man had splattered onto his face, so the features were readily visible.

The photograph was that of the corpse, clearly enough. Turenne scanned the text alongside the photograph. The meaning of much of it wasn't clear, but one item sprang immediately to his attention.

The man's name. *Quentin B. Underwood.*

Turenne drew in a sharp breath, almost a hiss. He recognized the name, from intelligence reports that Richelieu's *intendant* Servien had provided. An American, and one of those who had become quite prominent in manufacturing and financial circles. Estranged from most of the Grantvilliards, lately, and now attached to Wilhelm Wettin's party.

There would be political repercussions from this killing, obviously. But Turenne simply had no idea what they might be. He still found the inner workings of the political affairs of the United States of Europe often puzzling.

Mentally, he shrugged. Whatever the repercussions,

and however they might fall upon France, the man had been killed in the course of a military operation in which he'd been directly involved. He'd not been murdered; not been assassinated.

He looked now at the soldiers who were with the subaltern. One of them was holding an up-time rifle in his hands. The dead man's weapon, Turenne assumed.

"Were any of you directly involved?"

One of the soldiers lifted his chin. "Yes, Marshal. Me and"—a quick jab of the thumb at the man standing next to him—"Jules Lambert here, we shot him. Somebody else too, from the wounds, but I don't know who that was."

The soldier named Lambert was the one holding Underwood's rifle. He glared down at the corpse. "Fucking bastard killed François. We weren't even trying to shoot anybody any more, since they were all running away. Took us by surprise."

Turenne nodded. "Can either of you write?"

Both men looked dubious.

"Never mind, then. Just give your testimony to the subaltern here." To him, Turenne said, "Make up a report. It'll be something we can show the Americans, if need be, so keep it simple and factual. No rhetoric, you understand."

"Yes, Marshal. And what do you want done with the man's rifle?" The subaltern pointed to the up-time weapon in Lambert's hands.

There was a time when that rifle would have been almost invaluable. But that time was at least a year back, by now. Thibault and du Barry already had more than a dozen American guns in the workshop in Amiens. They didn't need another one, especially since this rifle looked to be a simple hunting weapon, and an old one at that.

"Was it your shot that killed him?" he asked Lambert. The soldier started to say something, then hesitated and looked at his mate. "Ah . . . hard to say, Marshal. Could have been either me or Édouard."

"The rifle's yours, then. I'll leave the two of you to decide how to divide it up." He gave them a smile. "I wouldn't advise sawing it in half, though. But you could certainly sell it and divide the money."

The two men looked at each other. Then Lambert hefted the rifle and studied it. "Better gun even than a Cardinal," he muttered. "Hate to sell it."

"Don't be foolish, Jules," said the other soldier. He stooped and plucked a small brass cylinder from the ground, lying not far from the corpse. "You have to have these to shoot the gun. Here, let me show you."

Édouard took the up-time rifle from his mate Lambert and operated the bolt, then showed him something that Turenne couldn't see from his vantage point. "See that?" the soldier demanded. "There's less than a handful left. Better to stick with a Cardinal. We'll sell it to some nobleman. Make a bundle."

Still smiling, Turenne walked off. Both soldiers were from rural areas, from their accents. The shrewd avarice of French country folk was a byword.

Shrewd in other ways than money, too. Turenne wondered by what happenstance a simple French cavalryman had become so familiar with up-time weapons. For a moment, he was tempted to go back and ask him.

But, he didn't. He knew the explanation would be

perfectly innocent—and incredibly tortuous. Three years had passed since the Ring of Fire. By now, knowledge of all sorts of things American had spread across Europe, following an untold number of pathways. That part of Europe, at least, that was west of the Vistula and north of the Pyrenees and the Balkans.

Turenne knew from Servien that part of the reason Richelieu had developed such a deep if grudging respect for the USE's prime minister was that Michael Stearns had never made any attempt to keep that American knowledge a secret, beyond a few specific items. It was a policy that looked foolish at first glance, but actually wasn't foolish at all.

First, because keeping it all a secret would have been impossible anyway. Leaving aside spying and outright theft, the prices people were often willing to pay for such knowledge and items were enormous. There were a lot of coffers in Europe, and many of them were very large—and Americans were no more saintly than anyone else.

And, second—the truly cunning aspect—was that Stearns understood something that Europe's rulers were only beginning to grasp. This part of what Servien had told Turenne, he'd said quite ruefully. Just as was true in many legends and folk tales, supping from a demon's broth was a dangerous business. Much of that American knowledge came with consequences attached. There was a political, social and economic reality lying beneath those alluring devices. It was impossible, often enough, to simply take the device and leave the reality behind. Willy-nilly, using those same untold number of pathways, Stearns was steadily forcing his opponents to cede ground. Not physical terrain, but the more insubstantial terrain of law and custom that was the ultimate battlefield.

It would be interesting to see how it all turned out. Turenne was still a very young man, so he'd have decades to observe the process—assuming, of course, he didn't get killed in one of the wars that were sure to accompany it. The truth was, although he generally kept it to himself, he didn't really care much any longer exactly what might result, so long as France was still there at the end.

Hearing a peculiar noise, he looked up. As the sound grew louder, his eyes looked for the source and soon found it.

He'd never seen one before, but it was what he'd been expecting. Had feared most, in fact, until the final moments when they launched the attack on the oil field.

Chapter 50

"They're trashing the whole place, Mike," Jesse's voice came over the speaker. *"There's a good two thousand of them. I think they're starting to pull out now. There's smoke everywhere. They're burning everything they can."*

Sighing, Mike lowered his head. "Can you get any sense of the casualties?"

"That's not too bad, from what I can tell. I think most people just ran off, rather than trying to put up a fight."

Mike didn't bother asking about Underwood. There was no way, even from a slow, low-flying Belle, that Jesse could see faces well enough to recognize anyone. He'd just have to hope that Quentin's stubbornness had given way soon enough to get him out of danger. Mike didn't like Underwood personally, but he didn't wish him any ill beyond political failure in the next election.

"Okay, Jesse, you may as well come on back."

"Give me a minute. They're all staring up at me, but I can't see any signs that anyone's getting ready to shoot. I want to take one really low pass, to see some more details."

"Jesse . . ." But Mike broke off the rest. Colonel Wood wasn't reckless. If Jesse thought it was safe to get within musket range, Mike wasn't going to second-guess him.

Seeing how low the airplane was coming this time, Turenne realized abruptly that he'd been so fascinated by watching the flying machine that he'd overlooked a simple duty. That was an *enemy* machine, after all.

But when he looked around, he saw at once that it was too late. All of his cavalrymen were mounted, and all of them were doing exactly what their commander had been doing: sitting in their saddles, staring up, their mouths half-open. Not more than one out of three even had a rifle in their hands any longer, most of them having scabbarded their Cardinals in preparation for the march.

On the other hand, Turenne's carelessness probably didn't matter anyway. Now that he'd finally had a chance to observe one of the fabled American aircraft in person, Turenne could see how much luck had been involved when the Danes shot down one of them in the battle at Wismar.

Luck—and the recklessness of the pilot himself, who'd flown directly at a warship with a company of marines mustered on deck and ready to fire a volley.

But this pilot had never given Turenne that chance, even if the marshal had been ready to take advantage of it. He'd stayed too high for muskets, and, even then, had never flown a straight path long enough for men on the ground to have been able to predict where his course might be intersected with a volley of musket balls.

And the thing was so *fast*. Turenne hadn't realized

that, at first, because of the airplane's altitude. But now
that the pilot was bringing it very low, the machine's
real speed was evident. Turenne had hunted birds with
a shotgun. He knew how difficult it was to track the
creatures and bring them down—and this plane was
coming faster than almost any bird could fly.

It swooped by, almost right over Turenne's head.
The marshal watched it go, off toward the Elbe.

"Mike, we've got a real problem on our hands."

Mike winced. "Yeah, no kidding. Our small petroleum industry just got a really big monkey wrench
tossed into it."

*"Worse than that, Mike. They couldn't really have
done that much damage to the oil field. We'll lose a
few weeks' production, that's all. Two months, tops."*

Mike's wince turned into an outright grimace. As
the air force commander, Jesse knew better than
almost anyone how tight the petroleum reserves were
for the campaign Gustav Adolf was about to launch.
They had enough in reserve to cover the needs of the
campaign itself, most likely. But the king of Sweden
had just had a lid placed on any further ambitions he
might have had. At least, if those ambitions required
anything that needed petroleum to operate on.

Which meant there had to be something *really*
bad on the way.

Sure enough:

*"They've got breechloaders, Mike. Carbines, I'm
pretty sure. Probably every damn one of them. I was
pretty sure they did, just from what I saw from higher
up. That's why I wanted to make that last low run. I
saw at least three of those cavalrymen reloading."*

Mike drew in a breath. "They might be flintlocks."

"Yeah, maybe. I couldn't see that much detail, of course. But I'm willing to bet you dollars for donuts that they're using percussion caps. Prepared cartridges, for damn sure, since no cavalryman wants to be fumbling with a powder flask. And whether they're flintlocks or percussion locks, Mike, there's no way in God's green earth those guns aren't rifled. I can't say I ever much cared for the French, but nobody ever accused them of being morons. Why bother with a smoothbore breechloader?"

Mike didn't doubt it himself. Which meant that if the French had been able to manufacture enough of those breechloaders to supply their whole army, one of the major technical advantages the USE had been counting on in the coming campaign had just vanished. Instead of being—by far—the best hand weapon on the field, the SRG rifled musket would be second-best. The French would have the same range, with the added advantage that their soldiers didn't need to stand up to reload.

"Thanks, Jesse. I'll get someone in there as fast as I can, to see what we can find out. In the meantime—I've already talked to him—General Torstensson is sending down three cavalry companies and a full regiment."

"You can tell him there's no point in sending the infantry regiment. He may as well keep them, with a battle looming. These guys are pulling out of here, Mike. The lead elements were already on the road by the time I got here. They'll be long gone before the cavalry arrives, much less the foot soldiers."

❖   ❖   ❖

After Jesse got off the air, Mike took another deep breath before he began a new round of radio calls. Gustav Adolf was not going to be a happy man.

After the plane finally disappeared, Turenne ordered the march to resume. He spent the rest of the day until they reached the bridge at Minden mulling over the airplane.

He came to two conclusions. The first was that, under the right circumstances, he was fairly certain that a large enough volley could bring down one of the aircraft, if it flew low enough. Muskets might even do it, but Turenne was sure that Thibault could figure out something better. Bombards of some sort, firing canister or perhaps grapeshot, that were specifically designed for the purpose.

The other conclusion was obvious. France *had* to get its own air force. Give it more than a few years, and no army without aircraft could possibly hope to win a war.

Turenne had never really understood that, until this raid. He'd read the reports compiled by French intelligence agents concerning the USE's use of airplanes in the fighting around Luebeck, of course. But, in truth, he hadn't been that impressed. The flying machines simply couldn't carry that great a load of munitions. Aside from the occasional lucky hit, they were more of a nuisance than anything else. The real damage they did was to the morale of the soldiers, since the pestiferous devices were so very hard to defend against.

After the past few days, Turenne understood how much he'd underestimated the things. True enough, as *weapons* they didn't amount to much. Not yet, at least. But he'd simply overlooked the monstrous advantage they provided an army in terms of reconnaissance.

Which should have been blindingly obvious from the beginning, especially to a cavalry officer like Turenne. Reconnaissance, after all, was one of the primary missions of cavalry.

By the end of the first day of the raid, Turenne had started peering nervously into the sky every few minutes. Realizing, finally, that all his plans could be wrecked by one airplane that flew overhead and spotted him. It wouldn't take any more than that. The aircraft didn't need to fire a single shot or drop so much as a stone or an empty bottle. All it had to do was pass along the word to the enemy's commanders—who, until the last day or two, could have gotten a large military force into position at the oil fields before Turenne arrived.

In the event, no enemy aircraft had made its appearance until it was too late to stymie the raid. The plane that came then hadn't even bothered to drop any of the small bombs it might have been carrying. Nor would there had been much point if it had, unless the pilot waited until the cavalry column had formed up. At the oil field, the men had been scattered into small groups. At most, a few small bombs couldn't have done more than injure or perhaps kill a few men. And what did that matter, really? There were always casualties in military operations, simply from accidents if nothing else. They'd suffered a few on this raid, even as smoothly as it had gone.

He'd given orders to maintain reconnaissance parties a bit farther out than he would have normally done, just in case the plane did come back. The signal would be three shots, fired in quick succession. That was probably an excessive precaution, but until he got more experience dealing with the flying machines, Turenne would rather err in that direction. Even without the outriders, he was pretty sure the machines made enough noise that his officers could disperse the column before the aircraft got close enough to bomb.

Bridges would be the trickiest places, of course, with nowhere to disperse. He could see that even two or three small bombs dropped on a column of men trapped on a bridge could be dangerous. Turenne decided to establish as new doctrine that soldiers crossing a bridge should always leave a wide space between the units, just in case an airplane appeared. That'd be something of a nuisance, and not always possible in any event. But anywhere within range of enemy aircraft, a nuisance worth tolerating.

What *was* their range, anyway? He was fairly certain that information had been included in the intelligence reports, but he couldn't remember the details. He hadn't paid much attention to that, because he'd known he would be within range during the entire operation—and had ignored the issue, because he'd assumed the enemy would concentrate the few aircraft they had near Luebeck.

And so, indeed, they had done. With hindsight, Turenne could now see that his luck had been mostly due to the fact that the enemy had so few aircraft to begin with. Literally, not more than a handful. With their resources so badly stretched, in that respect, they'd simply not bothered to devote any of them to patrolling so far southwest of the theater of operations.

A year from now, however—certainly two or three years from now—that would no longer be true. Once an enemy had enough aircraft, an army would have no choice but to assume at all times that its operations would always be under observation, unless it could match the enemy's aircraft with its own. The ability to operate unseen, at least much of the time, had been a central aspect to all military planning and generalship for millennia. Now, gone up in smoke!

The bridge at Minden finally came into sight. Even at a distance, it was obviously still under the control of Philippe de la Mothe-Houdancourt and his men. More than that, judging from the number of visible French soldiers. Jean de Gassion must have already returned from his feint at Hesse-Kassel.

The lead units of Turenne's cavalry force began cheering. But Turenne did not participate. He was glaring at the bridge, calculating how many men he could send across at a time.

"We have *got* to get our own air force," he muttered.

That evening, in the tavern at Minden that de la Mothe-Houdancourt had set up as their operational headquarters, Turenne was finally able to get full reports from all of his lieutenants.

"One of my men went missing entirely," reported one of the junior officers. "I have no idea what happened to him."

That turned out to be the only case of a man missing in action, in the end. Several killed and wounded.

It was unfortunate, of course. Not so much the absence of the man, as the absence of his carbine. Most likely, the enemy already had possession of one of the Cardinals. It wouldn't be long at all before they started duplicating the weapon.

But Turenne had never thought he could keep it a secret, anyway, once the weapon was used in operations. It was simply impossible to put together in one place thousands of energetic and aggressive young men without *something* going wrong. You couldn't do it even in big markets and trade fairs, much less on military campaigns. Only idiot fat generals like the ones claiming to lead the war from the comfort of the Louvre—most of whom hadn't seen combat in years, even decades—could contemplate such nonsense.

As it happened, the missing man's horse had thrown him during the raid, startled by one of the refinery's pots exploding. The French cavalryman had the bad luck to suffer a concussion as well as a broken arm.

Nothing worse than that, in the end. Bad luck had been followed by good luck, when the fire spreading from the pot hadn't moved in his direction. But by the time he recovered consciousness, not only had his own horse run off but he discovered he'd been left behind by the rest of the expedition. Apparently, no one had witnessed the accident.

So, more bad luck. But, again, followed by good luck. The soldiers who found him and took him prisoner turned out to be from a Hessian unit. They'd suffered no casualties at all from the marshal's raid, so they weren't in a particularly foul mood. A couple of mild butt-strokes, more as a matter of principle than passion, was all the cavalryman suffered beyond the broken arm itself.

Not so bad, really. The cavalryman came from a farm family. Who, like all such stock, were accustomed to the perils of farm work. One of his cousins had been killed simply plowing a field. Tripped, somehow, and gotten caught in the equipment the horse was pulling. His leg was so badly gashed he bled to death before he was found. His brother had lost three fingers; his father's shoulder had ached since he was fourteen; one of his uncles—

Why go on? Not the least of the reasons the man had joined the army was that it was generally safer work than farming.

He didn't give a single thought to the Cardinal. None of his business, that.

"You are overreacting, Michael," said the emperor. His tone of voice sounded completely calm. Mike didn't think that was an artifact of the radio, either. It was just the manner of Gustav Adolf. under pressure in a military situation.

Like millions of people, Mike had watched the Ken Burns documentary on the American Civil War, when it came out in 1990. He could remember being particularly struck by a comment made by the southern historian Shelby Foote, with regard to Ulysses Grant. He'd depicted Grant as one of those relatively rare generals who had "four o'clock in the morning courage." Even startled and caught by surprise, as he'd been at Shiloh, he'd remained unruffled and steady.

Gustav Adolf was another. As he'd shown less than three years earlier at Breitenfeld, when the entire

Saxon wing of his army had panicked and raced off the battlefield. The king of Sweden hadn't panicked at all—and had gone on to win the battle.

"I never expected we could maintain technological superiority everywhere," continued the emperor. *"Foolish to think so. And in this instance, I am quite sure that these new rifles are not in the possession of the forces that Torstensson and I are facing here. Not in significant numbers, at least. We have quite good intelligence in the enemy camps outside Luebeck, you know. There's been no report at all of anything beyond the usual muskets."*

There came an odd sound that Mike couldn't quite interpret. At a guess, Gustav Adolf had cleared his throat.

"I will admit—privately, and if you tell Axel I said so I will deny it vigorously—that the Committees of Correspondence have their uses. The point is, Michael, that while a sparrow may fall unnoticed in those enemy lines a short distance from here, I can assure you that no brilliantly designed new muskets could possibly do so. Flintlocks, percussion locks, it is irrelevant. They are not there, except possibly a few in the hands of officers."

Mike didn't doubt it. The ability of the CoCs to serve the USE as an informal intelligence agency was often uncanny, even when it came to purely military intelligence. That was usually because, quite unlike regular spy services with their limited funds, the CoCs could enlist—at no cost—the enthusiastic participation of all sorts of people who could move amongst the soldiers in a seventeenth-century army without being noticed. Servants for the officers, laundresses and cooks for the soldiers, even sometimes outright prostitutes. If nothing else, there was always a ten-year-old boy willing to go on an adventure—and who would pay any attention to such, as he scampered about a military camp playing games with his fellows? Armies of this day and age were always accompanied by camp followers.

That still left the possibility that the French were on the verge of sending a large shipment of the new weapons to their forces outside Luebeck. But before Mike could raise the possibility, Gustav Adolf did himself.

"Yes, I realize the situation might change, within a week or two. Although I doubt it, actually. If the French had that sort of production underway, they'd never have allowed one cavalry expedition to give away the secret on the eve of a major battle. But it doesn't matter. There won't be anything left worth talking about of the Ostender fleet in Luebeck Bay after today. Admiral Simpson's flotilla has already entered the bay and is preparing to engage the enemy. The Ostenders don't have one week left. They have one or two days. Three, at most. By tomorrow or the day after, the Danes will start pulling out of the siege lines. The French will have no choice but to follow. Watch and see if I'm not right."

Mike wasn't about to argue the matter. As the old saying went, his mama hadn't raised no fools. Granted, the advice Mike's mother had given him over the years hadn't included "and whatever else, you young scamp, don't argue military tactics with a general so famous he'll be remembered three and half centuries later." But she'd covered the basics, well enough.

"All right, Your Majesty. That does raise—"

"Yes, Michael, I know. Now that your timberclad has been repaired, what to do with it? Too late for the Achates to play any role in the Baltic, and while I might possibly have some use for it along the Elbe, it's not likely. Lennart has the French bastards trapped, now that he's cut their lines of retreat. They'll never get to the Elbe. Even if they do, I still have the five timberclads in Henderson's flotilla at Hamburg, if I need to use them.

"So go. You have my blessing. Try not to let the ship sink somewhere in the North Sea, would you? I don't want to have to listen to the admiral wailing and moaning about it."

Mike couldn't imagine John Chandler Simpson wailing and moaning about anything. Like most of Gustav Adolf's jests, this one was heavy-handed.

But he chuckled anyway. "London, here we come. Get me Melissa on the radio, please," he said to the radio operator. Doing his level best to sound as calm and unruffled as the man who, from time to time, he really didn't mind calling "Your Majesty."

Chapter 51

Luebeck Bay

The Bay of Luebeck was a dark blue sheet of polished marble, burnished with regular patterns of silver foam, sliding steadily north-northwest. The wind was brisker than it had been, and the visibility had cleared as SSIM *Constitution* led her squadron steadily south toward the city of Luebeck and the estuary of the Trave River.

It was chillier than it had been, too, Simpson reflected as he stood on the bridge wing once more, and the wind-over-deck generated by the ships' speed made it even chillier.

He looked astern, at the clouds of smoke belching from the timberclads' funnels, and wondered once more if he should have left them behind. It was a hard call. Steaming through the water as fast as their thrashing paddle wheels could drive them, they were making good a speed of almost thirteen knots. He couldn't drive them any faster than that, even under these relatively benign conditions, and the strain of maintaining that sort of speed was undoubtedly having its consequences in their engine rooms. Temperatures down there must be soaring, however brisk it might feel out here on the open bridge, and he was well aware that he was running the risk of severe injuries—possibly even *fatal* injuries—to his stokers and engine room personnel by driving them so hard.

Unfortunately, those two timberclads represented forty percent of his total carronade strength and a third of his total available hulls. He was going to need those guns—and those hulls—very shortly now.

His problem, like most problems war threw up, was fundamentally simple. It was the *solution* that was hard.

Colonel Woods' last reconnaissance report put the League of Ostend's naval strength in the Bay of Luebeck at thirty-plus men-of-war. Any one of Simpson's vessels should be able to demolish any seventeenth-century warship in no more than a few broadsides. What had happened to *Railleuse* constituted a sort of practical field test proof of that assumption. And, every one of Simpson's vessels was much faster—probably three times as fast, even the timberclads, under these weather conditions—than any of the League's ships could possibly be. The problem was that there were at least *five* times as many League ships as Simpson had, even with the timberclads. If they did the smart thing and scattered and ran for it the instant he arrived on the scene, he'd need as many weapons platforms as he could get his hands on just to chase them down. And he'd *also* need as many hours of daylight as he could get in which to accomplish the aforesaid chasing down, which meant he had to get there as quickly as he could.

On the other hand, he thought moodily, looking at the dark pillars of smoke coming along at the end of his line, *there's the little problem of smoke*.

The funnel smoke from *Achilles* and *Ajax* had to be visible for miles. The squadron had certainly outrun any Danish or French vessels that might have sighted them and tried to take warning to Luebeck. Unless Captain Admiral Overgaard's lookouts were blind, however, they were going to spot that smoke well before the squadron's ships themselves ever became visible. And unless Captain Admiral Overgaard was a complete and total idiot (which, manifestly, he was not), the instant anyone reported smoke rising out of the water somewhere to the north of him, he would know exactly what must be coming toward him from just over the horizon. Admittedly, he might not know exact numbers, and his estimate of Simpson's vessels' capabilities was undoubtedly problematical, at best. Aage Overgaard, however, had already been the recipient of several unpleasant surprises, courtesy of Gustav Adolf's former up-timer allies and current up-timer subjects. He was unlikely simply to sit around waiting for the next unpleasant surprise to be visited upon him.

What was it Clausewitz said? "In war, everything is very simple, but even the simplest things are very difficult," or something like that.

Well, he'd made up his mind, and one thing he'd learned long ago. Once you'd committed yourself to a course of action, trying to change course in the middle of things was a sure path to disaster.

So stop worrying about the damn smoke clouds, John, he told himself sternly.

Sure, no problem, himself replied sarcastically.

✦   ✦   ✦

"What's this all about, Jerome?" Captain Alain Lacrosse demanded testily as he stepped on to *Justine's* poop deck. The fifty-four-gun ship, one of only four French vessels still attached to the allied fleet off Luebeck, now that *Railleuse* had finally been allowed to escape, had been stationed quite a bit farther to leeward than the main body of that fleet. She was there specifically to maintain a lookout for likely threats, and Lacrosse's own standing order to his officers was that he was to be informed whenever such a threat might have been detected, but that made him no happier about the interruption of his lunch.

"I'm not certain, Captain," Jerome Bouvier, his first lieutenant, replied. Then he pointed toward the north. "The lookouts spotted that about five minutes ago, sir."

Lacrosse followed Bouvier's pointing finger, and his eyebrows furrowed as he saw the dark smear on the horizon. For a moment, he thought it was cloud. But only for a moment.

"Smoke, you think, Jerome?"

"Yes, sir," Bouvier said rather grimly, and Lacrosse pursed his lips.

"Well," he said after a moment, "I doubt there are very many houses out there to catch fire."

"The same thought had occurred to me, sir."

"In that case, I suppose we should inform the captain admiral. See to it, please."

"At once, sir."

Lacrosse watched as Bouvier began giving orders to the signal party. That was a new innovation, the handi-work of King Christian—and an innovation that had caused Lacrosse, unlike some of his fellow Frenchmen, to reconsider the notion that the king of Denmark was simply one more drunken sot.

So far as Lacrosse knew, no one outside the so-called "United States of Europe" actually had any real idea of how the mysterious up-timer "radio" worked. What they did know was that it had afforded the Americans and their allies an enormous advantage, time and again . . . and that it was an advantage *they* couldn't duplicate yet. King Christian, on the other hand, had decided to see what he might be able to come up with instead of radio, and one of his better investments had been in a book—a history book, even if much of the "history" it recounted had not yet happened—about the development of pre-radio means of communication. It had contained the details of something called "telegraphs" and "Morse code," and also a copy of the "international signal flags" and a technique for sending messages using "semaphore flags."

Several of Lacrosse's fellow French captains had dismissed the notion's practicality—and value—with the disdain properly accorded to anything Christian might have suggested. Captain Admiral Overgaard, on the other hand, had not, and he had not only issued complete sets of the appropriate flags to all of the ships under his command but also insisted that those ships train in their use.

Which was why it was possible for Captain Alain Lacrosse to inform his commanding officer that he had spotted funnel smoke on the northern horizon much more quickly than anyone on the other side had anticipated that he might.

❖   ❖   ❖

"Recon One, this is Navy One."

"Navy One, Recon One," a voice replied from the speaker in *Constitution's* radio room.

"We're ready for your situation report, Recon One."

"Understood, Admiral Simpson," said Lieutenant Ernst Weissenbach, the aircraft's pilot. *"I make it thirty-one—repeat, three-one—warships,"* he continued. *"There are several smaller vessels around, too. Another half-dozen, but I think most of them are supply or support ships. They aren't in formation with the others, at any rate."*

"In formation?" Simpson repeated in a rather sharper tone. "What sort of formation?"

"They're forming into what looks like it's supposed to be a column," Weissenbach replied. *"They're about fifteen miles south of you, four miles north of the estuary, course about two-eight-three true."*

"You say they're *forming* into a column?"

"Yes, sir."

"And how long have they been doing so?"

"They started shifting formation probably ten or fifteen minutes ago, Admiral."

"I see." Simpson frowned and rubbed his forehead thoughtfully. "Wait one, Recon One," he said, and looked at Captain Halberstat.

"I think something new has been added, Franz," he said. Halberstat cocked his head to one side, clearly not seeing exactly where his admiral was headed, and Simpson snorted.

"Assuming Lieutenant Weissenbach has his time interval right, then they started shifting formation just about the time one of them might have seen the timberclads' smoke if he'd been maintaining a particularly sharp lookout. Which raises the interesting question of exactly how whoever might have spotted the smoke got the word to Overgaard—and Overgaard got his orders back to everyone *else*—fast enough for them already to be altering formation in response to our arrival."

Halberstat's lack of comprehension disappeared abruptly, and he swore softly in German.

"I beg your pardon, Admiral," he apologized a moment later. "But you're right. Signal flags, do you think?"

"Most likely," Simpson agreed. "Could be semaphore, I suppose, but it's not going to be signal lamps. Not for daylight signaling, at least."

"But surely the reconnaissance flights should have reported that they were practicing using signal flags, sir!"

"Only if they realized that was what was going on," Simpson countered. Halberstat looked incredulous, and the admiral shrugged.

"Oh, you're right, Franz. They have to have spent time training with them, especially if they're responding this quickly. And Colonel Woods' pilots probably have been overhead when they were doing it, too. The problem is that, so far as I know, none of the air force's pilots know a damned thing about ships or navies. That was a problem we had back up-time, as well. Someone familiar with our own signal processes, or simply aware that you just can't maneuver squadrons of ships that way without some means of quick communication, probably would have recognized what he was seeing. The air force didn't."

"How much difference to you expect it to make today, sir?" Halberstat asked.

"That, I don't know," Simpson admitted. "The fact

that they appear to be forming up to offer battle—and in line-of-battle, too, now that I think about it, which is a considerable improvement on the sort of mob/melee tactics most people around here use—would seem to indicate Overgaard plans to fight. In that respect, it could be a good thing. Trying to fight is going to require him to concentrate his ships where we can get at them, instead of having to chase them all down individually. On the other hand, if he decides the time has come to break off and run, he can probably pass a specific order to that effect quickly."

"To be honest, sir," Halberstat said with a some-what nasty smile, "I don't really expect most of his 'gallant allies' to wait around for any *orders* to break off. Not once they see what's going to happen to them, at any rate."

"You're probably right about that," Simpson con-ceded, then frowned thoughtfully.

"You know, Franz," he said slowly, "we don't have those nice, tall masts and sails they do. And at this range, both sides are still hull-down from one another."

"Sir?" Halberstat said, when the admiral paused. Simpson quirked an eyebrow, and the flag captain smiled. "You appear to have something . . . unpleasant in mind, sir."

"I was just thinking about the wind, Franz. If you were one of those captains, and you decided to break and run away, what heading would you choose?"

"In this wind?" Halberstat pursed his lips thought-fully for a moment, then shrugged. "Northeast, sir. Maybe north-northeast. I wouldn't want to get too far east, for fear we might be coordinating our attack with the speedboats at Wismar. And I wouldn't want to head west, for fear we—the enemy, that is—might pin me against the land."

"That's exactly what I was just thinking," Simpson agreed. "And it occurred to me, while I was thinking that, that *all* they can see of us right now is the timberclads' smoke. Smoke which the *ironclads* don't happen to emit."

He gazed at Halberstat for several seconds, watching the flag captain work through it himself. Then Halberstat's eyes lit in sudden understanding.

"Due east, were you thinking, Admiral? And with how many?"

"*United States* and *Monitor*, I think. And we'll slow our own rate of advance to give them more time to get into position, too."

"I agree, sir," Halberstat said.

"Good." Simpson nodded, then returned his attention to the radio and keyed the mike. "Recon One, Navy One. Thanks for being patient. I'd like you to keep a close eye on them for me. Let me know when they finish getting themselves into that column—assuming they do—and if any of them decide to break off or wander away on their own."

"*Understood, Navy One. We'll orbit and advise you of any changes.*"

"Thank you, Recon One. Navy One, out."

Simpson looked down at the signalman manning the radio.

"Get me Captain Bollendorf, please."

Captain Markus Bollendorf, *Monitor*'s CO, was senior to Captain Samuel Thackeray, who commanded *United States*.

"Yes, sir."

❖   ❖   ❖

Captain Admiral Aage Overgaard stood on the poop deck of his flagship, the fifty-gun Danish ship *Freja,* and glared up at the signal flags streaming from the main topsail yard. Those flags allowed him to exercise a tighter central control over a squadron of ships than had ever before been possible for anyone . . . except for the never-to-be-sufficiently-damned Americans. Who, of course, happened to be the people heading toward him from the north.

He was grateful for *Justine*'s report, of course. For that matter, Captain Lacrosse was one of the few French captains he'd been able to stomach. The man not only had a brain, he was actually willing to *use* it, and he never gave Overgaard the impression that his nostrils had detected something that had been dead for several days when he arrived aboard *Freja* for a conference.

Of course, even Martignac is better than the damned English, Overgaard told himself. *On the other hand, the English aren't the ones playing puppetmaster. In fact, judging from reports about their king's idiocy, they're even more inept puppets for Richelieu than we are! Which,* he conceded, *takes some doing.*

He grimaced at the thought, then squared his shoulders and lowered his eyes to the smoke blurring the hard, blue horizon. The morning's mistiness had disappeared, for which he supposed he ought to be at least a little grateful. And he probably would have been, had he been less aware of how that improved visibility was going to help the Americans and—he spared a moment to glower up at the aircraft circling about his fleet—their damned flying spies.

What he really wanted to be doing was sailing in the opposite direction from that smoke just as quickly as he could go. In fact, if the king had paid any attention to Overgaard's advice, they would have withdrawn the blockading force from Luebeck Bay as soon as the reports that the "ironclads" were ready to depart from Magdeburg had been confirmed. Blockading the city—or trying to, at any rate—had made at least some sense, as long as the French army supposedly preparing to assail the city from the landward side was likely to do so before Gustav Adolf's half-tame Americans could sail to his relief, Overgaard supposed. Trying to maintain the blockade (such as it was, and what there was of it) made no sense at all, however, if his ships were even remotely as outclassed as he suspected they were.

Deep down inside somewhere, he shuddered as he remembered the merciless pattern of explosions marching through his anchored fleet when the American "scuba divers" managed to mine them from below. And the detachment that had been sent against Wismar had fared almost worse. In fact, its losses *had* been worse, as a proportion of its total strength, although it had also cost the Americans at least one of their airplanes and what had probably been their best speedboat. Despite what some people seemed to believe, Overgaard had come to the conclusion that the forces protecting Wismar had been hastily improvised out of whatever the Americans had been able to rush into the city quickly. If he'd had more naval strength available to him, he would have been tempted to press the attack on Wismar from the sea, if only to determine whether or not he was right about that.

But the important point at this particular moment was that whether the Wismar defense had been mounted by improvised forces or not, what was coming at Overgaard's command right now most definitely hadn't been improvised. It had been very carefully designed and built, and it was under the command of their Admiral Simpson. The name struck Overgaard's Swedish ear as outlandish, even after an entire winter spent with English captains and their subordinates flowing through his flagship. However peculiar it might sound, however, all of the reports he'd received, including those Richelieu's spies had deigned to share with him, agreed that Simpson was almost certainly the most competent of the up-timers as a military commander.

All of which helped to explain why Overgaard had no desire whatsoever to meet those ironclads in battle.

Unfortunately, his orders gave him very little choice. *Not, at least, until I've been able to determine that they represent a force too powerful for me to engage,* he reminded himself, and his eyes moved from the horizon to the signal party waiting to run up his next command.

It was probably bad form for an admiral to sail into battle already prepared to hoist the signal ordering his command to scatter and run, but Aage Overgaard intended to get no more people killed than he had to. He would carry out his orders to test the combat capabilities of the new warships, and then—

And then, he thought grimly, *I'll run like hell.*

Chapter 52

Commander Rudolph Klein stood on his timberclad's bridge and watched the weather-stained topsails rising steadily above the southern horizon. There were a lot of them, he noted, like a forest of worn canvas and spars.

He stepped to the rear of the bridge and looked aft through one of the vision slits. Commander Mülbers' *Ajax* steamed steadily along in the wake of his own *Achilles*. The thumping and thrashing of *Achilles'* big paddle wheel in its heavily timbered well vibrated through the deck under his feet, but it was less jarring than it had been, thanks to the reduction in speed Admiral Simpson had ordered when he shifted formation. The tall, ungainly, structure protecting the paddle wheel was the ugliest and clumsiest part of Klein's entire unlovely vessel's construction. It was also thin enough to make him nervous upon occasion. The paddle wheel, like a sailing ship's masts, was the *Achilles'* heel (Klein grimaced at the metaphor) of her design. Without it, she was dead in the water, the helpless hostage of wind and wave, not to mention enemy action. And its sheer size meant that it couldn't be as heavily protected as her broadside weapons, which meant it was more vulnerable, as well.

But not as vulnerable as those bastards are, he reminded himself, moving back to the front of the bridge and the steadily growing masts once more.

On the other hand, he hadn't expected for a moment to find *his* ship leading the squadron's attack. All of the original, preliminary planning had emphasized holding the timberclads back, letting the ironclads take the brunt of any initial embrace while Klein and Mülbers waited to "bat cleanup," as Admiral Simpson had put it.

Now, on the very brink of battle, the admiral had chosen to completely rearrange things. Rudolph Klein didn't like last-minute changes, especially not just before he took his ship into action for the very first time. Still, he had to admit that the deviousness of the admiral's thinking did appeal to him.

"Well, there they are, Jerome," Lacrosse observed as the USE warships finally appeared from their deck-level perspective, crawling over the horizon toward them.

"I see them, sir," Bouvier acknowledged. It was clear that *Justine*'s first lieutenant was doing his best to project a certain studied nonchalance, however unsuccessfully.

Lacrosse's lips twitched under his thin mustache at the thought, and he raised his heavy spyglass, peering through it at the oncoming vessels.

His temptation to smile faded as the glass brought them closer to hand. The lead ships didn't look at all like the sketches of the "ironclads" that their spies in Magdeburg had provided. In fact, what they looked

like were the so-called "timberclads," which was . . .
perplexing. All of the spies' reports agreed that the
ironclads were much better protected than the steam-
powered timberclads, and he would have anticipated
that a wise commander would have used his most
heavily protected ships first.

*Unless, of course, the wise commander in question
already knows that even his lightly protected ships aren't
in any particular danger,* he thought grimly. *And perhaps it does make sense, in a way. According to those
same spies, the timberclads have more of those short
guns—those "carronades." If Simpson is confident that
our guns can't hurt them, he might want to get the ones
with the heavier weight of broadside into action first.
Besides, the rumors indicate that the ironclads are probably faster. So maybe he wants to hold back his speediest
ships until he sees exactly how things work out.*

His thoughts didn't make him feel any happier, and
his mind ran back over the instructions the comte
de Martignac had very quietly given him for certain
contingencies. He hadn't cared for those orders at
the time, particularly not given the memory of what
had happened to their Dutch "allies" in the English
Channel last fall. Part of him still didn't care for them;
another part was beginning to consider how he might
best put them into effect.

"Any orders, sir?" Bouvier asked quietly.

"Not yet, Jerome." Lacrosse glanced to the south,
toward the fleet flagship. *Freja* held her position in
the rather clumsily formed line of battle, about a
third of the way back from *Justine*. Frankly, Lacrosse
was astonished that Overgaard's captains were managing to come as close to maintaining formation as

they were. It wasn't exactly something at which most navies' captains had much practice, after all. And it *would* have been nice, seeing that they'd managed to get into formation so well, if the looming battle had been one in which tactical formations were going to make very much difference.

"No, not yet," Lacrosse repeated very softly, under his breath.

"Navy One, Recon One," Weissenbach said. *"They're still holding formation, headed almost straight for you, Admiral."*

"Understood, Recon One. Thank you," Simpson replied, then left the radio room and climbed the short ladder to the conning tower, one deck level above. Halberstat looked at him as he stepped off the ladder, and he smiled thinly.

"According to Weissenbach, they're holding course and formation," he said. "For now, at least."

Halberstat returned his smile, then swung back to the forward vision slit, watching the timberclads' smoke swirl across the water ahead of him.

Simpson's formation change had put the remaining ironclads in line behind *Ajax* and *Achilles*, and Halberstat wondered if any of the League ships had actually spotted *Constitution* or *President* yet. Their lack of funnel smoke, coupled with the obscuration of the timberclads' smoke— not to mention the tendency of all that self-same smoke to attract the eye—made the odds no more than even that they had been sighted, he estimated.

Not that anyone would be overlooking them much longer, of course.

❖   ❖   ❖

"Sir, the masthead reports at least one more ship."

Lacrosse looked at Bouvier, arching one eyebrow, and the first lieutenant shrugged.

"We have a good man up there, sir. He says there's at least one ship—looks like the spies' sketches of the 'ironclads,' he says—following along behind the two we already knew about. And he *thinks* there's at least one more, coming along astern of that."

"Only one more?" Lacrosse murmured.

"That's what he says," Bouvier confirmed.

"Hmmm . . ." Lacrosse tugged on the tip of his nose thoughtfully. *Justine* was the third ship in Overgaard's formation, behind a pair of Swedish forty-gunners. That brought their lookouts close enough to the head of the somewhat ragged column to see the oncoming Americans fairly well. Certainly well enough to tell the difference between a timberclad and an ironclad, assuming the spies' sketches were even reasonably accurate. And, presumably, to get a reasonably accurate count, as well. But according to the spies, the Americans were supposed to have *four* ironclads ready for service, so where were the others?

Well, I suppose the most likely answer is that they didn't manage to get the monsters down the Elbe after all. They're supposed to be big bastards, and the reports of how they managed to set the damned river on fire certainly confirm they can make mistakes, just like anyone else. Maybe they underestimated problems and managed to put two of them aground somewhere. Hell, for that matter, maybe the damned Hamburgers actually managed to stop a couple of them!

The last possibility, Lacrosse admitted to himself,

was the one he found most attractive. After all, if the guns of Hamburg had managed to sink or disable an ironclad, maybe the guns of the blockade fleet could do the same thing.

However unlikely that outcome might be.

"If there are only two of them—the ironclads, I mean," he said to Bouvier, "that might explain why they don't have them in front. Especially if the timberclads have more guns to begin with."

Bouvier nodded, and Lacrosse shrugged.

"We should know something in about another fifteen minutes, I suppose," he said.

"Yes, sir. Shall we reduce sail?"

"Oh, I think not, Jerome." Lacrosse showed his teeth in a thin smile. "I believe I'd prefer to hang on to as much speed as we can instead of worrying about damage aloft."

Klein watched the range fall.

The closest ship was obviously Danish. Her guns were run out, and, as he watched, she altered course slightly to starboard, coming onto a northeasterly heading. She had more wind to work with than Captain Grosclaud's *Railleuse* had been able to count upon, and she got around more quickly, but he judged that her maximum speed couldn't be much more than four or five knots.

The turn also presented her port broadside to *Achilles*, and Klein felt his stomach muscles tighten involuntarily. Intellectually, he felt confident—well, *reasonably* confident—that his vessel's thick, wooden armor was proof against that ship's artillery. His emotions, however, were rather less certain of that.

"Pass the word to Lieutenant Gerhard," he said. "He may open fire when the range drops to one hundred yards."

"Lieutenant Gerhard can open fire at one hundred yards, aye, aye, sir!" the signalman on the voice pipes replied crisply.

"Helm," Klein continued, "come ten degrees to starboard."

"Interesting," Lacrosse murmured to himself.

Bouvier looked across at him, without speaking, but his curiosity showed in his eyes, and Lacrosse gave a slight shrug.

"If I were in command over there," he said, pointing with his chin at the leading American vessel, "I would have altered course to port, not starboard. With my speed advantage, I could easily have gotten around in front of *Monarch*. And I would have been better placed to cut the rest of us off, if we tried to break and run."

"I suppose we should be grateful for small favors, sir," Bouvier replied. "At the moment, however, I find that oddly difficult."

"Fire!"

His Danish Majesty's Ship *Monarch*'s portside vanished behind a thick, choking pall of smoke as her broadside thundered. The range was still a bit over a hundred yards, and most of her shots went comfortably wide of their target. At least one or two twelve-pounder round shot struck home, but without doing any noticeable damage.

Then *Achilles* fired back.

✧   ✧   ✧

"Mon Dieu!"

Lacrosse doubted Bouvier was even aware that he'd spoken aloud. Not that the captain blamed his subordinate for his shocked exclamation.

There were only six gun ports in the timberclad's broadside, compared to *Monarch*'s twenty. But whereas the few shots the Danish ship had managed to land had obviously bounced right off their target, the same could not be said of the return fire.

From *Justine*'s poop deck, it appeared that none of the American's fire had missed. And it certainly hadn't "bounced off," either. Instead, to Lacrosse's horror, the timberclad's massive projectiles smashed straight through *Monarch*'s timbers, buried themselves . . . and then exploded.

It was almost like hearing a double broadside. First there was the dull, ear-stunning thud of the firing guns; an instant later, came the oddly muffled, echoing thunder of the exploding shells. Huge splinters were blown out of *Monarch*'s side. More fragments—*large* fragments, individually visible even from Lacrosse's position—flew upward in lazy arcs that went spiraling outward until they plunged into the water in white feathers of foam. Smoke and flashes of flame erupted through the holes torn abruptly through the Danish ship's structure, and the French captain's blood ran chill as he contemplated the horrendous inferno explosions like that might ignite.

Monarch seemed to stagger under the blow, and then the second American ship slammed a second broadside into her. More jagged bits and pieces blasted out of her. Her mizzenmast staggered, then wobbled drunkenly. Somehow, it didn't quite come down . . . yet.

Smoke streamed from the Americans' gun ports, rolling steadily northward on the wind, and the lead ship's cannon—those "carronades" the spies had warned of—flashed fresh fire. It was preposterous for such heavy guns to fire so rapidly, but they managed quite handily, and *Monarch* literally began to disintegrate.

"I believe it's time to come hard to starboard, Jerome," Lacrosse heard himself say. The order was out of his mouth before he even realized he'd decided to speak, but he never contemplated changing his mind. Martignac had discussed exactly this contingency, after all.

"Yes, sir!"

Bouvier's fervent response made his own reaction to his orders abundantly clear, and he began snapping commands of his own.

I'm sorry, Captain Admiral Overgaard, Lacrosse thought, looking astern, *but it's time to save what we can from the wreck.*

Aage Overgaard swore with passionate inventiveness as his formation abruptly began shedding the vessels of his so-called "allies." He wasn't certain who'd turned away first, although he felt fairly confident that if he *had* been certain, it would have been a Frenchman. Not that it mattered. Once the first ship turned to flee, it would have taken the direct intervention of God Almighty to keep the others from following suit.

And for that matter, he told himself, fighting to get his fury under control, *what else could you expect them to do, Aage? In fact, it's what they* ought *to do.*

"Hoist the signal to scatter!" he snapped harshly. "New course, north-by-northeast."

❖   ❖   ❖

"Well, *that* didn't take very long, did it?" Admiral John Simpson murmured to himself, watching through his binoculars from *Constitution*'s open bridge as the League's column began to unravel. It was safe enough to stand out here in the open, at least for now, he reflected. None of Overgaard's ships were in a position to fire on *Constitution*, and none of them appeared to *want* to be, either.

Hard to blame them for that, he reflected. *There's absolutely no point in standing around and getting yourself blown out of the water when you can't even hurt the other side. Trying to fight wouldn't be showing guts, only stupidity.*

Achilles and *Ajax*'s first target was a broken ruin. In fact, Simpson was more than a little astonished that the Danish ship hadn't caught fire. Not that the lack of flames was going to make much difference to the broken wreck's ultimate fate. Wood reacted poorly to powerful explosions. Framing timbers, hull planking, masts . . . the very fabric of the vessel had shattered. Her port side was beaten in, as if it had been pounded with huge sledgehammers, and her decks were littered with dead and wounded.

"Alter course to port, Admiral?"

Simpson turned his head at the quiet question and found himself looking into Halberstat's steady gray eyes.

"No, Captain. Not yet, at any rate. Instruct Commander Klein to increase to ten knots. We'll circle around to the west and close the sack from behind."

❖   ❖   ❖

Overgaard watched in half-incredulous but vast relief as the preposterous USE vessels continued swinging around to the west.

Don't feel too grateful yet, Aage, he told himself. *They're devilishly fast. Even if you get a head start on them, they've probably got the speed to run you down. Unless, of course, you can keep away from them until dark, at least . . .*

The enemy's guns continued to bellow, and he felt his jaw clench as the ironclads began to fire, as well. The USE ships seemed to be moving more rapidly, and even from here he could hear those murderous shells exploding inside the hulls of his more laggard—or perhaps simply foolishly brave—warships.

He forced himself to turn around, look back. The timberclads' dense black funnel smoke merged with the dirty-gray clouds of powder smoke, billowing like some brimstone-born fog bank shot through with the lightning of muzzle flashes. At least two of his ships *were* on fire now, he noted grimly, and three more were obviously in severe distress. Under the circumstances—

"Fire!" Captain Markus Bollendorf barked, and SSIM *Monitor*'s starboard carronades thumped deafeningly.

Alain Lacrosse's head jerked around in sheer, shocked disbelief as the low, squat ironclad almost directly across *Justine*'s bows opened fire. The abrupt appearance of the enemy vessel stunned him. His attention—like that of every other man aboard his ship, a corner of his brain realized numbly—had been focused on the carnage astern of them, where the American timberclads and ironclads were now moving steadily in pursuit. The weight of their fire had been significantly reduced as they were forced to turn end-on to follow in the fleeing fleet's wake. That wasn't preventing them from scoring hits steadily, if not in enormous numbers, however, and they didn't *need* a lot of hits. Not when the accursed things kept exploding *inside* their targets!

But perhaps at least some of us should have been looking the other *way*, he thought with a clear sort of shock-induced detachment. *If we had, we might have noticed where the* other *ironclads had gotten to.*

The thought was still running through his brain when the first two eight-inch shells crashed into his command. One of them struck just to one side of *Justine*'s cutwater. It ripped into the cable tier and exploded deep inside the coiled heap of anchor hawsers, and a few, potentially deadly tendrils of smoke began to curl upward.

Lacrosse never noticed. He was still staring ahead, still trying to wrap his mind about what had happened, when the second shell streaked aft, somehow missing masts, spars, and rigging until it crashed directly into *Justine*'s poop deck.

The resultant explosion killed Jerome Bouvier, both helmsmen, and the sailing master. It did not kill Alain Lacrosse . . . but only because the shell itself had cut him cleanly in half before it detonated.

"It worked, Admiral!" Halberstat announced gleefully as he listened to Bollendorf's radio reports. "I never thought they'd get *that* close before anyone even saw them!"

"Neither did I, Franz," Simpson admitted.

The admiral tried to match his flag captain's jubilation, but it was hard. *Constitution* reeked of gunsmoke, despite the high-powered blowers he'd installed. She hadn't fired all that many shots, perhaps—certainly not for the amount of damage she'd inflicted—but each carronade shot spewed out truly extraordinary amounts of smoke.

And why are you thinking about that right now, John? he asked himself harshly. *Could it be to keep you from thinking about just how many dead and mangled men that "damage" represents?*

Perhaps it did. But whatever he might feel at the moment, it wasn't going to stop him from doing his duty.

"Let's get this over with, Franz." He'd thought his voice sounded completely calm, completely normal, but the expression in Halberstat's eyes told him that he hadn't. There was nothing he could do about that, and so he simply met the flag captain's gaze levelly.

"Take us in among them," he said.

"Aye, aye, sir," Halberstat acknowledged.

The flag captain turned to his helmsman, and Admiral John Chandler Simpson returned to his conning tower vision slit, gazing out into the hellish murk of gunsmoke and burning ships as his squadron closed to finish off its crippled, demoralized prey.

Please, Overgaard, he thought. *Please order your men to surrender before I have to kill them all.*

Chapter 53

London

Rita Simpson had been half-petrified that she wouldn't be able to pull it off. She'd always been a lousy actress, and she knew it. Leaving aside her one brief stab at amateur thespianism her sophomore year in college—what a disaster that had been!—there was the accumulated evidence of all those years as a kid and a teenager when her parents invariably saw through her fibs and lies while her brother Mike got away with everything.

But, by the time she got out from under the heavy staircase leading up to the White Tower's only entrance, she was in fact so thoroughly disgusted and angry that she had no trouble at all.

"You'll be lucky if you don't get an epidemic!" she snarled at Sir Francis Windebank. She half-turned and pointed a rigid finger at the staircase. More precisely, at the dark interior below the construction. "It's a cesspool in there! I don't care if the so-called toilets in the keep are completely inadequate for the number of soldiers you're billeting in it. They have *got* to

769

start using the latrines! It's insane to have them shitting right underneath the main entrance—no, I take that back! the *only* entrance—to their own lodgings. Are you all crazy? Do you have any idea how much bacteria that's generating?"

She lowered the Finger of Accusation and the hand that it belonged to—but only partway. As she was doing with her other hand, she kept it well away from her skirt. She still had hopes—faint hopes—that she might be able to salvage the garment. Her shoes, of course, were hopeless, and would have to be pitched into the moat. They were a cheap pair she'd bought yesterday from the Tower's saddler, though, not one of her good pairs.

"Look at me! I'm filthy! Just from going in there to set the bacteria monitors." Thankfully, she hadn't actually had to crawl at any point, which had been her other great fear. There was enough room under the staircase for her to move about in a half-crouch. Still, with an area that filthy—not to mention vile; gross; disgusting; nauseating—there was no way she could have managed the chore without bringing traces back out with her. An incredible stench, if nothing else.

The stench was bad enough that Windebank was trying to sidle away. But Rita would have none of it.

"No, you don't! Come here, Sir Francis!" She made an imperious and impatient gesture, waving at him to accompany her toward the stairs. "I want to show you the monitors, so you can make sure—I'm holding you responsible, sir!—that none of these idiots fiddle with them."

"Please, Lady Simpson," he murmured, raising his own hands. That was more in the way of a protective gesture than a protest. Just in case Rita might try to grab him and get his own fancy clothing filthy. "I assure you—"

"No, you don't, buster! *Look* at them." She'd reached the staircase and stooped over—careful to stay a couple of steps from where the real filth began—and once again pointed the Finger of Accusation. "You can see one of them from here. Not too easily, because it's dark, but you can see it. The other one, you'd have to go inside."

Reluctantly, Windebank followed, staying several steps behind. Now, he lowered his head in a very brief manner and began nodding vigorously. "Yes, yes, I see it."

That was pure nonsense, of course. Windebank couldn't possibly have spotted the package that Rita had affixed to one of the staircase's two main weight-bearing columns, not with that brief a glance. All the more so because Harry Lefferts' demolitions expert Gerd Whazzisname—and wait till she finally met the bastard personally and could give him a piece of her mind; him and Wild-Man Harry both!—had deliberately painted the things to make them hard to see in a dark place.

But it was good enough. She was so aggravated that she had to remind herself that the "bacteria monitors" were nothing of the sort, and she didn't *actually* want Windebank or anyone else looking at them closely.

"Fine, then," she muttered, coming away from the stairs again. "As I told you, they need to stay in place—undisturbed—for a full week. At that point, I'll have an accurate reading of how bad the situation is. But, in the meantime—station guards if you have to—nobody keeps using the place for an outhouse."

"Yes, Lady Simpson. Certainly. Not a problem."

He just wanted to get rid of her, obviously enough. But Rita was pretty sure she'd accomplished her goal, so she gave him a curt nod and began stalking off toward her quarters in St. Thomas' Tower.

Amazingly, it was done. What she'd labeled "Mission Impossible" when that maniac Lefferts had first proposed it, but would now label otherwise.

Mission Disgusting.

Mission Puke—no, best not dwell on that.

Mission Harry I Will Piss On Your Grave. That had a nice ring to it. She might even crap on the bastard's grave, she was so ticked off.

"See to it," Francis Windebank ordered the Lieutenant of the Tower, Sir Henry Langscarr, after the obnoxious American woman left. Langscarr served as Windebank's deputy, whenever the constable was not present in the Tower—which was most of the time, these days.

"Yes, Sir Francis. I will have to post guards, though."

Windebank frowned but said nothing. The mercenary companies that now made up most of the Tower's military force were as poorly disciplined as mercenaries usually were. He found it hard to imagine, himself, why any sane man would crawl into that horrid space to defecate when there were perfectly functional latrines not more than a minute's walk from the White Tower. But, surely, they did—giving proof yet again that Pope Gregory the Great and St. Thomas Aquinas had been correct in listing Sloth as one of the seven deadly sins.

"What is 'bakeria'?" Langscarr asked, as the two men walked away.

"I have no idea, Sir Henry. The woman's accent is wretched enough when she speaks English. I hate to think how she's mangling Latin. Something to do with disease."

"Ah." Langscarr's puzzled expression disappeared. Actually, he thought Sir Francis was being excessively harsh. Langscarr himself had found Lady Simpson quite pleasant to deal with, as a rule. Her behavior today had been untypical—not that he could blame her, given the circumstances.

More importantly, like many people who spent most of their time in the Tower, he'd come to respect the young American woman's medical knowledge. Even some of the mercenaries had started taking their injuries and ailments to her for healing. Whatever that mysterious bakeria was that her devices were monitoring, he was quite sure she knew what she was doing, even if she couldn't pronounce the Latin properly.

Or perhaps it was Greek. Hard to say. Her accent really was atrocious.

"You did good, hon," said her husband soothingly.

But he, too, held his hands up in that fending-off gesture. No loving embrace there, ha!

"I *stink*," Rita hissed at him.

"Well, yeah, you do," Tom allowed. "Reek to high heaven, in fact. But it's nothing a good long bath won't fix."

The dark expression on his wife's face didn't lighten a bit. "Yeah, right. A good long seventeenth-century plumbing so-called 'bath.'"

"Oh, come on, it isn't that bad."

She gave him a sweet-looking smile that would have looked appropriate on the face of a tarantula, if spiders could smile. "Really? In that case, I'm sure you won't mind scrubbing my back."

"Well . . ."

"She did it!" Harry exclaimed gleefully, slapping his hands together after he set the walkie-talkie down on the kitchen table. "I will be good goddamed."

"Probably," said Andrew Short. "Though not damned by the Almighty. But I'd recommend you keep your distance from Lady Simpson, once we're all piled into the boat. Or you'll likely find yourself swimming back to the Continent."

Harry grinned. "Yeah, I'll just bet she's spitting mad by now. But that's okay. Rita's like her brother Mike. They both got a temper—every Stearns I ever met does—but they don't actually hold grudges."

The two men who'd worked together to design and build the explosive devices Rita had placed under the White Tower's staircase were also smiling, in the way skilled craftsmen will when a difficult job is finished.

One skilled craftsman, rather—Gerd Fuhrmann, the wrecking crew's acknowledged demolitions expert. Jack Hayes, still only nineteen years old, had a natural aptitude for the work, not to mention an avid interest. But you couldn't really consider him more than a promising apprentice in the Art of Boom.

Despite his youth, he was the one member of the Hamilton-Short clan whom Gerd had deemed worth training. As tough as they undoubtedly were—the women, in their own way, as much as the men—the talents of the rest of the male members of the clan ran toward more personal forms of mayhem. You needed to have a finicky streak, working with explosives and incendiary materials. Jack was the only male member of the extended family who possessed that quality.

"That's it, then." Harry pulled out his chair and sat back down. "Two windfalls in a row, by damn. I didn't really think Gerd and Jack would be able to manage their job, either."

Fuhrmann shrugged. "You can thank Jack for that, really. The charges were straightforward enough, just like the ones that are sitting under the stairs of the White Tower. The real problem was the same. How do you plant the bloody things without being spotted?"

Gerd jabbed his thumb at the smallish young man sitting next to him, who was grinning with a combination of pride and embarrassment. "But he managed it, as neatly as you could ask for."

"It's because I look younger than my age," Hayes said modestly. "People don't think much of a youngster scampering where he shouldn't be."

Julie Mackay shook her head. "Naw, Jack, it's the freckles. I don't know what it is about freckles, but the minute people see 'em they figure the owner's an innocent fellow." She jabbed her own thumb at her husband, sitting next to her. "I can't tell you how many times I've seen that trick work for Alex. It's why I fell for him, prob'ly, until I learned what a devious mind lurked beneath. But by then, it was too late."

Alex Mackay arched his eyebrows but made no other comment. Not to Julie, at any rate. To Harry, he said, "Do keep in mind that if you set off those charges at the wrong time, a lot of innocent people are likely to be hurt. Killed, some of them. Deaths at the Tower, especially those of mercenary soldiers, won't matter. But killing a dozen civilians just going about their business is a different proposition altogether."

Harry looked smug. Gerd looked even smugger.

"Way ahead of you, Alex," said Lefferts. "Gerd and Jack planted a smoke bomb with the big charges."

"Stink bomb, too!" said Hayes. "It'll go off first, when we send the signal. Half a minute later, when the real bombs go off, you won't find anyone in the vicinity."

Mackay shook his head. "Instead of concocting spurious theories about freckles, people ought to be examining a true mystery. How is it that the same people obsessed with the crude business of blowing things up also have such twisted minds?"

"I had a warped childhood," said Fuhrmann.

"Stephen Hamilton is my uncle," was Jack's explanation. He gave his mentor a sly glance. "What's that American term, Gerd? 'You piker,' I think."

Stephen Hamilton shook his head. "No, lads, I'm firm on the matter. I'll accompany Darryl and Victoria into the Fens. Then, Scotland beyond. But I'll go alone. You and the rest of the family will go with Lady Mailey and Lady Simpson and their party, over to the Continent."

Given the nature of this subject, as opposed to some others, the senior female members of the family were present also, along with all the adult males. That was Isabel Short and Patricia Hayes. Isabel was the mother of Andrew and Victoria and their two surviving older brothers, William and John. Patricia was Isabel's half-sister, being the offspring of the same father, the now-deceased Henry Short, and his second wife Elizabeth. Her last name of Hayes came from her husband, Thomas Hayes, who'd been killed in an accident three years before.

Patricia had had four children by Thomas, all of whom had thankfully survived childhood. Their chances were good, now. Neddie, the oldest, was almost twenty-one years of age, and the youngest, Mary, had just turned twelve. In truth, Patricia was more worried about the health of her second-oldest child, Jack. Not from the danger of illness but from his new-found enthusiasm for explosives.

"You're certain about this, then?" asked John Short. He was the oldest of the three Short brothers, being almost forty. That gave him, along with Stephen Hamilton, the informal status of one of the two patriarchs of the little clan. In practice, it was normally the youngest of the three brothers who really exercised that function. That was due to Andrew's personality, which was more assertive and self-confident than those of his two older brothers. But for such a solemn matter as dividing the family, John's opinion and agreement were necessary.

Stephen Hamilton nodded. "Yes. It simply makes sense, John. We've all agreed, after discussing it at some length, that we'll accept his offer and enlist in Captain Lefferts' company once we make our escape. Formally speaking, that is, since for all that matters we've already done so. But the reality that remains is that the captain's military unit is really not well suited for families. Certainly not children."

Patricia made a face. "Tell that to my son!"

Andrew smiled. "The captain doesn't consider a nineteen-year-old lad to be a 'child,' Patricia. Neither do I, come down to it."

Isabel sniffed. "Sophistry, and you know it. Harry Lefferts wouldn't think twice about enlisting a twelve-year-old in his schemes if he saw a place for him."

"Or her," added John, chuckling, "and at the age of nine. Just last week I found out he'd put my little Mollie—Marian, as well—to the task of counting all the soldiers using the staircase below the White Tower in the early morning hours. Great fun, she thought it was. Marian, too. Those two girls! Whom their mother usually has to threaten with bodily harm to do any chores at all."

His brother William frowned. "I thought the only ones of us who'd ever met Captain Lefferts in person were Stephen, Andrew and Jack when they crossed over to Southwark."

John shrugged. "Oh, he didn't do it himself. Darryl was the go-between. But don't you doubt for a moment that the magic words were 'Captain Lefferts wants.' Mollie and Marian wouldn't normally do Darryl McCarthy's bidding any more than they do their mother's."

He turned his attention back to Hamilton. "But we interrupted you. Go on, Stephen."

Hamilton spread his hands. "For an occasional task, certainly, Captain Lefferts will employ a child. In fairness to the man, it won't be anything dangerous, as ruthless as he can be otherwise." The term "ruthless" was not spoken disparagingly. Rather the opposite, in fact.

"But as a rule, given the tasks his company gets

assigned, families would be a handicap. There's only one married couple in the entire unit, and they have no children. All of which comes down to this. The *official* duties of the captain's company include guarding the prime minister of the USE. And that's what most of our family will wind up doing. Staying in Magdeburg, not gadding all about Europe with the captain."

"But not you," said Patricia, eyeing her brother-in-law.

"No, not me," said Stephen Hamilton. "Jane and I had no children of our own. So there's really no reason I can't do a bit of the gadding about. And the captain asked me to. He's a bit concerned that the party which will be heading into the Fens and Scotland lacks a sufficient number of . . . ah, people."

That was the diplomatic way of putting it. What Harry Lefferts had actually said was: "*Stephen, there ain't no better rifle shot in the world than Julie, and her husband and my man Darryl are both solid guys. So's Gayle Mason, for that matter, even if she ain't a guy. And I got no reason to think otherwise of Cromwell. But the fact remains that they could really use a shooter. If you know what I mean. Not long-range, not stout-hearted, not any of that bullshit. Put a pistol in a man's face and blow his head off right now and not blink. That kind of shooter. I think they're going into a world of hurt and they'll need it.*"

He smiled a little, at the memory. Stephen Hamilton was coming to like Harry Lefferts, and he was a man who liked very few people. Perhaps that was because Harry reminded him of a younger version of himself.

He coughed, disguising the smile with his fist.

"Well . . . I should have said those are their official duties so long as Michael Stearns is the prime minister. It's quite unclear, actually, what will happen if Stearns loses that position. Knowing Captain Lefferts as I do now, I suspect the real allegiance is to the man, not the post."

"Oh, yes," murmured Andrew Short. He was smiling faintly also. Both men had come to the conclusion early on that they'd willingly exchange the formal security of their posts as Yeoman Warders for the considerably less stable positions of being—as the Americans might put it—"one of Harry's guys."

They were quite medieval themselves, in many ways, Stephen Hamilton and Andrew Short. Harry Lefferts commanded loyalty and trust from his people as naturally as he breathed, and one could only conclude that the same was true of the man he considered his own liege lord, Michael Stearns.

Stephen and Andrew had had their fill of overlords like King Charles and the earl of Cork and Sir Francis Windebank. They'd gladly trade them in for a very different sort, and leave the rest to Providence.

"So there it is," Hamilton concluded. "I'll go with them, the rest of you go across to the Continent. We'll see each other, soon enough."

The only clear memory Mike Stearns thought he'd ever retain of the *Achates'* voyage across the North Sea was that he was seasick the whole time. Whatever its other qualities, the shallow-draft, paddle-wheeled timberclad was a tub on the open sea.

No, he'd have two clear memories. The other was of Captain C.H. Baumgartner's lugubrious commentary.

"Blind luck the weather's holding up," he pointed out. "Sheer happenstance. This time of the year, a good channel gale would capsize us in a minute."

He made that statement on at least ten occasions, that Mike could recall. The first time, before they'd even finished casting off from the pier at Ritsenbuttel.

And that was among his cheerier comments. Some others were:

This thing was never designed for the open sea, you know. He's a fine man, the admiral, and a splendid commander. But an incorrigible optimist, all the same.

Very rough weather it has, the North Sea. Even seaworthy craft negotiate its waters at their peril.

Don't believe anyone who tells you drowning's a good way to die. Sheer nonsense. Your mind ruptures even before your lungs do. By the time life flees your body, your sanity's already gone.

Not too many sharks in these waters. But it hardly matters, with all the scavengers. Nothing but your bones will settle on the seafloor, you can be certain of that.

In between bouts of puking over the side and trying not to get pitched overboard in the process, Mike wondered where and when and how—most of all, *why?*—John Chandler Simpson had selected Baumgartner to be one of his ship captains. The miserable bastard could cast a pall of gloom over a wedding. Invite him to a christening, and all he'd talk about would be the baby's inevitable death. Of old age, if he was lucky—that would be accompanied by a long recitation of the ailments visited upon the elderly, in grisly detail—but more likely of some horrid childhood disease. Or an accident, as a teenager. Or syphilis, if he made it to his thirties.

If he'd had the strength, Mike would have strangled the captain and taken his chances in a court of law. Could you convict a nation's chief executive officer of mutiny for killing one of his own subordinates? He didn't think so. And a straightforward charge of homicide would fall flat on its face. Be laughed out of court, in fact, if he finagled himself a jury trial. Had history ever witnessed a clearer case of justifiable homicide? The jurors would carry him out of the courtroom on their shoulders.

His novel theories of jurisprudence would never be put to the test, however. Mike doubted if he could have strangled a mouse. Any good-sized rat would take him down, three falls out of three.

Baumgartner was a fountain of wisdom on that subject, too.

Oh, yes, the filthy creatures positively thrive here. God help a man who gets pitched on his head—which is easy to do, on this lubberly craft. If he lies unnoticed for more than five minutes, the rats will strip his flesh clean.

Mike would have been a lot better off if he'd accepted Captain Juan Hamers' offer to travel on his ship, one of the two merchant sailing vessels that were accompanying the paddle wheeler. Those vessels would carry off the people rescued from England. The timberclad's sole function was to serve as their bodyguard. Or bank robber, if might be better to say, with the merchant ships being the getaway vehicles.

But Mike had decided that would be unwise. Everyone knew that the real risk in crossing the North Sea, given the decent weather they were having, would be borne by the shallow-draft paddle wheeler alone.

Since he was the commander of the whole expedition, it would be bad for morale if he didn't go on the warship.

No, three clear memories. He'd also remember spending a fair amount of time, while puking over the side and trying not to get pitched overboard in the process, pondering a heretofore-unexamined philosophical problem.

Why was it that the expression "maintaining morale" was never applied to the *commander* of a military force?

Maybe he'd ask Gustav Adolf and John Chandler Simpson. If he survived the seasickness. He wasn't in the least bit worried about the other dangers of the expedition.

Then again, maybe he wouldn't. He had a dark suspicion—very dark; seasick heave your guts out dark—that they'd both just laugh at him.

Thomas Wentworth read the note one more time. Which was pointless, really, since by now he had it memorized. Perhaps some still-childlike part of his soul thought there might be some magic in the paper and ink itself, that would provide the answer for him.

From Samuel I, chapter 29, verse 10, this one:

> *Wherefore now rise up early in the morning with thy master's servants that are come with thee; and as soon as ye be up early in the morning, and have light, depart.*

He couldn't possibly be misreading it. So, finally, it was time to decide. Until this moment, he'd not had to do so. Not really. Thomas had been entirely a passive observer in the process, whose acquiescence had been simply a matter of silence rather than outright consent.

He still had no idea what the Americans were planning specifically. But he didn't have much doubt that, whatever their scheme, it had a good chance of succeeding. For all its formidable reputation, the Tower of London was by no means impossible to escape from. Several people had done so, over the centuries.

All of those escapes had had one feature in common—they'd had help both from inside and outside the fortress. They'd never been feats carried out by a prisoner on his own.

The help on the inside was now established. Somehow, the Americans had managed to suborn at least part of the Yeoman Warders. By what means, Thomas didn't know. It could be anything, from an offer of riches to simple personal allegiance, or any combination thereof.

That still left the help needed from the outside, but Thomas didn't have any doubt that would be there on the morrow. The people whom the crown of England had kept prisoner in St. Thomas' Tower were not friendless outlaws or despised heretics, after all. They were the embassy of a foreign power, and one which had great resources to draw upon. Whatever was going to happen tomorrow morning, he was quite sure it had been months in the planning.

So, finally, there was nothing left but the heart and soul of Thomas Wentworth, now the earl of Strafford. Was he prepared to go into exile? He'd be labeled a traitor, for a certainty—and this time, the charge would be very hard to deny. Given that his escape *would* involve colluding with a foreign and hostile nation.

He didn't know. He simply didn't know. He'd studied the message for hours, rather than tossing it into the fire as he'd done with all the others.

And he still didn't know. His mind seemed paralyzed.

He knew now that he'd go to bed not knowing. Toss through the night, and still not know come the morning. Thomas Wentworth had never felt so lost and helpless in his entire life. A man sure to a fault, who was now unsure of everything.

Chapter 54

London

"Here comes the barge," Anthony Leebrick murmured. He looked around the area from the small wharf on the south side of the Thames where they'd just finished setting up Julie's shooting bench. "And there's still no one about."

"'Cause they ain't crazy," said Julie. "The sun's just coming up. Damn, I'm cold."

She had her hands tucked into the pockets of her coat, to keep them warm. Unfortunately, it was a thin coat to begin with. She'd brought a heavier one to London, but it wasn't really suitable for good shooting.

However, she was mostly just grumbling to keep her nerves steady. She wasn't really worried that the early morning chill would affect her shooting. She wasn't *that* cold, after all—not to mention that her original plans, way back when, had been to compete for a position on the U.S. biathlon team in the Olympics. That meant skiing as well as shooting, and you didn't ski in mid-summer.

Alex was sitting on the bench next to her. Oddly,

given her husband's slender frame, Alex never seemed affected very much by low temperatures. Maybe because he'd been born and raised in Scotland, who knew? He not only had his hands out, he was holding the spotting scope, whose frame had to be downright icy.

His presence was a great comfort, though, more than enough to make up for the chill. Leaving aside all personal considerations, by now Alex had become the best spotter Julie had ever worked with.

Throughout, after that one glance around, Leebrick had kept his attention either on the barge slowly moving down the river or on the wharf directly across from them, right in front of the Tower of London. He'd leave it to Patrick and Liz, who were positioned ten yards back and to either side, to keep an eye out for awkward passers-by. Even if someone showed up, there shouldn't be any serious problems.

"Getting close to the wharf now, Julie," Leebrick said, still in that same soft and unhurried tone. "And Richard's got our own craft following not far behind."

A few seconds later, he added, "The gun crew's beginning to stir, it looks like."

Alex raised the scope to his eyes. "Indeed, they are. Get ready, love."

There were gun batteries on the Tower's wharf, but in time of peace they weren't normally manned at all. Since the mercenary companies took over handling the Tower's security from the Warders, however, they'd always maintained one gun crew on the wharf. Not for any practical purpose anyone could imagine, but simply as a means of mild punishment for miscreants. Spend a night shivering on the wharf instead of sleeping in a billet.

Needless to say, the gun crews always dozed off once enough time had passed after sundown for there to be no danger of an officer moving about on inspection. That posed a constant headache for the people in St. Thomas' Tower, because they couldn't extend the radio antenna out of the window until they were sure the gun crew wasn't paying attention. Sometimes that took long enough that they missed the evening window altogether.

But it was all about to come to an end. This night's gun crew was coming to life, finally, seeing a big barge approaching the wharf just as the dawn broke. The craft clearly intended to dock alongside. Right in front of the Traitor's Gate, in fact, with the bulk of St. Thomas' Tower looming above.

It had no business being there, certainly not at this time of day.

Julie brought the rifle into position. "Call it, Alex."

"Not yet. They're still just staring at the barge. Sluggish bastards. Take out the fellow with the plumed hat first. He's likely the sergeant."

Julie found him in the scope. "On your call."

"Just a bit longer."

Standing in the bow of the barge, Harry Lefferts gave the gun crew a cheery wave of the hand. That might hold them for another few seconds.

Not that he really cared. Not with Julie Mackay across the river.

Still, it'd be handy if they could finish tying up before the shit hit the fan.

He glanced back and saw that Matija and Paul had already hopped off the barge and were taking care of that. Now, he just had to wait until they cleared themselves off to the side. He didn't think the rubble from St. Thomas' Tower would hit the barge itself—although everyone on it was staying as far as they could to the stern or the bow, just in case—but it was sure and certain to land all over the wharf.

In the event, he didn't need to give the signal. The crack of Julie's rifle did it for him.

Harry didn't waste time looking to see if she'd hit her target. Or the next one—by the time he brought the walkie-talkie up to his lips, she'd fired a second round.

And Darryl didn't wait for him, either.

"I can't believe I'm doing this," Melissa Mailey hissed, crouched in the heavy stonework that held the machinery for the watergate below St. Thomas' Tower. All the members of the embassy were crouched there with her. Months ago, they'd decided that would provide them with a safe refuge from the blast.

Darryl McCarthy was the one nearest the entrance to the rest of the tower. He had an electrical detonating device in his hands and a truly disgusting grin plastered on his face. Melissa wasn't sure if the grin was because of the overall situation, which Darryl seemed to view as a great adventure, or the more specifically cheerful fact that the many weeks they'd had to delay their escape had had its side benefits. One of them being that, with the Shorts serving as the couriers and go-betweens, Darryl and Tom had been able to replace the primitive fuses they'd originally planned to use with much fancier mechanisms. Harry Lefferts seemed to be an endless cornucopia, when it came to anything that could wreak havoc and destruction.

Rita Simpson was crouched right next to her. "Never expected you'd wind up in a combat operation at your age, huh? Me neither, tell you the truth, and I'm still a spring chicken."

Melissa shook her head. "No, it's not that. It's—"

She heard a sharp cracking sound, coming from somewhere outside. That had to be a rifle shot. Glancing over, she saw that Darryl was already—

"Yee-*haaaaa!*" he shouted.

The noise was deafening. Even the heavy stonework seemed to shake.

Darryl was up and entering the main part of St. Thomas' Tower the instant the blast ended. "Oh, man!" she heard him shout. "You wanna talk about a beautiful sight!"

Melissa lowered her head. "I can't believe it. We just blew up the Tower of London." Her voice began to rise. "For God's sake, *it's a historical monument!*"

But Rita was already hauling her to her feet. "Come on, Melissa. Worry about it later. Besides, there's still plenty more blowing up to do."

"He still hasn't come out, Uncle," said Jack Hayes nervously.

Squatting next to him, in the shadows, Stephen Hamilton shrugged. "His problem, not ours. The stupid bastard was told not to shit under there."

He gave his young kin a look that was as sympathetic as anything Hamilton could manage. "I'll do it for you, if you'd rather."

Jack Hayes was still peering intently at the big

heavy wooden staircase that led up to the White Tower's second-floor entrance. The huge central keep of the Tower of London had been built more than six centuries earlier, and had been designed from the standpoint of early medieval warfare. Having only one entrance, and that one far above the ground, had undoubtedly made sense at the time. But once that staircase was destroyed, most of the Tower of London's mercenary soldiers would be trapped inside the keep, with no way to get out except a very risky jump or using a rope or jury-rigged ladder.

No harm would come to them, of course. Not, at least, so long as they stayed there. And they didn't even need to stay for all that long. Just long enough.

"No!" Jack suddenly exclaimed, almost yelling the word. His hands made an abrupt motion. The White Tower's staircase blew out at the upper corners and, a moment later, collapsed into a pile of wooden rubble. Thankfully for the sake of Jack's nerves, there was no sign of the corpse that had to be lying at the bottom of all that now.

It was the first time the nineteen-year-old had ever killed a man. Difficult, that was. Hamilton could remember his own first killing, which he'd done at a younger age and in a considerably messier manner. It had bothered him, even.

"You go with your uncle Andrew, remember," he told Jack. "He'll be in the dungeons."

Hamilton rose and hurried toward the Lieutenant's Lodging. The adult males of the family had been in position well before dawn. Now he could see the family's women already coming out, carrying their bundles, with the children following behind. Except for the one infant Griselda, who was being carried by her mother, all the children were carrying bundles also. Even little Jack and George were each carrying one—not very big, of course—toddling on their three-year-old legs.

For the past month, Sir Francis Windebank had ordered Cromwell guarded by mercenaries instead of Yeoman Warders. That had been just another of the many insults that, one piling on another, had led Andrew Short to return to that same dungeon. Not as a guard, but as a jailbreaker.

He was glad of it, now, though. He'd have found it very hard to kill Warders.

"There's an attack on the Tower!" Andrew shouted at the two soldiers, pointing back over his shoulder with his left hand. When their eyes followed, he drew his pistol and shot them both. Twice each. Their halberds clattered to the stone. One blade was chipped; the other, cushioned by landing on its owner's corpse.

All four shots had hit center mass. A bit below the ideal sniper's triangle, as Lefferts called it, but Andrew hadn't wanted to take the risk with an up-time pistol he still hadn't fired all that often. It didn't matter. The men were both dead, and it didn't take Andrew long to find the keys.

By the time he got the outer door open and was starting to work on the door to the actual cell, his nephew Jack had arrived. "Help me with these bolts, lad. There are a damn bloody lot of them, just to hold one man."

They got the ramp up to the great gaping hole that had been blown in the side of St. Thomas' Tower by the simple expedient of tossing up a rope. With one end of the rope attached to one end of the ramp and Tom Simpson pulling on the other end, there it was. Quick as that—all they had to do was help guide it and then anchor the bottom to the wharf. It took longer to muscle the damn thing out of the barge in the first place.

Melissa Mailey was the first one to appear at the top, hesitating as she looked down the very steep incline. Gutsy as she might be, she was still almost sixty years old, with the caution that had slowly seeped in over the years when it came to any sort of acrobatics. This was no shallow cruise ship ramp, either. It was more like a heavy ladder, pitched at no better than a forty-five degree angle.

She took her first awkward, gingerly step. Then retreated hastily, when she realized she'd have to go down backwards, as if she was using an actual ladder. She took her first awkward step in that pose, feeling behind her uncertainly for the first of the boards that had been nailed across the ramp to provide footing.

"Christ, this is gonna take forever," Harry muttered. He heard another shot from Julie's rifle, the first one since she'd killed the gun crew. That meant soldiers were starting to appear somewhere on the Outer Wall.

Tom Simpson's huge form appeared at the top of the ramp. The man was so big it was easy to forget he'd also been a top college athlete. More gracefully than Harry could have imagined, Tom eased himself down the ramp next to Melissa, picked her up in a fireman's carry—close enough, anyway—and had her down on the wharf in less than five seconds.

She only squawked once. Harry was impressed. Tough old bird.

As soon as the ramp was clear, Harry raced up. Don Ohde and Sherrilyn came behind him, moving more slowly since they were carrying rifles instead of pistols.

"Another one," said Alex Mackay. "No, two. To your left, by the Bell Tower."

Julie's aim shifted. Three seconds later, she fired. Three seconds later, fired again.

Neither Anthony nor Patrick was watching any longer for inconvenient passers-by, other than a quick glance every ten seconds or so. No need to, really. In Southwark, by now, any pedestrian who'd been ambling about in the vicinity was long gone.

But they'd probably have done the same, even if alertness had been necessary. Experienced soldiers both, they were simply too fascinated by what they were seeing. The concept of "marksmanship" was by no means unknown, in their day, to be sure. Some of Patrick's skirmishers were very good shots, with their rifled muskets.

But that was by a definition of "good shots" that now seemed as antiquated as the pharaohs. They'd heard the tales of the young American woman's ability to use a rifle, but hadn't really quite believed them.

They did, now. Reaching across an entire river, she was striking down any man who showed himself on the Outer Wall. Seven of them, all told, since she'd taken out the four men on the gun crew. She'd only missed once—and that was if you counted as a "miss" a man whose shoulder was shattered and was as surely out of the fray as if he'd been slain outright.

"Now, another. All the way over by the Well Tower."

A few more seconds passed, and the angel of death spread her wings again.

By the time Stephen Hamilton reached the entrance to the Lodging, all the women and children of the family were out and starting to pass through the gate into the Water Lane. And by then, of course—with two deafening explosions, one coming from the White Tower and one from St. Thomas' Tower—some of the Warders were coming out also.

Stephen stopped fifteen feet from the entrance and took out his pistol. One of the wonderful American automatic pistols, it was. Captain Lefferts had given one to him and one to Andrew, and then taken them out into the country a few weeks back to practice with the weapons.

The three Warders who'd come out included one of the other captains of the force, Charles Hardy. With his left hand, Hamilton pulled a small packet out of his coat pocket and tossed it to him.

"Here, you'll need this in a moment."

Confused, Hardy looked down at the object in his hand. "What's in it?"

"They're called sulfa drugs. I had Lady Simpson make up the packet for me. They're good for flesh wounds, keep them from getting infected. Just sprinkle the stuff on."

Hardy stared at him.

Hamilton made a face. "Sorry, Charles. But if you lads don't suffer any casualties at all, it'll look bad." He brought up the pistol and fired. Once, twice, thrice. All three Warders fell to the ground, yelling with shock and clutching their legs.

"They're just flesh wounds. Nasty ones, I admit. Remember—sprinkle the stuff on. Better do it quickly, too."

Hamilton left. Running now. He hadn't shot the three Warders in any hope that would stop the others from doing their duty. He'd simply done it out of a sense of duty of his own, as peculiar as others might think it to be.

The Bloody Tower, next. But when he arrived, he saw that John and William had already knifed the guard and were opening the door with the keys they'd found on him. So Stephen continued on, to check the progress with loading the family on the barge.

"Thank God I talked Windebank into letting her and the kids move into Wakefield Tower, last month, since he was hardly ever using it himself. I got no idea how we'd have gotten them out of the Lodging."

Harry listened to Rita Simpson with only part of his mind, as he peered across the walkway. "We'd have managed, somehow," he murmured. "Damn. I don't think the bastards are going to make it easy for us."

He'd hoped the officers quartered in Wakefield would have come to investigate the explosion right next door to them in St. Thomas' Tower, but no such luck. Cowards, sluggards, simply confused, it didn't make any difference. They'd have to blow their way in.

No problem. Sherrilyn and Don had taken positions to deal with anyone who tried to come into the Water Lane or showed up somewhere on the Inner Wall where Julie couldn't spot them. But their rifles wouldn't have been much use for this, anyway. And, in the meantime, George Sutherland and Paul Maczka had showed up.

Just in time, too. What seemed like a veritable flood of women and children had come up into St. Thomas' Tower and were making their way down the ramp to the wharf below. Felix and Darryl were helping them, while Matt stayed with the barge.

"Okay, guys," he said. "It's shotgun time and you're the two designated trolls." He pointed at the heavy door across the walkway. "Don't know if it's locked or not."

"What does it matter?" grunted Sutherland. "Just let me switch to slugs."

That didn't take long. Two blasts at close range into the door latch and it didn't matter if it had been locked or not. George's great bulk slammed against the door, and that was that. Harry wondered if he'd be able to sweet-talk Sutherland and Simpson into having an arm-wrestling match, just to pass the time as they crossed the North Sea.

Probably not a good idea, though. They might capsize the ship.

"Clear!" George bellowed from inside. Paul had already passed through, continuing into the next chamber. Harry heard him fire two rounds. At whatever, probably nothing. The sound alone, inside the stone walls of Wakefield, would be enough to stun anybody for a second or two.

"Clear!" Maczka shouted.

"Okay, Rita, let's go."

Once inside Wakefield, with George and Paul blasting their way ahead—they still hadn't actually shot anybody yet, since the Tower seemed to be deserted—Harry let Rita guide him.

"Here," she said, stopping at a door. "The poor woman's probably frightened out of her wits."

"Good thing I'm such a charmer then, huh?"

He rapped on the door with the butt of his fist. Not the one holding the pistol, of course.

"Mrs. Wentworth! Lady Strafford! Whatever! We're here to take you and your husband and your kids out of the Tower."

He thought he heard a whimpering sound. A kid, maybe. Other than that, nothing.

"Okay, let's try it again! If you and the kids aren't out here in ten seconds I'm going to come in and shoot every one of you deader'n doornails!"

"Harry!"

"Look, Rita, charm works in mysterious ways."

And so it proved. Perhaps five seconds later, the door opened and a terrified-looking young woman peered out.

Rita took it from there, pushing her way in. "Pay no attention to him, Elizabeth! But you do need to come, right now. No, don't take time to gather up anything. Just get the kids. Hi, Nan, how's tricks?"

A girl, maybe six or seven years old, barreled into Rita and clutched her. "Lady Simpson, I'm frightened! What's happening?"

"Everything's fine, sweetie. Where's—oh, there she is. Now where's William?"

"Here," came a squeaky little voice. A boy's face peeked from around a corner, staring at Harry as if he were an ogre.

"Well, come out, now! We've got to go."

The boy didn't budge, his eyes still fixed on Harry.

Rita turned her head and gave Harry a smile that would have looked good on a rattlesnake, if snakes could smile. "Why don't you just get lost, Captain Lefferts?

Go find an enemy somewhere you can practice your charm on. I'll handle this."

All things considered, that seemed like a good idea. Harry went to see what George and Paul were up to.

Blowing Wakefield Tower into pieces, it sounded like. They couldn't really manage that, of course, just with shotguns. The stonework looked downright ancient. Still, they were giving it their enthusiastic best.

Four soldiers appeared in the Water Lane, coming around the corner from Mint Street. Sherrilyn missed her first shot, cursed herself for buck fever, and took one of them down with her second. By then, Don Ohde was shooting too. The sole unscratched survivor vanished somewhere. The one who'd been wounded was slowly crawling his way back. From the amount of blood he was leaving behind, Sherrilyn didn't think he'd make it. But there was obviously no point in wasting a bullet on him.

Sherrilyn caught a glimpse of motion to her right. A body hurtled off the Outer Wall, just past Cradle Tower. The sharp sound of a distant rifle shot was followed by the much duller sound of the corpse landing on the stones below.

"She really is the best, isn't she?" Ohde said admiringly.

Cromwell wasted a few seconds snatching up one of the dead guard's halberds, then tossing it aside when he saw the badly chipped blade, in favor of the other. But Andrew didn't begrudge him the moment. If he'd been imprisoned under likely sentence of death for months, he'd probably have done the same. And his worst fear, that Cromwell wouldn't be able to move well after such a long confinement, proved to be unfounded. Darryl had told him that Cromwell was maintaining an exercise regimen, but Andrew had been skeptical.

"Quickly, now," he said, racing toward St. Thomas' Tower.

Tom Simpson had braced himself for the worst. Unfortunately, Windebank had left Laud under the guard of the Warders; figuring, presumably, that a short, dyspeptic and sixty-one year old archbishop posed no great threat of escaping, be the Warders still reliable or not.

Luckily, when he entered the Salt Tower and reached the chamber where Laud was held captive, he discovered that not only was there only one Warder on duty, but he knew him quite well. Michael Dunn, whose daughter Cecily had just barely managed to survive the winter, mostly due to Rita's medical care.

"Tom!" Dunn exclaimed. "What is the name of all that's holy is happening out there?"

The Warder was obviously not in the least bit suspicious, even though there was no logical reason for Tom to have entered the Salt Tower. Dunn's grip on his halberd was simply that of a man keeping a heavy weapon from toppling and hurting someone.

"Don't know, Michael. Some sort of robbery, I think."

Dunn frowned. "Robbery? But why—"

Tom's fist ended that. He sucker-punched the poor guy. Hit him pretty hard, too, although at least he'd been able to catch him while he fell and keep the halberd from gashing him.

Tom felt pretty guilty about the whole thing. But

nowhere nearly as guilty as he'd have felt if he'd had to kill a Warder.

There turned out to be a positive side to the whole thing, too. When Tom entered Laud's chambers to rescue him from captivity, he was in a peevish enough mood to handle the old man properly.

Red-faced and shrill, Laud protested and denounced him and flatly refused to go. So, Tom sucker-punched him too, and took him out over his shoulder.

"You *slugged* the archbishop of Canterbury?" Rita's mouth stayed wide open for seconds after she posed the question.

Grimacing, Tom passed Laud's still unconscious body over to Felix and Darryl, who'd get him down the ramp and into the barge.

"Yeah, 'fraid so. But look on the bright side, hon."

Her mouth gaped wider still. "There's a bright side to punching out the primate of your own church?"

"Sure is. I figure my chances of getting ordained as a priest just went down the tubes. Forget bishop."

Rita's jaw snapped shut. "Maybe you shoulda kicked him, too. Right in the nuts."

When they reached the gate that passed by the Bloody Tower, Cromwell stopped. "One moment, gentlemen." With no further ado, he hurried through the gate.

"What is he doing?" asked Jack.

Gritting his teeth, Andrew went after Cromwell. He didn't give Hayes an answer because he had no idea himself what the madman was doing.

He caught up with Cromwell just as he was going into the Bloody Tower.

"What do you think you're doing?" he demanded angrily.

Cromwell paused and looked down at Andrew. "I'm fairly certain Thomas Wentworth needs my assistance, right about now. Knowing the man as I do."

"And what if he does?" Andrew pointed back through the gate. "We need to get through St. Thomas' Tower and into the bloody barge!"

To his relief, he saw that Stephen Hamilton was coming through the gate.

"What the bloody hell is taking so long with Wentworth?" he half-shouted. "The soldiers'll be rallying any moment."

Cromwell nodded. "What I figured."

Hamilton glared at him. "And what are you doing here?"

"I believe I owe the man a debt, of sorts. Seeing as how I had him executed once, in another universe." And with that, Cromwell passed through the door.

Andrew stared at Hamilton. After a moment, with a rather odd look on his face, Stephen shrugged. "It makes sense, you know. If you look at it the right way."

"He just sits there. Won't move, won't say anything." William Short shook his head. "We haven't known what to do."

Cromwell moved around William and his brother, leaned the halberd against the fireplace, and came to face Wentworth. The earl of Strafford was slumped in a chair by the fireplace, looking very haggard, as if he'd barely slept that night. Which was probably the case, in fact.

"Thomas," Cromwell said gently. "Look at me."

Wentworth's eyes came up. Cromwell extended his hand.

"In how many worlds can you serve the same faithless king? Be it a hundred, Thomas—be it a thousand—he'll betray you in every one. Come, man. Let's try it a different way."

After a couple of seconds, hesitantly, Wentworth extended his own hand. Cromwell took it and drew him to his feet.

"Elizabeth," the earl of Strafford murmured. "My children."

"They're already on the barge," said Hamilton, who'd come into the chamber. "Now, let us *go.*"

They had to pass through gunfire on the way. But it was just matchlocks, fired at too great a range—and fired too hurriedly, at that. By now, the savage marksmanship of Donald and Sherrilyn had taken its toll on the Tower's mercenaries. And they all knew that to climb onto the Outer Wall was nothing but a death sentence.

"Okay, listen up, everybody!" Harry bellowed, once the barge cast loose and had gotten well out into the Thames. He pointed over his shoulder with a thumb. "Once we get out of London, we'll be coming alongside that small boat following us that none of you should be looking at right now even though I'm pointing to it myself. Just take my word for it. We'll do the switch then. So, Gayle—you and Oliver and Darryl and Vicky and Stephen make sure you're ready to go. Four people will be switching the other way, too."

He lowered his hand and planted it on his hip. Then, made a flourishing gesture with his other hand.

"For the moment, ladies and gents and kiddies, just relax and enjoy your cruise on the lovely Thames. The show is about to begin. Maestro Gerd, take it away!"

Melissa had been staring at the ruins they'd left behind of what had once been St. Thomas' Tower. Except for possibly the Bloody Tower and the White Tower, it had been the most famous part of the world-famous Tower of London. Her face seemed gaunt. Now, hearing Harry's last words, her head came snapping around.

"What are you talk—"

"And one!" cried Gerd gleefully, triggering the detonator. Less than a mile upstream, a goodly part of London Bridge was suddenly engulfed in smoke.

Melissa half-rose from her seat. "My God! *You blew up London Bridge!*"

"Nah," said Harry, waving his hand dismissively. "That's just the smoke bomb—"

"Stink bomb, too!" interjected Jack Hayes eagerly.

"—that we set off first. Make sure there's nobody around."

Melissa was just gaping at the sight of the bridge. Her face, pale by nature, now looked as white as a sheet.

After ten seconds or so, her head jerked, as if something had finally registered. "What do you mean—nobody around? Nobody around for *what?*"

Harry frowned at her. "What do you think? For when we—"

"And two!" Gerd cried gleefully, working the detonator again. In the distance, there seemed to be a much smaller puff of smoke emerging from within the larger cloud. Perhaps a second later, London Bridge—parts of it, rather—began collapsing into the river.

"*Actually* blow up the bridge," Harry concluded.

Sherrilyn began rocking her head back and forth. Then, started singing, in a rather pleasant mezzo-soprano but one that was noticeably off-key.

> "*London Bridge is falling down,*
> *Falling down, falling down,*
> *London Bridge is falling down,*
> *My fair Lady.*"

"I can't believe it, Harry!" Melissa shrieked. "*You blew up London Bridge!*"

"As a matter of fact, we didn't. We could've, but with all the people living in those shops on it we were afraid there'd be way too many casualties. So we just blew up some parts of it where nobody was living. Blew 'em up pretty good, too, so it'd look like we tried to drop the bridge but didn't quite manage to pull it off. Look, Ms. Mailey. I don't tell you how to do grammar, how's about you don't tell me how to do commando."

He pointed behind them. "We're on a barge that ain't exactly a speedboat, and we've got fifty miles to go, thereabouts, before we're in the clear. So, we need diversions. Keep the enemy confused. Make 'em think we're escaping a different way. First thing'll cross anybody's mind if you blow up London Bridge—or it looks like you tried to, anyway—is that you made your escape over to Southwark and you blew the bridge to stymie the pursuit. Which is the exact opposite of what we're actually doing. Especially when, just a short while later—"

He looked over to Gerd. "'Bout time, I'm thinking, huh?"

"And three!" whooped Gerd.

There was no loud noise, this time. Just what seemed to be a faint puff of smoke a considerable distance off, on the Southwark side of the Thames but a good ways to the west of the bridge.

Melissa squinted. "I can't see . . . what . . ."

"Just give it a minute. We didn't need no fancy big explosives for this one. Just some nice incendiaries. That great big honking idiot thatch roof will burn like nobody's business."

It took perhaps five seconds for the meaning of that to register on Melissa. By then, the first flames could be seen and she no longer seemed pale. She seemed positively translucent.

"You—you—you—"

She was actually gobbling, for just a moment there. But she rallied by seizing her hair in both hands.

"You burned down the Globe theater? You barbarian!"

Harry looked aggrieved. "Jeez, Ms. Mailey, ease up some, willya? It ain't like we're talking about Grauman's Chinese theater in Hollywood, you know."

"That was Shakespeare's theater, you—you—you—"

She was gobbling again.

"Yeah, well, and what of it?" said Harry, unimpressed. "Julie says the place was a dump and nobody seems to be able to agree who Shakespeare was in the first place. I *been* to Grauman's Chinese, Ms. Mailey. Seen Marilyn Monroe's handprints in the sidewalk with my own eyes."

"You burned down the Globe theater!"

Chapter 55

Luebeck

Colonel Nils Ekstrom didn't think he'd ever seen Gustav Adolf in this good a mood, not even after the birth of his daughter Kristina. Not in terms of sheer exuberance, at any rate. The king of Sweden and emperor of the United States of Europe was practically prancing on the walls of Luebeck.

"Ha! Ha!" he shouted, making gestures toward the Danish and French forces beginning to pull out of the siege lines surrounding Luebeck. Those gestures fell short of being technically obscene, but only because the emperor was too excited to take the time to shape them into anything coherent. But the spirit that infused them, as it did the tone of voice—he wasn't shouting anything too coherent, either—was completely and thoroughly derisive toward his opponents. If the enemy forces had been close enough, Nils suspected the emperor would have unlaced his trousers and urinated on them.

At the very moment that thought crossed the colonel's mind, the emperor *did* unlace his trousers. Unlaced them, shoved them down to his knees, turned around, bent over, and exposed his naked buttocks to the foe. That done, he pulled the trousers back up and gave Ekstrom a huge grin.

"Probably pointless, but who knows? Maybe that bastard de Valois is watching through an eyeglass."

Ekstrom wasn't quite sure how to respond. The protocol that governed discourse between a Swedish monarch and his subjects was less ornate than that favored in many kingdoms, but it was still fairly elaborate. Normally, that was a comfort for a man in the colonel's position, since it enabled him in a pinch to retreat into meaningless formalities. But nothing really seemed applicable to this particular display of royal prerogatives.

"Probably not, Your Majesty," seemed safe enough, though.

Gustav Adolf was still grinning as he laced back up the trousers. "No, I'm afraid not. That fat old bastard is probably squatting somewhere with his own trousers down, shitting all over the place. As well he should!"

The trousers restored to their proper condition, the emperor waved his hand in summons and began hurrying toward the stairs. "But come! Come! The radio room! There are orders to be given! Foes to smite! And smite again!"

He even broke into song, as they made their way down the stairs. No solemn hymn, either, of which Gustav Adolf had composed many for the Lutheran church. This seemed to be a pastiche that he was putting together on the spot. Most of it was from a well-known Swedish drinking song, but there were lines interspersed in English from something Ekstrom didn't recognize. Probably one of the American songs which he played on a peculiar device his daughter had sent him in December, as a gift in honor of Gustav Adolf's thirty-ninth birthday.

A "tape recorder," it was called, if Nils remembered correctly. He wasn't positive, though, because he tried to spend as little time as possible in the emperor's company whenever he used the device. Nils himself thought the music that emerged from it was hideously raucous. As a rule, the emperor had told him, he had much the same opinion—but he felt obliged to listen since Kristina had included some of her own favorite songs.

The emperor had quite a nice singing voice, actually, but it was still painful to listen to such musical bedlam. The portions from the drinking song came as a relief, for all that it was raucous in its own right. Extremely bawdy, too—but at least Ekstrom could make sense of it.

As it happened, the commander of the French forces outside Luebeck had been studying buttocks through an eyeglass. But they weren't the naked buttocks of a Swedish king, they were the still-trousered rear ends of thousand of Danish soldiers beginning their retreat back to Denmark.

"Those stinking Danes," snarled Charles de Valois, duc d'Angoulême, after he finished his study and returned to his headquarters. "Cowards!"

Standing toward the back of the tavern in the large inn that had served the duke of Angoulême as his headquarters over the course of the siege, one of his officers made very sure to keep his face expressionless. Months earlier, Jean-Baptiste Budes, comte de Guébriant, had begun coming to certain conclusions. As of today, he decided those conclusions could now be considered as firm.

His first conclusion—this one had actually become firm by the end of December—was that Charles de Valois was an ass. An old man with an unpleasant disposition, none too keen-witted with regard to anything, and particularly prone to stupidity when it came to military matters.

Of course the Danes were lifting the siege and returning to their defensive lines at the Danewerk. That wasn't cowardice, it was simply common sense. Now that the American admiral Simpson had shattered the blockade of Luebeck, how in the name of God did the duke of Angoulême think the siege *could* be maintained?—even leaving aside the not-small problem that the Swedish general Torstensson had brought an army north from Hamburg to relieve the siege. Even if Torstensson hadn't come, what difference would it make? How could any general with the sense of a goose think he could "besiege" a port when the enemy had control of the sea?

The real problem now was that army of Torstensson's, which had already reached Segeberg and thereby stood across the French line of retreat up the Trave. If d'Angoulême had had the sense of even a chicken, much less a goose, he would have ordered the French forces to begin their retreat before the Danish commander had done so. The Danes didn't have far to go, and they didn't have to worry about Torstensson intercepting them before they got back to Denmark.

It was a long way to France, and the way had just gotten a lot longer.

Jean-Baptiste's second conclusion was that, as much as he generally thought well of Cardinal Richelieu in political terms, France's effective ruler was woefully lacking when it came to providing the nation with military leadership. Unfortunately, Richelieu had a long history and habit of handing out military posts primarily for reasons having to do with France's internal—and seemingly interminable—political faction fights. In that sphere of combat, Richelieu was the master, no doubt of it. But the resultant damage to the French army could be severe.

In some instances, Richelieu's factional purposes wound up being beneficial. He'd appointed Charles de la Porte because he was Richelieu's cousin, for instance—but there was no question de la Porte was a good officer. Far more often, however, the results were insalubrious.

D'Angoulême was a case in point. French political factionalism was often closely tied to the influence wielded by the great families of the *princes légitimés*—the "legitimated princes" who amounted to royal bastards given official recognition, and were among the wealthiest and most powerful families in the French aristocracy. For years, Richelieu had maneuvered to crush the power of the Guise and Vendóme families. He'd done so, but his success had been due in large part to lavishly rewarding the other two great lines of the *princes légitimés*, the Angoulême and the Longueville.

A brilliant political maneuver, yes—but one of the side effects was that the French army laying siege to Luebeck had been given to Charles de Valois, a man whose principal qualification for high military command was that he was the bastard of King Charles IX. He was sixty-one years old but often seemed to think like an octogenarian. De Valois was firmly set in old ways of fighting wars; ways which might have made sense in the days of the wars of religion, but were now completely inadequate.

For d'Angoulême, as for most of France's top generals, war was essentially a matter of sieges. Capturing important cities and towns as part of the chess game of the factional struggles in France. The fact that the nearest major foreign war, for decades, had been the struggle between the Spanish crown and the Dutch rebels—a struggle in which, until the recent formation of the League of Ostend, the French had always sided with the Dutch—had simply reinforced that attitude. The struggle in the Netherlands was certainly a war of sieges, yes. But that was inevitable, given the nature of the terrain. It did not follow that a war fought on the open terrain of northern Europe was going to have the same characteristics.

Indeed, it most certainly didn't. Jean-Baptiste's friend Bernhard of Saxe-Weimar was openly derisive of the French military command. "Every other army in Europe," he'd pointed out to Jean-Baptiste, "tries to have as powerful a cavalry force as it does an infantry force. Why? Because the only way you can win battles on the open field is with cavalry."

He was right about that, Jean-Baptiste was pretty sure. Which would not be surprising, given that the youngest of the dukes of Saxe-Weimar was a veteran commander of the German wars. Unless you could mass enough artillery, as Gustav Adolf had managed to do at Breitenfeld, it was effectively impossible to shatter a large force of well-trained infantry on the field with other infantry. With pikes and muskets, it simply couldn't be done. What you *could* do, however, was use powerful cavalry forces on the flanks to drive off the enemy cavalry—at which point you could launch attacks on the great blocks of infantrymen from the rear or the flanks. The same tercio-style formations which were unbreakable when attacked from the front, were extremely fragile if attacked elsewhere.

But those were lessons that the duke of Angoulême had not only refused to learn, he'd even refused to study. What does a French prince need to learn from barbarous Germans and Swedes? War was siegecraft, and by God he'd come to lay siege to Luebeck—and any idiot knows that you fight a siege, on either side, with infantry and artillery.

So, France's army suffered from a severe shortage of cavalry units. The only powerful one that had been put together was Turenne's—and the enmity and animosity of the French military establishment to that young upstart was so intense that Richelieu had had no choice but to give him an independent command far distant from the main theater of war.

Being fair to Richelieu, Jean-Baptiste knew that the cardinal was aware of the problem, and had promoted a number of young officers in order to deal with it. But Turenne's appointment as a marshal had stirred up such a firestorm of protest that Richelieu had not been able to pursue the project as far as needed.

Which brought Jean-Baptiste Budes, the count of Guébriant, to his third firm conclusion.

He was himself an ass. A veritable idiot. An idiot twice over, in fact. Turenne had offered him a position in his small cavalry army, and Jean-Baptiste had declined.

The count of Guébriant had the normal ambition of any capable thirty-two year old officer, and he'd thought Turenne's forces would spend the whole war simply twiddling their thumbs.

Which, indeed, they might be. Jean-Baptiste was on cordial terms with Turenne, but they were not personally well acquainted, so he'd had little contact with the young marshal since the campaign at Luebeck began. He really had no idea what Turenne and his forces had been doing for the past few months. But at least Turenne wouldn't come out of the war with a major defeat on his record—and a major defeat was precisely what the situation looked like to Guébriant, here in northern Germany.

Then—twice an idiot!—he'd also declined Bernhard's offer to give him a commission in Saxe-Weimar's mercenary army defending the frontier in the Franche-Comté. Partly because Jean-Baptiste was reluctant to resign from the regular French forces, but mostly because his assessment was that Bernhard's army would not be playing a particularly glorious role in the war either.

Which, indeed, they probably wouldn't. But lack of glory, modest as it might be, was far superior to inglorious defeat.

"Cowards, I say! Cowards!" The duc d'Angoulême was still indulging himself in his denunciation of the Danes, which had now gone on for several minutes. Several more minutes in which an army of Germans led by the Swede Torstensson and armed with American military technology had closed still tighter the noose around the French army at Luebeck.

No, say better, inglorious and humiliating disaster.

✧   ✧   ✧

"Let the Danes go, Lennart," Gustav Adolf commanded over the radio. "You probably couldn't catch them anyway, but even if you could I'd still feel the same. At this point, I'm looking for a political settlement with Christian. Killing a lot of Danes for no good reason won't help that in the least. It's the French I care about now."

"Yes, Your Majesty. I can deal with the French."

"I want that French army crushed, Lennart. Defeated isn't good enough. I want it crushed. I want France—that bastard Richelieu—so thoroughly whipped that they'll hide in their holes for at least a year. Come next spring, I'll be giving John George of Saxony and that treacherous brother-in-law of mine in Brandenburg what they deserve—and I don't want to have to be watching over my shoulder for a French army coming, while I'm about it."

"Understood, Your Majesty. But I can't do anything about that cavalry force that overran the Wietze oil fields."

"No, of course not. But we've found out more about that. Turenne was in command, in turns out. A splendid commander, no question about it—but he's in very bad odor with the French high command. His success at Wietze combined with their humiliation here at Luebeck will tie the French army up in a faction fight that'll go on for . . . God knows how long. Nobody holds grudges like those arrogant French noblemen."

"True enough. Very well, Your Majesty. I'll be off to my work, then."

The Thames

"Just leave the boat," said Anthony Leebrick. "But make sure you tie it up properly, Richard. Adrift, it's likely to draw attention."

Towson gave him a look that was not filled with admiration. "Indeed. And what other sage advice do you have, O my captain? Make sure that I don't drive the wagon stark naked, shouting in every village we pass through that we're the ones who just carried out the biggest escape from the Tower of London in English history?"

Leebrick gave him a grin that was somewhat sheepish. "Well . . . point taken."

Gayle Mason, meanwhile, had been giving the wagon that Patrick Welch had brought out of the nearby village's stable a look that was even less admiring. "I thought Harry's coffers were the envy of Midas. He couldn't afford anything better than *this*?"

"Which is exactly why I'm riding one of the horses," Julie said. "No way I'm trusting my spine to that thing."

"Swell." Gayle gave the horses in question an equally skeptical examination. "But as I believe you know, 'Gayle Mason' and 'horseback' go together about as well as ham and—and—and—whatever. Not eggs. Maybe tofu. Or rutabagas."

Spotting the smile on Oliver Cromwell's face, Gayle asked him: "And what's so funny?" The expression on her face, however, removed the crossness of the words themselves. Now that she and Oliver had been able to spend some time together in person, the very peculiar quasi-romance that had developed over months of nothing but conversations on walkie-talkies seemed to be . . .

Coming along quite nicely, she thought. Still early days, of course.

"Actually, I think your Harry Lefferts is something of a genius at this work." Cromwell nodded toward the beat-up old wagon and the four nags that drew it. "This won't draw any attention at all. Not anywhere in the English countryside, and certainly not in the Fens."

Alex Mackay swung into the saddle of one of the other horses. Gayle thought there was something vaguely comical about the motion. He went into the saddle with all the ease and grace you'd expect from an experienced cavalry officer, of course. Much the way a champion motocross racer might climb onto a tricycle.

Those other horses weren't quite nags. Not quite. But she hoped they didn't pass any glue factories along the way, or the horses would head for it unerringly.

"All right, all right. Oliver—you too, Darryl—give me a hand loading the radio gear into this heap, will you?"

To Gayle's gratification, "give me a hand" meant that Oliver took one end of the heavy damn thing and Darryl took the other. To her was left the proper chore of giving orders.

"But be careful putting it into the wagon. Be very careful."

Cromwell grunted, as he helped lift the thing up to the wagon's bed. "Fragile, is it? You wouldn't think so."

"I'm not worried about the *radio*."

✧   ✧   ✧

By the time the *Achates* and its little flotilla reached the estuary of the Thames, Mike was starting to recover from his seasickness. So he was able to have an actual conversation with Greg Ferrara when the radio call came in, relayed from Amsterdam, instead of simply half-listening and being unable to speak in fear the effort would just make him vomit.

"Jesse freed up one of the Belles to fly me into the airfield at Wietze, Mike. By the time I got here, some of Hesse-Kassel's cavalrymen had already arrived and secured the area. What's left of it, anyway."

"How bad's the damage?"

"Well . . . in one sense, not all that bad. The French—it was Turenne in command, by the way; he left us a note—couldn't have carried enough in the way of explosives in a purely cavalry expedition to really demolish something like an oil field. So they didn't even try. They just wrecked or carried off as much equipment as they could and torched all the buildings."

"Turenne left us a *note*? Why?"

"That's part of the bad news, Mike. Quentin Underwood is dead. Shot by French soldiers. The gist of Turenne's note was an explanation that he was killed in the course of combat, and the French had no idea who he was until afterward. Turenne gives his word of honor that it was not an assassination and says he'll provide us with a full report later if we request it."

Mike took a deep breath, and let it out slowly. "Damn it. I was afraid of that. I tried to talk him into getting out, but . . ."

"Yeah, I know. Quentin Underwood. As pigheaded a man as any who ever lived."

"That he was. Where did Turenne leave the note?"

"He left it with one of his junior officers. The man showed up under a flag of truce early this morning, just a couple of hours before I got here. What do you want me to tell him?"

"Tell him we accept Marshal Turenne's explanation. No, better write a short note to that effect. But we'd appreciate it if he'd send us the report as soon as convenient. If for no other reason, because Quentin's family will want to know what happened."

"Okay, will do. But, Mike, the worst news isn't really what happened to the oil field. We'll lose a few weeks' production, but there's no permanent damage done. What matters a lot more is that we found a French soldier who'd gotten hurt in an accident and was left behind. More than that—we found his rifle. And Jesse's guess was right. It is a breechloader. In fact, it's basically just an American Sharps rifle from back in the middle of the nineteenth century."

There was a pause, on Ferrara's part, then, "Mike, I feel terrible about this. I really dropped the ball."

"Hey, look, Greg—"

"No, I mean I really dropped it big time. It's a percussion-cap design, Mike. The French somehow managed to mass produce production caps after I convinced everybody on our side it couldn't be done quickly enough for this war. On account of all the problems you have trying to work with fulminate of mercury."

"Yeah, I remember. So I guess the French were more willing to absorb a lot of casualties in their production force than—"

"Goddamit, Mike—I don't think they're using fulminate of mercury. I won't be sure until I get it into the lab, but I'm willing to bet they're using potassium chlorate."

Mike frowned. "I thought—"

"Yeah, yeah, I did think of it myself, back when. What I told you was that the production process would be way too complicated. But now that I'm looking at this . . . Oh, shit. I half-remember, now—now that it's too late—that I think you can probably make the stuff just by—"

From the way his voice was rising, it was obvious to Mike that Ferrara was on the edge of tears. "Greg! Stop it! For Christ's sake, man, you're a high school chemistry teacher who got the world dropped on your shoulders. We asked you to become a one-man military research and development team that would have employed thousands of people up-time and had a budget in the umpteen God-knows-how-many billions of dollars. You've worked miracles as it is. So, fine, maybe you dropped a stitch here. I'm just amazed you haven't dropped a hundred by now."

Mike broke off, giving Greg time to compose himself. A few seconds later, he continued. "It isn't the end of the world. So stop beating on yourself, will you? The way I look at it, the whole thing's just a salutary reminder to us not to drop the biggest stitch of all. And you want to know what that one is? It's the arrogant presumption that our side is the only one with any brains. We'll survive this one, well enough. We ever get in the habit of dropping the big stitch, our ass is grass. We *are* talking about the French, right? Correct me if I'm wrong, but aren't they the same people who produced Pasteur, the Curies, ah—hell, I can't remember—"

Ferrara's chuckle was quite audible. *"Oh, jeez, there's a whole slew of 'em, Mike. Cuvier, Berthelot, Becquerel—four generations of great physicists, in that family—Ampère, Foucault, Poincaré, the list goes on and on. If you include mathematicians and philosophers, you can start with René Descartes and Blaise Pascal—and let me tell you it feels really weird knowing they're both alive right now."*

"I rest my case. Just take a deep breath or three and relax, Greg. If they can make a Sharps, we ought to be able to catch up before too long. And they didn't make enough of them to make a qualitative difference in *this* war, so we've got the time. Right?"

When Ferrara spoke next, his tone was firm and resolute. *"Yes, we can. Damn right we can, in time for the next war."*

"That's assuming there's a 'next war' in the first place. Who knows? Maybe there will be and maybe there won't. Don't forget they're also the same nation that produced the Marquis de Lafayette and the Declaration of the Rights of Man and of the Citizen. Not all that far down the road from now, either, if you put it all in perspective. We're not trying to destroy France, Greg. We never were. We just want to hurry those folks along a bit, that's all."

"Yeah, you're right. Easy to forget sometimes, though, isn't it?"

Mike hesitated, not wanting to add another bruise to Ferrara's already battered spirit. But some things just had to be said, and damn the bruises.

"I've never forgotten it once, Greg," he said bluntly "That's what it's all about in the first place. The world doesn't need another fucking empire. They always come out of the mint looking bright and shiny, but the truth is they're a dime a dozen. The human race has been littering the landscape with them for thousands of years. The Mesopotamians alone must have produced a dozen, and nobody except specialists even remembers the names of more than a couple any longer. For every one that did some good, there were at least ten that were just pretentious garbage."

There was silence on the other end, for a moment. Then, quietly, Ferrara said, *"Okay, I'll sign off now. I've got things to do and you've got some of our people to rescue. But . . . ah, Mike . . ."*

"Yeah?"

"In case the chance never comes around again, I'd just like to tell you that I've been really glad, ever since it happened, that you came through the Ring of Fire with us. Most of us just floundered, but you were the one person who seemed made for this time and place."

Mike smiled. "Well, thanks. But you're forgetting Tom Stone, aren't you? Not to mention—talk about predestination—a certain gent by the name of Harry Lefferts."

"And there it is," said George Sutherland cheerfully. "The Tilbury fort. How d'you want it, Captain Lefferts? Scrambled or fried?"

Harry stood in the bow of the barge, his hands on his hips, gazing benignly upon the ramshackle old fort that had just come into view. "Aw, hell, those guys were friendly and polite when me and Don dropped by for a visit. I'd feel downright unneighborly if we went and ruined their day. As long as they don't mess with us, I figure we won't mess with them. Besides, we're getting low on munitions."

Melissa Mailey had seemed to be dozing off, but

her eyes popped wide open. "Oh, certainly. You need to save the stuff for more important work. Destroying Stonehenge. The Roman works at Bath. Better yet! I think we should sail back to London. You forgot to blow up Parliament. And as long as we're headed that way, we could hunt around and find the field at Runnymede. Plow it up and sow it with salt."

"Jeez, Ms. Mailey. How long are you gonna hold this grudge, anyway?"

Melissa's expression was dark, dark, dark. "They signed the Magna Carta a little over four hundred years ago. That seems about right."

Harry grinned. "I hate to be the one to break the news, but you aren't likely to live that long."

"You watch, young man. I'm starting an exercise regimen as soon as I get back. Eat nothing but healthy foods, too."

"Fine. *I* won't live that long."

"Won't do you any good. Might have, back up-time, but not here. Paracelsus and Nostradamus didn't die all that long ago, not to mention John Dee. I'll track down their disciples, find out how to raise the dead. If Dante were still alive, of course, I wouldn't bother. I'm sure I could talk him into adding a tenth level to the Inferno and immortalizing you for posterity."

Sitting on the deck next to her, Rita Simpson rolled her eyes. "Melissa, don't you think you're overreacting just a tad?"

"I most certainly am not. *He burned down the Globe theater!*"

Chapter 56

A field in Germany,
just south of the village of Ahrensbök

The most peculiar thing, thought Thorsten Engler, was
how magnificent a battle looked before it began. It was
a gigantic theatrical spectacle, with a cast numbering all
told something like fifty thousand men, complete with
precision marching, musical accompaniment, pennants
and banners flying, and horsemen galloping all over
carrying messages from commanders to subordinates.
Not even the wealthiest and most powerful emperor
of ancient Persia could have afforded to put on such
a spectacle for any purpose save the deadly one that
confronted them today.

Standing on the ground next to him—keeping a
certain distance from the horse—Eric Krenz planted
his hands on his hips and whistled softly.

"And will you *look* at that? Too bad we're not artists, eh, fellows? We could stay back here the whole
time and just paint the performance. Match deadly
brushes against fearsome canvas."

The crew of the nearest volley gun smiled. "Not

for the likes of us, Krenz," said the gunner, Olav Gjervan.

The volley gun battery had been positioned on a very slight rise on the southern side of the field, so they had a better view of the unfolding drama than most of the soldiers in either army. Gjervan pointed toward the center of the French army and said, "We'll be down there, soon enough, you watch. About all we'll be seeing are clouds of gunsmoke. What sort of stupid painting would that make?"

One of his mates grunted. That was Raymond Meincke, the crew's loader. "On the other hand, we'll have a better view of the real business. Guts spilled all over, rivers of blood, brains served up for the beetles."

Krenz made a face, but the two other crew members just responded with a little laugh. Meincke had a certain reputation. One of the up-time noncommissioned officers, Floyd Little, called him the regiment's "designated pessimist." His friend and fellow American sergeant John Dexter Ennis favored *Mr. Doom and Gloom*.

"Better make sure your ears are covered, Eric," said Gjervan, "seeing as how the helmets don't do it. Every crow in miles will have its eye on them."

That brought a much bigger laugh, even from Krenz himself. Eric had very big ears, it was just a fact. They were the frequent butt of rough humor, although usually along the lines of people wondering how a man with such big ears could somehow manage to not hear any order he found inconvenient.

Eric started to make a quip in response, but was cut off by the sound of a bugle. The USE's army had adopted that up-time version of a trumpet because it made a distinctive sound of its own, and one that couldn't be confused with the various horns being used by the enemy. For simpler commands, of course, they continued to use the fifes and drums that were common to most armies.

"Well, shit," said Krenz. "Looks like General Torstensson decided we'd make lousy artists. Here we go, boys."

That had been the order to advance. Thorsten turned his horse and began trotting down the line of the batteries' guns, making sure that every crew was following the signal. About halfway down he encountered Lieutenant Mark Reschly trotting his horse the other way, doing the same.

Since all the crews were going about their business properly, the two men took a moment to exchange a few words.

"I'm a little surprised the general's ordering an advance," said Thorsten. "I thought he'd have us keep this position." He made a little back-and-forth jerking motion with his head, indicating the surrounding terrain. "Here we've got the headwaters of the Trave anchoring our line on the right and the woods outside Ahrensbök on our left."

Mark smiled. "You'd make a good officer, Thorsten, as I've told you before. Sure you don't want a commission? I'm certain I can get you one. Ever since that mess crossing the Alster, Colonel Straley has had a very good opinion of you."

That *had* been a mess, when a hastily and poorly made bridge had collapsed. Thorsten had been able to get the men organized to deal with it quickly, though, and they'd only suffered two dead horses and

one man crippled. But he didn't really consider the
episode an indication of any special martial virtues on
his part. It was just a job that needed to be done,
and in truth he was a very good foreman. There was
nothing more to it than that.

Personally, Engler thought the real reason their
regiment's commander Len Straley had a good opinion
of him had far more to do with a personal situation
than anything involving the army. Stan Musial Wilson,
an up-time army sergeant who was the son of one of
Straley's close friends, had gotten very interested in a
German woman he'd encountered during their stay in
Hamburg. At Straley's diffident suggestion, Thorsten
had wound up becoming young Wilson's principal
adviser in the matter, which seemed to be developing
to everyone's satisfaction. He'd had a certain perspective on the situation, given that he'd faced it himself
from the other way around.

"No, thank you, Lieutenant. It's as I've told you
before. I'm only in the army for three years. After
that, I plan to become a psychologist. Germany's first
one, I think."

"As you wish," said Reschly. He pointed to the
field ahead of them. It widened out dramatically less
than thirty yards beyond, where the Trave—which
was more of a creek, here, not the river it was down
at Luebeck—made a sharp bend to the south. Once
the USE army moved past that point, it would be
entering a wide field instead of the narrow stretch
of clear land where Torstensson had first had it take
up position.

"Mind you, I'm just a lieutenant and not privy to
the general's plans. But I'm quite certain he's gotten

orders from the emperor to defeat the French here, not simply stand on the defensive. And to do that, he's got to get us some maneuvering room. Be nice, of course, if we could just stand where we are and let the French grind themselves up against us. But they're not that stupid, not even the duke of Angoulême."

Thorsten thought about it, for a moment, and then decided to play devil's advocate. Not out of any spirit of contrariness, but simply because he always found it very difficult not to ponder all sides of a problem once he got it into his head.

"Why not, Lieutenant? What I mean is, it doesn't matter whether the French are stupid or not. *They're* the ones—not us—who have to get somewhere. So why doesn't General Torstensson just stay on the defensive? If they try to move around us, we just move to block them. Sooner or later, they'd have to attack."

Reschly scratched his jaw. "Good point, in fact. I think the answer—though I'm not sure—is that the emperor wants this all done quickly. The sort of maneuvers and countermaneuvers you're talking about could take days, even as much as a week or two. And that brings up another problem, which is that we're getting low on supplies and the French have no supply lines at all. That means their army will have to start foraging almost immediately, and we'd probably have to follow suit soon enough, if the maneuvering took us very far from Luebeck. It'll still be some time before the TacRail units can catch up with us, even as fast as they work."

He cocked his head slightly, peering at Engler. "You're from a farm family, Sergeant Engler. You know better than most what 'foraging' really means."

Thorsten's jaws tightened a little. What it meant—at best—from a farmer's standpoint, was seeing his livestock and crops seized. Often enough, it also meant being killed and his womenfolk ravished. If they were lucky, the women would then be carried off as camp followers. If they weren't, their corpses would join those of their fathers and husbands and sons.

Farmers hated soldiers. It really didn't matter whose army they belonged to, even their own. Supposedly their own, rather—since from the standpoint of most farmers, as a rule, it hardly mattered. Let an army be badly beaten on a battlefield, and the survivors of the defeated side were likely to find themselves hunted if they couldn't reform their units. For a few miles, they'd be hunted down by the cavalry of the victors. Thereafter, by any farm villagers they ran across, who'd pursue them and murder them pitilessly.

"You see what I mean?" said Reschly. "The emperor plans to incorporate all of this area into the United States, even if he's never quite come out and said it in so many words. But you know it and I know it and probably even the local village idiots know it. So he'll not want the populace ravaged, and a quick decisive victory is the best way to make sure it doesn't happen."

Put that way, Thorsten could not only see the logic but he approved of it. The bugles blew again at that point, however, followed by the fifes and drums. He and Reschly fell silent for a while as they watched over the batteries' evolutions.

That went smoothly enough. The volunteer regiments of the new USE Army still didn't have much in the way of combat experience. But they'd been well trained, and trained for months—far more so than most armies of the day. So there were no major problems in simply carrying out a maneuver. How well they'd do once the fighting started, remained to be seen. But their morale was high and they were quite confident they'd do well. Thorsten thought so, himself.

A few minutes later, he asked Reschly another question. "They're putting us farther out on the flank than we usually go. Any idea why?"

In fact, the way Torstensson was ordering the formations, the three volley gun companies by now were almost at the very edge of his army's right flank. There were only a few units of skirmishers and a thin cavalry screen beyond them

Reschly sucked in a breath. His jaws weren't exactly clenched; but he had his teeth pressed together and his lips spread. It was an expression that was half-apprehensive and half-thoughtful.

"I'm guessing, Sergeant. But the way you break a big army on a battlefield is by tearing at their flanks with cavalry—and, unfortunately, we don't have enough cavalry for the purpose. We've got more than the French, but not enough. You really need to be able to hammer at them to manage it."

He closed his lips and blew the breath back out. "One of the problems, you know, with the way this army was created. We simply don't have enough mercenaries"—here he smiled almost gaily—"and we sure as hell don't have enough noblemen."

That was true enough too, once Thorsten thought about it. The regiments mainly drew their volunteers from the CoC strongholds. With some exceptions here and there, those were in the cities and big towns. Such recruits might have splendid morale and determination to fight, but it was just a fact that not too many of them were good horsemen. Not even most farmers were, really. Almost any man of the time had some familiarity with horses, including riding them. But there was a world of difference between being able to guide a stodgy cart-horse and being able to ride the sort of horses a cavalrymen needed, in the way they needed to be ridden, and using weapons at the same time.

Thorsten was rather unusual, that way. For whatever reason, he'd always had the knack with horses. Eric Krenz's attitude was on the opposite extreme, but the truth was that most soldiers in the regiments were a lot more like Krenz than they were like Engler.

Which meant—

He sucked in a breath of his own. "You think the general's going to use us up close, in a charge."

"Yes, I do," said Reschly. "And, yes, I know that's a real switch. We're mostly supposed to fend off cavalry, not substitute for them. But I'm pretty sure that's what Torstensson has in mind."

The French army had come to a halt, its commanders having apparently decided to stand on the defensive. Now, they seemed to be trying to get the big tercio-style formations on their left flank to wheel around and face the cavalry and volley gun regiments that Torstensson had kept moving farther and farther to the right.

It was still an incredible spectacle, but the sheer glory was fading from it rapidly. The tusked demon beneath was rising to the surface.

"They're not going to make it in time!" said Reschly, suddenly sounding excited and eager. He pointed at the French forces that were now less than half a mile away. "Look, they're too slow!"

He was right, Thorsten decided. Those bulky infantry formations were very hard to maneuver quickly. That was true even in a simple forward assault, much less the more difficult maneuver of trying to get them to square off to the flank. "Refuse the line," it was called. Gustav Adolf's Swedish army had managed to carry off the maneuver at Breitenfeld, thereby enabling them to fend off Tilly's assault long enough for the king of Sweden to bring his artillery to bear. But they'd been facing Tilly's slow-moving tercios, whereas a very large part of the training of the USE's new regiments had been designed to enable them to move quickly. As quickly, at least, as tightly formed infantry could.

Torstensson knew he was gambling, but he didn't think it a reckless one. From his position at the center of the USE army, he hadn't gotten as good a view of the ragged nature of the French left flank as a young lieutenant from the Moselle and a young sergeant from the Oberpfalz. But he hadn't needed it, either. He had far more experience at gauging battles than either Reschly or Engler—or a dozen of them put together, for that matter.

So, he'd keep the main body of the French army pinned with his infantry and artillery, and see if he could rout the enemy's left flank with a cavalry charge. More precisely, a charge of cavalrymen and the three volley gun companies he had in his force.

The only one of his subordinates who put up any sort of protest at all was Frank Jackson, and that wasn't so much of a protest as a cold-blooded observation.

"This is likely to get pretty rough on the volley gun crews, if the French don't break."

"Yes, it will," was Torstensson's reply. "But I haven't got enough cavalry for the purpose, and I think this maneuver will work because they'll be expecting regular light artillery. And if it comes down to it, I can afford to lose the volley guns, since the French have even less cavalry than I do."

Seeing the expression on Jackson's face, Torstensson gave him a thin smile. "Cold-blooded bastard, aren't I?"

After a moment, Frank shrugged. "The last war I was in was being run by a guy named Robert McNamara, who was even more cold-blooded than you are, General. The difference was, he didn't have a clue what he was doing."

Jean-Baptiste Budes, comte de Guébriant, wasn't giving any thought at all to the nature of the enemy's commanders. He was too busy cursing that of his own, under his breath. The evolution the French army was trying to carry out would have been difficult enough, under any conditions. Having as the commander of the left flank another one of Cardinal Richelieu's political appointments made it twice as hard. Jean-Baptiste didn't have any personal animus against Manassés de Pas, marquis de Feuquières, whom he'd found in person to be a pleasant and convivial sort of fellow. But the marquis was far more suited temperamentally to the life of a courtier than a cavalryman. He was just plain sluggish—and they were in a situation where quick reflexes were critical. Those enemy cavalry and flying artillery units were coming at them rapidly, and in very good order.

"So much for an undisciplined rabble, eh?" said his adjutant sarcastically, as he drew up his horse.

Guébriant scowled. Normally, he enjoyed Captain Gosling's dour Norman sense of humor, but today it grated a little. "They're *supposed* to be professional soldiers, Guilherme! Look at them! It's like herding geese."

Guilherme Gosling made a little placating and apologetic gesture. "Sorry. My quip was intended for the enemy." The gesture turned into a finger, pointing at the German forces moving to outflank them.

"Oh." Jean-Baptiste winced. "Yes. As I recall, the phrase the esteemed duke of Angoulême used last week was 'a mere militia.' They don't look like it, though, do they? What news from Feuquières?"

"He says he'll have the infantry units in place shortly."

Guébriant savored the term. It left a very acrid taste. "'Shortly.' How marvelously imprecise."

His lieutenant shrugged. "He *is* trying to move them along, Comte. The problem isn't so much the marquis as, well . . ."

"He surrounded himself with a gaggle of adjutants, not one of whom could find his ass in broad daylight, on a battlefield. Yes, I know." Guébriant was scowling fiercely. "Fine fellows in a salon in Paris, though, I have no doubt."

But there was no time for that, either. Jean-Baptiste pointed at the enemy's flying artillery units. They had fallen slightly behind the first line of cavalry, instead of moving to the front as they should have been. That was the only sign he'd seen yet of the insufficient experience of the enemy army. It was always hard to get light artillery to develop the iron nerve it took to set up at the very fore of a battle line. No point in having them anywhere else, though, since they could hardly fire through their own ranks.

By now, several of Guébriant's lieutenants had gathered around. "Pull together as many of our cavalry units as you can. We'll charge at once, while the enemy's artillery is still out of position."

"They've got somebody competent in charge over there," commented Torstensson. He lowered his eyeglass. "So now we'll find out just how good those volley gunners are. Have the buglers give the order."

Eric Krenz's face had been pale already, as he sat on the lead horse of the battery wagon. Now, hearing the command for *volley guns, forward,* it got paler still. Thorsten Engler almost managed a laugh. Not quite— since he might very well be dead in a few minutes.

"I *told* you," he hissed at Krenz as he swept by him. "*Flying* artillery."

He took up his position at the head of the batteries along with Lieutenant Reschly. The young officer from the Moselle already had his saber in hand and wasn't waving it so much as he was flourishing the weapon. It was all very dramatic.

Further down the line, Thorsten caught a glimpse of Colonel Straley doing the same thing.

Thorsten drew his own saber, feeling both awkward and foolish. It wasn't the sword that bothered him—it was just another tool, that's all, for a different purpose—but the need to pose histrionically with the damn thing. He was a *farmer,* for the love of God!

Just before the bugles blew again, though, he steadied his nerves. He even laughed. Caroline had described to him, in one of her letters, the manner in which Princess Kristina had finagled their way onto the army base.

Volley guns, charge!

So what a farmer might have found difficult, the count of Narnia managed quite easily. He flourished his own saber as splendidly as anyone could ask for and shouted "Forward, fellows!" loudly enough to be easily heard by all the gun crews in the company, and several of the ones in the companies on either side. Best of all, although he hadn't noticed himself, that sudden and impromptu laugh had been almost as loud. Steadied the men very nicely, it did.

"Forward, I say!"

Chapter 57

The count of Guébriant was astonished when he saw the enemy's cavalry peeling aside to let their flying artillery come forward. The maneuver itself was a standard one, of course, and they carried it out quite nicely. But they had to be insane to do it at this late stage. Jean-Baptiste's cavalry was already within a few hundred yards of their enemy. The USE artillery would be able to fire at most one volley before they'd be overwhelmed.

True, they'd be firing canister, and the French cavalry would suffer losses from that one volley. But there wouldn't even be that many casualties. As quickly as the enemy artillery was moving—they'd already almost gotten into position, he saw—those couldn't be anything more powerful than four-pounders.

Those thoughts came to him in chaotic fragments, though, and he didn't have time to consider the problem except on the half-instinctual basis of an experienced combat officer. Leading a cavalry charge was just about as insalubrious an activity as could be imagined, from the standpoint of careful and deliberate cogitation.

"En avant!" His own sword-flourishing was splendid, as you'd expect, and by now came to him as easily as breathing.

"Steady, fellows, steady!" Thorsten shouted, as he trotted down the line. "Don't pay any attention to them! Just do your job! You know how to do it!"

Thankfully, he didn't see any reason to maintain the silly sword-waving business, since he was now a few feet behind the volley gun crews. He did use the sword once, though, to point at a jittery-looking crewman who was glancing back and forth between the advancing enemy and the rear. The sword-thrusting gesture was a combination of an admonishment and a veiled threat.

"Stop worrying about them, Metzger! Pay attention to your job!"

Easy enough to say, of course. Thorsten had to struggle a bit himself not to just gape at the oncoming French. He was discovering—they all were—that what they'd been told in training was quite true. Cavalry charges are absolutely terrifying, if you let yourself dwell on them instead of concentrating on what you're planning to do to the enemy. Even at a few hundred yards distance, those armored men on horseback looked twice the size they actually were. As soon as they began to gallop, which they would very soon, they'd look larger still.

And there were thousands of them coming. Only a few thousand, true—Reschly's estimate had been no more than four thousand, and probably closer to three—but even three thousand horses make an incredible drumming din. They were still cantering, too, since the enemy commander was smart enough or experienced enough not to take the risk of winding the mounts. Once they started the gallop of the final charge—

Three hundred yards. Close enough. *"Charge!"* shouted Guébriant. A few paces behind him, the trumpeters sounded the command.

—they'd make the very earth seem to shake.
Which it did.
"Steady, fellows, steady!"
He saw that all the gun crews in his half of the battery were ready. Glancing over, he saw the same was true of Reschly's half. The lieutenant was already lowering his sword, having used it to give the colonel a signal. Straley had wanted the first magazines fired in a coordinated volley, although thereafter the gun crews would fire as ready. With the slightly duck-foot design of the volley guns, the rounds became too dispersed beyond two hundred and fifty yards, and the colonel didn't want nervous gun crews wasting that important first volley.

In the distance, Engler could see Straley's mouth open, shouting something. He couldn't hear a word of it, though, over the thunder of the horses' hooves.

That's why they used bugles, of course. The sharp sound of the instruments pierced through the noise quite easily.

Fire!

One of the cavalrymen right next to Jean-Baptiste was slammed back in the saddle, his helmet sailing off. The man stared blank-eyed at the sky for a moment, blood pouring down the back of his skull, before he slumped off onto the ground.

He was already dead, thankfully. Being in the front ranks of a massed charge like this, a minor wound was as surely fatal as anything, if a man fell off his mount. The horses coming behind would trample his body into a barely recognizable mass of pulp. They were galloping fairly slowly, with the weight of their armored riders—not more than fifteen or sixteen miles an hour—but that was more than fast enough for a big horse to be unable to avoid a man lying on the ground.

That was just a passing thought for Guébriant, however. The count was squinting, trying to see ahead through the huge cloud of gunsmoke that had now obscured the USE forces.

There had been something peculiar about that first enemy volley. It didn't sound quite right, even for four-pounders. The cloud of gunsmoke was a bit peculiar, too. It had seemed to emerge instantly across the entire ranks of the enemy artillery, instead of spreading out from the clumps emerging from cannon barrels. It looked a lot more like the sort of gunsmoke produced by musketeers, in fact.

Whatever, it didn't matter. They'd closed another fifty yards in those five or six seconds. By the time even four-pounders could fire again, the French cavalry would be upon them. Even if one or two crews managed to get off a second shot, they'd only do it at the last moment and canister lost much of its effectiveness at very close range. Deadly to anyone directly in front of the barrels, of course. But the shot simply didn't have time to spread out very far.

❖   ❖   ❖

Thorsten had come to a halt directly behind one of the volley guns. He watched as the three-man crew went smoothly through the sequence. The used ammunition strip was extracted and tossed into a thin-walled metal case lying on the ground nearby. They'd reload it later, when they had time. A new strip was brought out of another case and fitted into the barrels. A powder train was laid behind the ammunition strip and the side-mounted loading lever was shoved into position, securing the breech. A percussion cap was then placed on the nipple located in the center of the barrel array and would be fired by the gunner using a simple hammer mechanism.

The gunner gave the oncoming targets no more than a perfunctory glance, just to double-check that the gun's recoil shift had been corrected properly. The volley gun barrels were rifled, giving them much greater accuracy than smoothbore muskets. But the real advantage was the added range the rifling gave the bullets. With twenty-five barrels laid down in a row, angling slightly apart in a duck-foot design, there was no more point in "aiming" a volley gun than there was in aiming a smoothbore musket. Just point it in the direction of the enemy and close the hammer.

Which, he did. The twenty-five round magazine fired almost in unison with those of the other volley guns on the line. A trained crew could work the volley guns once every eight to ten seconds, where it took the crew of a four-pounder cannon much longer than that. Over time, that slight spread of skill would produce increasingly ragged fire, but this was only the second volley.

Twenty-five barrels to a gun, six guns to a battery, six batteries to a company—and on this field, today, Colonel Straley had three companies under his command. Within a space of one second, two thousand and seven hundred rounds were fired at an enemy now about one hundred and fifty yards away.

Bang.

Bang.

Two thousand, six hundred and fifty rounds, rather. Two gun crews had screwed up and fired a couple of seconds later. But they weren't any of the crews under Thorsten's command, so he didn't worry about it. And he was worrying a lot less about the oncoming enemy cavalry, too. They were starting to suffer heavy casualties already.

The enemy fired another volley, long before Jean-Baptiste expected. For the second time, the count of Guébriant was astonished.

Stunned, even—and quite literally. A round had struck his cuirass. Dead-on, a heavy three-ounce canister ball would have punched right through the armor and killed him. So would a musket ball weighing half as much, for that matter, if it hit straight on. A canister round could kill even with a glancing blow, with its greater weight. This bullet had struck a glancing blow, but the bullet wasn't any heavier than a musket ball.

Good for him at the moment, to be sure. He was a bit dazed and from the pain he knew he might have suffered a cracked rib. He'd certainly be badly bruised. But even through the shock and pain, Guébriant finally understood what he was facing, even though he still couldn't see the enemy clearly because of the gunsmoke. Those weren't artillery of any kind. They were organ guns!

But what sort of lunatic general would try to use organ guns against a cavalry charge? The weapons took as long to reload as cannons did. They weren't used that often, and then almost entirely in siege warfare for the purpose of suppressing enemy sharpshooters on the walls.

Another volley came, after they closed to seventy yards, and the count was struck again. A minor flesh wound on the back of his hand, but it was the right hand that held the sword. His weapon went flying.

That was three volleys in perhaps twenty seconds. Glancing from side to side, Guébriant realized they'd suffered casualties as bad as they would have taken against heavy artillery or massed infantry. It was incredible. He'd led his men into a trap.

Nothing for it now, however, but to press the charge through. Even with this horrendous enemy rate of fire, they were now within sixty yards. They wouldn't suffer more than one more volley.

That volley came when the French cavalry was not more than ten yards from the line of volley guns. Thorsten had been practically screaming at the gun crews, in his insistence that they stand their ground and keep firing. That wasn't easy, even with the huge clouds of gunsmoke obscuring the sight of the enemy. Unlike infantry units, the volley gun companies didn't have pikemen to fend off cavalry at the final moment. They'd be forced to fight with the ten-foot partisans they carried as hand weapons against men on horseback

armed with wheel locks and sabers. And lances, some
of them. It would be a slaughter, if it got that far.

But . . . it wouldn't. The gunsmoke had cleared
enough, in patches here and there, for Thorsten to
be able to see that the French cavalry charge was
already collapsing even before that final volley was
fired. There was still a solid group of perhaps two
hundred men at the center—coming almost right at
him, in fact—that was maintaining the charge. But
the rest were not. The casualties they'd suffered from
this head-on charge at ranked volley guns had simply
broken their spirit. They were already peeling away,
salving their wounded pride with a rather pointless
caracole-style firing of their wheel locks and then
racing to the rear. Very few volley gunners would be
hit by pistol shots fired in such a manner.

Thorsten ignored them. There were still that two
hundred or so thundering at his batteries. He'd never
relinquished his own saber, and now he made sure he
had it in a tight grip. Being one of the few men in the
batteries on horseback, he'd have to meet cavalrymen
directly and fight in their manner rather than his.

So be it. He had a fleeting and regretful thought
of Caroline, but pushed it aside. He'd die or he
wouldn't.

But it never came to that. That final volley shattered
what was left of the charge. Only a dozen French
cavalrymen made it into the ranks of the gunners, and
a good third of them were wounded. Even with their
superior weapons, they were simply too outnumbered
to put up much of a fight.

The officer leading them was bleeding badly and
half-slumped over his saddle before his horse passed

through the line. Fortunately for him, his half-panicked mount instinctively avoided the guns and so he passed just beyond the range of partisans being wielded on either side. Then, not thirty feet beyond, a sudden panicky lunge to the side by his horse spilled him from the saddle. He landed on the ground like a sack of meal, his helmet coming off and flipping over twice. Then, with a little spasm of an elbow motion, the officer managed to roll himself over on his back. Half of his face was covered in blood.

Thorsten trotted his horse over and saw that the man was still conscious. That head wound wasn't as bad as it looked. A lot of blood, as always with head wounds, but the wound was a gash across the side of his head just above his ear, not anything that had penetrated the skull. He'd been creased by a bullet, was all.

The French officer groaned and raised his right hand to the wound on his head. The hand was bleeding also.

Thorsten dismounted and came to one knee beside him. "Hold still," he said. "I'll get a bandage on as soon I can, so you don't lose too much blood."

Bleary-eyed, the officer stared up at him. Only then did it occur to Engler than he might not speak German.

Apparently he did, however. The critical phrase, anyway. That might be the only phrase in German he knew, which he'd have memorized as a young soldier.

"Je suis Jean-Baptiste Budes, comte de Guébriant," he whispered. Then added in German: "There is a ransom."

Eric Krenz had run over and arrived just in time to hear. He stooped, hands planted on knees, and gave Engler an evil-looking grin. "Not that it'll do you any good, Thorsten. You're neither a widow nor an orphan, and don't have any even if you'd gotten killed, since you didn't marry Caroline yet. Makes you long for the good old days, doesn't it?"

Thorsten gave him an exasperated glance. Leave it to Krenz to make wisecracks about an issue that had practically caused a mutiny in the army, back in training camp. The mercenary soldiers—who were few, in the ranks, but constituted almost half of the officers—had taken it for granted that any ransom for captured enemy officers would accrue personally to the soldiers who actually did the capture. With a rightful portion accruing to the officers in charge, naturally. That had been the established custom for centuries; the army's version of naval prize money.

But, led by their CoC component—very large component—the volunteers in the regiments would have none of it. Medieval barbarism, that was. Instead, in solemn assemblies that they technically had no right to hold but fuck the authorities if they didn't like it, the soldiers voted in their great majority that all ransom money should be turned over to a common pool, to be dispensed to the families of those soldiers who were slain or crippled in action.

The officers had tried to suppress the assemblies, the soldiers had taken up weapons, and things had gotten very tense. Fortunately, General Torstensson was able to keep the situation from escalating to actual violence long enough for the emperor in his siege at Luebeck to rule on the side of the soldiers.

A number of mercenary officers had resigned at that point. But since they were usually the ones who'd been foremost in trying to suppress the near-mutiny, it was just as well. Certainly for them. Very prominent among the American loan words that had made its way into Amideutsch—especially as spoken in the volunteer regiments—was the term "fragging."

Most of the mercenaries stayed, however, grumble as they might. In part, because Gustav Adolf sweetened the deal for them by saying that he'd pay bonuses out of his own imperial coffers to officers whose men did well in the fighting—and it was understood that one of the important determinations for "doing well" meant capturing enemy commanders, especially the noblemen who completely dominated the French officer corps.

So, the issue had died down. The soldiers were now arguing over exactly how to organize the disbursement. Some favored using the CoCs, but even most CoC members felt that would be inappropriate. Others wanted to set up special committees for the purpose in the regiments. But that had the disadvantage of impermanency, since the regiments were supposed to disband in three years—the men felt very strongly on *that* subject—and a widow or orphan was likely to need the money for a lot longer than that.

Of late, a new school of thought had emerged and was gaining many adherents. That was to turn the whole problem over to the settlement house in Magdeburg run by the Americanesses. They had a reputation for being honest and efficient; they were on good terms with the CoCs but not part of them; and, best of all, they maintained scrupulous neutrality with regard to sectarian and denominational disputes.

Thorsten was in favor of that solution, of course. As Krenz promptly alluded to with another stupid witticism.

"Caroline will be delighted, on the other hand. What's that up-time expression? 'Tickled pink,' I think. That's because you're 'bringing home the bacon,' as they say."

"Shut up. And find me something to make a bandage for the man's head wound."

"Good idea. If he bleeds to death, no ransom. Caroline will be furious. Might break off the engagement."

"Eric!"

"No sense of humor, any more. Exalted rank has ruined you, Thorsten." Shaking his head, Krenz went off.

While they'd been seeing to the wounded French officer, the USE's own cavalry had swept around the volley guns and was now pursuing the retreating French. Thorsten hadn't given much thought to the matter, once he saw that his own position was now secured.

The unconcern of a sergeant, engrossed in immediate tasks. General Torstensson, of course, was taking a much keener interest.

"That's it!" he exclaimed, handing the eyeglass to an aide. "General Jackson, my congratulations. I couldn't have asked anything better from your heavy weapons units. They broke the French cavalry on their own, leaving mine still fresh and ready to be used."

Frank grinned with pleasure. But Torstensson was already turning away, giving rapid-fire orders for the cavalry to press the charge against the French left flank—which would collapse, watch and see if

it wouldn't!—and for the infantry and artillery to
begin an assault against the enemy's main force. In
one hour, this battle would be over! As big a victory
as Breitenfeld!

The French left flank was not well organized, to
begin with. The routed French cavalry who poured into
their ranks with the USE cavalry in pursuit confused
and demoralized them still further. Coming less than
two minutes later, the impact of five thousand charging
enemy cavalrymen simply shattered the flank altogether
and sent the units reeling against Angoulême's forces
facing Torstensson directly.

By then, the USE's infantry had closed to within
four hundred yards and the USE artillery was in
position at the fore and firing steadily. The biggest
difficulty with green artillery units was giving them
the confidence to take positions far enough ahead of
their protective infantry to do any good in the first
place. The rout of the French left flank was obvious
to anyone on the field, by then, and that was enough
to do the trick, given that they'd been well trained
during the months in camp over the winter.

At three hundred and fifty yards, with a clear line
of fire and good level ground, the artillery was devastating. Grazing shots fired by four and six pounders
were just murderous against massed infantry. The
balls caroming off the ground would pass through the
enemy ranks at waist level, killing or wounding up to
a dozen men at a time.

The battle actually took almost three hours, not
the one hour that Torstensson had predicted. Once
his initial enthusiasm passed, Torstensson realized

he'd do better to take the time to use his artillery to pound the main forces of the French before he pushed through an infantry charge. Here on this field, as on every one that Gustav Adolf or his generals fought, they had a great superiority in artillery. That was counterbalanced by the usual enemy superiority in pikemen—Tilly had enjoyed that at Breitenfeld, too—but the counterbalance in practice was almost meaningless. Great masses of pikemen in tercio formations simply couldn't move fast enough to overwhelm massed artillery, unless their own cavalry could clear a way for them. And most of the French cavalry was somewhere on the road back to Luebeck.

It didn't help any that their commanding officer joined those cavalrymen less than an hour after the battle started. True, he didn't race off in a panic. Not officially, at least. Instead, he tried to lead a flanking maneuver of his own—so he described it—even though the maneuver bordered on insanity, coming as it did early in the afternoon in the middle of a battle. The duke of Angoulême proposed to lead his remaining cavalry forces down to the Trave at Reinfeld, then follow the river up to Segeberg and from there, fall upon Torstensson's army from the rear.

It was a total distance of at least thirty miles, which he'd be attempting with a force of two thousand cavalry traveling along narrow country roads across a terrain that was in parts heavily wooded. Even if the maneuver worked, it would be a miracle if he could bring his forces into play before nightfall.

Still, off he went. Leaving in command the thirty-one-year old Charles de la Porte, seigneur de Meilleraye, after having stripped him of all the cavalry forces that remained to the French army.

Not surprisingly, the first words spoken by de la Porte after Angoulême left were "that fucking bastard." So were the next three, and the three after that.

Chapter 58

"The poltroon!" snarled Torstensson. He handed the eyeglass back to the same aide. "Yes, you're right. That's got to be d'Angoulême, unless someone stole his personal banners—and why would anyone do that?"

Frank took off his hat and scratched his head. "What the hell does he think he's doing? All that's back there is Luebeck—and by now, the emperor's probably led the garrison out."

Gustav was doing much better than that—or, rather, was ordering Axel Oxenstierna to do it for him.

The chancellor of Sweden had accompanied Admiral Gyllenhjelm and his fleet. So had ten thousand Swedish soldiers, packed on its many ships.

"Axel, once you get them formed up, take them up the Trave to meet Torstensson. Between the two of you, you'll have d'Angoulême's army in a vise."

The chancellor gave Gustav Adolf a skeptical look. Not because of any hesitation on his own part—Oxenstierna was quite an experienced military commander himself—but simply because it was so out of character for the king of Sweden.

Seeing the look, Gustav Adolf smiled a bit ruefully. "Yes, yes, it's a great temptation. But the truth is, Axel, I'd do far better to leave for Copenhagen with Karl and his warships rather than lead this expedition myself. Judging from the last radio report, by the time you get there it may all be over, anyway. Torstensson seems to be doing quite well. Whereas there's only so much Admiral Simpson can do on his own. Those wonderful ironclads are splendid for blowing things up, but I need to make a settlement with the Danish king. Not so good for that, once he's softened up the drunken bastard. I need to deal with that business myself."

Oxenstierna nodded. "Oh, I don't disagree, Your Majesty. Especially when I reflect that less than two years ago, in another universe, you got yourself killed at Lützen leading a cavalry charge. It's amazing, really. You wouldn't think the difference between being thirty-eight and thirty-nine years old would produce such a drastic increase in wisdom. I'm fifty, myself, and I can't remember any such great transformation in my own life."

The emperor just responded with a grin. "It's yours, then!" He turned and clapped his half-brother Karl Gyllenhjelm on the shoulder. "Come, Admiral of Sweden! We don't want that upstart Simpson to get all the naval glory."

As they headed for the door leading out of Luebeck's Rathaus, Gyllenhjelm winced. "He really hasn't left us poor Swedes with much more than scraps, Gustav."

"All the more reason to grab the scraps! Before the greedy bastard takes them from us, too."

Torstensson was still snarling. "I'll be damned if he will! Thinks he can escape while leaving his army in the lurch, does he? Fuck that French shithead. Bryan, send a cavalry force after him."

Colonel Thorpe cleared his throat. "Ah, general. You've already thrown the cavalry we have against the French left. All that remains are two companies in reserve."

Torstensson frowned. "So I did. Well . . ."

He turned his head toward Jackson, smiling a little wickedly. "Let's see if you can make good on another boast, Frank. Now's your chance to prove those heavy weapons units can march as quickly as you claim, too."

Jackson returned the smile with one of his own, that was just as wicked. "A small wager, on the side?"

"Ha! Think me a fool? No, just see to it, please. Do the liaison with Colonel Straley personally, if you would. That'll be faster than sending a courier to try to explain it all."

As he'd been talking, Jackson had squatted down, so he could see the map spread over the ground better. It was held down by small rocks on each corner. Fortunately, there wasn't much wind. Somehow or other, the tent they'd planned to use for a command post had gotten lost along the way. It would probably turn up in a day or two—by which time, the way things were looking, they'd be comfortably set up in a nearby tavern anyway and wouldn't need it.

Such is war, as Frank remembered quite well from his days as a youngster in Vietnam. The plans of mice and men gang aft agley, and never more so than once the fighting started.

"I don't think there's any point in actually chasing after them, General." He pointed to a spot on the map and then shifted his finger. "The volley guns can move fast, but they can't move as fast as cavalry—and they'd lose more ground right at the start having to get around the French army. Better, I'm thinking, to figure out where Angoulême is going and cut him off at the pass. So to speak."

Torstensson squatted next to him, and studied the map for a moment. "Yes, I see your point. He can't go down to Luebeck, obviously, which means he's probably trying to reach the Trave somewhere around here." His own finger came down on the spot that marked the small town of Reinfeld, then slid along the line that marked the upper stretch of the Trave until his finger reached Segeberg.

"Somewhere between Reinfeld and Segeberg—but it would have to be much closer to Segeberg—he'll leave the Trave and make his way across to the headwaters of the Stör. Then follow it down the Elbe near Glückstadt and try to cross there."

"That's what I'm figuring," agreed Jackson. "So I think we'd do better to take the volley guns back to the headwaters of the Trave right here"—he pointed to the west—"and just follow it down until we run into Angoulême coming the other way. Should be somewhere around . . . here, I'm think. This village called Nutschel, if I'm reading this damn script properly." An aggrieved tone came into his voice. "I thought we'd agreed to use Roman lettering in the army, instead of this Fraktur crap."

Torstensson rose from the map. "Germans, you know. Most stubborn people on the face of the earth. All right, General Jackson. Be off, and Godspeed. Bring me back the head of Charles de Valois. And I don't care if it's attached to the rest of his body or not."

"*Again?*" whined Krenz.

"I told you to pay attention to your horsemanship." Thorsten had no sympathy at all with Krenz on this subject. "'Flying artillery,' remember? And now we'll really have to fly, if we're to catch up with that French general."

"Order an advance, all across the line," said Charles de la Porte. Before his lieutenants could start arguing the matter, he threw up his hands with exasperation. "Yes, I know! But what else can we do? If we continue to stand our ground, those fucking guns will just keep hammering us. Our own artillery is simply no match for them. And if we try to retreat—and where, exactly? Certainly not Luebeck!—we'll get cut to pieces without cavalry to screen us. We've got no other choice. We either win a straight-up battle or we surrender. That's it—and I don't want to hear any arguments."

At least the flight of Angoulême had left a decisive man in command of the French army. As they hurried off to prepare the advance, the lieutenants tried to take what confidence they could from that fact.

"His best option," said Torstensson, once he saw the enemy beginning its advance. "Not a good one—not with our artillery—but the best he's got. Who's in command over there, Bryan, do you think?"

His staff officer pondered the question, for a moment

or two. "Hard to know, General. If I had to guess, I'd say either Charles de la Porte or Gaspard de Coligny. Either one of them is supposed to be competent. Coligny has seniority, but de la Porte has better family ties. He's one of Richelieu's cousins. Given d'Angoulême, I'd think he'd ignore seniority and select for family ties. If nothing else, it'll help spread the blame better."

"Why not de la Valette, then?" asked another of Torstensson's lieutenants, who'd spent some time in the French colors. "His mother was a Montmorency, his wife a royal bastard, and now that she's dead the rumor is that he's courting one of Richelieu's nieces."

Thorpe barked a sarcastic little laugh. "Better for us if he had! But I don't think d'Angoulême is downright stupid."

As it happened, Bernard de Nogaret de la Valette had accompanied Angoulême's cavalry force, although no one had actually invited him to do so. He knew perfectly well that the so-called "flanking maneuver" was the best—probably the only—way to get out of the trap the French army was in. There'd be hell to pay when they got back to France, but de la Valette would deal with that when the time came. He was considerably more proficient in that field of battle than he was in this much cruder one.

By the time they reached the Trave near Reinfeld, however, scouts reported that lead elements of a new army were advancing from Luebeck. As the duke of Angoulême had guessed, Gustav Adolf was already leading out the city's garrison. There was no time to waste!

Somewhere between Reinfeld and the town of

Oldesloe, any pretense that the two thousand cavalrymen were engaged in a wide flanking maneuver crumbled. This was a simple retreat—and, as panic began spreading, it rapidly took on the features of a rout. With d'Angoulême himself setting the pace, the cavalrymen began running their mounts much faster than they should have been, given the great distance they still had to go before they'd reach the Elbe. Or even the headwaters of the Stör, for that matter.

De la Valette was relieved at first. That half-buried part of him that was an experienced horseman knew perfectly well that they couldn't maintain this pace for very long without winding the animals. But all he cared about at the moment was putting distance between himself and those two armies of the damned Swede.

Soon enough, though, his relief gave way to apprehension, and then fear. Let two thousand horsemen on a narrow country road lose control of themselves, and the sure result is what amounts to equestrian turbulence. It was like riding rapids on horseback instead of a boat.

About two miles past Oldesloe, another horseman jostled de la Valette's mount and forced the beast off the road. One of its hooves caught in something, the horse went down, breaking its own leg and one of de la Valette's in the bargain. Then, as it continued to thrash about hysterically with its rider unable to move away, broke the French nobleman's collarbone, cracked several of his ribs, and left lacerations and bruises over half his body. It only ended when a frantic de la Valette managed to extract one of his wheel-lock pistols and shoot the animal in the head.

At that point, he collapsed unconscious. When he came back to his senses, the sun was setting—and four very ruffianly-looking soldiers were grinning down at him. One of them had a dagger held to his throat.

The relief was immense. First, because he was alive, even if in great pain. Second, because his injuries along with his capture would help a great deal to alleviate suspicion once he got back to Paris. The awkward matter of the precise location where these unfortunate events occurred could probably be elided.

Finally, he was relieved that he'd been captured by soldiers. Just two miles from Oldesloe, he could have easily been found by villagers instead. In which case, the knife now being held to his throat to ensure his cooperation would already have slit it. And then moved on to his evisceration and probable emasculation— except most likely not in that sequence.

De la Valette knew the magic phrase also, of course. *"Je suis Bernard de Nogaret de la Valette, duc d' Épernon,"* he croaked. "There is a good ransom."

He said that last in German. Which, as it happened, not one of the soldiers understood, being Swedish country boys. But it didn't matter. They weren't such rural bumpkins that they didn't know that all four of them had just gotten rich, if they kept this fine fellow alive. Swedish troops, naturally, had no truck with that CoC foolishness about creating a common pool for widows and orphans—if they'd heard of it at all, which these new arrivals from Sweden hadn't. It wouldn't have mattered anyway, since they were soldiers of the king of Sweden, not the emperor of the United States of Europe.

❖   ❖   ❖

"Fire!" shouted Colonel Straley. Lying in what amounted to an open ambush across the road alongside the Trave and in the edges of the woods beyond, the volley gun batteries could hear the colonel's voice perfectly well. They were already starting to fire when the bugles blew.

With dozens of volley guns concentrating their fire on such a narrow frontage, the first ranks of the French cavalry force were simply shredded. To make things worse, the piled up bodies of the horses made it impossible for them to advance further—and the panicked cavalrymen from the rear were still pressing forward, making it impossible to retreat. They were like animals trapped in a cage.

The batteries fired four more volleys before one of the French officers managed to jury-rig a flag of surrender. By then, they'd suffered casualties that were every bit as bad as those being suffered by the main army still fighting on the field.

On that field, a considerably more courageous young French commander had finally had enough. "Send a surrender signal," gasped Charles de la Porte. He was so exhausted he didn't even notice the minor wound he'd taken to the hip. "This is hopeless."

Torstensson had been waiting for the signal, since the outcome of the battle had been obvious from the moment the only French units who managed to reach the USE infantry had been driven back in less than a minute. Since then, this had just been carnage.

"Cease fire!" he commanded. As the buglers blew the signal, Torstensson turned to Colonel Bryan Thorpe with a cheerful smile. "Well, I admit I misgauged the time. But it's still as good as Breitenfeld. Better!—if we catch that bastard d'Angoulême. At Breitenfeld, Tilly got away from us."

One of the French officers in the trap along the Trave tried to escape on his own, racing his horse toward the woods. He might even have made it—at least two hundred did— except that he passed too close to Engler's batteries. Thorsten spotted him, and since he was still on horseback went in pursuit.

He probably wasn't as good a horseman as the fleeing French officer, who was almost certainly a nobleman who'd been riding since he was a boy. But Engler was good enough, given that his mount had had time to rest and that of his prey was badly winded.

He caught up with him in less than half a mile. The fleeing officer's horse had finally stumbled from exhaustion. By then, fortunately, the horse had been moving so slowly that its fall was more in the way of a slow roll than a sudden spill. So its rider had the time to get out of the saddle before the huge beast fell on top of him and crushed him.

He was still badly bruised, of course. Horsefalls are always a dangerous experience and never a pleasant one. But he didn't even have his wind knocked out, so when Thorsten brought his horse alongside and aimed his wheel lock pistol at the man, he was able to speak.

"*Je suis Charles de Valois, duc d'Angoulême*. There is an excellent ransom."

As Colonel Nils Ekstrom worked his way through the various reports sent to Luebeck from Torstensson's adjutants, he spotted an oddity.

Coincidence, perhaps. Or a simple error.

Still, it was intriguing. He sent a courier to inquire.

The following day, the courier returned. No coincidence of names, and no error. The humble sergeant in Torstensson's volley gun units who had captured both the French cavalry commander Guébriant as well as the enemy's commander-in-chief d'Angoulême were, indeed, one and the same man. And, yes, he was the Thorsten Engler who was betrothed to an American woman in Magdeburg.

"Oh, splendid!" exclaimed Ekstrom. "That's one problem solved, at least."

Well . . . not quite. Imperial counts—at least, if they followed the Austrian model—didn't carry place names. And the princess was likely to be stubborn.

"Bring me a map," he commanded an aide. When the map was brought, Ekstrom studied it for a moment.

"Nutschel. That's about where the capture was made."

Frank Jackson happened to have come into the chamber of the Rathaus where Ekstrom was conducting his labors, while Ekstrom had been waiting for the map. "What's this about, Nils?"

Ekstrom explained, then said, "Silly name, anyway. We'll just inform the villagers that the emperor—their emperor, now—has decided to rename their village to honor the great victory."

"Rename it what?"

"Narnia, of course. That gives us a fallback position—that is the American term, yes?—in the not unlikely event the emperor capitulates to his daughter."

Frank stared at him. Then, at the map. "You've got to be kidding."

Ekstrom gave him a fish-eyed look. "You *have* met Princess Kristina, I believe."

Frank had grown a beard not long after the Ring of Fire, foreseeing the likely disappearance of safety razors, and long since had developed the common habit of tugging it. He did so now, wincing. "Good point. Yeah, I have met her."

He looked back at the map. "Narnia, huh? Well . . . as long as they don't spell it in Fraktur."

Chapter 59

The Øresund

SSIM *Constitution* moved steadily on a north-by-northwest heading. The gray-blue coast of the island of Falster lay to port, floating on the horizon like some distant bank of fog, as she led the rest of Simpson's squadron out of Luebeck Bay and towards Copenhagen. The dark, cold blue water of the Baltic stretched into hazy invisibility to starboard, and Simpson stood gazing out into that blue vastness while he considered what lay just over two hundred air miles north of his present position.

God knew King Christian was a stubborn fellow. He was as renowned for that as he was for his ability to . . . multitask enthusiastically. But surely even someone like Christian should recognize the inevitable when it dropped anchor off the waterfront of his capital city.

Of course, anyone *but* King Christian would have recognized that aligning himself with Catholic Europe against Protestant Germany and Sweden had not been the most effective possible technique for convincing his fellow Protestants to back his candidacy for their leadership. In which case, he wouldn't have had to worry about what the USE Navy might be about to do to his capital city, now would he?

He's not really an idiot, Simpson reminded himself. *He couldn't possibly have accomplished everything he's gotten done if his brain simply didn't work. In fact, his brain has to work better than most people's. But he's certainly managed to figure out how to look like an idiot this time.*

The admiral snorted at the thought, more in disgust than amusement.

At least he's a hell of a lot smarter than King Charles of England—not that "smarter than Charles" is any great recommendation of genius. And I suppose part of it is that we all end up comparing him to the other Scandinavian king, which would tend to make anyone look less than lifesize. But I still wish Railleuse *had managed to get there before we did. Grosclaud's report would've been a real douche of cold water. Unfortunately*—he looked back towards the south, where the squadron had passed the crippled French ship an hour or so earlier—*she didn't. But even without that*, he grinned thinly, *we should still be able to get Christian's attention when we get there. Now if only*—

"Message from Commander Klein, sir," a voice said respectfully from behind him, and Simpson turned. It was an indication of how lost he'd been in his own thoughts that he hadn't even noticed the bridge signalman's approach until the young rating spoke.

"Thank you, Ebert," he said, accepting the message flimsy. The youngster—he couldn't have been a day

over seventeen—smiled as the admiral called him by
name. Fortunately, Simpson had always been particularly good at remembering names. And the practice of
issuing nameplates for all personnel didn't hurt any,
of course, he acknowledged with an inner smile.

He opened the message slip and scanned it quickly,
then frowned.

"Give Captain Halberstat my respects and ask him to
join me here," he said and young Ebert saluted sharply
and scampered into the conning tower. Franz Halberstat
appeared on the bridge wing moments later.

"Yes, sir?"

"Message from Klein," Simpson said, holding up
the message slip. The paper's edges fluttered with
an almost popping sound in the brisk breeze. "He's
just carried out an inspection of his deck boat, and
it doesn't look good."

"Why not, sir? I was under the impression that
Achilles hadn't been hit at all."

"She wasn't. Apparently, it's blast damage from the
carronades."

Halberstat grimaced, then nodded in understanding.

Two of the motor boats that had scouted ahead of
the squadron on its passage down the Elbe River had
been put aboard *Achilles* and *Ajax* as deck cargo for
the passage from the Elbe River's estuary to Copenhagen. The timberclads had been chosen because they
could stow the boats higher, thanks to their taller
superstructures. And because they'd been supposed to
be committed to action against Overgaard's blockade
fleet only after the ironclads, which should have meant
they would have been less exposed to hostile fire.

On the other hand, the flag captain reminded himself,

from what the admiral had just said, it didn't sound like *hostile* fire had been responsible for the damage.

"How bad is it, sir?" he asked after a moment.

"From what Klein's saying, the actual damage doesn't sound all that bad. In fact, if it were a wooden hull, his ship's carpenter could probably fix it pretty quickly. Unfortunately, it's a *fiberglass* hull, since it's one of the up-time boats that came through the Ring of Fire. And someone"—Simpson tapped himself on the chest—"didn't insist on bringing along a patching kit."

"I see, sir." Halberstat carefully didn't point out to the admiral that no one else had thought to suggest that they bring one along, either. "What about *Ajax*'s boat, sir?"

"Mülbers is inspecting it now. But, first, he's got the smaller of the two. And, second, I've always had reservations about using them at Copenhagen at all. They're just too small, Franz. We can't put anywhere near as many men into either of them as the Danes can get aboard their galleys and gunboats. Without the second boat to support Mülbers', I'm even less inclined to risk letting the one of them we'd have get far enough ahead that we can't support it quickly. And if we're not going to let it operate any farther ahead of us than that, I'm afraid the scouting advantage isn't going to be great enough to do us much good."

"I suppose not, sir. Although there are those reports of minefields."

Simpson glanced at the flag captain and smiled very slightly. Halberstat's tone could not have been more respectful, but he'd managed to put exactly the right edge of cautionary question into it. And he had a point. Someone in one of the small, agile fishing boats would have a much better chance of spotting a moored mine than any lookout on *Constitution*'s bridge or mast. And a boat that small would be far less likely to hit a mine in the first place.

The admiral thought about it carefully, for the better part of a full minute, then shrugged.

"All right, Franz. If Mülbers' boat is in good shape, and if weather conditions are no worse than this"—he waved one hand at the relatively moderate swell—"then you can have your mine scouter. But only if the weather cooperates, mind you. Those flat-bottomed bastards are bitches in any sort of seaway, and a load of seasick Marines isn't going to be keeping the best lookout in the world. Besides, if it's too rough, they'll actually be slower than the other side's galleys."

"Of course, sir," Halberstat agreed.

"Your Highness!"

Prince Ulrik held up one hand, interrupting his current conference with Baldur Norddahl, as the messenger half-dashed into the room in Rosenborg Castle that Ulrik had taken over for what amounted to the headquarters of his naval force. In earlier times, the chamber had served his father's second wife Kirsten Munk as a living room.

"What?"

"Your Highness," the newcomer repeated, sliding to a stop and bending in a hasty, panting bow, "the Americans have arrived!"

"Where? When?" Ulrik demanded rather more sharply.

"They've anchored in the Øresund, Your Highness. About three-quarters of an hour ago."

"*Anchored?*"

"Yes, Your Highness. They've raised a white flag, and their Admiral Simpson has requested a truce. According to the messenger he sent ashore, he has messages for your father. The king sent me to tell you that he wants you there when he receives him in the Long Hall."

"Of course. Go back and tell my father I'm on my way. I'll be there immediately."

"Yes, Your Highness!"

The messenger disappeared, and Ulrik turned back to Norddahl.

"I have to go," he said quickly. "But, first, what do you make of it?"

"I don't imagine they'd be here unless they'd already raised the blockade." The piratical-looking Norwegian's expression was grim. "And I don't imagine they'd be wasting time sending in messages if they thought giving us additional time to prepare would make any difference in the end."

"Couldn't you at least *suggest* the possibility that they're so afraid to attack that they're trying to bluff us into giving up without a fight?" Ulrik demanded with a tight grin, and Norddahl chuckled.

"Well, no, I don't suppose you can," the prince continued, and drew a deep breath. He thought with obvious intensity for several seconds, then nodded briskly and looked back at Norddahl.

"All right. To be perfectly honest, there's nothing I'd like more than to settle this entire affair without anyone getting hurt. I'm afraid that's not going to happen, though. So, while I go find out what Admiral Simpson has to say, I think you need to be passing the word to get ready."

"Of course."

Norddahl nodded back, sharply, and Ulrik turned to hurry off after the vanished messenger.

King Christian was waiting with some impatience by the time Ulrik reached the Long Hall. The huge room had been the last one to be furnished in Rosenborg Castle, only completed in 1624. Its official purpose was to serve as a ballroom, but Ulrik's father often used it as an audience chamber when he was feeling too restless to sit in his own chamber. The floor gave him plenty of room to pace about, and if he did feel the urge to sit down he could select any one of the many silver chairs that lined the walls.

The king looked more like a bear than ever, but his normal ebullience was singularly absent. He seemed completely sober, thankfully, but the look on his face didn't exactly inspire Ulrik with boundless optimism. The prince found himself wishing that his brother Frederik were here to assist him in reining in their father's emotional nature. Unfortunately, Frederik had been with the Danish forces besieging Luebeck, and was now helping to lead the retreat back to the Danewerk.

The oldest of the three princes was absent also, due to illness, but Ulrik didn't miss him. Truth be told, he didn't have a very high opinion of his brother Christian.

Which meant it was all up to Ulrik.

"Took you long enough," the king observed, and Ulrik shrugged very slightly.

"I came as quickly as I could, Father. Norddahl and I had to alert the galleys if we expect them to accomplish anything. And," he pointed out, "I don't see any American messenger waiting for us."

"Of course not! We had to send back our agreement to talk to them."

It was a sign of his father's anxiety, Ulrik thought, that he appeared completely oblivious to the illogic inherent in criticizing his son's "tardiness" when both of them were fully aware that no message could possibly get back to the palace for at least another hour or so.

Not that the king wasn't completely capable of being equally illogical under other circumstances.

"Did they give any indication as to the nature of this 'message' of Simpson's, Father?" the prince asked.

"No, and I wish they had." Christian grimaced, fingers drumming on the hilt of his sword. Ulrik nodded. Simpson obviously had something special—and probably complicated, if not downright devious—in mind. Any *simple* message could have been delivered at the same time he sent his request for a truce ashore.

"I suppose we'll find out shortly," the prince observed.

Well, there's *a message all by itself,* Ulrik reflected some ninety minutes later, as Captain Admiral Overgaard followed the immaculately uniformed USE lieutenant into the Long Hall behind the chamberlain.

"Lieutenant Franz-Leo Chomse, Your Majesty, and . . . Captain Admiral Overgaard," the chamberlain announced in the voice of a man who devoutly wished he were elsewhere. Just about *any* elsewhere, if Ulrik was any judge.

For a long, smoldering moment, Christian simply stared at his two "visitors." Lieutenant Chomse advanced toward the king with a respectful expression and a stride that was rather impressively calm for a young man who—Ulrik was certain—had not a single drop of aristocratic blood in his veins.

"Your Majesty," he murmured, bending his head respectfully. Then he straightened his spine and met the king's eyes. "I have the honor to be Admiral Simpson's flag lieutenant, and on his behalf, I thank you for agreeing to speak with me."

For a few seconds, Ulrik thought his father was going to refuse to respond. Then Christian shook his head slightly, with a bemused belligerence which made him look more like a middle-aged bear than ever.

"Your thanks are scarcely necessary, Lieutenant Chomse," he said in a voice whose self-control surprised Ulrik more than a little. He took no apparent notice of Overgaard, however.

"Just what message did Admiral Simpson entrust to you?" he continued.

"With your permission, Your Majesty," Lieutenant Chomse replied, "the admiral instructed me to request that you allow me to deliver his message after Captain Admiral Overgaard has been able to give you his report on the outcome of the Battle of Luebeck Bay."

Christian's face tightened. His jaw muscles swelled momentarily, and his eyes hardened dangerously. But it appeared that the message inherent in Overgaard's mere presence was one which even Christian realized he could not ignore.

"Very well, Lieutenant," the king said frostily, and swiveled those hard eyes to the commander of his navy. "Captain Admiral?"

To his credit, Overgaard didn't even flinch from the

undeniable coldness of Christian's tone. Ulrik wasn't prepared to even guess how much it cost him, but he met the king's gaze levelly.

"Your Majesty," he said, "I deeply regret that I must inform you that the vessels under my command have been decisively defeated. Eleven of them have been sunk or burned. Six more are severely damaged, and our casualties have been heavy. Two French vessels and six English vessels are among those that have been destroyed."

Christian's eyes flickered. For a moment, pure, unadulterated shock peeked out of them as he heard the grim listing of the blockade fleet's losses.

"Despite the bravery of the men you entrusted to my command, we were unable to inflict equivalent damage upon the enemy. In fact—" He looked directly into Christian's eyes. "—to the best of my knowledge, we failed to inflict a single casualty. Under the circumstances, when Admiral Simpson summoned me to surrender to avoid further useless bloodshed, I felt there was no option but to accept his terms rather than see all of the ships under my command destroyed, along with their crews, with no chance of damaging the enemy in return.

"I apologize to you for this failure," Overgaard continued, bowing his head at last. "I also acknowledge that I personally am responsible for it, and that it was in no way the fault of the officers and men with whose command you honored me."

The captain admiral stopped speaking and stood silently before his monarch, and Christian glared at the crown of his bent head. Lieutenant Chomse allowed the silence to linger for several seconds, then cleared his throat discreetly, and Christian's eyes whipped back to the USE officer.

"If I may, Your Majesty," the lieutenant said gravely, "my admiral has instructed me to tell you that Captain Admiral Overgaard and his men fought with the utmost gallantry against insurmountable odds. Their artillery was completely unable to damage our vessels, yet they did not surrender until more than half of their own ships had been disabled or destroyed outright."

"I see," the king said after a moment. "May I ask what the terms of their surrender were?"

"Of course, Your Majesty." Chomse bowed slightly once again. "In light of their courage, and of the losses they suffered, Admiral Simpson permitted Captain Admiral Overgaard's remaining ships and men to sail for Svendborg, with the understanding that they would remain there, at anchor, taking no further part in the current conflict until the conclusion of a general peace or until they have been formally exchanged. At that time, unless the terms of any such general peace preclude it, they will be returned to the service of the Danish crown."

Christian's jaw muscles tightened once again, yet despite his evident anger, it was obvious even he recognized the liberality of Simpson's terms. Which didn't mean he liked them, of course.

"Somehow, Lieutenant," he said after a moment, "I feel certain your admiral didn't send you to my palace just to tell me the terms under which he permitted Captain Admiral Overgaard's surrender."

"You're correct, of course, Your Majesty," Chomse replied. "In fact, Admiral Simpson instructed me to inform you that he is under orders to proceed to the complete reduction of Denmark's ability to continue to wage war against His Imperial Majesty Gustav II Adolf and the United States of Europe. He regrets the fact that those orders require him to bombard and destroy the shipyards and fortifications of Copenhagen. In addition, he is deeply distressed by the potential for the loss of civilian lives when he carries out that bombardment."

Christian seemed to swell to an even larger and somehow denser size as Chomse delivered Simpson's message in a clear, respectful, but firm voice.

"Admiral Simpson would greatly prefer to avoid the necessity for any such bombardment, loss of life, and destruction of property. He therefore urges you, Your Majesty, to seriously consider the possibility of agreeing to withdraw from the so-called 'League of Ostend's' coalition against the United States. Should you agree to do so, the admiral will consider that his instructions from the emperor have been discharged without any further conflict."

"And what of reparations and indemnities?" the king demanded in a rasping voice. "What of reprisals?"

"Your Majesty, Admiral Simpson instructed me to tell you, should you raise that question, that he is unable to comment on those points. He would strongly urge the emperor to press no unreasonable demands upon you, and he believes the emperor would prefer to avoid doing so. However, the admiral also instructed me to reiterate that he is unable to speak for the emperor and has no official instructions on this point."

"Of course not." Christian snorted harshly. "And because he can't, his own conscience will be clear when the Swede dictates his demands!"

Chomse said nothing, but Ulrik felt his own heart sink. Like his father, he knew that Gustav Adolf cherished the design of restoring the Union of Kalmar—only, this time, under the crown of Sweden instead of Denmark. Despite that, the reasonableness—no, call it what it was; the *generosity*—of Simpson's terms was astonishing. Far better than anything Denmark might have reasonably anticipated out of an emperor fighting for his life against most of the rest of Europe, and now emerging triumphant.

From where Ulrik stood, it was obvious Gustav Adolf wanted to woo Denmark rather than club the kingdom into unwilling, surly submission. No doubt that was the result of cold, political calculation on his part, but did it really matter? Especially when Ulrik had no doubt at all that the emperor would bring out the club if Denmark—which was to say King Christian IV—declined his offer.

His father, he knew, was intelligent enough to understand that at least as well as he did. Unfortunately, his father was also stubborn enough—*obstinate* enough, one might better put it—to reject that offer anyway.

Now the king glared at Chomse, as if daring the flag lieutenant to disagree with his last statement. The naval officer, however, was clearly too smart to fall into any such trap and simply stood silently, respectfully, obviously awaiting the Danish monarch's formal response to Simpson's terms.

"I am, of course, aware of the . . . generosity of the admiral's offer," Christian said at last, his voice hard and flat. "Denmark is not yet destitute of means by which to defend herself, however. If Admiral Simpson wants to discover exactly what those means are, then by all means, he should attack my capital. But I warn him that if he does, he won't enjoy the experience."

"I see." Lieutenant Chomse gazed at him for several heartbeats, then gave his head an odd little toss. "Should I inform the admiral that you choose not to accept his proposed means of avoiding further destruction and loss of life?"

"You may inform Admiral Simpson that *I* will decide with whom to ally myself, Lieutenant. No one else will dictate that decision to me, and my capital is prepared to defend itself against any attack," Christian said with a cold, hard control Ulrik found far more disturbing than his father's normal roar of outrage would have been.

"Very well, Your Majesty." Chomse bowed deeply. "In that case, my admiral has instructed me to inform you, regretfully, that hostilities will resume as soon as I've returned aboard the flagship with your response."

"Fine!" Christian half-snapped while Ulrik's heart settled somewhere in the vicinity of his boot tops.

"If that's your final word, Your Majesty, I must beg leave to return to my ship now. Captain Admiral Overgaard has given my admiral his parole and promised to take no part in any fighting until he is exchanged or released from his parole's conditions."

"Of course," Christian agreed coldly, then looked to the chamberlain who had escorted the lieutenant into the throne room.

"See to it that the lieutenant and his boat are returned safely."

Ulrik wasted no time trying to convince his father to see reason. That, he'd known from the outset, would have been difficult, at best. Given the king's hard, controlled tone and the white-hot rage that lay beneath it, it would have been outright futile. So, instead, he took his leave quickly and went jogging off in search of Norddahl.

He found the Norwegian down by the waterfront, where their own response to the probable American attack had been prepared. Norddahl was busy shouting orders to their carefully chosen and trained crews, but he paused and looked over his shoulder, one eyebrow raised, as Ulrik appeared on the wharf behind him.

"Why do I suspect from your expression that Admiral Simpson's message failed to find a favorable reception, Your Highness?" he asked.

"Because you know my father," Ulrik growled, and Norddahl chuckled harshly.

"True," he conceded. "How much time do we have?"

"Not a lot, but long enough to get into position, I think." Ulrik shrugged. "It's going to take Lieutenant Chomse—that's Simpson's aide—another half-hour or so just to get back to the flagship. Then they're going to have to move into position. Call it another hour or so. Probably longer."

"Hmmm." Norddahl rubbed his chin thoughtfully. "At least the wind is out of the north. That's something. And the tide will be on our side, as well. You know,"—he grinned at the prince—"we might just actually accomplish something after all."

"I hope so." Ulrik's tone was enough grimmer that Norddahl looked at him with some surprise. The prince shrugged again. "There was someone else at the meeting, Baldur. Captain Admiral Overgaard."

Norddahl's lips pursed in a silent whistle as he considered the fresh information for a few seconds.

"Well," he said finally, "I suppose that answers any questions about the effectiveness of Simpson's ships. Do you know if Overgaard managed to inflict any damage in return?"

"Yes, I do, and the answer is no."

Norddahl sighed. "I wish I could say that surprised me."

"I feel the same way," Ulrik agreed. "On the other hand," his smile was thin, "unlike Overgaard, *we're* not going to be trying to batter our way through their armor, are we?"

Chapter 60

"I'm sorry, sir," Franz-Leo Chomse said. "His Majesty seemed disinclined to listen to reason."

"Not too surprising, sir," Captain Halberstat pointed out.

"Not surprising at all, actually," Simpson replied. He stood on the bridge wing once again, gazing up the body of water usually known in English as the Sound. He'd been here before the Ring of Fire, right after the Øresund suspension bridge's construction had finally been authorized. He would have liked to have seen the bridge completed, he thought.

There are a lot of things I would have liked to have done, come to that. And there are some things I'm not going to enjoy doing at all. Not that Christian's left me a lot of choice.

He considered delaying the attack until the turn of the tide. The channel between the island of Amager to the west and the shoal fringing the low-lying island of Saltholm to the east wasn't all that wide. Indeed, when Nelson attacked Copenhagen, several of his ships had gone aground on that shoal, Simpson recalled. The seaman in him was tempted to allow the incoming flood tide to give him the greatest depth of water possible over the shoal, but the admiral in him suspected that the temptation was simply one more subconscious effort to avoid the inevitable. Yes, some of Nelson's ships had grounded. But those ships had been wind-powered, far less maneuverable than any of his. And Nelson's ships had been deeper-draft than his, as well. Not to mention the fact that *his* ships boasted fathometers.

Stop delaying, John, he told himself sternly. *You have enough water for what you've got to do. And the more promptly you move in, the deeper the psychological impact is going to be. Maybe even deep enough to make an impression on Christian IV.*

"All right." He turned back to Halberstat. "If he won't listen to reason, then we're just going to have to convince him to reconsider his position, aren't we?"

"They're moving!"

Ulrik glanced up from his conversation with Norddahl. The man assigned to watch the dockyard signal flag mast was pointing at the mast, and the prince looked over his own shoulder. The agreed upon signal flag had been raised, and he felt his belly muscles tighten.

"I suppose it's time to go a-viking," he said, as lightly as he could.

"It is that," Norddahl agreed. The pirate was closer to the surface than Ulrik had ever seen it, and the burly Norwegian radiated a fierce readiness, an *eagerness*, which abruptly made even the most outrageous of his tales very believable.

To Ulrik's surprise, some of that same fierceness seemed to leap across the space between him and the older man, like sparks flying from a piece of rubbed amber.

"Then let's get started," he said, and oars thumped, then groaned in the oarlocks, as the crews ran out the sweeps and threw their weight on to them.

The shallow-draft, fifty-foot galleys—basically outsized open rowboats with three men on each sweep—gathered speed through the two-foot swell. Fifteen of them still carried their original eighteen-pounder cannon mounted in their bows, but the other ten had traded in their artillery for spar torpedoes, raised so that they looked like strange masts stepped all the way forward, swelling into ungainly pods at the business ends.

Half of the galleys towed rafts in addition to their weapons, and Ulrik jerked his head in their direction, then nodded to Norddahl.

"Whenever you think best, Baldur," he said.

Norddahl glanced at the water, obviously considering the state of the tide and wind. He waited a few more moments, then picked up the signal flag and waved it around his head with a quick, circling motion.

The galleys towing the rafts slowed briefly. Just long enough for the men carrying the lit oil lanterns to toss them into the carefully prepared rafts. Oil splashed over the piled combustibles. Flame followed, and the first tendrils of dense smoke began to rise.

"Smoke bearing three-five-five!"

Simpson raised his binoculars and peered in the indicated direction. At first, there wasn't a great deal to see, but the first smudge the sharp-eyed lookout had done remarkably well to spot grew quickly into something far denser and darker. The moderately stiff breeze blowing out of the north played with it, rolling it along on its breath, and he frowned as his binoculars picked out the first of several low-slung galleys.

"Ships bearing three-five-five!" the same lookout announced at almost exactly the same moment Simpson spotted them. "Many ships—galleys!"

Simpson's mouth tightened. His intelligence reports had warned him the Danes were assembling a fleet of oar-powered gunboats to defend Copenhagen. Even without those reports, he would have anticipated exactly the same thing. Galley fleets had lasted longer in the Baltic and the Black Sea than anywhere else, given the normal sailing conditions. They were also small enough that they could be turned out quickly in relatively large numbers, and they had frequently been manned by hastily impressed soldiers, rather than the trained seamen sailing ships required.

Set against that, they'd seldom proved very effective against larger warships. They were simply too fragile, and the best most of them could hope to mount was a single heavy gun in the bows, which could normally fire only straight ahead. True, some of the larger ones mounted a single gun aft, as well, but none of them were stable enough for broadside fire, which meant they could never bring more than one gun to bear at a time. As long as a sailing ship had enough wind to turn and keep its broadside directed at the oncoming galleys, they'd been able to accomplish very little. Against the tough hides of Simpson's ironclads and timberclads, galley gunboats—especially with seventeenth-century artillery—were going to be totally ineffectual.

Several of *these* galleys, however, carried what were obviously spar torpedoes, and those actually could damage or even sink any of his ships . . . if they managed to get close enough.

Which is exactly what that damned smokescreen of theirs is designed to bring about, he thought grimly. *Damn. Why couldn't they be stupid, as well as stubborn?*

Even as he watched, the steadily thickening pall of smoke was rolling down across the leading galleys, blotting them from sight like a dense, artificial fog bank.

He lowered the binoculars, eyes narrow as he contemplated his options. The probability of any one of those torpedo-armed galleys getting close enough, even under the protection of their smokescreen, wasn't very great. But he'd seen at least six or seven of them, and the odds of *at least* one of them getting through were substantially higher. What he needed to fend them off were lighter escorts of his own, but he didn't have those. Certainly the one undamaged bass boat he still had available would be useless floundering around out there in the smoke.

"Captain Halberstat!"

"Yes, sir?" the flag captain replied almost instantly.

"We're going to change formation," Simpson decided. "Have *Ajax* take the lead, then *Achilles*. The ironclads will follow behind them, and the squadron will assume Formation Charlie on a heading of zero-niner-five."

"Aye, aye, sir."

Halberstat disappeared back into the conning tower, and Simpson heard him calling down the interior ladder to the radio room. At almost the same instant, *Constitution* and her sister ships slowed, reducing speed to allow the timberclads to steam past them.

Simpson watched *Achilles* coming up to port, while *Ajax* steamed past to starboard and wondered what their crews were thinking. He wasn't sending them ahead because they were more expendable, although he supposed that was exactly what they were, in cold-blooded terms. But the main reason for sending them ahead was their heavier close-range firepower. They'd be much more capable of taking care of themselves in the sort of knife fight galleys with spar torpedoes would be seeking.

"Well, sir," Halberstat's voice observed at his elbow, "at least we can be fairly certain we're not sailing directly into one of those minefields of theirs. Not if their own galleys are crossing through it, at any rate."

"Probably," Simpson replied, but his own tone was more thoughtful, less assured, and Halberstat's eyebrows rose. Simpson turned his head in time to see the flag captain's expression, and he chuckled mirthlessly.

"First, those galleys probably don't draw much more water than the ironclads do when their ballast tanks are empty. They could be sailing right across the top of a minefield, if they were ballsy enough. Second, they *could* be deliberately showing themselves to us figuring that we'd charge right in to attack them, at which point we'd discover that there was a minefield *between* us and them."

"Do you seriously think there is one, sir?"

"No, not really," Simpson acknowledged. "Mining this channel would have closed Copenhagen's harbor completely, which obviously hasn't been the case. Not unless they somehow managed to work out a way to detonate mines from the shore after all, and I don't believe they could have. Even contact mines built with the tech currently available to them are going to be pretty damned problematical. Most of the mines employed prior to the 1900s had a very high failure rate, and I'd guess that anything they could cobble up on such relatively short notice would be . . . less than fully reliable, let's say.

"On the other hand, only one of them would have to work to put any one of our ships on the bottom. And the same is true for those spar torpedoes of theirs. Which is why we're going to Formation Charlie."

"Yes, sir."

The main problem with smoke screens, Ulrik discovered (not to his surprise, particularly) was that *neither* side could see through them. He knew approximately where the American warships had been when the reeking, choking, thoroughly filthy wall of smoke rolled down across the galleys. Unfortunately, he couldn't be certain they were still there. For that matter, it was all but impossible to be confident about his own vessels' heading. Fortunately, the breeze was strong enough and the smoke rolling along on it was thick enough to keep his sense of direction from becoming totally confused.

"Shouldn't we have made contact by now, Your Highness?" his galley's second-in-command asked. He sounded more than a little nervous, and Ulrik commanded himself to wait long enough to draw a deep breath and be positive he was in control of his own voice before he responded.

"We haven't gone as far as you think we have since we lost sight of them, Sven," he said then. "And if you were in command on the other side, would you

have continued charging straight ahead after you'd
sighted us coming? Especially if you'd noticed the
spar torpedoes, first?"

"Probably not, Your Highness," the other man
acknowledged after a moment. "I wish we did know
where they are, though."

"Well, so do I!" Ulrik assured him with a laugh.
"On the other hand, blind as we may be, they have
to be equally blind. And just between the two of us,
that suits me just fine."

Commander Wolfgang Mülbers muttered another
oath as the front edge of the smoke bank enveloped
Ajax. Mülbers' timberclad had turned hard to starboard, with *Achilles* astern of her. Their new heading
was at right angles to their earlier course, and they
had reduced speed to no more than six or seven
knots. He didn't like moving so slowly when he might
have to maneuver hard to avoid those dammed spar
torpedoes, but Formation Charlie was essentially a
defensive one. Admiral Simpson had worked it out
as one of the Navy's standard deployments specifically
designed to deal with the threat of torpedo attack in
poor visibility and narrow waters. In open water, or
with better visibility, they would almost certainly have
gone to Formation Delta. Delta called for all units
to maneuver at high speed, giving them the best
opportunity to evade, but that wouldn't have been very
practical here in the approaches to Copenhagen. And
at least the slow speed of Formation Charlie should
give them stable gun platforms.

The smoke grew thicker, and he heard members
of his bridge crew coughing. He also felt his muscles

tightening, and his nerves singing with tension. Below the bridge, the forward port mitrailleuse moved slightly, mounting squeaking as its crew trained it in the direction of the anticipated threat. The carronades were ready, as well, but they were also much slower firing.

Seconds dragged past, trickling away into minutes that seemed impossibly long, and still there was no sign of the Danes. What the hell where they up to?

"Think the smoke's reached the ironclads?" Ulrik asked. He kept his voice low, his mouth only inches from Norddahl's ear, as if he were afraid the Americans might hear him. Which was pretty silly, he supposed . . . not that he had any intention of raising his voice.

"Hard to say," Norddahl replied only slightly more loudly. The Norwegian frowned into the eye-watering murk, then shrugged with a certain fatalism. "Either it has, or it's about to, or it's never going to get there at all. In any case, it's probably time, Your Highness."

"That's what I was thinking, too," Ulrik said, and then he did raise his voice.

"All right, boys! Let's go!"

There were no cheers. He and Norddahl had been very firm about that part of their instructions during their training exercises. But Ulrik felt the sudden electric surge, the release of the tension of waiting transmuting itself into eagerness, as the sweeps groaned once more and the galleys, which had come almost completely to a halt, began to accelerate through the water again.

They'd stayed about as close together as they could get without fouling one another's sweeps. Even so,

Ulrik could see only the three or four closest galleys, and he was unhappily certain that his squadron was advancing unevenly. The other galleys, the ones far enough out from the center of his line to be unable to see his command galley, wouldn't know to begin advancing once more until one of the other galleys they *could* see started to move. Still, he'd factored that into his planning with Norddahl from the beginning. They couldn't hope to win an organized fight at any sort of extended range, so they'd planned from the outset to fight the opposite sort of battle: a close-in melee under the worst visibility conditions they could create.

Now it remained to be seen how well those plans were going to succeed.

"Ship on the port quarter!"

Commander Mülbers whipped around, peering aft through the filthy, greasy smoke. For a second or two, all he could see was more smoke. Then the bows of a gun-armed galley came thrusting into visibility.

The galley's crew obviously hadn't seen *Ajax* until the moment they were spotted in return. Its eighteen-pounder couldn't be brought to bear, and the slender craft began turning sharply, trying to point its bows toward its larger enemy.

There was no need for Mülbers to issue any orders. Or, rather, all the necessary orders had been issued long since. As the galley started its turn, the after mitrailleuse in the port broadside pivoted slightly behind its heavy splinter shield, and the gunner turned the crank.

The staccato explosions sounded like someone dragging the world's biggest stick down a picket fence made

of steel, Mülbers thought. The range was no more than
forty or fifty yards, close enough that a shot from the
galley's gun might well penetrate *Ajax*'s stout timbers,
or at least the thinner planking protecting the paddle
wheel. But that was also a low enough range for the
mitrailleuse's .50-caliber slugs to punch through the
galley's thin hull planking like sledgehammers.

The men clustered around the eighteen-pounder
went down first as the heavy bullets ripped through
them in a ghastly red fog. The same slugs, scarcely
even slowed by their passage through the gunners'
bodies, smashed into the rowers behind them. Men
screamed, others simply died, and splinter-fringed holes
perforated the galley as the mitrailleuse walked its fire
aft down the centerline of the Danish vessel.

A single magazine more than sufficed to cripple the
galley, but the mitrailleuse crew swung into polished
action. The intensive training Admiral Simpson and their
own officers had hammered into them went deep—so
deep they never really had to think about it at all. The
gunner released the expended magazine. One of his
assistants snatched it from the mitrailleuse's breech,
aligned it over the extractor's fingers, and shoved it
down, punching out the empty cartridges. Even as the
empties fell to the deck, the gunner's second assistant
had slammed a second magazine into the weapon. The
gunner threw the lever, locking the new magazine into
place, and then turned the crank again, traversing his fire
across the shattered slaughter pen of the galley, while
his third assistant reloaded the first magazine.

Fresh thunder sounded from the direction of *Ajax*'s
bows as the forward mitrailleuse opened fire, and then
number two port carronade bellowed. Mülbers had

turned back forward when the second mitrailleuse opened up, but he still hadn't found the carronade's target when the eight-inch shell smashed into it.

Fortunately for the galley's crew, the shell punched clear through both sides of their vessel before the fuse could initiate detonation. Unfortunately, it did so at a sharp downward angle, exiting through the boat's bilge and giving birth to an instant geyser. And, even more unfortunately, water wasn't very compressible. When the shell *did* explode, the force of its detonation was directed upward, right into the bottom of the galley's hull, with devastating consequences. The vessel's back broke instantly and it capsized, spilling men into the icy water, and the Sound was cold enough even in May for hypothermia to be a very real danger.

The after mitrailleuse was thundering again, and in the brief pause as its crew reloaded, Mülbers heard *Achilles* firing astern of him.

"It would be nice," John Chandler Simpson said through clenched teeth, "to have some fucking idea who's fucking shooting at what."

The admiral's tone was remarkably level, under the circumstances, Franz Halberstat thought. His language was something else, of course, and the flag captain felt an ignoble temptation to flee to the other side of the conning tower. The actual physical separation wouldn't have meant much, but every little bit helped.

He waited for Simpson to say something else, but despite the profanity, the admiral obviously had himself under tight control, which said quite a lot about his self-discipline. One concept he'd hammered home again and again was the absolute necessity of situation reports. "Never assume that your senior officers see and know what *you* see and know," he'd said over and over. Now he and Halberstat could both hear the stuttering bursts of mitrailleuse fire and the occasional deeper, harder coughs of carronades. Unfortunately, what they could actually *see* was absolutely nothing, and no one was using the radio to enlighten them.

"Ship on the port bow, bearing three-four-niner!"

Halberstat was out of the conning tower's protection and onto the port bridge wing in a flash. The need to see as clearly as possible dwarfed any consideration of the conning tower's armored protection, and he strained his eyes against the smoke.

The centerline mitrailleuse mounted on the foredeck in front of the main armored casement began to spit streaks of fire into the smoke. Halberstat followed their direction and finally found the galley the lookout had spotted. How that young man had managed to pick it out of this infernal fog was more than Halberstat was prepared to guess. He couldn't see it very clearly himself even now, but it looked as if it had actually been crossing ahead of the flagship when it was sighted. And even under these miserable visibility conditions, it was clear that the mitrailleuse's gunner had found his mark.

The galley slewed sideways, and an instant later at least one of the mitrailleuse's heavy bullets must have hit the spar standing upright in its bows. The torpedo mounted on the spar pitched over the side as the spar itself shattered. It plunged into the water, vanishing in a flash of white foam . . . then exploded with ear-stunning violence as its sinking weight jerked the firing lanyard taut.

The galley—and its entire crew—disappeared in a volcano of white water and splintered timbers.

"New ship, port quarter, two-seven-five!" another lookout shouted, and the after mitrailleuse began to fire.

Ulrik heard the rapid-sequence firing of what had to be the USE's "mitrailleuses," and the interspersed thunder of their cannon. He couldn't see a thing, and the tension in his own torpedo-armed galley twisted tighter and tighter as the crew continued to row straight ahead into the impenetrable smoke.

The gunfire seemed to be coming from every direction *but* directly ahead of them, he reflected bitterly, while his heart hammered at the base of his throat. Apparently everybody but him and the other two galleys somehow managing to stay in formation with him had made contact. It took all his willpower to keep from ordering his own galley to turn sharply, hunting back the way it had come for the prey it had obviously somehow missed.

"That was a torpedo!" someone unidentifiable through the smoke half-shouted as a deeper, somehow *longer* explosion roared.

Ulrik had no doubt that whoever had shouted was absolutely correct. The question was whether or not the explosion had accomplished anything. And, if it had, what—

"Ship dead ahead!" someone screamed.

Captain Markus Bollendorf's lookouts weren't as fortunate as *Constitution*'s had been. They picked up all three of the attackers, but not until the galleys were almost on top of SSIM *Monitor*.

The after mitrailleuse opened fire almost instantly, and the carronade crews started frantically training their guns toward the threat, but the forward mitrailleuse wouldn't bear at all, and there wasn't enough time to coordinate the ironclad's defensive fire power properly. The after mitrailleuse crew ripped one of the attacking gunboats into a splintered charnel house, and the forward carronade managed to get off a single shot which struck its target with devastating force. It hit just to one side of the galley's stem and punched directly aft until it exploded halfway down the vessel's length, killing virtually its entire crew.

The second carronade, unfortunately for *Monitor*, had been training around to engage the same target. When the first gun's shell exploded, the second gun captain instantly started slewing his weapon around to engage the remaining galley, but there simply wasn't enough time.

A corner of Ulrik's brain cringed.

Despite everything, his efforts to envision the effectiveness of the USE warships' weapons had come up short. The stabbing, staccato thunderbolts streaming from the mitrailleuse came faster and more accurately than he had ever anticipated. They had heaped the crew of one of his accompanying galleys in mounds of dead and wounded, and the shockwave from the volcanic eruption as the carronade shell disemboweled his second galley seemed to punch his entire body like some huge, immaterial fist.

But despite the carnage that had enveloped and devoured the other two galleys, his own swept forward, as if protected by some magic spell.

Norddahl manned the tiller, arrowing straight toward the fire-spitting behemoth of their target, and Ulrik's heart thundered louder than the enemy's guns as he lowered the spar. It dropped, angling sharply into the water, and drove straight toward the ironclad's flank. It was like a knight's lance driving into a dragon's side, and every ounce of Ulrik's being focused down to the firing lanyard in his fist.

The tip of his lance drove in under the ironclad's bilge. Despite the potentially lethal consequences if the spar shattered and drove back into his own body, Ulrik kept his free hand on the thick shaft, feeling for any telltale vibrations.

It quivered suddenly, jerking, flexing madly, and the prince visualized the torpedo on its other end. It was as if his eyes could pierce the blinding smoke, actually see down into the water. He *knew* the torpedo had gone exactly where it was supposed to go, under the turn of the bilge, grating along under the "roof" of the ship's flat bottom.

He jerked the lanyard.

Monitor heaved indescribably.

Bollendorf went to his knees as the entire ship bounced and *twisted* underfoot. Wooden planking shattered, framing members snapped, water poured in through a ton by-ten-foot breach, and the ship began listing sharply to port.

Any other vessel of *Monitor's* size would have sunk quickly. But *Monitor* had been designed by John Chandler Simpson with exactly this sort of situation in mind, and Bollendorf used the voice pipes to drag himself back upright.

"Pump the port trim tanks!" he shouted down the voice pipes to Engineering. "Shut down the port drive pump!"

"Aye, aye, sir!"

The disembodied reply coming back up out of the voice pipe was distorted, high-pitched with excitement and perfectly reasonable fear. It was also recognizable as that of Lieutenant Johannes Verlacht, *Monitor*'s senior engineer. Even better, Bollendorf heard the steady, pounding roar of the ironclad's big diesel still thundering along in the background. As long as they had power for the pumps, they had a chance.

Chapter 61

The first thing Prince Ulrik was aware of as he recovered a rather groggy consciousness, was the steel bar clamped across his chest. He blinked as he set his oddly drifting mind the task of figuring out what was happening.

He was in the water—*cold* water. Water so cold his extremities were already beginning to feel numb. Was that one of the reasons his brain seemed to be working so slowly, as well?

He blinked again, then coughed harshly. The top of his skull seemed to separate from the rest of him, and his throat burned as the saltwater came up. It was thoroughly unpleasant, but it also seemed to joggle his mind back to awareness.

He rolled his head. The steel bar across his chest, he discovered, was Baldur Norddahl's left forearm. The Norwegian was towing him through the water with a powerful sidestroke.

For a moment, Ulrik wondered what had happened to the galley. Then he remembered. The explosion had seemed muffled, almost silent. He couldn't really remember it as a *sound* at all, he realized. But he *did* remember the sudden, incredible *lifting* sensation—a sensation much like a stone hurled out of a catapult might have felt—as the galley's bows reared upward.

That was all he remembered, but as he looked back, he saw the shattered galley lying on its side, sinking rapidly. There was no sign of most of the crew. A handful of swimmers struggled through the water in Norddahl's wake—that was all he could see . . . out of a crew of seventy-six.

Ulrik gave himself a mental shake, then reached up and patted Norddahl's forearm with his right hand. The Norwegian stopped swimming for a moment, looking back at the prince, and his craggy face blossomed into a huge grin.

"Good!" he said. He released his grip, although it was obvious he was prepared to take Ulrik in tow again if the prince proved less recovered than he thought he was. Ulrik appreciated that, but he shook his head again and began treading water beside Norddahl.

"Good!" the Norwegian repeated, then turned and pointed. "And now, we go there, I think," he said.

Ulrik followed the pointing finger's direction and felt a sudden, undeniable flare of satisfaction as he saw the sharply listing ironclad. The ship was still afloat, and from the looks of things, it might well stay that way. A part of Ulrik was disappointed by that, but only a part. Whether it sank or not, the ship clearly wasn't going to be participating in any bombardments of Copenhagen this afternoon. And, on a more selfish level, if it managed to stay afloat, Prince Ulrik of Denmark might just survive the day, after all.

✧   ✧   ✧

"Captain Bollendorf is on the radio, Admiral."

"Good."

Simpson dropped quickly down the internal ladder to the radio room. The radioman looked up at him, then handed him the microphone.

"Markus?"

"Yes, Admiral." The voice coming back over the speaker was hoarse and rasping, but if there was any hint of despair in it, Simpson couldn't hear it.

"What's your situation?"

"Not good, sir, but a lot better than it could have been. We've been badly holed. The torpedo detonated underneath the left tunnel pod and the blast punched up through the bottom of the hull. The breach has to be at least ten feet across, and it's almost directly under the bulkhead between number two and number three trim tanks. They're both completely flooded, and so are three of the compartments inboard of the tanks. We've pumped out the other two trim tanks and all the ballast tanks, but we've still got a heavy list—Lieutenant Verlacht estimates it at around fifteen to twenty degrees. Some of the bulkheads around the flooded compartments have lost integrity, as well, but the pumps seem to be keeping up with any water we're taking on there. I don't think she's in any immediate danger of sinking, but we've definitely lost the port pump, and we're going to need major repairs."

"Casualties?" Simpson's flat, over-controlled tone shouted his own emotions

"So far, we have three dead and eight wounded," Bollendorf replied. He paused for a moment, then added, almost gently, "It could have been worse, Admiral. A lot worse."

"Understood," Simpson replied. He stood thinking for a moment, rubbing one eyebrow with a forefinger, then nodded to himself.

"Head for Saltholm Island," he said. "Beach her in the shallowest water you can. We'll see about pulling her out of the mud after we finish dealing with Copenhagen."

"Aye, aye, sir," Bollendorf replied. Then he seemed to hesitate for a moment before he continued. "Admiral, we've recovered the survivors of the galley which damaged us. There aren't many; the blast from their own torpedo sank them. But one of them says that he's King Christian's son, Prince Ulrik."

"You've got *Prince Ulrik* over there?" Simpson said very carefully.

"Yes, sir. We do."

"I see. Hang on for a minute, Markus, while I find out what sort of shape Mülbers' bass boat is in now."

"Welcome aboard, Your Highness."

It wasn't the first time Ulrik had ever seen Admiral Simpson, but it was the first time they'd actually been introduced. The American officer's grip was firm, and his eyes examined Ulrik's face intensely.

"Thank you, Admiral," Ulrik replied. "I'm very grateful to Captain Bollendorf for rescuing my men."

Simpson's free hand made a small waving-off gesture, and Ulrik smiled wryly. The journey from *Monitor* aboard the "bass boat" from one of the timberclads had been . . . lively. The wind had freshened further, dispersing the remnants of his smokescreen as the combustibles on the rafts finally burned out. The flat-bottomed boat had bounced across the steeper swell like a skipping stone from a child's hand. The fact that only three of his galleys were still afloat—and that two of those were clearly foundering—had tightened his mouth with pain. He doubted that very many of those galley crews had been as fortunate as he had.

Still, *Monitor* was a worthwhile prize. True, he hadn't managed to *sink* her, which would have been worth the entire cost of his galley squadron twice over, but he'd certainly demonstrated that not even the ironclads were truly invincible.

"I wish I could have welcomed you aboard under better circumstances, Your Highness," Simpson continued. "Unfortunately, just as you, I have orders to carry out. Would you come this way please?"

"Of course," Ulrik replied, and followed the American up the ladder on *Constitution*'s steep-sided casement to the open bridge wing. As he climbed, he was conscious of how much he missed Norddahl's solid, reassuring bulk at his back, but the Norwegian was still back on the *Monitor.*

They reached the bridge, and Simpson introduced Ulrik to *Constitution*'s captain and executive officer. It was the first time Ulrik had actually been aboard one of the USE's American-designed ships, and he was deeply impressed by the interior of the conning tower with its up-timer lighting and carefully thought out and arranged control stations.

"Very well, Captain," the admiral said to Captain Halberstat. "Let's get the squadron back underway."

"Aye, aye, sir."

Halberstat passed a quick sequence of orders, and the squadron resumed the steady advance Ulrik's attack had managed to at least delay.

The prince stood silently on the bridge, watching alertly. Everything he saw only impressed him more, and felt a deep temptation to chatter away to his captors about their marvelous equipment, but he suppressed it sternly. No doubt a lot of it was shock, and the result of sheer jubilation at finding himself still alive.

That wasn't the reason he made himself keep his mouth shut, however. He and Baldur had planned their defense of Copenhagen carefully, and they still had one last string to their bow, so to speak. So, Ulrik forced his expression to remain only interested and fascinated by his surroundings as the gunboats forged ahead once more.

Ajax led the reduced squadron toward Admiral Simpson's chosen firing point some hundred yards off Amager Island's defensive batteries. Captain Mülbers was back on his bridge wing, watching the white water foaming back from either side of *Ajax*'s blunt bow. He didn't like to admit just how frightening he'd found the Danish galleys' attack. Not so much for his own personal safety, as for the safety of his vessel and the men serving in her. What that single spar torpedo had managed to do to *Monitor* was grim evidence of what *could* have happened if they'd been even a little less lucky in that smoke-strangled melee.

He grimaced at the memory, then worked his shoulders from side to side, trying to flex the tension out of them. It helped, and he reached for his binoculars again. He'd just started to lift them toward his eyes when the corner of his attention noticed something floating in the water directly ahead of *Ajax*.

It wasn't very big. Obviously, it was a piece of

wreckage from one of the smashed galleys, or something of the sort. It couldn't be anything else, given the fact that they were heading back through the very area where the brief, madly confused engagement had taken place. Of course, it was remotely possible there were still survivors in the water, using some of that same wreckage for flotation, so—

Wolfgang Mülbers never completed the thought. The "wreckage" ahead of his ship was in fact one of the floating mines that had been towed along behind a dozen of Prince Ulrik's galleys. They'd been cut loose only after the smokescreen had hidden them from any observation, been left behind . . . which had put them squarely in the path of Admiral John Simpson's gunboats. Not only put them there, but left them in water that was obviously clear of mines because the galleys themselves had just passed through it.

Each mine was actually part of a cluster of *three* mines, roped together. The dot Mülbers had observed was part of one such cluster, but the dot that he *didn't* see was part of another cluster. One which SSIM *Ajax* had just run directly across.

The improvised detonators were less than reliable, just as Simpson had suggested might be the case in his earlier conversation with Captain Halberstat. Five of them completely failed to function. The *sixth* detonator, however, did exactly what it was supposed to. The mine to which it was attached exploded, and both of its companions went up in sympathetic detonation.

It was a thunderous burst of sound, but before it even truly registered, it was drowned by another, far more powerful blast as *Ajax's* magazine exploded.

✧   ✧   ✧

John Simpson stared at the expanding ball of fire and smoke that had once been one of his timberclads. Bits and pieces of wreckage lofted outward from the heart of the blast, trailing thin ribbons of smoke across the blue northern sky. He saw one of the ship's carronades sail at least sixty or seventy feet straight up, and his jaw clenched so tightly he was astonished his teeth didn't shatter.

I put the magazines as low as possible to protect them . . . which put them exactly where a bottom-contact explosion could get to them, didn't it?

He wrenched his attention away from the explosion, looking over his shoulder. The expression on young Prince Ulrik's face was all the confirmation he needed. He realized exactly what Ulrik must have done—and how the Danish prince had succeeded in drawing Simpson into exactly the mistake he'd wanted.

For an instant, white-hot rage blasted up inside John Simpson. He'd known all of the officers and men aboard that ship. None of them could have survived that cataclysmic blast, and the man responsible for arranging it stood less than five feet away from him, within easy reach.

But as quickly as it had come, his fury shrank back to merely mortal proportions.

He was only doing his duty, the admiral told himself, the thought harsh in his own mind. *Only doing his duty. And let's face it, he may have arranged it, but you're the one who walked straight into it. Which is exactly why you're so goddamned mad at him.*

He inhaled deeply, then made his white-knuckled grip on his binoculars relax and turned to Captain Halberstat.

"I think we'll have a use for the bass boat after all, Franz," he said. "Please signal Ensign Halvorsen that we need him to take point. And pass the same word by radio to the other gunboats. Bring the squadron forty-five degrees to starboard until we're well clear of the engagement area."

"Aye, aye, sir," Halberstat acknowledged. He nodded to one of the signalmen, and Simpson looked at Prince Ulrik as the signal lamp mounted on the front of the bridge began to flicker at Halvorsen's powerboat.

"I see your father was telling the truth when he said Copenhagen wasn't defenseless, Your Highness," he said. The column of gunboats altered course while simultaneously slowing sharply to let Halvorsen take up his new station. "I wish I could congratulate you on your accomplishment. I trust you'll understand why I find that rather too difficult to do at this particular moment."

Ulrik nodded, just a bit gingerly. His own emotions were mixed. Although the mines had been his idea, and even though he and Norddahl were the ones who had worked out the plan to bring them into action, he'd never really expected one of these ships to simply *blow up* like that. Never imagined he would kill *everyone* aboard one of them. The sudden flush of triumph he'd felt was tempered by the knowledge that there could have been no survivors, and he was guiltily delighted when he realized the Americans' change of course would take them safely clear of any of his remaining mines.

Well, of course you're delighted, Ulrik! he told himself. *After all, if they hadn't changed course, there's no reason this ship couldn't have been sunk, as well, and you've already been swimming once today.*

The gunboats steadied on a heading that would bring them to his chosen firing position in about twenty more minutes. "I think, however," Simpson continued, as the shore batteries began to thump smokily, "that Copenhagen's defenses—*effective* defenses, that is—are just about expended now. Under the circumstances, I'd like to invite you to take another message from me to your father."

"Thank God you're alive, Ulrik!" King Christian blurted, crushing his son in a rib-popping, eye-bulging embrace. If Ulrik had ever doubted that his father loved him, that doubt would have been vanquished forever, and he felt his own eyes burn as he hugged Christian back.

"I'm alive, Father," he said, "but most of my men aren't. We did our best, but we didn't stop them. That's why Admiral Simpson sent me ashore to tell you that his original terms still stand."

"No!"

Christian jerked back, his huge smile banished by an expression of ferocious determination.

"Father, they're ready to open fire. Trust me, the shore batteries aren't going to stop them, and my galleys are gone now."

"Maybe so," his father said half-sullenly. "But we've still got more of your floating mines, and wind and tide will carry them straight into those gunboats if we release them in the right spot."

"Father, there's no way to control the direction they'll drift if we turn them loose. They may get to the Americans, but they probably won't. And if they don't, then they'll be a menace to any other vessel that approaches Copenhagen. And even if we manage to sink another one of their ships, it's not going to change the fact that they're anchored right off the waterfront, ready to turn the shipyard—and the entire city, for that matter—into rubble."

"We won't sink *one* more of their ships; we'll sink *all* of them!"

"Father, I don't think we—"

"Yes, we can!" Christian thundered. "Can and *will*!"

It was a mark of his father's fury, thought Ulrik—almost mindless fury, now, even though the king was still completely sober—that he obviously hadn't given any thought at all to the most likely target of Admiral Simpson's guns. Being charitable about the matter, that could be explained by the fact that Rosenborg Castle, located in the center of the city, could not easily be fired upon by ship-mounted cannons. Not, at least, unless Simpson was prepared to have most of his shells missing the palace and landing in residential areas. But it was Ulrik's assessment that the American admiral was still doing his best to keep casualties down.

And why bother, anyway—when there was such a splendidly visible and obvious target right at the waterfront? Which, unfortunately, happened to be the very place that a prisoner was being kept—who, if he died, might very well send Simpson's temper soaring as high as that of the Danish king.

So, Ulrik left his father to his consultations with his gunnery captains and quietly slipped out of the Long Hall, then went first to his own chambers for the pouch of coins they'd be needing. For obvious reasons, he hadn't taken the pouch with him on the galleys.

He gave the trusted servant waiting there a little smile. "Since I'm still alive after all, I'll take care of the matter myself, Bent." The old man nodded stiffly, letting only a faint trace of his relief at the prince's survival show. He'd been Ulrik's manservant since the prince was four years old. They were very close.

"You're lucky you got here in time, Your Highness," Bent said gruffly, handing over the pouch. "I was about to leave."

Ulrik found Anne Cathrine where he'd told her to wait for him or Bent, if this plan proved necessary also. Not in her own chambers but in the king's so-called Golden Chamber, a small room Ulrik's father used for private meetings.

The moment he came into the room, Anne Cathrine seized him in a tight embrace. "Oh, Ulrik! I was so afraid you'd get killed!"

Despite the tension and anxiety of the moment, Ulrik felt himself awash with affection for his younger half-sister. The long winter months during which they'd slowly and carefully laid their plans—sometimes with their father's knowledge and agreement, sometimes behind his back—had brought the two siblings much closer than they'd ever been in times past.

But he didn't let the embrace last for long. There was very little time left.

"Here," he said, pressing the pouch of coins into his sister's hand. "There's plenty for whatever bribes you'll need to pay."

Anne Cathrine frowned. "They've *already* been paid," she protested.

Ulrik chuckled. "I'm trying to remember if I was

that naïve when I was fifteen years old. I don't think
so. Let me explain to you the secret of bribery, little
sister. The one being bribed *always* wants a little
extra at the very end, once he knows you really want
him to do what you're paying him to do. Or not do,
more often."

"That's rotten!" she snapped.

"Rotten or not, it's the way it is. Now go!"

She hurried toward the door, then stopped, just as
she was about to leave, and turned around.

"I want two days!" She held up two fingers. "Two
days, Ulrik, not an hour less. Before you tell Papà
where we are."

He grinned at her. "This is all supposed to be very
cold-blooded, little sister. High matters of state—your
sole and only motive."

She sniffed as haughtily as a fifteen-year-old could
manage. "Maybe for you. Not me. Not any more,
anyway. Remember—I want two full days. Not an
hour less!"

And she was gone.

"Damn the man!" John Simpson muttered as
the white flag flying over the central battery slowly
descended its pole. It was the agreed-upon sign to
indicate the rejection of his terms, but the Danes
waited punctiliously until it had been completely
lowered before fresh jets of smoke and flame spurted
from the defending artillery.

The Danish gunners were better shots than those
of Hamburg had been. Round shot slammed into the
three remaining ironclads' armor, skipping off in a
deafening clangor like some berserk chorus of bells.

More round shot made white circles in the water as they plunged deep, and others kicked up mud when they hit in particularly shallow water.

It was, Simpson was forced to admit, an impressive sight. In practical terms, however, it was accomplishing exactly nothing.

Unlike their frigging mines and torpedoes, he reminded himself.

That thought sent a flicker of uneasiness through him. Most of him was certain Copenhagen's defenders had shot their bolt. That this was simply Christian's typical bullheaded, bloody-minded obstinacy. But he wasn't about to ignore the possibility that Ulrik had contrived some additional deviltry that might yet cost Simpson more ships—and lives—if he allowed himself to be distracted.

I don't want to kill those poor damned gunners over there, either, though, he thought, glaring at the batteries and remembering the wreckage his guns had left behind at Hamburg. *It's not their idea, after all.*

His eyes narrowed suddenly, and his spine straightened.

Wait a minute. It isn't *their idea, John; it's Christian's. So why don't you just find yourself a target that can demonstrate the depth of his . . . unwisdom even to him? Something prominent, something royal . . .*

His eyes lit on the tall finger of the Blue Tower rising above Copenhagen Castle on Slotsholmen Island, and he smiled thinly.

Chapter 62

Almost mesmerized, Eddie stared at the distant ironclad that was bringing itself around to bring its big ten-inch guns to bear on Copenhagen Castle. The two pivot-mounted guns had been trained around to the port broadside from their normal fore and aft positions, so he got an excellent view of *three* of them. And judging from their elevation, Eddie had a pretty shrewd notion that their target was the castle's single most prominent feature: the Blue Tower.

The same Blue Tower, unfortunately, that contained Eddie himself—locked into a room on one of the upper floors.

That was the *USS Constitution*, to make things perfect—Simpson's own flagship. Even at the distance, Eddie could recognize the admiral's flag.

No, it'd be the *SSIM Constitution*, now. He'd learned that from Ulrik.

He would have been positive as to the ship's identity, even if it hadn't been for the admiral's flag. It was hard to distinguish the ironclads at a distance because they'd all been built according to the same design. They were certainly too far away for him to read the lettering on the hulls. Still, each ship tended to have slight variations of its own, and as much time as he'd spent working on them those variations had become as familiar to him as the features of different people's faces.

He could see the national colors they were flying, too, which was the new flag adopted by the United States of Europe after it was formed—by which time Eddie himself was a Danish prisoner of war—not the flag he'd been familiar with. That had been the flag of the New United States, which was an adaptation of the up-time flag of the USA. A different pattern for the stars, but the same familiar red and white stripes. Since the Confederated Principalities of Europe had been a loose confederation rather than having the federal structure of the USE, the CPE's Navy had actually been the NUS Navy. Just on loan, so to speak. The CPE had never had a flag of its own.

Eddie had never seen the USE flag up close, and Ulrik's depiction of its design had been rather vague. From this distance, it looked remarkably like a Confederate battle flag from the American Civil War. At least, it clearly had the same stars and bars design, even if Eddie couldn't really make out the stars that well. But the color scheme was quite different. The USE's colors were the traditional German red, black and gold, not the red, white and blue of American custom—whether Union or Confederate. And the black crossed bars on this new flag were considerably thinner than the blue crossed bars of the Confederate flag. The end result was that, from a distance, the USE flag mostly just looked like a big red flag.

Swell, thought Eddie. *Might as well just call it a*

bloody flag and be done with it, far as I'm concerned.
Within less than a minute, he was about to get a personal
introduction to the phenomenon known as "friendly fire."
Most likely, a very brief introduction. Even if none of
the shells struck his chamber directly, he knew that it
wouldn't take that many rounds from those huge guns to
bring down the whole Blue Tower in a heap of rubble.
With Eddie Cantrell's poor squished skinny little carcass
somewhere in the middle of it, oozing blood and—best
not dwell on that—at least maybe they'd be able to
identity the remains from the scraps of red hair still
sticking to this or that shredded piece of—

Oh, yuck.

But, since Eddie couldn't see anywhere he could
hide that would make any difference, he decided to
stay at the window. What the hell. Might as well enjoy
a good show, short and unfortunately truncated as it
would be, on his way out.

He heard something behind him and turned. To
his surprise, the door was being unlocked. A small
hope flared up. Could the guards have decided to
take him out?

But the person who came through the door was not
one of the palace guards, it was Anne Cathrine.

"Hurry, Eddie!" she hissed, waving at him. "We
don't have much time."

Eddie wasn't about to argue the point. He didn't
quite race for the door—not with a pegleg—but came
damn close. If he survived all this, maybe he'd look
into setting up a Special Olympics. He'd probably be a
cinch for the gold medal in the 100 Meter Stump.

"You aren't kidding we don't have much time," he
said, as he got to the door. "Won't be more than—"

Anne Cathrine was already hustling him down the corridor, her shoulder under one of his arms, carrying him as much as he was moving himself. Under other circumstances, he might have been irritated and he'd certainly have been embarrassed, but he wasn't going to worry about that now. The simple fact was that, as strong as she was, Anne Cathrine was getting him down that corridor faster than he'd have managed on his own.

"The guards only agreed to leave for twenty minutes," she hissed. "The greedy swine. Hurry!"

And, of course, the feel of that young and incredibly vigorous and healthy and very female body pressed so closely to him was half-scrambling his brains. As he had before, for what now seemed a million times, he tried to remind himself sternly that the girl was only fifteen. No cradle robber he, damnation.

Alas, his mind—as it had the same million times before—refused to cooperate.

Her birthday's August 10th, so she's actually fifteen and three-quarters years old, which is a lot closer to sixteen, and sixteen ain't so bad when you really start thinking about it—sweet sixteen, remember?—not to mention that it's the age of consent in West Virginia and even if it weren't, a quick car ride across the state line from where Grantville used to be puts you in either Pennsylvania or Ohio where it's also sixteen and in a real pinch Jimmy Andersen once told me he'd heard it was only fifteen or maybe even fourteen in South Carolina although he thought you had to get parental permission for that to apply and fat chance of that even leaving aside the fact that Papà in this case is the king of fucking Denmark and just because it wasn't all that long ago that the hypocritical Norse bastards were ravishing Irish virgins didn't mean they took the same attitude when it was THEIR virgin daughters involved—

By now, they'd reached one of the servants' narrow staircases and were working their way down to the next floor. An incredible explosion above them wiped Eddie's feverish reveries right out of his mind. He was almost relieved.

The whole staircase shook—and it was mostly stone. Fortunately, no rubble came down.

Yet.

"What was that?" cried out Anne Cathrine, stopping for a moment and staring back up the stairs.

"*That,*" said Eddie grimly, "was the first of what will be as many ten-inch explosive shells as my boss Admiral Simpson thinks it takes to turn this place into rubble. Let's get moving again, king's daughter."

She stared at him. "Your admiral is *shooting* at the Blue Tower?"

"Sure is. Please, Anne Cathrine, we *have* to get moving. This whole thing's going to come down. Trust me, it *will.* Even up-time construction couldn't stand up to what's coming."

She did as he bade her, moving even more quickly than before. It was pure Valkyrie now, with not even a trace of her former—none too elaborate, damn the girl—attempts to salve Eddie's pride whenever she helped him along. For all practical purposes, she'd more or less picked him up and had him half-slung over her hip—

Imminent death and destruction be damned, that hip kicked all his reveries back into full gear. How could one teenage girl so completely demolish an adult man's hold on reality?

—and was practically bounding down the stairs, her mane of red-gold hair coming loose and starting to spill over half of Eddie's face.

Okay, fine. He was only a twenty-year old adult man, not some kinda codger, and even the girl's *hair* was gorgeous. Still and all!

She reached the landing and kept going down the next flight of stairs. Another incredible concussion rattled the whole structure. There was no way, with the slow rate of fire of the big ten-inch guns, that the *Constitution* could have fired a second broadside that quickly. Which meant that Simpson must have ordered another ironclad to start firing on the castle.

"My father will be furious!" she yelped. "Your admiral will be in a lot of trouble!"

Eddie giggled. Literally giggled. He couldn't help himself.

"And what's so funny?" she demanded. Not, however, breaking any strides to do so, thank God.

"Ah, nothing," said Eddie. There was no point trying to explain. Not now, for sure. Like every royal Eddie had met except Prince Ulrik—not that he'd met all that many—there was one side to Anne Cathrine that just plain lived in a fantasy world. For the most part, the girl was level-headed and practical. More so than any of her sisters that Eddie had met, and certainly more so than her mother Kirsten Munk, from all reports. Anne Cathrine not only had the constitution of a Danish dairy maid, she actually *did* know how to milk a cow.

Still, being raised in a royal family was bound to

distort your sense of reality, unless you had the rare faculty that Ulrik possessed of being very clear-sighted and very ruthless with your own preconceptions. It was difficult to understand that the map was not the territory. Surrounded by the trappings of power, those became confused with the reality that lay beneath those trappings. Even to the point where a royal father's temper still seemed more powerful and potent than the ten-inch explosive shells that were bringing his capital city down around him.

So be it. Eddie didn't mind, actually. Why should he? Most of the teenage girls he'd known back up-time had been at least as prone to confusing fantasy with reality. Even if, in their case, the confusion was between a credit card and the money that had to pay the bills, instead of a confusion between castles and debris.

It wasn't a perfect world—and never had been, for a skinny and socially inept red-headed kid raised in a trailer park, even when he still had two feet. The fact was, Anne Cathrine just plain bowled him over. The only thing that *really* bothered him was that he just couldn't see any way to make a real romantic relationship between them work, even assuming she was willing. And the fact that she *did* seem to be willing just made it all the worse.

Her age wasn't even the problem. Eddie would wait, and be glad to do so. But you don't "wait" for a princess to get older, because it doesn't matter how old she gets. She'll always be a princess—fine; "king's daughter." Big fricking difference, when you're still a one-footed chump of a junior naval officer with no title to your name beyond "Lieutenant"—a dime a dozen, that title was, in this world even more than the one up-time—and no fancy family connections—no family left at all, actually—and the only influential human being you had any close connection to—

Oh, the icing on the cake!

—was the same admiral who was blowing Daddy's Place to smithereens.

Who ordered this?!

The one and only thing that kept Eddie and Anne Cathrine alive was the simple fact that, powerful as they were, those ten-inch guns took a long time to reload. So, they'd reached the bottom floor and were already out the door into the courtyard where a coach was waiting for them when the second broadside from the *Constitution* started finally collapsing the Blue Tower. Not completely, not yet—but looking back hurriedly Eddie could see that the top two stories had come down already and what remained beneath was looking very, very shaky. He also saw the cloud of dust and debris that blew out of the doorway they'd just emerged from, and knew that the interior staircase must have been brought down. If they'd been just a few seconds later getting out of there, they'd have been crushed.

"In," Anne Cathrine hissed, more or less tossing Eddie into the carriage. She clambered in behind him, then had to stretch to close the door. The coach driver had already had the team of horses moving before she'd gotten all the way in, and the door had been flung wide open.

"Idiot!" she muttered. Eddie, on the other hand, thought the driver was a genius. He leaned his head out the window and looked back. From the looks of it, the Blue Tower would be coming down on its own, soon enough, even if the ironclads didn't fire any more rounds. It was already on fire, of course. The explosive material in those ten-inch shells was simply black powder. They weren't designed to be incendiary rounds, as such. But firing into a castle full of flammable materials, it hardly made any practical difference.

Anne Cathrine's head came into the window right next to his, her cheek pressed against his cheek and the rest of her in a full-body press against his back and the back of his legs.

"Oh!" she gasped, staring up wide-eyed. "Papà will have a *fit*. Your admiral will be lucky if he keeps his head!"

Eddie would have giggled again, except his whole throat was constricted. He felt like a one-man hormone factory. A very, very *big* factory—and the only boss in charge seemed to have the intelligence of a rabbit. A tiny little scrap of a brain with only enough room in it for one thought, and that one as primitive as it gets.

And then, what little scrap remained shrank down to maybe four functioning neurons. Anne Cathrine pulled him out of the window and closed the curtains. "You musn't be seen," she murmured. Right into his ear, because her cheek was pressed more closely still. So was her full body press, except within seconds it wasn't pressed against his back.

"You musn't be seen," she repeated, still murmuring. "The driver and two coachmen probably know who you are, but they've been very well paid. Still,

the less they see, the less they have to remember to
lie about."

Then, *she* giggled. "Too bad it's not a very long
trip." She was nuzzling his ear, now. "But we'll have
lots of time when we get there."

Eddie tried to rally. His cortex did, anyway. The
rest of his nervous system seemed to be on autonomous mode, with his hands moving here and there of
their own volition. It didn't help that everywhere they
roamed, Anne Cathrine's body came to meet them.

"Where are we going?" he croaked.

"Frederiksborg Palace. Ulrik and I figured out a
good place to hide you. Good thing we did, too."

Eddie croaked a little laugh. "Yeah, I'd say so. Or
I'd be hamburger *a la Tower*."

"Oh, yes." She kissed him. "We were pretty sure
Papà would be angry. So we had to hide you from
him, for a while. Or he might take it out on you."

She kissed him again. "He *certainly* would now,
unless your admiral surrendered so Papà could cut
his head off instead."

The third kiss was long and slow. As were all the
ones that followed. They didn't speak again until the
coach finally came to a stop.

Regretfully, Anne Cathrine pulled away and opened
the trunk that served as the bench across from theirs.
She came out with some nondescript-looking garments.

"Put these on, quickly. We will pretend you are a
servant who came with me."

That was a ploy so threadbare it almost seemed
pointless. Mere servants did *not* ride in coaches with
king's daughters. Certainly not male ones, with all the
curtains drawn.

But Eddie didn't argue the point. First, because his brain was still not functioning that well and, second, because its level of functioning declined still further when he realized that Anne Cathrine had every intention—unabashed, almost gleeful; did the girl have *any* sense of shame at all?—of watching him get undressed.

Fortunately, since the curtains were still drawn, it was fairly dark inside the coach. But Eddie was still red-faced by the time he finished changing his clothes.

"You are *so* cute!" she said, then reached with her hand to pinch his cheek, and then brought him close enough for a quick kiss. "But, come! Place the old clothes in the trunk and close the lid. We must hurry!"

And out she went. As soon as she reached the ground, she drew herself up in a decent imitation of a haughty princess—well, imitation of a haughty one, since she *was* a princess—and began striding away. Completely ignoring Eddie—as, indeed, a royal scion would completely ignore a servant who was supposed to know what to do when his royal mistress hared off somewhere.

Hurriedly, he stuffed his old clothing into the trunk and got out of the carriage. A bit awkwardly, because of the pegleg, but easily enough. With months of experience, Eddie had learned how to get about fairly well.

Still, by the time he reached the ground, Anne Cathrine was already halfway to the nearest building. Eddie barely noticed the coach setting off again, as he peered around curiously.

The coach had let them out in a part of the extensive palace grounds he wasn't familiar with. From what he could tell, they were on the southernmost of the three islands in the lake that made up the palace grounds, and he'd always been kept in the big royal palace on the northern island.

Anne Cathrine was striding toward two round towers that looked much older than the part of Frederiksborg Castle he knew. Almost, if not quite, medieval construction.

But she didn't enter them. Just before she got there, she began to head around what looked like big stables. And smelled like it, for that matter. She stopped abruptly, half-turned, and gave Eddie a very disapproving look. Not a personal look, though, just the sort of generic princess-or-noblewoman's glare at a sluggish servant who wasn't keeping up.

Eddie could take a hint. He started hobbling toward her as fast as he could. He had to be a little careful, because a lot of the courtyard he was crossing was cobblestoned and he'd learned the hard way that peglegs with narrow tips did not do well on such paving. On the other hand, he wasn't at all tempted to go off to the side and walk through the unpaved surfaces, since those left no doubt at all that they were in horse-stable territory.

Just before he caught up with her, Anne Cathrine started striding off again. But she'd waited long enough so that Eddie could follow her. Once she got around the corner, she headed straight for a big and very new-looking building, which had both a small entrance door and, quite a bit further down, a set of double-doors that were even bigger than you'd find in a stable. As if something very large had to be periodically taken in or out of the edifice.

She went through the small door, however, still as haughtily as she'd been walking since she got out of the carriage. She didn't glance back once to see if the menial servant was still following. Obviously, he would be, since that's what servants *did*.

The door closed behind her. Muttering under his breath—very unkind words on the subject of snotty princesses—Eddie followed through.

The moment he got inside, all unkind thoughts about snotty princesses vanished immediately. Anne Cathrine was back to the full-body press business, complete with long and lingering kiss. Eddie forgave her all her sins and any she might accumulate in at least the next five lives.

"Come," she finally said. "Baldur dismissed all the workmen, for a week, but someone might still come in. We must hide."

Taking him by the hand, she led him through what Eddie quickly realized was some sort of peculiar workshop. Not any sort of workshop he'd ever seen before, though, except . . .

About halfway through, he finally realized what it was. Greg Ferrara had set up something like this in Grantville, right after the Ring of Fire. Call it the Early Modern Era's version of a Manhattan Project. Two and two came together soon thereafter, and Eddie knew this was the place where Baldur Norddahl—who *still* had no business, in a sane world, being a cross between Harald the Bloody-Handed and Herr Professor Doktor Doktor Über-Weaponsgeek—undertook his fiendish experiments in military hardware.

Anne Cathrine was heading toward some sort of very peculiar wooden contraption against the far wall of the workshop. *Big* contraption, too.

It was the wood that threw Eddie off, until he was almost in front of it. At which point he realized he was looking at a *submarine*.

A real live, no-kidding, submarine. Not completed, obviously—he could see where the holes for whatever propulsion device would drive it were still empty—but the hull seemed finished.

A *wooden* submarine? The idea seemed completely outlandish, but . . .

Now that he was reminded, Eddie had read somewhere—a long time ago, long before the Ring of Fire, when he'd still been in his oceanographer phase—that somebody had built a wooden submarine once, way back in the nineteenth century. A Spaniard, if he remembered right, who'd intended the thing to be used for commercial diving operations. Pearls, or maybe coral, he couldn't remember. The submarine had worked, too, although it had eventually been scrapped because the commercial enterprise hadn't worked out.

There was a small opening on the side, low enough that only a step stool was needed to pass through. Anne Cathrine was already doing so, stooping to get in. Once she was inside, her smiling face looked back. "Come in, Eddie! This is where we will hide. No one will think of it."

In for a penny, in for a pound. As he worked his way through the opening, which was a very tight fit—probably something Baldur eventually intended for a ballast mechanism, or possibly a big observation port—Eddie realized with genuine shock that the submarine had been designed with a double hull—exactly the way submarines would wind up being designed, centuries in the future.

"Baldur Norddahl is a freak of nature," he muttered. "A man like that has *no business* being this smart."

The much bigger shock, though, came after he got inside. He'd gauged the overall size of the submarine at somewhere around forty feet long and ten feet in diameter. With the double-walled design, of course, the interior was much smaller—about twenty-five to thirty feet long, and not much over six feet in diameter in the very center. Eddie could just manage to stand up straight with a bit of clearance, although he'd have to stoop if he moved more than seven or eight feet toward the bow or the stern.

The hull was tapered, too, and even had a stream-lined bulb-nose design that was probably a little fatter than it should be but not much. Given that Norddahl had been working from scratch with nothing more than maybe some photos to guide him and having to work with wood instead of metal, the only thing that really registered was how incredibly well designed it was. If Baldur could figure out a workable propulsion system, he'd probably be able to build a truly functional submarine. It was certainly way, way good enough, to move Norddahl to the very top of the *shoot-this-mad-genius-now-before he-goes-any-further* list.

But all that Eddie simply half-noted in passing. The real shock came from the interior furnishings, which he could see quite clearly because Anne Cathrine was lighting two lamps inside the submarine.

Whatever propulsive mechanism Baldur might have intended was unknowable, because the interior had been stripped clean—if there had ever been anything to begin with—and replaced with . . .

With . . .

The only thing Eddie could think of was a set from a movie. *The King and I,* maybe. Or . . .

Anne Cathrine was now lolling back on a pile of very expensive looking cushions and blankets. Lolling, as in lying on one hip and giving him a look that was at least two decades too sultry. Fifteen going on Scheherazade.

Or the set from *A Thousand and One Arabian Nights,* maybe, although he wasn't sure if they'd ever made a movie of that book. He'd read it, though.

She waved her hand, way more languidly than any girl her age ought to be able to, at a small stack of baskets toward the bow. "There is plenty of food. Breads, cheeses, delicacies. Plenty of wine, too. We may have to hide here for days, before we can be sure my father's temper will have subsided."

Some part of Eddie's brain—a tiny little cluster of neurons somewhere in the left cortex making a valiant last stand, but even now being overwhelmed by the thalamic hordes—was trying to gibber something on the subject of fathers and their tempers in general, and royal fathers and royal tempers in particular—but they were soon slaughtered mercilessly.

"Come here, Eddie," she said. "Now."

"Enough," said Christian IV, finally slumping into one of the silver chairs in the Long Hall. He gave his son Ulrik a haggard look. "So, you were right. Those guns are incredible. And our own fire simply bounces from the damned things."

Ulrik placed a hand on his father's big shoulder and gave it a squeeze. "The terms will not be bad, Father. I'm quite sure of that."

"Union of Kalmar," the king muttered. "A *Swedish* union."

Ulrik started to say something, but closed his mouth. Now was not the time to discuss with his father the opinion that Ulrik had come to develop on the subject. Partly as the simple result of being the vanquished party—but much more as a result of long months of thinking of this possibility ahead of time.

It was odd, really, the way Christian IV loved modern gadgetry and doted on having a splendid library, given that the king himself didn't like to read. But his son did, and Ulrik had spent many hours in the Winter Room studying the up-time encyclopedia.

It hadn't taken him long to come to a simple conclusion. The century they were in, the seventeenth century, was the heyday of Scandinavia, historically speaking. From here—well, perhaps a half century more—it would all be a downward slide. Disunited and divided, Scandinavians were simply too few in number to play a major role in world affairs. They'd only managed it in this century due to happenstance. But starting in the next, Scandinavia would be lucky if it was simply ignored by its more populous and powerful neighbors to the south.

France and Britain would dominate Denmark in the nineteenth century, and Germany would conquer it outright in the next. Norway, too. Sweden only stayed independent by being meek and mild.

To hell with it, as Eddie would say. A re-united Scandinavia seemed like a far better prospect to a young Danish prince, even if its initial master spoke Swedish. Languages evolve also, after all—he had only to look at the new dialect of German that was sweeping over central Europe to see the proof of it.

"Would you take my surrender to Simpson yourself, Ulrik?" asked the king, his tone—for a wonder—mild and meek. "I think that might work best."

"Yes, father, of course."

Chapter 63

The estuary of the Thames, at Sheerness

"This is going to be closer timing than I'd like," Mike Stearns said to Captain Baumgartner. "I just talked to Harry on the radio and he says there's only so much he can do to slow down the barge. The current alone will bring them alongside Sheerness in less than an hour."

The commander of the *Achates* issued a soft little grunting sound. "Should be enough, Prime Minister. We'll be in sight of whatever warships the English have stationed at the Royal Dockyard within ten or fifteen minutes. Once they see us, I doubt they'll be worrying too much about a mere barge."

The calm words, spoken in a calm and even tone, did much to alleviate Mike's anxiety. Now that action was looming, he was getting a better understanding of Simpson's reasons for selecting Baumgartner as a warship captain. As morose as the wretched fellow might be at other times, the nearer they came to possible conflict the more the captain just seemed to get phlegmatic. It was as if his gloomy expectations were strangely lightened by the prospect of mayhem.

Why not? Having predicted disaster at every moment since the crossing of the North Sea began, how could mere hostile enemy activity be any worse?

It was an upside-down sort of psychology, to someone with Mike's temperament. But . . .

"Different strokes for different folks," he muttered.

Baumgartner turned his head slightly. "What was that, Prime Minister? I'm afraid I didn't catch it."

"Ah, never mind, Captain. Just talking to myself."

"Okay, everybody!" Harry hollered. "Take battle stations! We'll be coming in sight of Sheerness any minute now!"

Melissa stared at Rita.

Rita stared at Harry.

"Hey, Captain!" Rita hollered. "Could you puh-leese explain a little more clearly exactly what 'battle stations' consists of? Y'know—for us women and kids?"

Harry gave her a quick grin. "Mostly, it means you keep your heads below the gunwales—or whatever you call 'em, on a barge like this—and get ready to jump overboard first, if she starts to sink."

"Sink," said Melissa. She leaned over the rail and looked at the waters of the Thames. "How deep is it here, anyway?"

"Got no idea, Ms. Mailey," replied Harry. "Look at it this way. There's good news and there's bad news. The good news is that this barge is probably heavy enough to absorb one or two rounds from whatever guns they've got on whatever ships they've got stationed at the dockyard. The bad news is that one or two rounds is about the limit, too. If Rita's brother ain't there in time to take out them warships, we're screwed."

Several of the Warder women were looking worried, now. "None of us can swim very well, Lady Mailey," said Patricia Hayes. "The children, not at all." She gave the distant shore of the river an apprehensive glance. "That's a far ways."

In point of fact, Melissa knew, if the barge sank then even very good swimmers would face a real challenge. They were now well into the estuary of the Thames, and you couldn't really call it a "river" any longer. It was more like a small bay. At a guess, although she wasn't particularly good at estimating distances, they were at least a mile from land.

"Right," said Rita, suddenly moving purposefully. "Let's set about rigging up some sort of rafts. Or flotation devices, at least. Harry, I suppose it'd be too much to ask if you brought life vests with you, amongst all that other stuff you somehow managed to smuggle into England."

"No, sorry." Harry's smile contained as much in the way of apology as that of a crocodile, admitting that, no, it hadn't thought to bring napkin rings to the feast. "We pretty much concentrated on stuff that goes bang and boom, y'know."

"Don't remind me," muttered Melissa, who was also rising from her seated position, though much more awkwardly than Rita. The combination of the adrenaline from the escape and the hours they'd spent since, crammed into a barge, had left her feeling every day of fifty-nine years old.

On the bright side, if you chose to look at it that way, the fact that they'd made their escape from the Tower at dawn meant that it was no later than midafternoon once they reached the estuary. So at least they weren't fumbling in the dark.

The flip side of that, of course, was that any enemy warships lying in wait at Sheerness wouldn't be fumbling in the dark, either.

One or two rounds, and down she goes. Melissa wondered how long it took a warship to fire two rounds from whatever cannons they carried. She wasn't about to ask, however, since she was darkly certain that whatever the answer was, it would be extremely depressing.

"And there's Sheerness," murmured Captain Baumgartner. He brought up his eyeglass. "Now let's see how many ships they've got that aren't still at anchor."

To Rita's surprise, Thomas Wentworth came to give her some assistance. That was the first thing she'd seen him do since the barge left the Tower except stare off into whatever inner space he'd gotten lost in.

True, he wasn't much help. Whatever skills the former chief minister of England's government possessed—a great many, of course—they clearly didn't include being a handyman. Not that it made much of a difference. Rita soon realized that the "flotation devices" she was jury-rigging out of whatever odds-and-ends she could find on the barge weren't going to be of much use beyond whatever psychological solace they brought to the Warder folks. She wouldn't have trusted these things in a swimming pool, back up-time. If they went into the water, most of them were going to drown, it was as simple as that.

Still, she was glad to see some spirit come back to the man. Now that it was all over, and especially with the sharp contrast that Sir Francis Windebank and his mercenary goons had provided during the final period, she looked back upon Wentworth's role in those long months of captivity and remembered simply his invariant courtesy and graciousness.

"I'm afraid it's not much," Wentworth said to her quietly, once they were done.

"No, it isn't. On the other hand, I don't think we'll need to find out, either."

He cocked an eyebrow at her. "You've that much confidence in your navy?"

Rita chuckled. "Not exactly. It's just that I grew up with my brother, you know. We're talking about a guy who, for a stretch there in his teens, used to hot-wire cars in Fairmont or Clarksburg and go joy-riding about every month with his buddies. Never got caught once, even though every cop in Marion County knew damn good and well who the culprit was."

Wentworth frowned, obviously trying to extract the gist from the indecipherable terms. "A successful petty criminal, you're saying?"

"Well . . . technically. But since he always returned the cars in perfect condition, with a full tank of gas—sometimes, he'd even give them a wash in the process—nobody really cared that much."

"Ah." After a moment, the earl of Strafford smiled. That was the first smile she'd seen on his face all day. "I see. A successful politician, in the making."

"Yeah, you could put it that way. The point is, I really don't think he's likely to screw up."

A sudden shout came from the bow. From Sherrilyn,

obviously. That feminine shriek of glee was quite
unmistakable.

She turned her head to look. Sherrilyn was perched
rather precariously, pointing at something ahead of
them in the distance. "Eat your heart out, Harry!
Now—any second now, they've already got the guns
run out—you're going to hear a *real* pick-up line!"

Maybe two seconds later, Rita heard the distant
sound of cannons being fired.

"Now you lads!" roared Baumgartner. "Smartly,
y'hear!"

The captain was bringing the *Achates* around so that
it would be able to fire a full broadside at the nearest
of the three Royal Navy ships that were moving to
intercept it, instead of just the lead carronade on a
pivot mount. Even someone as nautically-challenged as
Mike Stearns could see that the timberclad's paddle-
wheel design that had made it such a tub on the
open sea now gave it an enormous advantage over
the three sailing vessels facing it. Where their captains had to maneuver in the estuary by contending
with the complex cross-forces of tide and current and
wind, Baumgartner simply had to give his helmsman
an order.

Within seconds, the broadside was fired. Only one
of the three English ships was in position to do the
same—and it was out of range. The broadside of the
Achates was fired at the lead enemy ship, which was
still trying to come into position.

It helped, of course, that the disparity in ordnance
was so tremendous. The biggest guns on those English
ships would be culverins, firing eighteen-pound round

shot. Most of the guns, and perhaps all of them, would be no bigger than twelve-pounders. And they were going up against the *Achates*, whose four-foot thick wooden walls would shrug off their fire, while it replied with explosive rounds fired from sixty-eight-pound carronades. There were just six of them, on a broadside—but six was plenty.

Indeed it was. Only two rounds from that first broadside struck the English warship, but they were enough to shatter its bow. Worse still—this was always the real threat that explosive rounds posed to wooden warships—they'd started fires in several places. Even given that warship crews of the time were trained and ready to deal with shipboard fires, at least one of those fires was already too big to be extinguished.

In fact, the captain of that ship—or whichever officer had succeeded him, if he'd been killed—was already giving the order to abandon it. Seeing the boats being lowered over the side, Baumgartner ignored that ship altogether and ordered the *Achates* to steam toward the other two.

One of those two seemed to be trying to head back to the docks, from what Mike could tell. The other one . . .

Either that captain couldn't make up his mind, or his ship had somehow gotten stalled in mid-water by incorrect or cross-purpose orders. Whatever that was called, in nautical terms. Mike could see its sails flapping uselessly in the wind. *Caught up in stays,* or something. It had been years since he'd read C. S. Forester's Hornblower novels, and he'd never paid much attention to the technical details anyway.

"Incompetent bastard," he heard Baumgartner

murmur contemptuously. To the helmsman he said: "Come hard to port. Let's let the lads on the starboard guns get a bit of experience too."

He seemed utterly calm, cool and collected. Mike wasn't prepared to forgive the captain all his sins, yet. But he did allow to himself, privately, that his former thoughts of homicide had been a tad excessive.

Perhaps two minutes later, the starboard broadside went off. At what amounted to point-blank range, in this case; close enough that the English ship was able to fire a broadside of its own.

So far as Mike could tell, only two shots from that enemy broadside struck the *Achates*. One hit the paddle wheeler's hull and simply bounced off. Literally, *bounced*—like a pebble thrown against a tree. The other one smacked into one of the timberclad's tall funnels. Mike would have expected it to knock the funnel completely down, but it didn't. Instead, it simply punched straight through it, leaving a smoke-streaming hole in each side about eight feet above bridge height.

All that, however, he barely noted in passing. The effect of the *Achates*' broadside on the English ship was so incredible that it pretty much obliterated everything else as it obliterated the ship. It was honestly hard to think of any other term to describe what happened when those six shells struck it amidship, even before the magazine exploded perhaps half a minute later and destroyed it altogether.

"Jesus Christ," Mike said softly. "May God have mercy on their souls."

The sharp glance Baumgartner gave him made it clear that the captain of the *Achates* disapproved of blasphemy, first; and, second, thought the likelihood that the Almighty would look with favor upon the souls of dead enemies of the USE Navy was probably a blasphemous notion itself.

He really was something of a shithead, Mike concluded. On the other hand, as the old cynical saying went, he was *our* shithead—and very damn good at it. Very damn good indeed.

"I can catch up to that third ship and send it down, if you'd like, Prime Minister. Though I can't say there's probably much purpose to doing so."

"No, no. Let's just find Captain Lefferts' barge and finish what we came here to do."

Less than a minute later, the lookout spotted the barge. It took less than half an hour, thereafter, to transfer everyone from it onto one of the two merchant vessels that would carry them to Amsterdam.

"And you're sure about Amsterdam, Prime Minister?" asked Captain Baumgartner. "Given that the weather seems to be holding up well—and there's a miracle, in itself—I'm sure we can make it back to Hamburg." His innate essence, naturally, made him hastily add, "The merchant vessels, at least. Our chances in the *Achates*, you understand, remain as grim as ever."

"Yes, I'm sure. For three reasons. First, because I think it will have a very salutary effect on Don Fernando to see a warship of the United States of Europe steaming serenely into Amsterdam's harbor, thumbing its nose at his entire blockading fleet. Now that I've observed this ship in action, I don't have much doubt they'd be no match for you, if they were stupid enough to try it."

"In the sheltered waters of the Zuider Zee?" Baumgartner shook his head. "No match at all."

Mike was pretty sure the cardinal-infante wouldn't try to test the issue, anyway. Not with the news they'd just received concerning the outcome of the Battle of Ahrensbök, which Becky would be sure to pass along to the Spanish. An entire French army destroyed, with most of its officers and soldiers captured, was *such* a good incentive for finding a diplomatic resolution to the war.

"What I figured. My second reason is that it would be better to set Wentworth and Laud ashore on Dutch soil. Of course, if *they* choose to seek further sanctuary in the USE, we'll be glad to oblige them. But I'd rather it was clearly their own choice, and not something we forced them into."

"I understand, Prime Minister. And the third reason?"

Mike frowned, trying to remember why he'd said "three reasons" in the first place. He'd come up with the number more from a subconscious impulse than anything else.

After a moment, the answer came to him, with truly brilliant clarity. At which point, he cleared his throat.

"Ah . . . 'three,' did I say? Can't imagine what I was thinking. No, it's just those two."

Because I really miss my wife and I want to get laid was not, all things considered, the sort of answer people expect from a head of state explaining matters of high diplomacy.

"Very well, Prime Minister. In that case, we should see to transferring you aboard Captain Hamers' ship."

Mike's eyes widened. "I was planning to remain aboard the *Achates*. At least, until we've safely made the North Sea crossing again and are in sheltered waters."

Baumgartner gave him a smile, the first one Mike had ever seen on his sourpuss face. "Oh, I think there's no need for that. I'm sure the men appreciate as much as I do your willingness to share the risks with us on the voyage over, Prime Minister. But now that the task is accomplished, I would be remiss in my duties if I didn't insist that you make the voyage back in the security of the seagoing vessels. Besides, with Wentworth and Laud aboard, you've got diplomatic work to do."

Mike stared at him. "You're . . . ah . . . sure about this, Captain? I assure you—"

"No, I insist! If for no other reason, because Admiral Simpson would be furious with me if I did otherwise."

Blessedly, the unnatural smile disappeared and was replaced with Baumgartner's usual lugubrious visage. "That's in the unlikely event I survive the crossing, of course. The North Sea's a treacherous mistress, treacherous beyond belief. She can turn on you in an instant. Even Hamers in that real ship of his will likely have a struggle of it. I don't really expect the *Achates* to make it, although I have hopes that we might get close enough to the Waddensee Islands before we founder that the ship's company can find refuge there. Insofar as those bleak and barren strips of sand can be called 'refuge' at all. But, who knows? Enough of the rats may come ashore that we'd have some food for a day or two. More likely, though, they'll be dining on us."

The first thing Harry Lefferts said after Mike clambered aboard Hamers' ship and explained they were headed for Amsterdam was, "Jeez, boss, you're making major decisions of state just to get laid?"

Mike ignored that. The first thing Melissa Mailey said—pointing a rigid finger at Harry—was, "Does the United States of Europe have firm laws on the books prohibiting the destruction of historic monuments; and if not, why not?"

Mike decided to ignore that, too. The first thing his sister said—pointing a rigid finger at her husband Tom—was, "Dammit, Mike, you're his commander-in-chief. Tell him he can't do it!"

Hard to ignore your own sister. "Do what?"

"Become a goddam priest! Or maybe even a bishop!"

Mike now looked at his brother-in-law. Tom had a sheepish expression on his face, and was rubbing his jaw with a hand that looked almost the size of a dinner plate.

"Well . . . It's like this, Mike." He glanced at a small, elderly, red-faced man standing in the stern of the ship and engrossed in conversation with a tall younger fellow. From descriptions he'd gotten and their apparel, Mike assumed that was the archbishop of Canterbury and Thomas Wentworth.

"Rita's ticked off," Tom continued, "because she figured—so did I—that after I coldcocked Laud while rescuing him that my chances of getting ordained were about zero. But it turns out the archbishop doesn't remember any of that. I guess I slugged him harder than I thought. The only thing he seems to remember—vaguely—is that I'm the guy who got him out of captivity. And his mood's improving by the minute."

"Do something, Mike!" shrilled Rita.

Chapter 64

Düsseldorf
Duchy of Berg

"A complete, total, unmitigated disaster," concluded Francois Lefebvre, the cavalry officer who also served Turenne's small army as its de facto intelligence officer. He tossed the Düsseldorf newspaper onto the big table at the center of the tavern's main room. "That's assuming this account is reasonably accurate, but I'm pretty sure it is. Every item in it that we've been able to check against what few French reports we've gotten has proven to be so."

"And what exactly *are* those reports, Francois?" asked Jean de Gassion.

Lefebvre made a face. His lips, curled into a sarcastic sneer; his brows, wrinkled with exasperation. "Not much, Jean—and with only one exception, they're all reports coming from officers or soldiers passing through here in what they call a 'retreat.' Passing very quickly through, in a tearing hurry to get back to France."

"Deserters, in other words," snorted Philippe de la Mothe-Houdancourt.

Marshal Turenne waved his hand. "We should be a bit charitable here. If the reports are even halfway accurate, our army was shattered outside Luebeck. At—"

He leaned over in his chair and reached for the newspaper. "What are they calling it?"

"The Battle of Ahrensbök," Lefebvre supplied. "At least, that's what the Germans and Swedes are calling it."

Turenne picked up the newspaper and scanned the front page. "Well, they won it, so they get to pick the name."

"Just as well," said de la Mothe-Houdancourt, his tone of voice every bit as sarcastic as his snort had been. "If we named it, we'd have no choice but to call it the Battle of the duc d'Angoulême's Rear End."

That brought a laugh from most of the officers at the table or standing near it. Even Turenne couldn't help but smile.

"My point, Philippe," he continued, "is that any great defeat produces a flood of men—officers, too, don't ever think otherwise—racing to get out of the disaster. That's not quite the same thing as desertion, I don't think."

The marshal's tone of voice was very mild, as it had been throughout the discussion since it began. De Gassion cocked his head and gave his commander a long and considering look.

"Why so diplomatic?" he asked suddenly. "If you'll pardon me for asking, sir. Whatever else this terrible defeat produces, it'll lift your name in Paris. No need, any longer, to soothe the thin skins of men who've just demonstrated their complete incompetence."

Turenne smiled and laid the newspaper down. "So naïve, Jean! You're a good cavalry officer, but you've still got a lot to learn about the way factional battles are fought. Yes, it's certainly true that the results of Ahrensbök make the French army's top officers look like fumblers, at best. And it's also true that our raid on Wietze spares us from the same accusation. But if you think that will result in a calm and deliberate consideration of the reasons for the disaster, you are living in a fantastical world of your own. What it will *actually* do is fuel the factional disputes. What's that incomprehensible American expression? The one about the muscular poison?"

"Put the factional disputes on steroids," said Lefebvre. "They'd also say something about 'turbo-charged,' and when I find out exactly what a 'turbo' is I'll let you all know."

That brought another laugh, from everyone except de Gassion, who was now frowning. "Are you serious, Marshal? How can such as de Valois and de la Valette *possibly* do anything but hide their heads? That's after they ransom themselves from captivity, mind you."

One of the men at the table who'd hitherto been silent now spoke. That was Urbain de Maillé, one of the many relatives of Cardinal Richelieu who'd entered military service and had distinguished themselves. In his case, enough to have been made a marshal of France—the only one in the room besides Turenne himself. Being now at the age of thirty-seven, he was the oldest man in Turenne's inner circle of officers.

He was both liked and respected by Turenne's other officers. Liked, because he was a likeable man. Respected, in part for his talents but also because,

944 Eric Flint & David Weber

despite being much senior to Turenne and with great accomplishments of his own, he had never exhibited the hostility and jealousy toward their very young commander that so many other figures in the French military establishment had done. In fact, he'd volunteered for Turenne's force on his own initiative—a decision which most of the French officer corps had considered insane at the time, but which was now looking smarter and smarter by the day.

"I'm afraid our normally impetuous young commander has the right of it, Jean. This is, indeed, a time for great caution. True enough, we will now be the apple of Richelieu's eye, as the Americans would put it. But don't fool yourself—the moment our army at Ahrensbök surrendered, after suffering such terrible casualties, was the moment a new civil war began in France. For the next few years, my brother-in-law the cardinal will be fighting not just to retain power. He'll be fighting for his life."

Those sober—even somber—words brought silence to the table. De Maillé stretched out his hand and laid a finger on the newspaper on the table, then tapped the finger a few times.

"Please take note of the one name that is *not* included in this list of officers and great figures humiliated at Ahrensbök." Seeing the blank looks on the faces around him, he chuckled humorlessly. "Oh, come, gentlemen. It's obvious."

Francois Lefebvre sighed, and leaned back in his chair. "Monsieur Gaston."

The same little sigh was echoed elsewhere. *Monsieur Gaston* was the phrase commonly used in France to refer to Gaston Jean-Baptiste, duc d'Orléans—the younger brother of King Louis XIII. Thereby also, since the king had not yet produced a successor, being the immediate heir to the throne of France.

Monsieur Gaston was an inveterate and incorrigible schemer, whom many—including all of the men at that table—suspected to be guilty of treasonous actions in his pursuit of power. He was also Richelieu's chief antagonist in the nation's political struggles and maneuvers, and a man who hated the cardinal with a passion.

"But—" Still frowning, Jean de Gassion looked about in some confusion. The bluff Gascon cavalry commander really was notoriously thick-witted when it came to parsing his way through the intricacies of French factionalism. "I still don't understand."

He, too, reached out and tapped the newspaper. "Most of these idiots—these craven bastards—are partisans of Monsieur Gaston. Ah . . . aren't they?"

De Maillé issued that same, completely humorless chuckle. "No, as a matter of fact. Some were, some weren't. Charles de Valois himself, for instance, has normally been considered one of Richelieu's men. But you may rest assured, Jean, that from this moment forward—from the moment they yielded at Ahrensbök— every single one of them became Monsieur Gaston's fiercest enthusiast. They have no choice, really."

Lefebvre shook his head. "I think that's a bit too sweeping, Urbain. Not *every* French officer at Ahrens-bök covered himself with pig shit. I grant you, poor de la Porte will probably take the blame for the surrender itself, but what else could he do under the circumstances? And while his charge failed, the reports would seem to indicate that Guébriant con-ducted himself courageously."

De la Mothe-Houdancourt stroked his huge nose. "Much good that'll do them. The cardinal can probably save them from any other penalties, but their careers are still ruined. They may wind up joining Gaston's camp simply because they don't see any choice."

Both Lefebvre and de Maillé gave Turenne a sharp, meaningful glance. The young marshal cleared his throat. "This is all speculation, gentlemen. Interesting, but not of immediate concern. To go back a bit, Francois, you said there was one exception to the general run of reports."

"Ah, yes. In fact, they're waiting in a room upstairs. The two officers who commanded the attempt on the ironclads. They arrived this morning, and expressed a desire to speak to you."

"Privately, I imagine."

"Yes, Marshal."

"Well, I see no reason I shouldn't. While I'm about that business, gentlemen, the rest of you had best see to the preparations for the march."

Seeing their stares, he smiled thinly. "Our march tomorrow, back to France. Or has it escaped your attention that one of the many unfortunate results of Ahrensbök is certain to be the rapid withdrawal of Düsseldorf's hospitality?"

The officers looked about the big room, their eyes falling upon the tavern keeper. For his part, that worthy fellow had carefully remained at a great enough distance that no one could suspect him of eavesdropping. Now, seeing the officers staring at him, he paused in his vigorous wiping of the countertop and gave them a smile.

"That's a rather thin, tight smile," mused de la

Mothe-Houdancourt. "The sort a man has when he's desperately trying to keep from pissing his pants. If I recall correctly—and it wasn't but a week ago—that was a cheerful grin when we first arrived."

"So it was," agreed Lefebvre, scraping back his chair and rising to his feet. "And so it is. The marshal's right. This very moment, in fact, I suspect, the duke of Jülich-Berg is pissing his own pants. He'll want us out of here before we draw the attention of unfriendly and newly enlarged neighbors upon him."

"Fat lot of good it'll do him," murmured Gassion, also rising.

Upstairs, after hearing the reports provided by Anatole du Bouvard and Léandre Olier, Turenne nodded and gave du Bouvard a friendly clap on the shoulders. Then, for good measure, did the same for Olier.

"As you say, a desperate business, and one that was never likely to succeed anyway. No fault of yours, of course."

Seeing the strained expressions of the two young officers, Turenne gave them a serene smile in response. "You may rest assured I will say the same in my report to the cardinal. Now, have you given any thought to the future?"

When he came back downstairs, he said to Lefebvre, "I've given them commissions, but I'd actually like you to take them under your wing, François."

Lefebvre looked skeptical. "I have a feeling they're both something in the way of rogues, Marshal."

Turenne chuckled. "Oh, yes. But who better for the purpose? I'm thinking it's time we created a real intelligence division, instead of just relying on your own wits."

"I did, what, exactly, to deserve this honor?"

"You were too good at your job, of course. Haven't you learned by now that no worthy deed ever goes unpunished?"

"So it is." Lefebvre sighed. "There's more news, Marshal. The subaltern we left behind at Wietze has just returned. He's waiting for you outside. With a message from the USE prime minister himself, no less."

As they headed for the door, Turenne lifted his eyebrows. "*Stearns* came to Wietze? That soon?"

"Well, the note was written by someone else, but apparently it came by radio from Stearns."

"Ah, yes. That 'radio.' Has it struck you yet, Francois, that there's something—"

"Fishy about all that, as they'd say. Yes, Marshal. It has. In fact, there's a Russian word for it—not our Russia, theirs—that the Americans like to use themselves. '*Maskirovka.*' It means deception, disguise, a ruse, especially applied to war. I've come to suspect those giant stone towers they've built here and there are a fraud of sorts."

"Look into it, would you?"

"Certainly." By then, they'd passed out the door into the courtyard beyond. The subaltern waiting for him handed Turenne the note.

He read it quickly enough. It was written in both English and German, since apparently they'd had no one at Wietze who could translate into French. Not surprising, of course, given what must have been the chaos still there.

No matter. Turenne was not fluent in either language, especially when spoken, but he could read them well enough.

"So," he said, handing the note to Lefebvre. The intelligence officer read it more quickly, being quite fluent in both tongues.

"Most gracious," said Lefebvre approvingly, when he finished.

"Yes, it is. Gracious enough, I'm thinking, that it would be worth the effort to send a reply along with the report. A request, rather."

"The nature of which is . . ."

"That they pass along to two of their captives a personal letter from me. I feel obliged, under the circumstances, to send Charles de la Porte and the comte de Guébriant my admiration and respects for their valor at Ahrensbök. And I think we should include an offer—slightly veiled, you understand, nothing crude—of commissions should they find themselves unemployed elsewhere in the future, once they've been ransomed."

Lefebvre grinned, and lapsed for a moment into informality. "You're still only twenty-two years old, Henri. You've got no business thinking like this, yet."

Turenne shrugged. "Alas, life seems determined to age me quickly. What's that American expression? The witty curse, I mean."

Lefebvre understood immediately. "It's Chinese, actually. The Americans steal like magpies, when it comes to language. 'May you live in interesting times.'"

"Yes, that one. We're in interesting times, I'm thinking, Francois. So best we get more interesting than anyone. And do so very quickly."

The siege lines of the Spanish army in the Low Countries, outside the walls of Amsterdam

"All the troops are back in the trenches, Your Highness," said Miguel de Manrique. "It went very smoothly. No problems at all."

"Thank you, Miguel." The cardinal-infante nodded toward the man standing next to him, the artist Rubens. "Give the details later to Pieter. He can include them in the letter we'll be sending to my brother, the king of Spain. Explaining that, unfortunately, the mule-headed intransigence of the archbishop of Cologne prevented us from passing through Munster to come to the aid of the French at Ahrensbök."

Understanding that he'd been given a polite dismissal, the Spanish general bowed and withdrew. When he was gone, Don Fernando gave the walls of Amsterdam no more than a glance before he resumed his conversation with Rubens.

"*Months?* I'd had the impression all along that you wanted me to hasten the process, Pieter."

The artist pursed his lips. "Well . . . not exactly. I simply felt you were overly concerned with the reaction of the court in Madrid. Which—I will be blunt here, Your Highness—is going to be a furious one, no matter when you make public the formal decision. And would have been, at any time, and under any conditions. The count-duke of Olivares is probably the most flexible of that lot, but that's not saying much."

The Spanish prince smiled. "About like saying that oak is a bit less rigid than steel, yes. I grant you that.

But I still don't understand why you think we should keep delaying for several more months."

Rubens wagged his hand, back and forth. "I propose to delay only *some* things, Your Highness. You should propose an immediate and full cessation of hostilities. A cease-fire on all fronts. And when I say 'immediately,' I mean within the hour. By tomorrow morning, from what Rebecca Abrabanel told me yesterday evening, the *Achates* and its accompanying ships will arrive in Amsterdam. In fact, they've already entered the Zuider Zee. They could be here sometime tonight, from what she says, except that her husband is deliberately delaying their progress."

He gave the prince a quick glance. "The reason for which, I trust, is obvious."

Don Fernando scowled. "Obvious indeed. The ruthless bastard wants to sail into the harbor in broad daylight, just to rub salt into the wounds."

"Only if the wounds are still open, Your Highness. Yes, he's ruthless, but he's not actually a bastard. Had he chosen to, he could have left you no way to avoid the public humiliation."

"Well . . . true enough." For a moment, the young and bold prince surfaced. "Are you sure—I mean, we've had no direct reports—"

"Please, Your Highness. No direct reports? I remind you that you spoke yourself—just yesterday—to our ambassador in Copenhagen, when you crossed into Amsterdam under flag of truce. Or do you think American technical wizardry allows them to mimic voices over the radio?"

"Ha! The old donkey's voice, maybe. But not his irritating mannerisms, which I remember from when

I was a boy. But I wasn't referring to that, Pieter. I don't doubt one of their ironclads could ruin our fleet blockading Amsterdam—although I will remind you that the Danes did manage to sink one of them. But Stearns does not have an ironclad at his disposal. He only has . . . well . . ."

Don Fernando's voice trailed off, as the young and impetuous prince sank below the surface again, replaced by the canny scion of Europe's canniest royal family. "Well, fine. One of those paddle-wheeled things, that seem to be as dangerous to ships as the ironclads, if not to heavy fortifications. I grant you that."

"I'll add into the bargain that Stearns apparently sailed right up the Thames to get his people out, the English Navy be damned. And I'll also add that while, yes, the Danes managed to completely destroy one of the USE's ships and even disable one of the ironclads, they only did so because of the reckless-ness of a Danish prince who was *not* the heir to the throne. I trust . . ."

"Not likely!" the cardinal-infante barked, almost laughing. "No, I'm afraid my reckless days are now behind me. And at the tender age of twenty-three! Is there no justice?"

"Not for princes, not in these times," came the blunt reply. "You need to send that proposal for a cease-fire within the hour, Your Highness."

Don Fernando didn't hesitate for more than a second or two. "Yes, you're right. Done. But why postpone the rest for so long?"

Rubens went back to his hand-wagging. "Not *every-thing* works in the Swede's favor now, Your Highness. To start with, that daring French raid on their oil works probably means that their mechanical war devices won't have fuel much longer. Not for a while, at least. And without them, assaulting your works here in the Low Countries will be a costly business. If it could even succeed at all, for that matter. Gustav Adolf has other enemies, you know. He can't amass his entire army against you. Beyond that . . ."

The artist and diplomat paused for a moment, his eyes become slightly unfocused. "Beyond that, there's the more general problem he faces. He's just swallowed an enormous meal, you know—or is about to, I should say—and will need time to digest it."

"That Union of Kalmar business?"

"Yes. Scandinavia hasn't been effectively unified since the days of Queen Margaretha, back in the fourteenth century—and that didn't last very long. Norsemen are every bit as disputatious as Germans, you know. And now Gustav Adolf proposes to do it again, only this time effectively."

"Not likely!"

Rubens shrugged. "Not easily, for sure. Which means he'll be preoccupied with that business for some time. Months, certainly, until sometime in the autumn. The same months I recommend that you delay any final political settlement. Just leave the cease-fire in place, and bide your time."

"But for what reasons, Pieter? You just pointed out yourself that my older brother and his court are going to imitate a volcano, no matter when I move. So why wait?"

"To be honest, Your Highness, I don't have a clear answer to that. It's just a matter of my . . . diplomatic and political instincts, you could call it. Once the hostilities end—and given that no one is in position to threaten you any time soon—I simply think it's to your advantage to wait. If I had to give you a more precise answer, let me just say that a period of waiting will allow all parties involved to . . . 'warm up to each other,' is the way I think our nurse Anne Jefferson would put it. The same nurse—call her doctor, now, rather—whom you will immediately invite to come openly into our cities and towns to the south, to oversee medical and sanitary projects. Starting with Brussels."

Don Fernando winced. "If I let her come—openly, as you say—there will be no way to prevent Richter from coming either. Openly or not."

"Then make that invitation open also, Your Highness—since you can't prevent her from coming, anyway."

The prince's eyes almost bulged. "You *can't* be serious."

"Yes, I am. Be realistic, Your Highness. Sooner or later, you will have to deal with the Committees of Correspondence throughout a united Netherlands. That being the case, better to do it sooner and do it yourself—while you still have the chance to negotiate the terms of the forthcoming disputes."

"Ha! You schemer!" Don Fernando gave Rubens a jeering little smile. "And, by the same token, establish— they call it the 'ground rules,' I think—whereby that fledgling committee of yours and Scaglia's can join the dispute."

"Well. Yes. Better that than what they call a 'free-for-all.' A chaotic melee with no rules of any sort."

The young prince thought about it for a minute or so. Then, sighing a bit, he shrugged his shoulders. "I suppose you're right. New times, new methods. But—!"

He held up an admonishing finger. "I leave it to you—you, Pieter, not me!—to explain to my aunt how it comes to be that the troll-woman Richter has free passage in Brussels."

Rubens tugged at his beard. "Um. Her Grace is still a bit furious over that business, isn't she? Well, perhaps the archduchess Isabella and the agitator Gretchen Richter will warm up to each other, given time." After a moment, he added: "A very great deal of time, of course."

Besançon,
The Franche-Comté

"So we have more time, then, in other words," said Friedrich Kanoffski von Langendorff. He looked around the table at the other members of *Das Kloster* whom Bernhard of Saxe-Weimar had summoned to the salon in the town's Hotel de Ville, before his gaze returned to their commander.

"That's my assessment," said Bernhard. "Judging from the tone of his note that arrived this morning, Cardinal Richelieu is furious with me. But he maintained the veneer of civility, and formally—accepts my explanation that recent troop movements on the part of General Horn in Swabia made it impossible for me to send any significant forces as far north as Holstein."

The duke of Saxe-Weimar bestowed a cold grin on his assembled subordinates. "What choice does he have, really, after that catastrophe at Ahrensbök? True, we betrayed him—but we don't pose a direct threat, either. What's a small little stab in the back, compared to the fangs and talons of Monsieur Gaston, rising like a great bear in front of him?"

After the laughter died down, Bernhard shook his head. "No, we'll simply continue as before. Gather our strength, but keep our final goals obscure. Time works entirely on our side, for the next few months. Perhaps as much as a year, or even two."

He held up his hand, thumb and fingers widely spread. Then, closed down the thumb with the fingers of his other hand. "The Swede will be preoccupied with absorbing Denmark, and then come next year he'll turn his attention to Saxony and Brandenburg. That's bound to bring in the Austrians and the Poles, of course. His General Horn will be a nuisance, but Horn on his own can't threaten us."

The forefinger was closed. "Neither can Maximilian of Bavaria, without Austrian support, and the Austrians will most likely be preoccupied elsewhere."

Now, the middle finger. "Within a year, France may start dissolving into civil war. Even if Richelieu manages to prevent that, he'll be far too busy to pay much attention to us."

He closed the last two fingers. "That leaves the Spaniards and their possessions in Italy. Hard to know, yet, exactly how that situation will unfold. But the way things are looking in the Netherlands, more and more, I think the Spanish crown will also have bigger issues to deal with than what happens to a part of their Spanish Road—which they haven't been able to use in years, anyway."

He leaned back in his chair. "Patience, gentlemen. All we have to do now is keep attending properly to details. Such as—"

The cold grin returned. "Such as the letter I will write this evening, to my old friend Jean-Baptiste Budes, comte de Guébriant, now held in groaning captivity. Making clear to him—delicately, of course—that my offer of employment still stands."

Chapter 65

A stay in heaven, Eddie Cantrell discovered, lasts for two and a half days. On the evening of the third day, the Devil came to collect the bill—seeing as how Eddie had tried to cheat and get to heaven before he was actually dead.

An oversight which could easily be remedied, of course.

The soldiers who tried to clamber into the submarine eventually realized they'd have to leave their halberds behind. By then, Anne Cathrine was in full protest mode—they paid that no attention at all—and Eddie knew the jig was up.

So, he surrendered without a struggle.

Once he was hauled out of the submarine, with Anne Cathrine being hauled only a bit more gently behind him, he found himself standing face to face with King Christian IV.

The father in question. Whose temper, alas, showed no trace of subsidence. Not the least, tiniest, littlest bit.

"So!" bellowed the Danish monarch. As big as he was, he seemed to loom over Eddie like a mountain. Or a troll king.

Christian stomped over to the submarine. He was too fat to get in, but he did manage to stick his head in far enough to examine the interior.

"So!" he bellowed again, his voice sounding like it came from an echo chamber.

He came back out and gave Eddie a glare that dwarfed any glare in Eddie's experience. Admiral Simpson's glare, which he'd once thought ferocious, was like a candle to an arc light.

"So!" He pointed a rigid finger at Eddie. "Arrest him!"

That seemed a pointless sort of thing to say. Eddie already had two soldiers holding him by the arms, with two more prodding his back with halberd blades.

"Papà!" wailed Anne Cathrine. "You can't do this!"

"Watch me!"

Part Five

The labyrinth of the wind

Chapter 66

Copenhagen

June 1634

"How are the mighty fallen," grumbled Colonel Jesse Wood, taking off his leather jacket and hanging it on a hook in the shed-in-all-but-name that had been jury-rigged as the new "Command Headquarters" of the brand spanking new Union of Kalmar's brand spanking new first and only airfield, just outside Copenhagen. "Hi, Frank. What are you doing here?"

Sitting in a chair that was at least six degrees of separation from anything that belonged on an air field and would have cost a small fortune up-time—lounging in it luxuriously, rather—General Frank Jackson grinned up at him.

"Still grousing, huh? What's the matter, Jesse? Why does it offend your sensibilities to have the air force turned into a passenger service? Hell, I thought you were just a lowly trash-hauler up-time."

"Please. I flew a *tanker*. Big, big difference—and never mind what any stupid fighter pilot jock says."

He looked around and, seeing no alternative, sat in another chair that was every bit as absurd. "Where did they get these damn things, anyway? Every time I sit in one of them I expect a museum guard to start shouting at me."

Frank's cheerful grin seemed fixed in place. "Frederiksborg Palace, where else? You know how much King Christian loves this airfield. I think Gustav Adolf's offer to build it for him right away is what really turned the tide and finally reconciled him to the Union of Kalmar. Well, between that and agreeing to betroth Princess Kristina to Prince Ulrik. You're in the air most of the time, so you probably aren't aware of it, but Christian comes out here bright and early at least every third morning, all the way from the palace in Copenhagen. How he manages that, with the hangovers he must have, is a mystery to me. Hollow leg is one thing. That guy's got a quasi-dimensional leg, from what I can tell."

Frank half-rose from the chair, supporting himself with his left hand on one of the armrests, and pointed out the window with the other. More precisely, out of the three panes in the huge window that weren't stained glass. Like the chairs, the window was a preposterous thing to have in such a ramshackle and hastily constructed edifice.

"I hate to be the one to break the news to you, Jesse, but they've already started breaking the ground out there. Just past the perimeter fence."

"Breaking the ground? For what?"

"What do you think? Christian's new palace. He says it'll be a small one, though. A 'flying cottage,' he calls it."

Jesse rolled his eyes. "God help us. I've already had to give him four joyrides."

"Piker. He's pretty well adopted Woody. Who's given him at least a dozen joyrides—and is now trying to figure out how to fend off the increasingly royal insistence that we teach Christian how to fly."

Jesse didn't roll his eyes, this time. He closed them tightly shut, the way a man does when he's feeling intense pain. "God help us, again."

"He's pretty well coordinated, actually."

"Yeah, I know. So what? He's also half-drunk most of the time."

By the time he reopened his eyes, Frank was back to lounging in his chair. "But you never answered my question. Why are *you* here, Frank? Puh-leese don't tell me you want a joyride, too. I just got finished having to listen to a seven-year-old girl squealing with delight for hours."

Frank chuckled. "Yeah, I saw. What a mob, huh?"

He was referring to the huge crowd that had been at the airfield to greet Princess Kristina and her two companions when they landed. The emperor himself had been at the center of it, along with King Christian, surrounded by umpteen officials, officers and courtiers. Prince Ulrik had been there also, of course, to greet his new seven-year-old fiancée. Or rather, fiancée to be, since the betrothal wouldn't be official until the formal ceremony in a few days. But, by now, the news had even spread through most of the United States of Europe, much less Denmark. There'd been an even bigger crowd at the airfield in Magdeburg to cheer the princess on her way—although that one had mostly been made up of commoners.

Lady Ulrike and Caroline Platzer had spent the entire flight from Magdeburg in absolute silence, clutching anything available to clutch with knuckle-whitening intensity. Lady Ulrike had been terrified because it was the first time she'd ever flown. Caroline Platzer had been even more terrified because she'd flown many times—and therefore knew perfectly well how far removed Jesse's *Gustav* was from anything an up-time commercial airline company would have allowed to even taxi onto a landing strip. They wouldn't have trusted the damn thing to tow luggage carts to the ramps, for that matter.

Kristina had just been ecstatic. It was her first time flying, too, and so what? Fifteen minutes after they got into the air, she'd started pestering Jesse to teach her how to fly.

The odd thing was, he might very well wind up doing so. When the girl got bigger, of course. But in her case, the thought only caused him to wince a bit. The truth was—all you had to do was watch her on a horse—Kristina had the physical skills to do it. God knows, she had the attitude. The biggest problem would be to keep her from trying fancy acrobatics and dive-bombing routines the first time she went up behind the controls.

"To answer your question," said Frank, "I'm here on a private mission from our beloved prime minister. Things are still kinda dicey for Eddie Cantrell, and Mike wants to know if—in a real pinch—you could be ready to fly the scapegrace out of here on a moment's notice. 'Moment's notice' as in, just before the headsman's axe comes down. That's assuming Mike can figure out a way to get him out of the palace, but he's pretty sure he can manage that. Seeing as he sent for the experts. It's being kept very quiet, of course, but Harry Lefferts and his crew got here two days ago on a ship they swindled somebody out of. Mike's prepared to go to the mat on this one, if he really has no choice."

Jesse sighed. "Christ on a crutch. They still have the poor kid locked up?"

Frank shrugged. "Yeah, insofar as you can call being under house arrest in a room—suite, more like—in Rosenborg Castle 'locked up.' It ain't exactly a barren cell in Marion County jail. Even the plumbing's probably better."

"Still, it seems excessive as all hell. I mean, the kid's not charged with anything that up-time would have—"

Frank's grin was gone by now, and he interrupted Jesse forcefully. "We aren't up-time, Jesse, if you hadn't noticed—and the girl involved is royalty. You may not be aware of it, but Christian IV is actually considered a very tolerant monarch in the here and now. Even something of a wimp, when it comes to family stuff like this. The reason people think that is because he only had his second wife Kirsten Munk—she's the girl's mother, if you didn't know—imprisoned when she was suspected of adultery. Instead of having her head cut off on the grounds of treason. Which is what Henry VIII did—twice—not all that long ago."

Jesse made a face. "Seventeenth fucking century. I forget, sometimes."

"Yeah, we all do. But there it is. Mike thinks—*thinks*, mind you, he's not positive—that Christian's mainly insisting on the full royal treatment as part of all the bargaining maneuvers. To put it another way, he's not actually as outraged as he claims to be. But . . ."

"Yeah, but. Who knows?—and seventeenth-century 'bargaining' is every bit as much of a contact sport as everything political is in this day and age. It can get really rough."

Frank nodded. "Yep, sure can. As Christian IV proved when he agreed to let Eddie go in return for Prince Ulrik—and then dragged out the process until the emperor arrived, so he could demand that Gustav Adolf have him arrested. Drunk or sober, he ain't no dummy. He needed Gustav Adolf here to squelch the admiral, who was making loud noises by then about reducing the rest of Copenhagen to rubble if his lieutenant wasn't goddamit produced on his flagship right fucking now. Even then, Gustav had to do some truly imperial squelching before the admiral shut up."

There was silence for a time, as two men engaged in that ancient ritual whereby another man was finally allowed into their private comradeship.

"Simpson's okay," Jesse declared.

"Yeah, he is," Frank concurred.

After a moment, Jesse said, "I can get Eddie out of here. Now that all the fricking passengers have been shuttled to Copenhagen in time for the big shindig—have they come up with a name for it yet, by the way?—I've got a legitimate excuse to stick around for a while, instead of spending every waking hour in a cockpit."

He waved his hand toward the airfield beyond the closed door. "All of the Gustavs have to have those stupid passenger benches taken out and get re-fitted as fighting planes. Am I the only one who remembers that there's still a war going on? Supposed to be, anyway. Last I heard, the only ones who'd agreed to a cease-fire are the Spaniards—and then, only the ones under the cardinal-infante's command."

"Oquendo's agreed to it also," Frank said. "We just got the word yesterday. It seems the good admiral has decided his commission requires him to obey the commander of all Spanish forces in the Netherlands, and to hell with what Madrid says." Frank chuckled. "Of course, the count-duke of Olivares and the king of Spain himself aren't likely to agree, but nobody in this day and age can lawyer like Spanish hidalgos. Especially when the hidalgo in question has his fleet anchored in the Zuider Zee and the rest of the Spanish navy can't get to him without fighting their way through a big chunk of the USE's navy."

Jesse cocked an eyebrow. "The *Achates* is hardly what I'd call a 'big chunk.'"

Frank shook his head, looking smug. "You're way behind the curve, Jesse. Too much time spent staring through a windscreen, the last couple of weeks. Gustav Adolf ordered Commodore Henderson to take his flotilla into the Zuider Zee. There are now *six* of those paddle wheelers guarding Amsterdam—each and every one of which has a dozen sixty-eight pound carronades loaded with explosive shells, just in case anyone gets any screwy ideas."

He settled into his chair, very comfortably. "No, at least for the time being, Don Fernando and Don Antonio de Oquendo can thumb their noses at the Spanish crown around the clock, if they want to. As for the rest . . ."

He waved a hand, dismissively. "The Danes are out of it, obviously. The English are too, for all practical purposes. They never had much in the way of land forces involved in the war, and after the wreckage the *Achates* left in the Thames estuary it's not likely even that dimwit Charles I is going to order his navy into action. That leaves the French, who are *asking* for a cease-fire. But Gustav Adolf is ignoring their ambassador. He won't agree to it until his troops finish gobbling up as much territory as he figures he can digest. All those dinky little principalities in northwest Germany and what you and I would have called northeast France in the old days are falling like tenpins to Gustav's forces. Hesse-Kassel's done some nibbling of his own too. With the emperor's agreement, of course. Most of it, anyway—and a little after the fact, in some cases. But there's been hardly any fighting at all."

Jesse frowned. "I'd think—"

"You aren't a French cardinal staring at a civil war in the making, Jesse. The only reliable, intact and powerful force Richelieu has at his disposal is Turenne and his cavalry. And guess where they are, now? We just got word about that yesterday, too."

Jesse thought for a moment, and then chuckled himself. "Billeted in the Louvre, I imagine."

"You got it in one. Richelieu needs Turenne to keep the lid on Paris, so he's not about to send him off to fight us. Turenne's got the only French army worth talking about, at the moment, if you don't count Bernhard of Saxe-Weimar—and Mike thinks it's not all that clear how much Richelieu can count on Bernhard these days. The key thing, though, is that those dangerous damn Sharps breechloaders of Turenne's are out of it for while. So, Gustav Adolf figures now is a good time to let his eager commanders on the ground bring him a lot of little Floridas."

"Floridas?"

"Never mind. Inside joke, I'll explain it to you later. I heard it from Torstensson."

Frank planted his hands on the armrests and heaved himself to his feet, grimacing as if he were engaged in one of the labors of Hercules. "Damn, I love these chairs. Gotta see if I can wheedle the Danes into giving us a couple for army headquarters. Which—you got it rough, flyboy, you surely do—the rotten bastards made us put in what's left of Copenhagen Castle. Stumble over the rubble on your way in, which is probably just as well 'cause it takes your mind off the stench coming from the harbor."

Once erect, he ambled toward the door. "Okay, I'll tell Mike you're a go if we need a fast horse out of Copenhagen for Eddie."

"So, what did you think of him?" asked Caroline, once they were settled in their chambers in Rosenborg Castle.

Princess Kristina frowned. "I don't know yet. He's very quiet. I'm not sure I like that. And I'm still angry at him. He blew up one of our ships! Almost blew up another!"

"Which took a great deal of courage."

Kristina rubbed her nose. "Well. Okay. Still."

"He's good-looking, you know, in a quiet sort of way," chipped in Lady Ulrike.

Kristina continued to rub her nose. "I guess."

Caroline and Lady Ulrike exchanged an exasperated glance.

"Your *father* is not holding a grudge over the matter," pointed out Lady Ulrike.

Silence. Then, with a little sniff, Kristina took her hand away from her nose and peered up at Caroline. "And where's the count of Narnia? I wanted to say hello to him. Congratulate him, too, for being such a hero."

Caroline had to restrain a smile. She'd finally gotten some more letters from Thorsten and had gotten *his* viewpoint on that business. Which amounted to bemusement at being told that he was a "hero" for doing something that was considerably less dangerous than any number of farm chores. Capturing a badly wounded young officer and an exhausted old one? Try tending to a lame horse, sometime. *That* critter can cave your skull in. Break a shoulder, easily. Not to mention what an ox can do to you.

But all she said was, "He hasn't arrived yet. Sometime this afternoon, supposedly. No fancy flying for him, you understand. He's just a sergeant. They're bringing him here on a merchant ship."

"Well, they *shouldn't*. He's a count and he *should* be an officer."

The seven-year-old girl wandered to a nearby window and looked out over the gardens below. After a moment, she said, "He rides a horse well. The Danish prince, I mean. Really well. I watched him carefully."

"Well, thank the Lord," murmured Lady Ulrike.

Chapter 67

"I can remember when this was easy," muttered Ulrik. "Not more than—at most—one out of hundred people in Copenhagen recognized me, unless I was wearing court dress. Even then, it wasn't more than one in ten."

Walking next to him, in the same sort of cheap and utilitarian clothing, Baldur Norddahl smiled thinly. "You were just a prince, then. Not the Danish national hero."

Ulrik scowled. "I was prepared for death and dismemberment. *Not* the destruction of what little privacy I had left."

"Oh, stop complaining." Whatever traces of formality had still been left in their relationship had sunk into the Øresund somewhere in the course of the battle. And the prince didn't miss it at all. He'd had very few close friends in his life.

"Not more than four people stopped to take a second glance, Ulrik, and I don't think any of them decided it was really you."

"Still. It's annoying."

A few paces farther down, Baldur put a hand on his arm. "This is it."

Ulrik looked up at the tavern's sign. The nonexistent sign. Then, at what might be the entrance to a tavern. Maybe.

"Could they have found a more inconspicuous and wretched-looking place?" he asked.

"They are who they are. Which, if you've forgotten, is why we came here to begin with."

Ulrik waved him forward. "You first. You're the nerveless adventurer. I'm just a timid national hero. Better you than me, if the floor collapses or the roof falls down or giants rats come at us."

Smiling, still thinly, Baldur led the way.

Inside, the tavern wasn't quite as wretched-looking as its exterior had been. Which wasn't saying a lot, of course.

Aside from the tavern keeper, the only occupants of the room were a small crowd gathered around a large table toward the back. All men, except for two women. They were wearing the same sort of common apparel that Ulrik and Baldur were wearing, but they looked as completely out of place as a den of lions in a mousehole.

"Yes, that's them," murmured Baldur. As if Ulrik could have any doubts.

This time, Ulrik led the way. As he got nearer, he heard one of the men at the table whisper to another, "Heads up, Harry. We got trouble."

He spoke in English, perhaps thinking that a Danish prince wouldn't be familiar with the tongue. Which, indeed, most wouldn't.

Ulrik decided he might as well start there. He not only spoke the language—rather well, by now—he even had something of an Appalachian accent, according to Eddie. So, when he came to a stop, just a few feet away, he said in English:

"I am Prince Ulrik of Denmark. I believe I am speaking to Captain Harry Lefferts, of the USE Army."

He addressed the remarks to the man who had been the recipient of the whisper. Even without that clue, however, Ulrik would have known who their commander was. For someone like himself, born and raised in a position of power, it was quite obvious in ways he would have found difficult to explain in words—but obvious, nevertheless.

The man who gazed back at him was a handsome young fellow. Considerably more handsome—and certainly much younger—than Ulrik would have expected, from the reputation. He even had a boyish sort of grin, which he now put on display. The only real indication that Ulrik could see that this was *the* Captain Lefferts was something in his eyes. There were subtleties there, beneath the apparent insouciance.

Baldur spotted it also, judging from the way he became just that little bit more still, more watchful. Lefferts was a very dangerous man, did he choose to be; of that Ulrik was quite certain. Which was what he expected, of course. He wouldn't have come here, otherwise.

"Yup, that's me, Prince. What can I do for you?"

Ulrik wanted to clear his throat, which felt very dry, but managed to restrain himself. "I believe you have come here to Copenhagen to rescue Lieutenant Eddie Cantrell from captivity. And I believe it would be fruitful if we could discuss the matter, before you do anything."

Every person at the table became suddenly motionless. The aura of menace, heretofore present but subtle, was no longer subtle at all.

Captain Lefferts made a small motion with his hand. A little downward flap, as if to quiet restless monsters.

"Interesting theory, Prince. If you don't mind me asking, is it yours—or your father's?"

Ulrik pointed with his thumb to Baldur, standing next to him. "His, actually. This is Baldur Norddahl, my . . . ah, call him companion. Or 'sidekick,' to use American idiom."

The eyes of everyone at the table now went to Baldur. As impossible as it seemed, the motionless figures grew intensely motionless. In the manner that wary monsters will, encountering another.

"He's normally quite harmless," Ulrik said. "I assure you. And in answer to your real question, Captain Lefferts, my father does not know that you are here in Copenhagen. Nor does he know that I came here to speak to you. I came on my own, because I believe my father—not for the first time, alas—is gambling too recklessly."

After a moment, Lefferts nodded. "Have a seat, then, please. Paul and Don, clear a space for him."

As they did so, Baldur reached back and pulled up a chair for Ulrik from an adjoining empty table. By the time the prince sat down, the tension at the table had eased somewhat.

Not much, though.

Lefferts still had a smile on his face, but there was no trace of the humor that had been in his eyes earlier. "All right, Prince. I'll be blunt. Cut to the chase and do it quickly. Since your Americanese is damn good enough to understand the expression. Got that from Eddie, I take it?"

"Yes. He is, by now, a friend of mine."

"Ah." Lefferts glanced away, looking at the door. "The plot thickens."

"Excuse me?"

"Never mind. Yes, you're right. And if you're not here for the reason I'm guessing you're here, things are going to get really sticky between us. Really quick."

He glanced now at Baldur. "Meaning no offense, Mr. Norddahl, but there's only one of you."

The tension was back in full. Hastily, Ulrik said, "I came here because—in the event Eddie needs to be rescued, which I don't think he actually will—we can handle it in a better way than having you shoot up half a palace in the process."

"Really. And how is that?"

Now, Ulrik felt he could afford to clear his throat. "Well, I *am* a prince of Denmark. That means, among other things, that I have access to the palace keys."

"That's a step, sure enough. But it's a small step." Lefferts pointed toward a very large man seated down the table, next to one of the women. "You'd be amazed how fast George there can get through a locked door. Clickety-boom; clickety-boom; smash. That's how long it takes."

"Makes a lot of noise, though."

"True enough. But we'd have to get through the guards at the door, anyway. Which also doesn't take much time, although it's just as loud and one hell of a lot messier."

"Not if the guards are irrelevant. Which they would

be, if a Danish prince insisted he had to take the prisoner to a private meeting. Very quiet, very clean, in less than five minutes we are at one of the many side entrances to the castle, you have a wagon waiting, and it's done. Nobody is hurt at all."

Lefferts studied him, intently. "You'd catch—pardon the expression—royal hell, afterward."

Ulrik shrugged. "So I would. But it's not likely my father would have me executed, either. The worst he'll do is have me imprisoned for a year or two—and that, in very comfortable quarters."

After a moment, the cool smile on Lefferts' face broadened and became considerably warmer. "Well, I guess the stories about you aren't bullshit. I figured they probably were. Royal spin doctors at work, you could say."

One of the women spoke up. "Harry, this is awfully damn dicey." She gave Ulrik a quick hard glance. "All we've got is his word—"

"No we don't, Sherrilyn," said Lefferts brusquely. "He hasn't 'given his word,' to begin with. Just said what he would do. No solemn royal oaths, no bullshit sacred vows, nada. Just said what he would do."

When he looked back at Ulrik, the good humor had returned to his eyes as well. "I figure a prince of Denmark who charged one of the admiral's ironclads in a rowboat with nothing better than a bomb on the end of a stick has probably got the *cojones* to do this, too."

Clearly, the woman wasn't bashful. From her accent, Ulrik thought she was another American. "Yeah, fine, Harry, point taken. Which means he's a complete screwball. Meaning no offense, Your Highness or whatever you Danes call you." She was now looking at Ulrik directly. "I mean, Jesus. What're you? Fucking *crazy*?"

Suddenly, the room burst into laughter. No little round of laughs, either, but riotous laughter.

"I'll drink to that!" boomed one of the men who'd moved aside to make room for Ulrik. Paul, he thought. "Here's to crazy fucking princes!"

"Another round!" called out Lefferts, waving his hand at the tavern keeper. "And bring a couple of more mugs. Baldur, have a seat. Paul, you and Felix make room, this time."

Once the tavern keeper had carried out his tasks, Harry gave him a meaningful glance. Or so, at least, it seemed to Ulrik—a guess which was confirmed when he saw that the man quickly left the room, thereby eliminating any possible eavesdroppers.

In a peculiar way, he found that more impressive than anything else. He knew from Baldur that Lefferts and his team had only arrived in Copenhagen very recently. Yet somehow, in that short a time, they'd managed to find a tavern they could use as a headquarters, replete with a cooperative owner. How? he wondered.

Probably by waving money under his nose, along with the none-too-subtle suggestion that they were about some criminal enterprise. In a neighborhood like this, and with a tavern this run-down, that had probably not been difficult. It wouldn't occur to the tavern keeper, of course, that the criminal enterprise in question would have anything to do with infuriating the Danish crown.

Still, it was impressive. There were skills involved here that went far beyond the obvious.

❖   ❖   ❖

Developing the plan itself didn't take long. The biggest problem was simply timing the escape properly, so that whatever alarm was given wouldn't come in time to prevent a slow-moving wagon from getting to the harbor at Helsingør. Lefferts insisted on that, although it would obviously be much faster to get Eddie from the palace to a boat in Copenhagen's own harbor.

"Tell you what, Ulrik," he'd said, "I won't tell you how to prince, you don't tell me how to do my line of work. Misdirection's the key. We'll have a couple of our guys—Felix and Don, I'm thinking—make a big production out of smuggling somebody—that'll be Sherrilyn, all bundled up so you can't tell if she's a guy or a girl—onto a boat in Copenhagen's harbor. The kind of thing an eyewitness or two—or ten, more like—is bound to notice. That way, when your father's soldiers come searching—and where else would they start?—they'll think Eddie's on *that* boat. By the time they catch up to the boat and search it and find nobody, we've got Eddie on a boat in Helsingør and we're sailing around the Skaw. I figure we'll smuggle him back to Amsterdam, rather than trying for the USE. They won't expect that."

"He's got the right of it, Ulrik," said Baldur.

"Why me?" demanded Sherrilyn, a bit crossly.

Felix snorted. "To make it easy on *us,* once we get caught. What do you think? With you as the smugglee, we can claim one of us was your paramour and we were getting you out of Denmark to save you from the lecherous and slimy clutches of . . . Hmmm. Probably Harry himself, I'd say."

Harry grinned. Don did, too. "Which one of us, Felix, is what I want to know? 'Paramour' is one of those words that usually comes"—here, he leered at Sherrilyn—"with all sorts of perks and privileges."

"In your dreams, wise guy," was Sherrilyn's answer. But she immediately added, "Okay, that makes sense."

"Done, then." Harry rose and extended his hand to Ulrik and Baldur. "Prince, Baldur, it's been a pleasure. We'll stay in touch, probably using Juliet as our go-between."

As Ulrik and Baldur were about to go out the door, Harry called out. "Hey, Ulrik?"

He turned. "Yes?"

"If it ever happens—God forbid—that your royal line of work doesn't pan out right, and you find yourself unemployed, feel free to look me up. You too, Baldur."

Not knowing what to say, Ulrik simply nodded and left.

When they were gone, Don Ohde gave Harry a sly smile. "Speaking of misdirection, I notice you didn't tell the prince about the airplane we're really planning to use."

Harry shrugged. "Who says we are? The more I think about it, the more I like the idea of using a boat at Helsingør. Keep the whole USE out of it entirely, except for us. And—"

He gave his companions at the table a smile that was slyer by an order of magnitude. "It ain't like it'd be hard for Mike to claim we're a pack of goddam rogues, now would it?"

After the laughter died down, he added, "Especially as pissed as he'll be, when he realizes we misdirected him too. You wanna talk about plausible denial."

❖   ❖   ❖

As they started walking back toward the palace, Ulrik frowned. "I *think* that was a compliment."

"Oh, yes, indeed," murmured Baldur. He had a peculiar expression on his face, as if he were daydreaming. "I'm almost tempted . . . Ah, well, never mind. Although he *does* remind me a great deal of . . . ah, well, best leave that name buried. What adventures we had, though, while it lasted. Too bad the bards don't sing about . . . ah, well, never mind. Probably just as well. Empty half the sprightly lads out of Norway, it would, if they started singing about it. And then who'd do the farm work?"

In the quick way he had, Norddahl suddenly changed the subject. "So what did you think of the princess? Aside from the fact that she'll be ugly when she grows up. No worse than most princesses around, after all."

Ulrik gave him a half-scowl. "Kristina is all of seven years old, you lout. No way to know what she'll look like in ten years, even, much less twenty or thirty."

Baldur wasn't abashed. "And you should keep telling yourself that, I agree. Even if only a madman would think that big nose is someday going to shrink down to normal size."

Ulrik was a bit irritated, but there was no point arguing the matter. On the subject of women, it was just a fact that he and Norddahl were almost polar opposites. The Norwegian adventurer, as you might expect, liked women who were good-looking in a bland sort of way, with heftily female figures, and not much brighter than a cow. Given that his own intelligence on the subject was not much higher than a bull's.

Ulrik, on the other hand, had been a prince in line

of succession all his life. He couldn't remember a time when he hadn't been surrounded by young Danish noblewomen who were good-looking in a bland sort of way, with figures that ranged from hefty to slender but were usually quite attractive, and . . .

Well, it wouldn't be fair—not to some, anyway—to call them as stupid as cows. But even the bright ones had a very limited and incurious view of the world. Conversations with them were almost invariably dull, and often excruciatingly dull.

True, Princess Kristina had a outsized nose, which she'd probably retain her whole life. In old age, if she also had bad problems with her teeth, she might make a ferocious-looking crone. And while it was impossible to tell yet what her figure would be, once she passed childhood, he suspected it would remain on the scrawny side.

He could live with all that. Quite easily, in fact. What mattered was simply whether he and the Swedish princess could manage to get along. If they could—only time would tell—then all the rest would come into play.

Dear God, the girl was smart! Even with her only at the age of seven, on short acquaintance, it was obvious.

"She's adventurous, too," he murmured to himself. The average Danish noblewoman's idea of adventure was wearing a slightly daring new dress. Not learning how to fly—which he'd heard Kristina pestering the pilot about as she got off the airplane.

"What was that?" asked Baldur. "I didn't catch it."

"Never mind. And to hell with the nose. And we'd better start walking more quickly. I'm already going to be late for the congress."

Chapter 68

"Into the new USE province of Westphalia," Axel Oxenstierna droned on, "we propose to include the following: Muenster, Osnabrück, Schaumburg, Verden, Lippe, Lingen, Bremen, Hoya, Diepholz, and—"

He paused for a moment, here, and Mike Stearns was sure the Swedish chancellor had to force himself not to give King Christian a sharp glance.

"—Holstein."

But, except for a scowl that seemed more ritualistic than heartfelt, Christian IV made no objection. Seated almost across the huge table from Oxenstierna and right next to Gustav Adolf, he simply consoled himself with a royal quaff from his goblet of wine. Which, for its part, was royal-sized.

A bit hurriedly, Oxenstierna went on. "Said province, as we have already agreed, to be administered on behalf of Emperor Gustav II Adolf by Prince Frederik of Denmark."

Here he gave Christian's second oldest son in the line of succession a very friendly smile. The twenty-five-year old prince smiled back, in a semi-friendly manner.

That didn't surprise Mike, however. He was pretty sure that Prince Frederik was still smarting at having been passed over in favor of his younger brother for the really plum position, which was being the quite-likely eventual co-ruler of both the USE and the Union of Kalmar—and Sweden, for that matter, if it turned out that he and Kristina got along well enough. Instead, he was being offered the consolation prize of a newly formed USE province to administer. Yes, yes, it would be a big province, and unless Frederik was hopelessly stupid he'd easily be able to see to it that he was chosen as the permanent ruler once Westphalia was ready for full provincial status instead of being an administered territory. Still, it was very much a consolation prize, and very obviously so.

And why, exactly, *had* he been passed over? Mike had been told by those in the know that Christian's official excuse to his second-oldest son was that he'd insisted on the youngest of the three brothers because he'd been sure Gustav Adolf would refuse. The young-ster in question, of course, being the same fellow who'd inflicted the only major damage on the enemy in the course of the war.

No one was more astonished, went Christian's claim, when the damned Swede had immediately and enthusiastically agreed to have Ulrik betrothed to his daughter—and, of course, it was now too late to do anything about it. No way to withdraw the offer, under the circumstances. As gracious and generally lenient as Gustav Adolf was being about most everything, he was still the victor in the war. You could only take things so far.

The excuse was . . . plausible enough. But Mike

didn't believe it for a minute. Now that he'd finally met Christian IV and had been able to spend some time in his company, a few things had become clear to him.

First, the king was an alcoholic with a truly prodigious capacity for alcohol—but, like some alcoholics Mike had known, he was able to function much better than you'd imagine, at least until he got completely soused.

Second, he could play the buffoon like nobody's business.

Third, most of that was an act. Not all of it, especially when Christian was feeling the wind in his sails. But he was nowhere nearly as foolish as he could sometimes make himself out to be.

There was a fourth thing that Mike was not quite as sure about, but damn near. And that was that by far the most intelligent and capable of the Danish king's three sons in line of succession was the one who resembled Christian the least—his youngest, Prince Ulrik. And he also thought that the king himself knew it.

If he was right, in other words, there had been no error of judgment on Christian's part at all. He'd known, cold-bloodedly, that Gustav Adolf would accept Ulrik as Kristina's betrothed. For two reasons. First, just to close the deal. And second, because that would close it better than anything else.

Like most peoples in Europe in the early seventeenth century, Danes didn't really have a national consciousness yet. The roots of it were there and visible—it was indeed a unified nation and they were indeed its subjects, and accepted the fact willingly—but that still

987 : THE BALTIC WAR

wasn't the same thing as what a later age would call
"nationalism." If for no other reason than the inveterate particularism of most people in this era. Any
resident of any village or town or city could explain
to you in great detail why the inhabitants of a village
or town or city maybe forty miles away—twenty miles
away, for that matter—were a bunch of dolts with
lousy manners, stupid customs, and shaky morals. And
watch out, because they'll cheat you in a heartbeat.

All that said, every Dane since the battle in Copenhagen's harbor had adopted Prince Ulrik as their champion. Partly because there hadn't been much else for
Danes to cheer about in the war, and partly because
by this point lots of Danes had seen the ironclads for
themselves. Crippling and almost sinking one of those
seagoing dragons was indeed a prince's business, and
only a true prince could have done it.

And . . .

Obviously the Swedes, dumb and boorish and ill-
mannered and criminally-inclined as they might be,
were at least smart enough to know it. So, having no
prince of their own, they'd turned to the Danes to
provide them with one.

As salves for wounded pride went, this one . . . wasn't
bad, actually. It had certainly gone a long way to rec-
onciling the Danes to being frog-marched into Gustav
Adolf's Union of Kalmar.

What Mike still didn't know, and could only guess
at, was exactly why Christian had made that choice.
Did he want his sharpest son in that position to thwart
the project, over time? Or did he want him there to
make it succeed?

Mike's attention was drawn away from his musings,

for a moment, by the sight of the door to the chamber opening. A moment later—speak of the devil—Prince Ulrik himself slipped in and quietly and unobtrusively took a seat among the noblemen and officials watching the proceedings at the big table in ranked chairs along three of the four walls.

His gaze met Mike's for a moment, then slid away. As usual, the prince's expression was noncommittal. He was amazingly hard to read, for someone so young.

Which led Mike to another tentative conclusion, which was that in the long run it really didn't matter why Christian had chosen to act as he had. It would be his son, not he, who would determine how it all shaped up.

Interesting times.

Thankfully, it was also time for a break, and Gustav Adolf had just given the signal. Mike got up and headed for the toilets, after holding Becky's chair for her. She scurried for the toilets faster than he did, not surprisingly. Whatever else was different between the early seventeenth and late twentieth centuries, one thing had remained constant. The line at the women's toilet would move a lot slower than that at the men's.

You wouldn't think so, given how few women were attending the Congress of Copenhagen in an official capacity. But Danish concepts of "official capacity"—and Swedes and Germans were no different—were a lot more relaxed than those of the up-time world. So if, for instance—to take an example present right then and there—the count of Schwarzburg-Rudolstadt, Ludwig Guenther, who'd just celebrated his fifty-third birthday and *had* been officially invited to the Congress, chose to bring his nineteen-year-old wife and sit beside her, nobody was going to tell him he couldn't.

Normally, Mike would have waited for Becky to emerge before he went back into the big meeting chamber. But he needed to take care of some pressing business during this break.

Fortunately, the admiral hadn't moved from his chair. Mike had noticed before, in other long meetings, that John Chandler Simpson was one of those people who seemed to possess a cast-iron bladder. Probably a very handy thing to have, at long stockholder's meetings.

The chair next to Simpson's was vacant, for the moment, so Mike slid into it.

"It's set, John," he said softly. "If it goes to the wire, we'll get Eddie out of there. Let the chips fall where they may."

Stiffly, Simpson nodded. "Thank you." He paused, and swallowed. "It means a great deal to me. Not just personally, either. There's . . ." His eyes became grim. "Principles at stake."

"So there are. That said, John . . ."

Simpson raised his hand, his expression lightening a great deal. "Please, Mike. I'm fully aware of how bad the fallout is likely to be. And I'm just as aware that there's an easy solution to it all. But I'm still not going to force Eddie into it."

Mike smiled. "Who said anything about 'forcing' him? I simply point out two things to you. The first is that any man who successfully ran a major corporation for umpteen years has got to have some skill at getting people to do what he wants them to do, without breaking their heads. Am I right?"

"Well. Yes."

"Thought so. And the second thing I'll point out is that since he got put back under arrest, Eddie has clammed up completely. The only thing he says—so the Danes tell me—is that the only one he'll report to is his commanding officer, Admiral Simpson."

Simpson's lips quirked. It wasn't quite a smile. "Yes, I know. And, yes, I understand your point. I'll do what I can. But when are they going to allow me to speak to him?"

Mike coughed into his fist. "Well . . . actually, John, I've been the one dragging it out, not them. I wanted to make sure I had Harry in place, first. So . . ."

He glanced over and saw that Gustav Adolf and Christian were alone, for the moment. "Give me a minute."

It took two minutes, before he got back. "Right after the meeting. In fact, they'll have Eddie brought to one of the rooms off to the side."

Simpson nodded again. Even more stiffly than before. Then, very quietly, he said, "It is a pleasure to have you as my commander-in-chief, Prime Minister Stearns."

Axel Oxenstierna stood up. "The session will resume!"

Mike rose and went back to his chair at the table. Becky was already there. And if anybody wondered why a female who was merely a senator from one of the provinces of the United States enjoyed one of the coveted seats at The Table, they could kiss Mike's sweet ass. On some subjects, he and the seventeenth century saw eye to eye, thank you.

"—following principalities will henceforth be part of the province of Hesse-Kassel: Paderborn, the Duchy of Westphalen—"

"Someday," Mike muttered, "somebody is going to have to explain to me the logic of creating a new province called 'Westphalen'—and then incorporating the existing Duchy of Westphalen into a different province."

"It's a seventeenth-century thing," Becky whispered. "You wouldn't understand."

"—*Waldeck, Wittgenstein, the northern portions of Nassau-Siegen and Nassau-Dillenberg, Wied, Trier east of the Rhine, parts of Mark and Berg, Corvey—*"

"Smart ass," Mike complained. "And where the hell do you pick up all these Americanisms, anyway?"

"I hang out with a bad crowd at the mall," Becky whispered. "And you're muttering too loudly."

"—*into the new Upper Rhenish Province: The remnants of the Rhine-Palatinate, Pfalz-Zweibrücken, the Diocese of Speyer, Erbach, Saarbruecken—*"

"Let's have three cheers for coherent political geography. Free at last, free at last . . ."

"Michael—*hush.*" She slid her hand under the table and squeezed his knee. Since the squeeze turned into a caress, Mike decided to shut up. It never pays to irritate a very affectionate but political-junkie wife at a major political conference where she has a ringside seat.

"—*Saarwerden, Hagenau, Dagsberg, the northern portion of the Diocese of Strassburg, Obersalm, Landstuhl—*"

At the next break, Mike tracked down Prince Ulrik. It was time for a casual conversation, he figured.

That proved to be a lot harder. Not because Ulrik was hard to find, but because Mike had to fight his way through three circles of admiring young Danish noblewomen who surrounded him. There were some Germans in there too, he thought, and at least one Swedish girl.

Again, it would seem odd, if you didn't understand the time and place. Why, after all, would the fact that a young man was about to become betrothed to a princess make him attractive to other women? There was not a cold chance in hell that he'd abandon a match with Kristina for anything else.

But . . . there were wives, and there were mistresses, and nobody knew yet whether Ulrik was going to be one of those monarchs—Gustav Adolf being an example—who dallied little if at all. Or whether he'd prove to be a chip off the old block and follow his father's example. For an ambitious and enterprising young noblewoman, the status of royal mistress was a lot more exciting—not to mention probably remunerative—than that of a nobleman or rich merchant's wife. Especially when the prince was young, physically fit and rather good-looking, and the nobleman or merchant was likely to be a pot-bellied middle-aged man with flatulence and bad breath.

Mike didn't know himself, but he suspected the poor girls were wasting their time. Ulrik didn't seem like a cold fish, as such. But if Mike had assessed him correctly, he was far shrewder than his sire, and much less prone to impulsive behavior. In the short run, a royal mistress might be a veritable delight. In the long run, she was likely to become a monstrous headache—and her children, worse still. If anyone had any doubts, they had only to contemplate French politics.

The slight look of relief on Ulrik's face when he

spotted Mike muscling his way to the center gave support to that hypothesis, at least.

"Excuse me, ladies," the prince said smoothly, "but I must speak to the prime minister now."

After the little mob of young women went their regretful way, Ulrik gave Mike a nod. "Thank you. I felt like a city under siege. What are their mothers thinking, anyway? Do they really believe I'm that mindless?"

"Well . . . You might want to consider, Your Highness, that trying to ram an ironclad with a rowboat doesn't exactly give the impression of a cool and calculating fellow."

Ulrik smiled. "No, I suppose not. What may I do for you, Prime Minister?"

"Mike, please. This is more in the way of a personal conversation."

"In that case, please call me Ulrik. You're here with regard to Eddie, I assume."

"Yes."

Ulrik took a deep breath, glanced over to the table where his father was now talking to Chancellor Oxenstierna, and let it sigh out slowly. "I've done what I can, Mike, and I will continue to do so. But my father is set on his course. When he gets like this, it's impossible to budge him. Partly it's just childish; the fact that he enjoys drama—and he did, personally, catch the culprit . . . ah, what's your expression for it?"

"Red-handed." Mike made a little shrug. "Yes, that's understood. But I wasn't actually referring to that part of the business. I wanted to raise with you—open a discussion, rather—of what happens if Eddie, ah, sees his way clear."

"Oh." For a moment, the prince's face got an

actual expression. Very warm, it was. "I'd like that. I surely would."

Mike rubbed his chin. Doing so reminded him that he hadn't shaved that morning, and he'd best not let it go another day. Alas, however marvelous a wife Becky might be in most respects, she was not one of those broad-minded and jolly ladies who thought beards on a man's face were splendid. "Like kissing a dog," was the way she put it. She'd become downright adamant on the subject since some too-damn-enterprising fellows had figured out how to make safety razors a few months ago, so Mike no longer had the excuse of the deadly perils of using a straight razor.

"Well, good. But I trust you understand that the connection will work both ways?"

Ulrik smiled. "The 'conduit,' you might also say, if I've gotten the right term. Yes, of course." He swept the room with his finger. "Isn't that what we're about here, after all? Making connections and laying conduit."

The hypothesis was looking better and better, all the time.

But Oxenstierna was rising again.

"Nice talking to you, Ulrik. Let's do it again."

"Lunch tomorrow, perhaps."

He slid back into his seat just late enough to get a sharp glance from Becky.

"*—province of the Main will remain under direct imperial administration, between the Fulda region under Thuringian administration and the Rhine, down to Mainz. Franfurt-am-Main, however, remains an independent imperial city. As for Baden-Durlach and Strassburg—*"

Ulrik was right, of course—as was demonstrated by Oxenstierna's droning recitation. None of the business taken up this afternoon, after all, had anything to do with the Union of Kalmar. It was all internal matters for the United States of Europe. But Gustav Adolf had wanted the Congress of Copenhagen to be sweeping and authoritative, and he'd insisted that Christian sit in on all of its deliberations. His capable advice might be needed, for one thing—which the emperor said with a perfectly straight face, even solemnly—and, for another, his son Frederik was about to become one of the USE's top officials.

So, sit Christian did. And if he drank wine throughout, he also paid attention—and did, indeed, offer his advice and opinions. Much of which was quite good, and only a little of which was half-drunken nonsense.

"—be allotted to a future Province of Swabia once it is pacified, the administrator of which will be the margrave of Baden-Durlach, the following territories: everything east to the Lech and south to the borders of Switzerland and Tyrol, except for—"

Sweeping, indeed. Some of these areas the Swedish chancellor was now referring to were not actually under USE military control, and even in the ones that were, the control was still shaky. If for no other reason than that Bernhard of Saxe-Weimar still had a powerful army in the vicinity and Mike was more and more coming to think that Bernhard was not simply a mercenary working for the French. Which, if true, meant . . .

Interesting times just got a little more interesting.

"—imperial cities of Ulm and Augsburg. Count Ludwig Guenther has agreed to negotiate with Duke Anton of Oldenburg on the subject of merging Oldenburg into

the province of Westphalia voluntarily. Regretfully, Ostfriesland is apparently petitioning for admission to the United Provinces instead of the United States of Europe, as is Bentheim, a subject which will require firm discussions with the various authorities in the Netherlands at such time—"

That was likely to get interesting, too. But right now, he had more immediate concerns. "When's the dinner break?" he muttered.

"Michael, be quiet or I will put you on a strict regimen of bread, water and abstinence."

He could live on bread and water. The third threat, though, was downright scary. Becky might even do it. Real political junkies were unpredictable, that way. Turn on you like wild beasts.

So, he shut up again.

Finally, though, came the dinner break. And it would be the break for the rest of the day, because a banquet was being prepared.

Mike rose and began moving through the crowd toward Admiral Simpson. Before he got there, a Danish subaltern intercepted him and gave him the news. Lieutenant Cantrell been moved and was being held in—the subaltern pointed—that room over there.

"Thank you," Mike murmured. Looking up, he saw that Simpson was coming his way, so he just waited in place.

"He's in there," Mike said, indicating the room.

Simpson nodded. "This shouldn't—"

A booming voice interrupted him. "How long, Admiral?"

Mike hadn't seen Gustav Adolf coming. The fact

that he had done so was an indication by itself of how seriously the emperor took the matter. There was undoubtedly a comic-opera aspect to *l'affaire Eddie,* but . . .

Heads sometimes rolled in comic operas, too. There was a great deal at stake here, and the man who was simultaneously the king of Sweden, emperor of the United States of Europe, and the new ruler of the Union of Kalmar—they hadn't settled on a title yet, but "High King" seemed to be in the lead—wasn't about to see it start coming apart because a very junior American officer couldn't keep one organ of his body under control and, so far at least, had shown precious few signs that the organ between his ears was working at all.

Mike didn't blame him, not one bit. But that still wouldn't stop him from throwing his own monkey wrench into the works if push came to shove. Whatever disagreements he'd had with John Chandler Simpson in the past, he had none at all today. There were principles—and one of them was that you didn't let one of yours be hung out to dry just because a goddam king was having a royal snit. Piss on all the crowned heads of Europe, if that's what it came down to.

"I'd estimate about twenty minutes, Your Majesty," said Simpson smoothly. "My lieutenant's a good man. I'm sure this is all just a misunderstanding."

Gustav Adolf's ensuing *harrumph* was about what you'd expect from someone with all those titles. Majestic, it was.

A Danish official scurried up, with a document in his hand. "These are the formal charges, Admiral Simpson."

"Thank you. Well, then, I'll be off."

Chapter 69

Had he been asked a year earlier—even a few days earlier—Eddie Cantrell would have sworn that no human being could possibly stand at attention as rigidly as he was doing that very moment. As if, by imitating perfectly the absence of all life, those still alive in the vicinity might just possibly ignore him. Mistake him for a potted plant or a vase or something. Maybe a statue.

Alas, it didn't work.

"Let me get this straight, Lieutenant Cantrell," said Admiral Simpson, staring down at him from what seemed an impossibly imposing height, his hands clasped behind his back. "If I'm interpreting your incoherent mumbles correctly, the accusation leveled by the king of Denmark against one of my junior officers is indeed correct. Entirely correct, and in all its particulars."

"Well . . ."

"Please enlighten me as to any errors in detail."

"Ah . . . she's not actually a 'princess,' sir. Technically, she's just a 'king's daughter.'"

"Indeed." Simpson glanced back at the table in

the small salon in Rosenborg Castle where he and Eddie were meeting privately. On the table lay the very formal looking document—parchment, royal seal now broken, the whole nine yards—containing the king of Denmark's charges.

"Perhaps I misspoke, not being familiar with Danish custom. But I think it hardly matters, since the operative terms involved are two: 'daughter' being the first; 'of the king' being the second."

"Well. Yes, sir. Anne Cathrine is, ah . . . well, yes. She's the king's daughter."

Some mad impulse made him add: "His oldest daughter, sir."

"I recommend that you avoid issues of age, Lieutenant. That's because, in this instance, the operative term is not actually 'oldest.' The operative term is"—again, the admiral glanced back at the document—"fifteen. That *is*, I believe, the age of the princess. Excuse me, king's daughter."

"Ah. Well. Sir, she's *almost* sixteen."

Eddie wondered where in hell John Chandler Simpson had learned that piercing gaze. The one that belonged on some sort of weirdo Hawk God determined to penetrate to the truth, where any reasonable human being would settle for a decent fudge.

Since the gaze seemed unrelenting, Eddie was forced to add, "Well. In about two months. Her birthday's August 10."

"In other words, fifteen. As I said. Which brings us to the core of the matter. Did you or did you not—in a submarine, no less, which may speak well of your nautical interests but does not help you in the least in these circumstances—deflower the fifteen-year-old daughter of the king of Denmark?"

"Well." Eddie cleared his throat. "Well, sir."

"Perhaps you're unfamiliar with the term 'deflower.' The common and much coarser variant is 'popped her cherry.' So, I repeat. Lieutenant Cantrell, did you or did not pop the cherry of the king of Denmark's fifteen-year-old daughter?"

For a moment, wildly, Eddie's mind careened back to the memory of what had been—to hell with admirals, standing at attention, kings, and the whole damn world—easily the most wonderful moment of his life.

"Well. Yes, sir. I guess. In a manner of speaking."

Simpson's stone face finally moved. Slightly. His eyebrows went up perhaps a quarter of an inch.

"'In a manner of speaking.' Lieutenant Cantrell—since you force me to be clinical about it—that particular act is generally only carried out in one manner. The male involved inserts his penis into the female's vagina, which had not theretofore been penetrated in that manner and with that human organ, and does so fully. There may or may not be a hymen in the way, but whether there is or isn't does not actually affect the end result. The male usually but not always ejaculates inside the vagina when the act is concluded; but, again, whether he does or doesn't has no relevance here. Prior to the performance of this act, the female is considered a 'virgin.' Often, the term 'maiden' is used as well or instead. Thereafter, she is not."

He was back to that detestable piercing-gaze business. "So. I will rephrase the question, in the hopes that I might finally get a straight answer from a junior officer whom I have quite distinct recollections of being forthright even to the point of annoying the piss out of me. Is Anne Cathrine, the fifteen year old daughter of the king of Denmark, still a virgin?"

"Ah. Well." Eddie cleared his throat. "No, sir. She is not." He could have added—had the situation called for an imbecile hopping up and down in joyful remembrance of things past—*not by a country mile, sir. Not after two and a half days in that submarine.*

But he didn't. Not being actually an imbecile, even if he was probably doing a fair imitation.

"And you are responsible for this transformation in her status?"

"Well. Yes, sir."

The admiral looked away, finally—thankfully!—and spent perhaps a minute staring out the window. Eddie spent that minute wondering whether he'd just be struck by the admiral's lightning, or whether they'd actually turn him over to King Christian to be fitted into a diving suit for the world's grossest form of execution. Clearly enough, that was the question his commanding officer was contemplating.

In point of fact, John Chandler Simpson was waging a mighty struggle not to burst into laughter. Having been introduced to Anne Cathrine the day before, it wasn't as if he had any trouble understanding Eddie's actions. The girl's very evident concern and anxiety for Eddie's fate had actually been more impressive than her attractive physical appearance. Simpson didn't have any doubt that there was a lot more involved here than simply youthful hormones.

Even the girl's age didn't bother him, being honest about it. True enough, in most states back up-time, she'd not reached the age of consent. But that was more a matter of stubborn American legal tradition than anything in the real world, or anything Simpson cared about on a moral level. Most European countries even in the world he'd come from would have considered her of legal age. If he remembered correctly, Denmark and Sweden were among them.

Customs in the seventeenth century varied a great deal, as did the legal systems themselves. But the issue didn't usually revolve around the matter of age, as such.

Beyond that, John Chandler Simpson wasn't a hypocrite. Or liked to think not, at least. Like most Americans from upper class backgrounds—probably any backgrounds, although he wasn't sure about that—both he and his wife Mary had become sexually active in their mid-teens. Fifteen years old, in his case, with a high-school girlfriend he still remembered quite fondly. In Mary's case, the day after her sixteenth birthday, which she'd celebrated with a high school boyfriend she now claimed to detest.

Of course, what neither of those high-school paramours had been was *royalty*. Which was really what was at issue here. And, perhaps still more to the point, neither of them had been motivated by royal ruthlessness—whose presence here was quite apparent. Indeed, quite impressive, in its own way. He wouldn't have thought Christian IV to be that subtle. A good reminder, really, that simply because a man is an alcoholic doesn't mean he isn't shrewd and canny when he's sober.

"You realize you were played, don't you?" he asked Eddie, still looking out the window.

From the corner of his eye, Simpson could see Cantrell's little start of surprise. "Sir?"

He decided he could allow himself a smile, finally. Just a thin one, of course. Wise, stern, knowing, etc., etc. So it was with that expression on his face that he turned back to look at Eddie.

"Played. I'd say 'played for a fool' except that I don't actually think you've stumbled into outright folly. Not so far, anyway."

Eddie was practically gaping at him. Simpson was pleased to see, however, that the youngster was still standing at attention. By God, there was hope for him yet.

"For Pete's sake, Eddie. Are you so naïve as to think that a captured enemy officer would be allowed in close and continual proximity to the oldest daughter—princess or not, who cares?—of the king who holds him imprisoned? More than that! From your jumbled explanation earlier, it's blindingly obvious that the two of you were practically thrown at each other. And with the whole damn royal family in on the game. Her brother Ulrik, for certain. Her father, needless to say. And—"

It had to be said, and said bluntly. "And the girl herself, of course."

After a moment, Eddie swallowed. A hurt look seemed to creep into his eyes.

Simpson unclasped his hands and gave a little dismissive wave with the left. "Oh, don't misunderstand me. I don't have any doubt your prin—king's daughter—is genuinely fond of you. May even be in love with you, insofar as the term ever applies to royalty in this day and age. Royal or not, fifteen-year-old girls don't give up their virginity in cold blood. Not *that* one, at least; so much is clear enough to me, having met her. But the fact remains that this thing was set up from the very beginning. Literally, from the day you arrived here. By her father, with both her and Prince Ulrik as part of the . . ."

He shook his head, slightly. "I'm not sure what to call it. 'Plot' implies the intent to do harm, which isn't actually involved here. Not, at least, unless you're one of those idiots who thinks getting married is a fate worse than death. 'Scheme' comes closer, but it's still got too much of a sinister connotation. The best word is actually 'machination,' if you give it the proper Machiavellian twist. The way a smart king will, when he considers that the world of power can take many twists and turns, so he'd do well to make preparations for alternative outcomes. And however much alcohol he consumes, Christian IV is a very smart man."

Eddie swallowed again. "You're kidding. Uh, sir."

Simpson chuckled. "Oh, stand at ease, will you? Eddie, when have you *ever* known me to kid you? Or anyone, for that matter. I'm hardly what people think of as a jester."

"Ah . . . well, never. Sir. But . . ."

He was still in that same rigid pose. Simpson placed his right hand on the young man's shoulder and gave it a little shake. "At ease, I said. Eddie, it's not the end of the world. Not, at least, if you're willing to let a small modicum of intelligence enter into what has heretofore clearly been a matter guided only by . . .well. I won't say there were *no* brains involved, since there clearly were on the part of the Danish royal family. But there were certainly damn few on yours."

He moved over to the table and held up the royal document. "If you strip away the flowery language which is but a patina over a truly impressive list of dire consequences should the culprit—that's you, Lieutenant Cantrell—fail to make good on his crimes, what this amounts to is something any humble farmer back home could have said. With a shotgun in his hand. 'Marry my girl—betroth her, in this instance, the customs being different—or I'll blow your fucking head off.' That's pretty much the gist of it."

"But—can he *do* that, sir? I mean . . ." Eddie's shoulders sagged a bit. "I mean, jeepers, *we* won the war, not him."

"So? Have no illusions, Lieutenant. I can probably manage to spare you the worst of these consequences—by the way, did you really show him how to use a diving suit to—"

"Hell, no! Uh, sir."

"Well, that's a bit of a relief. But, as I was saying, I can almost certainly manage to get you executed in a reasonably civil manner. I think I even have a good chance of getting Gustav Adolf to insist on a mere exile to somewhere . . . oh, incredibly unpleasant. They have a lot of medieval fortresses around here, you know. Lock a man up, throw away the key, and let him fight it out with the rats. Probably in Norway, whose rats are famous."

Eddie was staring at him. "But . . ."

"But *what*? Do you suffer from the delusion that Gustav Adolf would intercede on your behalf? Right at the point where he's finally reached an agreement with Christian that Prince Ulrik will betroth his own daughter Kristina? Thereby—that was a shrewd move, as you'd expect—taking most of the sting out of Denmark being forced into a new Union of Kalmar. Now, Christian can console himself with the knowledge that at least his grandchild will continue to rule his kingdom—as well as Sweden and Norway and Iceland and Finland, for that matter. In the middle of all this, do you think the emperor is going to risk upsetting the deal because a junior naval officer is a complete dunce?"

"He *did*?"

Simpson frowned. "Did what?"

Eddie shook his head. "Sorry, sir. I was talking about Ulrik. Did he agree to marry—uh, betroth—Princess Kristina?"

"Well, *of course* he did. Why in the world wouldn't he? Even leaving aside the fact that every child of royalty—in the line of succession or not, it really doesn't matter—knows perfectly well that they'll wind up marrying someone for reasons of state, in this case it's an incredibly advantageous match for him."

"But—but—"

"But *what*? But his bride-to-be is only seven years old? But he only met her for the first time this morning? For God's sake, Eddie, the Ring of Fire was three years ago. Has it only just registered on you that we're in the seventeenth century?"

For whatever reason, it was that last remark by Simpson that cleared the whole thing up for Eddie. Not that there was any reason for the admiral to be so sarcastic!

Especially since he was wrong, anyway. Looking back on it all, Eddie could now see that it *hadn't* been set up from the beginning. What had actually drawn Anne Cathrine and him together in the beginning was that when he first encountered her she was being set up to marry a rich merchant, whom she disliked intensely. Eddie had helped her scheme her way out of the match— or so he thought. With hindsight, he could now see that that was when her father had gotten the idea of matching her with him instead.

And . . . yes, of course Anne Cathrine would have agreed. By then, at the very least, Eddie was sure she'd come to be quite fond of him. Far more so than she could realistically expect with any alternative prospect. You could call it "calculated," if you wanted to cast it in the worst possible light. Or "unromantic," if you wanted a milder term. But both terms were just stupid. She was what she was, that's all. And he thought she was the most terrific girl he'd ever met, and by that same country mile.

He was still puzzled by something, though. "But why *me*, sir? I mean, like you said, I'm just a junior naval officer—and in an enemy's service, at that."

"You need to be more precise. You are an *American* junior naval officer. One of that relative handful of people who have managed to turn Europe upside down in three years. From King Christian's standpoint, as the old saying gets paraphrased, he loses a daughter but gains a son who is not only a technical wizard but one of proven courage and determination, to boot. Might be a very handy fellow to have around, in the family business."

Eddie winced. "Uh, sir, I need to tell you that regardless of what the Danes may have told you I didn't actually ram the *Outlaw* into that ship. Not on purpose, I mean. It all just happened by accident after we got shot up and Larry and Bjorn got killed."

Simpson smiled. "I never thought you had, myself. But it takes nothing away from the courage you displayed at Wismar, Lieutenant. For which—quite properly—you were awarded the Navy Cross. Nor does it take anything away from the rest of it. From King Christian's viewpoint, since his oldest daughter isn't in the line of succession, she's not available for a major political match anyway. So why not marry her off to a young American officer, especially one with a great deal of technical knowledge? There are a lot fewer of those around these days than noblemen or rich merchants."

"But we're *enemies.*"

"Not any more—and don't think for a moment that Christian didn't have this possible outcome in mind. The war's over and now we're . . . you can't even say 'allies,' exactly. Well, you could from the standpoint of the emperor of the USE, but from the standpoint of the king of Sweden—we've got a dual monarchy here, never forget, and we're about to get a triple one—Denmark now belongs to him. As for Christian IV, he's now the greatest prince in the Union of Kalmar, second only to Gustav Adolf himself—and that, only for one generation. That being the case, the clear and certain duty of the ruler of the Union is to see to the suitable punishment of that scoundrel who beguiled and seduced and dishonored and debauched—oh, it's a long, long list, in those charges—the innocent and childlike daughter of his Number One Man."

The admiral's gaze was still piercing, but more like

that of a weirdo Owl God now, instead of a hawk. Of course, owls were still raptors, so fat lot of good that did Eddie.

"But—but—we *were* enemies. When it happened, I mean. Sir." His voice rose a little. "And that's not what happened anyway! I did not 'beguile' and 'seduce'—more like she did me, is the truth of it—and—and—okay, she's only fifteen years old— fifteen and five-sixths—but—well, okay, I won't say she's not pretty innocent—at least of anything that I care about—but—"

"You're babbling, Lieutenant."

Eddie shut his mouth. Then he took a deep breath and reminded himself of what was actually important. His eyes got a little teary.

"I love Anne Cathrine, sir. Whatever she thinks, and I don't really think she's as conniving as you do. Just . . . a seventeenth-century sort of girl. The point is, I've got no problem betrothing her. Uh . . . I mean, if that's what she wants, too."

To his astonishment, the admiral grinned. The first honest-to-God real grin Eddie had ever seen on Simpson's face.

"What a relief," said the admiral. "My lieutenant's two brain cells finally rubbed together."

He stepped forward, and once again placed his hand on Eddie's shoulder. "Are you sure, Eddie? I'm not going to force you into anything like this." His eyes seemed strangely intent. "Neither is Mike Stearns. If you don't want to do it . . . Well. Let's just say there are alternatives."

Eddie took a deep breath—not in order to think, simply in order to steady his nerves. Then he laughed softly. "The truth is, sir, I've spent most of the past few months trying to figure out any way I *could* get involved—really involved, I mean—with Anne Cathrine. I just figured it was hopeless—and now here it's being handed to me on a plate. Oh, yeah, I'm sure. Don't have any doubt about it at all."

Simpson smiled, and the hand on Eddie's shoulder now became a firm and guiding one. "Come along, then, Lieutenant." He began steering him toward the door.

"Where are we going now, sir?"

"Right outside."

Eddie frowned. "Right outside" would just be an empty room. One of those completely pointless huge rooms that seemed to be mandatory in palaces, and which had no function Eddie had ever been able to determine except to rub into the faces of anyone who wandered in that the guy who owned the palace was way, way, way, way richer than you were or ever would be.

But, as it turned out, the room *did* have a function. It was big enough to hold two kings, one prime minister, one senator, one prince—no, three; both of Ulrik's older brothers were there too—umpteen admirals and generals and officers and officials and noblemen.

And one king's daughter.

Gustav Adolf looked at his watch. "Twenty minutes, Admiral, and twenty-seven seconds. About what you predicted."

He then leaned over and glanced at the watch adorning the equally thick wrist of the man standing right next to him. "Exactly what yours says, to the second. I told you these up-time watches were perfect, Christian."

"Right you were." The king of Denmark had a

cheerful smile on his face. From long experience, Eddie interpreted this one as *the-king-is-half-plastered-but-only-half-and-he-can-drink-anyone-under-the-table-anyway* crossed with *God-I-love-gadgets*.

Good thing, too, because most of the faces in the room were unfriendly. Well, stern and solemn, at least. Okay, Mike Stearns and Rebecca were smiling at him. Sweetly, in the case of Rebecca; sorta, in the case of Mike. And he recognized Caroline Platzer over in a corner, although he didn't have a clue why she was here at all. She was standing next to some guy he didn't know, and she was smiling too.

Ulrik was standing not far from his father, and a little behind him. He was giving Eddie that inscrutable look that belonged on some sort of ancient Chinese mandarin or Tibetan monk instead of a Scandinavian prince almost his own age. Naturally, Baldur Norddahl was grinning. Any shark who saw that grin would swim as fast as it could the other way.

That left . . .

Anne Cathrine. When he finally looked at her, she was just staring at him, looking very wide-eyed and very apprehensive.

Simpson cleared his throat. "My lieutenant—"

There weren't many times—almost almost almost none at all—when it was a smart idea for a junior officer to interrupt his admiral. But this was one of them. Damn the sarcastic old fart. Eddie had at least *three* brain cells.

"There seems to be a misunderstanding, which I've just cleared up with my commanding officer." He was pleased to see that he managed to say all that firmly and coherently. Didn't stammer or hesitate at all, and never said "uh" or "well" even once.

"*As was my intention all along*—which simply got interrupted by the battle—I would like to ask the king of Denmark for his daughter's hand in marriage."

He didn't know if that was the right protocol. But screw it. The worst Christian would do for a lapse in protocol was make Eddie drink with him for three hours while he explained the right way to do it. He probably wouldn't even mention the diving suit.

As it happened, it didn't matter. As soon as he finished, Anne Cathrine drew herself up in as haughty a pose as a fifteen-and-five-sixths-year old could manage— not too good, really, although the out-thrust bosom was magnificent, even in formal court wear—and gave her father what would be called a "withering look" if she'd been twice the age and could pull it off.

But that didn't matter either. "I *told* you, Papà!" she exclaimed. Then she gathered her skirts, rushed to Eddie, threw her arms around him and planted a big kiss on his cheek.

"*Tonight,*" she whispered into his ear. "*Northwest corner room. Third floor. I'll open the window.*"

She glanced down at his feet. Foot and pegleg, rather. "*Oh, I forgot. Can you manage a rope?*"

Before Eddie could answer—or even catch his breath—her father was bellowing something about impropriety and Anne Cathrine scurried back.

Gustav Adolf drew his sword. "Come here, Lieutenant Cantrell."

Oh, shit.

The emperor leaned his head toward Christian IV. "I suppose I should properly do it elsewhere, since this is imperial and not Union business. But with your permission?"

The Danish king was still glaring at his daughter. "Oh, yes, certainly, brother. No need to stand on formalities."

Simpson's hand propelled Eddie forward. When he was just a few feet from the emperor, Gustav said, "Kneel, sir."

He then glanced at a man standing next to him. Eddie didn't recognize him, but he was wearing a Swedish army uniform. "Have we established any firm protocol yet, Nils?"

The Swedish officer shook his head. "Not really, Your Majesty. This is only the second, so it's all still rather malleable."

"In that case, I'll do it like in the movies. It's got more style."

By then, Eddie was on his knees, more-or-less driven down by Simpson's hand. The treacherous bastard.

Gustav frowned. "Something's not right."

"One knee only, Your Majesty."

"Ah, yes, of course. On one knee only, Lieutenant."

Confused, Eddie did as he was told. Did it really matter how many knees a man was on, when they chopped off his head?

At least it'd be quick. That was a real sword that had been wielded in real battles, and by a king who knew how to use it.

But Eddie was confused again when the sword simply came down, rapped him lightly on both shoulders, and was withdrawn.

"Rise, now, Imperial Count of Wismar!" boomed Gustav II Adolf.

"That calls for a drink!" boomed Christian IV. "In the banquet hall! Eddie, you sit next to me, of course, now that you're part of the family."

Chapter 70

It wasn't until nine o'clock that night before Eddie managed to weasel his way out of the banquet hall. He was a lot less sober than he wanted to be, but still sober enough to walk and—hopefully—skinny up a rope with only one foot.

It took him a while to find the right part of the palace, and when he did he was dismayed to see that another man was already standing there. He was looking up at the windows on the floors above, with a puzzled frown on his face.

As he got closer, Eddie recognized the man. His face, anyway, since he didn't know his name. It was the fellow who'd been standing next to Caroline Platzer in the big room.

Seeing nothing else to do, Eddie just marched up to him. Well, stumped up.

As he came near, the man looked at him and gave him a formal little bow. More in the way of an exaggerated nod, really.

"Good evening, Imperial Count of Wismar."

"Ah . . . Lieutenant Eddie Cantrell, please. That

count business was none of my doing and I'm not too comfortable with it."

The stranger's blocky face was suddenly creased by a smile. One of those genuinely friendly smiles that made Eddie instinctively sense he probably liked the guy.

"Yes, I know," the man chuckled. "They made me the imperial count of Narnia right after I arrived. But I'm actually just Thorsten Engler."

He stuck out his hand and Eddie shook it.

"What are you doing here, Thorsten, if I might ask? And are you kidding about the Narnia business?"

"To answer your questions in reverse order, the Narnia issue is still unsettled. My betrothed thinks that it's preposterous to force a whole town to change its name on a royal whim, and she's insisting that the princess tell her father to change it back. Princess Kristina, on the other hand, insists that 'count of Nutschel' sounds stupid and she likes Narnia and so there. In this instance, unlike many, I suspect the princess will win the contest of wills. As to the first . . ."

He looked up at the row of windows on the third floor of the palace. The very *many* windows on a palace the size you'd expect Christian IV to build. "As to the first, I'm faced with a quandary."

The proverbial lightbulb went off. "You're engaged to Caroline Platzer. Uh, betrothed, I mean."

"Yes, indeed. A simple farm boy, in my origins, who never expected he'd someday have to *figure out* which window . . . Ah!" He pointed an eager finger. "There!"

Looking up, Eddie saw that a window had been opened and a rope was being lowered. Thorsten began moving toward it.

Before he'd taken three steps, however, another window was opened and another rope began coming down.

The imperial count of Narnia came to an abrupt halt. "And now what?"

"Who ordered this?" demanded Eddie.

Cast of Characters

I. United States of Europe (USE)

USE GOVERNMENT

Abrabanel, Rebecca "Becky"	Wife of Mike Stearns; USE senator; head of USE embassy to the Netherlands
Grady, Maureen	Head of USE Department of Social Services
Hesse-Kassel, Wilhelm V	Landgrave of Hesse-Kassel
Hesse-Kassel, Amalie	Landgravine of Hesse-Kassel; wife of Wilhelm V
Mailey, Melissa	Senior advisor to Rita (Stearns) Simpson in USE embassy to England; prisoner in the Tower of London
Piazza, Edward Vincent "Ed"	Successor of Mike Stearns as president of the State of Thuringia-Franconia

Saxe-Weimar, Ernst, duke of	Brother of Wilhelm Wettin; regent for Gustav II Adolf in the Upper Palatinate
Saxe-Weimar, Wilhelm IV, duke of	See: Wettin, Wilhelm
Simpson, Rita	USE ambassador to England; wife of Tom Simpson; sister of Mike Stearns; prisoner in the Tower of London
Stearns, Mike	Prime minister of the USE; husband of Rebecca Abrabanel
Vasa, Gustav II Adolf	King of Sweden; Emperor of the United States of Europe; also known as Gustavus Adolphus
Vasa, Kristina	Daughter and heir of Gustav II Adolf
Wettin, Wilhelm	Formerly Wilhelm IV, duke of Saxe-Weimar; abdicated in favor of his brother Albrecht to run for the House of Commons in the USE Parliament; head of political opposition to Mike Stearns
Zimmermann, David	Secretary to Mike Stearns in Magdeburg; former professor of languages at the University of Jena

USE ARMY, REGULAR FORCES

Engler, Thorsten	Sergeant in USE Army; fiancé of Caroline Platzer; later Imperial Count of Narnia
Fey, Christopher "Kit"	USE Army, left as garrison commander at Hamburg
Gjervan, Olav	USE Army, gunner in flying artillery units
Higgins, Jeff	Soldier, USE Army, assigned to embassy to Amsterdam; husband of Gretchen Richter
Jackson, Frank	USE Army general, aide to General Torstensson
Krenz, Eric	USE Army, assigned to flying artillery units
Mason, Gayle	USE Army radio specialist with the USE embassy to England; imprisoned in the Tower of London
Mavrinac, Erik	USE Army officer
McCarthy, Darryl	USE Army soldier; member of USE embassy to England, imprisoned in the Tower of London; betrothed to Victoria Short
Meincke, Raymond	USE Army, gun crew member in flying artillery units;
Reschly, Markus "Mark"	USE Army, lieutenant in flying artillery units

Simpson, Thomas "Tom" III	USE Army captain, assigned to USE embassy in England; husband of Rita Stearns; son of John and Mary Simpson; prisoner in the Tower of London
Straley, Len	USE Army, colonel of flying artillery units
Thorpe, Bryan	Englishman, colonel serving under Torstensson
Torstensson, Lennart	Swedish general, top commander of the military forces of the United States of Europe
Witty, Carl	Captain, USE Army

USE ARMY, SPECIAL COMMANDO UNIT

Fuhrmann, Gerd	USE Army, member of Harry Lefferts' unit
Grabnar, Matija	USE Army, member of Harry Lefferts' unit
Lefferts, Harry	Captain, USE Army, head of commando team sent to the Tower of London
Kasza, Felix	USE Army, member of Harry Lefferts' unit
Maczka, Paul	USE Army, member of Harry Lefferts' unit
Maddox, Sherrilyn	USE Army, member of Harry Lefferts' unit

Ohde, Donald	USE Army, member of Harry Lefferts' unit
Sutherland, George	USE Army, member of Harry Lefferts' unit; husband of Juliet
Sutherland, Juliet	USE Army, member of Harry Lefferts' unit; wife of George

USE NAVY

Baumgartner, C.H.	Captain, USE Navy, commander of SSIM *Achates*
Cantrell, Edward "Eddie"	Lieutenant, USE Navy; prisoner in Denmark
Chomse, Franz-Leo	Lieutenant, USE Navy, aide to Admiral Simpson
Halberstat, Franz	USE Navy, captain of SSIM *Constitution*
Halvorsen, Kjell	USE Navy ensign
Henderson, Richard	USE Navy commodore
Mülbers, Wolfgang	USE Navy, captain of SSIM *Ajax*
Simpson, John Chandler	USE Navy admiral

USE AIR FORCE

Krueger, Friedrich "Freddy"	USE Air Force sergeant
Martin, Enterprise	USE Air Force pilot
Martin, Endeavor	USE Air Force pilot

Wood, Joseph Jesse "der Adler"	Colonel, in command of the USE Air Force
Woodsill, Eugene "Woody"	USE Air Force pilot
Weissenbach, Ernst	USE Air Force pilot

USE MARINE CORPS

Probst, Leberecht	USE Marine Corps lieutenant

USE CIVILIAN

Achterhof, Gunther	Leader of Committee of Correspondence in Magdeburg
Anhalt-Zerbst-Dessau, Anna Sophia of	The dowager countess of Schwarzburg-Rudolstadt, patroness of social work activities in Magdeburg
Ferrara, Greg	Chemist and industrialist; former high school chemistry teacher in Grantville
Hamers, Juan	Merchant ship captain
Jefferson, Anne	Nurse in Amsterdam, engaged to Adam Olearius
Mackay, Julie (Sims)	Sharpshooter; wife of Alex Mackay
Mackay, Alexander "Alex"	Cavalry officer in the army of Gustavus Adolphus; on extended leave in Scotland

Platzer, Caroline Ann Social worker in Magdeburg; companion for Princess Kristina; betrothed to Thorsten Engler

Richter, Gretchen CoC organizer; in Amsterdam; wife of Jeff Higgins

Schwarzburg-Rudolstadt, Emelie, countess of Wife of Count Ludwig Guenther of Schwarzburg-Rudolstadt; supporter of social work activities in Magdeburg

Schwarzburg-Rudolstadt, Ludwig Guenther, count of Conducting a Lutheran colloquy in Magdeburg on behalf of Gustav II Adolf

Simpson, Mary Wife of John Chandler Simpson; patron of the arts

Sims, Julie See: Mackay, Julie

Smith, Henry "Hal," Sr. Airplane manufacturer in Grantville

Stiteler, Robert Coal gas plant worker, Magdeburg

Ulrike, Lady Lady-in-waiting and governess of Princess Kristina

Underwood, Quentin B. Co-owner of coal gas works in Magdeburg; developer of the Wietze oil field; former mine manager in Grantville; political supporter of Wilhelm Wettin

II. Other Nations

SWEDEN

Banér, Johan Gustafsson	Swedish general
Ekstrom, Nils	Swedish colonel, aide-de-camp to Gustav II Adolf, brother to Sigvard
Ekstrom, Sigvard	Swedish colonel, aide-de-camp to Gustav II Adolf, brother to Nils
Oxenstierna, Axel	Swedish chancellor, chief advisor of Gustav II Adolf

DENMARK

Anne Cathrine	Oldest daughter of Christian IV by his morganatic marriage to Kirsten Munk; "king's daughter" but not "princess"
Christian IV	King of Denmark
Norddahl, Baldur	Norwegian adventurer and engineer in Danish service
Ulrik	Prince of Denmark; youngest son of Christian IV in the line of succession

ENGLAND

Boyle, Richard	Earl of Cork; English politician opposed to Thomas Wentworth
Charles I	King of England; member of the Stuart dynasty
Cork, earl of	See: Richard Boyle
Cromwell, Oliver	Prisoner in the Tower of London
Henrietta Maria	Queen of England; sister of Louis XIII of France
Hamilton, Stephen	Captain of the Yeomen Warders at the Tower of London; patriarch of the Short/Hayes family group
Hayes, Jack	Son of Patricia Hayes
Hayes, Patricia (Short)	Aunt of Andrew Short; sister-in-law of Stephen Hamilton
Langscarr, Henry	Lieutenant of the Tower of London, deputy of Sir Francis Windebank
Laud, William	Archbishop of Canterbury
Leebrick, Anthony	Mercenary captain employed by Charles I of England
Lytle, Elizabeth	Lover of Captain Anthony Leebrick
Pindar, Paul, Sir	English politician; supporter of Boyle
Porter, Endymion, Sir	English politician; supporter of Boyle

Short, Andrew	Yeoman Warder, Tower of London
Short, Elizabeth (Crane)	Wife of Andrew Short
Short, Isabel (Thurlow)	Mother of Andrew, John, William, Mary, Catherine, and Victoria Short; widow
Short, John	Yeoman Warder; brother of Andrew Short
Short, Victoria	Sister of Andrew Short; betrothed to Darryl McCarthy
Short, William	Yeoman Warder; brother of Andrew Short
Towson, Richard	Mercenary officer employed by Charles I of England
Welch, Patrick	Mercenary officer employed by Charles I of England
Wentworth, Elizabeth	Wife of Thomas Wentworth, earl of Strafford
Wentworth, Thomas, earl of Strafford	Head minister for Charles I of England
Windebank, Francis, Sir	English politician, opponent of Strafford; becomes Constable of the Tower of London

FRANCE

Angoulême	See: Valois, Charles de

Budes, Jean-Baptiste, comte de Guébriant	French army officer
De la Mothe-Houdancourt, Philippe	French cavalry officer serving under Turenne
De la Porte, Charles	French army general
De la Valette, Bernard de Nogaret, duc d'Epernon	French army general
Du Barry, Robert	French officer under Turenne, in charge of technological projects
Du Bouvard, Anatole	French officer supervising scuba divers on the Elbe
Gaston Jean-Baptiste, duc d'Orleans	Younger brother of King Louis XIII; heir to the throne so long as Louis has no children; opponent of Richelieu; commonly called "Monsieur Gaston"
Gassion, Jean de	French cavalry officer serving under Turenne
Gosling, Guilherme	French cavalry officer, adjutant to Guébriant
Guébriant, Jean Baptiste Budes, comte de	Budes, Jean-Baptiste Budes

Kanoffski von Langendorff, Friedrich Ludwig	Close associate of Bernhard of Saxe-Weimar
Lefebvre, Francois	French cavalry officer serving under Turenne
Louis XIII	King of France
Maillé, Urbain de	French officer, married to Cardinal Richelieu's sister
Olier, Léandre	French officer supervising scuba divers on the Elbe
Richelieu, Armand Jean du Plessis de	Cardinal; first minister of Louis XIII
Saxe-Weimar, Bernhard, duke of,	Brother of Wilhelm Wettin; in French employ with his army in Swabia, the Franche-Comte, and the Breisgau
Servien, Etienne	Intendant in the service of Richelieu
Thibault, Yves	French armaments designer and manufacturer
Turenne, Henri de la Tour d'Auvergne, vicomte de	French cavalry general
Valois, Charles de, duc d'Angoulême	French general, commander of the forces besieging Luebeck

NETHERLANDS AND SPAIN

Fernando, Don	Commander of Spanish military forces in the Netherlands; younger brother of King Philip IV of Spain; nephew of Infanta Isabella Clara Eugenia; known as the "cardinal-infante"
Fourment, Helena	Second wife of Pieter Paul Rubens
Fredrik Hendrik	Stadholder of the Netherlands; head of the House of Orange
Isabella Clara Eugenia	Infanta of Spain; Daughter of Philip II; widow of Archduke Albrecht of Austria; regent of the Spanish Netherlands
Manrique, Miguel de	Military adviser to Don Fernando, the cardinal-infante
O'Neill, Owen Roe	Irishman serving in the Spanish army in the Netherlands; adviser to Don Fernando
Olivares, Gaspar de Guzman, count-duke of	Head minister and favorite of Philip IV of Spain
Oquendo, Antonio de	Spanish admiral
Olearius, Adam	Diplomat in Amsterdam; fiancé of Anne Jefferson
Philip IV	King of Spain; older brother of Don Fernando

Rubens, Pieter Paul   Diplomat and artist; adviser of
                          Don Fernando

Scaglia, Alessandro   Diplomat; adviser to Infanta
                          Isabella Clara Eugenia

MISCELLANEOUS

Hempel, Rolf   Gunnery captain on Hamburg's
                    fortifications

John George I,   Opponent of Gustavus II
  elector of Saxony   Adolphus

Grantville Gazette

An electronic-only magazine of stories and fact articles based on Eric Flint's 1632 "Ring of Fire" universe

The *Grantville Gazette* can be purchased through Baen Books' Webscriptions service at www.baens.com (then select Webscriptions) or you can subscribe through www.grantvillegazette.com, which is an electronic magazine that publishes six issues per year.

Each electronic volume of the *Gazette* can be purchased individually for $6.00 from either site, or you can purchase them in packages from Webscriptions as follows:

- Volume 1. This volume is free and can be obtained from the Baen Free Library. (Once you're in the Baen web site at www.baen.com, select "Free Library" on the left hand side of the menu at the top. Then, select "The Books" and you'll find *Grantville Gazette Volume 1*.)
- Volumes 2–4, $15.
- Volumes 5–8, $15.
- Volumes 8–10, $15.
- Volumes 1–10, $40. This special offer allows all of our fans to read all of the stories published so far at a bargain rate.
- Volumes 11–13, $15.
- Volumes 14–16, $15.
- Volumes 17–19, $15. Volume 17 is already available with Volumes 18 and 19 in production.

The following is an excerpt from:

1635

THE DREESON INCIDENT

ERIC FLINT AND VIRGINIA DeMARCE

Available from Baen Books
December 2008
hardcover

Prologue

August 1634

Magdeburg
United States of Europe

Don Francisco Nasi, spymaster for the United States of Europe, pushed his glasses up his nose. "Michel Ducos moved on quickly, even before Peter Appel notified the Frankfurt authorities. He'd been gone a couple of days before they got the news to me. We can't just move in and arrest his lieutenant Guillaume Locquifier. Partly because then we'd lose the trail, but jurisdictionally because the crime didn't happen on USE soil and we don't have an 'arrest on sight and extradite' from the Papal States. It's better just to keep Locquifier under surveillance. Frankfurt says that he isn't doing anything active right now—just huddling in the back parlor of an inn with a few other men."

Ed Piazza scowled. Once a high school principal in Grantville, he was now the president of the State of Thuringia-Franconia. The SoTF, whose capital was Grantville, was one of the largest and most populous provinces of the United States of Europe. Ed was in Magdeburg for a few days consulting with Mike Stearns, the Prime Minister of the USE. "It's your call, I guess. Personally, I'd be happier if they were in jail, considering that mess at the Galileo hearing."

Sitting behind his desk not far away, Mike Stearns shrugged. "Mazarini cleaned up the mess around the assassination attempt on the pope very efficiently. Politically speaking, I mean—he didn't wash the blood off the floor of the church or dig the bullets out of the plaster himself, of course. Frank, Ron and Gerry Stone were all in big trouble right after the assassination attempt and things could have turned out a lot worse if he hadn't put in the fix."

"Nevertheless," said Nasi, "once they realized that Ducos was not really a member of the Committees of Correspondence, but had been using them for his own purposes, the Stone boys acted decisively. The assassination might very well have succeeded had it not been for them. Therefore they interest me."

"Tom Stone told me that his son Frank and his new wife Giovanna are staying in Venice," added Mike. "Frank's going to keep working with the Committee of Correspondence there. Maybe try to develop some in other places in Italy. In the *Italies*, I should say. It's as bad as 'the Germanies.' A patchwork of little duchies and principalities, the Papal States in the middle and the Spanish in the south in Naples."

Piazza shook his head. "Where's Garibaldi when we need him?"

"Not born yet. Never will be, in this universe," Nasi said practically.

"Tom and Magda are staying in Italy, too. His lectures at the Padua medical school are really catching on, and she's done very well negotiating the purchase of a lot of things we need for industrial development in the USE. But Tom's other two sons, Ron and Gerry, are coming back to Grantville when Simon Jones does. They're traveling with him and with the mother of Jabe McDougal's girlfriend. The painter. Artemisia Gentileschi. The mother, I mean—not the girlfriend."

Nasi smiled and looked at Ed. "I would appreciate an opportunity to speak with Signora Gentileschi, should one arise. She has been living in Naples, working for the Spanish. Her father is in England. She has ties to both the Barberini and the Tuscan court in Florence. Let me know when they get to Grantville. If she isn't coming to Magdeburg, I believe such a conversation would be worth my while, even if I need to make the trip to Grantville to have it. Jabe goes back and forth, I believe."

"Will do. I'll radio you as soon as she shows up. What about the boys?"

"How old are they, exactly?"

"Ron graduated from high school in 1633 on the accelerated program, right before they all left for Venice. He'd turned seventeen in December, so that would make him eighteen, now. Eighteen and a half. Gerry . . ." Piazza stopped and thought a minute. "He should be turning sixteen this month. Gus Heinzerling was supposed to be tutoring him while they were in Venice, so he didn't fall behind. But I'm told that he's not coming back to high school in Grantville. He's decided to finish up at the boys' school in Rudolstadt. I'm not sure why. But if they're willing to admit him over there, it means that Gus really did keep his nose to the grindstone, at least as far as Latin was concerned."

"Too young for my work, and he will be too busy.
Gerry, that is," Nasi said. "Would the older one have
anything to contribute?"

"You can debrief him, of course. If he's willing to
talk to you. He's a legal adult, so he can make his
own decision on that. Tom Stone's always been a
little . . . anti-authoritarian. More than a little. Magda's
a straight arrow, though, and she has that incredible
Lutheran sense of duty. Well, she grew up in Jena,
with all those theology professors in the town. She's
been their stepmother for close to three years now,
and they like her. So maybe . . . I can't make any
promises on his behalf."

Nasi dug into his briefcase and drew out a sheaf
of papers. "He submitted a written report to me.
Voluntarily, sent in the diplomatic pouch from Venice.
Detailing all of their contacts with Michel Ducos while
he was posing as a member of the Venice Committee of Correspondence. It's retrospective, of course.
Written with all the benefits of hindsight. He does
not spare himself or his brothers. Perhaps, he is even
too harsh in his judgment of them. We sent them
out with very little training and with no expectation
that they would encounter the developments that
occurred. Bedmar, d'Avaux, Ducos. The boys were,
as your baseball commentators would say, 'way out
of their league.' But, the self-condemnation aside,
his analysis of what happened is certainly competent.
More than competent."

"Tom and Magda seem to agree with you," said
Mike. "On the competence issue, that is. Karl Juergen
Edelman will stay available for consultation—Magda's
father has a keenly honed sense about the importance

of following the money—but he has his own businesses
to run and he's tired of being on the train between
Jena and Grantville every week and sometimes twice
a week. So Ron's going to be managing Lothlorien for
them when he gets back. Not just the *Farbenwerke*,
but the pharmaceuticals end of it, too."

Piazza nodded. "I'll keep an eye on him."

Padua

"Signora Gentileschi and her daughter arrived from
Rome last night," the doorman reported. "They send a
message that they are prepared to leave for Grantville
as soon as the rest of you can pack up. Unless there
is some delay here, they do not plan to unpack more
than they will need for a night or two."

Simon Jones stood up, taking the note from the
porter's hand. "Please let them know that all I still
have to do is put the clothes I wore yesterday into
my saddlebags. The rest of the stuff is ready for the
men to put on the pack horses any time."

Magda smiled. "I think the boys are ready, too.
More than ready."

The doorman bowed slightly and backed out of
the room. They'd never been able to break him of
that habit.

Simon looked at the note again and frowned. "Some-
times I wish that Larry and Gus hadn't had to stay in
Rome. Who's Joachim Sandrart, and why is he with the
Gentileschis? Why is he traveling with us, that is?"

Magda shrugged.

"Who would know?" Simon frowned. "If he's someone

who could be a problem, I should warn Ron and Gerry to keep their lips zipped when he's around."

"Signora Gentileschi is an artist. Perhaps he is another one. An . . . associate?"

Simon had no trouble interpreting Magda's disapproving tone. Cardinal Antonio Barberini, by way of Mazzare, had warned them. By the standards of a respectable Lutheran from Jena, Artemisia Gentileschi's past was as colorful as her canvases. It was by no means certain that her younger daughter, the one she was bringing with her, was the child of her husband.

"Not a lover, probably, if you're worried about bad influences on the boys. This," Simon waved the note in the air, "says he's in his twenties. She's fortyish and the little girl she has with her is only ten or eleven, I think. Probably some ambitious young artist who's finished putting in his practically mandatory time in Italy and is ready to go home and launch himself into a hopefully lucrative career of putting paint on canvas."

Magda snorted. "I will ask someone. I do have responsibilities, after all."

Lausanne
Switzerland

Duke Henri de Rohan put down his pen. He had finished today's letter to his brother Benjamin in England, but hadn't signed it yet, in case something else came to mind. He re-read. *After his assassination attempt on the Pope was foiled, Michel Ducos was last seen escaping by boat down the Tiber, presumably to*

*take ship from Ostia. I predict that he will not go
back to d'Avaux. In any case, Mazarini is ensuring
that d'Avaux will have only minimal chances to foment
mischief in the future. I am afraid that Ducos has
become the head of a small group of unpredictable
fanatics. Keep an eye out in England for any sign of
him and his followers. Though, of course, he may be
headed for Holland. Or Scotland. Or. . . .*

He picked up the pen again. *I am also writing to
our agent in Frankfurt am Main. If necessary, please
be prepared to make a rapid trip to Frankfurt. You
should find the burden of this bearable, since to a
considerable extent our associates there are also members of a network of international wine merchants.* He
paused a moment, then signed his name.

The duke moved on, to finish his outgoing correspondence for the day. Happily, his new assignment
from Venice, attempting to reconcile the feuding Swiss
cantons, significantly reduced the time it took for his
letters to reach their destinations. Instructions for his
wife in France; a shorter note to his father-in-law, also
in France; one to his brother Benjamin, in care of
Isaac de Ron in Frankfurt; a letter to Hugo Grotius,
another to the mathematician Descartes. One to the
city council of the Most Serene Republic of Venice,
which was dithering about whether or not to renew
his employment contract.

And one to Cardinal Richelieu, assuring him, with
the monotonous regularity he brought to such reas-
surances, that he remained a loyal and faithful subject
of the French monarchy.

The duke missed his long and faithful correspondence with his mother, who had died three years

earlier. If he was not concentrating, Rohan often still found himself thinking that he should mention something to her.

Now, a letter to his daughter Marguerite, in France with her mother. Marguerite had been born almost fifteen years after the wedding and was now seventeen years old. Of the nine children of his marriage, only she had survived. When he finished it, he started to put down his pen and then picked it up again.

One to Duke Bernhard of Saxe-Weimar. After Bernhard's successes this summer, it was time to consider the possibility that he might make a suitable son-in-law. He was thirty. It was time for him to be getting married. Marguerite had the splendid advantage that she was already old enough to bear children and still young enough to bear a lot of children, God willing.

The Austrians would probably try to pick Bernhard off with some minor Habsburg bride, of course, to protect their interests in Vorarlberg and the other territories dotted across southern Swabia to the Breisgau. But it would be a terrible pity, in Rohan's opinion, to waste a successful Protestant prince on a Catholic wife.

True, Bernhard was Lutheran, not Calvinist as was the duke himself. But Lutherans counted as Protestants, at least from the political perspective, the same way that members of the Church of England did. If not, quite, theologically. After all, the Lion of the North himself was a Lutheran. German-language Catholic popular pamphleteers, an imprecise group of people sadly lacking in perception where the nuances of doctrinal distinction among their opponents were concerned, tended to refer even to Calvinists and Anabaptists as *Lutheraner*.

Even the city council of Venice had been known to refer to Duke Henri de Rohan himself as a "Lutheran." The most prominent Huguenot in contemporary France shuddered slightly at such a lack of theological precision.

A match between Marguerite and Bernhard would not make King Louis XIII of France and Cardinal Richelieu at all happy, of course. But then neither would a match between Marguerite and young Turenne, which was also an attractive possibility. The only thing that would make Louis and Richelieu happy would be for Marguerite to convert to Catholicism and marry one of Richelieu's relatives.

Which wasn't going to happen. At least not as long as Henri de Rohan was alive.

Then he wrote directly to Isaac de Ron in Frankfurt, telling him to expect the arrival of Henri's brother Benjamin (letter to him enclosed) from England any day now.

Please take out a lease on a suitable town house and have it furnished and staffed with reliable people by the time he arrives, charging the cost to my account with the banker Milkau.

Benjamin liked his comforts. He accomplished more when he was comfortable.

Now for the inbox. On top of it, the latest report from Leopold Cavriani. A delightful man. He'd had a really fascinating summer. Leopold did not suffer from the constraints that were an inevitable part of having been born into the high nobility.

Occasionally, Henri de Rohan envied him.

But only occasionally.

Somewhere in Switzerland

"If he pontificates at me one more time," Ron Stone said, "I think I'll gag. I don't see how Gerry can stand to listen. Hour after hour, after hour."

"Your brother isn't listening, really. He's just . . . not bothering to avoid Joachim." Artemisia Gentileschi smiled patiently.

"How much more do we need to know about him? Hell, we already know more than enough." Ron grabbed onto the reins with one hand and waved the other in the air. "Talk, talk, talk, talk, talk, talk, jabber, pontificate, talk some more. We've already heard that he was born in Frankfurt, that his family are Calvinists who fled from the Spanish Netherlands because of religious persecution, that he apprenticed with Soreau and Stoskopff in Hanau and can't face a future limited to still-lifes so he'll probably have to work for Catholic patrons mostly, that he learned print making in Nürnberg, that the engraver he worked for in Prague advised him to specialize in painting, that he learned to paint from Gerard van Honthorst in Utrecht, that he toured Holland with Pieter Paul Rubens, that he worked at the English court for a while with Honthorst, that he has not only seen Florence, Rome, and Naples, but also Messina and Malta, that he thinks the war has ruined the career prospects of most German artists, that . . ." He stopped. "If I hear one more word about the trials, troubles, and travails of the 'Frankenthal exiles,' I think I'll spit. What's worse, the guy talks in capital letters." He groaned with disgust.

Simon Jones, riding on his other side, laughed out

loud. Joachim Sandrart *did* talk in capital letters. He didn't speak, he orated.

He was doing it now.

"Time and again Queen Germania has seen her Palaces and Churches, decorated with splendid Painting, go up in Flames, and her Eyes are so darkened with Smoke and Weeping that she no longer has the Desire or the Strength to pay Heed to this Art: Art that now seems to want only to enter into a long and eternal Night and there to sleep. Perhaps a man may find a short Contract with one Ruler. But as the Scene of War moves, so, perforce, does he, leaving his Efforts unfinished. And so such Things fall into Oblivion, and those that make Art their Profession fall into Poverty and Contempt. They put away their Palettes and Easels. They must take up the Pike, the Sword, or the Beggar's Staff instead of the Paintbrush, while the Gently Born are ashamed to apprentice their Children to such despicable Persons."

Are you planning to do anything about it, man? Ron thought sourly. *Like maybe try to end the war? Or do you just plan to complain and complain and complain?*

"Gently born?" Ron asked Artemisia Gentileschi. "Is the guy noble?"

"No." She twisted her lips. "Joachim is far more gently born than I, to be sure. The family was Walloon, certainly one of the more prominent commoner lineages in Hainaut. His father was—is, if he is still alive, but I haven't heard recently—a merchant. Very wealthy, but still a merchant. His mother was from a merchant family, also. Joachim's a cousin of Michel le Blon. Still, even in Frankfurt Laurentius Sandrart achieved some status. Certainly among the Walloons, if not among the native-born. Even though he was an immigrant into a city where the Lutheran council does not precisely make Calvinists welcome—they refused to grant permanent resident to Sebastian Stoskopff, which is why he went to Paris when he left Hanau.

"However, I'm sure that Joachim would not object if, some time in the future, a ruler chose to ennoble him for his many services to the cause of Art. Services which he has yet to perform, though I don't really doubt that he is capable of performing them. If he hadn't decided to return with me, Count Vincenzo Giustiniani in Rome had made him a very generous offer to manage his collection. So he should do well as an art dealer and promoter, at least, even if his own canvases do not display an immense amount of promise. Merely a high level of workmanlike competence. Both of my brothers, after all, have made their way quite successfully as dealers and agents. As has Hainhofer in Augsburg. The art world needs its intermediaries.

"Nor, I'm sure, would Joachim object if a ruler who employs him as a painter should also choose to utilize him as a diplomat, as the rulers of the Spanish Netherlands have done with Rubens. Everybody knows that his cousin le Blon—he's an engraver and goldsmith, a good twenty years older than Joachim, I think—operates out of Amsterdam as an agent for Oxenstierna." Artemisia frowned. "Of course, le Blon is a religious nut, too, quite taken with the writings of that Silesian, Jacob Böhme. Just because a man is successful in one field, it doesn't necessarily that he has common sense in any other.

"Joachim is an ambitious man. He is unlikely to become as great an artist as Rubens, but he doesn't lack high aspirations."

Grantville

"Denise!"

There were several Denises in town. She kept going.

"Denise Beasley, hey there!"

She slowed down, then stopped her motorcycle. Someone was running after her.

"Denise, if you're going downtown, can you give me a lift? Drop me off at the middle school. I'm going to be late for practice." It was Missy Jenkins, who worked in the "State Library" part of the libraries housed in the high school these days.

"What are you practicing?"

"I'm not. I'm coaching recreation league girls' soccer. I don't usually mind the run; it's only a couple of miles and good for me. But we had a VIP tour this afternoon and I got away a half hour after I should have."

"Sure. Climb on behind."

Missy did. "There are days that I would give my eyeteeth to be able to ride one of these. If I had one, that is."

Denise was a little surprised. "Compared to horses?" A lot of the girls her own age were totally horse crazy. A lot of the older ones, too, for that matter.

"Horses don't speak to me," Missy said.

"I can see that. Horses don't speak to me, either.

I don't speak to them, if I can avoid it. Do you mind if we stop at the funeral home first, for a second? I'll take you all over and get you there on time."

"No problem. But why?"

"Minnie Hugelmair garages her cycle there, behind the hearse. It's more secure than the old shed behind Benny's house. They had a few problems. Some vandalism and at least once somebody tried to break in and steal it, we think. At the funeral home, there's always someone up and around, every day, all around the clock. It's safer, and Jenny doesn't charge much."

They headed down Route 250 in silence.

Until Missy, the wind whipping through her hair since she didn't have a helmet, asked, "Would you teach me to ride this thing? We could figure out the costs of the lessons. Your time, the fuel, wear and tear, all that."

Joe Pallavicino sat in the principal's office at the middle school, cleaning his fingernails while he waited to talk to Archie Clinter about their common problems. Denise Beasley had gone on to high school this fall. There had already, less than a month into the academic year, been trouble in regard to a boy who tried to hit on her after she told him to beat it. Senior on freshman. He'd recover.

It looked like Minnie Hugelmair would probably finish sixth grade by Thanksgiving, according to Tina Sebastian. By spring, at this rate, she would get her eighth grade diploma—earlier, if she tested out. Then, if she went to summer school and Denise didn't, she'd finish ninth grade in August of '35 and they'd both be sophomores the fall of 1636. In the class of '38.

There was no question that Minnie did her own school work. She wasn't in ESOL at all any more. She seemed to regard textbooks as obstacles on a course she was running and scaled them with determination.

There was no question that she still attracted trouble like a magnet.

Especially . . .

Especially given the increasing level of "anti-Kraut" muttering here and there around Grantville. Considering that she was still best friends with Denise Beasley. Considering that Denise's uncle Ken owned the 250 Club, which was the center of most of the muttering.

High school was one of the ages that started a lot of the trouble, with up-time and down-time boys competing for the attention of the same girls.

Minnie was not a beauty. She probably hadn't been before the riot in Jena. With the addition of the scar and the slightly mismatched artificial eye, she never would be.

But Denise was. She always would be. At the age of ninety, if she lived that long. Somehow, she managed to combine her mother Christin's delicate build and brunette vividness with Buster's sheer vigor. Trouble also, if a different kind of trouble. With Minnie there to take her part, next year. And there were too many up-time kids who would classify any retaliation by Minnie as "Kraut trouble."

Minnie wasn't likely to be as gentle as Denise herself had been. Denise never did more than was necessary to make her point.

Of course, any boy who wasn't a total idiot knew that she would, in a pinch, call on her father for backup. Buster Beasley was an ex-biker whose seventeen-inch biceps were only partly obscured by the tattoos that covered them. He constituted significant backup for a girl.

Some boys, on the other hand, were total idiots.

Joe decided he'd better talk to a few people besides Archie. Benny and Buster. Preston Richards at the police department. Lisa Dailey and Vic Saluzzo at the high school. Henry Dreeson and Enoch Wiley. Mary Ellen Jones, maybe. If they had some lead time, maybe they could arrange things so that Denise and Minnie could finish high school without triggering some kind of mudslide.

Words and music came wafting up the high school corridor.

"You know," Victor Saluzzo said, leaning against the library circulation desk. "I could have lived my life a lot more happily if Benny Pierce hadn't decided to teach Minnie Hugelmair that old turkey of a song and she hadn't spread it to our incoming freshmen."

> *"School days, school days,*
> *Dear old Golden Rule days.*
> *Reading and writing and 'rithmetic,*
> *Taught to the tune of a hickory stick . . ."*

Missy Jenkins giggled. She was there on temporary loan from the state library for a couple of weeks while the school went through the agonies of starting a new semester. "I hope you know that Minnie herself has every intention of finishing sixth grade the first semester and showing up on your doorstep before Christmas."

Pam Hardesty, also on loan from the state library, grinned. "Then you'll have both of them, Victor. Not just Denise, but Minnie, too. They do sort of have a tendency to cut out of school on the slightest excuse, don't they?"

Victor shook his head. "The real problem is that they're both bright enough to do it without really hurting their grades. But a lot of other kids aren't that smart, so it's a bad example." He paused. "Maybe we should try providing them with mentors." He pushed himself upright. "If anybody comes looking for me, I'll be down in the guidance counseling office."

Pam watched him go and sighed.

"What's the matter."

"Reproaching myself, I guess. When he mentioned Minnie, what hit me first was *Schadenfreude*. And that's terrible. Taking pleasure in somebody else's troubles. But, honest to God, Missy. The great Velma Hardesty soap opera continues. Given the way Mom's been behaving lately, hanging around with that gorgeous garbage man . . . You've seen him, haven't you? Jacques-Pierre Dumais? I guess it's sort of comforting to realize that other people have troubles, too."

"Yeah. Like Winnie the Pooh called honey. 'Sustaining.' You're not alone, though. Neither is Mr. Saluzzo. Think of what Mr. Dreeson has to deal with, every single day."

Chapter 1

"We could do it, you know," Gui Ancelin said. He threw the newspaper down on the table in the private parlor at Isaac de Ron's inn. "The woman, this Dreeson's wife, has turned up in Basel, it says. Logically, to return to the USE, she will shortly be traveling right through Frankfurt. An old woman. How hard could it be to intercept her?

"We will not violate the trust Michel has placed in us!" Guillaume Locquifier said forcefully. He even went so far as to make a fist at the other man.

Mathurin Brillard blinked. That was not part of Guillaume's usual repertoire of gestures, but he was unusually furious this morning. Possessed by all of the classical furies. Even more immovable and stubborn than usual.

The table was covered with newspapers, and their headlines. Headlines about the new king in the Netherlands and the prospect that Frederik Hendrik, the Calvinist Prince of Orange, would betray his Protestant allies by compromising with the Spaniard—formerly the Cardinal Infante. Headlines about airplanes. Headlines about the archduchess Maria Anna of Austria, who was going to marry that Spanish conqueror after having fled from her intended husband, the Duke of Bavaria, on the eve of her wedding.

There were also headlines about the up-time woman, Simpson's wife. Headlines about Admiral Simpson, who apparently had plans to install a major naval facility within the lands surrounded by those that the Spanish conqueror had already occupied.

There were even headlines about the Grantville mayor's wife, Veronica Richter, who had accompanied Simpson's wife and the former Austrian archduchess in their adventures.

Admittedly, it was maddening. So far, Michel Ducos had not given the people he left behind in Frankfurt permission to do anything at all. Brillard sometimes suspected that Michel was trying to hog all the glory for himself.

But Ducos and Antoine Delerue had placed Guillaume Locquifier in charge of the group in Frankfurt—and as far as Locquifier was concerned, Michel Ducos was The Great Leader. A brilliant leader; an inspiring leader. If seeing him that way would not amount to idolatry, almost a semi-divine leader.

Not to mention a somewhat intimidating leader.

In Brillard's personal opinion, Ducos was also a leader who was more than halfway to becoming insane. He never mentioned that to Guillaume, of course.

So, no matter how furious Locquifier became at the news in the papers, he would wait. Which was precisely what he was proclaiming now.

"Michel has never mentioned this woman. We do

not have time to get his permission by way of Mauger's commercial contacts before she will have come and gone. She may not be part of his greater plan. We do not *know* all the details of his greater plan. He has not chosen to impart them to us."

Fortunat Deneau reached over and picked the paper up. "She will have guards around her if she comes on a Rhine boat. There are still so many different jurisdictions along the Rhine that no one would let her travel without guards. If she travels by river at all, of course. Once she reaches Mainz, however, it is all within the USE to Frankfurt. Is she important enough that any of them would be detailed to accompany her to Frankfurt?"

"We cannot initiate anything without Michel's approval," Guillaume insisted. "Nothing. We will do nothing. *Absolutement!*"

Robert Ouvrard looked a little mutinous. "If and when we know for certain that she will follow this route, are we to sit around all winter, then, doing nothing but talk? Then maybe talk some more?"

"We may watch her," Locquifier conceded. "Once we know that she has left Basel, if she is coming this way, some of us may go down to Mainz. When she arrives there, we can observe her land. See where she stays. Find out how many people are in her party. Surely she will not be traveling entirely without companions for the rest of her trip, though she is unlikely to have bodyguards." He turned to Ancelin. "You and—he looked around the room—Deneau. Get on the same boat on which she comes to Frankfurt. Observe her. Hear anything useful that is to be heard. But . . . Do . . . Nothing."

"Why don't we at least write to Michel?" Ancelin picked up the paper again. "Ask for a sort of blanket approval that we can make some decisions here. Get his agreement that we can take out easy targets if and when we identify any, if they fit in with the prospect of destabilizing Richelieu. We wouldn't have to mention this particular woman. Just ask for something general."

"*Non!*" Ouvrard shook his head. "Tell Michel who this woman is. She makes a good example. Point out what a splendid opportunity we may be missing because of our obedience to his directives." He stood up, waving his hands in the air. "Michel is the leader, Guillaume, but he simply isn't *here*. Since we don't have, and won't have, one of the almost magical radios, not any time soon, we can't afford to wait for his approval of every single action. Even our Lord Christ, when he sent out the seventy to convert the world, did not reserve approval of every minor thing they decided to do to himself."

"I will write him," Locquifier said finally. "But I will not do any more than ask. I will not urge. Remember what he told me in Italy. 'Don't be stupid, Guillaume. Do you propose to curse every soldier who stands against us? Divert ourselves at each instant in order to punish lackeys?' I, personally, have no intention of letting him call me 'stupid' again."

Brillard shrugged. It was more than he had expected Ancelin and Ouvrard to accomplish. Michel Ducos w[as] not a man to be pushed. Guillaume Locquifier wa[s] a man to try.

—end excerpt—

from *1635: The Dreeson In[cident]*
available in hardco[ver]
December 2008, from [Baen Books]

DID YOU KNOW YOU CAN DO ALL THESE THINGS AT THE
BAEN BOOKS WEBSITE ?

‡ Read free sample chapters of books   `SCHEDULE`

‡ See what new books are upcoming   `SCHEDULE`

‡ Read entire Baen Books for free   `FREE LIBRARY`

‡ Check out your favorite author's titles   `CATALOG`

‡ Catch up on the latest Baen news & author events   `NEWS` or `EVENTS`

‡ Buy any Baen book   `SCHEDULE` or `CATALOG`

‡ Read interviews with authors and artists   `INTERVIEWS`

‡ Buy almost any Baen book as an e-book individually or an entire month at a time   `WEBSCRIPTIONS`

or young adults   `YOUNG ADULT LISTS`

the coolest fans in science minds on the planet   `BAEN'S BAR`

TO
AEN.COM

approval that we can make some decisions here. Get his agreement that we can take out easy targets if and when we identify any, if they fit in with the prospect of destabilizing Richelieu. We wouldn't have to mention this particular woman. Just ask for something general."

"*Non!*" Ouvrard shook his head. "Tell Michel who this woman is. She makes a good example. Point out what a splendid opportunity we may be missing because of our obedience to his directives." He stood up, waving his hands in the air. "Michel is the leader, Guillaume, but he simply isn't *here.* Since we don't have, and won't have, one of the almost magical radios, not any time soon, we can't afford to wait for his approval of every single action. Even our Lord Christ, when he sent out the seventy to convert the world, did not reserve approval of every minor thing they decided to do to himself."

"I will write him," Locquifier said finally. "But I will not do any more than ask. I will not urge. Remember what he told me in Italy. 'Don't be stupid, Guillaume. Do you propose to curse every soldier who stands against us? Divert ourselves at each instant in order to punish lackeys?' I, personally, have no intention of letting him call me 'stupid' again."

Brillard shrugged. It was more than he had expected Ancelin and Ouvrard to accomplish. Michel Ducos was not a man to be pushed. Guillaume Locquifier was not a man to try.

—end excerpt—

from *1635: The Dreeson Incident*
available in hardcover,
December 2008, from Baen Books

DID YOU KNOW YOU CAN DO ALL THESE THINGS AT THE
BAEN BOOKS WEBSITE ?

+ Read free sample chapters of books   `SCHEDULE`

+ See what new books are upcoming   `SCHEDULE`

+ Read entire Baen Books for free   `FREE LIBRARY`

+ Check out your favorite author's titles   `CATALOG`

+ Catch up on the latest Baen news & author events
  `NEWS` or `EVENTS`

+ Buy any Baen book   `SCHEDULE` or `CATALOG`

+ Read interviews with authors and artists   `INTERVIEWS`

+ Buy almost any Baen book as an e-book individually or an entire month at a time   `WEBSCRIPTIONS`

+ Find a list of titles suitable for young adults   `YOUNG ADULT LISTS`

+ Communicate with some of the coolest fans in science fiction & some of the best minds on the planet   `BAEN'S BAR`

GO TO
WWW.BAEN.COM